# FILM ART

## AN INTRODUCTION

# FILM ART

# AN INTRODUCTION

THIRD EDITION

## DAVID BORDWELL
## KRISTIN THOMPSON

*University of Wisconsin*

**McGraw-Hill Publishing Company**

*New York   St. Louis   San Francisco   Auckland   Bogotá
Caracas   Hamburg   Lisbon   London   Madrid
Mexico   Milan   Montreal   New Delhi   Oklahoma City   Paris
San Juan   São Paulo   Singapore   Sydney   Tokyo   Toronto*

# FILM ART: AN INTRODUCTION

1 2 3 4 5 6 7 8 9 0   VNH   VNH   8 9 4 3 2 1 0 9

ISBN 0-07-006439-3

This book was set in Bodoni Book by Ruttle, Shaw & Wetherill, Inc.
The editors were Peter Labella and Curt Berkowitz;
the designer was Joan E. O'Connor;
the production supervisor was Laura Lamorte.
Von Hoffmann Press, Inc., was printer and binder.

Cover photos (*clockwise from upper right*): George Méliès in his
*The Man with the Rubber Head* (France, 1902); Cary Grant in
Alfred Hitchcock's *North by Northwest* (USA, 1959), © 1969
Loew's Inc., renewed 1987 Turner Entertainment Company; Dziga
Vertov's *Man with a Movie Camera* (USSR, 1929); Mariko Okada
in Yasujiro Ozu's *An Autumn Afternoon* (Japan, 1962), courtesy
New Yorker Films.

Library of Congress Cataloging-in-Publication Data

Bordwell, David.
    Film art: an introduction / David Bordwell, Kristin Thompson.
    3rd ed.
    p.   cm.
    Includes bibliographies and index.
    ISBN 0-07-006439-3
    1. Motion picture—Aesthetics.    I. Thompson, Kristin, (date).
II. Title.
PN1995.B617    1990
791.43'01—dc20                                 89-12702

# ABOUT
# THE AUTHORS

David Bordwell and Kristin Thompson are married and live in Madison, Wisconsin.

**David Bordwell** is Professor of Communication Arts at the University of Wisconsin—Madison. He holds a master's degree and a doctorate in film from the University of Iowa. His books include *The Films of Carl-Theodor Dreyer* (University of California Press, 1981), *Narration in the Fiction Film* (University of Wisconsin Press, 1985), *Ozu and the Poetics of Cinema* (British Film Institute/Princeton University Press, 1988), and *Making Meaning: Inference and Rhetoric in the Interpretation of Cinema* (Harvard University Press, 1989). He has won a University Distinguished Teaching Award.

**Kristin Thompson** is an Honorary Fellow at the University of Wisconsin—Madison. She holds a master's degree in film from the University of Iowa and a doctorate in film from the University of Wisconsin—Madison. She has published *Eisenstein's Ivan the Terrible* (Princeton University Press, 1981), *Exporting Entertainment: America's Place in World Film Markets, 1907–1934* (British Film Institute, 1985), *Breaking the Glass Armor: Neoformalist Film Analysis* (Princeton University Press, 1988), and numerous articles on film. She is currently at work on a history of European avant-garde film styles of the 1920s. In her spare time she does research on the work of P. G. Wodehouse.

The authors have previously collaborated, with Janet Staiger, on *The Classical Hollywood Cinema: Film Style and Mode of Production to 1960* (Columbia University Press, 1985).

To our parents
Marjorie and Jay Bordwell
and Jean and Roger Thompson

# CONTENTS

# PART III

# FILM STYLE

# PART IV

## CRITICAL ANALYSIS OF FILMS

# PART V

## FILM HISTORY

# PREFACE

This book seeks to introduce the reader to the aesthetics of film. It assumes that the reader has no knowledge of cinema beyond the experience of moviegoing. Although some aspects of the book may prove useful for people with considerable knowledge of film, our aim is to survey the fundamental aspects of cinema as an art form.

By stressing film as art, we necessarily ignore certain aspects of the medium. Industrial documentaries, instructional filmmaking, the social history of cinema or its impact as a mass medium—all these are important dimensions of film, and each would require a separate book for adequate treatment. Instead, this book seeks to isolate those basic features of film which can constitute it as an art. The book therefore directs itself at the person interested in how the film medium may give us experiences akin to those offered by painting, sculpture, music, literature, theater, architecture, or dance.

As we wrote this book, we envisioned readers of three particular sorts. First is the interested general reader, who wants to know a little more about the movies. Second is the student in a course in film appreciation, introduction to film, film criticism, or film aesthetics; for this reader, the book can function as a textbook. Third is the more advanced student of film, who may find here a convenient outline of principal issues and concepts and a set of suggestions for more specialized work.

Organizationally, *Film Art: An Introduction* offers a distinct approach to studying its topic. It might be possible to survey, willy-nilly, all contemporary approaches to film aesthetics, but we judged this to be too eclectic. Instead, we have sought an approach that would lead the reader in logical steps through various aspects of film aesthetics. Crucial to this approach is an emphasis on *the whole film*. Audiences experience entire films, not snippets. If the particular film is the irreducible center of our inquiry, we need an approach that will help us understand it. The approach we have chosen emphasizes the film as an artifact—made in particular ways, having a certain wholeness and unity, existing in history. We can outline the approach in a series of questions.

*How is a film created?* To understand film as art demands that we first understand how human labor creates the artifact. This leads to a study of *film production* (Part I).

*How does an entire film function?* This book assumes that like all artworks, a film may be understood as a *formal* construct. This leads to a consideration of what form is and how it affects us, of basic principles of film form, and of narrative and nonnarrative forms in cinema (Part II). Matters of film form also demand that we consider the *techniques* which are characteristic of the film medium, for such techniques function within the form of the total film. Thus we will analyze the artistic possibilities of the four primary film techniques: mise-en-scene, cinematography, editing, and sound (Part III).

*How may we analyze a film critically?* Armed with both a conception of film form and a knowledge of film technique, we can go on to analyze *specific films* as artworks. We analyze several such films as examples (Part IV).

*How does film art change through history?* Although a thorough history of cinema would require many volumes, here we can suggest how the formal aspects of film do not exist outside determinable historical contexts. We survey the most noteworthy *periods and movements in film history* to show how understanding form helps us locate films within history (Part V).

It is worth noting that this approach to the entire film came from several years of teaching introductory film courses. As teachers, we wanted students to see and hear more in the films we studied, but it was evident that simply providing the "lecturer's view" would not teach students how to analyze films on their own. Ideally, we decided, students should master a repertory of *principles* which would help them examine films more closely. We became convinced that the best way to understand cinema is to use general principles of film form to help analyze specific films. Our success with this approach led us to decide that this book should be skills centered. By learning basic concepts of film form and film technique, the reader can sharpen his or her perception of any specific film.

The stress on skills has another consequence. You will note that the book's examples and evidence are quite varied; we refer to a great many films. We expect that very few readers will have seen all of the films we mention, and certainly no teacher of a film course could possibly show every title. But we have varied our examples in the interests of clarity, vividness, and accessibility. If some titles seem unfamiliar, it is partly because film study over the past five years has opened up new areas of inquiry which any textbook must address. (Those areas, incidentally, are within the reach of film courses. Ozu's *The Only Son* is just as accessible as Bergman's *The Silence* and is in fact cheaper to rent; Antonioni's *Story of a Love Affair* is no harder to obtain than is his *Red Desert*. Almost every film we cite is available for rental or purchase or both.) Moreover, because the book stresses the acquisition of conceptual skills, the reader need not see all of the films we mention in order to grasp the general principles. Many other films can be used to make the same points. For instance, the possibilities of camera movement can be as easily illustrated with *La Ronde* as with *La Grande Illusion;* to exemplify narrative ambiguity, *Shadow of a Doubt* will serve as well as *Day of Wrath*. Indeed, although the book can serve as a syllabus for a course in cinema, it is also possible for a teacher to use different films to illustrate the book's ideas. (It would then be a useful exercise for the class to *contrast* the text example with the film shown, so as to specify even more clearly particular aspects of the film.) The book rests not on titles, but on concepts.

*Film Art: An Introduction* has certain unusual features. A book on film must be heavily illustrated, and most are. Virtually all film books, however, utilize so-called production skills—photographs taken during filming, but usually not from the position of the motion picture camera. The result is a picture that does not correspond to any image in the finished film. We have used very few production stills. Instead, the illustrations in this book are virtually all frame enlargements—magnified photographs from the actual film. Most of these illustrations come from 35-mm prints of the films, and with the exception of the shots from *Daisies*, all of the color illustrations are taken from 35-mm prints or negatives.

Another unusual feature is the Notes and Queries section at the end of almost every chapter. In these sections we attempt to raise issues, provoke discussion, and suggest further reading and research. As chapter supplements, the Notes and Queries sections constitute a resource for the advanced undergraduate, the graduate student, and the interested general reader.

In all, we hope that this book will help readers to watch a greater variety of films with keener attention and to ask precise questions about the art of cinema.

This edition of *Film Art: An Introduction* seeks to enrich and refine the ideas set forth in the first edition a decade ago. Once again we have tried to make the book more comprehensive, flexible, and up to date.

By and large the concepts pertaining to film form and film technique remain constant from the second edition. We have updated the *Notes and Queries* sections to reflect recent developments in more advanced cinema studies, and Chapter 11's treatment of film history has been revised in the light of contemporary scholarship. In the interests of greater clarity of exposition, we have reordered the chapters within Part II. Now it begins with our discussion of narrative form, the variety most familiar to students. The survey of nonnarrative forms follows.

In many respects the book's range of coverage has expanded. We have included more material on animation, documentary, and experimental cinema. We have added critical analyses of *Man with a Movie Camera* and a trio of animated films. In acknowledgment of the persistent importance of Hitchcock's American films to introductory film studies courses, we have replaced our analysis of the British version of *The Man Who Knew Too Much* with a study of *North by Northwest*. We have drawn examples from recent films such as Wenders's *Wings of Desire* and Sayles's *Matewan*, and we have devoted a lengthy analysis to Woody Allen's *Hannah and Her Sisters*. In addition, Chapters 1 and 6 take more notice of video as a significant distribution/exhibition outlet. Finally, the opening chapter has been thoroughly revised to provide a more detailed account of both large-scale studio production and of independent filmmaking. In all, the book now includes a great many fresh examples and several dozen new illustrations.

Because of the increasing importance of developing college students' writing skills, Part IV now includes a guide to writing critical essays on films. This is not meant as a replacement for basic wok in expository and argumentative writing, but it does suggest how general principles of composition apply to the specific tasks of planning, organizing, and writing critical analyses.

Over the years, many people have helped us improve *Film Art: An Introduction*. For previous editions, our thanks go to David Allen, Tino Balio, Eileen Bowser, Martin Bresnick, Michael Budd, Peter Bukalski, Richard B. Byrne, Kent Carroll,

Bruce Conner, Mary Corliss, Susan Dalton, Robert E. Davis, Dorothy Desmond, Maxine Fleckner-Ducey, Don Fredericksen, Jon Gartenberg, Ernie Gehr, J. Douglas Gomery, Claudia Gorbman, Ron Gottesman, Don Larsson, José Lopez of New Yorker Films, Roger L. Mayer of MGM Inc., Norman McLaren, Kazuto Ohira of Toho Films, Badia Rahman, Leo Salzman, Rob Silberman, Michael Snow, John C. Stubbs, Dan Talbot of New Yorker Films, Edyth von Slyck of Pennebaker Films, and Chuck Wolfe. For this edition, we are grateful to John Belton, Edward Branigan, Jerome Carolfi, Charles Keil, Laura Kipnis, Mark Macauley of Films, Inc., and Paul Rayton. We would also like to express our appreciation to the following people, who reviewed the manuscript for this edition of *Film Art: An Introduction* and gave constructive comments and suggestions.

Ralph Berets, University of Missouri—Kansas City

Corbin Carnell, University of Florida

Jeffrey Chown, Northern Illinois University

Kathe Geist, Illinois State University

Howard Harper, University of North Carolina

Barbara Klinger, Indiana University

Thomas M. Leitch, University of Delaware

Joseph Evans Slate, University of Texas

Charles Wolfe, University of California—Santa Barbara

As always, we also thank our editors at McGraw-Hill: Roth Wilkofsky, Kathleen Domenig, Curt Berkowitz, and especially Peter Labella.

David Bordwell
Kristin Thompson

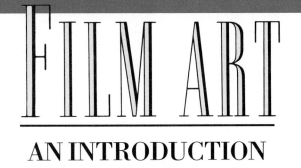

# FILM ART

## AN INTRODUCTION

# PART I

## FILM PRODUCTION

# ONE

# THE WORK
# OF FILM
# PRODUCTION

On sober reflection, we readily admit that films are like buildings, books, and symphonies—artifacts made by humans for human purposes. Yet, as part of an audience watching an enthralling movie, we may find it difficult to remember that what we are seeing is not a natural object, like a flower or an asteroid. Cinema is so captivating that we tend to forget that movies are *made*. An understanding of the art of cinema depends initially on a recognition that a film is produced by both machines and human labor.

## TECHNICAL FACTORS IN FILM PRODUCTION

Watching a film differs from viewing a painting, a stage performance, or even a slide show. A film presents us with *images* in *illusory* motion. What creates this specific effect, this sense of "moving pictures"? For cinema to exist, a series of images must be displayed to a viewer by means of a mechanism which presents each image for a very short period and which inserts between successive images an interval of blackness. If a series of slightly different images of the same object is displayed under these conditions, physiological and psychological processes in the viewer will create the illusion of seeing a moving image. Such conditions for "moving pictures" exist only rarely in nature. Like most human artifacts, a film depends on particular technological factors.

**Fig. 1.1**

**Fig. 1.2**

First, the images must be capable of being displayed in a *series*. They might be on a row of cards, as in the Mutoscope (Fig. 1.1), and flipped past the viewer to create the illusion of movement. More commonly, the images are inscribed on a strip of some flexible material. Optical toys such as the Zoetrope put their images on strips of paper (Fig. 1.2), but cinema as we know it uses a strip of celluloid as support for the series of images, which are called **frames.** If the images are to be put on a strip of film, cinema usually requires three machines to create and display those images. All three share a basic principle: a mechanism controls how light is admitted to the film, advances the strip of film a frame at a time, and exposes it to light for the proper interval. The three machines are:

1. *The camera* (Fig. 1.3). In a light-tight chamber, a drive mechanism feeds the motion picture film from a reel (a) past a lens (b) and aperture (c) to a take-up reel (d). The lens focuses light reflected from a scene onto each frame of film (e). The mechanism moves the film intermittently, with a brief pause while each frame is held in the aperture. A shutter (f) admits light through the lens only when each frame is unmoving and ready for exposure. The standard shooting rate for sound film is 24 frames per second (fps).

2. *The printer* (Figs. 1.4, 1.5). Printers exist in various designs, but all consist of light-tight chambers that drive a negative or positive roll of film from a reel (a) past an aperture (b) to a take-up reel (c). Simultaneously, a roll of unexposed film (a′, c′) moves through the aperture (b or b′), either intermittently or continuously. By means of a lens (d), light beamed through the aperture prints the image (e) on the unexposed film (e′). The two rolls of film may come into contact and pass through the aperture simultaneously (Fig. 1.4 diagrams a contact printer). Or, light coming through the original may be beamed to the unexposed roll through lenses, mirrors, or prisms (as in (f), in the optical printer, Fig. 1.5).

3. *The projector* (Fig. 1.6). A drive mechanism feeds the exposed and developed film from a reel (a) past a lens (b) and aperture (c) to a take-up reel (d). Light is beamed through the images (e) and magnified by the lens for projection on a screen. Again, a mechanism moves the film intermittently past the aperture, while a shutter (f) admits light only when each frame is pausing. For the movement effect to occur, the film must display at least 12 frames per second; the shutter must also block and reveal each frame at least twice in order to reduce the flicker effect on the screen. The standard projection rate for sound film is 24 frames per second, with two shutter flashes per frame.

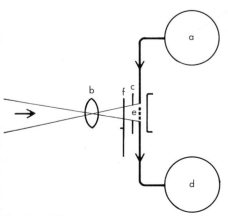

**Fig. 1.3   The camera.**

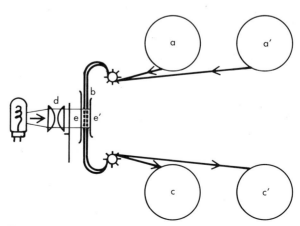

**Fig. 1.4   The contact printer.**

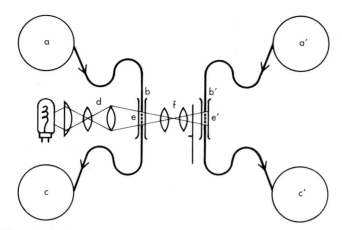

**Fig. 1.5**   The optical printer.

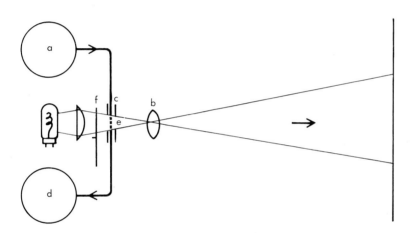

**Fig. 1.6**   The projector.

Camera, printer, and projector are all variants of the same basic machine. The camera and the projector both control the intermittent movement of the film past a light source. The crucial difference is that the camera gathers light from outside the machine and focuses it onto the film, whereas in the projector the reverse happens: the machine produces the light which shines through the film onto a surface outside. The printer combines both other devices: like a projector, it controls the passage of light through exposed film (the original negative or positive); like a camera, it gathers light to form an image (on the unexposed roll of film).

These three machines induce the film viewer to see static pictures as moving. But what perceptual processes cause this illusion? In the nineteenth century, some thinkers proposed the concept of "persistence of vision," the phenomenon by which an image lingered on the retina for a fraction of a second after the source had vanished. But this does not in itself explain why we would see movement rather than a succession of still images. Twentieth-century research has shown the problem to be more complex. We still do not know for certain how illusory movement is generated by cinema, but at least two features of the human visual system would seem to be involved.

First is what is called *critical flicker fusion,* a term that describes the results of increasing the rate at which a light is flashed. If a beam of light is broken by more than 50 flashes per second, the viewer no longer sees pulses or bursts but rather the illusion of continuous light. A film is usually shot and projected at a rate of 24 frames per second. Then the projector shutter breaks the light beam two or three times per frame. This raises the number of flashes to the threshold of flicker fusion. Early silent films were shot at a lower rate (often 16, 18, or 20 fps), and until engineers devised shutters that could break the beam more than once per frame, the projected image had pronounced flicker. (Hence the early slang term for movies, "flickers," which survives today when people talk about a film as a "flick.")

A second factor in creating cinema's illusion is *apparent motion.* This is the tendency of human vision to see movement when there is in fact no moving object. In 1912, the Gestalt psychologist Max Wertheimer discovered that when two side-by-side lights were flashed at certain intervals, viewers perceived not two flashing lights but a single moving light. (The same effect can be seen on many neon advertising signs.) For a time researchers hypothesized that the viewer might be using some process of unconscious thought in creating the illusion of movement. Recent experimental work, however, suggests that apparent motion may owe something to specific "motion analyzers" in the human visual system. Any displacements, whether real or only projected on a screen, may trigger certain cells in the eye or brain, and these automatically assign movement to the stimuli.

*The Photographic process*

Whatever the physiological or psychological causes, the images that we see in movement are usually created photographically. Like photographic film, motion picture film consists of a transparent *base* (formerly of nitrate, now of acetate), which supports an *emulsion* (a layer of gelatin containing light-sensitive materials). Black-and-white film emulsion contains grains of silver halide. When light from the environment strikes them, they register a latent image. Chemical processing makes the latent image visible as a configuration of black grains on a white ground. The resulting image is either a negative one, from which positive prints can be struck, or a positive one (called a reversal image).

Color film emulsion consists of three layers, each one containing not only silver halides but also a chemical dye sensitive to one primary color (red, green, or blue). With color negative film, the developing process yields an image that is complementary to the original color values. Color reversal processing yields a positive image with colors conforming to the original scene. Most professional filmmaking uses negative emulsion so as to allow greater control of print quality and larger numbers of positive prints to be made. The reversal process is chiefly confined to amateur work, such as home movies. Although the filmmaker can create *non*photographic images on the film strip by drawing, cutting or punching holes, etching, or painting, most filmmakers have relied on the camera, the printer, and other photographic technology.

*× gauges*

In order to run satisfactorily through camera, printer, and projector, the strip of film must have certain standardized features. The film strip is perforated along one or both edges, so that small teeth (sprockets) in the machines can seize the perforations (sprocket holes) and pull the film at a uniform rate and smoothness. Space is also reserved along one or both edges for an optical or magnetic sound track. The physical dimensions of the film have necessarily been standardized, with width being the crucial variable. Motion picture film widths, called **gauges,** are measured in millimeters. Although many gauges have been experimented with, the internationally standardized ones are super 8 mm, 16 mm, 35 mm, and 70 mm.

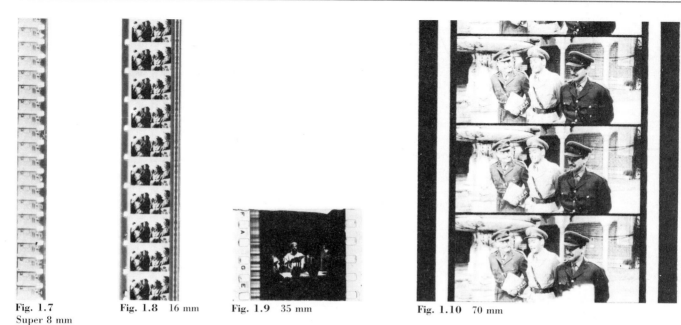

Fig. 1.7
Super 8 mm

Fig. 1.8   16 mm

Fig. 1.9   35 mm

Fig. 1.10   70 mm

Super 8 mm (Fig. 1.7) was for several years a popular gauge for amateurs and experimental filmmakers, but currently it is in decline. Portable video formats have by and large eclipsed it. Figure 1.8 shows 16-mm film, which is used for both amateur and professional film work. Most film study courses show 16-mm prints of films. The standard professional gauge is 35 mm. Most commercial theaters show 35-mm prints. Figure 1.9 shows a frame from *The Jazz Singer* (1927). Another professional gauge is 70-mm film, which was in the 1960s often used for "spectacular" projects (e.g., Fig. 1.10, frames from *Lawrence of Arabia*).

Image quality varies directly with the width of the film; normally, the higher the gauge, the better defined and more detailed the image. The print we see of a film, however, may not be in the gauge of the original. Most films shot in 70 mm are also distributed in 35-mm prints, whereas most films studied in cinema courses were originally shot in 35 mm but are shown in 16 mm. Often, quality deteriorates when a film shot on one gauge is transferred to another. Thus a 35-mm print of Keaton's *The General* will almost certainly be photographically superior to a 16-mm print, whereas a film shot on super 8 mm will look fuzzy and grainy if printed and projected in 35 mm.

There are some exceptions to this generalization. Today films released in 70 mm are shot on 35-mm negative film that is blown up to make prints in the larger format. Due to improved film stocks, there is no significant decline in image quality. Also, complicated special effects are sometimes shot on 70 mm for better definition or control. These portions are then copied to 35-mm negative for inclusion in the finished film.

Usually a recording of the sound accompanies the images. The sound track may be either *magnetic* or *optical*. In the magnetic type, one or more strips of magnetic recording tape run along the film's edges. During projection, the film's track is "read" by a sound head similar to that on a tape recorder. The 70-mm frames in Figure 1.10 have a stereophonic magnetic sound track (running along both edges of the film strip). An optical sound track encodes sonic information in the form of patches of light and dark in a parallel line running alongside the frames. During production, electrical impulses from a microphone are translated into pulsations of light which are photographically inscribed on the moving film strip. (Modern optical sound recording usually records on magnetic tape initially, then transfers the taped sound onto film.) When the film is projected, the optical track produces varying intensities of light which are translated back into electrical impulses and then into sound waves. An optical sound track may encode the sound as *variable area* (a wavy contour of black and white within the sound image) or as *variable density* (gradations of black and white). The 16-mm frame in Figure 1.8 has a variable-area optical sound track on the right side; the 35-mm frame in Figure 1.9 utilizes a variable-density optical track, on the left.

Specific machines, then, create a film from a raw material—a photochemically sensitive strip of perforated celluloid of a standardized gauge. Important as technology is, however, it is only part of the story.

## SOCIAL FACTORS IN FILM PRODUCTION

Machines don't make movies by themselves. Film production transforms raw materials into a product through the application of machinery *and* human labor. But human labor may be utilized in different ways, and the options are affected by economic and social factors.

Most films go through three general phases of production.

1. *Preparation.* The idea for the film is developed and usually committed to paper in some form. At this phase, the filmmaker or filmmakers usually acquire funds to make, publicize, and distribute the film.

2. *Shooting.* At this stage, images and sounds are created on the film strip. More specifically, the filmmaker produces **shots** and discrete sounds (dialogue, noises, or whatever). A shot is a series of frames produced by the camera in an uninterrupted operation. In shooting, the separate shots are often filmed "out of continuity"—that is, in the most convenient order for production. (They will be assembled in proper order later.)

3. *Assembly.* At this stage, which may overlap with the shooting phase, the images and sounds are put together in their final form.

Not every film goes through every step. A home movie might involve very little preparation and might never undergo any final assembly. A compilation documentary might not require the shooting of any new footage, only the assembly of existing clips from library and archives. On the whole, though, most films go through these production phases.

The organization of production tasks at each phase can vary significantly. It is possible for one person to do everything: plan the film, finance it, perform in it, run the camera, record the sound, and put it all together. More commonly, though, different tasks are assigned to different people, making each job more or less specialized. This is the phenomenon of *division of labor,* a process that occurs in most of the tasks any society undertakes. Various jobs are assigned to different individuals. Even a single job may be broken down into smaller tasks, which then may be assigned to specialists. In the framework of filmmaking, the principle of

**Fig. 1.11**

division of labor yields different *modes,* or social organizations, of film production and different *roles* for individuals within those modes. The overall preparation, shooting, and assembly stages remain, but they take place within different social contexts.

## ■ MODES OF PRODUCTION: THE STUDIO PROCESS

We can conveniently start by looking at the most detailed and specialized division of labor—that present in the *studio* mode of production. This will allow us to trace the amazing variety of tasks that a film can require. We will then be in a better position to understand how those tasks can be accomplished in other modes of production.

A studio is a company in the business of manufacturing films. The most famous examples are the studios that flourished in Hollywood between the 1910s and the 1960s—Paramount, Warner Bros., Columbia, and so on. Under the classic studio system, the company owned its own filmmaking equipment and an extensive physical plant, and it retained most of its workers on long-term contract. (In Fig. 1.11, a World War II–era publicity photo, MGM studio head Louis B. Mayer, front row center, shows off his stable of stars under contract.) The studio central management planned the projects, then delegated authority to individual supervisors, who in turn assembled casts and crews from the studio's pool of workers.

The classic studio system has frequently been compared to industrial assembly-line manufacture, in which a manager supervises a number of workers, each repeating a particular task at a rigid rate and in fixed order. The analogy suggests that the Hollywood studios of the 1930s cranked out films the way that General Motors turns out cars. But the analogy is not exact, since each film is different, *serial manufacture.*

not a replica of a prototype. A better term for studio mass-production filmmaking is probably *serial manufacture*. Here skilled specialists collaborate to create a unique product while still adhering to a blueprint prepared by management.

While the centralized studio production system remains viable in some parts of the world (such as China, India, and Hong Kong), the American production companies of today do not usually oversee a film to the degree they once did. Now each film is planned as a unique "package," with director, actors, staff, and technicians gathered specifically for this project and hired for a limited term. The production company may have a physical plant that can be used for the project, as many of the surviving studios still do, but other companies will require the producer to rent or acquire facilities for the project. Nevertheless, despite the growth of a "package" system, the specific production stages and the assignment of roles remain virtually the same as they were in the heyday of more centralized studio production.

## ■ THE PREPRODUCTION PHASE

In studio filmmaking, the preparation phase is usually known as *preproduction*. At this point, two roles emerge as most critical: that of producer and that of writer.

The role of the *producer* is chiefly financial and organizational. She or he may be an "independent" producer, unearthing film projects and trying to convince production companies or distributors to finance the film. Or the producer may work for a studio and have as his or her job the discovery of ideas for films. The producer may even be hired by a studio to put together the "package."

The producer's job is to develop the project through the script process, to obtain financial support, and to arrange for the personnel who will work on the film. During shooting and assembly, the producer usually acts as the liaison between the writer or director and the production company that is financing the film. After the film is completed, the producer will often have the task of arranging the distribution, promotion, and marketing of the film and of monitoring the paying back of the funds that underwrite the production.

The chief task of the *writer* is to prepare the script. Sometimes the writer will set the process in motion by sending a script to his or her agent, who submits it to an independent producer or a production company for consideration. Alternatively, an experienced screenwriter meets with a producer in a "pitch session," where the writer can propose several ideas that might become scripts. And sometimes the producer has an idea for a film and hires a script writer to work it up. The latter course of action is particularly common if the producer, ever on the lookout for ideas, has bought the rights to a novel or play and wants it *adapted* into a film.

In mass-production filmmaking the script writer usually is expected to follow traditional storytelling patterns. For several decades, Hollywood studio production has called for scripts about strong central characters who struggle to achieve well-defined goals. It is also generally believed that a script ought to have a "three-act" structure, with the climax of the first act coming about a quarter of the way into the film, the climax of the second act appearing about two-thirds of the way through, and the climax of the final act bringing about the resolution of the protagonist's problem. Writers will also be expected to include *plot points*, twists that intensify the action.

The script will go through several stages. These stages include a *treatment*, a synopsis summarizing the basic action; one or more full-length scripts; and a final version, the *shooting script*. Extensive rewriting is common. Often the director will

TREATMENT!

**Fig. 1.12**

want to shape the film in certain directions. For example, the protagonist of the original script of *Witness* was Rachel, the Amish widow with whom John Book falls in love. The romance, and Rachel's confused feelings about Book, formed the central plot line. But the director, Peter Weir, wanted to emphasize the clash between pacifism and violence. So William Kelley and Earl Wallace revised their script to emphasize the mystery plot line and to center the action on Book, who brings urban crime into the peaceful Amish community.

Even the shooting script is not sacrosanct. It may be altered during the shooting phase. During the filming of the 1954 *A Star Is Born*, the scene in which Judy Garland sings "The Man That Got Away" was reshot at several points in the production, each time with different dialogue supplied by the script writer, Moss Hart. Script scenes that have been shot may also be condensed, rearranged, or dropped entirely in the assembly stage. Figure 1.12 is a publicity still for Alfred Hitchcock's *Notorious*, showing a scene which does not appear in the final version. (Indeed, the actress sitting next to Cary Grant does not appear in the film at all.)

If the producer or director finds one writer's script unsatisfactory, other writers may be hired to revise it. As you may imagine, this often leads to conflicts about which writer or writers deserve screen credit for the film. In the American film industry, these disputes are adjudicated by the Screen Writers' Guild.

When the script reaches its final state, the producer will need to start planning the film's finances. He or she will have sought out a director and perhaps also stars to make the package a promising investment. (In some cases, the director will initiate the project, but this is more common in "independent" production.) The producer must now prepare a budget spelling out *above-the-line costs* (essentially the costs of script writer, director, and major performers) and *below-the-line costs* (the expenses allocated for the rest of the cast, the crew, the shooting and assembly phases, and the advertising).

The producer must also prepare a daily schedule for shooting and assembling the film. This will be done with an eye on the budget. For example, since the film will be shot out of continuity, all shots using a certain setting or certain personnel can be filmed during one period. If a star is forced to join the production late or leave it at intervals, the producer must plan to "shoot around" the performer. Keeping all such contingencies in mind, the producer and his or her staff are expected to come up with a schedule of several weeks or months that juggles cast, crew, locations, and even seasons and geography for the most efficient use of resources.

## ■ THE PRODUCTION PHASE

In Hollywood parlance, the shooting phase is usually called **production** (even though "production" is also the term for the entire process of making a film).

Although the *director* may be involved at various stages of preproduction, he or she is primarily responsible for overseeing the shooting and assembly phases. Traditionally, the director puts the script on film by coordinating the various aspects of the film medium.

Because of the specialized division of labor in large-scale production, many aspects of the task of shooting the film must be delegated to other workers who will consult with the director.

1. In the preparation phase, the director has already begun work with the *set* unit. This is headed by a *production designer*. The production designer creates drawings and plans that determine the architecture and the color schemes of the sets. Under the production designer's supervision, an *art director* supervises the construction and painting of the sets. The *set decorator*, often someone with experience in interior decoration, modifies the sets for specific filming purposes, supervising a staff who finds props and a *set dresser* who arranges things on the set during shooting.

Working with the production designer, a graphic artist may be assigned to produce a **storyboard**, a series of comic-strip-like sketches of the shots in each scene, including notations about costume, lighting, camera work, and other matters. Figure 1.13 is taken from the storyboard for Hitchcock's film *The Birds*. The storyboard, useful for any film, is especially important for films relying heavily on special effects, since it gives the cinematography unit and the special-effects unit a preliminary sense of what the finished shots should look like.

2. During the shooting, the director will rely on what is called the *director's crew*. This includes:

  a. The *script supervisor* or *continuity person*, known in the classic studio era as a "script girl." Today one-fifth of Hollywood script supervisors are male.

  b. The *first assistant director*, who, with the director, plans out each day's shooting schedule and sets up each shot for the director's approval.

  c. The *second assistant director*, who is the liaison among the first assistant director, the camera crew, and the electricians' crew.

  d. The *third assistant director*, who serves as messenger for director and staff.

  e. The *dialogue coach*, who may feed performers their lines but who more often than not speaks the lines of offscreen characters during shots of other performers.

473-B  FOUR GULLS DIVE TOWARDS HIGHWAY

473-C

474  GULL MISSES ATTENDANT.

Fig. 1.13

f. The *second unit director*, who films stunts, location footage, action scenes, and the like, at a distance from where principal shooting is taking place.

3. The most publicly visible group of workers is the *cast.* The cast will likely include *stars*, well-known players assigned to major roles and likely to attract audiences. Figure 1.14 shows 1930s star Greta Garbo in a *screen test*, a procedure used to determine casting and to try out lighting, costume, make-up, and camera positions in relation to the actor. The cast also includes *supporting players*, or performers in secondary roles; *minor players;* and *extras*, those anonymous persons who pass by in the street, mass for crowd scenes, and fill distant desks in large office sets. One of the director's major jobs is to shape the performances of the cast, and most directors will spend a good deal of time explaining how a line or gesture should be rendered, reminding the actor of the place of this scene in the overall film, and helping the actor create a coherent performance. The first assistant director usually works with the extras and takes charge of arranging crowd scenes for the director's approval. On some productions, more specialized cast members require particular coordination. *Stunt persons* will probably be supervised by a *stunt coordinator;* professional dancers will work with a *choreographer*. If animals join the cast, they will be handled by a *wrangler*. (*Mad Max beyond Thunderdome* carried the memorable credit line "Pig Wrangler.")

4. Another unit of specialized labor is the *photography unit*. The leader here is the *cinematographer*, also known as the *director of photography* or "DP." The cinematographer is an expert on photographic processes, lighting, and manipulation of the camera. The cinematographer consults with the director on how each scene will be lit and filmed. In Figure 1.15, on the set of *Citizen Kane*, Orson Welles directs from his wheelchair on the far right, cinematographer Gregg Toland crouches below the camera, and actress Dorothy Comingore kneels at the left. (The "script girl," now known as the script supervisor, can be seen in the background left.) The cinematographer supervises:

Fig. 1.14

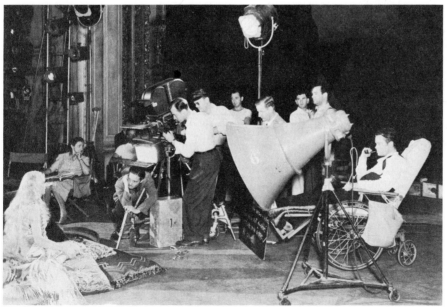

Fig. 1.15

a. The *camera operator*, who runs the machine and who may also have assistants to load the camera, adjust and follow focus, push a dolly, and so on.

b. The *key grip*, the person who supervises the *grips*. These workers carry and arrange equipment, props, and elements of the setting and lighting.

c. The *gaffer*, the head electrician who supervises the placement and rigging of the lights. In Hollywood production the gaffer's assistant is called the *best boy*.

5. Parallel to the photography unit is the *sound unit*. This is headed by the *production recordist* (also called the *sound mixer*). The recordist's principal responsibility is to record dialogue during shooting. Typically the recordist will use a portable tape recorder, several sorts of microphones, and a console to balance and combine the inputs from various microphones. The recordist will also usually attempt to tape some ambient sound when no actors are speaking; these bits of "room tone" will later be inserted to fill pauses in the dialogue. The recordist's staff includes:

a. The *boom operator*, who manipulates the boom microphone and conceals radio microphones on the actors.

b. The *"third man,"* who places other microphones, lays sound cables, and is in charge of controlling ambient sound. Some productions have a "sound designer" who enters the process during the preparation phase and who, like the production designer, plans a "sonic style" appropriate for the entire film.

6. A *special-effects* unit is charged with preparing and executing process shots, miniatures, matte work, computer-generated graphics, and other technical shots. Figure 1.16 shows a miniature used in the making of *The Comedians*. During the planning phase, the director and the production designer will have determined what effects will be needed, and the special-effects unit consults with the director and the cinematographer on an ongoing basis.

7. A miscellaneous unit includes a *make-up* staff, a *costume* staff, *hairdressers*, and *drivers* (who transport cast and crew).

8. During shooting, the producer is represented by a unit often called the *producer's crew*. This consists of the *production manager*, also known as the *production coordinator* or the *associate producer*. This person will manage daily orga-

Fig. 1.16

# SOME TERMS AND ROLES
# IN FILM PRODUCTION

The rise of "packaged" productions, pressures from unionized workers, and other factors have led producers to credit everyone who worked on a film. (The credits for *Who Framed Roger Rabbit?* contained 771 names.) Moreover, the specialization of mass-production filmmaking has created its own jargon. Some of the most colorful terms ("gaffer," "best boy") are explained in the text. Here are some other terms that you might see in a film's credits.

*ACE:* After the name of the editor; abbreviation for the American Cinema Editors, a professional association.

*ASC:* After the name of the director of photography; abbreviation for the American Society of Cinematographers, a professional association. The British equivalent is the BSC.

*Additional photography:* A crew shooting footage apart from the *principal photography* supervised by the director of photography.

*Clapper boy:* Crew member who operates the clapboard that identifies each take.

*Dolly grip:* Crew member who pushes the dolly that carries the camera, either from one setup to another or during a take for moving camera shots.

*Foley artist:* A sound-effects specialist who creates sounds of body movement by walking or by moving materials across large trays of different substances (sand, earth, glass, and so on). Named for Jack Foley, a pioneer in postproduction sound.

*Greenery man:* Crew member who chooses and maintains trees, shrubs, and grass in settings.

*Lead man:* Member of set crew responsible for tracking down various props and items of decor for the set.

*Loader:* Member of photography unit who loads and unloads camera magazines, as well as logging the shots taken and sending the film to the laboratory.

*Optical effects:* Laboratory workers responsible for such effects as fades and dissolves.

*Property master:* Member of set crew who supervises the use of all *props*, or movable objects in the film.

*Publicist, Unit publicist:* Member of producer's crew who creates and distributes promotional material regarding the production. The publicist may arrange for press and television interviews with the director and stars, and for coverage of the production in the mass media.

*Scenic artist:* Member of set crew responsible for painting surfaces of set.

*Still photographer:* Member of crew who takes photographs of scenes and "behind-the-scenes" shots of cast members and others. These photographs may be used for checking lighting or set design or color, and many will be used in promoting and publicizing the film.

*Timer, Color timer:* Laboratory worker who inspects the negative film and who adjusts the printer light to achieve consistency of color across the finished print.

*Video assist:* The use of a video camera mounted alongside the motion picture camera to check lighting, framing, or performances. In this way, the director and the cinematographer can try out a shot or scene on tape before committing it to film.

nizational business, such as arranging for meals and accommodations. A *production accountant* (or *production auditor*) will monitor expenditures, a *production secretary* will coordinate telephone communication among units and with the producer, and *production assistants* will run errands. (Newcomers to the film industry often start out working as production assistants.)

All this coordinated effort, involving perhaps hundreds of workers, results in many thousands of feet of exposed film and recorded sound-on-tape. Every shot called for in the script or storyboard or decided on by the director will have several **takes,** or unique versions of that shot. For instance, if the finished film requires one shot of an actor saying a line, the director may make several takes of the speech, each time asking the actor to vary the expression or posture. Only some

Fig. 1.17

takes will be printed, and typically only one of those will become the shot included in the finished film.

Because shooting usually proceeds out of continuity, the director and crew must have some way of labeling each take. During filming, one of the cinematographer's staff holds a *clapboard* up before the camera at the start of each shot. The clapboard records the production, scene, shot, and take. The clapboard's hinged arm makes a cracking sound that helps the editor to synchronize sound and picture later. (See Fig. 1.17, from Jean-Luc Godard's *La Chinoise*. The white "X" marks this as the exact frame with which the cracking sound should synchronize.) Thus every take is identified for future reference.

## ■ POSTPRODUCTION

Members of the film industry today call the assembly phase of filmmaking *postproduction*. Yet this phase does not begin simply when shooting is completed. Postproduction staff members work steadily, if sometimes behind the scenes, throughout shooting.

Before the shooting has begun, the director or producer has probably hired an *editor* (also known as the *supervising editor*). This person is charged with cataloguing and assembling the various takes produced during shooting. Typically, the editor receives the processed footage from the laboratory as quickly as possible; this footage is known as the *dailies*, or the *rushes*. The editor inspects the dailies, leaving it to the *assistant editor* to synchronize image and sound and to sort the takes by scene. The editor will meet with the director to examine the dailies or, if the production is filming far away, the editor will call to inform the director of how the footage looks. Since retaking shots is costly and troublesome, constant checking of the dailies is important for spotting any problems with focus, exposure, framing, or other visual factors.

As the footage accumulates, the editor assembles the shots into a *rough cut*— the film loosely strung in sequence, without sound effects or music. From this the editor, in consultation with the director, builds toward a *fine cut* or *final cut*. At the same time, further laboratory work or special-effects work may be done.

Once the shots are arranged in something approaching final form, the *sound editor* (also known as the *sound-effects editor*), takes charge of building up the sound track. First, the editor will add sound effects. Most of the sound effects the audience hears in a studio-produced film are not recorded at the moment the image is shot. The sound editor may draw on a library of stock sounds, utilize effects recorded "wild" on location, or create particular effects for this film. Sound editors routinely manufacture footsteps, cars crashing, doors closing, pistol shots, a fist thudding into flesh (often produced by whacking a watermelon with an axe).

The sound editor will also supervise a practice that has become standard in the American film industry: rerecording dialogue after filming. By and large, dialogue recorded on the set serves only as a guide track. The actors are brought into the recording studio to rerecord their lines (a process called **dubbing** or "looping"), and the sound-effects editor supervises this process. In addition, the sound editor will loop alternative lines of dialogue in order to eliminate language that would not be permitted on broadcast television, where the film will eventually be shown. (This procedure avoids the older methods of simply cutting the offending words out, leaving a noticeable silence on the track.)

At about the same time as the sound editor begins work, the *composer* enters the process. The composer sees a fairly advanced cut of the film and decides, along with the producer, director, editor, and sound editor, where music should be inserted. (This is called *spotting*.) On the basis of these plans, the composer compiles cue sheets that list exactly where the music will go and how long it should run. The composer proceeds to write the score, although she or he will probably not orchestrate it personally. With the aid of a "click track," which synchronizes the beat of the music to the finished film, the score will be recorded and form part of the sound editor's material.

All these sounds are recorded on distinct tracks: voice tracks, music tracks, and effects tracks. Dozens of tracks may be used in a production. At a final mixing session, the director, editor, and sound-effects editor put all the separate tracks together into a single master track. When the film negative is cut in accordance with the final cut, this master track will be synchronized with it. Then positive "married" prints, with both picture and sound, will be printed for distribution and exhibition.

Many fictional films, such as *Singin' in the Rain*, have been made about the studio mode of production. Some films set their action at particular phases of the process. Federico Fellini's *8½* concerns itself with the preparation, or preproduction, stage of a film that is abandoned before shooting starts. François Truffaut's *Day for Night* takes place during the shooting phase of a production marred by the death of one of the cast. The action of Brian De Palma's *Blow Out* occurs during the sound editing process of a low-budget slasher movie.

The studio mode of production is characterized by a minute breakdown of labor. With this comes an attempt to control every aspect of the filmmaking process. A paper trail testifies to the importance of exhaustive calculation. At the start there will be versions of the script; during shooting reports will be written on camera footage, sound recording, special-effects work, and laboratory results; in the assembly phase there will be logs of shots catalogued in editing, and a variety of cue sheets for music, mixing, looping, and title layout. Once something is on paper, either before or after filming, the production workers can eliminate, or at least control, any intrusion of unplanned events.

This is never wholly successful. Every case study of a large-scale studio production will attest to the compromises, accidents, and foul-ups that plague the process. Weather may throw the shooting off schedule. Disagreements about the script may result in a director's being fired. Last-minute changes demanded by the producer or director may require that some scenes be reshot. Studio production is a constant struggle between the desire to plan the film completely and the inevitable "noise" created by the sheer complexity of such a detailed division of labor.

Not all films that use the studio mode of production are large-budget projects financed by major companies. In recent years, it has proven possible for some filmmakers to initiate their own projects and retain a considerable degree of independence in the course of the production. Such a filmmaker is John Sayles, director of *The Return of the Secaucus Seven*, *The Brother from Another Planet*, and *Eight Men Out*. Sayles's script for *Matewan* was based on labor struggles in the West Virginia coal fields after World War I. It was budgeted at $4 million at a period when the average studio-financed feature ran almost three times that. Sayles's producers financed the film with funds from private investors, from a distributor, and from a presale to home video. Working on a smaller budget and with his own selection of cast and crew, Sayles was able to retain more control over his project than might have been possible under the auspices of a major studio. Nevertheless, in making *Matewan* Sayles generally adhered to the detailed breakdown of labor characteristic of the studio mode of production.

## ■ MODES OF PRODUCTION: INDIVIDUAL AND COLLECTIVE

Our survey of the studio mode of production demonstrates how precisely production tasks can be broken down. But not all filmmaking demands such a detailed division of labor. In general, two alternative modes of production treat the preparation, shooting, and assembly phases differently.

In *individual* film production the filmmaker functions as an artisan. He or she may own or rent the necessary equipment. Financial backing can be obtained on a film-by-film basis, and the production is generally on a small scale. The preferred format is 16 mm. There is very little division of labor: the filmmaker typically oversees every production task, from obtaining financing to final editing, and will actually perform many of them. Although technicians or performers may make distinct contributions, the principal creative decisions rest with the filmmaker.

Documentary production offers many examples of the individual mode. Jean Rouch, a French anthropologist, has made several films alone or with a small crew in his efforts to document the lives of marginal people, often members of minorities, living in an alien culture. Rouch wrote, directed, and photographed *Les Maîtres fous* (1955), his first widely seen film. Here he examined the ceremonies of a Ghanian cult whose members lived a double life: most of the time they worked as low-paid laborers, but in their rituals they passed into a frenzied trance and assumed the identities of their colonial rulers. Other documentary filmmakers will work on a scale only somewhat larger than that of Rouch. Frederick Wiseman, whose *High School* we examine in Chapter 10, produces, plans, and distributes his own films. During filmmaking he often serves as sound recordist while a cinematographer runs the camera.

Politically activist documentary offers another example of individual film production. Barbara Koppel devoted four years to the production stages of *Harlan County, U.S.A.*, a record of Kentucky coal miners' struggles for union representation. After eventually obtaining funding from foundations, she and a very small crew spent 13 months living with miners during the workers' strike. A large crew was ruled out not only by Koppel's budget but also by the need to be absorbed as naturally as possible into the community. During filming Koppel acted as sound recordist, working with cameraman Hart Perry and sometimes also a lighting person. Like the miners, the filmmakers were constantly threatened with violence from strikebreakers. Some of these incidents are recorded on film, as when the driver of a passing truck fired a gun at the crew (Fig. 1.18).

The individual mode of film production is also exemplified by the work of many experimental filmmakers. Maya Deren, one of the most important American experimentalists, made several films in the 1940s (*Meshes of the Afternoon, Choreography for Camera, Ritual in Transfigured Time*) which she scripted, directed, performed in, and edited. In some cases the shooting was done by her husband, Alexander Hammid. A comparable example is the work of Stan Brakhage, whose films are among the most directly personal ever made. Some, like *Window Water Baby Moving* and *Scenes from under Childhood*, are lyrical studies of his family life; others, such as *Dog Star Man*, are mythic treatments of nature; still others, such as *23rd Psalm Branch* and *The Act of Seeing with One's Own Eyes* are quasi-documentary studies of war and death. Funded by grants and his personal finances, Brakhage prepares, shoots, and edits his films virtually unaided. For a time, while he was working in a film laboratory, he also personally developed and printed his footage. The work of Brakhage, which now comprises over 150 films, demonstrates that in the individual mode of production the filmmaker can become an artisan, a

Fig. 1.18

solitary worker executing all the basic production tasks. In later chapters, we will be examining films by other experimental directors, such as Bruce Conner, Michael Snow, Robert Breer, and Ernie Gehr, who have likewise fulfilled several production roles in the making of their films.

In *collective* film production several film workers participate equally in the project. Like individual filmmakers, the group may own or rent its equipment. The production is on a small scale, and financing may come from foundations or members' personal resources. But although there may be a detailed division of labor, the group shares common goals and makes production decisions collectively. Roles may also be rotated: the sound recordist one day may serve as cinematographer on the next. The collective mode of production attempts to replace the authority vested in the producer and director with a more broadly distributed responsibility for the film.

Not surprisingly, the political movements of the late 1960s fostered many efforts toward collective film production. In France, several such groups were formed, the most noteworthy being SLON (an acronym for a name that translates as Society for the Launching of New Works). SLON was a cooperative that sought to make films about contemporary political struggles around the world. Financed chiefly by foreign television companies, SLON filmmakers often collaborated with factory workers in documenting strikes and union activities.

In the United States, the most famous and long-lived collective unit has been the Newsreel group, which was founded in 1967 as an effort to document the student protest movement. Newsreel attempted to create not only a collective production situation, with a central coordinating committee answerable to the complete membership, but also a community distribution network that would make Newsreel films available for local activists around the country. During the late 1960s and early 1970s, the collective produced dozens of works, including *Finally Got the News* and *The Woman's Film*. Newsreel branches sprang up in many cities, with those in San Francisco (now known as California Newsreel) and in New York (known as Third World Newsreel) surviving into the 1980s. After the mid-1970s, Newsreel moved somewhat away from purely collective production, but it retains certain policies characteristic of the collective mode, such as equal pay for all participants in a film. Important Newsreel films of recent years are *Controlling Interest, The Business of America . . .* (funded largely by American public television), and *Chronicle of Hope: Nicaragua*. Members of Newsreel such as Robert Kramer, Barbara Koppel, and Christine Choy have gone on to make films on their own, individually.

Small-budget production, individual production, and collective production may all be known, somewhat confusingly, as "independent" filmmaking. The drawbacks of independent production consist, chiefly, in financing, distribution, and exhibition. Studios and large distribution firms have ready access to large amounts of capital and usually can ensure the distribution and exhibition of the films they decide to back. The independent filmmaker or group usually has trouble gaining access to money and to audiences.

But many filmmakers believe the advantages of independence outweigh the drawbacks. Independent production can treat subjects that large-scale studio production ignores. Few film studios would have initiated Sayles's *Matewan*, and no film studio would have made *Stranger than Paradise* (made by independent director Jim Jarmusch) or Spike Lee's *She's Gotta Have It* (a comedy about a black woman and the various men who pursue her). Because the independent film does not need as large an audience to repay its costs, it can be more personal, more unusual, and perhaps more controversial. The filmmaker need not tailor the script to the Hollywood three-act, plot-point pattern. (Indeed, the independent filmmaker may not use a script at all.) Independent filmmaking is thus often on the cutting edge of new possibilities of the film medium.

Film production requires some division of labor, but how that division is carried out, and how power is allocated to various roles, will differ from project to project. The process of film production will thus reflect different conceptions of what a film is, and the finished film will inevitably bear traces of the mode of production behind it.

## AFTER PRODUCTION: DISTRIBUTION AND EXHIBITION

Film production has been our principal concern, but the social institution of cinema also depends on distribution and exhibition. Feature films are usually distributed through companies set up for this purpose, and most exhibition occurs within theater circuits. When a firm owns the production facility, a distribution company, and exhibition outlets, it is said to be *vertically integrated*. Vertical integration is a common business practice in most film-producing countries. In the 1920s, for example, Paramount already consisted of production and distribution branches, and it went on to buy and build hundreds of theaters, thus guaranteeing itself a market for its products. In 1948, United States courts declared vertical integration monopolistic, but in this country the major production firms have remained the most important distributors. Recently some theater chains, such as Cineplex Odeon, have become involved in distribution.

Production has always affected exhibition and distribution. In the heyday of Hollywood, studios produced a variety of films (cartoons, comedy shorts, newsreels) which accompanied the feature film and made up a package with specific exhibition appeal. Nowadays the extra material on a cinema program is more likely to include advertisements, movie previews, announcements of no-smoking laws, and pleas for patrons not to litter the theater or to talk during the film.

The way in which a theater exhibits a film can have a profound effect on our movie-going experience. Most patrons are aware that it is more rewarding to see a film made with a stereo sound track in a theater equipped with a sound system capable of playing back the stereo, and thus theaters add "in stereo" to their advertisements. Throughout cinema history, the individual exhibitor has controlled how the patrons see films. In the earliest days of the cinema, when films were only a few minutes long, the exhibitor could arrange a program in a certain order and might even lecture during some of the films. With the move to longer and longer features in the teens and twenties, some exhibitors found ways to shorten their programs to squeeze in an extra show or two a day—by having the projectionist either cut out portions of the print or run the hand-cranked projector a bit faster than standard speed.

The introduction of sound discouraged such practices, but we should not assume that today we always see the film exactly as its makers intended. For one thing, since the 1950s, films have been shot in a variety of shapes, or aspect ratios. Some are very wide rectangles, others slightly narrower, and some are closer to the shape of a television screen. Theater projectors are equipped with a variety of *aperture plates*, whose rectangular slots enable the film to be projected in various proportions. The screen is also usually framed by a dark masking, which can be adjusted to match the shape of the image. In many cases, however, projectionists do not bother to change their projector's plates or move the masking to suit the film. If you see a film that, say, cuts off the tops of the actors' heads, the problem is most likely in the projection, not in the original cinematographer's work.

One reason why such mistakes occur is that in recent years theaters have tried to cut expenses by redefining the projectionist's job. In a "multiplex" cinema complex, a single projectionist might be responsible for supervising a half dozen films running simultaneously, from one central booth or from several. This works well as long as nothing goes wrong, but if the film goes out of focus, there may be no one in the projection booth to notice the problem for minutes on end. On the other hand, more and more theater chains are striving to improve the quality of their screenings, and many projectionists take immense pride in smoothly run shows. It is worth noticing which theaters provide the best presentation of films and trying to patronize them whenever possible.

Broadly speaking, there are three types of exhibition of new films in the United States. Mainstream commercial cinemas are the most common, showing popularly oriented feature films. Films with a more limited appeal are more likely to show in "art houses," which cater to those interested in foreign-language films, feature-length documentaries, festivals of animation, independently produced films, and the like. Like mainstream commercial theaters, art theaters are oriented toward making a profit, and they do so by appealing to a steady, loyal audience in such places as large cities and college towns. Finally, experimental films are usually shown in special exhibition situations intended for them. Museums and archives often sponsor film series, as do local filmmaking cooperatives. There are a few theaters devoted exclusively to showing experimental films, though these can survive only in the largest cities. Virtually all exhibition of experimental films receives some sort of outside support to supplement ticket sales—from grants, foundations, corporate sponsors, and so on.

A comparable division exists among the distributors that supply such exhibitors. Typically the large national distribution firms cater to the commercial cinemas, often having standing contracts with a certain theater chain in each given area. Smaller distributors may pick up independent productions or imported films for the art-house market. Experimental films also have their own alternative distribution system, consisting of outlets such as the Film-Makers' Cooperative in New York and Canyon Cinema Cooperative in San Francisco.

These distinctions among types of exhibition and distribution are not hard and fast. Some art cinemas show experimental films as shorts before their features. Independent filmmakers may try to break into the studio distribution and exhibition structure (as Emile de Antonio did with *Millhouse* and Andy Warhol did with several films he produced). In recent years there has been a trend toward taking foreign films that are initially very successful in an art-house context and moving them into mainstream commercial cinemas for a second run; this has happened, for example, with the Swedish film *My Life as a Dog* and the English import *Hope and Glory*. Italian director Bernardo Bertolucci's *Last Emperor* ordinarily might have played in art cinemas, but its spectacular sets and costumes helped it get a wide release in commercial cinemas instead, and its subsequent sweep of the Oscar awards made it a considerable popular success.

Mainstream theaters, art houses, and venues for experimental cinema are all instances of *theatrical* exhibition. *Nontheatrical* exhibition includes screenings in viewers' homes, classrooms, hospitals, public libraries, and similar institutional circumstances.

## ■ FILM AND VIDEO

By far the most significant nontheatrical means of exhibition is video, in the form of broadcast transmission, cable television, or home videocassette. Since the mid-1970s the number of films seen on video has steadily increased. By 1988, the American film industry had garnered twice as much income from nontheatrical video as from domestic theater returns. Because of the enormously widespread use of this new exhibition format, we should recognize the important differences between film and video.

Certain differences depend on technological factors. Video creates its images by bombarding light-sensitive phosphors on the surface of the picture tube. A "gun" at the rear of the tube scans the surface, activating the phosphors one by one. In the U.S. standard established by the National Television Systems Committee, the picture tube has 525 scan lines, each with about 500 separate dots, or picture elements (pixels). (In practice, the number of lines available on a home television monitor is significantly smaller.) By comparison, motion picture film can carry far more visual information. Estimates vary, but recent experiments suggest that a 16-mm color negative image is the equivalent of over 1100 video scan lines, while 35-mm color negative equals 2300 to 3000 lines. A similar disparity exists in contrast ratio, a term for the relation of the brightest area of the scene to the darkest area. While the video camera can reproduce a maximum contrast ratio of 30:1, color film negative can reproduce a contrast radio of 128:1.

The result of such differences is that the 35-mm film image can be far more detailed and can display a much greater range of tonalities. When a film is transferred to video, its detail and contrast ratio are sharply reduced. It may also fall prey to other video defects, such as color impurities or "comet tailing," streaks of light that trail movements of bright objects against a dark background.

There are other important differences between the media. An obvious one is scale. A 35-mm film image is designed to be displayed on a screen area of hundreds of square feet. Video images look faint and stippled when projected on even a 6-by-8-foot area. Another difference between the two media is long-term storage capacity. Film has been a notably perishable medium, but it can last far longer than videotape. By current estimates, images on a tape in the 1-inch format can start to degrade in 10 to 15 years, and images on a ½-inch videocassette will fall into jeopardy in half that time.

More than technological differences separate the two media. Certain customs of video exhibition have also created significant disparities between the original film and what the viewer sees. Most television viewers know that films are usually edited for broadcast and that sound tracks are reworked to eliminate potentially offensive dialogue. In recent years, viewers have also been made aware of "color-ization," a process that uses computer analysis to add color to black-and-white films. Less well known is the tactic of "time compression." Here a device speeds up the film past its original 24 fps. Local television stations fill the extra time with commercials.

The most widespread alteration of the original film, though, comes in the process of "panning and scanning." Here a film that is made in a widescreen ratio is "cropped" to fit the narrower television frame. Since most films made after 1965 or so have been intended to be shown in a wide format, pan-and-scan processes are very common. The results are often dramatic. The moviegoer who sees *River of No Return* in a 16-mm print sees an image like that in Figure 1.19. The home-video viewer sees what is in Figure 1.20. Sometimes the results can be quite

Fig. 1.19

Fig. 1.20

Fig. 1.21

hilarious, as when the television image includes an actor's nose sticking into the frame. (See Fig. 1.21, from a 16-mm television print of Douglas Sirk's *Tarnished Angels*.) To avoid such awkward compositions, panning and scanning will sometimes make separate shots out of what is actually a single shot. In any case, the video shot usually eliminates 25 to 50 percent of the original image.

All of which is not to say that motion pictures should not be watched on video. Video has undoubtedly aroused viewers' interest in a wider range of films than is usually available in local theaters. If a film is no longer in circulation or is prohibitively expensive to rent, watching it on video is certainly better than not seeing it at all.

Video can also be a useful tool in film study, but we suggest that it serve as an adjunct to the viewing of a film copy. Ideally, the first viewing of a film should be in a film-exhibition situation, and close analysis should be done using a film print. If a film print is unavailable for study, the scholar or student can fall back on the videocassette version. This is chiefly valuable for examining dialogue, music, performances, script construction, and other factors not crucially dependent upon visual qualities.

At present, some widescreen films are being transferred to video in the "letterbox" format, which eliminates panning and scanning by leaving a black band across the top and bottom of the frame. (Even here, however, the extreme edges of the widescreen frame are not visible.) As the television image improves, chiefly through the development of high-definition video, it may compete with 16 mm (see Notes and Queries). Like all media technologies, video has advantages as well as disadvantages, and in studying film we need to be aware of both.

## IMPLICATIONS OF DIFFERENT MODES OF FILM PRODUCTION

Since much of cinema's uniqueness rests on the technical and social factors that produce it, the modes and stages of film production have considerable implications for the study of film as an art. For one thing, a film is often classified on the basis of assumptions about how it was produced. How we think a film was made is relevant to how we categorize it. We often distinguish a *documentary* film from a *fiction* film on the basis of production. Typically, the documentary filmmaker controls only certain variables of preparation, shooting, and assembly; some variables (e.g., script, rehearsal) may be omitted, whereas others (e.g., setting, lighting, behavior of the figures) are present but often uncontrolled. For example, in interviewing an eyewitness to an event, the filmmaker will control camera work and editing, but will not tell the witness what to say or how to act. The fiction film, on the other hand, is characterized by much more control over script and other aspects of the preparation and shooting phases.

Similarly, we identify the category of *compilation* film by the fact that such a film is produced primarily by assembling images that record certain historical evidence about a topic. Gathering visual and auditory material from archives and other sources, the compilation filmmaker may skip the shooting stage of production and simply assemble newsreel footage to create a film dossier on a given subject, for example, television series such as "Victory at Sea" and "The World at War." A recent instance of a successful compilation film was the David Wolper film about John Lennon, *Imagine*.

One more kind of film is distinguished by features of its production: the *animated* film. Here the film does not record an independent, continuously existing stream of action; Daffy Duck and Mickey Mouse do not exist to be filmed. An animated film is produced frame by frame. Either images are drawn right on the film itself, or, more often, the camera photographs a series of drawings or three-dimensional models. In either case animation is characterized by unusual production work at the shooting stage. We shall examine the type of animation that uses drawings in Chapter 10.

Film production not only defines particular types of films, but is also tied to modes of production in the society as a whole. Because of the technological requisites of production, cinema began in the most highly industrialized societies—the United States, Germany, France, and England. In these countries filmmaking quickly became a business for both individual filmmakers and firms. Studio film production tends to occur when countries have achieved division of labor in other manufacturing industries. In American and European industry, for instance, the separation of production planning from execution had been accomplished by 1900, and the same separation emerged in the film industry in the subsequent decade.

Once film and equipment become more widely available, minority modes of production are possible. With access to 8-mm, 16-mm, and portable video equipment, people can engage in individual and collective film production. But this access rests in turn on the existence of social groups that can afford to purchase such machines and that know how to operate them. Just as MGM could not have developed in the Middle Ages, so independent film production cannot indigenously spring up among preindustrial societies today. Film production has historically modeled its practices on economic production in other industries, and the overall economic nature of a society constrains the modes of film production which can develop there.

Finally, the mode of film production affects how we view the filmmaker as artist. This is the issue of authorship. Who, it is often asked, is the "author," the artist responsible for the film?

For some modes of film production, the question is easily answered. In individual production the author must be the solitary filmmaker—Stan Brakhage, Louis Lumière, yourself. Collective film production creates collective authorship; the author is the entire group (Third World Newsreel or SLON). The question of authorship becomes difficult to answer only when asked about studio production.

In the earlier instances authorship is defined by control and decision making, whether by an individual or a collective. But studio film production delegates tasks to so many individuals that it is often difficult to determine who decides what. Is the producer the author? In the prime years of the Hollywood studio system, the producer might have had little or nothing to do with shooting. The writer? Again, in Hollywood, the writer's scripts might be completely transformed in filming. So is this situation like collective production, with group authorship? No, since studio division of labor denies film workers common goals and shared decision making. Moreover, if we consider not only control and decision making, but also "individual style," it must be admitted that certain studio workers leave recognizable and unique traces on the films they make. Cinematographers such as Hal Mohr and Gregg Toland, set designers such as Hermann Warm, costumers such as Edith Head, choreographers such as Gene Kelly—the contributions of these people usually stand out within the films they made. So where does the studio-produced film leave the idea of authorship?

In recent years the most commonly accepted solution has been to regard the director as the "author" of most studio films. Although the writer prepares a script, that script does not define the finished film, since later phases of production can modify the script beyond recognition. (Indeed, writers are famous for complaining about how directors mutilate scripts.) In general, the director's role comes closest to orchestrating all of those stages of production which most directly affect how a movie looks and sounds.

For a director to orchestrate the labor of shooting and assembly does not mean that he or she is expert at every job or even overtly orders this or that. Within the studio mode of production, the director can delegate tasks to trusted and competent personnel; hence the tendency of directors to work habitually with certain actors, cinematographers, composers, and so on. Alfred Hitchcock reportedly sat on the set during filming, never looking through the camera's viewfinder; yet he sketched out every shot beforehand and thoroughly explained to his cinematographer what he wanted. Even in the assembly phase, the director can exercise remote-control power. Hollywood studios would usually not permit the director to supervise the editing of the film. But John Ford, for example, got around this by simply making only one take of each shot whenever possible, with very little overlap of action from shot to shot. By precutting the film "in his head," Ford gave the editor the bare minimum and had no need to set foot in an editing room. Finally, the importance of the director's role is confirmed by the recent trend for the director to operate on a free-lance basis, organizing his or her chosen project.

For all of these reasons, in what follows we will generally identify the director as the author of the film in question. There are exceptions, but usually it is through the director's control of the shooting and assembly phases that the film's form and style crystallize. These two aspects of a film are central to film art and thus to the concerns of the rest of this book.

## NOTES AND QUERIES

### ■ THE ILLUSION OF MOVEMENT IN THE CINEMA

A good discussion of the illusion of movement in film is Susan J. Lederman and Bill Nichols, "Flicker and Motion in Film," in Nichols, *Ideology and the Image* (Bloomington: Indiana University Press, 1981), pp. 293–301. A more recent technical treatment is Julian E. Hochberg, "Representation of Motion and Space in Video and Cinematic Displays," in Kenneth R. Boff, Lloyd Kaufman, and James P. Thomas, eds., *Handbook of Perception and Human Performance*, vol. 1, "Sensory

Processes and Perception" (New York: John Wiley, 1986), chap. 22. A general introduction to visual perception is John P. Frisby, *Seeing: Illusion, Brain and Mind* (New York: Oxford University Press, 1980). Stuart Liebman uses the perceptual mechanisms of illusion to analyze an experimental film in "Apparent Motion and Film Structure: Paul Sharits's *Shutter Interface*," *Millennium Film Journal* **1**, 2 (Spring–Summer 1978): 101–109.

## ■ THE TECHNICAL BASIS OF CINEMA

André Bazin suggests that humankind dreamed of cinema long before it actually appeared: "The concept men had of it existed so to speak fully armed in their minds, as if in some platonic heaven" (*What Is Cinema?* vol. 1 [Berkeley: University of California Press, 1967], p. 17). But the fact of the matter is that whatever its antecedents in Greece and the Renaissance, the cinema became technically feasible only in the nineteenth century. Motion pictures depended on many discoveries in various scientific and industrial fields: optics and lens making, the control of light (especially by means of arc lamps), chemistry (involving particularly the production of cellulose), steel production, precision machining, and other areas. The cinema machine is closely related to other machines of the period. For example, engineers in the nineteenth century designed machines that could intermittently unwind, advance, perforate, advance again, and wind up a strip of material at a constant rate. The drive apparatus on cameras and projectors is a late development of a technology which had already made feasible the sewing machine, the telegraph tape, and the machine gun. The nineteenth-century origins of film are even more apparent today; compare cinema technology's mechanical and chemical basis with image systems such as television and holography, which depend on electronics and lasers.

On the history of film technology, see Barry Salt's *Film Style and Technology: History and Analysis* (London: Starwood, 1983); David Bordwell, Janet Staiger, and Kristin Thompson's *The Classical Hollywood Cinema: Film Style and Mode of Production to 1960* (New York: Columbia University Press, 1985), parts 4 and 6; and many essays in Elisabeth Weis and John Belton, eds., *Film Sound: Theory and Practice* (New York: Columbia University Press, 1985). Primary sources of technological information are included in Raymond Fielding, ed., *A Technological History of Motion Pictures and Television* (Berkeley: University of California Press, 1967). Douglas Gomery has pioneered the economic history of film technology; for a survey, see Robert C. Allen and Douglas Gomery, *Film History: Theory and Practice* (New York: Knopf, 1985). In *Basic Motion Picture Technology* (New York: Hastings House, 1975), L. Bernard Happé includes some historical background; the book as a whole constitutes a solid introduction to the technical basis of cinema. The most comprehensive and up-to-date reference book on the subject is Ira Konigsberg, *The Complete Film Dictionary* (New York: New American Library, 1987).

## ■ MODES OF FILM PRODUCTION

Many "how-to-do-it" books discuss basic stages and roles of film production. Especially good are William B. Adams, *Handbook of Motion Picture Production* (New York: Wiley, 1977); Lenny Lipton, *Independent Filmmaking* (San Francisco: Straight Arrow, 1972); and Edward Pincus, *Guide to Filmmaking* (New York: Signet, 1969). The Focal Press series contains many useful titles, including Alec Nisbett's

*The Technique of the Sound Studio* (New York: Hastings House, 1974); L. Bernard Happé's *Your Film and the Lab* (New York: Hastings House, 1974); and Pat P. Miller, *Script Supervising and Film Continuity* (Boston: Focal Press, 1986). Norman Hollyn's *The Film Editing Room Handbook* (New York: Arco, 1984) offers a detailed account of image and sound editing procedures. See also "Designed for Film," *Film Comment* **14,** 3 (May–June 1978): 25–60, on the set designer's role.

The techniques of special effects receive detailed discussion in a superbly designed magazine, *Cinefex*. The role of the screenwriter has been a recurrent subject of discussion in such works as Eugene Vale, *The Technique of Screenplay Writing* (New York: Grosset & Dunlap, 1972); Lewis Herman, *A Practical Manual of Screen Playwriting for Theater and Television Films* (New York: New American Library, 1974); Syd Field, *Screenplay: The Foundations of Screenwriting* (New York: Delta, 1979); and Linda Seger, *Making a Good Script Great* (New York: Dodd, Mead, 1987). Information about the script versions of *Witness* can be found in Seger's book.

Anecdotal biographies and chatty memoirs of stars, directors, producers, and other personnel offer some insight into historical aspects of production. But there are some excellent, detailed case studies of the making of particular films. See Rudy Behlmer, *America's Favorite Movies: Behind the Scenes* (New York: Ungar, 1982); Aljean Harmetz, *The Making of "The Wizard of Oz"* (New York: Limelight, 1984); François Truffaut's "Diary of the Making of *Fahrenheit 451*," in *Cahiers du cinéma in English* **5, 6,** and **7** (1966); Ronald Haver, *A Star Is Born: The Making of the 1954 Movie and Its 1985 Restoration* (New York: Knopf, 1988); Spike Lee, *Uplift the Race: The Construction of "School Daze"* (New York: Simon and Schuster, 1988); and John Sayles, *Thinking in Pictures: The Making of the Movie "Matewan"* (Boston: Houghton Mifflin, 1987).

There are fewer studies of individual and collective film production, but here are some informative works. On Jean Rouch, see Mick Eaton, ed., *Anthropology— Reality—Cinema: The Films of Jean Rouch* (London: British Film Institute, 1979). The makers of *Harlan County, U.S.A.* and other independent documentaries discuss their production methods in Alan Rosenthal, *The Documentary Conscience: A Casebook in Film Making* (Berkeley: University of California Press, 1980). Maya Deren's work is discussed in P. Adams Sitney, *Visionary Film: The American Avant-Garde, 1943–1978*, 2d ed. (New York: Oxford University Press, 1979). Stan Brakhage ruminates on his approach to filmmaking in *Brakhage Scrapbook: Collected Writings* (New Paltz, N.Y.: Documentext, 1982). For information on other experimentalists, see Scott MacDonald, *A Critical Cinema: Interviews with Independent Filmmakers* (Berkeley: University of California Press, 1988). Collective film production is the subject of Guy Hennebelle, "*SLON:* Working Class Cinema in France," *Cinéaste* **5,** 2 (Spring 1972): 15–17; Bill Nichols, *Newsreel: Documentary Filmmaking on the American Left* (New York: Arno, 1980); Michael Renov, "Newsreel: Old and New—Towards an Historical Profile," *Film Quarterly* **41,** 1 (Fall 1987): 20–33. Collective production in film and other media is discussed in John Downing, *Radical Media: The Political Experience of Alternative Communication* (Boston: South End Press, 1984).

Historians are beginning to study film production seriously. For the American film industry we have economic accounts such as Douglas Gomery's *The Hollywood Studio System* (London: Macmillan, 1985), which deals with production in relation to distribution and exhibition. Bordwell, Staiger, and Thompson's *The Classical Hollywood Cinema* (cited in the previous section) discusses the history of studio production practices and their relation to the development of American industry.

For an examination of an early period, see Janet Staiger, " 'Tame' Authors and the Corporate Laboratory: Stories, Writers, and Scenarios in Hollywood," *Quarterly Review of Film Studies* **8,** 4 (Fall 1983): 33–45; a historical overview is Tom Stempel, *FrameWork: A History of Screenwriting in the American Film* (New York: Continuum, 1988).

Other writers are turning their attention to current film production practices. An excellent overview of contemporary studio filmmaking is provided by David Pirie, ed., *Anatomy of the Movies* (New York: Macmillan, 1981). Other discussions include David Lees and Stan Berkowitz, *The Movie Business* (New York: Vintage, 1981); Jason E. Squire, ed., *The Movie Business Book* (Englewood Cliffs, N.J.: Prentice-Hall, 1982); Eric Taub, *Gaffers, Grips, and Best Boys* (New York: St. Martin's, 1987); and David Chell, *Moviemakers at Work* (Redmond, Wash.: Microsoft, 1987). See also Douglas Gomery, "The American Film Industry of the 1970s," *Wide Angle* **5,** 4 (1983): 52–59.

Types of films distinguished by their production practices include documentary, compilation, and animated films. For documentaries, see Richard Meran Barsam, *Nonfiction Films: A Critical History* (New York: Dutton, 1973); Erik Barnouw, *Documentary: A History of the Nonfiction Film* (New York: Oxford University Press, 1974); and John Grierson, *Grierson on Documentary* (London: Faber and Faber, 1966). A history of the compilation film may be found in Jay Leyda, *Films Beget Films* (New York: Hill & Wang, 1964). The standard works on film animation are John Halas and Roger Manvell, *The Technique of Film Animation* (New York: Hastings House, 1968), and Ralph Stephenson, *Animation in the Cinema* (New York: Barnes, 1967). More recent studies include Donald Crafton, *Before Mickey: The Animated Film, 1898–1928* (Cambridge: MIT Press, 1982), and Leonard Maltin, *Of Mice and Magic: A History of American Animated Cartoons* (New York: New American Library, 1980).

The relation between modes of film production and social organization as a whole has been explored very little. Ian Jarvie's *Movies and Society* (New York: Basic Books, 1970) compares methods of socialization in studio film production with those in other areas of life. A good introduction to twentieth-century modes of production is Harry Braverman's *Labor and Monopoly Capital* (New York: Monthly Review Press, 1974).

Issues of reception are addressed in Bruce A. Austin's *Immediate Seating: A Look at Movie Audiences* (Belmont, Calif.: Wadsworth, 1988).

## ■ FILM AND VIDEO

Roy Armes's *On Video* (New York: Routledge, 1988) provides a general consideration of film and video on technical, aesthetic, and cultural grounds. A detailed comparison of film and video technology can be found in Harry Mathias and Richard Patterson, *Electronic Cinematography: Achieving Photographic Control over the Video Image* (Belmont, Calif.: Wadsworth, 1985). John Belton has written several essays on pan-and-scan practices; two of the most informative are "Pan and Scan Scandals," *The Perfect Vision* **1,** 3 (Indian summer 1987): 40–49, and "The Shape of Money," *Sight and Sound* **51,** 1 (Winter 1987/88): 44–47. Paolo Cherchai Usai sums up many of the problems of watching film on video in "The Unfortunate Spectator," *Sight and Sound* **56,** 3 (Summer 1987): 170–174.

What of the future? In 1981, the Japanese broadcasting company NHK demonstrated a video system composed of 1125 lines, a remarkable gain in definition (that is, sharpness and detail). Several different high-definition TV (HDTV) systems have now been developed, some of which may be tried out in tape or disc formats before one is adopted for broadcast and cable transmission. In the fall of 1988, the United States Federal Communications Commission announced that any high-definition system to be used in broadcast must be compatible with the 525-line standard. It is possible that in the United States a system using 1050 lines will eventually be settled on. HDTV is coming, and it will markedly improve the video image, perhaps raising it to the level of 16-mm projection. Still, any system currently under consideration falls short of the definition available on 35-mm color negative film, and even a 2000-line video display exhibits significant "breakup" in highlights and details. In addition, film technology will continue to advance; today's 16-mm film stocks have the quality of 35-mm stocks of a decade ago.

Good discussions of HDTV prospects are in Nicholas Bedworth's and Ray Trumbull's articles, "High Definition Television" (parts I and II), *The Perfect Vision* **1,** 3 (Indian summer 1987): 75–81.

## ■ AUTHORSHIP

Among students of film, no question starts an argument faster than "Who is the author of a studio-produced film?" Many disputes arise because the concept of authorship has at least three different meanings.

**Author as production worker.** This is the concern of this chapter. Some film scholars believe that the director of a studio film cannot be the author unless he or she seeks to fulfill every role personally. (An example is Charles Chaplin, who was producer, writer, director, composer, and star of his later films.) Other scholars maintain that although the director cannot do all those tasks, he or she must at least have overt veto control at every stage of production (as, say, Jacques Tati did and Federico Fellini does). In the view of still other scholars, the director's role provides the closest thing to a grasp of the totality of the shooting and assembly phases. Not that the director can do everything or make every choice. But the director's role is defined as a synthetic one, combining various contributions into a whole. This is the position we have taken in this book. A defense of the "director as orchestrator" view may be found in V. F. Perkins's *Film as Film* (Baltimore: Penguin, 1972), chapter 8.

**Author as personality.** In France in the 1950s young writers grouped around the magazine *Cahiers du cinéma* began to discover traces of "personal style" in Hollywood films. Attributing this personality to the director, they stressed the "Howard Hawks" flavor (love of action and professional stoicism), the "Alfred Hitchcock" flavor (suspense but also a brooding Catholic guilt), etc. This became known as the *politique des auteurs,* the "position of being for authors." The idea was taken up by Andrew Sarris in a series of now famous essays. "The strong director imposes his own personality on a film. . . . The auteur theory values the personality of a director precisely because of the barriers to its expression." (*The American Cinema* [New York: Dutton, 1968], p. 31.) Auteurism also became an evaluative method, enabling the *Cahiers du cinéma* critics and Sarris to establish rankings of auteurs and nonauteurs. (Sarris: Fred Zinneman has only a superficial "personal commitment" to direction, David Lean's *Doctor Zhivago* is a work of "the most impeccable impersonality.")

The *politique des auteurs* made a major step toward our understanding of film as art, but according to this conception, what constitutes "personality"? Film form and style? Certain preferred themes, stories, actors, genres? More recent Anglo-American auteur criticism tends to speak of the director's "personal vision" and recurrent "concerns." For a vigorous statement, see William Cadbury and Leland Poague, *Film Criticism: A Counter Theory* (Ames: Iowa State University Press, 1983). The major progenitor of this emphasis is Robin Wood's remarkable body of work on various directors; he defends his stance in *Personal Views* (London: Gordon Fraser, 1976).

**Author as a group of films.** In reaction to the notion of "personality," some have suggested that we regard the idea of the "author" as simply a critical construct. On this account, the critic would group films by *signature* of director, producer, screenwriter, or whatever. Thus *Citizen Kane* could belong to the "Orson Welles" group *and* to the "Herman Mankiewicz" group *and* to the "Gregg Toland" group, etc. The critic would then analyze the patterns of relations within a given group. This would mean that certain aspects of *Citizen Kane* interact with aspects of other films directed by Welles, or of other films written by Mankiewicz, or of other films photographed by Toland. The "author" is no longer a person, but, for the sake of analysis, a system of relations among several films bearing the same signature. Implications of this position are developed by Peter Wollen in *Signs and Meanings in the Cinema* (Bloomington: Indiana University Press, 1972): "Fuller or Hawks or Hitchcock, the directors, are quite separate from 'Fuller' or 'Hawks' or 'Hitchcock,' the structures named after them" (p. 168). This approach, of course, could be applied to independent works as well as to studio-produced films.

The 1960s and 1970s saw a great many disputes over the concept of authorship, such as the argument between proponents of the "director as auteur," led by Andrew Sarris (in *The American Cinema* and elsewhere) and proponents of the "screenwriter as auteur," led by Richard Corliss (in *The Hollywood Screenwriters* [New York: Avon, 1972] and *Talking Pictures* [New York: Penguin, 1974]). It is interesting that the Sarris–Corliss dispute does not distinguish among author as production worker, as personality, or as critical label, so at times the two critics are not talking about the same thing. After the initial interest in authorship in the cinema, many critics have taken a step back to differentiate and compare assumptions as we have here. John Caughie's useful anthology *Ideas of Authorship* (London: Routledge & Kegan Paul, 1981) and Steve Crofts's "Authorship and Hollywood," *Wide Angle* **5,** 3 (1983): 16–22, both categorize various approaches to authorship. Despite the difficulties and varieties of approach, some version of the director-as-author position remains probably the most widely shared assumption in film studies today. Most critical studios of cinema put the director at center stage, and so do several reference books: see, for example, Richard Roud, ed., *Cinema: A Critical Dictionary: The Major Film-Makers*, 2 vols. (New York: Viking, 1980) and Jean-Pierre Coursodon, ed., *American Directors*, 2 vols. (New York: McGraw-Hill, 1982).

A detailed consideration of how the personal life of the independent filmmaker can be a source of creative material is P. Adams Sitney, "Autobiography in Avant-Garde Film," *Millennium Film Journal* **1,** 1 (Winter 1977–78): 60–105.

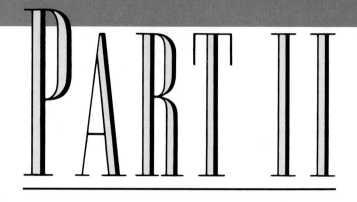

# PART II

## FILM FORM

"How are films made?" is an ambiguous question. We have given one answer: Films are made by people working with technology. But the question can also mean "By what principles is a film put together? How do the various parts relate to one another to create a whole?" These questions will take us into problems of cinema as an artistic medium.

In the next three chapters we will start to answer such aesthetic questions. We assume that a film is not a random collection of elements. If it were, people would not care if they missed the beginnings or endings of films or if films were projected out of sequence. But people do care. When you describe a book as "hard to put down" or a piece of music as "absorbing," you are implying that a pattern exists there, that an internal system governs the relations among parts and engages your interest. This system of relationships among parts we shall call form. Chapter 2 examines form in film to see what makes that concept so important to the understanding of cinema as an art.

One formal feature that commonly seizes our interest while viewing a film is its "story." Chapters 3 and 4 examine the different types of form that may occur in films—both narrative and nonnarrative form. We shall see there that not all films tell stories, and that whether or not a film does, we can examine that film's form; we can, that is, analyze how its parts relate to one another in ways which fascinate us.

# THE
# SIGNIFICANCE
# OF FILM FORM

If you are listening closely to a song on a tape and the tape is abruptly switched off, you are likely to feel frustrated. If you start reading a novel, become engrossed in it, and then misplace the book, you will probably feel the same way. Such feelings arise because our experience of artworks is patterned and structured; the mind craves form. For this reason, form is of central importance in any artwork, regardless of its medium. The entire study of the nature of artistic form is the province of the aesthetician; it is too large a question for us to deal with extensively here. (See the first part of the Notes and Queries to this chapter for pertinent readings.) But some ideas about aesthetic form are indispensible in analyzing films.

## ■ FORM AS SYSTEM

Artistic form is best thought of in relation to a perceiver, the human being who watches the play, reads the novel, listens to the piece of music, or views the film. Perception in all phases of life is an *activity*. As you walk down the street, you scan your surroundings for salient aspects—a friend's face, a familiar landmark, a sign of rain. The mind is never at rest; it is constantly seeking order and significance, testing the world for breaks in the habitual pattern. Artworks rely on this dynamic, unifying quality of the human mind. They provide organized occasions in which we exercise and develop our ability to pay attention, to anticipate upcoming events, to draw conclusions, and to construct a whole out of parts. Every novel leaves something to the imagination; every song asks us to expect a certain melody;

*Perception as activity*

every film coaxes us to connect sequences into a larger whole. But how does this process work? How does an inert object, the poem on a piece of paper or the sculpture in the park, draw us into such activities?

Some answers to this question are clearly inadequate. Our activity cannot be *in* the artwork itself. A poem is only words on paper; a song, just acoustic vibrations; a film, merely patterns of light and dark on a screen. Objects do nothing. On the other hand, the experience of the artwork cannot be completely private, locked in the mind of each perceiver. You cannot react to a poem unless you read it, or dance to a song without hearing it. Evidently, then, the artwork and the perceiver depend on one another. The best answer to our question would seem to be that the artwork *cues* us to perform a specific activity. Without the artwork's prompting, we could not start or maintain the process; without our playing along and picking up the cues, the artwork remains only an artifact. A painting uses color, line, and other techniques to invite us to imagine the space portrayed, to recall the moment before the one depicted or to anticipate the next one, to compare color and texture, to run our eye over the composition in a certain direction. A poem's words may guide us to imagine a scene, or to notice a break in rhythm, or to expect a rhyme. A piece of sculpture's shape, volume, and materials prompt us to move around it, anticipating and recalling how its mass may fill the space it occupies. In general, any work of art presents cues that can elicit a particular activity from the perceiver.

We can go further in describing how an artwork cues us to perform activities. These cues are not simply random; they are organized into *systems*. The idea of a system is straightforward: it is any set of elements that depend on and affect one another. The human body is one such system; if one component, the heart, ceases to function, all of the other parts will be in danger as well. Within the body there are individual, smaller systems, such as the nervous system or the optical system. A single small malfunction in a car's workings may bring the whole machine to a standstill; the other parts may not need repair, but the whole system depends on the operation of each part. Other, more abstract sets of relationships also constitute systems: a body of laws governing a country, for example, or the ecological balance of the wildlife in a lake.

As with each of these instances, a film is not simply a random batch of elements. Like all artworks, a film has **form.** By film form, in its broadest sense, we mean the total system that the viewer perceives in the film. Form is the overall system of relations that we can perceive among the elements in the whole film. In this part of the book and in Part III (on film style), we shall be surveying the sorts of elements a film may contain. Since the viewer makes sense of the film by recognizing these elements and reacting to them in various ways, we shall also be considering how form and style involve the spectator's activity.

This description of form is still very abstract, so let us draw some examples from one film that many people have seen. In *The Wizard of Oz* the perceiver can notice many particular elements. There is, most obviously, a set of *narrative* elements, which comprise the film's story. Dorothy dreams that a tornado blows her to Oz, where she encounters certain characters, and the narrative continues to the point when Dorothy awakens from her dream to find herself home in Kansas. We can also perceive a set of **stylistic** elements: the way the camera moves, the patterns of color in the frame, the use of music, and other devices. Stylistic elements derive from the various film techniques we shall be considering in later chapters.

Because *The Wizard of Oz* is a system and not just a hodgepodge, the perceiver actively relates the elements within each set to one another. We link and compare narrative elements: we see the tornado as causing Dorothy's trip to Oz; we identify

the characters in Oz as similar to characters in Dorothy's Kansas life. The stylistic elements can also be connected. For instance, we recognize the "We're Off to See the Wizard" tune whenever Dorothy picks up a new companion. We attribute unity to the film by positing two subsystems—a narrative one and a stylistic one—within the larger system of the total film.

Moreover, our minds seek to tie these subsystems to one another. In *The Wizard of Oz*, the narrative subsystem can be linked to the stylistic subsystem. Film colors identify prominent landmarks, such as Kansas (in black and white) and the Yellow Brick Road. Movements of the camera call our attention to story action. And the music serves to describe certain characters and actions. It is the overall pattern of relationships among the various subsystems of elements that makes up the form of the *The Wizard of Oz*.

## ■ "FORM VERSUS CONTENT"

Very often people assume that "form" as a concept is the opposite of something called "content." This assumption implies that a poem or a musical piece or a film is like a jug; an external shape, the jug, *contains* something that could just as easily be held in a cup or a pail. Under this assumption, form becomes less important than whatever it is presumed to contain.

We do not accept this assumption. If form is the total system which the viewer attributes to the film, there is no inside or outside. Every component *functions as part of* the overall pattern that is perceived. Thus we shall treat as formal elements many things that some people consider content. From our standpoint, subject matter and abstract ideas all enter into the total system of the artwork. They may cue us to frame certain expectations or draw certain inferences. The perceiver relates such elements to one another and makes them interact dynamically. Consequently, subject matter and ideas become somewhat different from what they might be outside the work.

For example, consider a historical subject, such as the United States Civil War. The real Civil War may be studied, its causes and consequences disputed. But in a film such as D. W. Griffith's *The Birth of a Nation* the Civil War is not neutral "content." It enters into relationships with other elements: a story about two families, political ideas about Reconstruction, and the epic film style of the battle scenes. The form of Griffith's film includes elements depicting the Civil War in a way that is coordinated with other elements in the film. A different film by another filmmaker might draw on the same subject matter, the Civil War, but there the subject would play a different role in a different formal system. In *Gone with the Wind* the Civil War functions as a backdrop for the heroine's romance, but in *The Good, the Bad, and the Ugly* the war aids three cynical men in their search for gold. Thus subject matter is shaped by the film's formal context and our perceptions of it.

## ■ FORMAL EXPECTATIONS

We are now in a better position to see how film form guides the audience's activity. An interrupted song or an uncompleted story brings frustration because of our urge for form; we realize that the system of relationships within the work has not yet been completed. Something more is needed to make the form whole and satisfying. We have been caught up in the interrelations among elements and want to understand how the cues prompt us to develop and complete the patterns.

How does form affect our experience of an artwork? For one thing, form creates the sense that "everything is there." Why is it satisfying when a character glimpsed early in a film reappears an hour later or when a shape in the frame is balanced by another shape? Because such relations among parts suggest that the film has its own organizing laws or rules—its own system.

Moreover, form intensely involves the audience. The appeal of form can be very great. In everyday life, we perceive things around us in a practical way. But in a film the things that happen on the screen serve no such practical end for us. We can see them differently. In life if a person fell down on the street, we would probably hurry to help the person up. But in a film when Buster Keaton or Charlie Chaplin falls, we laugh. We shall see in Chapter 6 how even as basic an act of filmmaking as framing a shot creates a new way of seeing. We watch a pattern which is no longer just "out there" in the everyday world, but which has become a calculated part within a self-contained whole. Film form can even make us perceive things anew, shaking us out of our accustomed habits and suggesting fresh ways of hearing, seeing, feeling, and thinking.

Try the following experiment (suggested by Barbara Herrnstein Smith). Assume that "A" is the first letter of a series. What follows?

1. AB

   "A" was a cue, and on this basis you made a formal hypothesis, probably that the letters would run in alphabetical order. Your expectation was confirmed. What follows AB? Most people say "C." But form does not always follow our initial expectation.

2. ABA

   Here form takes us by surprise, puzzles us. If we are puzzled by a formal development, we readjust our expectations and try again. What follows ABA?

3. ABAC

   Here the possibilities were chiefly two: ABAB or ABAC. (Note that your expectations *limit* possibilities as well as select them.) If you expected ABAC, your expectation was gratified and you can confidently predict the next letter. If you expected ABAB, you still should be able to make a strong hypothesis about the next letter.

4. ABACA

   Simple as this game is, it illustrates the involving power of form. You as a viewer or listener don't simply let the parts parade past you. You enter into an active participation with them, proposing and readjusting expectations about form as the experience develops.

Now consider a story in a film. *The Wizard of Oz* begins with Dorothy clutching her dog, Toto, and running down a road. Immediately, we form expectations: perhaps she will meet another character, or arrive at her destination. Even such a simple action asks that the audience participate actively in the ongoing process by making certain hypotheses about "what will happen next" and readjusting expectations accordingly.

Expectation pervades our experience of art. In reading a mystery story, we expect that a solution will be offered at some point, usually the end. In listening to a piece of music, we expect repetition of a melody or a motif. (Many musical pieces, in fact, follow the AB, ABA, and ABACA patterns we have just outlined.) In looking at a painting, we search for what we expect to be the most significant features, then scan the less prominent portions. From beginning to end, our involvement with a work of art depends largely on expectations.

This does not mean that the expectations must be immediately satisfied. The satisfaction of our expectations may be *delayed*. In our alphabet exercise, instead of presenting ABA we might have presented this:

AB . . . .

The series of periods postpones the revelation of the next letter, and you must wait to find it out. What we normally call *suspense* is simply a delay in fulfilling an established expectation. As the term implies, suspense leaves something "suspended"—not only the next phase in the pattern of elements but also our urge for completion.

Expectations may also be cheated, as when we expect ABC but get ABA. In general, *surprise* is a result of an expectation that is revealed to be incorrect. We do not expect that a gangster in 1930s Chicago will find a rocket ship in his garage; if he does, our reaction may require us to readjust our assumptions about what can happen in this story. (The example suggests that comedy often depends on cheating expectations.)

One more path of our expectations needs tracing. Sometimes an artwork will cue us to hazard guesses about what has come *before* this point in the work. When Dorothy runs down the road at the beginning of *The Wizard of Oz*, we wonder not only where she is going but where she has been and what she is fleeing from. Similarly, a painting or photograph may depict a scene that asks the viewer to speculate on some earlier event. Let us call this ability of the spectator to frame hypotheses about prior events *curiosity*. As Chapter 3 will show, curiosity is an important factor in narrative form.

It should be evident that artistic form may cue us to make expectations and then gratify them, either quickly or eventually. Or form may work to disturb our expectations. We often associate art with peace and serenity, but many artworks offer us conflict, tension, and shock. An artwork's form may even strike us as unpleasant because of its imbalances or contradictions. Many people find atonal music, abstract or surrealist painting, and experimental writing highly disturbing. Similarly, there are many important directors whose films jar rather than soothe us. As we shall see in examining the editing of Eisenstein's *October* (Chapter 7) or the ambiguous narrative in Resnais's *Last Year at Marienbad* (Chapter 10), a film may rely on contradictions and gaps. The point is not to condemn or wish away such films, but to understand that in disturbing us, such films still arouse *formal* expectations. Indeed, if we can adjust our expectations to a disturbing work, we may even become more deeply involved in our viewing of it than we would be with a work that gratifies our expectations easily. Such disturbing artworks may display new kinds of form to which we are not accustomed. Our initial disturbance may diminish as we grasp the work's unique formal system. Or some of these disturbing works may be less coherent than more traditional ones, but they reward analysis partly because they reveal to us our normal, implicit expectations about form. There are no limits to the number of possible formal arrangements which films can create, and our enjoyment of the cinema as a whole can only increase if we are prepared to explore the less familiar kinds of cues which challenging films offer us.

## ■ CONVENTIONS AND EXPERIENCE

Our ABAC example illustrates still another point. One guide to your hunches was *prior experience*. Your knowledge of the alphabet makes ABAX an unlikely alternative. This fact suggests that aesthetic form is not a pure activity isolated from other experiences. The idea that our perception of form depends on prior experience has important implications for both artist and spectator.

Precisely because artworks are human artifacts and because the artist lives in history and society, he or she cannot avoid relating the work, in some way, to other works and to aspects of the world in general. A tradition, a dominant style, a popular form—some such elements will be common to several different artworks. Such common traits are usually called *conventions*. For example, it is a convention of the musical film genre that characters sing and dance—a convention which (to return to our initial example) *The Wizard of Oz* firmly accepts. It is one convention of narrative form that the narrative solves the problems the characters confront, and the film likewise accepts this convention by letting Dorothy return to Kansas. Bodies of conventions constitute *norms* of what is appropriate or expected in a particular tradition. Through obeying or violating norms, artists relate their works to other works.

From the spectator's standpoint, the perception of artistic form will arise from cues within the work and from prior experiences. But although our *ability* to recognize formal cues may be innate, the *particular* habits and expectations we bring to the artwork will be guided by other experiences—experiences derived from everyday life and from other artworks. You were able to play the ABAC game because you had learned the English alphabet. You may have learned it in everyday life (in a classroom, from your parents) or from an artwork (as some children now learn the alphabet from television cartoons). Similarly, we are able to recognize the "journey" pattern in *The Wizard of Oz* because we have taken trips and because we have seen other films organized around this pattern (e.g., *Stagecoach* or *North by Northwest*), and because the pattern is to be found in other artworks, such as the *Odyssey* or *Alice's Adventures in Wonderland*. Our ability to spot cues, to see them as forming systems, and to create expectations is guided by our real-life experiences and our knowledge of formal conventions.

In recognizing film form, then, the audience must be prepared to understand formal cues through knowledge of life and of other artworks. But what if the two principles come into conflict? In ordinary life people don't simply start to sing and dance, as they do in *The Wizard of Oz*. Very often conventions demarcate art from life, saying implicitly, "In artworks of this sort the laws of everyday reality don't operate. By the rules of *this* game, something 'unreal' *can* happen." All stylized art, from opera, ballet, and pantomime to comedy and other genres, depends on the audience's willingness to suspend the laws of ordinary experience and to accept particular conventions. It is simply beside the point to insist that such conventions are unreal or to ask why Tristan sings to Isolde or why Buster Keaton doesn't smile. Very often the most relevant prior experience for perceiving form is not everyday experience but previous encounters with works having similar conventions.

**Genres,** or *types* of artworks, offer a persuasive set of examples of widely accepted conventional usage. If we expect a mystery story to eventually reveal a solution, this is not because of life experience—many real-life mysteries go unsolved—but because one "rule" of the mystery genre is that the puzzle will be solved at the end. Similarly, *The Wizard of Oz* is a musical, and this genre utilizes the convention that characters will sing and dance. Like other art media, film often asks us to adjust our expectations to the conventions which a particular genre uses.

Finally, we must recognize the extent to which artworks can create new conventions. A highly innovative work can at first seem odd because it refuses to conform to the rules we expect. Cubist painting, twelve-tone music, and the French "New Novel" of the 1950s seemed difficult initially because of their refusal to adhere to conventions. But a closer look may show that the unusual artwork has its own rules, creating an unorthodox formal system, which we can learn to recognize and respond to. Eventually, the new systems offered by such unusual works may themselves become models or new conventions and thus create new expectations.

## ■ FORM AND FEELING

Certainly emotion plays a large role in our experience of form. To understand this role, let us distinguish between emotions *represented in* the artwork and an emotional *response felt by* the spectator. If an actor grimaces in agony, the emotion of pain is *represented within the film*. If, on the other hand, the viewer who sees the painful expression laughs (as the viewer of a comedy might), the emotion of amusement is *felt by the spectator*. Both types of emotion have formal implications.

Emotions represented within the film interact as parts of the film's total system. For example, that grimace of pain might be reaffirmed by the contortions of the comedian's body. A character's sly expression may prepare us for the later revelation of his or her villainous side. Or a cheerful scene might stand in contrast to a mournful one. A tragic event might be undercut by humorous editing or music. All emotions present in a film may be seen as systematically related to one another through that film's form.

The spectator's emotional response to the film is related to form as well. We have just seen how cues in the artwork interact with our prior experience, especially our experience of artistic conventions. Often form in artworks appeals to ready-made reactions, already formulated emotions: fear of darkness or heights, or even stereotyped reactions to certain images (sexuality, race, social class). But form can create new responses instead of harping on old ones. Just as formal conventions often lead us to suspend our normal sense of real-life experience, so form may lead us to override our everyday emotional responses. People whom we would despise in life may become spellbinding as characters in a film. We can watch a film about a subject that normally repels us and find it fascinating. One cause of these experiences lies in the systematic way we become involved in form. In *The Wizard of Oz* we might, for example, find the land of Oz far more attractive than Kansas. But because the film's form leads us to sympathize with Dorothy in her desire to go home, we feel great satisfaction when she finally returns to Kansas.

It is first and foremost the dynamic aspect of form that engages our feelings. Expectation, for instance, spurs emotion. To make an expectation about "what happens next" is to invest some emotion in the situation. Delayed fulfillment of an expectation—suspense—may produce anxiety or sympathy. (Will the detective find the criminal? Will boy get girl? Will the melody return?) Cheated expectations and curiosity about past material may produce puzzlement or keener interest. (So he isn't the detective? This isn't a romance story? Has a second melody replaced the first one?) Gratified expectations may produce a feeling of satisfaction or relief. (The mystery is solved, boy does get girl, the melody returns one more time.) Note that all of these possibilities *may* occur. There is no general recipe by which a novel or film can be concocted to produce the "correct" emotional response. It is all a matter of context—that is, of the particular system that is each artwork's overall form. All we can say for certain is that the emotion felt by the spectator will emerge from the totality of formal relationships she or he perceives in the work. This is one reason why we should try to perceive as many formal relations as possible in a film; the richer our perception, the more exact and complex our response may become.

Taken in context, the relations between the feelings represented in the film and those felt by the spectator can be quite complex. Many people believe that no more sorrowful event can occur than the death of a child. In most films this event would be represented so as to summon up the sadness we would also feel in life. But the power of artistic form can alter the emotional tenor of even this event. In Jean Renoir's *The Crime of M. Lange* the cynical publisher, Batala, rapes and abandons the young laundress, Estelle. After Batala disappears, Estelle becomes integrated into the courtyard community and returns to her former fiancé. But Estelle is pregnant by Batala and bears his child. The scene when Estelle's employer, Valentine, announces that the child was born dead is one of the most emotionally complex in cinema. The first emotions represented are solemn sorrow: the characters display grief. Suddenly Batala's cousin remarks, "Too bad. It was a relative." In the film's context this is taken as a joke, and the other characters break out in smiles and laughter. The shift in the emotion represented in the film catches us off guard. Since these characters are not heartless, we must readjust our reaction to the death and respond as they do—with relief. That Estelle has survived is far more important than the death of Batala's child. The film's formal development has rendered appropriate a reaction that might be perverse in ordinary life. This is a daring, extreme example, but it dramatically illustrates how both emotions onscreen and our responses are dependent on the context created by form.

### ■ FORM AND MEANING

Like emotion, meaning is important to our experience of artworks. As an active perceiver, the spectator is constantly testing the work for significance. The sorts of meanings that the spectator attributes to the work may vary considerably. Let us look at four assertions about the meaning of *The Wizard of Oz*.

1. *In the Depression, a cyclone takes a girl from her family's Kansas farm to the mythical land of Oz; after a series of adventures, she returns home.*

This is very concrete, close to a bare-bones plot summary. Here the significance depends on the spectator's ability to identify specific items: a period of American history called the Depression, a place known as Kansas, features of midwestern climate. A viewer who was unacquainted with such information would miss some of the meaning cued by the film. We can call such tangible meanings **referential,** since the film *refers* to things or places already invested with significance. A film's subject matter—in *The Wizard of Oz*, American Midwestern farm life in the 1930s—is often established through referential meaning. And, as one would expect, referential meaning functions within the film's overall form, in the way that we have argued that the subject of the Civil War functions within *The Birth of a Nation*. Suppose that instead of having Dorothy live in flat, spare, rural Kansas, the film made Dorothy a child living in Beverly Hills. When she got to Oz (transported there, perhaps, by a hillside flash flood), the contrast between the crowded opulence of Oz and her home would not be nearly so sharp. Here the referential meanings of "Kansas" play a definite role in the overall contrast of settings that the film's form creates.

2. *A girl dreams of leaving home to escape her troubles; only after she leaves does she realize how much her home means to her.*

This assertion is still fairly concrete in the meaning it attributes to the film. If someone were to ask you the "point" of the film—what it seems to be trying to "get across"—you might answer with something like this. Perhaps you would also mention Dorothy's closing line, "There's no place like home," as a summary of what she learns. Let us call this sort of openly asserted meaning an *explicit* meaning.

Like referential meanings, explicit meanings function within the film's overall form; they are defined by context. For instance, we are inclined to take "There's no place like home" as a statement of the meaning of the entire film. But, first, *why* do we feel that as a strongly meaningful line? In ordinary conversation it is a cliché. In context, however, the line is uttered in close-up, it comes at the end of the film (a formally privileged moment), and it refers back to all of Dorothy's desires and ordeals, recalling the film's narrative development toward her achievement of her goal. It is the *form* of the film that gives the familiar saying an unfamiliar weight.

This example suggests that we must examine how explicit meanings in a film interact with other elements of the overall system. If "There's no place like home" adequately and exhaustively summarizes the meaning of *The Wizard of Oz*, no one need ever see the film; the summary would suffice. But like feelings, meanings are formal entities; they play a part along with other elements to make up the total system. We usually cannot isolate a particularly significant moment and declare it to be *the* meaning of the whole film. Even Dorothy's "There's no place like home," however strong as a summary of *one* meaningful element in *The Wizard of Oz*, must be placed in the context of the film's entire beguiling Oz fantasy. If "There's no place like home" were the whole point of the film, why is there so much that is pleasant in Oz? The explicit meanings of a film arise from the *whole* film and are set in dynamic formal relation to one another.

In trying to see the meaningful moments of a film as parts of a larger whole, it is useful to set individually significant moments against one another. Thus Dorothy's final line could be juxtaposed to the scene of the characters getting spruced up after their arrival at the Emerald City. We can try to see the film as not "about" one or the other but rather about the relation of the two—the risk and delight of a fantasy world versus the comfort and stability of home. Thus the film's total system will be larger than any one explicit meaning we find in it. Instead of asking, "What is this film's meaning?" we can ask, "How do *all* the film's meanings interrelate formally?"

**3.** *An adolescent who must soon face the adult world yearns for a return to the simple world of childhood, but she eventually accepts the demands of adulthood.*

This is considerably more abstract than the first two statements. It assumes something that goes beyond what is explicitly stated in the film: that *The Wizard of Oz* is in some sense "about" the passage from childhood to adulthood. On this view, the film suggests or *implies* that, in adolescence, people may desire to return to the apparently uncomplicated world of childhood. Dorothy's frustration with her aunt and uncle and her urge to flee to a place "over the rainbow" are used to illustrate a general conception of adolescence. Let us call this suggested meaning an *implicit* one. When perceivers produce implicit meanings from an artwork, they are usually said to be *interpreting* it.

Clearly, interpretations vary. One viewer might propose that *The Wizard of Oz* is really about adolescence; another might suggest that it is really about courage and persistence; or that it is a satire on the adult world. One of the appeals of artworks is that they seem to ask us to interpret them, often in several ways at once. Again, the artwork cues the spectator to perform certain activities—here, the teasing out of implicit meanings. But once again the artwork's overall form shapes the search for implicit meanings.

Some viewers approach a film expecting to learn great lessons about life. They may admire a film because it conveys a profound or relevant message. Important as meaning is, though, this attitude often errs by splitting the film into the content portion (the meaning) and the form (the vehicle for the content). The abstract quality of implicit meanings can lead to very broad concepts (often called *themes*): This film is about courage, that film is about love. Such descriptions have some value, but they are very general; hundreds of films fit them. To summarize *The Wizard of Oz* as being simply about the problems of adolescence does not do justice to the specific qualities of the film as an experience. The search for implicit meanings should not leave behind the *particular* and *concrete* features of a film.

This is not to say that we should not interpret films. But we should strive to make our interpretations precise by seeing how each film's thematic meanings are suggested by the film's total system. In a film, both explicit and implicit meanings depend closely on the relations among the elements of narrative and style. In *The Wizard of Oz* the visual element called "the Yellow Brick Road" has no meaning in and of itself. But if we examine the function it fulfills in relation to the narrative, the music, the colors, and so on, we can see that the Yellow Brick Road does indeed function meaningfully. Dorothy's strong desire to go home makes the Road represent that desire. We want Dorothy to be successful in getting to the end of the Road, as well as in getting back to Kansas; thus the Road participates in the theme of the desirability of home.

But interpretation of meaning need not be an end in itself; it helps in understanding the overall form of the film. Nor does interpretation exhaust the possibilities of a device. We can say many things about the Yellow Brick Road other than how its meaning relates to the film's thematic material. We could analyze how the Road becomes the stage for dances and songs along the way; we could see how it is narratively important because an indecision at a crossroads delays Dorothy long enough to meet the Scarecrow; we could work out a color scheme for the film, contrasting the yellow road, the red slippers, the green Emerald City, and so forth. From this standpoint, interpretation may be seen as one kind of formal analysis, one that seeks to analyze a film's implicit meanings. But those meanings should be constantly tested by reimmersing them in the concrete texture of the whole film.

4.  *In a society where human worth is measured by money, home and family may seem to be the last refuge of human values. This belief is especially strong in times of economic crisis, such as that in the United States in the 1930s.*

Like the third statement, this is abstract and general. It situates the film within a trend of thought which is assumed to be characteristic of American society during the 1930s. The claim could apply equally well to many other films, as well as to many novels, plays, poems, paintings, advertisements, radio shows, political speeches, and a host of cultural products of the period. But there is something worth noticing beyond the sweep of the statement. It treats an explicit meaning in *The Wizard of Oz* ("There's no place like home") as a manifestation of a wider set of values characteristic of a whole society. We could treat implicit meanings the same way. If we say the film implies something about adolescence as a crucial time of transition, we could suggest that this emphasis on adolescence as a special period of life is also a recurrent concern of American society. In other words, it is possible to understand a film's explicit or implicit meanings as bearing traces of a particular set of social values. We can call this sort of meaning **symptomatic meaning**, and the set of values that get revealed can be considered to be a social **ideology.**

*symptomatic meanings.*

The possibility of noticing symptomatic meanings reminds us that all meaning, whether referential, explicit, or implicit, is a social phenomenon. Many meanings in a film are ultimately ideological; that is, they spring from systems of culturally specific beliefs about the world. Religious beliefs, political opinions, conceptions of race or sex or social class, even our most unconsciously held, deep-seated notions of life—all these constitute our ideological frame of reference. Although we live as if our beliefs were the only true and real explanations of how the world is, we need only compare our own ideology with that of another group or culture or historical period to see how historically and socially shaped those views are. In other times or places, "Kansas" or "home" or "adolescence" do not carry the meanings they carry in twentieth-century America.

*ideological frame of reference.*

Thus films, like other artworks, can be subject to viewers' searches for symptomatic meanings. Again, however, the abstract and general quality of such meanings can lead us away from the concrete form of the film. Just as when analyzing implicit meanings, the viewer should strive to ground symptomatic meaning in the film's specific aspects. A film *enacts* ideological meanings through its particular and unique formal system. We shall see in Part IV how the narrative and stylistic systems of *Meet Me in St. Louis* and *Tout va bien* can be analyzed for ideological implications.

In short, films "have" meaning only because we attribute meanings to them. We cannot therefore regard meaning as a simple product to be extracted from the film. Our minds will probe an artwork for significance at several levels, seeking referential meanings, explicit meanings, implicit meanings, and symptomatic meanings. The more abstract and general our attributions of meaning, the more we risk loosening our grasp on the film's specific formal system. As analysts, we must balance our concern for that concrete system with our urge to assign it wider significance.

## ■ EVALUATION

In talking about an artwork, people often *evaluate* it, that is, they make claims about its goodness or badness. Reviews in popular magazines exist almost solely to tell us whether a film is worth seeing; our friends often urge us to go to their latest favorite. But all too often we discover that the film that someone else esteemed appears only mediocre to us. At that point we may bemoan the fact that most people evaluate films only on the basis of their own, often idiosyncratic, tastes.

How, then, are we to evaluate films with any degree of objectivity? We can start by realizing that there is a difference between personal taste and evaluative judgment. To say "I like this film" or "I hated it" is not equal to saying "It's a good film" or "It's wretched." There are very few people in the world whose enjoyment is limited only to the greatest works. Most people can enjoy a film they know is not particularly good. This is perfectly reasonable—unless they start trying to convince people that these pleasant films actually rank among the undying masterpieces. At that point others will probably stop listening to their judgments at all.

We may set aside, therefore, personal preference as the sole basis for judging a film's quality. Instead, the critic who wishes to make a relatively objective evaluation will use specific *criteria*. A criterion is a standard which can be applied in the judgment of many works; in this way, the critic gains a basis for comparing films for relative quality.

There are many different criteria. Some people evaluate films on "realistic" criteria, that is, whether the film conforms to their view of reality. Aficionados of military history might judge a film entirely on whether the battle scenes use historically accurate weaponry; the narrative, editing, characterization, sound, and visual style might be of little interest to them. Other people condemn films because they don't find the action plausible; they will dismiss a scene by saying, "Who'd really believe that X would meet Y just at the right moment?" But we have already seen that artworks often violate laws of reality and operate by their own conventions and internal rules.

Viewers can also use moral criteria to evaluate films. Most narrowly, aspects of the film can be judged outside their context in the film's formal system. Some viewers might feel any film with nudity or profanity is bad, while other viewers might find just these aspects praiseworthy. More broadly, viewers and critics may employ moral criteria to evaluate a film's overall significance, and here the film's complete formal system becomes pertinent. A film might be judged moral because of its overall view of life, its willingness to show opposed points of view, or its emotional range.

While "realistic" and moral criteria are well-suited to particular purposes, this book will suggest criteria that assess films as artistic wholes. Such criteria should allow us to take each film's form into account as much as possible; we can see whether the film succeeds, on its own terms, in creating a set of formal relationships.

One such criterion is *complexity*. We can argue that complex films (*not* simply complicated films) are good insofar as they engage our perception on many levels, create a multiplicity of relations among many separate formal elements, and tend to create interesting formal patterns. A second formal criterion might be *originality*. Originality for its own sake is pointless, of course; just because something is different does not mean that it is good. But if an artist takes a familiar convention and uses it in a way that makes it fresh again or creates a new set of formal possibilities, then (all other things being equal) the resulting work may be considered good from an aesthetic standpoint.

*Coherence* is yet another criterion; unity has traditionally been held to be a positive factor of artworks. So too has *intensity of effect:* if an artwork is vivid, striking, and emotionally engaging, it may be considered more valuable.

Note that all these criteria are matters of degree. One film may be more complex than another, but the second film may be more complex than a third one. Moreover, there is often a give and take among the criteria. A film might be very complex but lacking in coherence or intensity; ninety minutes of a black screen would make for an original film but not a very complex one; a "slasher" movie may create great intensity in certain scenes but be wholly unoriginal, as well as disorganized and simplistic. In applying the criteria, the analyst must often weigh one against another.

Evaluation can serve many useful ends. It can call attention to neglected artworks or make us rethink our attitudes toward accepted classics. But just as the discovery of meanings is not the end point of formal analysis, we ought not to see ourselves as primarily setting out to establish what the great films are. General statements ("This is a masterpiece") seldom enlighten us very much. Usually an evaluation is helpful insofar as it points to aspects of the film and shows us relations and qualities we have missed. Like interpretation, evaluation is most useful when it drives us back to the film itself as a formal system, helping us to understand that system better.

In reading this book, you will find that we have generally minimized evaluation. We think that most of the films and sequences we analyze are more or less good on the formal criteria we mentioned, but the purpose of this book is not to persuade you to accept a list of cinema masterpieces. Rather, we believe that if we show in detail how films may be understood as artistic systems, you will have an informed basis for whatever evaluations you wish to make.

## ■ SUMMARY

If one issue has governed our treatment of aesthetic form, it might be said to be concreteness. Form is a specific system of patterned relationships we perceive in any artwork. Such a concept lets us see how even elements of what is normally considered "content"—subject matter, or abstract ideas—take on specific and unique functions within any artwork. Our experience of an artwork is also a concrete one. Picking up cues in the work, we create specific expectations which are aroused, guided, delayed, cheated, satisfied, or disturbed. We undergo curiosity, suspense, and surprise. We compare the particular aspects of the artwork with general conventions which we know from life and from art. Emotions and meanings become specified and qualified through the concrete context of the artwork. And even when we apply general criteria in evaluating artworks, we ought to use those criteria to help us discriminate more, to penetrate more deeply into the particular aspects of the artwork. The rest of this book is devoted to studying these properties of aesthetic form in cinema.

## PRINCIPLES OF FILM FORM

Because film form is a system—that is, a unified set of related, interdependent elements—there must be some principles which help create the relationships among the parts. In disciplines other than the arts, principles may be sets of rules. In the physical sciences principles may take the form of mathematical propositions. For example, the design of an airplane must take into account principles of aerodynamics. The designer needs to determine the plane's form in relation to his or her knowledge of these principles.

In the arts, however, there are no absolute principles of form which all artists must follow. Artworks are products of culture; hence many of the principles of artistic form are matters of convention. For example, films that follow one particular set of formal principles are widely recognized as "Westerns." The artist obeys (or disobeys) norms, bodies of conventions, not laws.

But within these social conventions, each artwork tends to set up its own specific formal principles. The forms of different films can vary enormously. We can distinguish, however, five general principles which the spectator perceives in a film's formal system: function, similarity and repetition, difference and variation, development, and unity/disunity.

## ■ FUNCTION

If form in cinema is the overall interrelation among various systems of elements, we can assume that every element in this totality has one or more **functions.**

That is, every element will be seen as fulfilling one or more roles within the whole system.

Of any element within a film we can ask: What are its functions? In our example of *The Wizard of Oz*, every element in the film fulfills one or more roles. For instance, Miss Gulch, the woman who wants to take Toto from Dorothy, reappears in the Oz section as the Witch. In the opening portion of the film Miss Gulch causes Dorothy to run away from home; in Oz the Witch seeks to prevent Dorothy from returning home by keeping her away from the Emerald City and by trying to take the ruby slippers. Even an element as apparently minor as the dog Toto serves many functions. The dispute over Toto causes Dorothy to run away from home and to get back too late to take shelter from the cyclone; and later Toto's chasing of a cat makes Dorothy jump out of the ascending balloon and miss her chance to go back to Kansas. Even Toto's gray color, set off against the brightness of Oz, creates a link to the black and white of the Kansas episodes at the film's beginning. Functions, then, are almost always multiple; both narrative and stylistic elements have functions.

One useful way to grasp the function of an element is to ask what other elements demand that it be present. Thus the narrative requires that Dorothy run away from home, so Toto functions to motivate this action. Or, to take another example, Dorothy must be distinguished from the Wicked Witch, so costume, age, voice, and other characteristics function to contrast the two. Finally, the switch from black and white to color film functions to signal the arrival in the bright fantasy land of Oz.

Note that the concept of function does not depend on the filmmaker's intention. Often discussions of films get bogged down in the question of whether the filmmaker "knew what he or she was doing" in including this or that element. In asking about function, we do not ask for a production history. From the standpoint of intention, Dorothy may sing "Over the Rainbow" because singing a song was in Judy Garland's MGM contract. But, from the standpoint of function, we can say that Dorothy's singing that song fulfills certain narrative and stylistic functions. (It establishes her desire to leave home, its reference to the rainbow foreshadows her trip through the air to the color Oz sequences, etc.) In asking about formal function, therefore, we ask not, "How did this element get there?" but rather, "What is this element *doing* there?"

One way to notice the functions of an element is to consider the element's **motivation.** Because films are human constructs, we can expect that any one element in a film will have some logical justification for being there. This justification is the motivation for that element. For example, when Miss Gulch appears as the Witch in Oz, we justify her new incarnation by appealing to the fact that early scenes in Kansas have established her as a threat to Dorothy. When Toto jumps from the balloon to chase a cat, we motivate his action by appealing to notions of how dogs are likely to act when cats are around.

Sometimes people use the word "motivation" to apply only to reasons for characters' actions, as when a murderer acts from motives such as hatred. Here, however, we will use "motivation" to apply to any element in the film which the viewer justifies on some grounds. A costume, for example, needs motivation. If we see a man in beggar's clothes in the middle of an elegant society ball, we will ask why he is dressed in this way. He could be the victim of practical jokers who have deluded him into believing that this is a masquerade. He could be an eccentric millionaire out to shock his friends. Such a scene does occur in *My Man Godfrey*. The motivation for the beggar's presence at the ball is a scavenger hunt; the young society people have been assigned to bring back, among other things, a beggar. An event, the hunt, *motivates* the presence of an inappropriately dressed character.

Motivation is so common in films that spectators tend to take it for granted. The presence of a candle in a room motivates the fact that we can see the characters. (We may be aware that the source of the light is actually not just the candle, but the candle is the ostensible source and motivates the light.) The movement of a character across a room may motivate the moving of the camera to follow the action and keep the character within the frame. When we study principles of narrative form (Chapter 3) and nonnarrative form (Chapter 4), we will look more closely at how motivation works to give elements specific functions.

## ■ SIMILARITY AND REPETITION

In our example of the ABACA pattern, we saw how we were able to predict the next steps in the series. One reason for this was that there was a regular pattern of repeated elements. Like beats in music or meter in poetry, the repetition of the A's in our pattern established and satisfied formal expectations. Similarity and repetition, then, compose an important principle of film form.

Repetition is basic to our understanding any film. For instance, we must be able to recall and identify characters and settings each time they reappear. More subtly, throughout any film we can observe repetitions of everything from lines of dialogue and bits of music to camera positions, characters' behavior, and story action. It is useful to have a term to help describe formal repetitions, and the most common term is **motif.** We shall call *any significant repeated element in a film a motif.* A motif may be an object, a color, a place, a person, a sound, or even a character trait. We may call a pattern of lighting or camera position a motif if it is repeated through the course of a film. The form of *The Wizard of Oz* utilizes all of these kinds of motifs. Even in such a relatively simple film, we can see the pervasive presence of similarity and repetition as formal principles.

Film form utilizes general similarities as well as exact duplication. To understand *The Wizard of Oz*, we must see the similarities between the three Kansas farmhands and the three figures Dorothy meets along the Yellow Brick Road; we must notice that the itinerant Kansas fortune teller bears a striking resemblance to the old charlatan posing as the Wizard of Oz. The duplication is not perfect, but the similarity is very strong. This is an example of *parallelism,* the process whereby the film cues the spectator to compare two or more distinct elements by highlighting some similarity. Motifs can assist in creating parallelism. The viewer will notice, and even come to expect, that every time Dorothy meets a character in Oz, the scene will end with the song "We're Off to See the Wizard." Our recognition of parallelism provides part of our pleasure in watching a film, much as the echo of rhymes contributes to the power of poetry.

## ■ DIFFERENCE AND VARIATION

The form of a film could hardly be composed only of repetitions. AAAAAA is pretty boring. There must also be some changes or variations, however small. Thus difference is another fundamental principle of film form.

We can readily understand the need for variety, contrast, and change in films. Characters must be distinguished, environments must be delineated, different times or activities must be established. Even within the image, we must distinguish differences in tonality, texture, direction and speed of movement, and so on. Form needs its stable "background" of similarity and repetition, but it also demands that differences be created.

This means that although motifs (scenes, settings, actions, objects, stylistic devices) may be repeated, those motifs will seldom be repeated *exactly*. Variation will appear. In our chief example, *The Wizard of Oz*, the three Kansas hired hands are not exactly the same as their "twins" in Oz. (Parallelism thus requires a degree of difference, as well as striking similarity.) The repeated motif of Toto's disruption of a situation does not always function in the same way either: in Kansas it disturbs Miss Gulch and induces Dorothy to take Toto away, but in Oz Toto's disruption *prevents* Dorothy from going away. Even though Dorothy's determination to return home is a stable and recurrent motif, it expresses itself in varied ways because of the different obstacles she encounters.

Differences among the elements may often sharpen into downright opposition among them. We are most familiar with formal oppositions as conflicts among characters. It is true that character conflict is an important formal phenomenon, but we can situate it within the larger formal principle of difference. Thus not only characters but also settings, actions, and other elements may be opposed. In *The Wizard of Oz* Dorothy's desires are opposed, at various points, by the differing desires of Aunt Em, Miss Gulch, the Wicked Witch, and the Wizard, so that the film's formal system derives many dynamics from characters in conflict. But there are also color oppositions: black-and-white Kansas versus colorful Oz, Dorothy in red, white, and blue versus the Witch in black, and so on. Settings are opposed as well—not only Oz versus Kansas but also the various locales within Oz and especially the Emerald City versus the Witch's castle. Voice quality, musical tunes, and a host of other elements play off against one another, demonstrating that any motif may be opposed by any other motif.

Not all differences are simple oppositions, of course. Dorothy's three Oz friends—the Scarecrow, the Tin Woodman, and the Lion—are distinguished not only by external features but by means of a three-term comparison of what they lack (brains, a heart, courage). Other films may rely on less sharp differences, suggesting a scale of gradations among the characters, as in Jean Renoir's *Rules of the Game*. At the extreme, an abstract film may create minimal variations among its parts, such as in the very slight changes that accompany each return of the same footage in J. J. Murphy's *Print Generation*.

Repetition and variation are two sides of the same coin. To notice one is to notice the other. In analyzing films we ought to look for similarities *and* differences. Constantly poised between the two, we can point out motifs and contrast the changes they undergo, recognize parallelisms as a repetition and still spot the crucial variations.

## ■ DEVELOPMENT

One way to keep ourselves aware of how similarity and difference operate in film form is to look for principles of development from part to part of the film. Development will constitute some patterning of similar and differing elements. Our pattern ABACA is based not only on repetition (the recurring motif of A) and difference (the varied insertion of B and C) but also on a principle of *progression* which we could state as a rule (alternate A with successive letters in alphabetical order). Though simple, this is a principle of *development*, governing the form of the whole series.

Think of formal development as *a progression moving from X through Y to Z*. For example, the story of *The Wizard of Oz* shows development in many ways. It

is, first, a *journey:* from Kansas through Oz to Kansas. Many films possess such a journey plot. *The Wizard of Oz* is not only a journey, but also a *search* beginning with an initial separation from home, tracing a series of efforts to find a way home (e.g., to convince the Wizard to help), and ending with the object (Kansas, home) being found. Within the film there is also a pattern of *mystery,* which usually has the same from-X-through-Y-to-Z pattern: We begin with a question (Who is the Wizard of Oz?), pass through attempts to answer it, and conclude with the question answered (The Wizard is a fraud). Thus even such an apparently simple film is composed of several developmental patterns.

In order to analyze a film's pattern of development, it is usually a good idea to make a **segmentation.** A segmentation is simply a written outline of the film that breaks it into its major and minor parts, with the parts marked by consecutive numbers or letters. If a narrative film has ten scenes, then we can label each scene with a number running from one to ten. It may be useful to divide some parts further (for example, scenes 6a and 6b). Segmenting a film enables us not only to notice similarities and differences among parts but also to plot the overall progression of the form. A diagram may be a further help. In Chapters 3 and 4 we will consider how to segment different types of films.

Another way to size up how a film develops formally is to *compare the beginning with the ending.* By looking at the similarities and differences between the beginning and ending, we can start to understand the overall pattern of the film. We can test this advice on *The Wizard of Oz.* A comparison of the beginning and ending on the level of narrative reveals that the journey on which Dorothy initially sets out ends with her return home; the journey has been a search for an ideal place "over the rainbow" and has turned into a search for a way back to Kansas. The final scene repeats and develops the narrative elements of the opening. Stylistically, the beginning and ending are the only parts that use black-and-white film stock. This repetition supports the contrast the narrative creates between the dreamland of Oz and the bleak landscape of Kansas. The fortune teller, Professor Marvel, comes to visit Dorothy, reversing the situation of her visit to him when she had tried to run away. At the beginning he had convinced her to return home; then, as the Wizard in the Oz section, he had also represented her hopes to return home. Finally, when she recognizes Professor Marvel and the farmhands as the basis of the characters in her dream, she remembers how much she had wanted to come home from Oz.

Earlier, we suggested that film form engages our emotions and expectations in a dynamic way; now we are in a better position to see why. The constant interplay between similarity and difference, repetition and variation, leads the viewer to an active, developing awareness of the film's formal system. The film's development may be visualized in static terms, but we ought not to forget that formal development is a *process.*

## ■ UNITY/DISUNITY

All of the relationships among elements in a film create the total filmic system. Even if an element seems utterly out of place in relation to the rest of the film, we cannot really say that it "isn't part of the film." At most, the unrelated element is enigmatic or incoherent; it may be a flaw in the otherwise integrated system of the film—but it *does affect* the whole film.

When all of the relationships we perceive within a film are clear and economically interwoven, we say that the film has **unity.** We call a unified film "tight," because there seem to be no gaps in the formal relationships. Every element present has a specific set of functions, similarities and differences are determinable, the form develops logically, and there are no superfluous elements. Unity is, however, a matter of degree. Almost no film is so tight as to leave no end dangling, but if a film largely manages to create clear relations throughout its form, we tend to find it unified.

But some films may also introduce a degree of disunity. A film may simply fail to achieve unity; its formal system introduces elements and then fails to create clear relationships between them and the rest of the film. Such disunities are particularly noticeable when the filmic system as a whole is striving for unity. At one point in *The Wizard of Oz*, the Witch refers to her having attacked Dorothy and her friends with bees, yet we have never seen them, and the mention becomes puzzling. The sequence of the bee attack was shot but then cut from the finished film. The Witch's line now lacks motivation. More striking is a dangling element at the film's end. We never find out what happens to Miss Gulch; presumably she still has her legal order to take Toto away, but no one refers to this in the last scene. The viewer may be inclined to overlook this disunity, however, because Miss Gulch's parallel character, the Witch, has been killed off in the Oz fantasy and we do not expect to see her alive again.

But suppose we saw a film in which several characters die mysteriously, and we never find out how or why. This film leaves a number of loose ends, but the repetition suggests that the omission of clear explanations is not just a mistake. Our impression of a deliberate disunity would be reinforced if other elements of the film also failed to relate clearly to one another. Some films, then, create disunity as a positive quality of their form. This does not mean that these films become incoherent. Their disunity is *systematic,* and it is brought so consistently to our attention as to constitute a basic feature of the film. Inevitably such films will be formally disunified only to a relative degree; they have less unity than we may be used to but do not simply fall apart before our eyes. Later we shall see how films such as *Innocence Unprotected, Last Year at Marienbad,* and *Tout va bien* utilize formal disunity.

## SUMMARY

We can summarize the principles of film form as a set of questions which you can ask about any film.

1.  Of any element in the film, you can ask: What are its functions in the overall form? How is it motivated?
2.  Are elements or patterns repeated throughout the film? If so, how and at what points? Are motifs and parallelisms asking us to compare elements?
3.  How are elements contrasted and differentiated from one another? How are different elements opposed to one another?
4.  What principles of progression or development are at work throughout the form of the film? More specifically, how does a comparison of the beginning and ending reveal the overall form of a film?
5.  What degree of unity is present in the film's overall form? Is disunity subordinate to the overall unity, or does disunity dominate?

In this chapter we have examined some abstract and basic principles of film form. Armed with these general principles, we can press on to distinguish more specific *types* of form, the recognition of which is central for understanding film art.

## NOTES AND QUERIES

### ■ FORM IN VARIOUS ARTS

Many of the ideas in this chapter are based on ideas of form to be found in other arts. All of the following constitute helpful further reading: Monroe Beardsley, *Aesthetics* (New York: Harcourt Brace and World, 1958), especially chapters 4 and 5; Rudolf Arnheim, *Art and Visual Perception* (Berkeley: University of California Press, 1974), especially chapters 2, 3, and 9; Leonard Meyer, *Emotion and Meaning in Music* (Chicago: University of Chicago Press, 1956); Tzvetan Todorov, *Introduction to Poetics* (Minneapolis: University of Minnesota Press, 1981); Thomas Munro, *Form and Style in the Arts: An Introduction to Aesthetic Morphology* (Cleveland: Case Western Reserve University Press, 1970); René Wellek and Austin Warren, *Theory of Literature* (New York: Harcourt Brace and World, 1956); Victor Erlich, *Russian Formalism: History, Doctrine* (The Hague: Mouton, 1965); E. H. Gombrich, *Art and Illusion* (Princeton, N.J.: Princeton University Press, 1961).

### ■ THE CONCEPT OF FORM IN FILM

On the relation of form to the audience, see the book by Meyer mentioned above. The ABACA example is borrowed from Barbara Herrnstein Smith's excellent study of literary form, *Poetic Closure* (Chicago: University of Chicago Press, 1968). Compare Kenneth Burke's claim: "Form is the creation of an appetite in the mind of the auditor and the adequate satisfying of that appetite." (See Kenneth Burke, "Psychology and Form," *Counter-Statement* [Chicago: University of Chicago Press, 1957], pp. 29–44.) Gestalt psychology posited that the mind has innate form-making capacities, and this has made Gestalt thinkers strong contributors to conceptions of film form that stress audience response. See Rudolf Arnheim, *Film as Art* (Berkeley: University of California Press, 1957). For a more updated survey, see Julian Hochberg and Virginia Brooks, "The Perception of Motion Pictures," in Edward C. Carterette and Morton P. Freidman, eds., *Handbook of Perception*, vol. 10: *Perceptual Ecology* (New York: Academic Press, 1978), pp. 259–304.

Cognitive psychology, with its assumption that humans seek to make sense out of their environment by testing hypotheses and drawing inferences, offers many intriguing leads for an account of the spectator's activity. See Edward Branigan, *Point of View in the Cinema* (New York: Mouton, 1984), chapter 3, and David Bordwell, *Narration in the Fiction Film* (Madison: University of Wisconsin Press, 1985), chapter 3.

The dominant psychological paradigm for the spectator's absorption in the process of film form derives from Freudian psychoanalysis or its offshoots. A sampling of diverse approaches would include Christian Metz, *The Imaginary Signifier* (Bloomington: Indiana University Press, 1982); Robert T. Eberwein, *Film and the Dream Screen* (Princeton: Princeton University Press, 1984); Stephen

Heath, *Questions of Cinema* (Bloomington: Indiana University Press, 1981); Christine Gledhill, "Recent Developments in Feminist Film Theory," *Quarterly Review of Film Studies* **3,** 4 (Fall 1978): 457–493; Charles F. Altman, "Psychoanalysis and Cinema: The Imaginary Discourse," *Quarterly Review of Film Studies,* **2,** 3 (August 1977): 257–272; and Claude Bailblé, "Programming the Look," *Screen Education* 32/33 (Autumn/Winter 1979/80): 99–131. Dudley Andrew provides a rapid overview of such theories in *Concepts of Film Theory* (New York: Oxford University Press, 1984).

## ■ FORM, MEANING, AND FEELING

Some psychoanalytical theories of the spectator characterize the emotional appeal of cinema as involving "pleasure" and "unpleasure": an example is Laura Mulvey, "Visual Pleasure and Narrative Cinema," *Screen* **16,** 3 (Autumn 1975): 6–18. A somewhat different line of argument is pursued in Charles Affron, *Cinema and Sentiment* (Chicago: University of Chicago Press, 1982), which concentrates on how narrative structures create identification with the characters or their situations.

Many critics concentrate upon ascribing implicit meanings to films—that is, intepreting them. (Indeed, critics sometimes do this so habitually that they forget that other things can be done too.) An instructive collection of essays around *Red River* in *Ciné-tracts* **10** (Spring 1980): 54–87, shows how different critics can find varying implicit meanings in the same film. Other critics have objected to making interpretation the main goal of analysis. Susan Sontag's essay "Against Interpretation," in a collection of the same title (New York: Delta, 1966), pleads for "more attention to form in art" and "essays which reveal the sensuous surface of art without mucking about in it" (pp. 12–13). Jonathan Culler's *Structuralist Poetics* (Ithaca: Cornell University Press, 1975) emphasizes studying the functions and effects of art without always interpreting it.

The classic example of symptomatic criticism of a film is the 1970 essay "John Ford's *Young Mr. Lincoln,*" by the editors of *Cahiers du cinéma,* available in John Ellis, ed., *Screen Reader 1* (London: SEFT, 1977), and Bill Nichols, ed., *Movies and Methods* (Berkeley: University of California Press, 1976). Relying heavily on psychoanalytic interpretation, the authors bring out aspects of the film which suggest latent contradictions in American ideologies of family roles, romance, and the law. A subtle recent example of symptomatic criticism is Thomas Elsaesser's "Myth as the Phantasmagoria of History: H. J. Syberberg, Cinema and Representation," *New German Critique* **24–25** (Fall/Winter 1981/82): 108–154.

## ■ "AGGRESSIVE" FORMS

Strange as it may seem, many films seek to disturb the viewer, and we should try to understand how this happens. Our study must go beyond a form/content conception, e.g., "graphic depiction of sex or violence," to examine how a film's total system may deeply affect the viewer. Surrealist cinema offers one alternative, and its conception of cinematic form is discussed in J. H. Matthews, *Surrealism and Film* (Ann Arbor: University of Michigan Press, 1971) and in the critical studies devoted to Luis Buñuel. The Surrealists' own writings on cinema are available in Paul Hammond, ed., *The Shadow and Its Shadow* (London: British Film Institute, 1978). Recent avant-garde work has made displeasure an important goal; see Annette Michelson, ed., *New Forms in Film* (Montreux, 1974), and Peter Gidal, ed., *Structural Film Anthology* (London: British Film Institute, 1976). Some recent conceptions of aggressive form are discussed in Gregory Battcock, ed., *The New American Cinema* (New York: Dutton, 1967), and in Susan Sontag, "The Aesthetics of Silence," *Styles of Radical Will* (New York: Delta, 1970), pp. 3–34. More generally, the definitive study of "aggresive form" in film remains chapters 7 and 8 of Noël Burch's *Theory of Film Practice* (Princeton, N.J.: Princeton University Press, 1981).

## ■ SIMILARITY AND DIFFERENCE

No systematic study has been made of how films may be based on repetitions and variations, but most critics implicitly recognize the importance of these processes. A valuable exercise would be to read a critical essay on a film you have seen and to ask how the critic points out similarities and differences crisscrossing the whole film.

Some theorists have pointed out the play of similarity and difference quite explicitly. After an analysis of one sequence from *The Big Sleep*, Raymond Bellour ("The Obvious and the Code," *Screen* **15,** 4 [Winter 1975]: 7–17) concludes that a specific pattern of similarities and differences of shots makes the narrative intelligible to us. Stephen Heath attributes a great importance to the "rhyming" effect of certain scenes in *Jaws* ("*Jaws*, Ideology and Film Theory," *Times Higher Education Supplement*, no. 231 [March 26, 1976]: 11).

The strangeness of some films may come from their playing up of *differences* within their formal systems. Two theorists have devoted considerable attention to the functions of tension and conflict in cinematic form. See S. M. Eisenstein, *Writings, 1922–34*, vol. 1, ed. and trans. Richard Taylor (London: British Film Institute, 1988), and Noël Burch's *Theory of Film Practice*, mentioned above. Both theorists use the term *dialectics* of form, but in different ways. How would you define the differences between these theorists?

## ■ LINEAR SEGMENTATION AND DIAGRAMMING

Dividing a film into sequences in order to analyze its form is usually called segmentation. It is usually not difficult to do, though most often we do it intuitively. Recent film theory has devoted some consideration to the principles by which we segment a film. See Raymond Bellour, "To Analyze, to Segment," *Quarterly Review of Film Studies* **1,** 3 (August 1976): 331–354.

The most influential explanation of how to segment a narrative film has been Christian Metz's famous "Grand Syntagmatic of the Image Track." Metz suggests that there are eight basic sorts of sequences (with some subdivisions and exceptions). See Christian Metz, *Film Language,* trans. M. Taylor (New York: Oxford University Press, 1974), and Stephen Heath, "Film/Cinetext/Text," *Screen* **14,** 1/2 (Spring/Summer 1973): 102–127.

Usually a feature-length film will have no more than 40 sequences and no fewer than 5, so if you find yourself dividing the film into tiny bits or huge chunks, you may want to shift to a different level of generality. Of course, sequences and scenes can also be further subdivided into subsegments. In segmenting any film, an outline format or a linear diagram may help you visualize formal relations (beginnings and endings, parallels, patterns of development, etc.). We employ an outline format in discussing the nonnarrative films in Chapter 4 and a diagram in discussing *Citizen Kane* (pp. 74–75).

# THREE

## NARRATIVE AS A FORMAL SYSTEM

### PRINCIPLES OF NARRATIVE CONSTRUCTION

Stories surround us. In childhood we learn fairy tales and myths. As we grow up, we read short stories, novels, history, and biography. Religion, philosophy, and science often present their doctrines through exemplary stories: the Judeo-Christian tradition has its Bible and its Torah (huge collections of narratives), while a scientific discovery is often presented as the tale of an experimenter's trials and breakthroughs. Plays tell stories, as do films, television shows, comic books, paintings, dance, and many other cultural phenomena. Much of our conversation is taken up with stories of one sort or another—recalling an event from the past or telling a joke. Even newspaper articles are called stories, and when we ask for an explanation of something, we may say, "What's the story?" We cannot escape even by going to sleep, since we often experience our dreams as little narratives, and we recall and retell the dreams in the shape of stories. Perhaps narrative is a fundamental way that humans make sense of the world.

The prevalence of stories in our lives is one reason that we need to take a close look at how films may embody **narrative form.** When we speak of "going to the movies," we almost always mean that we are going to see a narrative film. Since most of the narrative films we see are fictitious, we will concentrate on fictional narratives. Much of what follows, however, also applies to factual narratives—for example, documentary films that choose narrative form rather than rhetorical form. In Chapter 4, we shall examine the alternative types of form that films may draw on.

Because stories are all around us, spectators approach a narrative film with definite expectations. We may know a great deal about the particular story the film will tell: perhaps we have read the book on which a film is based, or we have seen the film to which this is a sequel. More generally, though, we have anticipations that are characteristic of narrative form itself. We assume that there will be characters and some action that will involve them with one another. We expect a series of incidents that will be connected in some way. We also probably expect that the problems or conflicts arising in the course of the action will achieve some final state—either they will be resolved, or at least a new light will be cast on them. We have many other assumptions and expectations, but these broad ones suggest the degree to which a spectator comes prepared to make sense of a narrative film.

As the viewer watches the film, she or he picks up cues, recalls information, anticipates what will follow, and generally participates in the creation of the film's form. The film shapes particular expectations by summoning up curiosity, suspense, and surprise. The viewer also develops specific hunches about the outcome of the action, and these may control our expectations right up to the end. The ending has the task of satisfying or cheating the expectations prompted by the film as a whole. The ending may also call on the viewer's memory by cueing the spectator to review earlier events, possibly considering them in a new light. As we examine narrative form, we will consider at various points how it engages the viewer in a dynamic activity.

## ■ PLOT AND STORY

A narrative is *a chain of events in cause-effect relationship occurring in time and space.* A narrative is thus what we usually mean by the term "story," although we shall be using that term in a slightly different way later. A narrative begins with one situation; a series of changes occurs according to a pattern of cause and effect; finally, a new situation arises that brings about the end of the narrative.

All the components of our definition—causality, time, and space—are important to narratives in most media, but causality and time are central. A random string of events is hard to perceive as a story. Consider the following actions: "A man tosses and turns, unable to sleep. A mirror breaks. A telephone rings." We have trouble grasping this as a narrative because we are unable to guess at causal or temporal relations among the events.

Now consider a new description of these same events. "A man has a fight with his boss; he tosses and turns that night, unable to sleep. In the morning, he is still so angry that he smashes the mirror while shaving. Then his telephone rings; his boss has called to apologize."

We now have a narrative. We can connect the events spatially: the man is in the office, then in his bed; the mirror is in the bathroom; the phone is somewhere else in his home. More important, we can understand that the three events are part of a series of causes and effects. The argument with the boss causes the sleeplessness and the broken mirror. A phone call from the boss resolves the conflict; the narrative ends. In this example, time is also important. The sleepless night occurs before the breaking of the mirror, which in turn occurs before the phone call; all of the action runs from one day to the following morning. The narrative develops from an initial situation of conflict between employee and boss, through a series of events caused by the conflict, to the resolution of the conflict. Simple as it is, our example shows how important causality, space, and time are to narrative form.

The fact that a narrative relies on causality, time, and space does not mean that other formal principles cannot enter the film. For instance, a narrative may make use of parallelism. As Chapter 2 points out (pp. 47–48), parallelism posits a basic similarity among different elements. Our example was the way that *The Wizard of Oz* made the three Kansas farmhands parallel to Dorothy's three Oz companions. A narrative may cue us to draw parallels among characters, settings, situations, times of day, or any other elements. In Věrá Chytilová's *Something Different*, scenes from the life of a housewife and from the career of a gymnast are presented in alternation. Since the two women never meet and lead entirely separate lives, there is no way that we can connect the two stories causally. Instead, we compare and contrast the two women's actions and situations—that is, we draw parallels. But *Something Different* is still a narrative film because within each woman's life, we make sense of the action by applying notions of causality, time, and space. A more complex mixture of parallelism with other narrative principles is present in D. W. Griffith's *Intolerance*, in which four separate but parallel alternating stories are set in four different historical periods.

We make sense of a narrative, then, by identifying its events and linking them by cause and effect, time, and space. As viewers we do other things as well. We often infer events that are not explicitly presented, and we recognize the presence of material that is extraneous to the story world. In order to describe how we perform such activities, we can draw a distinction between **story** and **plot** (sometimes called story and "discourse"). Since this distinction is basic to understanding narrative form, we need to examine it in a little more detail.

We often make many assumptions and inferences about events in a narrative. For instance, at the start of Alfred Hitchcock's *North by Northwest* we know we are in Manhattan at rush hour. The cues stand out clearly: skyscrapers, congested traffic, hurrying pedestrians. Then we watch Roger Thornhill as he leaves an elevator with his secretary, Maggie, and strides through the lobby, dictating memos as she takes them down. On the basis of these cues, we start to draw some conclusions. Thornhill is an executive who leads a busy life. We infer that before we saw Thornhill and Maggie he was also dictating to her; we have come in on the middle of a string of events in time. We also assume that the dictating began in the office, before they got on the elevator. In other words, we infer causes, a temporal sequence, and another locale—none of which has been directly presented. We are probably not aware of having made these inferences, but they are no less firm for going unnoticed.

The set of all the events in a narrative, both the ones explicitly presented and those the viewer infers, composes the *story*. In our example, the story would consist of at least two depicted events and two inferred ones. (The inferred events are in parentheses.)

(Roger Thornhill has a busy day at his office.)
Rush hour hits Manhattan.
(Still dictating to his secretary, Maggie, Roger leaves the office and they take the elevator.)
Roger and Maggie get off the elevator and stride through the lobby.

The total world of the story action is sometimes called the film's **diegesis** (the Greek word for "recounted story"). In the opening of *North by Northwest*, the traffic, streets, skyscrapers, and people we see, as well as the traffic, streets, skyscrapers, and people we assume to be offscreen, are all diegetic because they are assumed to exist in the world that the film depicts.

The term *plot* is used to describe everything visibly and audibly present in the film before us. The plot includes, first, all the story events that are directly depicted. In our *North by Northwest* example, only two story events are explicitly presented: rush hour and Roger Thornhill dictating to Maggie as they leave the elevator. Secondly, the film's plot may contain material that is extraneous to the story world. For example, while the opening of *North by Northwest* is portraying rush hour in Manhattan, we also see the film's credits and hear orchestral music. Neither of these elements is diegetic, since they are brought in from outside the story world. (The characters cannot read the credits or hear the music.) Credits and such extraneous music are thus *nondiegetic* elements, and in Chapters 7 and 8 we will consider how editing and sound can function nondiegetically. At this point, we need only notice that the film's plot—the totality of the film—can bring in nondiegetic material.

Nondiegetic material may not be restricted to credit sequences. In *The Band Wagon*, we see the premiere of a hopelessly pretentious musical play. Eager patrons file into the theater; there then appears a pair of black-and-white drawings of bleak landscapes, followed by a third drawing of an egg. The three images are accompanied by a brooding, chanting chorus. These images and sounds are clearly nondiegetic, inserted from outside the story world in order to signal that the production was catastrophic and "laid an egg." The plot has added material to the story for comic effect.

In sum, story and plot overlap in one respect and diverge in others. The plot explicitly presents certain story events, so these events are common to both domains. The story goes beyond the plot in suggesting some events which we never witness. The plot goes beyond the story world by presenting nondiegetic images and sounds which may affect our understanding of the story. A diagram of the situation would look like this:

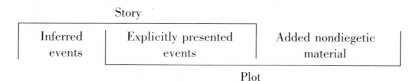

We can think about these differences between story and plot from two perspectives. From the standpoint of the storyteller, the filmmaker, the story is the sum total of all the events in the narrative. The storyteller can present some of these events directly (that is, make them part of the plot), can hint at events that are not presented, and can simply ignore other events. (For instance, though we learn later in *North by Northwest* that Roger has a mother, we never learn what happened to his father.) The filmmaker can also add nondiegetic material. In a sense, then, the filmmaker makes a story into a plot.

From the perceiver's standpoint, things look somewhat different. All we have before us is the plot—the arrangement of material in the film as it stands. We create the story in our minds on the basis of cues in the plot. We also recognize when the plot presents nondiegetic material. This suggests that if you want to give someone a synopsis of a narrative film, you can either summarize the story, starting from the very earliest incident the plot cues you to infer and running straight through to the end, or you can tell the plot, starting with the first incident you encountered in watching the film.

Our initial definition of narrative and the distinction between plot and story constitute a set of tools for analyzing how narrative works. We shall see that the plot-story distinction affects all three aspects of narrative: causality, time, and space.

## ■ CAUSE AND EFFECT

If narrative depends so heavily on cause and effect, what kinds of things can function as causes in a narrative? Usually the agents of cause and effect are *characters*. Characters in narratives are *not* real people (even when the characters are based on historical personages, like Napoleon in *War and Peace*). Characters are constructed in a narrative; they are collections of character *traits*. When we say that a character in a film was "complex" or "well developed," we really mean that the character was a collection of several or varying traits. A rich character such as Sherlock Holmes is a mass of traits (his love of music, his addiction to cocaine, his skill in disguise, and so on). On the other hand, a minor character may have only one or two traits.

In general, a character will have the number and kind of traits needed to function causally in the narrative. The second scene of Alfred Hitchcock's *The Man Who Knew Too Much* (1934) shows that the heroine, Jill, possesses the trait of being an excellent shot with a rifle. For much of the film, this trait seems irrelevant to the narrative, but in the last scene Jill is able to shoot one of the villains when a police marksman cannot do it. This skill with a rifle is not a natural part of a person named Jill; it is a trait that helps make up a character named Jill, and it serves a specific narrative function. Character traits can involve attitudes, skills, preferences, psychological drives, details of dress and appearance, and any other specific quality the film creates for a character.

But some causes and effects in narratives do not originate with characters. Causes may be supernatural. In the book of Genesis, God causes the earth to form; in Greek plays, gods bring about events. Causes may also be natural. In the so-called disaster movies, an earthquake or tidal wave may be the cause that precipitates a series of actions on the parts of the characters. The same principle holds when wild animals, like the shark in *Jaws*, terrorize a community. (The film may tend to anthropomorphize these natural causes by assigning human traits, for example, malevolence, to them. Indeed, this is what happens in *Jaws*: the shark becomes personified as vengeful and cunning.) But once these natural occurrences set the situation up, human desires and goals usually enter the action to develop the narrative. For example, a man escaping from a flood may be placed in the situation of having to decide whether to rescue his worst enemy.

In general, the spectator actively seeks to connect events by means of cause and effect. Given an incident, we tend to hypothesize what might have caused it, or what it might in turn cause. That is, we look for causal motivation. We have mentioned an instance of this in Chapter 2: in the scene from *My Man Godfrey*, a scavenger hunt serves as a cause that justifies the presence of a beggar at a society ball (see p. 46). Causal motivation often involves the "planting" of information in advance of a scene. In one film we shall be examining, John Ford's *Stagecoach*, there is a last-minute rescue from Indians by a cavalry troop. If these soldiers appeared from nowhere, we would most likely find the rescue a weak resolution of the battle scene. But *Stagecoach* begins with a scene of the cavalry discovering that Geronimo is on the warpath. Several later scenes involve the cavalry, and at one of their stops the passengers on the coach learn that the soldiers have had a skirmish with the Indians. These previous scenes of cavalry troops causally motivate their appearance in the final rescue scene.

Most of what we have said about causality pertains to the plot's direct presentation of causes and effects. In *The Man Who Knew Too Much*, Jill is shown to be a good shot, and because of this she can save her daughter. The townsfolk in *Jaws* respond to the shark attack that is shown at the start of the film. But the plot can lead us to *infer* causes and effects and thus build up a total story. The detective film furnishes the best example of how this active construction of the story may work.

A murder has been committed; that is, we know an effect but not the causal factors—the killer, the motive, perhaps also the method. The mystery tale thus depends strongly on curiosity, our desire to know events that have occurred before the plot action begins. It is the detective's job to disclose, at the end, the missing causes—to name the killer, explain the motive, and reveal the method. That is, in the detective film the climax of the plot (the action that we see) is a revelation of the earliest incidents in the story (events which we did not see). We can diagram this.

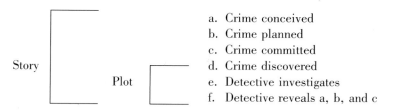

| Story | Plot | a. Crime conceived |
| | | b. Crime planned |
| | | c. Crime committed |
| | | d. Crime discovered |
| | | e. Detective investigates |
| | | f. Detective reveals a, b, and c |

Although this pattern is most common in detective narratives, any film's plot can withhold causes and thus arouse our curiosity. Horror and science-fiction films often leave us in the dark about what forces are behind certain events. We shall see that the plot of *Citizen Kane* delays revealing what causes the hero to say "Rosebud" on his deathbed. In general, whenever any film creates a mystery, it does so by suppressing certain story causes and by presenting only effects in the plot.

The plot may also present causes but withhold story effects, prompting the viewer to imagine them. During the final battle in *Jaws*, the young scientist, Hooper, is last seen hiding on the ocean bottom after the shark has smashed his protective cage open. Although we are not shown the outcome, we might assume that Hooper is dead. Later, after Brody has destroyed the shark, Hooper surfaces: he has escaped after all. A plot's withholding of effects is most noticeable at the end of the film. A famous example occurs in the final moments of François Truffaut's *The 400 Blows*. The boy Antoine Doinel has escaped from a reformatory and runs along the seashore. The camera zooms in on his face and the frame freezes. The plot does not reveal whether he is captured and brought back, leaving us to speculate on what might happen next.

## ■ TIME

Causes and their effects are basic to narrative, but they take place in time. Here again our story-plot distinction is of some help. As we watch a film, we construct story time on the basis of what the plot presents. For example, the plot may present events out of chronological order. In *Citizen Kane*, we see a man's death before we see his life, and we must build up a chronological version of his life. Alternatively, the plot may present only certain periods of time; the viewer thus infers that some story duration has been skipped over. Still another possibility is to have the plot present the same story event many times, as when a character repeatedly recalls a traumatic incident. This means that in constructing the film's story out of its plot, the viewer tries to put events in chronological **order** and to assign them some **duration** and **frequency**. We can look at each of these temporal factors separately.

**Temporal order.**   We are quite accustomed to films that present events out of story order. A flashback is simply a portion of a story that the plot presents out of chronological order. Suppose we see a shot of a woman thinking about her childhood, then a second shot depicting her as a girl; we understand that the second shot actually shows an earlier story event than the first one did. This does not confuse us, because we mentally rearrange the events into the order in which they would logically have to occur: childhood comes before adulthood. From the plot order, we infer the story order. If story events can be thought of as ABCD, then the plot that uses a flashback presents something like BACD. Similarly, a flashforward—that is, moving from present to future then back to the present—would also be an instance of how plot can shuffle story order. A flashforward could be represented as ABDC.

Our example of the detective film is also pertinent here. A detective film not only manipulates story causality by holding back key events, the film also juggles story order by presenting events surrounding the crime out of their chronological sequence, when the detective reveals them at the climax.

**Temporal duration.**   The plot of *North by Northwest* presents four crowded days and nights in the life of Roger Thornhill, but the story stretches back far before that, since information about the past is revealed in the course of the plot. The story events include Roger's past marriages, the U.S. Intelligence Agency's plot to create a false agent named George Kaplan, and Van Damm's series of smuggling activities. In general, a film's overall plot duration consists of highlighting certain stretches of story duration. This could involve selecting a short, relatively cohesive time span, as *North by Northwest* does, or by presenting significant stretches of time from a period of many years, as *Citizen Kane* does when it shows us the protagonist in his youth, skips over some time to show him as a young man, skips over more time to show him middle aged, and so forth.

But we need one more distinction. Watching a movie takes time—twenty minutes, two hours, eight hours (for example, Hans Jürgen Syberberg's *Our Hitler: A Film from Germany*). There is thus a third duration involved in a narrative film, which we can call *screen duration*. The relationships among story duration, plot duration, and screen duration are complex (see Notes and Queries for further discussion), but for our purposes we can say that the filmmaker can manipulate screen duration independently of the overall story duration and plot duration. For example, *North by Northwest* has an overall story duration of several years (including all relevant prior events), an overall plot duration of four days and nights, and a screen duration of about 136 minutes. Just as plot duration selects from story duration, so screen duration selects from overall plot duration. In *North by Northwest*, only portions of the film's four days and nights are shown to us. An interesting counterexample is *High Noon*, which is celebrated for making its screen duration identical with its plot duration: the 85 minutes of the movie approximate the same continuous stretch of time in its characters' lives.

At a more specific level, the plot can use screen duration to override story time. For example, screen duration can *expand* story duration. The most famous

*screen duration*

instance is that of the raising of the bridges in Sergei Eisenstein's *October*. Here an event that takes only a few moments in the story is stretched out to several minutes of screen time by means of the technique of film editing. As a result, this action gains a tremendous emphasis. The plot can also use screen duration to compress story time, as when a lengthy process is condensed into a rapid series of shots. These examples suggest that film techniques play a central role in creating screen duration. We shall consider this in more detail in Chapters 6 and 7.

**Temporal frequency.** A film's plot may change story frequency in several ways. If the story contains a habitual action that happens several times, the plot will present *one or a few* occurrences and let these sum up the rest. In Buster Keaton's *Battling Butler*, the unathletic hero is mistaken for a famous boxer and has to train for a big fight. The training period is a month, but we see only a few grueling exercise sessions and sparring matches; these serve to suggest the many repeated ordeals the hero must undergo during that month.

Occasionally, a single *story* event may appear twice or even more in the *plot* treatment. If we see an event early in a film and then there is a flashback to that event later on, we see that same event twice. Some films use multiple narrators, each of whom describes the same event; again, we see it occur several times. This may allow us to see the same action in different ways. The plot may also provide us with more information, so that we understand the event in a new context when it reappears. We shall see an example of this in *Citizen Kane*.

The various ways that a film's plot may manipulate story order, duration, and frequency illustrate how the spectator must actively participate in making sense of the narrative film. The plot supplies cues about chronological sequence, the time span of the actions, and the number of times an event occurs, and it is up to the spectator to make inferences and form expectations. Often we must motivate manipulations of time by the all-important principle of cause and effect. For instance, a flashback will often be justified as caused by some incident that triggers a character's recalling some event in the past. The plot may skip over years of story duration if they contain nothing important to the chains of cause and effect. The repetition of actions may be motivated by the plot's need to communicate certain key causes very clearly to the spectator.

## ■ SPACE

In some media, a given narrative might emphasize only causality and time; many anecdotes do not specify where the action takes place. In film narrative, however, space is usually an important factor. Events tend to occur in particular locales such as Kansas or Oz, or the Manhattan of *North by Northwest*'s opening. We shall consider setting in more detail when we examine mise-en-scène in Chapter 5, but we ought briefly to note how plot and story can manipulate space. Normally, the place of the story action is also that of the plot, but sometimes the plot leads us to infer other locales as part of the story. We never see Roger Thornhill's home or the colleges that kicked Kane out. Thus the narrative may ask us to imagine spaces and actions that are never shown. In Otto Preminger's *Exodus*, one scene is devoted to Dov Landau's interrogation by a terrorist organization he wants to join. Dov reluctantly tells his questioners of life in a Nazi concentration camp. Although the film never shows this locale through a flashback, much of the scene's effect depends on our using our imagination to fill in Dov's sketchy description of the camp.

Finally, we can introduce an idea akin to the concept of screen duration. Besides story space and plot space, cinema employs *screen space*: the visible space within the frame. We shall consider screen space and offscreen space in more detail in Chapter 6, when we analyze framing as a cinematographic technique. For now, it is enough to say that just as screen duration selects certain plot spans for presentation, so screen space selects portions of plot space.

### ■ OPENINGS, CLOSINGS, AND PATTERNS OF DEVELOPMENT

In Chapter 2 our discussion of formal development within the film suggested that it is often useful to compare beginnings and endings. This holds true for narrative form as well, since a narrative's use of causality, time, and space usually involves a change from an initial situation to a final situation.

A film does not just start, it *begins*. The opening provides a basis for what is to come and integrates us into the narrative. Typically, the plot will seek to arouse curiosity by bringing us into a series of actions that has already started. (This is called opening *in medias res*, a Latin phrase meaning "in the middle of things.") The viewer speculates on possible causes of the events presented. Typically, some of the actions that took place before the plot started will be stated or suggested so that we can start to construct the whole story, filling in prior events. The portion of the plot that sets out the story events and character traits important in the opening situation is called the *exposition*. In general, the opening raises our expectations by setting up a specific range of possible causes for and effects of what we see.

*Exposition*

No film can explore all the possibilities hovering in our mind at the start. As the plot proceeds, the causes and effects will define narrower patterns of development. There is no exhaustive list of possible plot patterns, but several kinds crop up frequently enough to be worth mentioning.

Most patterns of plot development depend heavily upon the ways that causes and effects create a change in a character's situation. The most common general pattern is a *change in knowledge*. Very often, a character learns something in the course of the action, with the most crucial knowledge coming at the turning point of the plot. A little more specifically, there are *goal-oriented* plots, in which a character takes steps to achieve a desired object or state of affairs. Plots based on *searches* would be instances of the goal plot: in *Raiders of the Lost Ark*, the protagonists try to find the Ark of the Covenant; in *Le Million*, characters compete for a missing lottery ticket; in *North by Northwest*, Roger Thornhill searches for George Kaplan. A variation on the goal-oriented plot pattern is the *investigation*, so typical of detective films, in which the protagonist's goal is not an object, but information, usually about mysterious causes. In more strongly psychological films such as Fellini's *8½*, the search and the investigation become internalized as the protagonist, a noted film director, attempts to discover the source of his creative problems.

Time or space may also provide plot patterns. A framing situation may bracket a series of shifts in temporal order, as in *Citizen Kane*'s flashbacks. The plot may set up a specific duration for the action, a deadline; in *Back to the Future*, the hero must synchronize his time machine with a bolt of lightning at a specific moment in order to get back to his life in the present. Or the plot may create patterns of repeated action via cycles of events: the familiar "here we go again" pattern. Such a pattern occurs in Woody Allen's *Zelig*, where the chameleonlike hero repeatedly loses his own identity by imitating the people around him. Space can also become the basis for a plot pattern, as when a film confines itself to a single locale, such as a train (Anthony Mann's *The Tall Target*) or a home (Sidney Lumet's *Long Day's Journey into Night*).

A given plot can, of course, combine these patterns. Any film built around a journey, such as *The Wizard of Oz* or *North by Northwest*, involves both a timetable and an itinerary. Jacques Tati's *Mr. Hulot's Holiday* uses both spatial and temporal patterns to structure its comic plot. The plot confines itself to a beachside resort and its neighboring areas, and it consumes one week of a summer vacation. Frequency is involved as well, since each day certain routines recur: morning exercise, lunch, afternoon outings, dinner, evening entertainment. Much of the film's humor relies on the way that Mr. Hulot alienates the other guests by disrupting their too-habitual routines. Although cause and effect still operate in *Mr. Hulot's Holiday*, time and space are central to the plot's formal patterning.

For any pattern of development, the spectator will create specific expectations, and these become more and more precise as the film "trains" the viewer in its particular form. Once we comprehend Dorothy's desire to get home, we see her every action as furthering or delaying her progress toward her goal. Thus her trip through Oz is hardly a sightseeing tour. Each step of her journey (to the Emerald City, to the Witch's castle, to the Emerald City again) is governed by the same principle—her desire to go home. In any film, the pattern of development in the middle may exploit suspense, the delay of an expected outcome. When Dorothy at last reaches the Wizard, he sets up a new obstacle for her by demanding the Witch's broom. Similarly, in *North by Northwest*, Hitchcock's journey plot constantly postpones Roger Thornhill's discovery of the Kaplan hoax, and this, too, creates suspense. The pattern of development may also create surprise, the cheating of an expectation, as when Dorothy discovers that the Wizard is a fraud or when Thornhill sees the minion Leonard fire point-blank at his boss Van Damm. The whole point of patterns of development is to engage the spectator in making long-term expectations that can be delayed, cheated, or gratified.

A film also does not simply stop; it *ends*. By the time we reach the end, there may be very few possibilities for further development. In a mystery, for instance, the clues may eliminate all but a few suspects. Or, the climax of a Western may involve a shoot-out in which we know that one of the two participants will die. Very often the ending will resolve, or "close off," the chains of cause and effect—the hero wins, everyone lives happily ever after, our expectations are eventually satisfied. But not all films offer such a sense of finality. An ending can be relatively "open," as our example from *The 400 Blows* suggests (p. 59). In other words, the plot presents story events that leave us uncertain as to the nature of the final consequences. In a mystery film, if we learn who the criminal is, the film has closure, but if it leaves a doubt about that person's guilt, it remains relatively open. Our response also becomes less firm. The form may thus encourage us to reflect on various ways our expectations might have been fulfilled.

## NARRATION: THE FLOW OF STORY INFORMATION

One of the functions that a plot performs is to present or imply story information. The opening of *North by Northwest* presents Manhattan at rush hour and Roger Thornhill as an executive; it also suggests that he has been busily dictating before we see him. Filmmakers have long realized that the spectator's interest can be whetted and manipulated by a film that carefully divulges story information at various points. In general, when we go to a film, we know relatively little about the story; by the end we know a lot more, usually the whole story. What happens in between?

*narration*

The plot may arrange cues in ways that withhold information for the sake of curiosity or surprise. Or the plot may supply information in such a way as to create expectations or increase suspense. All these processes constitute **narration,** the plot's way of distributing story information in order to achieve specific effects. Narration is the moment-by-moment process that guides us in turning the plot into a story. Many factors enter into narration (see Notes and Queries), but the most important ones for our purposes involve the *range* and the *depth* of story information that the plot presents.

### ■ RANGE OF STORY INFORMATION

The plot of D. W. Griffith's *The Birth of a Nation* begins by recounting how slaves were brought to America and how people debated the need to free them. The plot then shows two families, the northern Stoneman family and the southern Camerons. The plot also dwells on political matters, including Lincoln's hope of averting civil war. From the start, then, our range of knowledge is very broad. The plot moves across historical periods, regions of the country, and various groups of characters. This breadth of story information continues throughout the film. When Ben Cameron founds the Ku Klux Klan, we know about it at the moment the idea strikes him, long before the other characters learn of it. At the climax, we know that the Klan is riding to rescue several characters besieged in a cabin, but the besieged people do not know this. On the whole, in *The Birth of a Nation* the narration is very *unrestricted*: we know more, we see and hear more, than any or all of the characters can. Such extremely knowledgeable narration is often called *omniscient* narration.

*omniscient narration*

Now consider the plot of Howard Hawks's *The Big Sleep*. The film begins with the detective Philip Marlowe calling on General Sternwood to learn of his assignment. We learn about it as he does. Throughout the rest of the film, Marlowe is present in every scene. With hardly any exceptions, we see or hear nothing that he is not there to see and hear too. The narration is thus *restricted* to what Marlowe knows.

*Restricted narration*

Note the functional advantages of each choice. *The Birth of a Nation* seeks to present a panoramic vision of a period in American history (seen through peculiarly racist spectacles). Omniscient narration is thus essential to creating the sense of many destinies intertwined with the fate of the country. Had Griffith restricted narration the way *The Big Sleep* does, we would have learned story information solely through one character—say, Ben Cameron. We could not witness the prologue scene or the scenes in Lincoln's office or most of the battle episodes or the scene of Lincoln's assassination, since Ben is present at none of these events. The plot would now concentrate on one man's experience of the Civil War and Reconstruction.

Similarly, *The Big Sleep* derives functional advantages from its restricted narration. By confining our range of knowledge to Marlowe's, the film can create curiosity and surprise. Restriction is important to mystery films, since the films engage our interest by hiding certain important causes. Confining the plot to an investigator's range of knowledge realistically motivates concealing other story information. *The Big Sleep* could have been less restricted by, say, alternating scenes of Marlowe's investigation with scenes that show the gambling boss, Eddie

Mars, planning his crimes, but this would have given away some of the mystery. In each of the two films, the narration's range of knowledge functions to achieve specific effects on the viewer.

Unrestricted and restricted narration are not watertight categories but rather two ends of a continuum. Range is a matter of degree. A film may present a broader range of knowledge than does *The Big Sleep* and still not attain the omniscience of *The Birth of a Nation*. In *North by Northwest*, for instance, the early scenes confine us pretty much to what Roger Thornhill sees and knows. After he flees from the United Nations building, however, the narration moves to Washington, where the members of the United States Intelligence Agency discuss the situation. In this scene we learn something that Roger will not learn for some time: the man he seeks, George Kaplan, does not exist. Thereafter, we have a greater range of knowledge than Roger does. In at least one respect we also know more than the agency's staff: we know how the mix-up took place. But we still do not know many other things that the narration could have divulged in this scene. For instance, the intelligence agency's staff do not identify the agent they do have working under Van Damm's nose. In this way, any film may oscillate between restricted and unrestricted presentation of story information. (For more on narration in *North by Northwest*, see pp. 310–315.)

In fact, across a whole film, narration is never completely unrestricted. There is always something we are not told, even if it is only how the film will end. Usually, therefore, we think of a typical unrestricted narration as operating in the way that it does in *The Birth of a Nation*: the plot shifts constantly from character to character to change our source of information. Similarly, a completely restricted narration is not common. Even if the plot is built around a single character, the narration will present a few scenes that the character is not present to witness. The plot's range of story information creates a *hierarchy of knowledge*, and this may vary somewhat depending on the film. At any given moment, we can ask if the viewer knows more than, less than, or as much as the characters do. For instance, here is how hierarchies would look for the three films we have been discussing. The higher someone is on the scale, the greater his or her range of knowledge:

| The Birth of a Nation (unrestricted narration) | The Big Sleep (restricted) | North by Northwest (mixed and fluctuating) |
|---|---|---|
| viewer | viewer—Marlowe | the Agency |
| all characters | | viewer |
| | | Thornhill |

An easy way to analyze the range of narration is to ask, "Who knows what when?" The spectator must be included among the "whos," not only because we may get more knowledge than any one character but also because we may get knowledge that *no* character possesses. We shall see this happen at the end of *Citizen Kane*.

Our examples suggest the powerful effects that narration can achieve by manipulating the range of story information. Restricted narration tends to create greater curiosity and surprise. For instance, if a character is exploring a sinister house and we see and hear no more than the character does, a sudden revelation of a hand thrusting out from a door will surprise us. By contrast, as Alfred Hitchcock pointed out, unrestricted narration is better suited for maximal suspense. He explained it this way to François Truffaut:

> We are now having a very innocent little chat. Let us suppose that there is a bomb underneath this table between us. Nothing happens, and then all of a sudden, "Boom!"

There is an explosion. The public is surprised, but prior to this surprise, it has seen an absolutely ordinary scene, of no special consequence. Now, let us take a suspense situation. The bomb is underneath the table and the public knows it, probably because they have seen the anarchist place it there. The public is aware that the bomb is going to explode at one o'clock and there is a clock in the decor. The public can see that it is a quarter to one. In these conditions this innocuous conversation becomes fascinating because the public is participating in the scene. The audience is longing to warn the characters on the screen: "You shouldn't be talking about such trivial matters. There's a bomb beneath you and it's about to explode!"

In the first case we have given the public fifteen seconds of surprise at the moment of the explosion. In the second case we have provided them with fifteen minutes of suspense. The conclusion is that whenever possible the public must be informed. (François Truffaut, *Hitchcock* [New York: Simon and Schuster, 1967], p. 52)

Hitchcock lived up to his belief. In *Psycho*, Lila Crane explores the Bates mansion in much the same way as our hypothetical character is doing above. There are isolated moments of surprise as she discovers odd information about Norman and his mother. But the overall effect of the sequence is built on suspense because we know, as Lila does not, that Mrs. Bates is in the house, in the fruit cellar. (Actually, as in *North by Northwest*, our knowledge is not completely accurate, but during Lila's investigation we believe it to be accurate.) As in Hitchcock's anecdote, our superior range of knowledge creates suspense because we can anticipate effects that the character cannot.

## ■ DEPTH OF STORY INFORMATION

A film's narration not only manipulates degrees of knowledge, it manipulates the depth of our knowledge. Here we are referring to how "deeply" the plot plunges into characters' psychological states. Just as there is a spectrum between restricted and unrestricted narration, so is there a continuum between objectivity and subjectivity.

A plot might confine us wholly to information about what characters say and do: their external behavior. Here the narration is relatively *objective*. Or a film's plot may give us access to what characters see and hear. We might see shots taken from a character's optical standpoint (the **point-of-view shot**) or hear sounds as the character would hear them (what sound recordists call "sound perspective"). This would offer a greater degree of subjectivity, one we might call *perceptual subjectivity*. There is the possibility of still greater depth if the plot plunges into the character's mind. We might hear an internal commentary reporting the character's thoughts, or we might see the character's "inner images," representing memory, fantasy, dreams, or hallucinations. This can be called *mental subjectivity*. In short, narrative films can present story information at various depths of the characters' psychological life.

You might think that the more restricted the narration's range of knowledge is, the greater the subjective depth. This is not necessarily true. *The Big Sleep* is quite restricted in its range of knowledge, but we very seldom see or hear things from Marlowe's perceptual vantage point, and we never get direct access to his mind. *The Big Sleep* uses almost completely objective narration. The omniscient narration of *The Birth of a Nation*, on the other hand, plunges to considerable depth with optical point-of-view shots, flashbacks, and a final fantasy vision of a world without war. In Hitchcock's films, he delights in giving us greater knowledge than his characters, but then at certain moments he confines us to their perceptual

*what the*
*character sees*

subjectivity (for instance, through point-of-view shots). Range and depth of knowledge are independent variables.

Incidentally, this is one reason why the term "point of view" is ambiguous. It can refer to range of knowledge (as when a critic speaks of an "omniscient point of view") or to depth (as in the term "subjective point of view"). In this book, we will use "point of view" only to refer to perceptual subjectivity, as in the phrase "optical point-of-view shot."

Manipulating the depth of knowledge can have many functions and effects. Plunging to the depths of mental subjectivity can increase our identification with a character and can cue stable expectations about what the characters will later say or do. The memory sequences in Alain Resnais's *Hiroshima mon amour* and the fantasy sequences in Fellini's *8½* yield information about the protagonists' traits and possible future actions that would be less vivid if presented objectively. A subjectively motivated flashback can create parallels among characters, as does the flashback shared by mother and son in Kenji Mizoguchi's *Sansho the Bailiff*. A plot can create curiosity about a character's motives and then use some degree of subjectivity—for example, inner commentary, or subjective flashback—to explain the cause of the behavior.

On the other hand, objectivity can be an effective way of withholding information. One reason that *The Big Sleep* does not treat Marlowe subjectively is that the detective genre demands that the detective's reasoning must be concealed from the viewer. The mystery is more mysterious if we do not know his inferences and deductions before he reveals them at the end. At any moment in a film we can ask, "How deeply do I know the characters' perceptions, feelings, and thoughts?" The answer will point directly to how the narration is presenting or withholding story information in order to achieve a formal function or a specific effect on the viewer.

Fig. 3.1

Fig. 3.2

One final point about the depth of knowledge that the narration presents: Most films insert subjective moments into an overall framework of objectivity. For instance, in *North by Northwest*, we see Roger Thornhill crawl up to Van Damm's window and look in (objective narration); cut to a shot from Roger's optical point of view (perceptual subjectivity); cut back to a shot of Roger looking (objectivity again). (See Figs. 3.1 to 3.3.) Similarly, a dream sequence will often be bracketed by shots of the sleeper in bed. Flashbacks offer a fascinating instance of the overarching power of objective narration. They are usually motivated as mental subjectivity, since the events we see are triggered by a character's recalling the past. Yet, once we are "inside" the flashback, events will typically be presented from a wholly objective standpoint. (They will usually be presented in an unrestricted fashion too, and may even include action that the remembering character could have no way of knowing!) In other words, most films take "objective" narration as a baseline from which we may depart in search of subjective depth but to which we will return. There are, however, other films which refuse this convention and which mix objectivity and subjectivity in ambiguous ways. *8½*, Buñuel's *Belle de jour* and *That Obscure Object of Desire,* and Resnais's *Last Year at Marienbad* are good examples, and we shall examine this process more closely in Chapter 10.

Fig. 3.3

## ■ THE NARRATOR

Narration, then, is the process by which the plot presents story information to the spectator. This process may shift between restricted and unrestricted ranges of knowledge, and greater and lesser degrees of subjectivity. Narration may also utilize

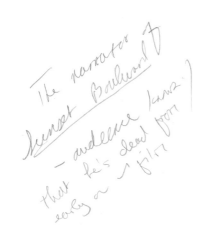

*The narrator isn't Bakhvool? — audience knows that he's dead from early on in film?*

a *narrator*, some specific agent who purports to be telling us the story. The narrator may be a *character* in the story. We are familiar with this convention from literature, as when Huck Finn or Jane Eyre recounts a novel's action. Edward Dymytrk's film *Murder My Sweet* makes the detective tell his story in flashbacks, addressing the information to inquiring policemen. A film may also employ a *noncharacter narrator*, such as the anonymous voice-over commentator of Truffaut's *Jules and Jim.*

Note that either sort of narrator may present various sorts of narration. A character narrator is not necessarily restricted and may tell of events that she or he did not witness. A noncharacter narrator need not be omniscient and could confine the commentary to what a single character knows. A character narrator might be highly subjective, telling us details of his or her inner life, or might be objective, confining his or her recounting strictly to externals. A noncharacter narrator might give us access to subjective depths (as in *Jules and Jim*) or might stick simply to surface events. In any case, the viewer's process of picking up cues, erecting expectations, and constructing an ongoing story out of the plot will be governed by what the narrator tells or does not tell.

## ■ SUMMARY

We can summarize the shaping power of narration by considering George Miller's *Road Warrior* (also known as *Mad Max II*). The film's plot opens with an offscreen commentary by an elderly male narrator who recalls "the warrior Max." After presenting an exposition telling of the worldwide wars that led society to degenerate into gangs of scavengers, the narrator falls silent. The question of his identity is left open. The bulk of the plot is organized around Max's encounter with a group of peaceful desert people who want to flee to the south but who are under siege by a horde of vicious marauders. The cause-and-effect chain involves Max's agreement to work for the settlers in exchange for gasoline. Later, after a brush with the gang leaves him wounded, his dog dead, and his car demolished, Max commits himself to helping the people escape their compound. The struggle against the encircling gangs comes to its climax in an attempt to escape with a truck full of gas, with Max at the wheel.

*Mad Max I*

Max is not only at the center of the causal chain; after the anonymous narrator's prologue, most of the film is restricted to his range of knowledge. Like Philip Marlowe in *The Big Sleep*, Max is present in every scene and virtually everything we learn gets funneled through him. The depth of story information is also consistent. The narration provides optical point-of-view shots as Max drives his car or watches a skirmish through a telescope. When he is rescued after his car crash, his delirium is rendered as mental subjectivity, using the conventional cues of slow-motion, superimposed imagery, and slowed-down sound. All of these narrational devices encourage us to identify with Max. At certain points, however, the narration becomes more unrestricted. This occurs principally during chases and battle scenes, where we witness events Max probably does not know about. In such scenes, unrestricted narration functions to build up suspense by showing both pursuers and pursued, or different aspects of the battle. At the climax, Max's truck successfully draws the gangs away from the desert people, who escape to the south. But when his truck overturns, Max—and we—learn that the truck holds only sand, that it has been only a decoy. Thus our restriction to Max's range of knowledge creates a surprise.

There is still more to learn, however. At the very end, the elderly narrator's voice returns to tell us that he was the feral boy whom Max had befriended. The desert people drive off, and Max is left alone in the middle of the highway. The film's final image—a shot of the solitary Max growing smaller as we pull back—suggests both a perceptual subjectivity (the boy's point of view as he rides away from Max) and a mental subjectivity (the memory of Max dimming for the narrator). In *The Road Warrior*, then, the plot's form is achieved not only by causality, time, and space but by a unified use of narration. The middle portion of the film channels our expectations by an identification with Max alternating with more unrestricted portions; but this middle section is "framed" by the mysterious narrator who puts all the events into the distant past. The narrator's presence at the opening leads us to expect him to return at the end, perhaps explaining who he is. Thus the film achieves closure both of cause and effect and of its narrational patterning.

## NARRATIVE CONVENTIONS

You may have noticed that we have often used the words "typically" or "usually" when describing certain aspects of narrative form. These are shorthand terms for various conventions that have developed over film history. We can appropriately close our survey of narrative form by looking at two common ways in which film critics discuss certain bodies of narrative conventions.

### ■ GENRES

As we have seen in Chapter 2, **genres,** or *types* of films, are a major source of audience expectations. If you know you are going to see a science-fiction film, you have fairly strong hunches about what you might encounter. Genres are based on a tacit agreement between filmmakers and audiences. In a musical, the audience expects musical numbers, either realistically integrated into the story's context (as are the dances in *Saturday Night Fever*) or presented with less realistic motivation (as in *The Wizard of Oz* or *An American in Paris*). Basically, a genre forms a set of "rules" for narrative construction that both filmmaker and audience know.

There is no single principle by which genres can be defined. Some genres are distinguished chiefly by shared subject matter. A science-fiction film is usually about advanced technology, a Western is usually about life on some frontier. Other genres are distinguished by certain objects or settings: a samurai film includes swords, a gangster film usually requires a city. Comedies and disaster films seem to be defined chiefly by a type of story situation. Musicals share only a style of performance, singing and/or dancing. The detective film, as we have seen, is partly defined by the plot pattern of an investigation that brings mysterious early causes to light at the climax. The flexibility of genre definitions is shown by the ability of genres to crossbreed freely. You can have a musical Western (*Cat Ballou*) or gangster film (*Bugsy Malone*), a melodrama that is also a mystery (*The Spiral Staircase*), a combination of science fiction and horror (*Alien*), a science-fiction detective tale (*Blade Runner*), even a horror Western (*Billy the Kid Meets Dracula*). The fact that genres can intermingle does not, however, mean that there is no difference between them. Instead of abstract definition, the best way to identify a genre is to recognize how audiences and filmmakers, at different historical periods and places, have intuitively distinguished one sort of movie from another. The combination of genres still implicitly recognizes that there are distinct genres, with different rules on which filmmakers and film viewers have agreed.

# ■ THE CLASSICAL HOLLYWOOD CINEMA

The number of possible narratives is unlimited. Historically, however, the cinema has tended to be dominated by a single mode of narrative form. In the course of this book we shall refer to this dominant mode as the "classical Hollywood cinema"—"classical" because of its wide and long history, "Hollywood" because the mode assumed its definitive shape in American studio films. The same mode, however, governs many narrative films made in other countries. For example, *The Road Warrior*, though an Australian film, is constructed along classical Hollywood lines.

This conception of narrative depends on the assumption that the action will spring primarily from *individual characters as causal agents*. Natural causes (floods, earthquakes) or societal causes (institutions, wars, economic depressions) may serve as catalysts or preconditions for the action, but the narrative invariably centers on personal psychological causes: decisions, choices, and traits of character.

Often an important trait that functions to get the narrative moving is a *desire*. The character wants something. The desire sets up a goal, and the course of the narrative's development will most likely involve the process of achieving that goal. In *The Wizard of Oz* Dorothy has a series of goals, as we have seen: first to save Toto from Miss Gulch, then to get home from Oz. The latter goal creates short-term goals along the way: getting to the Emerald City and then killing the Witch. We shall see in *Stagecoach* how the central character has a goal of revenge, whereas the subsidiary characters have goals of their own.

If this desire to reach a goal were the only element present, there would be nothing to stop the character from achieving the goal immediately. But there is a counterforce in the classical narrative: an opposition that creates conflict. The protagonist comes up against a character whose traits and goals are opposed to his or hers. As a result, the protagonist must seek to change the situation so that he or she can achieve the goal. Dorothy's desire to return to Kansas is opposed by the Wicked Witch, whose goal is to obtain the ruby slippers. Dorothy must eventually eliminate the Witch before she is able to use the slippers to go home. In *Stagecoach* the protagonist, who is under arrest by the marshal, has to prove himself trustworthy before the marshal finally allows him to participate in the shootout that gains him his revenge.

Cause and effect imply *change*. If the characters did not desire something to be different from the way it is at the beginning of the narrative, change would not occur. Therefore characters and their traits, particularly desire, are a strong source of causes and effects.

But don't all narratives have protagonists of this sort? Actually not. In 1920s Soviet films, such as Sergei Eisenstein's *Potemkin*, *October*, and *Strike*, no *individual* serves as protagonist. More recently, Jacques Rivette's *Out One Spectre* and Robert Altman's *Nashville* experiment with eliminating protagonists. In films like those of Eisenstein and Yasujiro Ozu, many events are seen as caused not by characters, but by larger forces (social dynamics in the former, an overarching Nature in the second). In many other narratives such as Antonioni's *L'Avventura*, the protagonist is not active but passive. So the active, goal-oriented protagonist, though common, does not appear in every narrative film.

In the classical Hollywood narrative mode the chain of actions that results from predominantly psychological causes tends to motivate most or all other narrative events. Time is subordinated to the cause-effect chain in a host of ways. The plot will omit significant durations in order to show only events of causal importance.

(The hours Dorothy and her entourage spend walking on the Road are omitted, but the moments during which she meets a new character are presented.) The plot will order story chronology so as to present the cause-effect chain most strikingly. Thus if a character acts peculiarly, we may get a flashback to reveal the cause of the odd behavior. Special devices weld plot time to the story's cause-effect chain: the appointment (which motivates characters' encountering each other at a specific moment) and the deadline (which makes plot duration dependent on the cause-effect chain). Motivation in the classical narrative film will strive to be as clear and complete as possible—even in the fanciful genre of the musical, in which song and dance numbers become motivated as either expressions of the characters' emotions or stage shows mounted by the characters.

Narration in the classical Hollywood cinema exploits a variety of options, but there is a strong tendency for it to be "objective" in the way discussed on page 66. That is, there is a basically "objective" story reality, against which various degrees of perceptual or mental subjectivity can be measured. Classical cinema also tends to put narration on the unrestricted end of the scale. Even if we follow a single character, there are portions of the film giving us access to things the character does not see, hear, or know. (*The Road Warrior* remains a good example of this.) This tendency is overridden only in genres that depend heavily on mystery, such as the detective film, with its reliance on the sort of restrictiveness we saw at work in *The Big Sleep*.

Finally, most classical narrative films display strong degrees of closure at the end. Leaving no loose ends unresolved, these films seek to end their causal chains with a final effect. We usually learn the fate of each character, the answer to each mystery, and the outcome of each conflict.

Again, none of these features is necessary to narrative form in general. There is nothing to prevent a filmmaker from presenting the "dead time" or narratively unmotivated intervals between more significant events. (François Truffaut, Jean-Luc Godard, Carl Dreyer, and Andy Warhol do this frequently, albeit in very different ways.) The filmmaker's plot can also reorder story chronology to make the causal chain *more* perplexing. For example, Jean-Marie Straub and Danièle Huillet's *Not Reconciled* moves back and forth among three widely different time periods without clearly signaling the shifts. Dušan Makavejev's *Love Affair, or the Case of the Missing Switchboard Operator* uses flashforwards interspersed with the main plot action; only gradually do we come to understand the causal relations of these flashforwards to the "present-time" events. The filmmaker can also include material that is unmotivated by narrative cause and effect, such as the chance meetings in Truffaut's films, the political monologues and interviews in Godard's films, the "intellectual montage" sequences in Eisenstein's films, the transitional shots in Ozu's work, and so on. Narration may be completely subjective, as in *The Cabinet of Dr. Caligari*, or it may hover ambiguously between objectivity and subjectivity, as in *Last Year at Marienbad*. Finally, the filmmaker need not resolve all of the action at the close; films made outside the classical tradition tend to have quite "open" endings.

We shall see in Chapter 7 how the classical Hollywood mode also makes cinematic space subservient to causality by means of continuity editing. For now it suffices to note how the classical mode tends to treat narrative elements and narrational processes in specific and unique ways. The classical Hollywood mode is, however, only one system among many that have been and could be used for constructing films.

## NARRATIVE FORM IN *CITIZEN KANE*

*Citizen Kane* is a useful film with which to begin film analysis, because it is unusual in form and varied in style. In what follows we shall examine *Citizen Kane* to discover how principles of narrative form may function in a particular film. *Kane*'s investigation plot carries us toward analyzing how causality and goal-oriented characters may operate in narratives. The film's manipulations of our knowledge shed light on the story-plot distinction. *Kane* also shows how ambiguity may arise when certain elements are not clearly motivated. Furthermore, the comparison of *Kane*'s beginning with its ending shows how a film may deviate from the patterns of classical Hollywood narrative construction. Finally, the film's use of narration clearly shows how our experience can be shaped by the way that narration governs the flow of story information.

### ■ OVERALL NARRATIVE EXPECTATIONS

Fig. 3.4

We have seen in Chapter 2 that our experience of a film depends heavily upon the expectations we bring to it and the extent to which the film confirms them. Before you saw *Citizen Kane*, you may have known only that it is regarded as a film classic. Such an evaluation would not give us a very specific set of expectations. A 1941 audience would have had a keener sense of anticipation. For one thing, the film was widely regarded as a disguised version of the life of the newspaper publisher William Randolph Hearst. Spectators would thus be looking for events and references keyed to Hearst's life. Moreover, the advertising campaign for the film (see Fig. 3.4), while not specifying any real-life correspondences, does prepare us for a story about a single man, a colossus seen from different vantage points.

After a few minutes of the film have gone by, the viewer can form more specific expectations about pertinent genre conventions. The early "News on the March" sequence suggests that this film may be a fictional biography, and this hint is confirmed once the reporter, Thompson, begins his inquiry into Kane's life. The film does indeed follow the conventional outline of the biography, which typically covers an individual's whole life and dramatizes certain episodes in the period. Examples of this genre would be *Anthony Adverse* (1936) and *The Power and the Glory* (1933). (The latter film is often cited as an influence on *Citizen Kane* because of its complex use of flashbacks.) The viewer can also quickly identify the film's use of conventions of the newspaper-reporter genre. Thompson's colleagues resemble the wisecracking reporters in *Picture Snatcher* (1933), *Five-Star Final* (1931), and *His Girl Friday* (1939). In this genre, the action usually depends on a reporter's dogged pursuit of a story against great odds. We are therefore prepared to expect not only Thompson's investigation but also his triumphant discovery of the truth. In the scenes devoted to Susan, there are also some conventions typical of the musical film: frantic rehearsals, backstage preparations, and most specifically, the montage of her opera career, which parodies the conventional montage of singing success in films like *Maytime* (1937). More broadly, the film evidently owes something to the detective genre, since Thompson is aiming to solve a mystery (what is "Rosebud"?) and his interviews resemble those of a detective questioning suspects in search of clues.

Note, however, that *Kane*'s use of genre conventions is somewhat equivocal. As a biographical film, *Kane* is more concerned with psychological states and relationships than with the hero's public deeds or adventures, as in *Anthony Adverse*. As a newspaper film, *Kane* is unusual in that the reporter does not get his story. As a mystery film, *Kane* answers some questions but suspends some too. *Citizen Kane* is a good example of a film that relies on genre conventions but often thwarts the expectations they arouse.

The same sort of equivocal qualities can be found in *Kane's* relation to the classical Hollywood cinema. Even without specific prior knowledge about this film, we expect that, as an American studio product of 1941, it will obey norms and rules of that tradition. In most ways it does. We shall see that desire propels the narrative, that causality is defined around traits and goals, that conflicts lead to consequences, that time is motivated by plot necessity, and that narration is objective, mixing restricted and unrestricted passages. We shall also see some ways in which *Citizen Kane* is more ambiguous than most films in this tradition. Desires, traits, and goals are not always spelled out; the conflicts sometimes have an uncertain outcome; at the end, the omniscience is emphasized to a rare degree. The ending in particular does not provide the degree of closure that one would expect in a classical film. Our analysis will show how *Citizen Kane* draws upon Hollywood narrative conventions but also violates some of the expectations that we have in watching a Hollywood film.

## ◼ PLOT AND STORY IN *CITIZEN KANE*

The first step in analyzing any film is to segment it into sequences. Sequences are often demarcated by cinematic devices (fades, dissolves, cuts, black screen, etc.) and form meaningful units. In a narrative film, the sequences constitute the parts of the plot. Most sequences in a narrative film are called **scenes**. The term is used in its theatrical sense, to refer to distinct phases of the action occurring within a relatively unified space and time. Our segmentation of *Citizen Kane* is below. (In segmenting films, we will label the opening credits with a "C," the end title with an "E," and all other segments with numbers.) In this outline, Arabic numerals refer to major parts, some of which are only one scene long. In most cases, however, the major parts consist of several scenes, and each of these is identified by a lowercase letter. Many of these segments could be further divided, but this segmentation suffices for our purposes.

Our segmentation lets us see at a glance the major divisions of the plot and how scenes are organized within them. The outline also introduces matters of how the plot organizes story causality and story time. Let us look at these more closely.

## ◼ *CITIZEN KANE'S* CAUSALITY

In *Citizen Kane*, two distinct sets of characters cause events to occur. On the one hand, a group of reporters seeks information about Kane; on the other hand, Kane and the characters who know him provide the subject of the reporters' investigations. The initial causal connection between the two groups is Kane's death, which leads the reporters to make a newsreel summing up his career. But the newsreel is already finished when the plot introduces the reporters; the boss, Rawlston, supplies the cause that initiates the investigation of Kane's life. Thompson's newsreel fails to satisfy him; Rawlston's desire for "an angle" for the newsreel gets the search for "Rosebud" under way. Thompson thus gains a goal, which sets him delving into Kane's past. His investigation constitutes one main line of the plot.

But another line of action, Kane's life, has already taken place in the past. There too a group of characters has caused actions to occur. Many years before, a poverty-stricken boarder at Kane's mother's boardinghouse has paid her with a deed to a silver mine. The wealth provided by this mine causes Mrs. Kane to appoint Thatcher as young Charles's guardian; Thatcher's guardianship results (in somewhat unspecified ways) in Kane's growing up into a spoiled, rebellious young man.

*Citizen Kane* is an unusual film in that the object of the investigator's search is a set of character traits. Thompson seeks to know what traits in Kane's personality led him to say "Rosebud" on his deathbed; this "mystery" motivates Thompson's detectivelike investigation. Kane, a very complex character, has many traits that influence the other characters' actions. As we shall see, however, *Citizen Kane*'s narrative does not ultimately define all of Kane's character traits.

## *CITIZEN KANE*: PLOT SEGMENTATION

C.   Credit title

1.   Xanadu: Kane dies

2.   Projection room:
        a. "News on the March"
        b. Reporters discuss "Rosebud"

3.   El Rancho nightclub: Thompson tries to interview Susan

4.   Thatcher Library:
        a. Thompson enters and reads Thatcher's manuscript

*First flashback*
        b. Kane's mother sends the boy off with Thatcher
        c. Kane grows up and buys the *Inquirer*
        d. Kane launches the *Inquirer*'s attack on big business
        e. The Depression: Kane sells Thatcher his newspaper chain
        f. Thompson leaves library

5.   Bernstein's office:
        a. Thompson visits Bernstein

*Second flashback*
        b. Kane takes over the *Inquirer*
        c. Montage: the *Inquirer*'s growth
        d. Party: the *Inquirer* celebrates getting the *Chronicle* staff
        e. Leland and Bernstein discuss Kane's trip abroad
        f. Kane returns with his fiancée Emily
        g. Bernstein concludes his reminiscence

6.   Nursing home:
        a. Thompson talks with Leland

*Third flashback*
        b. Breakfast table montage: Kane's marriage deteriorates
        c. Leland continues his recollections
        d. Kane meets Susan and goes to her room
        e. Kane's political campaign culminates in his speech

*Third flashback (cont.)*
        f. Kane confronts Gettys, Emily, and Susan
        g. Kane loses election and Leland asks to be transferred
        h. Kane marries Susan
        i. Susan's opera premiere
        j. Because Leland is drunk, Kane finishes Leland's review
        k. Leland concludes his reminiscence

7. El Rancho nightclub:

        a. Thompson talks with Susan

*Fourth flashback*
        b. Susan rehearses her singing
        c. Susan's opera premiere
        d. Kane insists that Susan go on singing
        e. Montage: Susan's opera career
        f. Susan attempts suicide and Kane promises she can quit singing
        g. Xanadu: Susan bored
        h. Montage: Susan plays with jigsaw puzzles
        i. Xanadu: Kane proposes a picnic
        j. Picnic: Kane slaps Susan
        k. Xanadu: Susan leaves Kane
        l. Susan concludes her reminiscence

8. Xanadu:

        a. Thompson talks with Raymond

*Fifth flashback*
        b. Kane destroys Susan's room and picks up paperweight, murmuring "Rosebud"
        c. Raymond concludes his reminiscence; Thompson talks with the other reporters; all leave
        d. Survey of Kane's possessions leads to a revelation of Rosebud; exterior of gate and of castle; the end

E. End Credits

Kane himself has a goal; he too seems to be searching for something related to "Rosebud." At several points characters speculate that Rosebud was something that Kane lost or never was able to get. Again, the fact that Kane's goal remains so vague makes this an unusual narrative.

Other characters in Kane's life provide causal material for the narrative. The presence of several characters who knew Kane well makes Thompson's investigation possible, even though Kane himself has died. Significantly, the characters provide a range of information that spans Kane's entire life. This is important if we are to be able to reconstruct the progression of story events in the film. Thatcher knew Kane as a child; Bernstein, his manager, knew his business dealings; his best friend, Leland, knew of his personal life (his first marriage in particular); Susan Alexander, his second wife, knew him in middle age; and the butler, Raymond, managed Kane's affairs during his last years. Each of these characters has a causal role in Kane's life, as well as in Thompson's investigation. Note that Kane's wife, Emily, does not tell a story, since Emily's story would simply duplicate Leland's and would contribute no additional information to the "present-day" part of the narrative, the investigation; hence the plot simply eliminates her (via a car accident).

## ◼ TIME

The order, duration, and frequency of story events differ greatly from the way the plot of *Citizen Kane* presents those events. Much of the film's power arises from the complex ways in which the plot cues us to construct the story.

To understand the story in its chronological order and assumed duration and frequency, the spectator must follow an intricate tapestry of plot events. For example, in the first flashback, Thatcher's diary tells of a scene in which Kane loses control of his newspapers during the Depression (4e); by this time Kane is a middle-aged man. Yet in the second flashback Bernstein describes Kane's youthful arrival at the *Inquirer* and his engagement to Emily (5b, 5f). We mentally reverse these plot events into a correct chronological (story) order, then continue to rearrange other events as we learn of them.

Similarly, the earliest *story* event about which we learn is Mrs. Kane's acquisition of a deed to a valuable mine; we get this information during the newsreel, in the second sequence. But the first event in the *plot* is Kane's death. Just to illustrate the maneuvers we must execute in order to construct the film's story, let us assume that Kane's life consists of these phases:

Boyhood
Youthful newspaper editing
Life as a newlywed
Middle age
Old age

Significantly, the early portions of the plot tend to roam over many phases of Kane's life, while later portions tend to concentrate more on particular phases. The "News on the March" sequence (2a) gives us glimpses of all periods, and Thatcher's manuscript (4) shows us Kane in boyhood, youth, and middle age. Then the flashbacks become primarily chronological. Bernstein's recounting (5) concentrates on episodes showing Kane as newspaper editor and fiancé of Emily. Leland's recollections (6) run from newlywed life to middle age. Susan (7) tells of Kane as a middle-aged man and an old man. Raymond's perfunctory anecdote (8b) concentrates on Kane in old age. The plot becomes more "linear" in its ordering as it goes along. This is functional: if every character's flashback skipped around Kane's life as much as the newsreel or Thatcher's account does, the story would be much harder to reconstruct. As it is, the early portions of the plot show us the results of events we have not seen, while the later portions confirm or modify the expectations that we formed earlier.

By arranging story events out of order, the plot cues us to form very specific anticipations. In beginning with Kane's death and the newsreel version of his life, the plot creates strong curiosity about two issues: What does "Rosebud" mean? And what could have happened to make so powerful a man so solitary at the end of his life? There is also a degree of suspense. We already have quite firm knowledge when the plot goes back to the past: we know that neither of Kane's marriages will last, that his friends will drift away, and so on. The plot encourages us to focus our interest on *how and when* a particular thing will happen. Thus many scenes function to delay an outcome that we already know is certain. For example, we know that Susan will abandon Kane at some point, so we are constantly expecting her to do so each time he bullies her. For several scenes (7b–7j) she comes close to leaving him, though at one moment he mollifies her (after her suicide attempt). The plot could have shown her walking out (7k) much earlier, but then the ups and downs of their relations would have been less vivid, and there would have been no suspense.

This process of mentally rearranging plot events into story order might be quite difficult in *Citizen Kane* were it not for the presence of the "News on the March" newsreel. The first sequence in Xanadu disorients us, for it shows the death of a character about whom we so far know almost nothing. But the newsreel gives us a great deal of information quickly. Moreover, the newsreel uses a narrative parallel to give us a miniature introduction to the plot of the ensuing film.

**A.** Shots of Xanadu
**B.** Funeral; headlines announcing Kane's death
**C.** Growth of financial empire
**D.** Silver mine and Mrs. Kane's boardinghouse
**E.** Thatcher testimony at congressional committee
**F.** Political career
**G.** Private life; weddings, divorces
**H.** Opera house and Xanadu
**I.** Political campaign
**J.** Depression
**K.** 1935: Kane's old age
**L.** Isolation at Xanadu
**M.** Death announced

A comparison of this outline with the one for the whole film shows some striking formal similarities. "News on the March" begins by emphasizing Kane as "Xanadu's Landlord"; a short segment (A) presents shots of the house, its grounds, and its contents. This is a variation on the opening of the whole film (1), which consisted of a series of shots of the grounds, moving progressively closer to the house. That opening sequence had ended with Kane's death; now the newsreel follows the shots of the house with Kane's funeral (B). Next comes a series of newspaper headlines announcing Kane's death. In a comparison with the plot diagram of *Citizen Kane*, these headlines occupy the approximate formal position of the whole newsreel itself (2a). Even the title card that follows the headlines ("To forty-four million U.S. news buyers, more newsworthy than the names in his own headlines was Kane himself . . .") is a brief parallel to the scene in the projection room, in which the reporters decide that Thompson should continue to investigate Kane's "newsworthy" life.

The order of the newsreel's presentation of Kane's life roughly parallels the order of scenes in the flashbacks related to Thompson. "News on the March" moves from Kane's death to summarize the building of Kane's newspaper empire (C), with a description of the boardinghouse deed and the silver mine (including an old photograph of Charles with his mother, as well as the first mention of the sled). Similarly, the first flashback (4) tells how Thatcher took over the young Kane's guardianship from his mother and how Kane first attempted to run the *Inquirer*. The rough parallel continues: the newsreel tells of Kane's political ambitions (F), his marriages (G), his building of the opera house (H), his political campaign (I), and so on. In the main plot Thatcher's flashback describes his own clashes with Kane on political matters. Leland's flashback (6) covers the first marriage, the affair with Susan, the political campaign, and the premiere of *Salammbo*. These are not all of the similarities between the newsreel and the overall film; you can tease out many more by comparing the two closely.

In general, the newsreel provides us with a "map" at the beginning of the investigation into Kane's life. As we see the various scenes of the flashbacks, we already expect certain events and have a rough chronological basis for fitting them into our story reconstruction.

*Kane*'s plot not only manipulates story order, it also cues us to construct story duration and frequency. The total *story duration* which the viewer infers consists of the 75 years of Kane's life plus a week after his death. This entire period is presented in a *plot duration* consisting of the week of Thompson's investigation. The use of flashbacks allows the plot to concentrate its revelation of story material into this short a period. But there is also *screen duration*, or running time—almost exactly 120 minutes. As in most films, ellipsis has been used. The plot skips over years of story time, and the running time omits even more, skipping over many hours of Thompson's week of investigation. But screen duration also compresses time, through "montage sequences," such as those showing the *Inquirer*'s campaign against big business (4d), the growth of the paper's circulation (5c), Susan's opera career (7e), and Susan's bored playing with jigsaw puzzles (7h). Here long passages of story time are condensed into brief summaries quite different from ordinary narrative scenes. We will discuss montage sequences in more detail in Chapter 7, but we can already see the value of such segments in clarifying story duration for the spectator.

*Citizen Kane* also provides a clear demonstration of how events that occur only once in the story may appear several times in the plot. In their respective flashbacks, both Leland and Susan Alexander describe the latter's debut in the Chicago premiere of *Salammbo*. Watching Leland's account (6i), we see the performance from the front; we witness the audience reacting with distaste. Susan's version (7c) shows us the performance from behind and on the stage, to suggest her humiliation. This repeated presentation of Susan's debut in the plot does not confuse us, for we recognize the two scenes as depicting the same story event. ("News on the March" has also referred to Susan's opera career, in parts G and H.)

Overall, *Citizen Kane*'s narrative dramatizes Thompson's search by means of flashbacks that encourage us to seek the sources of Kane's failure and to try to identify "Rosebud." As in a detective film, we must locate missing causes and arrange events into a coherent story pattern. Through manipulations of order, duration, and frequency, the plot both assists our search and complicates it in order to provoke curiosity and suspense.

## ■ MOTIVATION

Some critics have argued that Welles's use of the search for "Rosebud" is a flaw in *Citizen Kane*, because the identification of the word proves it to be a trivial gimmick. If indeed we assume that the whole point of *Citizen Kane* is really to identify "Rosebud," this charge might be valid. But in fact, "Rosebud" serves a very important motivating function in the film; it serves to create Thompson's goal and to focus our attention on his delving into the lives of Kane and his associates. *Citizen Kane* becomes a mystery story; but instead of investigating a crime, the reporter investigates a character. So the "Rosebud" clues provide the basic motivation necessary for the plot to progress. (Of course, the "Rosebud" device serves other functions as well; for instance, the little sled provides a transition from the boardinghouse scene to the cheerless Christmas when Thatcher gives Charles a new sled.)

*Citizen Kane*'s narrative revolves around an investigation into traits of character; as a result, these traits provide many of the motivations for events. (In this respect, the film obeys principles of the classical Hollywood narrative model.) Kane's desire to prove that Susan is really a singer and not just his mistress motivates his manipulation of her opera career. His mother's overly protective desire to remove her son from what she considers to be a bad environment motivates her appointment of Thatcher as the boy's guardian. The interested reader will be able to find dozens of actions that are motivated by character traits and desires.

At the end of the film, Thompson gives up his search for the meaning of "Rosebud," saying he doesn't "think any word can explain a man's life." Up to a point Thompson's statement motivates his acceptance of his failure. But if we as spectators are to accept this idea that no key can unlock the secrets of a life, we need further motivation, and the film provides this. In the scene in the newsreel projection room, Rawlston suggests that "maybe he told us all about himself on his deathbed"; one of the reporters says, "Yeah, and maybe he didn't." Already the suggestion is planted that "Rosebud" may not provide any adequate answers about Kane. Later Leland scornfully dismisses the "Rosebud" issue and goes on to talk of other things. These brief references to "Rosebud" help justify Thompson's pessimistic lines in the final sequence.

The presence of the scene in which Thompson first visits Susan Alexander at the El Rancho nightclub (3) might seem puzzling at first. Unlike the other scenes in which he visits people, no flashback occurs here. Thompson learns from the waiter that Susan knows nothing about "Rosebud"; he could easily learn this on his second visit to her. So why should the film include the scene at all? One reason is that it evokes curiosity and deepens the mystery around Kane. Moreover, Susan's story, when she does tell it, covers events relatively late in Kane's career. As we have seen, the flashbacks go through Kane's life roughly in order. If Susan had told her story first, we would not have all of the material necessary to understand it. But it is plausible that Thompson should start his search with Kane's ex-wife, presumably the surviving person closest to him. In Thompson's first visit, Susan's drunken refusal to speak to him motivates the fact that her flashback comes later; by that point, Bernstein and Leland have filled in enough of Kane's personal life to prepare the way for Susan's flashback. This first scene functions partly to provide motivation for postponing Susan's flashback until a later part of the plot.

Motivation makes us take things for granted in narratives. Mrs. Kane's desire for her son to be rich and successful motivates her decision to entrust him to Thatcher, a powerful banker, as his guardian. We may be inclined to think it is just natural that Thatcher is a rich businessman; this fact, however, in turn provides several important motivations. It motivates Thatcher's presence in the newsreel; he is powerful enough to have been asked to testify at a congressional hearing. More important, Thatcher's success motivates the fact that he has kept a journal now on deposit at a memorial library that Thompson visits. This, in turn, justifies the fact that Thompson is able to find information from a source who knew Kane as a child.

But *Citizen Kane* departs somewhat from the usual practice of the classical Hollywood narrative by leaving some motivations ambiguous. The ambiguities relate primarily to Kane's character. The other characters who tell Thompson their stories all have definite opinions of Kane, but these do not always tally. Bernstein still looks on Kane with sympathy and affection, whereas Leland is cynical about his own relationship with Kane. The reasons for some of Kane's actions remain unclear. Does he send Leland the $25,000 check in firing him because of a lingering sentiment over their old friendship or from a proud desire to prove himself more generous than Leland? Why does he insist on stuffing Xanadu with hundreds of artworks which he never even unpacks?

## ▪ PARALLELISM

Parallelism does not provide the entire basis of *Citizen Kane*'s narrative form, but several parallel structures are present. We have already seen important formal parallels between the newsreel and the film's plot as a whole. We have also noticed a parallel between the two major lines of action: Kane's life and Thompson's search. "Rosebud" serves as a summary of the things Kane strives for through his adult life; we see him repeatedly fail to find love and friendship, living alone at Xanadu in the end. His inability to find happiness parallels Thompson's failure to locate the significance of the word "Rosebud." This parallel does not imply that Kane and Thompson share similar character traits. Rather, it allows both lines of action to develop simultaneously in similar directions.

Another narrative parallel juxtaposes Kane's political campaign as he runs for governor with his attempt to build up Susan's career as an opera star. In each case he seeks to inflate his reputation by influencing public opinion. In trying to achieve success for Susan, Kane forces his newspaper employees to write favorable reviews of her performances; this parallels the moment when he loses the election and the *Inquirer* automatically proclaims fraud at the polls. In both cases Kane fails to realize that his power over the public is not great enough to hide the flaws in his projects: first his affair with Susan, which ruins his campaign, then her lack of singing ability, which Kane refuses to admit. Here the parallel points up how Kane continues to make the same kinds of mistakes throughout his life.

## ■ PATTERNS OF PLOT DEVELOPMENT

The progression from beginning to ending in *Citizen Kane* leads us through two lines of action, as we have seen: Kane's life story and Thompson's investigation of it. Each of Thompson's visits in his investigation leads to a flashback that gives us a further look at Kane. The order of Thompson's visits allows the series of flashbacks to have a clear pattern of progression. Thompson moves from people who knew Kane early in his life to those who knew him as an old man. Moreover, each flashback contains a distinct type of information about Kane. Thatcher establishes Kane's political stance; next Bernstein gives an account of the business dealings of the newspaper. These provide the background to Kane's early success and lead into Leland's stories of Kane's personal life, where we get the first real indications of Kane's failure. Susan continues the description of his decline with her account of how he had manipulated her life. Finally, in Raymond's flashback Kane becomes a pitiable old man.

Thus even though the order, duration, and frequency of events in the story vary greatly from those in the plot of *Citizen Kane*, the film presents Kane's life through a steady pattern of development. The "present-day" portions of the narrative—Thompson's scenes—also follow their own pattern of a search. By the ending this search has failed (as Kane's own search for happiness or personal success had also failed).

Because of this failure, the ending of *Citizen Kane* remains somewhat more open than was the rule in Hollywood in 1941. True, Thompson does resolve the question of "Rosebud" for himself by saying that it would not have explained Kane's life, so we have the common pattern of action leading to greater knowledge. But, in most classical narrative films, the main character reaches his or her initial goal (and Thompson is the main character of this one line of action).

The line of action involving Kane himself has even less closure. Not only does Kane apparently not reach his goal, but the film never specifies what that goal is to start with. Most classical narratives create a situation of conflict. The character must struggle with a problem and solve it by the ending. Kane begins his adult life in a highly successful position (happily running the *Inquirer*), then gradually falls into a lonely, failed existence. We are never sure exactly what, if anything, it would take to make Kane happy. *Citizen Kane*'s lack of closure in this line of action made it a very unusual narrative for its day.

The search for "Rosebud" does lead to a certain resolution at the end: we the audience discover what "Rosebud" was. The ending of the film, which follows this discovery, strongly echoes the beginning. The beginning had moved past fences toward the house; now a series of shots takes us away from the house and back outside the fences, with the "No Trespassing" sign and large K insignia.

But even at this point, when we learn the answer to Thompson's question, a degree of uncertainty remains. Just because we have learned what Kane's dying word meant, do we now have the key to his entire character? Or is Thompson's final statement *correct*—that no one word can explain a person's life? It is tempting to declare that all of Kane's problems arose from the loss of his sled and his home life as a child, but the film also suggests that this is too easy a solution. It is the kind of solution that the slick editor Rawlston would pounce on as an "angle" for his newsreel.

For years critics have debated whether "Rosebud's" solution does give us a key that resolves the entire narrative. This debate should suggest the ambiguity at work in *Citizen Kane*. The film itself provides evidence for both views and hence avoids complete closure. (You might contrast this slightly open ending with the tightly closed narratives of *His Girl Friday*, *North by Northwest*, and *Stagecoach*, in Part IV. You might also compare *Citizen Kane*'s narrative with two other films that contain ambiguities: *Day of Wrath* and *Last Year at Marienbad*, also discussed in Part IV.)

## ■ NARRATION IN *CITIZEN KANE*

In considering how *Kane*'s plot manipulates the flow of story information, it is useful to consider a remarkable fact: the only time we see Kane directly and in the present is when he dies. On all other occasions, he is presented at one remove— in the newsreel, in various characters' memories. This unusual treatment makes the film something of a portrait, a study of a man seen from different perspectives.

The film employs five narrators, the people whom Thompson tracks down: Thatcher (whose account is in writing), Bernstein, Leland, Susan, and the butler, Raymond. The plot thus motivates a series of more or less restricted views of Kane. In Thatcher's account (4b–4e), we see only scenes at which he is present. Even Kane's newspaper crusade is rendered as Thatcher learns of it, through buying copies of the *Inquirer*. In Bernstein's flashback (5b–5f), there is some deviation from what Bernstein witnesses, but in general his range of knowledge is respected. At the *Inquirer* party, for example, we are confined to following Bernstein and Leland's conversation while Kane dances in the background. Similarly, we never see Kane in Europe, we merely hear the contents of Kane's telegram, which Bernstein delivers to Leland. Leland's flashbacks (6b, 6d–6j) deviate most markedly from the narrator's range of knowledge. Here we see Kane and Emily at a series of morning breakfasts, Kane's meeting with Susan, and the confrontation of Kane with Boss Gettys at Susan's apartment. In scene 6j, Leland is present but unconscious most of the time. (The plot motivates Leland's knowledge of Kane's affair with Susan by having Leland suggest that Kane told him about it, but the scenes present detailed knowledge that Leland is unlikely to possess.) By the time we get to Susan's flashback (7b–7k), however, this range of knowledge fits the character more snugly. (There remains one scene, 7f, in which Susan is unconscious for part of the action.) The last flashback (8b) is recounted by Raymond and plausibly accords with his range of knowledge; he is standing outside as Kane wrecks Susan's room.

Using several narrators to transmit story information fulfills several functions. It offers itself as a "realistic" depiction of the process of investigation, since we expect any reporter to hunt down his information through a series of inquiries. More deeply, the plot's portrayal of Kane himself becomes more complex by showing somewhat different sides of him on the basis of who's talking about him. Moreover, the use of multiple narrators makes the film like one of Susan's jigsaw puzzles. We must put things together piece by piece. The pattern of gradual revelation enhances curiosity—what is it in Kane's past that he associates with Rosebud?—and suspense—how will he lose his friends and his wives?

This strategy has important implications for film form. While Thompson uses the various narrators to gather data, the plot uses them both to furnish us with story information and to *conceal* information. We can motivate gaps in knowledge about Kane by appealing to the fact that no informant can know everything about anyone. If we were able to enter Kane's consciousness, we might discover the meaning of "Rosebud" much sooner. The multiple narrator format thus appeals to expectations we derive from real life in order to motivate the gradual and piecemeal transmission of story information, the withholding of key pieces of information, and the arousing of curiosity and suspense.

Although each narrator's account is predominantly restricted to his or her range of knowledge, the plot does not treat each flashback in much subjective depth. Most of the flashbacks are rendered objectively. Some transitions from the framing episodes use a voice-over commentary to lead us into the flashbacks, but these do not represent the narrators' subjective states. Only in Susan's flashbacks are there some attempts to render subjectivity. In scene 7c we see Leland as if from her optical point of view on stage, and the phantasmagoric montage of her career (7e) suggests some mental subjectivity that renders her fatigue and frustration. On the whole, however, the film adheres to the classical Hollywood convention of objective presentation. This, too, is functional. If we are to pursue the Rosebud mystery and to watch the unraveling of Kane's personal relationships, we need to believe that what we see and hear actually occurred.

Against the five character narrators, the film's plot sets another purveyor of knowledge, the "News on the March" short. We have already seen the crucial function of the newsreel in introducing us both to Kane's story and to its plot construction, with the newsreel's parts echoing the parts of the film as a whole. The newsreel also gives us an initial expanse of knowledge—Kane's life and death—that will be filled in by the more restricted "behind-the-scenes" accounts offered by the narrators. The newsreel is also highly "objective," even more so than the rest of the film; it reveals nothing about Kane's inner life. Rawlston acknowledges this: "It isn't enough to tell us what a man did, you've got to tell us who he was." In effect, Thompson's aim is to add depth to the newsreel's superficial version of Kane's life.

Yet we are still not through with the narrational manipulations in this complex and daring film. For one thing, all the localized sources of knowledge—"News on the March" and the five narrators—are linked together by the shadowy reporter Thompson. To some extent, he is our surrogate in the film, gathering and assembling the puzzle pieces. Note too that Thompson is barely characterized; we cannot even identify his face. This, as usual, has a function. If we saw him clearly, if the plot gave him more traits or a background or a past, he would become the protagonist. But *Citizen Kane* is less about Thompson than about his *search*. The plot's handling of Thompson makes him a neutral conduit for the story information that he gathers (though his conclusion at the end, "I don't think any word can explain a man's life," suggests that he has been changed by his investigation).

Thompson is not, however, a perfect surrogate for us because the film's narration inserts the newsreel, the narrators, and Thompson within a still broader range of knowledge. The flashback portions are predominantly restricted, but there are other passages that reveal an overall narrational omniscience. From the very start we are given a god's-eye-view of the action. We move into a mysterious setting that we will later learn is Kane's estate, Xanadu. We might have learned about this locale through a character's journey, the way we acquaint ourselves with Oz by means of Dorothy's adventures there. Here, however, an omniscient narration conducts the tour. Eventually we enter a darkened bedroom. A hand holds a paperweight, and over this is superimposed a flurry of snow (Fig. 9.8, p. 281). The image teases us. Is the narration making a lyrical comment, or is the image subjective, a glimpse into the dying man's mind or vision? In either case, the narration reveals its ability to command a great deal of story information. Our sense of omniscience is enhanced when, after the man dies, a nurse scurries into the room: apparently no character knows what we know.

At other points in the film the omniscient narration calls attention to itself. For instance, during Susan's opera debut in Leland's flashback (6i), we see stage-hands high above her reacting to her performance. (Such omniscient "asides" tend to be associated with camera movements, as we shall see in Chapter 9.) Most vivid, however, is the omniscient narration at the very end of the film. Thompson and the other reporters leave, never having learned the meaning of "Rosebud." But we linger in the vast storeroom of Xanadu. And, thanks to the narration, we learn that "Rosebud" is the name of Kane's childhood toy. We can now associate the opening's emphasis on the little paperweight with the scene's revelation of the sled. This narration is truly omniscient: it "knew" a key piece of story information at the outset, teased us with hints (the snow, the tiny cottage in the paperweight), and has finally revealed at least part of the answer to the question posed at the outset. A return to the "No Trespassing" sign reminds us of our initial point of departure for the film. Like *The Road Warrior*, then, the film derives its unity not only from principles of causality and time but also from a patterned narration that arouses curiosity and suspense and yields a surprise at the very end.

## SUMMARY

Not every narrative analysis goes through the categories of cause-effect, story-plot differences, motivations, parallelism, progression from opening to closing, and narrational range and depth in that exact order, as we have done here. Our purpose in this examination of *Citizen Kane* has been as much to illustrate these concepts as to analyze the film's narrative. With practice, the critic becomes more familiar with these analytical tools and can use them flexibly, suiting his or her approach to the specific film at hand.

In looking at any narrative film, such questions as these may help in understanding its formal structures:

1. Which story events are directly presented to us in the plot, and which must we infer? Is there any nondiegetic material given in the plot?

2. What is the earliest story event of which we learn? How does it relate through a series of causes and effects to later events?

3. What is the temporal relationship of story events? Has temporal order, frequency, or duration been manipulated in the plot to affect our understanding of events?

4. Does the closing reflect a clear-cut pattern of development that relates it to the beginning? Do all narrative lines achieve closure, or are some left open?

5. How does the narration present story information to us? Is it restricted to one or a few characters' knowledge, or does it range freely among the characters in different spaces? Does it give us considerable depth of story information by exploring the characters' mental states?

6. Does this film belong to a familiar genre? If so, what conventions of that genre does the narrative employ in order to guide our expectations?

7. How closely does the film follow the standard traits of the classical Hollywood cinema? If it departs significantly from those traits, what formal principle does it use instead?

Though narrative films are the type we see most often when we "go to the movies" in a theater, many other possibilities exist for structuring the overall form in a film. We shall explore the basic types of nonnarrative form in the next chapter.

## NOTES AND QUERIES

### ■ NARRATIVE FORM

A fine overview of the history and functions of narrative in human culture is Robert Scholes and Robert Kellogg, *The Nature of Narrative* (New York: Oxford University Press, 1966). Most conceptions of narrative are drawn from literary theory, which in the last two decades has made remarkable contributions to the study of this type of form. Three good introductions are Seymour Chatman, *Story and Discourse: Narrative Structure in Fiction and Film* (Ithaca: Cornell University Press, 1978); Gerald Prince, *Narratology: The Form and Function of Narrative* (Berlin: Mouton, 1982); and Shlomith Rimmon-Kenan, *Narrative Fiction: Contemporary Poetics* (New York: Methuen, 1983). A more difficult but nonetheless seminal study is Gérard Genette, *Narrative Discourse: An Essay in Method* (Ithaca: Cornell University Press, 1980). The concepts we discuss in this chapter are congruent with this trend of contemporary theory. For other examples, see Ladislav Matejka and Krystyna Pomorska, eds., *Readings in Russian Poetics* (Cambridge, Mass: MIT Press, 1971); Roland Barthes, "An Introduction to the Structural Analysis of Narrative," in Stephen Heath, ed. and trans., *Image, Music, Text* (New York: Hill and Wang, 1977); Tzvetan Todorov, *The Poetics of Prose* (Ithaca: Cornell University Press, 1977); and Jonathan Culler, *Structuralist Poetics* (Ithaca: Cornell University Press, 1976). Many of the assumptions underlying this trend are challenged in Barbara Herrnstein Smith's essay "Narrative Versions, Narrative Theories," *Critical Inquiry* 7, 1 (Autumn 1980): 213–236.

For discussions centered on film narrative's debt to literature and other arts, see John L. Fell, *Film and the Narrative Tradition* (Norman: University of Oklahoma Press, 1974); Charles Musser, "The Early Cinema of Edwin Porter," *Cinema Journal*

**19**, 1 (Fall 1979): 1–38; and "Film/Narrative/The Novel," special number of *Ciné-tracts* **13** (Spring 1981). Specific discussions of particular problems of film narrative may be found in Noël Burch, "Narrative/Diegesis—Thresholds, Limits," *Screen* **23**, 2 (July–August 1982): 16–33; Colin MacCabe, "Realism and the Cinema: Notes on Some Brechtian Theses," *Screen* **14**, 2 (Summer 1974): 7–27; and Gill Davies, "Teaching about Narrative," *Screen Education* **29** (Winter 1978/79): 56–76.

## ■ THE SPECTATOR

What does the spectator *do* in making sense of a narrative? Various theorists have sought to characterize the perceiver's activity. In literature, two valuable studies are Horst Ruthrof, *The Reader's Construction of Narrative* (London: Routledge & Kegan Paul, 1981), and Peter Brooks, *Reading for the Plot: Design and Intention in Narrative* (New York: Knopf, 1984). Meir Sternberg emphasizes expectation, hypotheses, and inference in his *Expositional Modes and Temporal Ordering in Fiction* (Baltimore: Johns Hopkins University Press, 1978). Sternberg's approach is close to our own assumptions in this chapter. In "Styles of Reading," *Poetics Today* **3**, 3 (Spring 1982): 77–88, George L. Dillon distinguishes among the "Character-Action-Moral" approach, the "Digger for secrets" approach, and the "Anthropologist" approach. A brief suggestion about the narrative spectator is advanced by Christian Metz in "Histoire/Discours: A Note on Two Voyeurisms," *The Imaginary Signifier* (Bloomington: Indiana University Press, 1982). From a different standpoint, David Bordwell proposes a model of the spectator's story-comprehending activities in chapter 3 of *Narration in the Fiction Film* (Madison: University of Wisconsin Press, 1985).

## ■ NARRATIVE TIME

Most theorists agree that cause-effect relations and chronology are central to narrative. In a traditional narrative, the French novelist Alain Robbe-Grillet asserts, "The succession of facts, the narrative concatenation, as is said today, is based entirely on a system of causalities: what follows phenomenon A is phenomenon B, the consequence of the first; thus, the chain of events in the novel" ("Order and Disorder in Film and Fiction," *Critical Inquiry* **4**, 1 [Autumn 1977]: 5). A good analysis of causality and temporality may be found in Roland Barthes, "Action Sequences," in Joseph Strelka, ed., *Patterns of Literary Style* (University Park: State University of Pennsylvania Press, 1971). For specifically cinematic discussions, see Jan Mukařovský, "Time in Film," in John Burbank and Peter Steiner, eds., *Structure, Sign, and Function: Selected Essays by Jan Mukařovský* (New Haven, Conn.: Yale University Press, 1977), pp. 191–200; and Brian Henderson, "Tense, Mood, and Voice in Film (Notes After Genette)," *Film Quarterly* **26**, 4 (Summer 1983): 4–17.

Our discussion of the differences between plot duration, story duration, and screen duration is necessarily simplified. The distinctions hold good at a theoretical level, but the differences may sometimes vanish in particular cases. Story and plot duration differ most drastically at the level of the *whole* film, as when two years of action (story duration) are shown or told about in scenes that occur across a week (plot duration) and then that week is itself rendered in two hours (screen duration). At the level of a smaller *part*, say a shot or a scene, we usually assume story and plot duration to be equal, and screen duration may or may not be equal to them.

The matter is discussed at greater length in chapter 5 of Bordwell, *Narration in the Fiction Film* (cited above).

## ■ NARRATION

One approach to narration has been to draw analogies between film and literature. Novels have first-person narration ("Call me Ishmael") and third-person narration ("Maigret puffed his pipe as he walked along slowly, hands clasped behind his back"); perhaps film does as well? The argument for applying the linguistic category of "person" to cinema is discussed most fully in Bruce F. Kawin, *Mindscreen: Bergman, Godard and First-Person Film* (Princeton, N.J.: Princeton University Press, 1978). Kawin does not confine his discussion to character narrators, such as Kane's associates, who are obviously telling their tale in the first person; he suggests that entire films can be seen as proceeding from the mind of a narrator and thus warrant the label "first person." This analogy seems to assume the more basic categories of range and depth, which we discuss in this chapter. See also Don Fredericksen, "Modes of Reflexive Film," *Quarterly Review of Film Studies* **4**, 3 (Summer 1979): 299–320.

Another literary analogy is that of "point of view." The best survey in English is Susan Sniader Lanser, *The Narrative Act: Point of View in Prose Fiction* (Princeton, N.J.: Princeton University Press, 1981). The applicability of point of view to film is discussed in detail in Edward Branigan, *Point of View in the Cinema: A Theory of Narration and Subjectivity in Classical Film* (New York: Mouton, 1984). See also Chapter 6 of Kristin Thompson's "Closure within a Dream? Point-of-view in *Laura*," in *Breaking the Glass Armor: Neoformalist Film Analysis* (Princeton, N.J.: Princeton University Press, 1988), pp. 162–194. A special issue of *Film Reader* (**4** [1979]) considers various meanings of the concept.

In "A Scene at the 'Movies,'" *Screen* **23**, 2 (July–August 1982), Ben Brewster discusses how the hierarchy of knowledge can operate in a single "simple" film. The implicit moral values at work in narration are considered in Nick Browne, *The Rhetoric of Filmic Narration* (Ann Arbor, Mich.: UMI Research Press, 1982). For general discussion, see Bordwell, *Narration in the Fiction Film* (cited above).

## ■ NARRATIVE CONVENTIONS: GENRE AND OTHER GROUPINGS

A quick overview of genre theory in literature is Heather Dubrow's *Genre* (London: Methuen, 1982); a particular application that considers the reader's activity is Tzvetan Todorov, *The Fantastic: A Structuralist Approach to a Literary Genre* (Ithaca, N.Y.: Cornell University Press, 1975). Thomas Schatz's *American Film Genres* (New York: Random House, 1981) is a readable introduction to a myth-based approach to genre narrative. See also "Film Genre," a special number of *Film Reader* **3** (1978) for many varying analyses of genre films. In *Sixguns and Society* (Berkeley: University of California Press, 1975), Will Wright discusses how the narrative structure of Westerns relates to social forces of different periods. Studies of narrative and narration in the musical film are Rick Altman, ed., *Genre: The Musical* (London: Routledge & Kegan Paul, 1981); Jane Feuer, *The Hollywood Musical* (Bloomington: Indiana University Press, 1982); and Rick Altman, *The American Musical* (Bloomington: Indiana University Press, 1987).

Study of the narrative conventions of the classical Hollywood cinema has yielded many detailed analyses. An early and still important theoretical statement is Thomas Elsaesser, "Why Hollywood," *Monogram* **1** (April 1971): 4–10. Further discussion and bibliography will be found in David Bordwell, Janet Staiger, and Kristin Thompson, *The Classical Hollywood Cinema: Film Style and Mode of Production to 1960* (New York: Columbia University Press, 1985).

## ■ THE IDEOLOGY OF FORM

We are used to looking for various sorts of meaning in formal processes, but can the very type of form that a film uses itself be imbued with ideological implications? Is there an ideological significance to narrative patterning itself? For instance, does the Hollywood conception of causality itself embody a notion of individual action as the only effective sort? Such questions have come to the forefront of film studies in recent years. Many scholars have started to consider how a society's ways of constructing narratives can be interpreted as bearing ideological meaning. The most significant work has been done within a feminist frame of reference. Outstanding examples are Janet Bergstrom's "Enunciation and Sexual Difference," *Camera Obscura* **3–4** (Summer 1979): 33–69; E. Ann Kaplan, *Women and Film: Both Sides of the Camera* (New York: Methuen, 1983); and Annette Kuhn, *Women's Pictures: Feminism and Cinema* (London: Routledge & Kegan Paul, 1982).

## ■ NARRATIVE ANALYSES OF FILMS

Sample narrative analyses of films may be found in Alan Williams, "Narrative Patterns in *Only Angels Have Wings*," *Quarterly Review of Film Studies* **1**, 4 (November 1976): 357–372; Kristin Thompson, *Breaking the Glass Armor*, cited above; Joyce Nelson, "*Mildred Pierce* Reconsidered," *Film Reader* **2** (1977): 65–70; and Roy Armes, *The Films of Alain Robbe-Grillet* (Amsterdam: John Benjamins B. V., 1981). The Indiana University Press Filmguide series tended to emphasize narrative form, and these monographs are often good introductions to problems of film analysis. Typical are these: James Naremore, *Filmguide to Psycho* (Bloomington: Indiana University Press, 1973); E. Rubinstein, *Filmguide to The General* (Bloomington: Indiana University Press, 1973); and Ted Perry, *Filmguide to 8½* (Bloomington: Indiana University Press, 1975).

For advanced study, a difficult but rewarding analysis of Welles's *Touch of Evil* has been done by Stephen Heath in "Film and System: Terms of Analysis," *Screen* **16**, 1 (Spring 1975): 7–77, and **16**, 2 (Summer 1975): 91–113.

## ■ "ROSEBUD"

Critics have scrutinized few films as closely as *Citizen Kane*. For a sampling, see Joseph McBride, *Orson Welles* (New York: Viking, 1972); Charles Higham, *The Films of Orson Welles* (Berkeley: University of California Press, 1970); David Bordwell, "*Citizen Kane*," in Bill Nichols, ed., *Movies and Methods* (Berkeley: University of California Press, 1976); Robert Carringer, "Rosebud, Dead or Alive: Narrative and Symbolic Structure in *Citizen Kane*," *PMLA* (March 1976): 185–193; and James Naremore, *The Magic World of Orson Welles* (New York: Oxford University Press, 1978).

Pauline Kael, in a famous essay on the making of the film, finds "Rosebud" a naïve gimmick. Interestingly, her discussion emphasizes *Citizen Kane* as part of the journalist-film genre and tends not to go beyond the detective-story aspect. See *The Citizen Kane Book* (Boston: Little, Brown, 1971), pp. 1–84. In contrast, other critics find "Rosebud" an incomplete answer to Thompson's search; compare particularly the Naremore, Bordwell, and Carringer analyses above. A very different account of the film is offered by Peter Bogdanovich, in "The Kane Mutiny," *Esquire* **78**, 4 (October 1972): 99–105, 180–190. For a balanced account of *Kane*'s classical and modern features, see Peter Wollen, "Introduction to *Citizen Kane*," *Film Reader* **1** (1975): 9–15. Half of this issue of *Film Reader* is devoted to analyzing *Citizen Kane*. Robert L. Carringer's *Making of Citizen Kane* (Berkeley: University of California Press, 1985) offers the most extensive account of the film's production.

# FOUR

# NONNARRATIVE FORMAL SYSTEMS

In examining the general characteristics of film form in Chapter 2, we used *The Wizard of Oz* as our main example. The formal principles we saw at work in it—function and motivation, similarity and repetition, difference and variation, development, and unity and disunity—apply to all films. Because narrative films are so important in our film-viewing experience, we devoted Chapter 3 to this type of form, using *Citizen Kane* as our example.

But there are other types of film form, and these are as important in our lives as are narratives. Instructional films, political advertisements, the experimental films we may watch in a local art museum auditorium—such films may not contain any stories at all. They have *nonnarrative* formal systems.

We can distinguish four broad types of nonnarrative form: *categorical*, *rhetorical*, *abstract*, and *associational*. In this chapter we will look at the traits of each type of form, examining one example of each type closely.

How do these four types of nonnarrative form differ from each other? Before looking at each of these types in detail, let us differentiate them briefly by showing how each could treat the same subject matter differently. Suppose we are setting out to make a film about our local grocery store and are considering different ways of organizing its form. We could use narrative form by, say, showing a typical day in the store. But there are other, nonnarrative ways of constructing such a film.

**Categorical** films, as the name suggests, divide a subject into parts, or categories. In our hypothetical film, the grocery store would be our overall subject.

We could go through the store and film each portion, to show what sorts of things the store contains. We might show the meat section, the produce section, the checkout counters, and other categories within the store.

But this is not the only way to treat this subject. We might instead set out to convince our audience of something about the grocery store. In that case we would employ **rhetorical** form, which presents an argument and lays out evidence to support it. We might state the idea that a locally owned grocery store gives its customers better service than does a chain store. For this version, we might film the owner of the store giving the customers personal help; we might interview him or her about the services that the store tries to provide; we might interview customers about their opinions on the store; we might try to show that the food carried by the store is of superior quality. Overall, we would organize our film to give our audience reasons to believe that this locally owned store is a better place to shop.

We could, however, decide on a third alternative, to make a film about the grocery store using **abstract** form. In this type of organization, the audience's attention is drawn to abstract visual and sonic qualities of the things depicted—shape, color, aural rhythm, and the like. Hence we would try to film the store, which most people would consider quite mundane, in interesting and striking ways. Unusual camera positions could distort the shapes of cans and boxes on the shelves, close framings could bring out large areas of bright color, an incongruous musical track could affect the audience's reaction to the images, and so on.

Finally, we might wish to suggest an attitude toward the store, or to elicit a mood in relation to it. **Associational** form would be appropriate here, for it works through the juxtaposition of loosely connected images to suggest an emotion or a concept to the spectator. Perhaps we find grocery stores cramped and oppressive. We could film the store's contents to look bleak, and we could insert metaphorical material to cue the audience to respond negatively to what they see. For example, a shot of long lines of shopping carts at a checkout counter might be compared to a shot of a rush-hour traffic jam. Through a series of such associations between aspects of the store and other types of things, the film could create a certain tone or attitude toward the store.

We do not intend to suggest that filmmakers typically choose a subject and then cast about for an appropriate sort of organization; usually the type of form chosen is related to the purposes and interests of the filmmaker and to the choices available in a production context. The point is that each of these films would create a very different view of the same grocery store. The differences among types of nonnarrative form are important because each type will call upon different viewing conventions and will cue different types of expectations in the spectator. If we know we are watching a rhetorical film that is trying to convince us to support a certain governmental policy, we may adopt a skeptical attitude, testing the evidence and perhaps ultimately rejecting it. But as we watch an abstract film, we may become more contemplative, watching shapes and colors pass before us. Even though we may seldom consciously classify the films we watch as "rhetorical" or "associational," we do differentiate among different types of films, and we have a range of viewing skills upon which we can draw, depending on which is appropriate.

With our basic distinctions among the four types of nonnarrative form, we are ready to look at each in greater detail, with examples from actual films. For each example, we will segment the film, as described in Chapter 2. The emphasis of our analysis will then be on how these parts relate to each other in each type of nonnarrative organization.

## CATEGORICAL FORMAL SYSTEMS

### ■ PRINCIPLES OF CATEGORICAL FORM

*Categories* are groupings that individuals or societies create to organize their knowledge of the world. These categories can be more or less logical. Some are based on scientific theory and experiment, and these will often attempt to account exhaustively for all the data in question. For example, scientists have developed an elaborate system of categories to classify every known animal and plant into genus and species. Similarly, the Table of Elements establishes one category for each known element, depending on the number of particles in its atom. This table attempts to be exhaustive in its coverage: all matter on earth should fall into one or more of the categories, and when new types of matter are found, new categories must be created.

Most of the categories we use in our daily life are less scientific, less neat, and less exhaustive than these examples. We tend to group the things around us based on a common-sense, practical approach, or on ideological views of the world. Ordinarily, for example, we do not group animals we see by genus or species, but use such rough categories as "pets," "wild animals," "farm animals," "zoo animals," and so on. Such groupings are not logically exclusive or exhaustive (at one time or another, some animals might fit into most or all of these categories), yet they suffice for our usual purposes. Ideologically based categories are also seldom strictly logical. Societies do not "naturally" fall into such categories as "primitive" or "advanced," for example. These are groupings that have been developed out of complex sets of beliefs, and they may well not stand up to logical scrutiny.

If a filmmaker wants to convey some information about the world to audiences, categories may provide a basis for organizing the film's form. Usually the categories chosen will be conventional ones that exist in society and are widely recognizable. A documentary film about butterflies might use scientific groupings, showing one type of butterfly and giving information about its habits, then showing another, with more information, and so on. Similarly, a travelogue about Switzerland would give a sampling of local sights and customs. These might be things stereotypically associated with that country: skiing, clocks, chocolate, cheese, native costumes, and so on. The filmmaker might also devise new categories. The Swiss travelogue, for example, might be a portrait of little-known aspects of the country that the filmmaker found interesting; such a film might still convey a great deal of information but would offer the possibility of avoiding the clock-and-cheese clichés.

One important thing to note is that different sets of categories overlap. Any one thing or situation in the world can fit into many categories. A single building might be an example of the style of architect *X*, a post office in the United States, a source for stamp-collecting material, a target of political demonstrators, a site under consideration by condominium developers, or any number of other concepts. Similarly, a chicken could be classified as something to eat, an unusual pet, an animal found on a farm, an easily hypnotized creature, a state bird, and so on. As a result, the filmmaker, when faced with a certain subject matter, may have a broad range of choices as to what set of categories to use.

The formal organization of a categorical film will often be simple, since it is based upon repetition with slight variation. All the types of things in the film must in some way be alike, yet each type must be distinguishable from the others. Typically, the film will have one large subject that organizes its overall form, and then it will introduce categories to break the film up into segments. In our travelogue, the general subject was Switzerland, while categories would be clock making (one segment in a clock factory or store), skiing (a segment in the Alps), and so forth. The formal organization will often involve an introduction of the general category, followed by a series of segments, each devoted to one or more examples of the category. Typically the ending will return to the general topic as a summary.

Patterns of development will usually be simple as well: small to large, local to national, personal to public, and so on. The film on butterflies, for example, might begin with smaller species and work up to large ones, or it might go from drab to colorful types.

Because categorical form tends to develop in fairly simple ways, it presents potential problems for keeping the spectator interested. If the progression from segment to segment depends too much on repetition, our expectations will be easily satisfied, and we may become bored. To make the categories more interesting, the filmmaker may try to introduce variations and to make us keep adjusting our expectations. This variation may simply involve the introduction of an unusual category. But often the filmmaker may organize individual segments within the film around other types of formal systems: abstract, rhetorical, associational, or narrative. The butterfly film might exploit the colors and shapes of the various examples to add abstract visual interest. But such abstract interest will remain subordinate to the overall categorical form of the film. After all, if we grew so interested in the colors that we forgot to notice the differences among categories, the point of the film would be lost. (Of course, a filmmaker might use butterflies deliberately to make an abstract film. Stan Brakhage did so with moths in his *Mothlight*, where he attached real moth wings to a strip of film to create abstract patterns. But such a film would clearly be created for a very different purpose and would elicit different responses from us.)

Similarly, a rhetorical argument could be made within a segment. The film might deal with one endangered species of butterfly, arguing that certain governmental policies had created the threat. Or, the film could use narrative form in one segment, with a narrator telling an anecdote: "Now this is a very unusual specimen. I remember the day I caught it. . . ." But in either case, the overall organization of the film would be categorical, with these segments providing variation to hold our interest.

Such potential for variety suggests that in spite of the simplicity of categorical form, filmmakers can use it to create complex and interesting films. Our example, *Olympia*, Part 2, shows how this can be done.

## ■ AN EXAMPLE OF CATEGORICAL FORM: *OLYMPIA*, PART 2

Today we are used to seeing the Olympic games broadcast live on television, with the cameras and announcers picking out certain events from the several that are going on simultaneously. The series of broadcasts takes place over days and therefore has a somewhat loose organization. It takes the form of the Olympic games themselves, with opening and closing ceremonies to mark the beginning and end, and a series of events between. But even with such a rough formal pattern, we can reasonably expect certain patterns of repetitions: instant replays after events, interviews with the winners, and so on.

*Olympia*, the two-part film made of the 1936 Olympic games held in Berlin, has a more careful and varied formal structure than the television broadcasts of the Olympic games. Its director, Leni Riefenstahl, had to take the vast amount of footage of many events shot by over 40 cameras, and reduce it to two films of under two hours each. Since the events were not being shown live, her films could contain patterns of development that would link the individual events together into a unified whole. We will be analyzing only Part 2 of *Olympia* here, because its formal organization is more complex and varied than Part 1, which shows a series of games with little pattern of development across the film. Part 2, on the other hand, has distinct patterns of development and is a self-contained film that one can follow without having seen the first part.

Riefenstahl's overall category was dictated by the subject with which she was to deal: the 1936 Olympics. But there could be many ways to arrange the individual segments treating various categories. She could, for example, have gone chronologically through the games from their beginning to their end, as television does now. Instead, Riefenstahl rearranged events according to a distinctive structure of development that forms a sort of ABA pattern.

*Olympia* and the 1936 Olympic games were among the last efforts by the Nazi party to present a cooperative attitude to the world. To placate the International Olympic Committee and to avoid adverse reactions and boycotts by other countries, Hitler agreed to suppress anti-Semitic campaigns in Germany (though these campaigns resumed after the games ended). To demonstrate this apparent cooperativeness, the film stresses the comradeship among the athletes of various countries, and its pattern of development supports this explicit meaning. The early part of the film concentrates on the games as such, rather than on the competition among athletes and countries. Then gradually, toward the middle and latter parts of the film, we begin to learn the identities of the players, and suspense builds up about who will win the events. Finally, in the diving sequence at the end, the form turns back to the beginning, and we watch the diving without any differentiation being made among the participants, simply for the sheer beauty of the event itself. The film thus achieves variety and also places the competition in the context of the games themselves as the main focus of attention.

Accompanying this pattern of development are parallel changes that reinforce it. Most notably, the film begins by showing the athletes and crowds in an impersonal way during the games; individuals' appearances and reactions are not stressed. Then, as the competition becomes more important, we begin to see a personalized view of the athletes—even, at one point, a subjective one. Then, in the diving sequence, the personal emphasis drains away once more, and we watch a series of abstract, birdlike bodies flying through the air. Similarly, the athletes' participation in the events is made to look effortless at first; then, as the athletes are personalized, we see more of the stress and struggle they undergo; and finally the diving sequence returns us to the effortlessness of the original segments. Lastly, there is a move from nonnarrative form at the beginning, toward an introduction of little narratives within segments. Some of the central segments are like stories, with the athletes as characters, and the film builds suspense as to which of them will win. But such plot structures also disappear by the film's end.

Despite the simplicity of its subject, then, *Olympia*, Part 2, is a highly structured film with a variety of ways of presenting its categories. Its segments are clearly marked off within the film by fade-outs and frequently by musical fanfares as well.

**C.** Credits, with Olympic flag
**1.** Nature and the Olympians: morning exercise and swimming
**2.** Gymnastics
**3.** Yacht races
**4.** Pentathlon
**5.** Women exercising
**6.** Decathlon
**7.** Field games: field hockey, polo, soccer
**8.** Bicycle race
**9.** Cross-country riding
**10.** Crew
**11.** Diving and swimming, with epilogue in stadium

The individual games provide one set of categories for the film. Since the nationalities of the participants also are a set of categories, Riefenstahl can vary the relative emphasis placed upon each set in the course of the film. The participating countries are of less importance in the opening and closing games, but they come forward strongly in the central, personalized segments. Again, the result is a considerable degree of variety in a film that potentially could have become quite repetitious.

The opening credits introduce the main category of the film in a direct way, not only by the film's title itself but with flags bearing the Olympic emblem (Fig. 4.1). Yet the first segment of the film seems initially to cheat our expectations. Instead of athletes or a stadium, we see lyrical, almost static shots of foliage and a pond. Slow, Wagnerian music complements this passage. But soon we see a line of running figures in the misty morning air, and our expectations are belatedly fulfilled. Riefenstahl links the Olympian athletes to nature by introducing them in this woodland setting, and she also plays down their different nationalities at first. The whole first segment, in the woods and bathhouse, and later by the Olympians' club, centers around preparations for the games, rather than on the games themselves. The filmmaker has chosen to begin with a prologue centering around the one element that joins together all the athletes, whatever their sport—exercise. Thus the initial emphasis is on camaraderie rather than competition. At the same time, we begin to see indications of the athletes' nationalities; shirts with "Italia" on them (Fig. 4.2) and other similar cues introduce one set of categories—the countries represented at the games. The motif of comparing the athletes with nature continues as well, with shots of athletes exercising juxtaposed with shots of animals. The scene's ending brings all the segment's motifs together. A shot with flowers in the foreground (Fig. 4.3) shifts its focus to reveal an athlete in the background (Fig. 4.4)—nature and the games are compared once more. In the next, and final, shot of the segment, a row of flags (Fig. 4.5) summarizes the categories of nations participating.

Segment 2, the gymnastics, opens by picking up a motif from Segment 1, juxtaposing a branch in the foreground with the crowded stadium at the rear (Fig. 4.6). A parade of athletes with flags picks up the motif of nations. But, as the competition begins, we do not learn the participants' nationalities or names. The emphasis here is on skill, not the competition among countries, and this, too, follows directly from Segment 1. Of all the events shown, gymnastics is the closest in appearance to the calisthenics that we have just seen the athletes doing; now the spirit of fellowship we had seen before continues. The men seem to be cooperating rather than competing. The emotional reactions of both participants and

Fig. 4.1

Fig. 4.2

Fig. 4.3

Fig. 4.4

Fig. 4.5

Fig. 4.6

Fig. 4.7

Fig. 4.8

Fig. 4.9

onlookers are deemphasized. We see the crowds only at a distance, as the backdrop for the action (Fig. 4.7). And the next shot places the gymnast against the sky (Fig. 4.8), seeming to move with effortless grace. Indeed, in the final shot of the segment, an athlete goes soaring off the bar in slow motion (Fig. 4.9), with a fade-out as he drifts gracefully out of the frame to the right. In this and other shots of this segment, we see athletes flying off the bar, but not landing. The soaring, effortless action by bodies suspended in space will be a motif picked up by the diving sequence at the end.

Over the next few segments, *Olympia* emphasizes more and more the idea of competition among individual countries and athletes. Segment 3 shows a series of yacht races, and we see many quick shots of the individual crews and boats. Yet we cannot tell one crew from another. The emphasis is on the dynamic action of the race itself. While the boats are still skimming across the water, an announcer's voice tells us which country won each event, but we do not see the ends of the

Fig. 4.10

Fig. 4.11

Fig. 4.12

Fig. 4.13

races, the winners' reactions, or anything else that would individualize this international competition.

But in Segment 4, the pentathlon, the film's tactics change considerably. The announcer's voice gives us more information about the countries involved in the event: "Swedish officers have monopolized it since 1912." The contestants are introduced to us by name: Handrick, the German; Leonhard, the American; and so on. Shots of each with the names repeated come in at intervals during the various races, so that we can for the first time recognize the individuals. Moreover, the events of the pentathlon are shown in chronological order (though some are skipped and just summarized by the announcer). Thus we follow the event as a narrative; the participants are like characters, and we are in suspense about who will win. When the German wins the gold medal and the American the silver, there is much emphasis on their reactions during the awards ceremony. Moreover, we see the crowd's reaction, as boys in uniform applaud (Fig. 4.10), and then we see the winners and officials at the ceremony (Fig. 4.11).

We should note that, in spite of *Olympia* being a Nazi-financed film, its ideology downplays racism to a surprising extent; in a film destined for screenings around the world, the Nazis wanted to put on a show of international cooperation. (Different versions of *Olympia* were distributed with German, French, and English sound tracks; these, according to historians, differed only slightly. Riefenstahl made no attempt to deemphasize the fact that many black athletes won medals in Berlin in 1936. Despite Hitler's disapproval, in Part I she chose to concentrate on Jesse Owens more than any other athlete.) In some segments, however, a considerable amount of militarism is in evidence. The comparison of the uniformed boys to German officers in these two shots (Figs. 4.10 and 4.11) is particularly striking. Both the pentathlon and the riding events in Segment 9 involve military officers as participants and officials, and an occasional swastika armband is visible. Thus, though Nazi ideology is muted in the film, it could be considered an implicit meaning.

After the highly dramatic pentathlon, Riefenstahl provides an interlude, a brief series of shots of thousands of women doing calisthenics in unison on a field before the stadium. Beginning with close views of a few women, the scene takes us through a series of more distant views to a point high above the field, gradually revealing the enormous number of people taking part. This impressive segment depends partly on the abstract patterns of the dancelike movements and reiterates the exercise motif of the opening. For a short span the emphasis returns to cooperation among countries, before the film goes on to the next segment, which deals again with competition.

Segment 6, the decathlon, uses narrative form to a greater extent than any other part of the film. An announcer is shown standing before microphones (Fig. 4.12), and a voice (dubbed into English in American prints) introduces the participants. Although there are a number of athletes named, our attention is focused from the start on Glen Morris, described as "a hitherto unknown American." The "hitherto" cues us that he will probably win the event, and the rest of the segment concentrates on him. In each field event shown, the camera favors Morris, and suspense is generated by our sense of his tension and great effort. The announcer emphasizes this; over a shot of Morris's intense preparation for the shot put (Fig. 4.13), the voice declares, "He must try to catch up on Clark," the player currently ahead. We see Morris and his competitors' facial reactions to their performances in each event. This treatment is very different from the distant, objective, noncompetitive treatment of the gymnastics in Segment 2, and the decathlon marks the

Fig. 4.14

Fig. 4.15

Fig. 4.16

Fig. 4.17

Fig. 4.18

Fig. 4.19

height of this attempt to involve us with the athletes as characters. The segment ends by reiterating the flag motif, with Morris's laurel-crowned face superimposed briefly over an American flag.

Segment 7, the field games, goes back to a simple categorical presentation of three events: field hockey (in which an announcer tells us the winning country over general shots of play), polo (which is accompanied only by music, without our knowing who is playing), and soccer (which is presented as a chronological series of highlights of the game from beginning to end). Thus, even within a straightforward segment with three categories, the film manages to introduce variation to maintain our interest.

Segment 8, the bike race, is shorter than the pentathlon or decathlon segments, but there is some attempt to dramatize events here, too. At first we see only general shots of the race, but as the end approaches, the announcer tells us that various national teams are striving to pull ahead. This generates suspense, and the film involves us in the finish by actually giving us hints of the subjective experiences of the cyclists: we see a French cyclist (Fig. 4.14), then a tree whizzing by, as he might be seeing it (Fig. 4.15), and then a tree and road superimposed over a close view of a cyclist (Fig. 4.16). From the distant, depersonalized view of the athletes in the early parts of the film, we have progressed to a point where we are right with the cyclists, seeing things as they do. The ending of the segment brings back the flag motif as the cyclists are given their awards in the stadium (Fig. 4.17).

The next segments retreat from this strong subjectivity. The cross-country riding events are handled in Segment 9 in a fashion somewhat parallel to the pentathlon. We see the individual riders and know their nationalities, but there is little treatment of them as individuals. (The militarism of the pentathlon segment also returns here.) Similarly, the rowing races in Segment 10 put the stress on the teams' nationalities and the winners. We see close shots of crew members (Fig. 4.18) and onlookers, but there are no continuing "characters," as Glen Morris had been. In these segments, the film moves further along its pattern of development, starting back toward the eventual return to a more objective, depersonalized treatment.

The final segment climaxes this pattern. We see women's diving and do get brief views of the winners' reactions: for example, a woman embraced by her father and signing autographs. Similarly, the swimming races, though mostly covered by distant moving camera shots, do show us glimpses of the athletes' emotions, as when a Japanese contestant learns that he has won (Fig. 4.19). But by the final diving sequence, the emphasis on the competition between individuals and countries is nearly gone. Early in the diving sequence we briefly see the faces of the divers

Fig. 4.20

Fig. 4.21

Fig. 4.22

and audience (Fig. 4.20). But before long the divers' bodies simply plunge, one after another in a long series, into or toward the water. As in the gymnasts' segment, there is no announcer's voice, no information on identity or country—simply a sense of the beauty and dynamism of the sport itself. As with the gymnasts, we see less and less of the crowd; later shots isolate the divers as shapes against the sky (Fig. 4.21). Thus the film comes full circle in its pattern of development: back to treating the event as graceful, impersonal, and effortless action, drained of any sense of competition or narrative progress toward a winner. The emphasis rests wholly on the mastery of the body and on a feeling of flight.

At the end of Segment 11 a brief epilogue again summarizes the overall topic—the Olympics—and brings back some motifs. The sky behind the final divers changes to billowing clouds, and the camera moves down to reveal the stadium, with floodlights beaming into the sky. The Olympic flame, a bell, and rows of flags (Fig. 4.22) combine to reiterate the general idea of the Olympics, and the cloudy sky suggests once more the initial linking of the games to nature. The film ends as the camera moves up the beams of the searchlights to the bright point where they meet in the clouds above. And, although this triumphant moment brings the Olympics themselves to a climax, it also suggests the propaganda purpose behind the film itself: a display of Nazi power disguised by a show of cooperation with other nations.

Because of *Olympia*'s double purpose—as a record of the games and as subtle Nazi propaganda—the film provides a good example of all four types of meaning discussed in Chapter 2. On its referential level, we recognize it as coverage of the games, and some of its segments are straightforward accounts of who participated and won. The fact that we are often not given this information, and the beauty of the treatment of the events, also cues us to understand an explicit meaning: these games involve a peaceful, cooperative struggle among athletes of various countries to discipline their bodies and carry on a great international tradition.

There are further meanings involving the Nazi sponsorship of the games and the way those games, and the film's treatment of them, reflect a more general Nazi ideology. (The Nazi government financed the film, but to avoid antagonizing the International Olympic Committee, the film was treated as an independent production by Riefenstahl. See Notes and Queries for more information.) The implicit meaning, which we can interpret fairly easily, especially looking back from a modern perspective, involves an emphasis on Nazi power. In *Olympia*, Part 1, there had been numerous reaction shots of Hitler in the audience; in Part 2, as we have seen, the militarism and swastika armbands frequently remind us of the powers behind these games. More generally, we can find symptomatic meaning in the film's whole treatment of the Olympics with its stress on discipline, on regimenting mass activity (especially the calisthenics in Segments 2 and 5), on a sort of mystical bond between humans and nature, and so on. As we shall see in Chapter 9, the film's style supports all these levels of meaning. These meanings suggest that a categorically organized film can be as subject to ideological coloring as can any other sort of film.

## RHETORICAL FORMAL SYSTEMS

### ■ PRINCIPLES OF RHETORICAL FORM

Another type of film uses *rhetorical* form, in which the filmmaker presents a persuasive argument. The goal in such a film is to make the audience hold an opinion about the subject matter and perhaps to act upon that opinion. This type of film goes beyond the categorical type in that it tries to convince the viewer of some quality about the subject; it does not simply provide information about it.

Rhetorical form is common in all the media. We encounter it frequently in daily life, not just in formal speeches but also in conversation. People often try to persuade each other by argument. Salespeople use persuasion in their jobs, and friends may argue politics over lunch. Television bombards us with one of the most pervasive uses of rhetorical form in film—commercials, which try to persuade viewers to buy products or vote for candidates.

We can define rhetorical form in film by four basic attributes. First, it addresses the viewer, trying to move him or her to a new intellectual conviction, to a new emotional attitude, or to action. (In the latter case, we may already believe something but may need to be persuaded that the belief is important enough to act upon.) Second, the subject of the film will usually not be an issue of scientific truth but a matter of opinion, toward which a person may take a number of equally plausible attitudes. The filmmaker will try to make his or her position seem the most plausible by presenting different types of arguments and evidence. Yet, because the issue cannot be absolutely proven, we may decide upon our opinion simply because the filmmaker has made a convincing case for one position. Because rhetorical films deal with beliefs and arguments, they involve the expression of ideology; indeed, perhaps no type of film form centers so consistently around explicit meaning and ideological implications.

A third aspect of rhetorical form follows from this. If the conclusion cannot be proven beyond question, the filmmaker often appeals to our emotions, rather than presenting only factual evidence. And, fourth, the film will often attempt to persuade the viewer to make a choice that will have an effect on his or her everyday, practical life. This may be as simple as what shampoo to use, or it may involve decisions about which political candidate to support, or even whether a young person will fight in a war.

Films can use all sorts of arguments to persuade us to make such choices. Often, however, these arguments are not presented to us *as* arguments. The film will frequently present arguments as if they were simply true and will not point out other options. There are three main types of arguments the film may use: relating to the source, to the subject, and to the viewer.

**Arguments from source.** Some of the film's arguments will usually relate to the film itself, suggesting how reliable it is. The people who made it and those who narrate it try to give the audience the impression that they are intelligent, well informed, sincere, trustworthy, and so on. These seem just to be objective traits, but they imply an argument: this film comes from reliable people, therefore you should allow yourself to be persuaded by it. For example, a film may use a narrator whose voice is strong and clear, rather than soft and hesitating, because if we hear a voice that seems to carry conviction, we may be more likely to take it as a reliable source of information.

**Subject-centered arguments.** The film will also employ arguments about its subject matter. These arguments may not be *really* logical, but they will be made to seem so. Sometimes the film appeals to beliefs common at the time in a culture. For example, in contemporary America, a large segment of the population is said to believe that most politicians are cynical and corrupt. This may or may not be true of any one politician, but someone running for public office may appeal to that belief and tell potential voters that he or she will bring a new honesty to government. This is not a logical argument, but it may nevertheless persuade some voters. A second approach the film may take is to use examples that support its point. Such evidence may be more or less strong. A taste-test commercial that shows one person choosing the advertiser's product seems to imply that the product really tastes better; yet there is no mention of the other people—perhaps a majority—who preferred the other brand. Finally, filmmakers can back up an argument by exploiting familiar, easily accepted argumentative patterns. Students of rhetoric call such patterns *enthymemes*, arguments that rely on widespread opinion and usually conceal some crucial premises. For example, we might make a film to persuade you that a problem has been solved correctly. We would show that the problem had existed, then show that some action had been taken which solved it. The movement from problem to solution is such a familiar pattern of inference that you might assume that we had proven logically that the right thing was done. On closer analysis, however, you might discover that the film had a hidden premise, such as "On the assumption that this was the best solution, a particular course of action was taken." Perhaps other solutions would have been better, but the film does not examine them. The solution presented is not the logically necessary one that the problem-solution pattern would seem to suggest. Shortly we shall see such enthymematic patterns at work in *The River*.

**Viewer-centered arguments.** Lastly, the film may make an argument that appeals to the emotions of the viewer. We are all familiar with politicians who pose with flag, family, and pets to play upon the sympathies of potential voters. Appeals to patriotism, romantic sentimentality, and other emotions are common in rhetorical films. Filmmakers often use conventions familiar from other films to provoke the desired reaction. Sometimes such appeals can disguise the weakness of other arguments of the film and can persuade the more susceptible audience members to accept the film's outlook.

Rhetorical form in a film can organize these arguments and appeals in a variety of ways. Some filmmakers will present their basic arguments first, then go on to show evidence of the problems and how they would be solved by the solutions argued for in the film. Other films will start with the problem and describe it in detail, then let the viewer know late in the film what change is being advocated. This second approach may create more curiosity and suspense, leading the viewer to reflect on and anticipate possible solutions. Which overall approach the filmmaker chooses will depend on the subject and how it can be most effectively presented.

One standard description of rhetorical form suggests that it begins with an introduction of the situation, goes on to a discussion of the relevant facts, then presents proofs that a given solution fits those facts, and ends with an epilogue that summarizes what has come before. *The River*, made in 1937 by Pare Lorentz, will be our main example of rhetorical form. As we shall see, it presents the situation and problem first, reserving a proposal of a solution until near the end. In laying out its overall form, it adheres to the four-part structure just outlined.

## ■ AN EXAMPLE OF RHETORICAL FORM: *THE RIVER*

Lorentz made *The River* for the U.S. government's Farm Security Administration. In 1937, the country was making progress toward pulling out of the Depression. Under the administration of Franklin Delano Roosevelt, the federal government used its powers extensively to create public works programs in order to provide jobs for the large number of unemployed workers, as well as to correct various social problems. Although many people tend now to think of Roosevelt's policies as the right ones and to credit him with bringing America out of the Depression, we should not forget that there was much political opposition to those policies at the time. *The River*, which hails the Tennessee Valley Authority (TVA) as the solution to problems of flooding, agricultural depletion, and electrification, had a definite ideological slant: promoting Roosevelt's policies. Thus the film's argument was controversial at the time. Let us look at how this film sets out to persuade its audience that the TVA is a good program.

*The River* has eleven segments:

**C.** The credits
**1.** A prologue title setting forth the subject of the film
**2.** A description of the rivers that flow into the Mississippi and then into the Gulf of Mexico
**3.** A history of the early agricultural use of the river
**4.** The problems caused in the South by the Civil War
**5.** A section on lumbering and steel mills in the North and the building of urban areas
**6.** The flooding caused by careless exploitation of the land
**7.** The current effects of these cumulative problems on people: poverty and ignorance
**8.** A map and description of the TVA project
**9.** The dams of the TVA and the benefits they bring
**E.** An end title

The film seems at first just to be giving us information about the Mississippi, and we go quite a way into the film before its argument becomes apparent. But, by the careful use of repetition, variation, and development, Lorentz builds up a case that really depends on all the segments working together as a unified whole.

The opening credits initiate the introductory section of the film; they are shown over an old-fashioned picture of steamboats on the Mississippi, then over a map of the United States with the Mississippi River and its tributaries exaggerated in size (Fig. 4.23). The film immediately suggests to us that its makers are reliable and

Fig. 4.23

Fig. 4.24

knowledgeable, and that this will be an account based on both historical and geographical facts. The same map returns under the prologue writing in the brief opening segment, which states that "This is the story of a river." Such a statement disguises the rhetorical purpose of the film, implying that the film will be an objectively told "story"—that is, it will be presented in narrative form.

Segment 2 continues the introduction with images of the sky, mountains, and rivers, with a man's voice telling us facts about how water flows into the Mississippi from as far away as Idaho and Pennsylvania. The narrator's voice is deep and authoritative, playing on culturally conventional notions of what a trustworthy person sounds like. (The narrator, who was carefully chosen for these qualities, was Thomas Chalmers, formerly a baritone with the Metropolitan Opera.) As the images show the rivers growing in size as they join together (Fig. 4.24), the narrator begins to intone: "Down the Yellowstone, the Milk, the White, and Cheyenne . . . the Cannonball, the Musselshell, the James, and the Sioux." Many other river names follow in a rhythmic list that sounds like poetry. (Indeed, the technique is based on the work of Walt Whitman and other American poets.) Moreover, the voice combines at most points in the film with the distinctively American musical score written by Virgil Thomson, often employing familiar folk songs. Thus the film deliberately adopts an "American" tone throughout. This not only appeals to the spectator's patriotic and sentimental feelings, but also implies that the whole country should be united in dealing with problems that only seem to be regional.

Segment 2 has set up an idyllic situation, with its beautiful images of mountain and river landscapes, and we shall find that the overall development of the film will be toward a restoration of this beauty, but with a difference. The scene also sets up techniques to be repeated and varied in other segments.

With Segment 3, we move into the section of the film's form devoted to the discussion of the relevant facts of American history relating to the Mississippi and the problems it causes. Segment 3 begins much as Segment 2 had, with a view of clouds. But now things begin to change; in contrast to the mountains we saw before, we see mule teams and drivers. Again the narrator's voice begins a list: "New Orleans to Baton Rouge . . . Baton Rouge to Natchez . . . Natchez to Vicksburg." This list is part of the brief recounting of the history of the dikes built along the Mississippi in pre–Civil War days to control flooding. The narrator is confirmed as trustworthy and knowledgeable, giving us facts and dates in the nation's history. We see cotton bales loaded onto steamboats, giving a sense of the country's early strength as an exporter of goods.

So far the film has seemed to follow its initial purpose of telling a story of the river. But in Segment 4, it begins to introduce the problems that the TVA will eventually solve. The film shows the results of the Civil War: destroyed houses and dispossessed landowners, the land worn out by the cultivation of cotton, and people forced to move west. The moral tone of the film here becomes apparent, and it is an appealing one. Over images of impoverished people, bleak music plays. It is based on a familiar folk tune, "Go Tell Aunt Rhody," which, with its line "the old gray goose is dead," underscores the losses of the farm dwellers. The narrator's voice expresses compassion as he speaks of the South's "tragedy of land impover-ished." This attitude of sympathy may incline us to accept as true what the film tells us. The narrator also refers to the people of the period as "we": "We mined the soil for cotton until it would yield no more." Here the film's persuasive intent becomes evident. It was not literally *we*, you and I and the narrator, who grew this cotton. The use of the word "we" is a rhetorical strategy to make us feel that all Americans have a responsibility for this problem and for finding a solution.

Later segments repeat the strategies of these earlier ones. In Segment 5 the film again uses the poetically repetitious narration to describe the lumbering industry's growth after the Civil War, listing "Black spruce and Norway pine" and other trees. In the images, we see the pines against the sky, echoing the cloud motif that had opened Segments 2 and 3 (Fig. 4.25). This creates a parallel between the riches of the agricultural and the industrial areas. A sprightly sequence of logging, accompanied by music based on the tune "Hot Time in the Old Town Tonight," again gives us a sense of America's strength. A section on coal mining and steel mills follows and enhances this impression. This segment ends with references to the growing urban centers: "We built a hundred cities and a thousand towns," and we hear a brief list of their names.

Fig. 4.25

Up to this point we have seen the strengths of America associated with the river valley, with just a hint of the problems that growth has sparked. But Segment 6 switches over and creates a lengthy series of contrasts to the earlier parts. It begins with the same list of trees—"Black spruce and Norway pine," but now we see stumps against fog instead of trees against clouds (Fig. 4.26). Another line returns, but with a new phrase added: "We built a hundred cities and a thousand towns . . . but at what a cost." Beginning with the barren hilltops, we are shown how melting ice runs off, and how the run-off gradually erodes hillsides and swells rivers into flooding torrents. Once more we hear the list of rivers from Segment 2, but now the music is bleak and the rivers are no longer idyllic. Again there is a parallel presented between the soil erosion here and the soil depletion in the South after the Civil War. The film has gradually brought us from a situation of natural beauty and developed the central problem around which its argument is based. Now we see scenes of real flooding, with sandbagging, destruction, people rescued and living in tent camps, and other flood problems. And, as we watch these scenes, we hear sirens and the turbulent roar of water, building up a sense of onrushing disaster. There is a considerable emotional appeal here, as we are given a sense of the people being utterly unable to control the water.

Fig. 4.26

By this point we understand the information the film is presenting about flooding and erosion, but it withholds the solution and presents the effects of the floods on people's lives in contemporary America. Segment 7 describes government aid to flood victims in 1937 but points out that the basic problem still exists. *The River* employs a striking enthymeme here: "And poor land makes poor people— poor people make poor land." This sounds reasonable on the surface, but upon examination its meaning becomes unclear. (Didn't the rich southern plantation owners whose ruined mansions we saw in Segment 4 have a lot to do with the impoverishment of the soil?) Such statements are employed more for their poetic sound and emotional appeal than for any tight logic they may contain. Scenes of tenant farmer families (Fig. 4.27) appeal directly to our emotional response to such poverty. This segment picks up on motifs introduced in Segment 4, on the Civil War; now, the film tells us, these people cannot just pick up and go west—there is no more open land there.

Fig. 4.27

Now the problem has been introduced and discussed, and emotional appeals have prepared the audience to accept a solution. Segment 8 presents that solution and begins the part of the film devoted to the proofs that this solution is an effective one. In Segment 8, the map of the opening titles returns, and the narrator says, "There is no such thing as an ideal river in nature, but the Mississippi River is out of joint." Here we have another example of an enthymeme—an opinion assumed to be logically valid and factually accurate. The Mississippi may be "out of joint" for certain people's uses, but would it present a problem to the animals and plants in its ecological system? This statement assumes that an "ideal" river would be one perfectly suited to *our* needs and purposes. The narrator goes on to give the film's most clear-cut statement of its argument: "The old River *can* be controlled. We had the power to take the Valley apart. We have the power to put it together again."

Now we can see why the film's form has been organized as it has. In early segments, especially 3 and 5, we saw how the American population built up great agricultural and industrial strengths. At the time, we might have just taken these events as simple facts of history. But now they turn out to be crucial to the film's argument. That argument might be summarized this way: we have seen that the American people have the power to build and to destroy; therefore they have the power to build again. This argument is yet another enthymeme. Perhaps the people destroyed something incapable of being rebuilt, or maybe they have lost their former power. But the film does not consider these possibilities.

The narrator continues: "In 1933 we started . . . ," going on to describe how Congress formed the TVA. This segment presents the TVA as an already implemented solution to the problem, and presents no other possible solutions. Thus something that was actually controversial seems to be a matter of simple implementation. Here is a case where one solution, because it has been effective in dealing with a problem, is taken to be *the* solution. Yet, in retrospect, it is not certain that the massive series of dams built by the TVA was the single best solution to flooding. Perhaps a less radical plan combining reforesting with conservation-oriented farming would have created fewer new problems (such as the displacement of people from the land flooded by the dams). Perhaps local governments rather than the federal government would have been more efficient problem solvers. *The River* does not bother to rebut these alternatives, relying instead on our habitual inference from problem to solution.

Segment 9 contains similarities to and differences from several earlier parts of *The River*. It begins with a list of dams, which we see in progress or finished. This echoes the lists of rivers, trees, towns, and so on, that we have heard at intervals. The serene shots of the artificial lakes that follow link the ending to the beginning, recalling the lyrical river shots of Segment 2 (Fig. 4.28). The displaced, flooded-out, and unemployed people from Segment 6 seem now to be happily at work, building planned model towns on government loans. Electricity generated by the dams links these rural communities to those "hundred cities and thousand towns" we heard about earlier, bringing to the countryside "the advantages of urban life." Many motifs planted in a simple fashion are now picked up and woven together to act as proofs of the TVA's benefits. The ending shows life as being parallel to the way it was in the beginning—beautiful nature, productive people—but enhanced by modern government planning.

An upswell of music and a burst of views of the dams and rushing water create a brief epilogue summarizing the factors that have brought about the change—the TVA dams. Under the ending titles and credits, we see the map again. A list tells us the names of the various government agencies that sponsored the film or assisted in its making; these again seem to lend authority to the source of the arguments in the film.

*The River* was successful in achieving its purposes. Favorable initial response led a major American studio, Paramount, to agree to distribute the film—something rare for an independently made documentary short at that time. Reviewers and public alike responded favorably to the film. A contemporary critic's review testifies to the power of the film's rhetorical form. After describing the early portions, Gilbert Seldes wrote, "And so, without your knowing it, you arrive at the Tennessee

Fig. 4.28

Valley—and if this is propaganda, make the most of it, because it is masterly. It is as if the pictures which Mr. Lorentz took arranged themselves in such an order that they supplied their own argument, not as if an argument conceived in advance dictated the order of the pictures."

Roosevelt himself saw *The River* and liked it. He helped get congressional support to start a separate government agency, the U.S. Film Service, to make other documentaries like it. But not everyone was in favor of Roosevelt's policies or believed that the government should set itself up to make films that essentially espoused the views of the administration currently in office. By 1940, the Congress had taken away the U.S. Film Service's support, and documentary films were once again made only within the separate sections of the government. Such a series of results shows that rhetorical films can lead both to direct actions and to controversy.

## ABSTRACT FORMAL SYSTEMS

### ■ PRINCIPLES OF ABSTRACT FORM

Some films are organized around abstract principles, with the filmmaker juxtaposing components to compare or contrast qualities like color, shape, rhythm, and size. As viewers, we do not look for causally linked events that make up a narrative or for propositional claims that might add up to an argument, as in rhetorical organization. Similarly, the motifs used will not necessarily fit into substantive categories. A ball and a balloon might be put side by side, not because they are both toys but because they are both round or both of an orange color. To see the connection between the ball and the balloon, we must recognize the similarity of the abstract qualities of the objects.

Of course, all films contain objects with color, shape, and size, and their sounds have rhythm and other sonic qualities. We have seen how *Olympia* contains some segments, like the diving sequence, where our attention is drawn to abstract elements of the actions shown. Similarly, the lyrical beauty of the river and lake shots in *The River* function to create parallels, and the rhythm of its musical score enhances our emotional involvement in the argument being made. But in each of these cases, an abstract pattern becomes a means to an end, always subordinate to the overall purposes—categorical or rhetorical—of the films. They are not organized around abstract qualities but only make occasional prominent use of them. In abstract organization, the whole film's form will be determined by such qualities.

Abstract films are often organized in a way that we might call "theme and variations." This term usually applies to music, where a melody or other type of motif is introduced, and then a series of different versions of that same melody follows—often with such extreme differences of key and rhythm that the original melody becomes difficult to recognize. An abstract film's form may work in a similar fashion. An introductory section will typically show us in a relatively simple way the kinds of relationships the film will use as its basic material. Then other segments will go on to present similar kinds of relationships but with changes. The changes may be slight, depending on our noticing that the similarities are still greater than the differences. But abstract films also usually depend on building up greater and greater differences from the introductory material. Thus we may find considerable contrast coming into the film, and sudden differences can help us to sense when a new segment has started. If the film's formal organization has been created with care, the similarities and differences will not be random. There will be some underlying principle that runs through the film. Sometimes that principle will be a mathematically precise idea. In J. J. Murphy's *Print Generation*, for example, the filmmaker took a length of random color shots, then began to rephotograph it over and over again on an optical printer. Each succeeding duplication loses some of the original photographic quality, until the last images are unrecognizable. Murphy repeats the same length of film twenty-five times, then reverses the process and shows the segments again, until we build up in quality again to the original footage. On the sound track the progression is exactly the opposite; Murphy recorded and rerecorded the sound twenty-five times, but he begins with the fuzziest version over the original visual images; then as the image deteriorates, the sound gets better. The fascination of the film comes in discovering the pattern Murphy has used and in watching the effects of reduplication on the original images, turning them into blobs of abstract color.

Other abstract films use a more general idea as an organizing principle. Stan Brakhage's *Mothlight* was made by taping dead moths' wings to a strip of clear film, then duplicating the results on a negative. No mathematical principle is behind this. Rather, the varied and random positions of the wings from frame to frame create an interesting effect of flicker and changing shapes. Some animators, such as Oskar Fischinger and Norman McLaren, choose a piece of music and draw shapes that move in rhythm to the sound track. There are an infinite number of ways of organizing an abstract film, but most filmmakers will consider not just how to string images together but how to create overall forms for their films. Abstract films gain much of their complexity from their organization, and part of their interest for the viewer comes in discovering how the individual motifs function in relation to the overall organization.

When we call films abstract here, we do not mean that they have no recognizable objects in them. It is true that many abstract films use pure shapes and colors, created by the filmmaker by drawing, cutting out pieces of colored paper, animating clay shapes, and the like. There is an alternative approach, however, and that is to use real objects and to isolate them from their everyday context in such a way that their abstract qualities come forward. After all, shapes, colors, rhythmic movements, and every abstract quality that the filmmaker uses, exist both in nature and in human-made objects. Markings on animals, bird songs, cloud formations, and other such natural phenomena often attract us because they seem beautiful or striking—qualities similar to those that we look for in artworks. Moreover, even those objects that we create for very practical and mundane uses may have pleasing contours or textures. Chairs are made to sit on, but we will usually try to furnish our home with chairs that also look attractive to us—that have "good design."

Because abstract qualities are common in the world, filmmakers often start by photographing real objects. But, since they then juxtapose the resulting images in terms of shape, color, and so on, the film is still using abstract organization, in spite of the fact that we can still recognize the objects as a bird, a face, or a spoon. And, because the abstract qualities in films do resemble those present in real objects, such films call upon skills we use in everyday life. We are familiar with repetition from life—eating three meals a day, for example, or coming to the same class at a certain time. We also have practical experience of variation—as with winter versus summer activities, or day versus night. We use our ability to recognize shapes and colors in very practical ways, as when we drive and have to interpret traffic signs and lights quickly. But, in watching an abstract film, we do not need to use the shapes, colors, or repetitions that we see and hear for practical purposes. Consequently we can notice them more fully and see relationships that we would seldom bother to look for during the practical activities of everyday life. In a film these abstract qualities become interesting for their own sake.

This abstract, impractical interest has led some critics and viewers to think of abstract films as frivolous. They do not teach us a series of facts (as a categorical film might) or make a practical argument about events in the world (as rhetorical films do). Critics may call them "art for art's sake," since all they seem to do is present us with a series of interesting shapes and sounds. Yet in doing so, such films often make us more aware of such shapes and sounds, and we may be better able to notice them in the everyday world as well—in nature and in practical objects. In this sense we perceive not only the film but the world around us more fully through an awareness of abstract qualities. In talking about abstract films, we might amend the phrase to "art for life's sake"—for such films enhance our lives as much as do the films of other formal types.

## ■ AN EXAMPLE OF ABSTRACT FORM: *BALLET MÉCANIQUE*

*Ballet mécanique* ("Mechanical Ballet"), one of the earliest abstract films ever made, was also one of the most influential. It remains a highly enjoyable film and a classic example of how mundane objects can be transformed when their abstract qualities are used as the basis for a film's form.

Two filmmakers collaborated on *Ballet mécanique* during 1923–24. They were Dudley Murphy, a young American journalist and aspiring film producer, and Fernand Léger, a major French painter. Léger had developed his own distinctive variation of Cubism in his paintings, often using stylized machine parts. His interest in machines transferred well into the cinema, and it contributed to the central formal principles of *Ballet mécanique*.

This title suggests the paradox the filmmakers employ in creating their film's thematic material and variations. We expect a ballet to be rhythmic and flowing, with human dancers performing it. A classical ballet seems the opposite of a machine's movements—yet what we are to see is a series of movements and rhythms that create a dance out of machines and other objects that are made to move mechanically. Relatively few of the many objects we see in the film are actually machines; it mostly uses hats, faces, bottles, kitchen utensils, and the like. But, through juxtaposition with machines and through visual and temporal rhythms, we are cued to see even a woman's moving eyes and mouth as being like machine parts.

We cannot segment *Ballet mécanique* by tracing its arguments or dividing it into scenes of narrative action. Rather, we must look for changes in the types of abstract qualities being used at different points in the film. Going by this principle, we can find nine segments in *Ballet mécanique*:

**C.** A credits sequence with a stylized, animated figure of Charlie Chaplin introducing the film's title (The word "Charlot" in this introduction is Chaplin's character's name in France.)

**1.** The introduction of the film's rhythmic elements

**2.** A treatment of similar elements with views taken through prisms

**3.** Rhythmic movements

Fig. 4.29

Fig. 4.30

Fig. 4.31

4. A comparison of people and machines
5. Rhythmic movements of intertitles and pictures
6. More rhythmic movements, mostly of circular objects
7. Quick dances of objects
8. A return to Charlot and the opening elements

*Ballet mécanique* uses the theme and variations approach in a complex way, introducing many individual motifs in rapid succession, then bringing them back at various intervals and in different combinations. There is a definite pattern of development out of the elements of the earlier segments. Each new segment picks up on a limited number of the abstract qualities from the previous one and plays with these for a while.

The last segments pick up elements from early in the film once again, and the ending strongly echoes the opening. The film throws a great deal of material at us in a short time, and we must actively seek to make connections among motifs if we are to perceive these repetitions and variations.

As we have suggested, the introductory portion of an abstract film will usually give us strong cues as to what we can expect to see developed later. *Ballet mécanique*'s animated figure of Chaplin begins this process. The figure is highly abstract—recognizably human, but also made up of abstract shapes that move about in a jerky fashion (Fig. 4.29). Already we have the human figure as an object. Segment 1 surprises us by beginning with a woman swinging in a garden (Fig. 4.30). This seems to be a realistic scene, yet the film's title may lead us to notice the regular rhythm of the swinging, and the puppetlike gestures as the woman repeatedly lifts her eyes and head, then lowers them, a fixed smile on her face. Certain abstract qualities already have become prominent. Suddenly a rapid succession of images appears, passing too quickly for us to be able to do more than glimpse some objects: a hat, bottles, an abstract white triangle, and so on. Next a woman's mouth appears, smiling, then not smiling, then smiling again. The hat returns, then the smiling mouth again, then some spinning gears, then a shiny ball circles close to the camera. Next we see the woman in the swing and the camera moves back and forth with her—but now she is upside down (Fig. 4.31). This segment ends with the shiny ball, now swinging back and forth directly toward the camera, and we are invited to compare its movement with that of the woman in the swing. We are thus confirmed in our expectation that she is not a character but an object, like the bottles or the shiny ball. The same is true of that smiling mouth; it does not suggest an emotion—rather we primarily watch its changing shape as such. Shapes of objects (a round hat, vertical bottles), direction of movement (the

Fig. 4.32

Fig. 4.33

swing, the shiny ball), textures (the shininess of both the ball and the bottles), and especially the rhythms of these objects' movement, and of the changes from object to object, will be qualities which the film calls to our attention.

With these expectations set up in the short introductory section, the film goes on to vary its elements. Segment 2 sticks fairly closely to the elements just introduced by beginning with another view of the shiny ball, now seen through a prism—the same object, seen differently. There follow other shots of household objects, similar to the ball in that they are also shiny and are seen through a prism. One of these is recognizable as a pot lid (Fig. 4.32), its round shape picking up that of both the ball and the hat of the previous segment. Here is a good example of how a very mundane object can be taken out of its everyday use and its abstract qualities employed to create formal relations. In the middle of the series of prism shots, we see a rapid burst of shots, alternating a white circle and white triangle. This is yet another motif that will return at intervals, with variations. In a sense, these shapes, which are not recognizable objects, contrast with the kitchen utensils of the other shots. But they also invite us to make comparisons: the pot lid is also round, the prismatic facets are somewhat triangular. During the rest of Segment 2 we see more prism shots, interspersed with another rapid series of circles and triangles, and also with views of a woman's eyes opening and closing, a woman's eyes partially masked off by dark shapes (Fig. 4.33), and finally the smiling/ unsmiling mouth from Segment 1.

Segment 2 has further confirmed our expectations that the film will concentrate on comparisons of shapes, rhythms, or textures. We also begin to see a pattern of surprising interruptions of the segments with brief bursts of short shots: in Segment 1 it had been objects with one triangle; now we have twice seen a circle and triangle alternate. The rhythm of changing views is as important as the rhythm of movements within individual shots.

Now that such patterns are well established, the film begins to introduce greater variations to vary and sometimes overturn our expectations. Segment 3 begins with shots of rows of platelike round objects, alternating with spinning objects, like a fairground game wheel. Will round shapes and movements provide the main principle of development in this segment? Suddenly the camera is moving rapidly down a twisty slide in a fair; we see elements like marching feet, cars going over the camera, and rapid shots of a carnival ride's cars spinning past. Here different rhythms succeed each other, and common shape seems less important. Relatively few of the elements from Segments 1 and 2 return. We do not see the parts of the woman's face, and many of the objects are new ones, seen out of doors. Yet, after the carnival cars, we see a relatively lengthy shot of a spinning shiny

Fig. 4.34

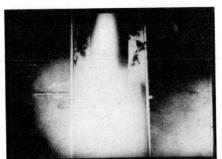

Fig. 4.35

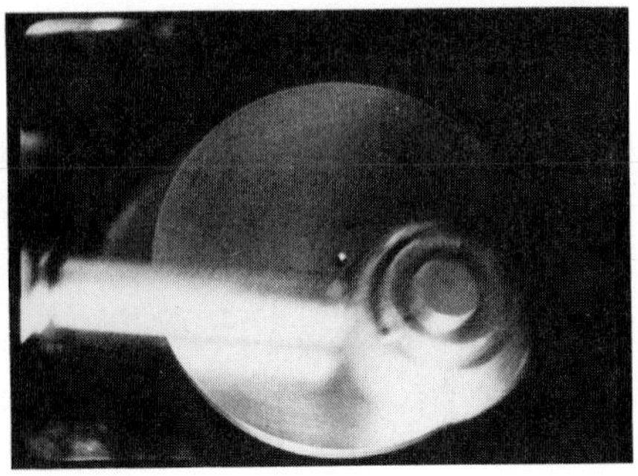

Fig. 4.36

object—not in a prism view but at least recalling the image of the kitchen utensils seen earlier. The segment ends with the familiar rapid alternation of circle and triangle.

Segment 4 gives us the film's most explicit comparison of humans and machines. We first see a carnival slide from above, picking up on an element from Segment 3 (though here the camera does not move down the slide). The slide stretches horizontally across the screen, and in quick succession a man's silhouette whizzes down it four times (Fig. 4.34). This may seem a continuation of Segment 3's concentration on rhythm, but next we see a machine part, strongly vertical on the screen (Fig. 4.35), with a piston moving up and down rhythmically. Again we see similarities—a tubelike object with another object moving along it—and differences—the compositions use opposing directions, and the four movements of the man are done in different shots, while the camera holds as the piston moves up and down within one shot. More shots compare the slide and machine parts, ending with one machine seen through a prism. The familiar alternating circle and triangle return, but with differences: now the triangle is sometimes upside down, and each shape remains on the screen slightly longer. The segment continues with more spinning shiny objects and machine parts, then reintroduces the motif of the woman's masked eye (similar to Fig. 4.33). Now the motions of this eye are compared to machine parts.

Segment 4 closes with one of *Ballet mécanique*'s most famous and daring moments. After a shot of a rotating machine part (Fig. 4.36), we see seven identically repeated shots of a washerwoman climbing a stair and gesturing (Fig. 4.37). The segment returns to the smiling mouth, then gives us eleven more shots of the same view of the washerwoman, a shot of a large piston, and five more repetitions of the washerwoman shot. This insistent repetition makes the woman's movements as precise as those of the machine; even though she is seen in a real place, we cannot see her as a character, but must concentrate on her movements' rhythms. (The filmmakers have taken advantage of the cinema's own mechanical ability to multiply exactly the same image.) Segment 4 is quite different from earlier ones, but it does bring back motifs: the prism recurs briefly (from Segment 2), spinning shiny objects recall those of Segment 3, and the woman's eyes and mouth (Segments 1 and 2) return, having been absent from Segment 3.

Segment 4 has been the culmination of the film's comparison of mechanical objects with people. Now Segment 5 introduces a strong contrast by concentrating on printed intertitles. Unlike other segments, this one begins with a black screen, which is gradually revealed to be a dark card upon which a white zero is painted; we see this first as a prismed shot (again recalling Segment 2). An unprismed view

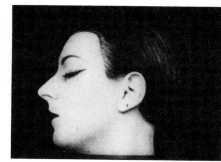

**Fig. 4.37**                    **Fig. 4.38**                    **Fig. 4.39**

of the zero shows it shrinking. Then, unexpectedly, an intertitle appears: "*ON A VOLÉ UN COLLIER DE PERLES DE 5 MILLIONS*" ("A pearl necklace worth 5 million has been stolen"). In a narrative film this might give us story information, but the filmmakers use the printed language as one more visual motif for rhythmic variation. There follows a series of quick shots, with large zeros, sometimes one, sometimes three, appearing and disappearing, shrinking and growing. Parts of the intertitle appear in isolation ("*ON A VOLÉ*"), participating in this "dance" of letters. The film plays with an ambiguity: is the zero really an "O," the first letter of the sentence, or is it part of the number 5,000,000, or is it a stylized representation of the pearl necklace itself? Beyond this sort of play with a visual pun, the zero recalls and varies the circle motif that has been so prominent in the film. More

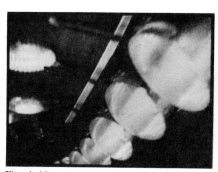

**Fig. 4.40**

punning occurs as the zero gives way to a picture of a horse collar—which resembles the zero visually, but also refers to the word "*collier*" (which in French can mean either "necklace" or "collar"). The collar bobs about in its own little dance, and alternates with moving zeros and parts of the intertitle sentence, sometimes printed backward—to emphasize their graphic, rather than informative, function. This segment has been very different from earlier ones, but even here a couple of motifs are repeated: just before the horse collar is introduced we see the masked woman's eye briefly, and in the course of the rapid shots of intertitles, one tiny shot of a machine part is inserted.

After this point, the film begins to move toward variations that are closer to the elements of the opening segments. Segment 6 shows us rhythmic movements involving mostly circular shapes. It begins with a woman's head, eyes closed, turning (Fig. 4.38). Directly after this we see a wooden statue swing toward and away from the camera (Fig. 4.39). Once again the comparison of person and object comes forward. An abstract circular shape grows, cueing us to watch for the recurrence of this shape. A woman's face appears in a prismed view; she passes a cardboard with holes cut in it before her face, with her expression continually changing in a mechanical fashion. We see the circles and triangles alternate again, but this time these shapes are presented in four different sizes. A quick series of shots of rows of shiny kitchen utensils follows (Fig. 4.40), with short bursts of black film interspersed. This blackness picks up and varies the dark backgrounds of the intertitles in Segment 5, and the shiny pots and other utensils reintroduce a motif which has appeared in every segment *except* 5. The motif of rows of objects had come in Segment 3, while the swinging motion of the utensils in many of these shots picks up the swinging of the woman and the shiny ball from way back in Segment 1. Now we may have a definite sense that the film's development is turning back toward its beginning, and Segment 7 intensifies that sense.

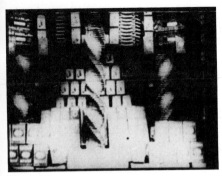

Fig. 4.41

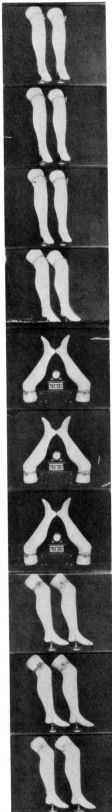

Fig. 4.42

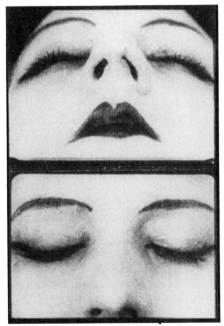

Fig. 4.43

Fig. 4.44

Segment 7 begins with a shot of a display window, with spiral shapes that seem to freeze the gyrating motions that have made up so much of the film's rhythmic play (Fig. 4.41). The circle motif returns, leading into a series of "dances" that vary key motifs. Short shots make a pair of mannequin legs seem to dance (Fig. 4.42); then the legs begin to spin within the shots. The shiny ball motif returns, but now two balls spin in opposite directions. Two very different shapes—a hat and shoe—alternate quickly (Fig. 4.43), creating a conflict of shapes similar to the juxtaposition of circle and triangle earlier. The prismed shot of a woman changing expressions follows, then a profile shot similar to the one in Figure 4.38. Two slightly different views of a face (Fig. 4.44) quickly alternated induce us to see the head as "nodding" mechanically. Finally, quick shots of bottles make them seem to change position in another dancelike rhythm.

**Fig. 4.45**

Interestingly, the motifs used in Segment 7 come primarily from Segments 1 and 2 (the shiny balls, hat, bottles) and from 6 (the prismed face, the growing circle). Here, where the "mechanical ballet" becomes most explicit, the film draws together elements from its beginning, and from the previous segment, where the recall of the earlier segments had begun. Segment 7 avoids motifs from the center of the film—3 through 5—and thus gives us a sense both that the film is continuing to develop and that it is coming full circle.

The final segment makes this return more obvious by showing us the Chaplin figure again. Now its movements are even less "human," and at the end most of its parts seem to fall away, leaving the head alone on the screen. The spinning head may remind us of the woman's profile (Fig. 4.38) seen earlier. But the film is not quite over yet. Its last shot brings back the woman from the swing in Segment 1, now standing in the same garden smelling a flower and looking around. Seen in another context, her gestures might seem ordinary to us (Fig. 4.45). But by now the film has "trained" us sufficiently to permit us to make the connection between this shot and what has preceded it. Our expectations have been so strongly geared to seeing rhythmic, mechanical movement that we will probably see her smiles and head gestures as *un*natural, and as similar to other motifs we have seen in the film. Léger and Murphy end their film by emphasizing how much they have altered our perception of ordinary objects and people.

## ASSOCIATIONAL FORMAL SYSTEMS

### ■ PRINCIPLES OF ASSOCIATIONAL FORM

Associational formal systems suggest expressive qualities and concepts by juxtaposing series of seemingly unlike things. The things used will not necessarily be of similar types, as in categorical systems; they will not present an argument, as in rhetorical systems; and their abstract qualities need not be the basis for the comparison, as in abstract systems. But, because the unlike things are placed together, we will look for a connection. The process is somewhat comparable to the techniques we find in lyric poetry, in which metaphors and other imagery are used. When the poet Robert Burns says, "My love is like a red, red rose," we do not leap to the conclusion that his love is literally prickly to touch, bright red, or subject to aphids. Rather, we look for the possible conceptual links: her beauty is more likely the reason for the comparison.

A similar process goes on in associational films. Here the lyric imagery, which poetry conveys through language, is presented in a more direct fashion. A filmmaker could film a woman he loved in a garden and suggest by visual juxtaposition that she is like the flowers that surround her. (Indeed, this might be an implicit meaning viewers could assign to *Ballet mécanique*'s last shot, if it were taken out of context.)

The imagery used in associational form may range from conventional to strikingly original, and the conceptual connections can be readily apparent or downright mystifying. (These possibilities are not necessarily linked—a highly original juxtaposition could easily have an obvious emotional or conceptual implication.) Again, poetry offers examples. Many religious, patriotic, romantic, and laudatory poems use strings of images to create their tone. In "America the Beautiful," the images of "spacious skies," "purple mountains' majesty," and "fruited plain" add up to suggest the patriotic fervor expressed in the chorus, "God shed His grace on thee." Here the words of the poem guide us to create the associations among the images.

Another poem might be more elusive in its effect, giving us less explicit statements of the associative qualities of its imagery. The Japanese poetic form called the *haiku* often juxtaposes two images usually in a brief three-line form, in order to create an immediate emotion in the reader. Here, for example, is a *haiku* by Bashō:

> The eleventh moon—
> Storks listlessly
> Standing in a row.

Here the images used are less obvious and the purpose for connecting them somewhat mysterious. Yet, if we are willing to fill in with our imaginations, as one is supposed to do with *haiku*, the effect should be an emotion or idea—one which is not present in either individual image but which results from the juxtaposition of the two.

Associational organization, when it is complex and original, depends greatly on the activities of the viewer. The filmmaker will not necessarily give us obvious cues as to the emotion or concept appropriate to the film. He or she may simply create a series of unusual and striking combinations and leave it up to us to tease out their relations. We must speculate on possible connections. In a sense, we try to retrace the leap of logic that created a certain juxtaposition. We cannot be sure that the connection we find is the same one the filmmaker had in mind. Nevertheless our emotional and conceptual satisfaction comes when we realize that the things do have an intriguing connection of some sort.

Associations can be made on the basis of any type of relations between objects. There is no need for geographical proximity: images can be brought together from anywhere. They do not have to be of the same type or look alike, although the filmmaker may use categorical or abstract similarities to compare things. But these qualities are not the basis for the organization of the film's form. Usually we are also led to compare the objects for their emotional or conceptual links in addition to these surface similarities. Because associational formal systems are so unlimited in their subjects and means of organization, it is impossible to define a conventional set of parts into which an associational film will fall. In categorical form, the individual categories must be distinct or the purpose is defeated. If we cannot follow the stages of a rhetorical film's argument, it would be pointless. And an abstract film's variations on a theme present us with visual and sonic qualities that are directly perceivable as such. But associational systems can be loose, using any type of organization at all. Many associational films will build their own individual formal systems with little attention paid to conventions. In many such films, we must be prepared to change our expectations frequently. As a result, many of the films that use associational form come under the heading of what are called "experimental" films, made by independent filmmakers working outside the mainstream commercial film industry.

Although the associational film may use striking, original, even puzzling, juxtapositions, it will usually elicit a fairly simple and familiar emotion or idea. Some films will show us a series of visual puns to create amusement; others may offer us frightening series of objects that put us in suspense. Associational form offers a handy way for filmmakers to convey their own subjective fantasies and states of mind through imagery. Even in the most complex and original films, our response is likely to involve only a few emotions and ideas, and these will be familiar from everyday life. The point of the film will usually be to make that familiar emotion or concept vivid by eliciting it through interesting new means.

Because associational form is so loose in its conventions, it is perhaps best defined by example. Bruce Conner's film *A Movie* well illustrates how associational form can confront us with elusive and mysterious juxtapositions, yet can at the same time organize its images into a clear and unified shape.

## ■ AN EXAMPLE OF ASSOCIATIONAL FORM: *A MOVIE*

Bruce Conner made *A Movie*, his first film, in 1958. Like Léger, he worked in the visual and plastic arts and was noted for his "assemblage" pieces—collages built up of miscellaneous found objects. Conner chose a comparable approach to filmmaking. He typically uses footage shot by a variety of earlier filmmakers. His shots come from old newsreels, Hollywood movies, soft-core pornography, and the like. As a result, Conner can find two shots from widely different sources that apparently have nothing in common. Yet, if we see the two shots together, we will strive to find some connection between them. From a series of juxtapositions, our activity can create an overall emotion or concept.

*A Movie* uses a musical accompaniment that helps establish these emotions and ideas. As with the images, Conner chose music that already existed: three portions of Respighi's well-known tone poem *The Pines of Rome*. The music is important to the film's form, since it has distinct sections, and the segments of the film are partly organized around these same sections. Moreover, the overall tone of each segment is different, corresponding to the music.

We can differentiate four segments in *A Movie*, each distinctly marked off from the others by filmic techniques:

1. An introductory portion with the film's title and director's name and various projectionists' markings
2. Quick, dynamic music with images of moving animals and vehicles on land
3. A more mysterious, tense section stressing precariously balanced objects in air and water
4. Frightening images of disaster and war interspersed with more lyrical, mysterious scenes.

Within a brief 12-minute span, *A Movie* leads us through a variety of emotions and ideas, and it also creates a distinct developmental thread running through Segments 3 and 4. Many of the shots show accidents or aggressive actions, and while some of these seem funny or trivial at first, they gradually accumulate and become more serious. By Segment 4 we see practically an apocalyptic vision through a series of war scenes, accidents, and natural disasters. Finally, *A Movie*'s tone eases in its epilogue's underwater scenes.

**Segment 1.**    This segment does far more than give us the title and filmmaker's name, and for that reason we have numbered it as the first segment rather than separating it off as a credits sequence. At first we see blank black leader, over which the dynamic, quick opening of *The Pines of Rome* begins. This stresses the importance of the music in the film, since we hear it before seeing any images. Then the words "Bruce Conner" appear, remaining on the screen for many seconds. As we do not need that much time to read the name, we may begin to sense that this film will playfully thwart our expectations. After the name we see black leader, then white leader, then a quick flicker effect rapidly alternating two frames of the word "A" with blank white leader, and then the word "Movie." The word "By" appears, with more white frames, then "Bruce Conner," as before. Now a black leader appears, with various markings that usually appear on the first portion of the film strip, but which are seldom projected on the screen for the audience to see: splice cues, dots, and other signs. Then, suddenly, "End of Part Four" flashes on the screen.

We might think that Conner is simply playing with the graphic qualities of titles and leader marks, as Léger and Murphy had done in Segment 5 of *Ballet mécanique* with their "dance" of intertitles and zeros. But here Conner uses graphics with conventional meanings: leaders and credits usually signal the beginning, while "End of Part Four" implies we have already seen a considerable part of the film. Once again *A Movie* signals us that it will not be a conventional film—not one where the parts will follow in logical order. We must prepare our expectations for odd juxtapositions. Moreover, the flicker and leader markings stress the physical qualities of the film medium itself: the title *A Movie* reinforces this reference to the medium, cueing us to watch this assemblage of shots *as* bits of film. This segment also suggests the implicit meaning that this opening is mocking the opening portions of most films.

The opening continues with a countdown leader, beginning with "12" and flashing other numbers at one-second intervals—again, more signals to the projectionist, but seldom seen by the audience. Is *this* the beginning, then? But after "4," we are startled to see the film's first moving image: a "nudie" shot of a woman taking off her stockings. The film is very worn, with lines and scratches, and we surmise that Conner took it from an old stag film. Here *A Movie* helps us to focus our expectations by suggesting that it will involve more "found footage" of this type. After the nude shot, the countdown leader continues to "1," then the words "The End" appear. Another joke: the end of the leader, not of the film. Yet even this is untrue, since more leader appears, with "Movie" backward, more projectionists' signals, and a repeating number "1" that flickers in time to the music's quick tempo, then goes to black.

**Segment 2.**    Although the music runs continuously over the transition, in Segment 2 we begin to see a very different kind of image. A series of twelve shots shows us mounted Indians on a hill, then chasing a fleeing wagon train, with Hopalong Cassidy recognizable as one of the cowboys. More old film footage follows, this time a clip suggesting a story situation continuing from shot to shot: a fight between Indians and settlers. But Conner shows us this scene only to refer briefly to the

Fig. 4.46

Fig. 4.47

conventional kind of movie he is *not* making. Suddenly, from a shot of horses pulling a wagon (Fig. 4.46), he cuts to similar horses—but pulling a fire engine on a city street (Fig. 4.47). The association here seems clear enough; we move from horses to more horses—but specifically horses in rapid motion. The same is true of the next change, to a troop of cavalry. The associations are simple to follow so far. But next we see a shaky shot of a charging elephant. Now we must stretch our associations to account for this: maybe the link is through a series of rapidly moving animals? This seems safe enough to assume, as we see two more shots of horses' running legs. But the next shot shows a speeding locomotive's wheels. We must generalize the terms of the association still further—the rapid motion of animals and vehicles on land. (The "on land" idea may not seem important at this point, but it will become significant in contrast to the later segments, which often emphasize air and water.) The next series of shots, repeating these motifs and introducing a military tank, seems to confirm this overall idea of rushing movement. The segment so far has been very dynamic, with short shots, fast-moving objects, and a loud musical accompaniment in a quick tempo.

This sense of rapid activity continues into the later part of Segment 2, which moves from the tank to a series of shots of race cars speeding around tracks. Since these shots initially confirm our expectations about moving animals and vehicles, they are less challenging to us—at first. Then one race car crashes, followed by two other similar crashes; and the segment ends with the long, spectacular fall of an old-fashioned car off a cliff. The sense of movement has become less funny and exhilarating, more uncontrolled and frightening in these final shots. The music has built up to a frenzied climax by the final crash and cuts off abruptly as a "The End" title flashes on the screen. This parody of the ending of a conventional film suggests that the crashes have resulted from all that rushing motion earlier in the segment. At this point, we might begin to sense that there was an underlying tone of threatening aggression and danger from the start: the attacking Indians, the cavalry, the charging elephant, the tank, and so on. This element will be intensified in Segments 3 and 4.

**Segment 3.**    More black leader continues the transition set up by the "The End" title, and there is a pause before the music of Segment 3 begins. (As at the film's

Fig. 4.48

Fig. 4.49

opening, it plays at first over the darkness.) But this time the music is slow, bleak, and slightly ominous. The "Movie" title and more black leader move us into a series of shots very different from those of Segment 2. Two Polynesian women carry large, mysterious, totemlike objects on their heads. More leader and a title interrupt once more, introducing a short series of shots of a large dirigible in flight (Fig. 4.48) and of an acrobat couple performing on a small platform and tightrope high above a street (Fig. 4.49). If the women and the dirigible are associated through balancing, the dirigible is linked to the acrobats not only by that but by an emphasis on heights and danger. This portion of the segment ends with a shot of a small plane plunging downward through fleecy clouds, as if, having lost its balance, it is falling. Slow, mysterious music has cued us how to react to these floating and falling objects; without the music, we might take them to be lyrical, but in context they suggest a vague threat. This passage ends with more titles: "A," "Movie," "By," and "Bruce Conner," followed by black leader.

The next part of the segment begins with an apparent incongruity between music and image. A series of shots shows parts of a submarine, including an officer looking through a periscope (Fig. 4.50). The next shot seems to suggest that he sees a bikini-clad woman (Fig. 4.51). This shot picks up the stag-film motif from Segment 1, and points up the paradox of this juxtaposition. We know the shots of the officer and the woman come from different films—yet at the same time we cannot help but interpret the shots as showing him "looking" at her, and thus we find the moment funny. The same principle underlies the next shots, as the officer orders a torpedo fired, and we see it seeming to race toward the woman, creating a sexual pun. This, too, is funny, as is the atomic-bomb orgasm that seems to result. But, as in the first segment, there is an overtone of threat and aggression— now specifically sexual aggression—in these images. They move quickly from humor to disaster as additional mushroom-cloud shots undercut the joke. Moreover, the music that plays through the submarine-woman series is slow, quiet, and ethereal— *not* appropriate to the silly punning scene, but more suited to the images of the bomb blasts.

This music carries us into a series of shots of waves and wavelike movements that seem to "result" from the bomb: a ship engulfed by fog or smoke, surfers and rowing teams battered by heavy waves, water skiers and motorboaters falling during stunts. During this, the music's ethereal quality gives way to a slow melody with a dynamic tempo, played on low stringed instruments; this creates a more ominous tone. The first accidents seem trivial, as when water skiers fall over. But gradually things become more grotesque: a motorboat driver deliberately plows into a pile of debris and is hurled out. Then we switch abruptly to people riding odd bicycles (Fig. 4.52). The move from the boat to the bikes takes us briefly away from the "accident" series to a string of shots showing people deliberately doing things that look grotesque. Additional shots show motorcyclists riding through deep mud and water and a plane without floats trying to land on a lake and flipping over.

This whole segment has developed steadily, introducing tension at the beginning, and then juxtaposing the humorous (the submarine-woman scene) with the disastrous (the bomb), and trivial accidents with grotesque actions. It ends in an odd way. Black leader appears after the plane crash, with music over building up toward a climax; this is followed by a close view of Theodore Roosevelt speaking, seemingly angry, with bared teeth (Fig. 4.53). Immediately, there follows a shot of

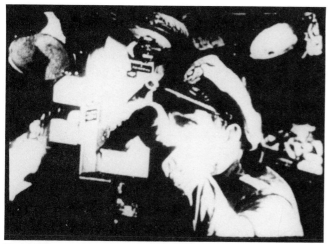

Fig. 4.50

Fig. 4.51

Fig. 4.52

Fig. 4.53

Fig. 4.54

Fig. 4.55

Fig. 4.56

Fig. 4.57

Fig. 4.58

Fig. 4.59

a collapsing suspension bridge, with the music swelling up exactly as the pieces fall (Fig. 4.54), then ending more quietly. Although these shots are difficult to interpret, the association of human-caused disasters with one of America's most belligerent presidents would seem to link even the toppling bridge to human, especially political, aggression.

**Segment 4.**   Once again *A Movie* marks off its segments clearly, with black leader once more accompanying the opening of the third portion of *The Pines of Rome*. An eerie gong and low, slow rhythmic chords create a distinctly ominous mood. Segments 2 and 3 had both built up toward accidents and disasters; now Segment 4 begins with a series of images of military planes being shot out of the sky and firing on the ground, then a series of explosions against a dark sky. But the next subsegment juxtaposes some shots of disasters with some shots that are inexplicable in this context. All the shots of planes and explosions seem associated through war and disaster. Then we see two planes flying past an Egyptian pyramid (Fig. 4.55). As with so many of the earlier juxtapositions, we must abruptly switch our assumptions about how these shots relate to one another—now we see *nonmilitary* planes. But immediately two shots of an erupting volcano appear. Clearly, the connection between them and the previous shot is mainly created by the similarity in appearance of mountains and pyramids. Are we back to disasters again? Seemingly not, for we next see an elaborate church ceremony of a coronation, and all our expectations are thwarted. But, immediately, the disaster motif returns as strongly as ever: the burning dirigible *Hindenburg*, tanks, more race-car crashes, and tumbling bodies. All these images create tension, but the next shots we see are of people parachuting from a plane. Interestingly, this action is not threatening, and the people here are not hurt—yet in the context of the earlier accidents and because of the ominous music, we have begun to expect some sort of disaster as the most likely subject of each shot. Now even these innocent actions seem threatening and again may be seen as linked to military and political aggression.

The next series of shots is equally innocent in itself but takes on mysterious and ominous overtones as part of the overall segment. We see a burning balloon floating to earth, reminding us of the floating dirigible and *Hindenburg* footage; then shots of palm trees, cattle, and other glimpses follow that suggest some idyllic Middle Eastern or African setting (Fig. 4.56). This brief respite, however, leads into one of the film's eeriest and most striking moments, three shots of a suspension bridge writhing and buckling as if shaken by a giant hand (Fig. 4.57). This is followed by the most intense disaster images in the whole film, including the burning *Hindenburg*, a sinking ship (Fig. 4.58), a firing-squad execution, bodies hanging on a scaffold, dead soldiers, and a mushroom cloud. A shot of a dead elephant and hunters introduces a brief series of shots of suffering Africans. The music has built up during this, becoming steadily less ominous and more triumphant with fanfares of brass instruments.

After the climactic series of disaster shots, the tone shifts one final time. We see a relatively lengthy series of underwater shots of a scuba diver. He explores a large sunken ship, encrusted with barnacles (Fig. 4.59). It recalls the disasters just witnessed—especially the sinking ship (Fig. 4.58). The music builds to a triumphant climax as the diver swims into the ship's interior. The film ends on a long-held musical chord over more black leader and a final shot looking up toward the surface of the sea. Ironically, there is no "The End" title at this point.

*A Movie* has taken us through its disparate footage almost entirely by means of associations. There is no argument about why we should find these images disturbing or why we should link volcanos and earthquakes to sexual or military aggression. There are no categorical similarities between many of the things juxtaposed and no story told about them. Occasionally, as we shall see in Chapter 9, Conner does use abstract qualities to compare objects, but this is only a small-scale strategy, not one that organizes the whole film.

In building its associations, *A Movie* uses the familiar formal principles of repetition and variation. Even though the images come from different films, certain kinds of objects are repeated, as with the series of horse shots in Segment 1 or the various airplanes. These repetitions form motifs that unify the segments into a whole, and there is a distinct pattern to the return of those motifs. We have seen how the titles and leader of the opening come back in some way in all the segments, and how the "nudie" shot of Segment 1 is similar to the one used with the submarine footage in Segment 3. Interestingly, not a single motif that appears in Segment 2 returns in Segment 3, creating a strong contrast between the two. But then Segment 4 picks up and varies many of the motifs of both 2 and 3. As in so many films, the ending thus seems a development of and return to earlier portions. The dead elephant, the tanks, and the race cars all hark back to Segment 2, while the natives, the *Hindenburg* disaster, the planes, the ships, and the bridge collapse all continue motifs begun in 3. Also, those juxtapositions that have obvious associations play on repetition, while startling and obscure ones create contrast. Thus Conner has created a unified work from what would seem to be a disunified mass of footage.

The pattern of development is also strikingly unified. Segment 1 is primarily funny, and a sense of play and exhilaration also carries through most of Segment 2, up to the car crashes. But we have seen that the subjects of all the shots in Segment 2 could also suggest aggression and violence, and they all relate in some way to the disasters to come. Segment 3 makes this more explicit, but uses some humor and playfulness as well. By Segment 4, the mixture of tones has largely disappeared and an intensifying sense of tension and doom replaces it; even odd or neutral events take on an ominous appearance.

As with many films organized associationally, it is hard to identify a clear-cut explicit meaning. Still, *A Movie*'s constantly shifting associations invite us to reflect on their implicit meanings. From one standpoint, the film can be interpreted as presenting the devastating consequences of unbridled aggressive energy. The horrors of the modern world—warfare and the hydrogen bomb—are linked with more trivial pastimes, like sports and risky stunts. We are asked to reflect on whether both may spring from the same impulse, perhaps a kind of death wish. This impulse may in turn be tied to sexual drives (the pornographic motif) and political repression (the recurring images of people of developing countries). Another interpretation might see the film as commenting on how cinema stirs our emotions through sex, violence, and exotic spectacle. In this sense, *A Movie* is "a movie" like any other, with the important difference that its thrills and disasters are actual parts of our world.

What of the ending? The scuba diver epilogue also offers a wide range of implicit meanings. It returns to the beginning in a formal sense: along with the Hopalong Cassidy segment, it is the longest continuous action we get. It might offer a kind of hope, perhaps an escape from the world's horrors. Or the images may suggest humankind's final death: after despoiling the planet, the human can only return to the primeval sea. Like much of *A Movie*, the ending is ambiguous, saying little but suggesting much. Certainly we can say that it serves to relax the tension aroused by the mounting disasters. In this respect, it demonstrates the power of an associational formal system: its ability to guide our emotions and to arouse our thinking simply by juxtaposing different images and sounds.

## SUMMARY

As we have seen in looking at some of our individual examples, films may mix types of form, and it is not always easy to tell which type any one film uses. *Olympia* uses categorical form but creates short narratives within a few of its segments. *The River* has some sections that employ associations between music and imagery to cue the spectator to adopt a certain attitude. *A Movie* exploits some abstract links between objects in different shots. Usually, however, one type of form dominates, providing the overall organization. In trying to identify a film's basic organizational principle, it is often helpful to look at the beginning and ending because films tend to put their strongest cues at these points. In addition, the development that has occurred between the beginning and end will usually help to define the large-scale formal relations within the work.

In looking at different types of films, you can ask questions like these:

1. What sort of response does the film seem to call forth? Is it trying to inform its audience about categories of things? to make a convincing argument? to elicit the contemplation of artistic properties? to evoke an emotion or concept?

2. If the form is categorical, what is the overall subject and how is it introduced? What are the categories, and how does the film progress from the first to the last?

3. If the form is rhetorical, what is the argument being made? What pieces of evidence are given, and how convincing are they? How does the film make itself seem authoritative and reliable?

4. If the form is abstract, what are the main visual and aural motifs set forth and varied? What is the pattern of their recurrence?

5. If the form is associational, what are the shifts in emotions or concepts through the course of the film? What types of imagery cue us to respond in a certain way?

In this portion of the book, we have tried to show how narrative and nonnarrative formal systems work within the total film. Understanding both types of form becomes important as we move into a consideration of film techniques because narrative or nonnarrative structure and cinematic techniques work together to create the overall formal system of a film. The analytical tools presented here in Part II, in combination with an ability to analyze the function of the techniques to be defined in Part III, should help us understand whole films. At the end of our survey of film techniques, we shall return to the films considered in the last two chapters and analyze how they use features of the film medium to create stylistic systems.

## NOTES AND QUERIES

### ■ TYPES OF FORM

Of all the types of formal organization, categorical structure has received the least discussion. As one preferred model for instructional and educational films, it warrants further reflection. Rhetorical form can be seen as a variant of verbal argument, and we can understand it through such studies of rhetoric as Stephen Toulmin's *The Uses of Argument* (Cambridge: Cambridge University Press, 1958). Many films may have a "layout of arguments" similar to Toulmin's. For a concrete analysis of one film's rhetorical form, see Steve Neale, "Propaganda," *Screen* **18**, 3 (Autumn 1977): 9–40. Categorical and rhetorical form seem to be subsumed under "expository form" in Bill Nichols's discussion of documentary structures in chapters 6–8 of *Ideology and the Image* (Bloomington: Indiana University Press, 1981).

Associational form may be studied by comparison to such poetic genres as the lyric; see Northrop Frye, "The Rhythm of Association: Lyric," in his *Anatomy of Criticism* (Princeton, N.J.: Princeton University Press, 1957), and Paul Goodman, "Lyrical Poems: Speech, Feeling, Motion of Thought," in his *The Structure of Literature* (Chicago: University of Chicago Press, 1954). A good example of a critic's discussion of associational form is Ken Kelman's "The Anti-Information Film (Conner's *Report*)," in P. Adams Sitney, ed., *The Essential Cinema: Essays on the Films in the Collection of Anthology Film Archives* (New York: New York University Press, 1975), pp. 240–244.

Abstract form is often best examined in the light of principles of musical form or abstract visual design. For the former, see parts 3 and 4 of William S. Newman's *Understanding Music* (New York: Harper, 1967). For the latter, see E. H. Gombrich, *The Sense of Order: A Study in the Psychology of Decorative Art* (Ithaca, N.Y.: Cornell University Press, 1979), and Rudolph Arnheim, *Art and Visual Perception*, 2d ed. (Berkeley: University of California Press, 1974). Noël Carroll considers qualities of abstract form in "Causation, the Ampliation of Movement and Avant-Garde Film," *Millennium Film Journal* **10/11** (Fall/Winter 1981/82): 61–82.

Both associational and abstract form are characteristic of what is usually called experimental or avant-garde filmmaking. In the early 1970s, Gene Youngblood's book *Expanded Cinema* (New York: E. P. Dutton, 1970) aroused many readers' interest in abstract filmmaking, but such films have a long history. Three significant accounts are Malcolm Le Grice, *Abstract Film and Beyond* (Cambridge, Mass.: MIT Press, 1977); P. Adams Sitney, *Visionary Film: The American Avant-Garde, 1943–1978*, 2d ed. (New York: Oxford University Press, 1979); and *Film as Film: Formal Experiment in Film, 1910–1975* (London: Arts Council of Great Britain, 1979). The latter two volumes also address films that employ associational form. A rich and valuable anthology is P. Adams Sitney, ed., *The Avant-Garde Film: A Reader of Theory and Criticism* (New York: New York University Press, 1978), in which one may find suggestions like that of Peter Kubelka: cinema is not essentially movement but rather "the quick projection of light impulses" (p. 140). (It would be hard to come closer to a purely abstract aesthetic.) The principal English-language journals of experimental cinema are *Film Culture*, *Afterimage*, and *Millennium Film Journal* (all U.S.A.) and *Afterimage* and *Undercut* (England).

# PART III

## FILM STYLE

We are still seeking to understand the principles by which a film is put together. Chapter 2 showed that the concept of film form offers a way to do this. Chapters 3 and 4 went on to look at two sorts of formal systems operating in films—narrative and nonnarrative systems.

When we see a film, though, we do not engage with only a narrative or a nonnarrative pattern. We experience a film—not a painting or a novel. Analyzing a painting demands a knowledge of color, shape, and composition; analyzing a novel demands knowledge of language. To understand form in any art, we must be familiar with the medium which that art utilizes. Consequently, our understanding of a film must also include features of the film medium. Part III of this book investigates just this area. We shall look at four sets of cinematic techniques: two techniques of the shot, mise-en-scene and cinematography; the technique that relates shot to shot, editing; and the relation of sound to film images.

Each chapter will introduce a single technique, surveying the choices it offers to the filmmaker. We will suggest how you can recognize the technique and its uses. Most importantly, we shall concentrate on the formal functions of each technique. We will try to answer such questions as these: How may a technique guide expectations or furnish motifs for the film? How may it develop across a film? How may it direct our attention, clarify or emphasize meanings, shape our emotional response?

In Part III, we will also discover that in any film, certain techniques tend to create a formal system of their own. Every film develops specific techniques in patterned ways. This unified, developed, and significant use of particular technical choices we shall call style. In our study of certain films, we shall see how each filmmaker creates a distinctive stylistic system. We can visualize the result in a diagram:

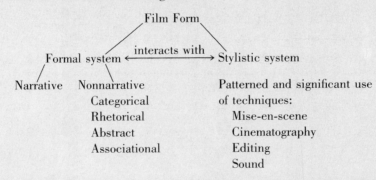

Film Form

Formal system ←——— interacts with ———→ Stylistic system

| Narrative | Nonnarrative | Patterned and significant use |
|---|---|---|
| | Categorical | of techniques: |
| | Rhetorical | Mise-en-scene |
| | Abstract | Cinematography |
| | Associational | Editing |
| | | Sound |

The use a film makes of the medium—the film's style—cannot be studied apart from the film's use of narrative or nonnarrative form. We shall find that film style interacts with the formal system. Often film techniques support and enhance nonnarrative or narrative form. In a narrative film, style can function to advance the cause-effect chain, create parallels, manipulate story-plot relations, or sustain the narration's flow of information. But also, film style may become separate from narrative or non-narrative form, attracting our attention in its own right. Some uses of film technique can call attention to patterns of style. In either event, the chapters that follow will continually return to the problem of relations between narrative and nonnarrative formal systems and the stylistic system.

# THE SHOT:
# MISE-EN-SCENE

Of all the techniques of cinema, mise-en-scene is the one with which we are most familiar. After seeing a film, we may not recall the cutting or the camera movements, the dissolves or offscreen sound, but we will almost surely recall items of mise-en-scene. We remember the costumes in *Gone with the Wind* or the bleak, chilly lighting in Charles Foster Kane's Xanadu. We retain vivid memories of the rainy, gloomy settings in *The Big Sleep* or the cozy family home in *Meet Me in St. Louis*. We recall Harpo Marx clambering over Edgar Kennedy's peanut wagon (*Duck Soup*) and Katharine Hepburn defiantly splintering Cary Grant's golf clubs (*The Phila-delphia Story*). In short, many of our most sharply etched memories of the cinema turn out to be of this or that element of mise-en-scene.

## WHAT IS MISE-EN-SCENE?

In the original French, **mise-en-scene** (pronounced "meez-ahn-sen") means "stag-ing an action," and it was first applied to the practice of directing plays. Film scholars, extending the term to film direction as well, use the term to signify the director's control over what appears in the film frame. As you would expect from the term's theatrical origins, mise-en-scene includes those aspects that overlap with the art of the theater: setting, lighting, costume, and the behavior of the figures. In controlling the mise-en-scene, the director *stages the event* for the camera.

## REALISM

Before we analyze mise-en-scene in detail, one preconception must be brought to light. Just as viewers often remember this or that bit of mise-en-scene from a film, so viewers often judge mise-en-scene by standards of "realism." A car seems to be "realistic" for the period the film depicts, or a gesture does not seem realistic because "real people don't act that way."

Realism as a standard of value, however, involves several problems. Notions of realism vary across cultures, through time, and even among individuals. Marlon Brando's acclaimed "realist" performance in the 1954 film *On the Waterfront* looks stylized today. To American critics of the 1910s, William S. Hart's Westerns seemed realistic, but to French critics of the 1920s, the same films appeared as artificial as a medieval epic. Moreover, realism has become one of the most problematic issues in the philosophy of art. (See Notes and Queries for examples.) Most important, to insist rigidly on realism for all films can blind us to the great range of mise-en-scene possibilities.

Look, for instance, at the frame from *The Cabinet of Dr. Caligari* (Fig. 5.1). The jagged rooftops and slanted chimneys certainly do not accord with our conception of normal reality. Yet to condemn the film for lacking realism would be foolish, because the film uses stylization to present a madman's fantasy.

It is better, then, to examine the *functions* of mise-en-scene than to dismiss this or that element that happens not to match our conception of realism. This means that the filmmaker may use *any* system of mise-en-scene and that we should analyze its function in the total film—how mise-en-scene is motivated, how it varies or develops, how it works in relation to narrative and nonnarrative forms.

## THE POWER OF MISE-EN-SCENE

To confine the cinema to some notion of realism would indeed impoverish mise-en-scene. This technique has the power to transcend normal conceptions of reality, as we can see from a glance at the cinema's first master of the technique, Georges Méliès. Méliès's mise-en-scene enabled him to create a totally imaginary world on film.

A caricaturist and magician, Méliès became fascinated by the Lumière brothers' demonstration of their short films in 1895. (For more on the Lumières, see pp. 167–168 and 373–374.) After building a camera similar to the Lumière machine, Méliès began filming unstaged street scenes and moments of passing daily life. One day, the story goes, he was filming at the Place de l'Opéra and his camera jammed as a bus was passing. After some tinkering, he was able to resume filming, but by this time the bus had gone and a hearse was passing in front of his lens. When Méliès screened the film, he discovered something unexpected: a moving bus seemed to transform itself instantly into a hearse. Whether apocryphal or not, the tale at least illustrates dramatically Méliès's recognition of the magical powers of mise-en-scene. He would devote most of his efforts to cinematic conjuring.

But to do so would require preparation, since Méliès could not count on lucky accidents like the bus-hearse transformation. He would have to plan and stage action for the camera. Drawing on his experience in theater, Méliès built one of the first film studios—a small, crammed affair bristling with theatrical machinery,

Fig. 5.1

Fig. 5.2

Fig. 5.3

Fig. 5.4

Fig. 5.5

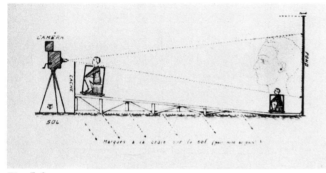

Fig. 5.6

balconies, trapdoors, and sliding backdrops. His talent as a cartoonist enabled him to sketch detailed shots beforehand and to design sets and costumes. Figures 5.2 and 5.3 illustrate the correspondence between his planning drawings and the finished shots. As if this were not enough, Méliès starred in his own films (often in several roles per film). His desire to create magical effects led Méliès to control the mise-en-scene of his films down to the last detail.

Such control was necessary to create the fantasy world he envisioned. Only in a studio could Méliès produce *The Mermaid*, in which an undersea world is created out of an actress in costume, a fish tank placed in front of the camera, some sets, and "carts for monsters" (see Fig. 5.4). Only by careful preparation and setting design could he present the illusion of *The Man with the Rubber Head*, in which Méliès inflates the disembodied head of Méliès. Figures 5.5 and 5.6 show that the trick depended on double exposure and Méliès in a cart rolling toward the camera.

Méliès's "Star-Film" studio made hundreds of short fantasy and trick films based on such a control over every element in the frame, and the first master of mise-en-scene demonstrated the great range of technical possibilities it offers. The legacy of Méliès's magic is a delightfully unreal world wholly obedient to the whims of the imagination.

## ASPECTS OF MISE-EN-SCENE

What possibilities for selection and control does mise-en-scene offer the director? We can mark out four general areas and indicate some potential uses of each.

### ■ SETTING

Since the earliest days of cinema, critics and audiences have understood that setting plays a more active role in cinema than in most theatrical styles. André Bazin writes:

> The human being is all-important in the theatre. The drama on the screen can exist without actors. A banging door, a leaf in the wind, waves beating on the shore can heighten the dramatic effect. Some film masterpieces use man only as an accessory, like an extra, or in counterpoint to nature, which is the true leading character.

Cinema setting, then, can come to the forefront; it need not be only a container for the action but can dynamically enter into the narrative action. (See Plates 8, 14, 15, and 16 for examples of settings without characters.)

The filmmaker may control setting in many ways. One way is to select an already existing locale in which to stage the action, a practice stretching back to the earliest films. Louis Lumière shot his short comedy *L'Arroseur arrosé* ("The Waterer Watered," Fig. 5.7) in a garden, and Victor Sjöstrom filmed *The Outlaw and His Wife* in the splendor of the Swedish countryside (production still, Fig. 5.8). Similarly we see the desert in *Lawrence of Arabia*, Gaudí buildings in the Barcelona scenes of Antonioni's *The Passenger*, and Times Square in *Desperately Seeking Susan*.

Fig. 5.7

Fig. 5.8

On the other hand, the filmmaker may choose to construct the setting. Méliès understood the increased control yielded by shooting in a studio, and many subsequent filmmakers followed his lead. In France, Germany, and especially the United States, the possibility of creating a wholly artificial world on film led to the development of several approaches to constructing setting. Some directors have emphasized historical authenticity. For example, Erich Von Stroheim prided himself on meticulous research into details of locale, as the production still from *Greed* (1924) illustrates (Fig. 5.9). *All the President's Men* (1976) took a similar tack, seeking to duplicate the *Washington Post* office on a sound stage by reproducing every detail of the original newsroom; even waste paper from the actual office was scattered around the set. We should remember, however, that "realism" in settings is a matter of viewing conventions. *Greed* and *All the President's Men*, each a model of realism for its day, now seem very different, and what strikes us as realistic today may well seem highly stylized to future audiences. Realism through historical authenticity is far from being the only possible approach.

Other films have not been so committed to historical verisimilitude. Though D. W. Griffith studied the various historical periods presented in *Intolerance*, his Babylon—part Assyrian, part Egyptian, part American—constitutes a personal image of that city (production still, Fig. 5.10). Similarly, in *Ivan the Terrible* Sergei Eisenstein freely stylized the decor of the czar's palace to harmonize with the lighting, costume, and figure movement, so that characters crawl through doorways that resemble mouseholes and stand frozen before allegorical murals.

Setting can crowd the actors, as in the cluttered production still from *The Scarlet Empress* (Fig. 5.11), or it can be reduced to zero, to a striking *absence*, as in many animated films and in Godard's *Le Gai Savoir* and Dreyer's *La Passion de Jeanne d'Arc* (Figs. 5.12 and 5.13), respectively. Setting can be convulsed and contorted, like the angular streets and tilting buildings of *The Cabinet of Dr. Caligari* (a film heavily influenced by German expressionist art).

Films can also use color to enhance the functions of their settings. For example, Jacques Tati's *Play Time* uses changing color schemes as part of its principles of

Fig. 5.9

Fig. 5.11

Fig. 5.10

Fig. 5.12

development in its narrative. In the first portion of *Play Time*, the settings (and costumes) are mostly gray, brown, and black—cold, steely colors (see Plate 3). Later in the film, however, beginning in the restaurant scene, the settings start to sport cheery reds, pinks, and greens, as in the flowers in Plate 4. This change in the settings' colors functions to support a narrative development, from an inhuman city landscape to one based on spontaneity.

Whether selected or constructed, historically authentic or stylized, color or black and white, settings can function in a virtually infinite number of ways.

We should note here that a full-size setting need not always be built. To save money or to create fantasy effects, the filmmakers may build miniature settings, and these too have the range of possibilities we have discussed for regular sets. (See Fig. 1.16 for an example of a miniature set.) Parts of settings may also be done as paintings which are then photographed to combine with full-size objects; we will look at how this is done in the next chapter.

Fig. 5.13

Fig. 5.14

Fig. 5.15

Fig. 5.16

Fig. 5.17

The manipulation of a shot's setting for narrative functions also implies that the setting may create props—another term indicating the overlap between cinematic and theatrical mise-en-scene. When part of the setting is motivated to operate actively within the ongoing action, we are justified in calling it a prop. Needless to say, films teem with examples: the snowstorm paperweight that shatters at the beginning of *Citizen Kane*, the little girl's balloon in *M*, the cactus rose in *The Man Who Shot Liberty Valance*, Cesare's coffin in *The Cabinet of Dr. Caligari*. In the shower murder in *Psycho* the shower curtain is at first an innocuous part of the setting, but when the killer enters the bathroom, the curtain screens her (him?) from our sight. Later, after the murder, Norman Bates uses the curtain to wrap up the victim's body. In *The Crime of M. Lange* a poster outside Batala's publishing house advertises its new dime-novel series "Javert" (Fig. 5.14), but after Batala has left the company, Lange and his associates pull the poster down to reveal the window and room that have for so long been blocked from sunlight (Figs. 5.15 and 5.16). Later we shall examine in more detail how elements of setting can weave through an entire film to form motifs within the narrative.

### ■ COSTUME AND MAKE-UP

Like setting, costume can have specific functions in the total film, and the range of possibilities is huge. Erich Von Stroheim, for instance, was as passionately committed to authenticity of dress as of setting, and he was said to have created underwear that would instill the proper mood in his actors even though it was never to be seen in the film. In Griffith's *Musketeers of Pig Alley* Lillian Gish appears in a faded and threadbare dress, which summarizes the poverty in which her character lives. Costumes may, on the other hand, be quite stylized, calling attention to their purely graphic qualities. In *The Cabinet of Dr. Caligari* the somnambulist Cesare wears a jet-black leotard, whereas the woman he abducts wears a white nightgown. Throughout *Ivan the Terrible* costumes are carefully orchestrated with one another in their colors, their textures, and even their movements. Note, for instance, the plastic sweep and dynamism of the robes in the shot of Ivan and Philip (Fig. 5.17). In *Meet Me in St. Louis* characters become associated with specific costume colors. And costume may in fact be so sparse as to bleed into the setting: in one scene of *THX 1138* George Lucas strips both locale and clothing to stark white on white.

Just as settings may furnish props for the film's ongoing narrative system, so may costume. To think of Dracula is to think of how his billowing cape enwraps him, unfolds, and closes decisively around a victim. To recall the film director Guido in Fellini's *8½* is to recall those sunglasses which he persistently uses to shield himself from the world outside. In cinema any portion of a costume may become a prop: a pince-nez (*Potemkin*), a pair of shoes *(Strangers on a Train, The Wizard of Oz)*, a cross pendant (*Ivan the Terrible*), a jacket (*Le Million*). When Hildy Johnson, in *His Girl Friday*, switches from her role of aspiring housewife to that of reporter, her stylish hat with its low-dipping brim is replaced by a "masculine" hat with its brim pushed up, journalist style (Figs. 5.18 and 5.19). Film genres make extensive use of costume props—the six-gun, the automatic pistol, the top hat and cane. Every major film comedian has turned a specific costume into a panoply of props: Chaplin's cane and derby, Fields's cigar and top hat, Laurel and Hardy's derbies and too-tight suits, Harpo Marx's capacious pockets, Jacques Tati's pipe, raincoat, and suede shoes. Examples could be multiplied indefinitely, but the crucial point is that costume motifs may function to unify the film's overall form.

Fig. 5.18

Fig. 5.19

Fig. 5.20

All these points about costumes apply equally to a closely related area of mise-en-scene, the actors' make-up. Make-up was originally necessary because actors' faces would not register well on early film stocks. And, up to the present, it has been used in various ways to enhance the appearance of actors on the screen. But a huge range of possibilities has grown up. Dreyer's *La Passion de Jeanne d'Arc* was famous for its complete avoidance of make-up when it appeared in 1928 (Fig. 5.13). This film relied on close-ups and tiny facial changes to create an intense religious drama. On the other hand, Nikolai Cherkasov did not look particularly like Eisenstein's conception of Czar Ivan IV, so he wore a wig and false beard, nose, and eyebrows for *Ivan the Terrible* (Fig. 5.23). Changing actors to look like historical personages has been one common function of make-up.

Make-up can aim at complete realism. When Laurence Olivier blackened his skin and hair to make a film of *Othello*, he strove to be as convincing a Moor as possible. Women often wear make-up that looks like the ordinary street cosmetics currently in fashion, and most men's make-up is designed to look on the screen as if they were not wearing any. Yet it is equally possible to use make-up in nonrealistic ways. Dracula's flapping cloak combines with his long, pointed incisors to create the image of a vampire, and in general, bizarre make-up plays a big role in the conventions of the horror genre. In *The Cabinet of Dr. Caligari* (Fig. 5.20), the actors' faces are heavily painted with unshaded areas of light and dark colors, and this fits in with a similar treatment of the other aspects of mise-en-scene in that film. Make-up, like costume, should be analyzed in terms of how it contributes to a unified characterization.

## ■ LIGHTING

The manipulation of an image's lighting controls much of its impact. In cinema, lighting is more than just illumination that permits us to see the action. Lighter and darker areas within the frame help create the overall composition of each shot and hence guide our eyes to certain objects and actions. A brightly illuminated patch may draw our attention and reveal a key gesture, while a shadow may conceal a detail and build up our suspense about what may be present there. Lighting can also articulate textures: the soft curve of a face, the rough grain of a piece of wood, the delicate tracery of a spider's web, the sheen of glass, the sparkle of a faceted gem.

Lighting shapes objects by creating highlights and shadows. A highlight is a patch of brightness on a surface; the man's face in Figure 5.21 or the edge of the fingers in Figure 5.22 are examples of highlights. There are two basic types of

Fig. 5.21

Fig. 5.22

Fig. 5.23

Fig. 5.24

shadows, each of which is important in filmic composition: *attached* shadows and *cast* shadows. An attached shadow occurs when part of an object blocks the light falling on another part of it. When you face a candle in a darkened room, your back is not illuminated—it is covered by an attached shadow. But the candle also shines past your body and creates a shadow on the wall behind; that is a cast shadow, because it is your body, not the wall, which blocks out the light. The shadows in Figure 5.21, for example, are cast shadows, made by bars between the actor and the light source. But, in Figure 5.22, the small shadows on portions of the hand are attached, for they are created by the three-dimensional curves and ridges of the hand itself. As these samples suggest, highlights and shadows help create our sense of a scene's space. In Figure 5.21, from De Mille's *The Cheat*, a few shadows imply an entire prison cell.

Lighting also shapes our understanding of the shot's composition. If a ball is lit from the front, it will appear round. If the same ball is lit from the side, we will see a half-circle. Hollis Frampton's short film *Lemon* consists primarily of gradually changing light patterns on a lemon, and the yellow and black areas of the screen shift accordingly. This film almost seems designed to prove the truth of a remark made by Josef von Sternberg, one of the cinema's great masters of film lighting: "The proper use of light can embellish and dramatize every object."

For our purposes, we can isolate four major features of film lighting: its *quality*, *direction*, *source*, and *color*.

Lighting *quality* refers to the relative intensity of the illumination. "Hard" lighting creates clearly defined shadows, whereas "soft" lighting creates a diffused illumination. The terms are relative, and many lighting situations will fall in between the extremes, but we can in practice easily recognize the differences. Hard lighting creates bold shadows and crisp textures and edges. In Figure 5.22, a close-up from Robert Bresson's *Pickpocket*, the veins in the hand are emphasized by the hard lighting. In Figure 5.23, a shot from *Ivan the Terrible*, softer lighting blurs contours and textures and makes for more diffusion and gentler contrasts between light and shade.

The *direction* of lighting in a shot refers to the path of light from its source(s) to the object lit. "Every light," wrote von Sternberg, "has a point where it is brightest and a point toward which it wanders to lose itself completely. . . . The journey of rays from that central core to the outposts of blackness is the adventure and drama of light." For convenience we can distinguish among frontal lighting, sidelighting, backlighting, underlighting, and top lighting.

**Frontal lighting** can be recognized by its tendency to eliminate shadows. In Plate 1, a shot from Godard's *La Chinoise*, the result of such frontal lighting is a fairly flat-looking image.

In *Touch of Evil*, Welles uses a hard **sidelight** to sculpt the characters' features. Note the sharp shadows cast by noses, cheekbones, and lips, as well as the shadows cast on the left wall (Fig. 5.24).

The illumination of only the edges of the figure is characteristic of **backlighting.** In Figure 5.25, a frame from Welles's *Citizen Kane*, the man is almost a silhouette. Backlighting defines depth by sharply distinguishing an object from its background.

**Underlighting** suggests that the light comes from below the subject. In Figure 5.26 (from Ivan Mosjoukin's *Le Brasier ardent*), the underlighting suggests an offscreen fire. Since underlighting tends to distort features, it is often used to create dramatic horror effects, but it may also simply indicate a realistic light source, such as a fireplace. As usual, several functions are possible.

Fig. 5.25

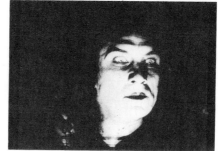

Fig. 5.26

Fig. 5.27

Fig. 5.28

Fig. 5.29

Fig. 5.30

**Top lighting** usually appears along with light coming from other directions. In the shot from Mosjoukin's *Le Brasier ardent* shown in Figure 5.27, the spotlight shines from above.

A shot will seldom have only one *source* of light. Lighting specialists have developed a versatile range of standardized sources, but two will suffice for our purposes: the **key light** and the **fill light.** The key light is the primary lighting source of the image, providing the dominant illumination and casting the dominant shadows. A fill light may then be used to "fill in," to soften or eliminate shadows cast by the key light. Through a combination of the two, the exact degree of lighting can be controlled. The key lighting source may be aimed into the space from any direction, as our examples have indicated. Plate 5 shows an example where the underlighting is the key source, while a less bright light falls on the setting behind the figure.

In Figure 5.28 the key light is hard and comes from the side. No fill light softens the shadows, as is often the case in this film, Welles's *Touch of Evil*.

*Touch of Evil.*

Figure 5.29 shows a frame from Gance's *La Roue*. The bold backlighting is complemented by a key light from the left (casting attached shadows on the left side of the actress's face, notably by the nose and eye) and a fill light from the right (which ensures that this side of her face will not appear completely dark, as the faces do in Figures 5.24 and 5.28).

Figure 5.30 shows a shot from *Bezhin Meadow*, in which Eisenstein uses a number of light sources and directions. The key light falling on the figures comes from the left side, but it is hard on the face of the old woman in the foreground and softened on the face of the man by a fill light from the right. The thin rims of light on the folds of the old woman's scarf indicate some backlighting as well.

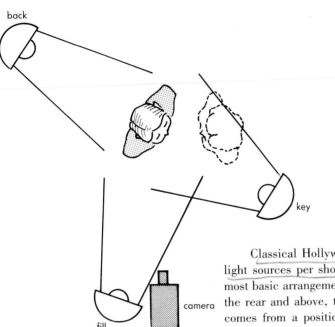

Fig. 5.31

Fig. 5.32

Classical Hollywood filmmaking developed the custom of using at least *three* light sources per shot: key light, fill light, and backlight. Figure 5.31 shows the most basic arrangement of these lights on a single figure. The backlight comes from the rear and above, the key light comes diagonally from the front, and a fill light comes from a position near the camera. The key will typically be closer to the figure or brighter than the fill, while the brightness of the backlight is between those of the other two. If another actor is added (as in the dotted figure in Fig. 5.31), the key light for one can be altered slightly to form the backlight for the other and vice versa, with a fill light on either side of the camera. Typically, each major character in a scene will have his or her own key, fill, and backlight (though some lamps may do double duty as key for one and backlight for another, as in this example).

In Figure 5.32, the Bette Davis character in *Jezebel* is the most important figure present, and the three-point lighting centers attention on her. A bright backlight from the rear upper right highlights her hair and outlines her left arm. The key light is off left here, with her right arm brightly illuminated. Note that although her face is fairly evenly lit, the nose is molded by an attached shadow on the left cheek. Thus even though a fill light comes in from just to the right of the camera, it is less bright than the key—not bright enough to wash out the nose shadow. This balanced lighting gives the face a modeled effect rather than a flat one. (Davis's back and key lights serve to illuminate the woman behind her at the right, but less prominently. Other fill lights, called "background" lighting, fall on the set and on the crowd at the left rear.)

You may have already noticed that this "three-point" lighting system implies that the arrangement of the lamps would have to be changed every time the camera position is shifted for a new framing of the scene. This is, in fact, the case. In spite of the great cost involved, most Hollywood films will have a different lighting arrangement for each camera position. Again, such shifting light sources do not conform to reality, but they do enable filmmakers to create clear compositions for each shot and to guide our eye by means of lighting.

We tend to think of film lighting being the white of sunlight or the soft yellow of incandescent interior lamps, but by shining motion picture lamps through a transparent colored filter, the filmmaker can make the illumination of a scene any color at all. There may be a realistic source in the scene to motivate the coloration of the light, as in a nightclub where a color wheel plays over musicians on a stage (as in Anthony Mann's *The Glenn Miller Story*). But color can just as easily be nonrealistic. In *Ivan the Terrible,* Part 2, Eisenstein uses a blue light suddenly cast on an actor, nondiegetically, to suggest the character's terror as he realizes an assassin is waiting to kill him (see Plates 5 and 6). Such a technique—using colored light to perform a function usually confined to the acting—is all the more effective because it is so unusual and hence unexpected.

All of these examples illustrate the cinema's ability to control the look and functions of a shot through light quality, direction, source, and color. Each of these aspects of light can be manipulated separately and combined to enhance the expressive potential of the film. No component of mise-en-scene is more important than "the drama and adventure of light."

## ■ FIGURE EXPRESSION AND MOVEMENT

The director may also control the behavior of various figures in the mise-en-scene. Here the word "figures" covers a wide range of possibilities, since the figure may represent a person but could also be an animal (Lassie, the donkey Balthasar, Donald Duck), a robot (R2D2 and C3PO in the *Star Wars* series), an object (as in *Ballet mécanique*'s choreography of bottles, straw hats, and kitchen utensils), or even a pure shape (as in *Ballet mécanique*'s circles and triangles). Mise-en-scene can give such figures the power to express feelings and thoughts; it can also dynamize them to create various kinetic patterns.

In Figure 5.33 (from *Seven Samurai*) the samurai have won the battle with the bandits. Virtually the only movement in the frame is the driving rain, but the slouching postures of the men leaning on their spears express their tense weariness.

In *White Heat* figure expression and movement cooperate to present an image of psychotic rage. In Figure 5.34 Cody Jarrett (James Cagney), after learning of his mother's death, hurls himself up from the prison mess table.

Although abstract shapes can become a part of the mise-en-scene, we usually think of figure expression and movement as "acting." Too often viewers (and critics) tend to treat actors as representing real people in a story. Yet, as we have seen, filmmakers who control mise-en-scene do not "capture" already existing events; rather, they create the event to be filmed. An actor's performance in a film consists of visual elements (appearance, gestures, facial expressions) and sound (voice, effects). At times, of course, an actor may contribute only visual aspects, as in the silent period of film history. Similarly, an actor's performance may sometimes exist only on the sound track of the film; in *A Letter to Three Wives*, Celeste Holm's character, Addie Ross, speaks a narration over the images but never appears on the screen.

Fig. 5.33

Fig. 5.34

Since the character the actor creates is in part a figure in the mise-en-scene, films may contain a wide variety of acting styles. It is not always fruitful to judge an actor's performance by its "believability" in relation to some view we may have of reality. Nothing illustrates the futility of demanding uniformly "realistic" performances so well as the changing fashions in what is considered to *be* "realism." Today, we may think the acting of Jane Fonda and Jon Voight in *Coming Home* or Dustin Hoffman and Jessica Lange in *Tootsie* to be the height of realism. Their behavior is quiet and restrained. They hesitate and occasionally stammer, as they might if speaking in real-life conversations. Yet in the early 1950s, the New York Actors Studio style, as exemplified by Marlon Brando's performances in *On the Waterfront* and *A Streetcar Named Desire*, were thought to be extremely realistic. Fine though we may still find Brando's work in these films, it seems deliberate, heightened, and quite unrealistic. The same might be said of the performances, by professional and amateur actors alike, in post–World War II Italian neorealist films, which were hailed when they first appeared as almost documentary depictions of Italian life but many of which now seem to us to contain polished performances suitable to Hollywood films. (In fact, one of the main neorealist actors, Anna Magnani, went to Hollywood and won an Oscar there.) Who can say what the acting in *Coming Home*, *Tootsie*, and other recent films will look like in a few decades? We should be cautious in using "realism" as a criterion for examining acting.

Changing views of realism are not the only reason to be wary of this as a concept for analyzing acting. Often when people say that acting was "unrealistic," they are evaluating it as bad. But not all films try to achieve realism. Instead of assuming that acting must be realistic, we should try to understand what kind of acting style the film is cueing us to accept. If the functions of acting in the film are best served by a nonrealistic performance, that is the kind that the skillful actor will strive to present. Obvious examples of nonrealistic acting style occur constantly in *The Wizard of Oz*, for fantasy purposes. (How would a "realistic" Wicked Witch behave?) Moreover, when we watch a film, we are inevitably aware that the performances on the screen are the results of the actors' skills, not of real people's actions in everyday life. The great stress placed upon acting awards—Oscars, actors' prizes at the Cannes Film Festival, and so on—suggest that we recognize acting as a craft, however realistic or stylized the outstanding performance may be. A considerable controversy was stirred up in Hollywood in 1985 because Steve Martin was not even nominated for an Oscar for his acting in the comedy *All of Me*. In that film, Martin portrays a man whose body is suddenly inhabited, on the right side, by the soul of a woman who has just died. Martin used sudden changes of voice, along with acrobatic pantomime, to suggest a "split" body. His performance is not realistic, since the situation he portrays could not exist in the real world. Yet in the context of this fantasy-comedy, Martin's acting is not only virtuosic but completely appropriate. There are many ways a film might motivate nonrealistic acting. In any type of very stylized film, an attempt to give a "realistic" performance would make the character stand out as inappropriate to his or her place in the context of the film's total mise-en-scene.

This fact indicates a clue for analyzing actors' performances. If the actor looks and behaves in a manner *appropriate* to his or her character's *function* in the context of the film, the actor has given a good performance—*whether or not* he or she has behaved as a real person might in such circumstances.

A few examples will serve to demonstrate how many acting styles can exist. Each may be appropriate to its context because cinema itself has so many different types of mise-en-scene. A film may strive for a certain resemblance to "realistic"

Fig. 5.35

Fig. 5.36

Fig. 5.37

behavior by attributing character behavior to psychological motivation. Thus in *Winchester 73* James Stewart plays a man driven by a desire for revenge that borders on psychosis; his extremes of gesture and facial expression are acceptable because they fit the traits which have been assigned to his character earlier in the film (see Fig. 5.35).

Psychological motivation is less important in a film like *Trouble in Paradise*, a sophisticated comedy of manners in which the main concern is with broad character *types* in a comic situation. In Figure 5.36 two rivals for the affections of the same man pretend to be friends, although they actually wish to trick each other. Their exaggerated smiles and polite gestures are amusing because we know the underlying situation. Again, the performances are perfectly appropriate to the style of the film.

Fig. 5.38

Comedy does not provide the only motivation for stylization. *Ivan the Terrible* is a film that heightens every element—music, costume, setting—to create a larger-than-life portrait of its hero; Nikolai Cherkasov's broad, abrupt gestures fit in perfectly with all of these other elements to create an overall unity of composition (Fig. 5.37).

The actor is always a graphic element in the film, but some films underline this fact. In *The Cabinet of Dr. Caligari*, Conrad Veidt's portrayal of the somnambulist resembles a dance; his behavior blends in with the graphic elements of the setting—his body echoes the tilted tree trunks, his arms and hands their branches and leaves (Fig. 5.38). As we shall see in our examination of the history of film styles, the graphic design of this scene in *Caligari* typifies the systematic distortion characteristic of German expressionism.

In *Breathless*, director Jean-Luc Godard juxtaposes Jean Seberg's face with a print of a Renoir painting (Fig. 5.39). We might think that Seberg is giving a wooden performance, for she simply poses in the frame and turns her head; indeed, her acting in the entire film is not conventionally expressive. Yet her face and general appearance are visually appropriate for her function in the film.

Fig. 5.39

By now it has become a cliché to point out that film acting differs from theatrical acting. Famous stars who move from one medium to another never tire of telling talk-show hosts that film acting must be more restrained, because the camera shows small gestures that would never be seen on the stage. Let us try to be a bit more precise in defining the difference.

In a theater, we are usually at a considerable distance from the actor; even if he or she comes to the front of the stage, we may be seated in the back of the balcony and will not see anything but broad gestures. We certainly can never get as close to the theater actor as the camera can put us in a film. But, in a film, we are not necessarily seeing close views of the actor at every moment either. The camera can be at any distance from the figure—far away, so that the actor is only a dot on the screen (farther away than even our balcony theater seat, in fact), or very close, showing us the tiniest details of an eye movement. Thus the film actor must behave differently than the stage actor but not always just by being more restrained. Rather, she or he must be able to adjust to each type of camera distance. If the actor is a mere dot far from the camera, he or she will have to gesture broadly or move around to be seen as acting at all. But, if the camera and actor are inches apart, a twitch of a mouth muscle will come across clearly. In between these extremes, there is a whole range of adjustments to be made.

Basically, we can distinguish between two types of emphasis in film acting: on facial expression and on pantomimic gestures of the body. Clearly, the closer the actor is to the camera, the more the facial expression will be visible and the more important it will be (although the filmmaker may choose to concentrate on another part of the body, excluding the face and emphasizing gesture). But if the actor is far away from the camera, or turned to conceal the face, his or her bodily gestures become the center of the performance.

Such differences depend on the distance of the camera from the actor, which we shall be examining in the next chapter as *shot scale*. Similarly, the staging, or the way in which the actors are arranged within the space being photographed, determines how we will see their performances. Many shots in Bernardo Bertolucci's *The Spider's Stratagem* show the two main characters from a distance, so that their manner of walking, combined with such details as how the heroine holds her parasol stiffly upright, constitute the actors' performances (Fig. 5.40); in conversation scenes, however, we see their faces clearly, as in Figure 5.41. In Figure 5.7, the actors are placed at either side of the garden, back from the camera, so that the broad movements of their arms, legs, and bodies are the main emphasis of the film. The actors are so distant in Figure 5.10 that we see each person only as part of a crowd of moving actors. Figures 5.17, 5.25, 5.33, 5.37, and 5.38 are all examples of shots where bodily gesture rather than facial expression forms the basis for the acting. Contrast these with Figures 5.13, 5.18, 5.19, 5.23, 5.29, 5.30, 5.32, and 5.39, where the faces are close enough for small changes to be visible. A performance may combine facial expression and bodily gesture, of course, as is evident in Figure 5.41; see also Figures 5.12, 5.24, 5.34, 5.35, and 5.36. In Figure 5.22, small bodily gestures become crucial. Thus film acting demands a great range of adjustments from its performers, and the truly skillful film actor would seem to be one who can gauge his or her performance according to how far away the camera is.

Sometimes film acting is denigrated because its practitioners do not have to sustain a performance. In the theater, the actor must be able to give a single, often lengthy presentation of a character. But a film, because it is shot over a period of time, breaks that performance up into bits. This can work to the filmmaker's advantage, since these bits can be selected and combined to build up a performance in ways that could never be accomplished on the stage. Most simply, if a shot has been done over and over, the editor may select the best gestures and expressions and create a composite performance better than any one sustained performance would be. (A similar process takes place when a musical performance is recorded.) Through the careful addition of music and the combination of the shots of one actor with shots of other things, the performance can be built up still further. The director may simply tell an actor to widen his or her eyes and stare offscreen. If the next shot shows a hand with a gun, we are likely to think the actor is depicting fear.

Fig. 5.40

Fig. 5.41

Thus acting in the cinema depends upon the combination of actual figure behavior with many other filmic techniques.

Before leaving the subject of acting, we should note that "great" performances are not the center of every narrative film. We tend to think of stars and their performances as being the most important elements of the films we normally see. Yet some directors counter this convention and deliberately instruct their actors to behave in a way that will create "flat," extremely restrained performances. Robert Bresson is noted for doing this; he chooses nonactors whose appearances fit the roles as he conceives them. Rather than giving them detailed information about the psychological traits of their characters, he tells them where to walk or look, and when to speak. The result is disconcerting in terms of our expectations, yet we soon realize that such restraint focuses our attention very intently on tiny gestures and on the other filmic techniques of the scenes. As a result, Bresson's films contain highly original and complex acting. Jean-Marie Straub and Danièle Huillet go even further in this direction. Their *Not Reconciled* and *Chronicle of Anna Magdalena Bach* also utilize nonactors who speak their lines in a rather wooden fashion or simply have no lines at all. (In *Chronicle* the emphasis is largely on lengthy musical performances, and hence the parts are played by real musicians.) In Straub and Huillet films, we are given some distance on what we are watching. We do not see the actors as complex psychological beings but as reciters of written dialogue; thus we become actively aware of our own conventional expectations about film acting, and perhaps those expectations are broadened a bit. In this way acting may be as stylized and sparse as the setting or lighting may be.

As with every element of a film, acting offers an unlimited range of various possibilities. It cannot be judged on a universal scale that is separate from the concrete context of the entire film's form.

## MISE-EN-SCENE IN SPACE AND TIME

Setting, costume, lighting, and figure expression and movement—these are the elements of mise-en-scene. Yet one element seldom appears in isolation. Each element usually combines with others to create a specific system in every film. The general formal principles of unity/disunity, similarity, difference, and development will guide us in analyzing how specific elements of mise-en-scene can function together. What are some ways in which mise-en-scene affects our attention? What pulls our eye to a portion of the frame at a given moment?

Looking is purposeful; what we look *at* is guided by our assumptions and expectations about what to look *for*. These, in turn, are based upon our previous experiences of artworks and of the real world. In viewing a film image, we make hypotheses on the basis of many factors.

One general factor is the total organization of the film's form. In a narrative film, characters and their actions offer strong cues. If a shot shows a crowd, we will tend to scan it looking for a character we recognize from earlier scenes. A second important controlling factor is sound. As we shall see in Chapter 8, sound can draw attention to areas of the image in various ways. A third source of control is written language, as when an intertitle cues us what to look for in the following shot. Fourth, mise-en-scene contains a host of purely spatial and temporal factors to guide our expectations and hence our viewing of the image.

Fig. 5.42

Fig. 5.43

Fig. 5.44

## ■ SPACE

We have already hinted at the different kinds of space in a film. The image projected on a screen is flat, of course, and it has a composition within a frame, just as a still photograph or a painting would. The arrangement of the mise-en-scene creates the light and dark shapes that make up the composition in the screen space. But, in most films, those shapes also represent a three-dimensional space in which the action occurs. Since the image is flat, the mise-en-scene must give us cues that will enable us to infer the three-dimensionality of the scene. Thus the movements of our eyes and attention across the screen are guided by a complex interaction of the flat composition and the represented depth.

In the flat screen space, our eyes will follow certain aspects of *movement*, *color*, *balance*, and *size*. Almost invariably, a moving shape will draw our attention more than will static shapes—even if the movement is far off to one edge of the screen. In Figure 5.42 (from Yasujiro Ozu's *Record of a Tenement Gentleman*), there are many shapes competing for our attention. But when a small bit of newspaper flaps, it immediately draws the eye, because it is the only motion in the frame. When several moving elements appear on the screen, as in a ballroom dance, we are likely to shift our attention among them, according to other cues or depending on our expectations about which one is most salient to the narrative action.

We are all familiar from our experiences with painting with the importance of color in a composition. Bright colors draw the eye more than do subdued ones. "Warm" colors in the red-orange-yellow range seem to come forward to us, while "cool" colors from purple to green recede. The filmmaker can take advantage of these principles. In Plates 14 and 15, for example, Yasujiro Ozu places bright red objects against cooler colors, and our eyes move irresistibly to the upper left of each composition. Compare Plate 10, with its subdued, predominantly cool colors, with the crowded composition of warm colors in Plate 11. In the latter the red and white at the top, the yellow in the foreground, and the spots of red clothing, keep us busy scanning the image. Note also how in Plates 1 and 2 Jean-Luc Godard keeps our attention on the whole composition rather than just the heads by using prominent background colors. In Plate 1, the pictures behind the actor's head lead us to scan the various small shapes quickly, while the bright red in Plate 2 comes forward strongly, making us aware of the background even if we stare intently at the face.

Black-and-white films use color in a different but comparable way. The colors register on the film as brighter or darker areas, and these in turn provide cues for us as we scan the image. Here whiter shapes will come forward, darker ones recede. Note how in Figure 5.43, from Pudovkin's *Mother*, your eye concentrates on the man's face rather than on the darkness surrounding it; the same principle works in Figures 5.25 through 5.30. Where two light areas compete in the composition (Fig. 5.39), we will most likely shift our attention back and forth, and the same holds for a cluttered composition with many bright elements. Dark shapes may become quite prominent as well, if they are clearly defined and placed against a light background. In Figure 5.38, the actor and the trees draw our eyes instantly because they stand out so starkly from the bright area.

Balance is crucial in determining whether we will concentrate on one area of the screen or scan it. Many shots place a single figure at the center of the frame and minimize other distracting elements at the sides, as in Figure 5.44, from *The Rules of the Game*; many of the illustrations we have just been examining show this

Plate 1  *La Chinoise*

Plate 2  *La Chinoise*

Plate 3  *Play Time*

Plate 4  *Play Time*

Plate 5  *Ivan the Terrible*

Plate 6  *Ivan the Terrible*

Plate 7  *An Autumn Afternoon*

Plate 8  *An Autumn Afternoon*

Plate 9  *Lancelot du Lac*

Plate 10  *Meet Me in St. Louis*

Plate 11  *Meet Me in St. Louis*

Plate 12  *Daisies*

Plate 13  *Innocence Unprotected*

Plate 14  *Ohayu*

Plate 15  *Ohayu*

Plate 16  *Daisies*

5.33

clearly (for example, Figs. 5.13, 5.26, and 5.37). Others may balance two or more elements on either side, encouraging our eye to move back and forth as in Figure 5.45, also from *The Rules of the Game*. (For other examples, see Figs. 5.30, 5.36, 5.39). The balance can be generally equal, as in Figure 5.36, or unequal; in Figure 5.31 we will most likely see the two standing men, since they are at the center, before noticing the crouching villagers at the far left.

Fig. 5.45

The effect of size is fairly obvious. Unless some other quality like color or movement emphasizes a small shape on the screen, we will look at the larger shapes first and then scan for their relations to smaller ones. In Figure 5.10, the huge pillars and statues of the Babylon set contribute more to our sense of the overall composition than do either the individual actors or the light and dark patches on the steps near the bottom. In Figure 5.24 we are likely to look first at the actor's face and the paper he holds, rather than at the small white labels on the file drawers—even though the labels are just as bright and in the same general centered area of the screen. But movement, color, and balance can easily override size as compositional cues and can draw our attention quickly to very small areas of the screen. For example, if one of those labels suddenly fell to the floor, we would almost certainly notice it.

In many abstract films, qualities of the screen space provide the most important cues for our attention. But in narrative and other types of films, composition works along with represented three-dimensional space.

In such films, we get a sense of three-dimensional space through *depth cues*. Here the spectator's active participation is very important. There is no real space extending behind the screen, but by noticing depth cues and imagining that space as existing, we create our understanding of the action. Depth cues are given by lighting, setting, costumes, and figure behavior. They suggest that a space has *volume* and *depth*. Again, we gain our understanding of depth cues from our experience of space in the real world and from conventions of space in such other arts as painting and theater.

Fig. 5.46

When we speak of an object as having volume, we mean that it is solid and occupies space, not just from side to side and top to bottom but from front to back as well. A film suggests volume by shape, shading, and movement. In Figures 5.39 and 5.46 (the latter from *La Passion de Jeanne d'Arc*), we do not think of the actors' faces as flat cutouts, like paper dolls. The shapes of those heads and shoulders suggest solid people. The attached shadows on the faces suggest the curves and recesses of the features and give a modeling effect. We assume that if the actor in Figure 5.39 turned her head, we would see a profile. Yet we know also that the painting on the wall behind her is flat. We see its edges against the white wall; it does not move. If it were turned to the side, we would just see the edge of the picture as a straight line rather than as a solid profile. Thus we use our knowledge of objects in the world to discern volume in filmic space. An abstract film, because it can use shapes that are not everyday objects, can create compositions without a sense of volume. The shapes in Figure 5.47, a frame from Norman McLaren's *Begone, Dull Care*, give us no depth cues for volume—they are unshaded, do not have a recognizable shape, and do not move in such a way as to reveal new views which suggest roundness.

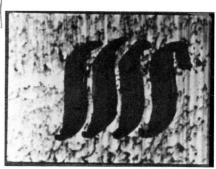

Fig. 5.47

When we speak of *planes* in a film, we are referring to the overall relation of foreground to background. The distance from the foreground plane to the background plane may seem shallow or deep, and other planes in between may create a middle ground as well. Depth cues pick out different planes in the shot and thus enable us to distinguish foreground from background.

**Fig. 5.48**

**Fig. 5.49**

**Fig. 5.50**

Only a completely blank screen has a single plane. Whenever a shape—even an abstract one—appears, we will perceive it as being in front of a background. In Figure 5.47, the four dark shapes are actually painted right on the frame surface along with the lighter, textured area. Yet the latter area seems to be behind the four shapes. The space here has only two planes, as in an abstract painting.

In *La Passion de Jeanne d'Arc*, the shots often suggest only two planes—a foreground (occupied by a face) and a neutral background (a wall or the sky). In Figure 5.46 the only depth cue is **overlap** of edges—the face's edge stands out against the setting.

Plate 2, a shot from *La Chinoise*, adds one more plane—drifting cigarette smoke—to the other two (face and setting). This illustrates that in cinema *movement* is an important depth cue for planes as well as volume (the shifting smoke indicates another plane in the foreground). Note also the *cast shadow* in the background, which is yet another depth cue.

**Aerial perspective,** or the hazing of more distant planes, is another depth cue; we tend to see clearer elements as belonging to the foreground. In William Wyler's *Jezebel*, as in many Hollywood films, lighting (and lens focus) blur the setting to make the closer objects stand out more (Fig. 5.48).

In Straub and Huillet's *Chronicle of Anna Magdalena Bach* the mise-en-scene provides several depth cues: overlap of edges, cast shadows, and **size diminution.** That is, figures and objects farther away from us are seen to get proportionally smaller; the smaller the figure appears, the farther away we believe it to be (Fig. 5.49). This reinforces our sense of there being a deep space with considerable distances between the various planes.

At this point, you might want to return to shots illustrated earlier in this chapter to compare how different images use depth cues in the mise-en-scene to create different foreground-background relations.

Spatial cues of both screen and story space interact within each shot, functioning in relation to the narrative action. To see how such factors work together to guide our attention, let's examine two examples from Carl Dreyer's film *Day of Wrath*.

In the first shot, Anne is standing before a grillwork panel (Fig. 5.50). She is not speaking, but since she is a major character in the film, the narrative already directs us to her. Setting, lighting, costume, and figure expression create pictorial cues that confirm our expectations. The setting yields a network of intersecting lines against which the delicate curves of her face and shoulders stand out for our notice. The lighting creates a patch of brightness on the right half of the frame and a patch of darkness at the left. Anne's face is precisely at the intersection of these two areas, and her face becomes sculpted by the relatively strong key lighting from the right, a little backlighting on her hair, and almost no fill light.

Coordinated with the lighting in creating the pattern of light and dark is Anne's costume—black dress punctuated by white collar, black cap edged with white—which again emphasizes her face. Given the two major planes of the shot, the geometrical background distinguishes the more important foreground element, Anne. Moreover, Anne's slightly sad face, the most expressive element in this frame, ensures that our scanning of the frame will pause there. Thus, although there is no motion in the frame, Dreyer has controlled our attention through the lines and shapes, the lights and darks, and the foreground and background relations set up by the overall mise-en-scene.

In the second shot, Dreyer sets up a to-and-fro movement of our eye from the couple to the cart (Fig. 5.51). Again, the plot guides us, since the characters and cart are crucial narrative elements. Sound helps too, since Martin is at the moment explaining to Anne the function of the cart. But mise-en-scene also plays a role. The foreground-background relations set up a unified interplay between Anne and Martin on the front plane and the cart of wood on the rear plane. The prominence of the couple and the cart is reinforced by line and shape, light and dark: the elements are defined by hard-edged lines and by dark costumes within the predominantly bright lighting and setting. The cart is near the top of the frame, balanced against the couple near the bottom, thus encouraging us to glance at each in turn.

Fig. 5.51

The same factors are at work in color films as well. In one shot from Ozu's *Autumn Afternoon* (Plate 7), our attention is concentrated on the woman in the center foreground. Here many depth cues are at work: overlap (with the two figures in two foreground planes set against a series of more distant planes), aerial perspective (the tree foliage is slightly out of focus), movement (the bride lowers her head), and perspective diminution (objects get smaller as they get more distant). The centered figure and the red, silver, and gold bridal costume stand out strikingly against the muted, cool colors of the background planes. Moreover, the colors have been part of a motif of red and silver hues that began in the very first shot of the film (Plate 8).

In all these cases, compositional and depth cues have functioned to focus our attention on the narrative elements. But this need not be the case. Robert Bresson's *Lancelot du Lac* uses a very sparse and muted color scheme throughout, and bright colors tend to stand out. In one scene (Plate 9), the narrative action involves the conversation among characters centered and balanced in the foreground planes; yet a bright saddle blanket on a passing horse draws our eyes *away* from this action momentarily. Such usage becomes a stylistic motif in this film.

Fig. 5.52

## ■ TIME

So far we have examined some spatial factors that guide our viewing of an image. But our viewing takes time, too. Only a very short shot forces us to grasp the image "all at once." In most shots we get an initial overall impression that creates formal expectations. These expectations are quickly modified as our eye roams around the frame. A static composition, such as our first shot from *Day of Wrath* (Fig. 5.50), may keep pulling our eye back to a single element (here, Anne's face). A composition emphasizing movement becomes more "time-bound" because our glance may be directed from place to place by various speeds, directions, and rhythms of movements. In the second image from *Day of Wrath* (Fig. 5.51) Anne and Martin are turned from us (so that expression and gesture are minimized), and they are standing still. Thus the single movement in the frame—the cart—catches our attention. But when Martin speaks and turns, we look back at the couple, then back at the cart, and so on, in a shuttling, dynamic shift of attention. In such ways mise-en-scene can control not only *what* we look at but also *when* we look at it.

Indeed, a film's mise-en-scene may set up its own unique sense of movement in time. Normally, for instance, we ignore the movement of scratches and dust on a film. But in David Rimmer's *Watching for the Queen*, in which the first image is an absolutely static photograph, the jumping bits of dust on the film draw our attention. Consider the varying qualities of movement in these three shots:

1. Stasis dominates in Figure 5.52, a shot from Chantal Akerman's *Jeanne Dielman, 23 quai du Commerce, 1080 Bruxelles*, in which the protagonist simply

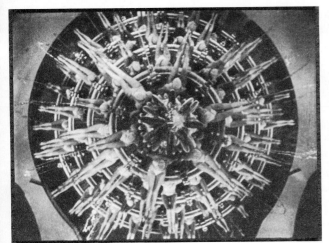

Fig. 5.53

Fig. 5.54

sits, unmoving, in her living room. This feminist film emphasizes the daily routine of a Belgian housewife, and many of its shots contain only small movements, in order to focus the viewer's attention sharply on details and on minute variations in that routine.

2. In Figure 5.53, from Busby Berkeley's *Footlight Parade*, there are strongly opposed movements in foreground, middle-ground, and background planes; alternating tiers of dancers swing their legs in opposite directions. The result is a partially abstract composition and a quick, steady tempo—appropriate to the shot's placement as part of a musical number.

3. In Figure 5.54, from Tati's *Play Time*, the frame contains movements of differing speeds and directions, in various planes. These movements compete for our attention, forcing us to scan the frame in order to notice as much as possible. Such "busy" tempos are important to many of Tati's compositions, which he crams with simultaneous gags for us to catch.

Mise-en-scene as a whole, then, helps compose the film shot in space and time. Setting, lighting, costume, and figure behavior interact to create patterns of foreground and background, line and shape, light and dark, and movements. These patterns are systems—unified, developing systems that not only guide our perception from frame to frame but also help create the overall form of the film.

## NARRATIVE FUNCTIONS OF MISE-EN-SCENE: *OUR HOSPITALITY*

Up to now we have looked at the general stylistic possibilities offered by mise-en-scene. Its potential for creating graphic compositions is vital to the abstract film, and can be useful as well to the other types of formal organization. Categorical, rhetorical, and associational films use mise-en-scene to guide our attention, our understanding, and our inferences about what we see. Now let us look specifically at how mise-en-scene can function in narrative films.

In order to understand story information presented to us in a narrative film, we must perform such activities as comparing locales, identifying characters by their appearances, and noticing salient gestures as the mise-en-scene presents them to us. Many motifs that recur in the course of the plot's unfolding are visual elements of the mise-en-scene, and such motifs can contribute significantly to the fundamental formal principles of the film's overall organization: its unity and its patterns of similarity, difference, and development.

Mise-en-scene contributes to the plot action, of course, because events we see directly constitute the plot. But elements of mise-en-scene can also imply story information. If a detective discovers a corpse, we may imagine the murder; if a woman tells a friend about an important event in her past and shows the friend a picture of her parents, the picture contributes information about earlier story events not shown in the film itself. Similarly, mise-en-scene can help present a more or less restricted narration. This may go to an extreme, as when all the mise-en-scene elements of *The Cabinet of Dr. Caligari* show us the distorted outlook of a madman's subjective vision (see Figs. 5.1 and 5.38). Few films go this far, but many will occasionally show us something only one character knows about, thus restricting our knowledge to that character's visual subjectivity—as when we see the words written in a diary or letter, or a view from a window.

Mise-en-scene usually cues our expectations about narrative events almost continuously. If we watch someone hide a box of jewelry early in the story, we wait to see if someone will eventually discover it. Such expectations often depend on genre conventions: a bakery full of pies in a slapstick comedy implies a sticky fight will break out at some point; a piano tucked away in the corner of a room in a Judy Garland–Mickey Rooney musical will almost certainly end up being played to accompany a song. But there are no hard-and-fast rules, and a narrative film may also frequently surprise us with unconventional mise-en-scene.

Mise-en-scene functions, not in isolated moments, but in relation to the narrative system of the entire film. *Our Hospitality*, like most of Buster Keaton's films, exemplifies how mise-en-scene can economically advance the narrative and create a pattern of motifs. Since the film is a comedy, we shall find that the mise-en-scene also creates gags. *Our Hospitality*, then, exemplifies what we shall find in our study of every film technique: an individual element will almost always have *several* functions, not just one.

Consider, for example, how the settings function within the narrative of *Our Hospitality*. They help divide the film into scenes and to contrast those scenes. The film begins with a prologue showing how the feud between the McKays and the Canfields results in the deaths of the young Canfield and the husband of the McKay family. We see the McKays living in a shack and are left in suspense about the fate of the baby, Willie. Willie's mother flees with her son from their southern home to the North (action narrated to us mainly by an intertitle). The main action begins years later, with the grown-up Willie living in New York. There are a number of gags concerning early nineteenth-century life in the metropolis, contrasting sharply with the prologue scene. We are led to wonder how this locale will relate to the southern scenes, and soon Willie receives word that he has inherited his parents' home in the South. A series of amusing short scenes follows as he takes a primitive train back to his birthplace. During these scenes Keaton uses real landscapes, but by laying the railroad tracks in different ways, he exploits the landscapes for surprising and unusual comic effects. The rest of the film deals with Willie's movements in the southern town and in the vicinity. On the day of his arrival he wanders around and gets into a number of comic situations. That night he stays in the Canfield house itself, since the law of hospitality has made it the only safe place for him. And, finally, an extended chase occurs the next day, moving through the countryside and back to the Canfield house for the end of the feud. Thus the action depends heavily on shifts of setting that establish Willie's two journeys, as baby and as man, and later his wanderings around to escape his enemies' pursuit. The narration is relatively unrestricted once Willie reaches the South, moving between him and members of the Canfield family. We usually know more about where they are than Willie does, and the narrative generates suspense by showing them coming toward the places where Willie is hiding.

Specific settings fulfill distinct narrative functions. The McKay "estate," which Willie envisions as a mansion, turns out to be a tumbledown shack. The McKay house is paralleled to (contrasted with) the Canfields' palatial plantation home. In narrative terms the Canfield home gains even more functional importance when the Canfield father forbids his sons to kill Willie on the premises: "Our code of honor forbids us to shoot him while he is a guest in our house." (Once Willie overhears this, he determines *never* to leave.) Thus, ironically, the home of Willie's enemies becomes the only safe spot in town, and many scenes are organized around the Canfield brothers' attempts to lure Willie outside. At the end of the film another setting takes on significance: the meadows, mountains, river banks, rapids, and waterfalls across which the Canfields pursue Willie. Finally, the feud ends back in the Canfield house itself, with Willie now welcomed as the daughter's husband. The pattern of development is clear: from the opening shoot-out at the McKay house that breaks up Willie's home, to the final scene in the Canfield house with Willie becoming part of a new family. In such ways every setting becomes highly motivated by the narrative's system of causes and effects, parallels and contrasts, and overall development.

The same narrative motivation marks the film's use of costume. Willie is characterized as a city boy through his dandified suit, whereas the southern gentility of the elder Canfield is represented through his white planter's suit. Props become important here: Willie's suitcase and umbrella succinctly summarize his role as visitor and wanderer, and the Canfields' ever-present pistols remind us of their goals of continuing the feud. Note also that a change of costume (Willie's disguising himself as a woman) enables him to escape from the Canfield household. At the end, the putting aside of the various guns by the characters signals the end of the feud.

Fig. 5.55

Like setting, lighting in *Our Hospitality* has both general and specific functions. The film systematically alternates scenes in darkness with scenes in daylight. The feuding in the prologue takes place at night; Willie's trip south and wanderings through the town occur in daylight; that night Willie comes to dinner at the Canfields' and stays as a guest; next day, the Canfields pursue him; and the film ends that night with the marriage of Willie and the Canfield daughter. More specifically, the somber action of the prologue is distinguished from the rest of the film by its hard, side key lighting. When the elder McKay flings off his hat to douse the lamp, the illumination changes from a soft blend of key, fill, and backlight to a stark key light from the fireplace (see Figs. 5.55 and 5.56). Later, the murder scene is played out in flashes of light—lightning, gunfire—which fitfully punctuate the overall darkness. Because this sporadic lighting hides part of the action from us, it helps build suspense. The shots themselves are seen only as flashes in the darkness, and we must wait to learn the outcome—the deaths of both opponents—until the next flash of lightning. The bulk of the film, however, is evenly lit in the three-point method.

Fig. 5.56

Fig. 5.57

Fig. 5.58

Fig. 5.59

Most economically of all, virtually every bit of the behavior of the figures functions to support and advance the cause-effect chain of the narrative. The way Canfield sips and savors his julep establishes his southern ways; his southern hospitality in turn will not allow him to shoot a guest in his house. Similarly, Willie's every move expresses his diffidence or resourcefulness. Even more concise is the way in which the film uses the arrangement of figures and setting in depth to present two narrative events simultaneously. While the engineer drives the locomotive, the other cars pass him on a parallel track (Fig. 5.57). Here we see cause (the engineer's cheerful ignorance) and effect (the runaway disconnected cars) juxtaposed in the same frame. Or, in another shot, the Canfield boys in the foreground make plans to shoot Willie, while in the background Willie overhears them and starts to flee (Fig. 5.58). In yet another shot, while Willie ambles along unsuspectingly in the background, one Canfield waits in the foreground to ambush him (Fig. 5.59). Thanks to depth in the spatial arrangement, Keaton is able to pack together and connect two story events, resulting in a tight narrative construction, and in a relatively unrestricted narration. In Figure 5.58, we know what Willie does and more than the Canfield sons do, enough to anticipate events: Willie will probably flee now that he knows the sons' plans. But in Figure 5.59, we are aware, as Willie is not, that danger lurks around the corner; suspense results, as we wonder whether the Canfield boy's ambush will succeed.

All of these devices for narrative economy considerably unify the film, but some other elements of mise-en-scene function as specific motifs. For one thing, there is the repeated squabble between the anonymous husband and wife. On his way to his "estate," Willie passes a husband beating his wife. Willie intervenes to protect her; the wife proceeds to thrash Willie for butting in. On Willie's way back, he passes the same couple, still fighting, but studiously avoids them; nevertheless, the wife aims a kick at him as he passes. The mere repetition of the motif strengthens the film's narrative unity, but it functions thematically, too, as another joke on the contradictions surrounding the idea of hospitality.

Other motifs recur. Willie's first hat is too tall to wear in a jouncing railway coach. (When it gets crushed, he trades it for the familiar Keaton trademark, a porkpie hat.) Willie's second hat serves to distract the Canfields when Willie coaxes his dog to fetch it. There is also a pronounced water motif in the film. Water as *rain* conceals from us the murders in the prologue and later saves Willie from leaving the Canfield home after dinner ("It would be the death of anyone to go out on a night like this!"). Water as a *river* functions significantly in the final chase. And water as a *waterfall* appears soon after Willie's arrival in the South; after an explosion demolishes a dam, the water spills over a cliff and creates a waterfall

Fig. 5.60

Fig. 5.61

Fig. 5.62

(Fig. 5.60); this waterfall initially protects Willie by hiding him (Figs. 5.61, 5.62), but later threatens both him and the Canfield daughter as they are nearly swept over it (see Fig. 5.68).

Two specific motifs of setting powerfully unify the narrative. First there is the recurrence of an embroidered sampler hanging on the Canfield wall: "Love Thy Neighbor." It appears initially in the prologue of the film, when seeing it motivates Canfield's attempt to stop the feud. It then plays a significant role in linking the ending back to the beginning. The sampler reappears at the end when Canfield, enraged that Willie has married his daughter, glances at the wall, reads the inscription, and resolves to end the years of feuding. His change in attitude is motivated by the earlier appearance of the motif.

The film also has a "gun rack" motif. In the prologue each feuder goes to his mantelpiece to get his pistol. Later, when Willie arrives in town, the Canfields hurry to their gun rack and begin to load their pistols. Near the end of the film, when the Canfields return home after failing to find Willie, one of the sons notices that the gun rack is now empty. And in the final shot, when the Canfields accept the marriage and lay down their arms, Willie produces from all over his person a staggering assortment of pistols taken (as a precaution) from the Canfields' own supply. Thus mise-en-scene motifs unify the film through their repetition, variation, and development.

Yet *Our Hospitality* is more than a film whose narrative system relates economically to patterns of mise-en-scene. It is a comedy, and one of the funniest. We should not be surprised to find, then, that Keaton uses mise-en-scene for gags. Indeed, so unified is the film that most of the elements that create narrative economy also function to yield comic effects.

The mise-en-scene bristles with many individually comic elements. Settings are exploited for amusement—the ramshackle McKay estate, the Broadway of 1830, the specially cut train tunnel that just fits the old-fashioned train and its smokestack (Fig. 5.63). Costume gags also stand out. Willie's disguise as a woman is divulged by a gap in the rear of his skirt; later, Willie puts the same costume on a horse to distract the Canfields. Most strongly, comedy arises from the behavior of the figures. The railroad engineer's high kick unexpectedly swipes off his conductor's hat (Fig. 5.64). (Keaton's father, Joe, played this role, and the gag was one of his famous vaudeville stunts.) The elder Canfield sharpens his carving knife with ferocious energy, just inches from Willie's head. When Willie lands at the bottom of the river, he stands there looking left and right, his hand shading his eyes, before he

Fig. 5.63

Fig. 5.64

Fig. 5.65

realizes where he is. Later, Willie scuds down the river, leaping out of the water like a fish and skidding across the rocks.

Perhaps the only aspect of mise-en-scene that competes with the comic brilliance of the figures' behavior is the film's use of deep space for gags. Many of the shots we have already examined function to create comedy as well: the engineer stands firmly oblivious to the separation of train cars from engine (see Fig. 5.57), just as Willie is unaware that the Canfield boy is lurking murderously in the foreground (see Fig. 5.59).

Even more striking, though, is the deep-space gag that follows the demolition of the dam. The Canfield boys have been searching the town for Willie. In the meantime, Willie sits on a ledge, fishing. As the water bursts from the dam and sweeps over the cliff, it completely engulfs Willie (Fig. 5.61). At that very instant, the Canfield brothers step into the foreground from either side of the frame, still looking for their victim (Fig. 5.62). The water's concealment of Willie reduces him to a neutral background for the movement of the Canfields. This sudden eruption of new action into the scene surprises us, rather than generating suspense, since we were not aware that the Canfield sons were so close by. Here surprise is crucial to the comedy. Keaton's erasure of the background plane and the sudden revelation of a new foreground plane confirms André Bazin's observation that slapstick comedy succeeded because "most of its gags derived from a comedy of space, from the relation of men to things and to the surrounding world."

However appealing the individual gags are, *Our Hospitality* patterns its comic motifs as strictly as it does its other motifs. The film's journey pattern often arranges a series of gags according to a formal principle of theme and variations. For instance, during the train trip south, a string of gags is based on the idea of people encountering the train: several people turn out to watch it pass, a tramp rides the rods, and an old man chunks rocks at the engine. Another swift series of gags takes the train tracks themselves as its "theme." The variations include a humped track, a donkey blocking the tracks, curled and rippled tracks, and finally no tracks at all.

But the most complex theme-and-variations series can be seen in the motif of "the fish on the line." Early in *Our Hospitality* Willie is angling and hauls up a minuscule fish. Shortly afterward, a huge fish yanks him into the water (Fig. 5.65). Later in the film, through a series of mishaps, Willie becomes tied by a rope to one of the Canfield sons. Many gags arise from this umbilical-cord linkage, especially one that results in Canfield's being pulled into the water as Willie was earlier.

Fig. 5.66

Fig. 5.67

Fig. 5.68

Perhaps the single funniest moment in the film occurs when Willie realizes that since the Canfield boy has fallen off the rocks, so must he (see two phases of this shot in Figs. 5.66 and 5.67). But even after Willie gets free of Canfield, the rope remains tied around him. So in the film's climax Willie is dangling from a log over the waterfall like the fish on the end of his fishing pole (Fig. 5.68). Here again, one element fulfills multiple functions: the fish-on-the-line device advances the narrative, becomes a motif unifying the film, and takes its place in a pattern of parallel gags involving variations of Willie on the rope. In such ways *Our Hospitality* becomes an outstanding example of the integration of cinematic mise-en-scene with narrative form.

## SUMMARY

The viewer who wants to study mise-en-scene should look for it systematically. Watch, first of all, for how setting, costume, lighting, and the behavior of the figures present themselves in a given film. (As a start, try to trace only one sort of element—say, setting or lighting—through an entire film.) We should also reflect on the patterning of mise-en-scene elements. How do they function? How do they constitute motifs that weave their ways through the film? In addition, we should notice how mise-en-scene is patterned in space and time to attract and guide the viewer's attention through the process of watching the film, and to create suspense or surprise. Finally, we should try to relate the system of mise-en-scene to the narrative system of the film. Hard-and-fast prejudices about realism are of less value here than an openness to the great variety of mise-en-scene possibilities. Awareness of those possibilities will better help us to determine the narrative functions of mise-en-scene.

## NOTES AND QUERIES

### ■ ON THE ORIGINS OF MISE-EN-SCENE

As a theatrical concept, mise-en-scene reaches back into the nineteenth-century theater. For a historical introduction that is relevant to film, see Oscar G. Brockett and Robert R. Findlay, *Century of Innovation* (Englewood Cliffs, N.J.: Prentice-Hall, 1973). More specialized are Brooks McNamara, "The Scenography of Popular Entertainment," *The Drama Review* **18**, 1 (March 1974): 16–24; and Martin Meisel, *Realizations: Narrative, Pictorial, and Theatrical Arts in Nineteenth-Century England* (Princeton, N.J.: Princeton University Press, 1983). The standard film work remains Nicolas Vardac, *Stage to Screen* (Cambridge, Mass.: Harvard University Press, 1949).

### ■ ON "REALISM" IN MISE-EN-SCENE

Many film theorists have seen film as a realistic medium par excellence. For such theorists as Siegfried Kracauer, André Bazin, and V. F. Perkins, cinema's power lies in its ability to present a recognizable reality. The realist theorist thus often values authenticity in costume and setting, "naturalistic" acting, and unstylized lighting. "The primary function of decor," writes V. F. Perkins, "is to provide a believable environment for the action" (*Film as Film* [Baltimore: Penguin, 1972], p. 94). André Bazin praises the Italian neorealist films of the 1940s for "faithfulness to everyday life in the scenario, truth to his part in an actor" (*What Is Cinema?* vol. 2 [Berkeley: University of California Press, 1970], p. 25).

Though mise-en-scene is always a product of selection and choice, the realist theorist may value the filmmaker who creates a mise-en-scene that *appears* to be reality. Kracauer suggests that even apparently "unrealistic" song and dance numbers in a musical can seem impromptu (*Theory of Film* [New York: Oxford University Press, 1965]), and Bazin considers a fantasy film such as *The Red Balloon* realistic because here "what is imaginary on the screen has the spatial density of something real" (*What Is Cinema?* vol. 1 [Berkeley: University of California Press, 1966], p. 48).

These theorists, then, set the filmmaker the task of representing some historical, social, or aesthetic reality through the selection and arrangement of mise-en-scene. Though this book postpones the consideration of this problem—it lies more strictly in the domain of film theory—the "realist" controversy is worth your examination. For arguments against a realist theory of mise-en-scene, see Noël Burch, *Theory of Film Practice* (Princeton, N.J.: Princeton University Press, 1981), and Sergei Eisenstein, "An Unexpected Juncture," in Richard Taylor, ed., *Writings 1922–1934* (Bloomington: Indiana University Press, 1988), pp. 115–122. Christopher Williams, in *Realism and the Cinema* (London: Routledge & Kegan Paul, 1980) reviews many issues in the area.

## ■ THE STAGED AND THE UNSTAGED IN MISE-EN-SCENE

The distinction between "documentary" and "fiction" films often rests on the difference between the staged and the unstaged. In a fiction film the filmmaker controls the mise-en-scene completely, but the documentary film purports to present unstaged events. For example, in *A Hard Day's Night*, Richard Lester staged a Beatles concert and was able to control setting, lighting, costumes, and figure behavior. But in *Monterey Pop* and *Woodstock* the filmmakers had no such control over the event and exercised their choices by means of other techniques—editing, camera work, and sound. Does the concept of documentary assume that the filmed event retains at least some of its "rawness" as an unstaged part of the world?

Interestingly, disputes periodically arise about faked documentaries, which use actors, rehearse shots, or falsify time and place. These disputes often revolve around the assumption that documentary should not rely on mise-en-scene. The most famous "borderline" documentary is Leni Riefenstahl's *Triumph of the Will*. Controversy still rages as to whether the film simply documented the 1934 Nazi Party Congress or whether the event was staged especially for the film. If the latter is true, the film would be the most stupendous effort of mise-en-scene in film history.

Most films we see, however, utilize mise-en-scene, and the technique is used not only in live-action films but also in animated and abstract films. Indeed, the animated film constitutes the extreme limit of the director's control of mise-en-scene—the most controlled sort of film there is. A good introduction to the subject is John Halas and Roger Manvell, *The Technique of Film Animation* (London: Focal Press, 1968).

## ■ PARTICULAR ASPECTS OF MISE-EN-SCENE

On costume, see Elizabeth Leese, *Costume Design in the Movies* (London: BCW, 1976), and Edward Maeder, ed., *Hollywood and History: Costume Design in Film* (New York: Thames and Hudson, 1987). Leon Barsacq, with careful assistance by Elliott Stein, has produced the best history of setting to date, *Caligari's Cabinet and Other Grand Illusions: A History of Film Design* (New York: New American Library, 1976). Other major studies of decor in the cinema are Donald Albrecht's *Designing Dreams: Modern Architecture in the Movies* (New York: Harper & Row, 1986); John Hambley and Patrick Donning, *The Art of Hollywood: Fifty Years of Art Direction* (London: Thames Television, 1979); and Howard Mandelbaum and Eric Myers, *Screen Deco: A Celebration of High Style in Hollywood* (New York: St. Martin's, 1985). A special issue of *Film Comment* (May/June 1978) deals with the work of the art director. The memoirs of a major set designer who worked extensively with Jean Renoir have been published: Eugene Lourie's *My Work in Films* (San Diego: Harcourt Brace Jovanovich, 1985).

The most commonly discussed type of figure behavior is, of course, acting. An excellent discussion of performance in film is Richard Dyer, *Stars* (London: British Film Institute, 1979), which is complemented by Charles Affron's *Star Acting: Gish, Garbo, Davis* (New York: Dutton, 1977) and James Naremore's *Acting in the Cinema* (Berkeley: University of California Press, 1988). See also the special number of *Cinema Journal* **20**, 1 (Fall 1980).

One of the most fascinating aspects of mise-en-scene is lighting. John Alton's *Painting with Light* (New York: Macmillan, 1949) and Gerald Millerson's *Technique of Lighting for Television and Motion Pictures* (New York: Hastings House, 1972) are fine surveys of the techniques as practiced in the Hollywood cinema. See also James Wong Howe, "Lighting," and Victor Milner, "Painting with Light," in *Cinematographic Annual* **I** (1930) (New York: Arno Press, 1972), pp. 47–60 and 91–108, for older but informative discussions.

One of the cinema's masters of lighting, Josef von Sternberg, has much to say on the subject in his entertaining autobiography, *Fun in a Chinese Laundry* (New York: Macmillan, 1965). Raoul Coutard discusses a different notion of lighting in "Light of Day," in Toby Mussmann, ed., *Jean-Luc Godard* (New York: Dutton, 1968), pp. 232–239. Hollywood cinematographers recall their lighting experiments in Charles Higham, *Hollywood Cameramen* (London: Thames & Hudson, 1970).

## ■ DEPTH

Though film directors have of course manipulated depth and flatness of the shot since the beginning of cinema, critical understanding of these spatial qualities did not emerge until the 1940s. It was then that André Bazin called attention to the fact that certain directors staged their shots in unusually deep space. Bazin singled out F. W. Murnau (for *Nosferatu* and *Sunrise*), Orson Welles (for *Citizen Kane* and *The Magnificent Ambersons*), William Wyler (for *The Little Foxes* and *The Best Years of Our Lives*), and Jean Renoir (for practically all of his 1930s work). Today we would add Kenji Mizoguchi (for *Osaka Elegy, Sisters of Gion*, and others) and even Sergei Eisenstein (for *Old and New, Ivan the Terrible*, and the unreleased *Bezhin Meadow*). By offering us depth and flatness as analytical categories, Bazin increased our understanding of mise-en-scene. (See "The Evolution of the Language of Cinema," in *What Is Cinema?* vol. 1.) Interestingly, Sergei Eisenstein, who is often contrasted with Bazin, explicitly discussed principles of deep-space staging in the

1930s, as recorded by his faithful pupil, Vladimir Nizhny, in *Lessons with Eisenstein* (New York: Hill & Wang, 1962). Eisenstein asked his class to stage a murder scene in a single shot and without camera movement; the result was a startling use of extreme depth and dynamic movement toward the spectator. For a discussion, see David Bordwell, "Narration and Scenography in the Later Eisenstein," *Millennium Film Journal* **13** (Fall/Winter 1983/84): 62–80. A general discussion of deep space and deep focus is Charles Henry Harpole, *Gradients of Depth in the Cinema Image* (New York: Arno, 1978).

## ■ FRAME COMPOSITION AND THE VIEWER'S EYE

The film shot is in a sense like the painter's canvas: it must be filled up, and in ways that cue the spectator to notice certain things (and not to notice others). For this reason, composition in film owes much to principles developed in the graphic arts. A good basic study of composition is Donald L. Weismann, *The Visual Arts as Human Experience* (Englewood Cliffs, N.J.: Prentice-Hall, 1974), which has many interesting things to say about depth as well. More elaborate discussions are to be found in Rudolf Arnheim, *Art and Visual Perception: A Psychology of the Creative Eye*, rev. ed. (Berkeley: University of California Press, 1974), and his *The Power of the Center: A Study of Composition in the Visual Arts* (Berkeley: University of California Press, 1982). Application of such principles to film is exemplified in Maureen Turim's "Symmetry/Asymmetry and Visual Fascination," *Wide Angle* **4**, 3 (1980): 38–47.

André Bazin suggested that shots staged in depth and shot in deep focus give the viewer's eye greater freedom than do flatter, shallower shots: the viewer's eye can roam across the screen. (See Bazin, *Orson Welles* [New York: Harper & Row, 1978].) Noël Burch takes issue: "All the elements in any given film image are perceived as equal in importance" (*Theory of Film Practice*, p. 34). Psychological research on pictorial perception suggests, however, that viewers do indeed scan images according to specific cues. A good review of the subject, with bibliography, may be found in Julian Hochberg, "The Representation of Things and People," in E. H. Gombrich et al., *Art, Perception, and Reality* (Baltimore: Johns Hopkins University Press, 1972), pp. 47–94. In cinema, static visual cues for "when to look where" are reinforced or undermined by movement of figures or of camera, by sound track and editing, and by the overall form of the film. The psychological research is outlined in Ralph Norman Haber and Maurice Hershenson, *The Psychology of Visual Perception*, 2d ed. (New York: Holt, Rinehart and Winston, 1980), pp. 141–157, 326–344.

# THE SHOT:
# CINEMATOGRAPHIC
# PROPERTIES

Mise-en-scene is at bottom a theatrical notion: the filmmaker stages an event to be filmed. But a comprehensive account of cinema as an art cannot stop with simply what is put in front of the camera. The "shot" does not exist until light and dark patterns are inscribed on a strip of film. The filmmaker also controls what we will call the *cinematographic* qualities of the shot—not only what is filmed but also *how* it is filmed. This consists of control over three features: (1) the photographic qualities of the shot; (2) the framing of the shot; and (3) the duration of the shot. This chapter surveys these three areas of control.

## THE PHOTOGRAPHIC IMAGE

**Cinematography** (literally, "writing in movement") depends to a large extent on photography ("writing in light"). Sometimes the filmmaker will eliminate the camera and simply work on the film itself, but even when drawing, painting, or scratching directly on film, punching holes in it, or growing mold on it, the filmmaker is etching patterns of light onto celluloid for the eye of the viewer. Most often the filmmaker uses a camera to regulate how light from some object will be photochemically registered on the sensitized film. In any event, the filmmaker can select the range of tonalities, manipulate the speed of motion, and transform perspective.

### ■ THE RANGE OF TONALITIES

An image may seem all grays or stark black and white. It may display a range of colors. Textures may stand out clearly or recede into a haze. The filmmaker may control all these visual qualities by manipulating film stock and exposure.

*Godard — fast*

Fig. 6.1

*— Renoir*
*— slow stock*

Fig. 6.2

**Film stocks**, or the different types of photographic film, vary in their light sensitivity. Some are "slow"—that is, they are not as sensitive to light as "faster" film stocks. This means that more light is needed to produce an image on a slower stock than is needed to produce an equally bright image on a faster stock.

The choice of film stock has many artistic implications, for the relative "speed" of the stock affects the image's appearance. A slower black-and-white film stock will usually produce a larger range of grays, more detail in textures, and softer contrasts. A faster black-and-white film stock tends toward a narrower gray range, less well-defined details, and a more contrasty look. In *Les Carabiniers* (Fig. 6.1), Jean-Luc Godard chose a very fast film stock, which yielded a grainy, contrasty, almost bleached-out look. But in *The Crime of M. Lange* (Fig. 6.2), Jean Renoir used a significantly slower film stock, which rendered many more grays as well as details of line and texture.

The choice of film stock need not work only with blacks, whites, and shades of gray. As everyone knows, color film stocks may produce a wider range of the spectrum. In fact, different color stocks yield different color qualities. Technicolor (as used in *Meet Me in St. Louis*, Plates 10 and 11), Agfa color stock (which Eisenstein used to film part of *Ivan the Terrible*, Plates 5 and 6, and which Ozu used for *An Autumn Afternoon*, Plates 7 and 8), Eastmancolor (Plates 1, 2, 3, 4, and 9), and others—all have different visual features, and filmmakers working in color tend to select film stocks with great care.

Types of film stocks have changed over history. Before the mid-1920s, most films were shot on a type of black-and-white stock called "orthochromatic." It was sensitive to the purple-to-green portion of the spectrum: light bouncing off objects of those colors would affect the film strongly and would show up as white or gray in the final shot. But orthochromatic stock was not sensitive to yellow or red; objects of those colors, no matter how brightly lit, would look black or dark gray in the film. Watching silent films, you can see how blue skies tend to look white and flat (white clouds do not even show up in the sky) and blond hair, unless brightly backlit, looks dark. Similarly, when actors wear red lipstick as part of their make-up, their lips look black. Buster Keaton sometimes exploited the effects of ortho-chromatic stock by making his face look white and his lips black, giving him a slightly clownlike appearance to enhance the film's humor.

Panchromatic film stock was introduced in America in 1913, but its speed was too slow and its cost too high to make it a serious rival to orthochromatic.

*orthochromatic Stock.*

*Iry*

*PANCHROMATIC*

Finally, when its speed was increased and its price came down in the 1920s, panchromatic became more popular, largely replacing orthochromatic by 1927. As its name implies, panchromatic was sensitive to all colors of the visible spectrum, rendering them in shades of gray. This new flexibility meant some loss of the sharp definition of orthochromatic. Since fewer of the light rays coming through the lens would affect orthochromatic stock, it was easier to focus the image very sharply; when panchromatic came in, images were inevitably a bit fuzzier.

The tonalities of the photographic image can also be affected by the control of how the film is developed in the laboratory. Again, orthochromatic offered an advantage. Since red light did not register on orthochromatic, the film could be inspected during developing under a red safelight. This meant that during processing the film could be manipulated for different photographic effects. During the 1920s, for example, it became popular to overexpose the film and then develop it for only a short time to give the image a soft, low-contrast look. But panchromatic film did not permit the use of any light for inspection during the developing stage, so such manipulation was impossible for a time.

Over the years, however, various ways of manipulating modern film stocks in the laboratory have emerged. Different chemicals can alter the look of the image, and manipulation on the optical printer can also change the initial appearance of film stocks. A good example is the *Les Carabiniers* frame (Fig. 6.1). Its "newsreel" quality is heightened by both the film stock and lab work that increased contrast. "The positive prints," Godard has explained, "were simply made on a special Kodak high contrast stock. . . . Several shots, intrinsically too gray, were duped again sometimes two or three times, always to their highest contrast." The effect suggests old war footage that has been recopied or shot under bad lighting conditions; for a film about the grubbiness of war, the high-contrast look was exactly what Godard wanted.

Needless to say, the laboratory process of developing and printing may alter the tonalities of the color stock just as it alters black and white. (Early Technicolor films are now often printed on Eastmancolor stock, which results in a slight loss of brightness in the hues.) But various procedures may also add color to footage originally shot in black and white. *Tinting* casts a uniform hue of any chosen color over the image, with the blacks remaining black and the white areas picking up the color. *Toning* (see Plate 12, from Věrá Chytilová's *Daisies*) does just the opposite; it reproduces the image's gray scale in the desired color (the whites are white, the grays slightly colored, the blacks heavily colored). Both tinting and toning were common in the silent cinema. Night scenes were colored blue, firelight red, and so on.

Rarest of all is the difficult process of *hand coloring*, whereby portions of black-and-white images are painted in colors, frame by frame. The ship's flag in Eisenstein's *Potemkin* was originally hand colored red against a blue sky. A modern use of hand coloring may be seen in Makavejev's *Innocence Unprotected* (see Plate 13). Other color laboratory possibilities include developing a film in a solution intended for another film stock or exposing a film to light before or during development (the latter process being called solarization). One result of such laboratory manipulations of color can be seen in Plate 16, from Chytilová's *Daisies*.

The range of tonalities in the image is also affected by the **exposure** of the image in the course of the photographic process. The filmmaker usually controls exposure by regulating how much light passes through the camera lens, though images shot with "correct" exposure can also be overexposed or underexposed in developing and printing. We commonly think that a photograph should be "well exposed"—neither underexposed (too dark, not enough light admitted through the lens) or overexposed (too bright, too much light admitted through the lens). But even "correct exposure" usually offers some latitude for choice; it is not an absolute. Moreover, the filmmaker can use overexposure or underexposure for specific effects. In *Ordet* Carl Dreyer has deliberately overexposed the windows, washing out the upper portion of the image (Fig. 6.3). And, in the American **films noirs** of the 1940s, the cinematographer sometimes underexposed the image to increase a pervasive darkness.

Fig. 6.3

Exposure can in turn be affected by **filters**—slices of glass or gelatin put in front of the lens of the camera or printer to reduce certain frequencies of light reaching the film. Filters thus alter the range of tonalities in quite radical ways. A filter can block out part of the light and thus make footage shot by sunlight seem to be shot by moonlight ("day-for-night" filming). Hollywood cinematographers since the 1920s sought to add glamor to close-ups of women by means of diffusion filters and silks. Filters applied during shooting or during printing can drastically alter the color image. In all, both in filming and in laboratory work the choice of both film stock and exposure powerfully affects the image that we see on the screen.

## ■ SPEED OF MOTION

A gymnast's performance seen in slurred slow-motion, ordinary action accelerated to comic speed, a tennis serve stopped in a freeze frame—we are all familiar with the effects of the control of the speed of motion. Of course, the filmmaker who stages the event to be filmed can (within limits) dictate the pace of the action. But that pace can also be controlled by a photographic power unique to cinema: the control of the depicted speed of movement.

The speed of the motion we see on the screen depends on the relation between the rate of the film as shot and printed and the rate of projection. Both rates are calculated in frames per second. The standard rate of shooting and projection for the sound cinema is 24 frames per second. This means that during shooting, the camera will normally expose 24 separate frames per second, that that rate will not be altered by printing, and that in theaters the projector will show the film at the same rate. Hence the depicted movement will look "normal."

But as far as speed of movement is concerned, any particular rate of shooting and projection is less important than the *uniformity* among shooting, printing, and projection rates. It would not affect speed of movement if a film were shot and printed at 16 frames per second, as long as it was also projected at 16 frames per second. For example, we are so used to seeing silent films with jerky, accelerated movements that we assume that the films always looked that way. But, in the silent era, most cinematographers cranked the film strip through the camera by hand and thus they could easily vary the speed somewhat. Silent films were shot at a variety of speeds, usually ranging from 16 to 20 frames per second, gradually getting a bit faster in the mid-1920s. Whatever the shooting rate, if the projection rate corresponded, the action would look smooth and "realistic." Shooting rates could also be a matter of artistic choice for the cinematographer; a comedy scene could be shot to move quickly on the screen. Once sound was adopted during the period from 1926 to 1929, it was necessary to record both sound and image at a standardized and uniform speed, so that they could be synchronized.

If naturalness of depicted movement depends on uniformity among shooting, printing, and projection rates, the speed of that depicted movement can be altered by varying any of the three factors. We are most used to projection's effects on movement speed, because although most silent projectors could vary their speeds, most contemporary film projectors cannot. Thus a film shot at 16 frames per second will often be shown at 24 frames per second ("sound speed"), accelerating the action with adverse results. Some modern projectors can show films at various speeds, run them in reverse, or freeze a single frame on the screen. (Many film classes use either "analysis" projectors or videotape machines that have the capacity to alter the intended speed of showing in order to permit close study of films.)

Projection usually lies outside the filmmaker's control, but he or she can control the rate of the film during shooting and laboratory printing. The camera's drive mechanism can be adjusted to vary the shooting rate. Assuming a constant projection speed, the fewer frames per second shot, the greater the acceleration of the screen action. The more frames per second shot, the slower the screen action. This may sound inconsistent, but it makes sense. Filming at 12 frames per second yields only those 12 frames for every second the action lasts. If we project that film at the standard 24 frames per second, the 12 frames will be onscreen for only half a second—the action will seem twice as fast as it originally was. Such "fast-motion" effects are achieved by slowing the rate of the film passing through the camera. In the silent era the cameraperson simply cranked the camera drive handle more slowly, causing fewer frames to pass through the aperture every second. The result was often a comic effect; the chief experiment in the use of undercranking for noncomic purposes occurs in F. W. Murnau's *Nosferatu*, in which the vampire's accelerated motion represents his supernatural power.

On the other hand, if we film a one-second action at 48 frames per second and project it at 24 frames per second, the event the audience sees will consume two seconds onscreen—it will be slowed down. Overcranking, or cranking quite quickly, was used notably in Dziga Vertov's *Man with a Movie Camera* to render sports events in detailed slow motion, a function that of course persists today.

When cameras became motorized, most still had a variable-drive control. In Rouben Mamoulian's *Love Me Tonight* the members of a hunt decide to ride quietly home to avoid waking the sleeping deer; their ride is filmed is slow motion to create a comic depiction of quietness. By knowing the final projection speed, the filmmaker can vary the shooting speed and create a wide range of depicted speeds of action.

Although 24 frames per second became the normal shooting speed, special cameras were designed to accomplish specialized tasks. For *time-lapse* cinematography, which permits us to see the sun set in seconds or a flower sprout, bud, and bloom in a minute, a very low shooting speed is required—perhaps one frame per minute, hour, or even day. For *high-speed* cinematography, which may seek to record a bullet shattering glass, the camera may expose more than 1000 frames per second. A common range on 35-mm cameras today is between 8 and 64 frames per second.

After filming, the filmmaker can still control the speed of movement on the screen through various laboratory procedures. The most common means used is the optical printer (see Fig. 1.5), which rephotographs an already processed film, copying all or part of each original frame onto another reel of film. Still assuming a constant speed of projection, the filmmaker can use the optical printer to skip frames (accelerating the action when projected), reprint a frame at desired intervals (slowing the action by *stretch printing*), stop the action (repeat a frame over and over, to freeze the projected image for seconds or minutes), or even reverse the action. Nowadays some silent films are stretch-printed with every other frame repeated, so that they may run more smoothly at sound speed. We are familiar with freeze-framing, slow-motion, and reverse-motion printing effects from the "instant replays" of sports films and investigative documentaries. Many experimental films have made striking use of the optical printer's possibilities, such as Ken Jacobs's *Tom Tom the Piper's Son.*

## ■ PERSPECTIVE RELATIONS

You are standing on railroad tracks, looking toward the horizon. The tracks not only recede but also seem to meet at the horizon. You glance at the trees and buildings along the tracks. They diminish by a simple, systematic rule: the closer objects look larger, the farther objects look smaller—even if they are actually of uniform size. The optical system of your eye, registering light rays reflected from the scene, supplies a host of information about scale, depth, and spatial relations among parts of the scene. Such relations are called *perspective* relations.

The lens of a photographic camera does roughly what your eye does. It gathers light from the scene and transmits that light onto the flat surface of the film to form an image that represents size, depth, and other dimensions of the scene. The focal plane for the lens is usually the film in the camera. One difference between the eye and the camera, though, is that photographic lenses may be changed and each type of lens will render perspective relations in different ways. If two different lenses photograph the same scene, the perspective relations in the resulting image could be drastically different. A wide-angle lens could exaggerate the depth you see down the track or could make the trees and buildings seem to bulge; a telephoto lens could drastically reduce the depth, making the trees seem very close together and nearly the same size.

**The lens: focal length.**   Control of perspective relations in the image is obviously very important to the filmmaker. The chief variable in the process is the **focal length** of the lens. In technical terms the focal length is the distance from the center of the lens to the point where light rays converge to a point of focus. The focal length of the lens can affect perspective relations in several ways.

The focal length alters the perceived magnification, depth, and scale of things in the image. We usually distinguish three sorts of lenses on the basis of their effects on perspective.

Fig. 6.4

1. *The wide-angle, or short-focal-length, lens.* Depending on aperture setting, the focal length, and subject-to-camera distance, this lens tends to distort straight lines toward the edges of the screen, bulging them outward. Depth is also exaggerated. In Figure 6.4, from *The Little Foxes,* the wide-angle lens makes the characters seem farther from each other than we would expect in so relatively small a locale. When a wide-angle lens is used for a medium shot or close-up, the distortion of shape becomes very evident. (See Fig. 6.5, from Ilya Trauberg's *China Express.*) The wide-angle lens also makes movement to or from the camera seem more rapid in that it takes less time to cover what looks like a greater distance. In 35-mm-gauge cinematography, a wide-angle lens is less than 35 mm in focal length.

2. *The normal, or middle-focal-length, lens.* The normal lens seeks to avoid noticeable perspective distortion. With a normal lens, horizontal and vertical lines are rendered as straight and perpendicular. (Compare the bulging effect of the wide-angle lens.) Parallel lines should recede to distant vanishing points, as in our railroad-tracks example. Foreground and background should seem neither stretched apart (as with the wide-angle lens) nor squashed together (as with the telephoto

Fig. 6.5

Fig. 6.6

Fig. 6.7

Fig. 6.8

Fig. 6.9

Fig. 6.10

lens). Figure 6.6, from *His Girl Friday*, is a shot made with the normal lens; contrast the sense of distance among the figures achieved in Figure 6.4. And contrast the rendering of the face in Figure 6.7, from *Goldwyn Follies*, with the wide-angle view of Figure 6.5. Today the average normal lens is 35–50 mm in focal length.

3. *The telephoto, or long-focal-length, lens.* The onscreen effects of longer lenses are usually as noticeable as those of wide-angle lenses. Generally, the space of the shot is flattened; depth is reduced and the planes seem squashed together. The most familiar uses of telephoto lenses are in the filming or televising of sports events. In a baseball game there will invariably be shots taken from almost directly behind the umpire. You have probably noticed that such telephoto shots make catcher, batter, and pitcher look unnaturally close to one another. Akira Kurosawa was famous for introducing extensive use of telephoto lenses into his films, as Figure 6.8, a still from *Seven Samurai*, shows. Note how the figures seem very close together and almost the same size, even though the two facing front are actually quite far behind the third. A telephoto lens also affects subject movement. Movement toward or away from the camera seems to be prolonged, since the flattening effect of the telephoto makes the figure take more time to cover what looks like a small distance. (The clichéd "running-in-place" shots in *The Graduate* and other films of the 1960s and 1970s were produced by lenses of very long focal length.) Note also that a telephoto lens creates reversed perspective: parallel lines do not recede to vanishing points in the background but rather seem to meet "in front of" the image. (See Fig. 6.9, from Samuel Fuller's *Dead Pigeon on Beethoven Street*.) The flattening effect of a telephoto lens on a closer view can be gauged by Figure 6.10, from *A Midsummer Night's Dream*. Today, telephoto lenses range from around 75 mm to 200 mm or more.

Lens length can distinctly affect the spectator's experience. Our expectations about how the action will develop will be quite different if a wide-angle lens makes the figures look yards apart or if a telephoto puts them virtually side by side (Figs. 6.4 and 6.8). A character or object can stand out in sharp relief (Fig. 6.5) or can seem to blend more into the setting (Fig. 6.10). A director can use lens length to surprise us, as Kurosawa does in *Red Beard*. When the mad woman patient comes into the intern's room, a long-focal-length lens filming from behind him initially makes her look quite close to him (Fig. 6.11). But a cut to a more perpendicular angle shows that they are actually several feet apart, and that he is not yet in danger (Fig. 6.12). And expressive qualities can be suggested by lenses which distort objects or characters; we can hardly see the man in Figure 6.5 as anything but sinister.

Fig. 6.11

Fig. 6.12

Fig. 6.13

*Zoom lens*

There is one sort of lens that offers the director a chance to manipulate focal length and to transform perspective relations during a single shot. This lens is the **zoom lens**. A zoom lens is optically designed to permit the continuous varying of focal length. Zoom lenses were originally designed for aerial and reconnaissance photography; they gradually became a standard tool for newsreel filming. It was not, however, the general practice to zoom during shooting. The camera operator varied the focal length as desired and then started filming. In the late 1950s, however, the increased portability of cameras led to a trend toward zooming while filming. Now the zoom lens is sometimes used to substitute for moving the camera forward or backward. Onscreen, the zoom shot magnifies or demagnifies the objects filmed, excluding or including surrounding space. The zoom, however, is not a genuine movement of the camera, since the camera remains stationary and the lens simply increases or decreases its focal length. Nevertheless, the zoom can produce very interesting and peculiar transformations of scale and depth, as we shall see when we examine Michael Snow's *Wavelength*; another example occurs in the opening scene of Francis Ford Coppola's *The Conversation*.

The impact that focal length can have on the image's perspective qualities is dramatically illustrated in Ernie Gehr's *Serene Velocity*. The scene is an empty corridor. Gehr shot the film with a zoom lens, which permitted him to change the lens's focal length. Gehr explains that he

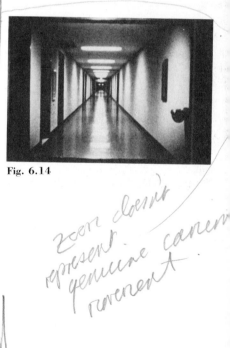

Fig. 6.14

divided the mm range of the zoom lens in half and starting from the middle I recorded changes in mm positions. . . . The camera was not moved at all. The zoom lens was not moved during recording either. Each frame was recorded individually as a still. Four frames to each position. To give an example: I shot the first four frames at 50 mm. The next four frames I shot at 55 mm. And then, for a certain duration, approximately 60 feet, I went back and forth, four frames at 50 mm, four frames at 55 mm; four frames at 50 mm, four frames at 55 mm; etc. . . . for about 60 feet. Then I went to 45–60 [mm] and did the same for about 60 feet. Then to 40–65, and so on.

*zoom doesn't represent genuine camera movement*

The resulting film presents an image whose perspective relations pulsate rhythmically—first with little difference in size and scale, but gradually with a greater tension between a telephoto image and a wide-angle one (see Figs. 6.13 and 6.14). In a sense *Serene Velocity* takes as its subject the effect of focal length on perspective.

**The lens: depth of field and focus.** Focal length not only affects how shape and scale are magnified or distorted. It also determines the lens's **depth of field.** Depth of field is the range of distances before the lens within which objects can be

Fig. 6.15

Fig. 6.16

Fig. 6.17

Fig. 6.18

photographed in sharp **focus.** A lens with a depth of field of ten feet to infinity will render any object in that range clearly, but the sharpness of the image will decrease when the object moves closer to the lens (say, to four feet). A wide-angle (short-focal-length) lens has a relatively greater depth of field than does a telephoto (long-focal-length) lens.

Depth of field should not be confused with the concept of deep space, used in Chapter 5. "Deep space" is a term for the way the filmmaker has established the action of the scene as taking place on several different planes, *regardless of whether or not all of these planes are in focus.* In the case of *Our Hospitality* those planes usually *are* in sharp focus, but in other films not every plane of deep space is in focus. Consider Figure 6.15. In this shot from *The Crime of M. Lange,* the action is staged in three planes of deep space: Valentine in the foreground, Batala going out the door, and the concierge passing in the distance. But the shot does not display great depth of field. The foreground plane (Valentine) is markedly out of focus, the middle ground (Batala) is slightly out of focus, and the distant plane (the concierge) is in sharp focus. Deep space is a property of mise-en-scene, affecting how the image is staged; depth of field is a property of the photographic lens, affecting what planes of the image are in focus.

If depth of field controls perspective relations by choosing what planes will be in focus, what choices are open to the filmmaker? He or she may opt for what is usually called **shallow focus**—choosing to focus on only one plane and letting the other planes blur. Before 1940 it was common Hollywood practice to shoot close-ups in shallow focus, making the faces sharp and the foreground and background planes hazy. (See Fig. 6.16, from *The Front Page.*) Sometimes objects near the camera were thrown out of focus so that the sharper middle ground would claim the viewer's attention. But in the 1940s, partly due to the influence of *Citizen Kane,* Hollywood filmmakers began using faster film, shorter-focal-length lenses, and more intense lighting to yield a greater depth of field. The contract-signing scene from *Citizen Kane* (Fig. 6.17) offers a famous example: from one plane near the lens (Bernstein's head) through several planes in the middle ground to the wall far in the distance, everything is in sharp focus. This practice came to be called **deep focus.**

Since the lens may be refocused at various points, the filmmaker may also adjust perspective relations while filming by **racking** or *pulling* **focus.** A shot may begin on an object close to the lens and rack-focus so that something in the distance springs into crisp focus. One shot in Miklós Jancsó's *Red Psalm* uses an opposite sort of rack focus. The lens focuses initially on a soldier striding to the right; in the foreground a peasant woman's hand is out of focus (Fig. 6.18). As he continues to walk, the lens racks focus to the hand and throws his figure out of focus (Fig. 6.19).

**Special effects.**   The image's perspective relations may also be created by means of certain "special effects." We have already seen (p. 14) that the filmmaker can create setting by use of models and miniatures. The filmmaker can also use a *glass shot.* Here portions of the setting are painted onto a pane of glass and the camera shoots through it to film action supposedly occurring in the painted setting. As another alternative, separately photographed planes of action may be combined on the same strip of film to create the illusion that the two planes are adjacent. The simplest way to do this is through **superimposition;** here, either by double exposure in the camera or in laboratory printing, one image is laid over another. This is most evident in scenes of ghosts or other spectral figures. More complex techniques for combining strips of film to create a single shot are usually called **process** or *composite* **shots,** and they can be divided into *projection* process work and *matte* process work.

In projection process work, the filmmaker projects footage of a setting onto a screen, then films actors performing in front of the screen. Classical Hollywood filmmaking began this process in the late 1920s, as a way to avoid taking cast and crew on location. (Both the cost of location filming and the difficulty of achieving acceptable sound were factors in the decision.) The Hollywood technique involved placing the actors against a translucent screen and projecting a film of the setting from behind the screen. The whole ensemble could then be filmed from the front. (See Fig. 6.20, from *The Sands of Iwo Jima*.) **Rear projection,** as this system was known, is still widely used, but it does not create a very convincing set of depth cues. Foreground and background tend to look starkly separate, partly because of the absence of cast shadows from foreground to background, and partly because all background planes seem equally diffuse. (See Fig. 6.21, from *Bwana Devil*.)

**Front projection,** which came into use in the late 1960s, projected the setting onto a two-way mirror, angled to throw the image onto a high-reflectance screen. The camera photographs the actors against the screen by shooting through the mirror (Fig. 6.22). The results of front projection can be clearly seen in the "Dawn of Man" sequence of *2001: A Space Odyssey*, the first film to use front projection extensively. (At one moment, a saber-toothed tiger's eyes glow, reflecting the projector's light.) Because of the sharper focus of the projected footage, front projection blends foreground and background planes somewhat better.

Composite filming can also be accomplished by **matte** work. A matte is a portion of the setting photographed on a strip of film, usually with a part of the frame empty. Through laboratory printing, the matte is joined with another strip of film containing the actors. One sort of matte involves a painting of the desired areas of setting, which is then filmed. This footage is combined with footage of action, segregated in the blank portions of the painted scenery. In this way, a matte can

**Fig. 6.19**

**Fig. 6.20**

**Fig. 6.21**

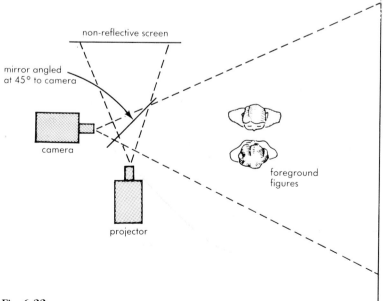

non-reflective screen

mirror angled
at 45° to camera

camera

projector

foreground
figures

high-reflectance
screen

**Fig. 6.22**

Fig. 6.23

Fig. 6.24

Fig. 6.25

create an entire imaginary setting for the film. (See Figs. 6.23 and 6.24, showing the live action and the finished frame from *Her Jungle Love*.) Stationary mattes of this sort have made glass shots virtually obsolete.

With a matte painting, however, the actor cannot move into the painted portions of the frame without creating a ghostly double exposure. To solve this problem, the filmmaker can use a *traveling matte*. Here the actor is photographed against a blank, usually blue, background. In laboratory printing, the moving outline of the actor is "cut out" of footage of the desired background. After further lab work, the shot of the actor is "jigsawed" into the moving gap in the background footage. It is traveling mattes that present shots of Superman's flight or of spaceships hurtling through space. In Figure 6.25, a production still from *2001*, the spacecraft visible through the porthole is a model that has been matted into a shot of the astronaut in the control cabin. The bird attacks in Alfred Hitchcock's *The Birds* required dozens of traveling mattes. You can often detect traveling mattes on the screen, because even the most expensive and carefully executed special effects do not always manage to join the various portions of the shot together perfectly. A thin dark line, called a *matte line*, may shimmer around the moving sections. In *The Empire Strikes Back*, matte lines are particularly evident during the battle with the Empire's "walkers."

se·nes / cuere s together

You may have noticed that glass shots, superimpositions, projection process work, and matte work all straddle two general bodies of film techniques. To the extent that these special effects all require arrangement of the material before the camera, they are aspects of mise-en-scene. But since they also require control of photographic choices (e.g., refilming, laboratory adjustments) and affect perspectivic relations, these special effects fall under cinematography as well.

Fig. 6.26

Like other film techniques, photographic manipulations of the shot are not ends in themselves. They function within the overall context of the film. Specific treatments of tonalities, speed of motion, or perspective should be judged less on criteria of "realism" than on criteria of function. For instance, many Hollywood filmmakers strive to make their rear-projection shots unnoticeable. But in Jean-Marie Straub and Danièle Huillet's *The Chronicle of Anna Magdalena Bach*, the perspective relations are yanked out of kilter by an inconsistent rear projection (Fig. 6.26). Bach stands playing a harpsichord, shot straight-on. Yet the building behind him is seen from a low angle. Since the film's other shots have been filmed on location in correct perspective, this blatantly artificial rear projection calls our attention to the visual style of the entire film. Similarly, Figure 6.27, a shot from *Daisies*, looks unrealistic (unless we posit the man as being about two feet long), but Chytilová has used setting, character position, and deep focus to make a comic point about the two women's treatment of men. The filmmaker chooses not only how to register light and movement photographically but also how those photographic qualities will function within the overall formal system of the film. But the fact that the man seems to lie directly on top of the screen against which the women are leaning depends upon another factor as well: the precise **framing** of the image.

Fig. 6.27

## FRAMING

It may seem odd to talk of something as elusive as the border of the image, since it may seem a sheerly negative feature, a simple edge or break. (After all, literary critics do not talk of the margins of the pages in *Moby Dick*.) But, in a film, the frame is not simply a neutral border; it produces a *certain vantage point* onto the material within the image. In cinema the frame is important because it actively *defines* the image for us.

Fig. 6.28

If proof were required of the power of framing, we need only turn to the first major filmmaker in history, Louis Lumière. An inventor and businessman, Lumière and his brother Auguste devised one of the first practical cinema cameras (Fig. 6.28). The Lumière camera, the most flexible of its day, doubled as a projector and as a developing tank. Whereas the bulky American camera invented by W. K. L. Dickson was about the size of an office desk (Fig. 6.29), the Lumière camera weighed only 12 pounds and was small and portable. As a result of its lightness, the Lumière camera could be taken outside and could be simply and quickly set up. Louis Lumière's earliest films presented simple events—workers leaving his father's factory, a game of cards, a family meal. But even at so early a stage of film history, Lumière was able to use framing to transform everyday reality into cinematic events.

Consider one of the most famous Lumière films, *The Arrival of a Train at La Ciotat Station* (1895). Had Lumière followed theatrical practice, he might have

Fig. 6.29

Fig. 6.30

Fig. 6.31

framed the shot by setting the camera perpendicular to the platform, letting the train enter the frame from one side, broadside to the spectator. Instead, Lumière positioned the camera at an oblique angle. The result is a dynamic composition, with the train arriving on a diagonal (Fig. 6.30). If the scene had been shot perpendicularly, we would have seen only a string of passengers' backs climbing aboard. Here, however, Lumière's oblique angle brings out many aspects of the passengers' bodies and several planes of action. We see some figures in the foreground, some in the distance. Simple as it is, this single-shot film, less than a minute long, aptly illustrates how choosing a position for the camera makes a drastic difference in the framing of the image and how we perceive the filmed event.

Consider another Lumière short, *Baby's Meal* (1895) (Fig. 6.31). Lumière selected a camera position that would emphasize certain aspects of the event. A long shot would have situated the family in its garden, but Lumière frames the figures at a medium distance, which downplays the setting but emphasizes the family's gestures and facial expressions. The frame's control of the scale of the event has also controlled our understanding of the event itself.

Framing can powerfully affect the image by means of (1) the size and shape of the frame; (2) the way the frame defines onscreen and offscreen space; (3) the way framing controls the distance, angle, and height of a vantage point onto the image; and (4) the way framing can be mobile in relation to the mise-en-scene.

## ■ FRAME DIMENSIONS AND SHAPE

We are so accustomed to the frame as a rectangle that we should remember that it need not be one. In painting and photography, of course, images have frames of various sizes and shapes: narrow rectangles, ovals, vertical panels, even triangles and parallelograms. In cinema the choice has been more limited.

The ratio of the length of one side of the frame to the length of the top or bottom is called the **aspect ratio**. The rough dimensions of the ratio were set quite early in the history of cinema by Edison, Dickson, Lumière, and other inventors. The film frame was to be rectangular, its aspect ratio approximately two to three. Nonetheless, there was no absolute agreement as to the exact dimensions. Many early sound films (e.g., F. W. Murnau's *Sunrise*, René Clair's *Le Million*) were shot in an almost square frame. Some silent filmmakers adventurously experimented with aspect ratios. Abel Gance shot and projected sequences of *Napoleon* (1927) in a format he called "triptychs." This was a widescreen effect composed of three normal frames side by side. Gance sometimes used the effect to show a single huge expanse, sometimes to put three distinct images side by side (Fig. 6.32). In contrast, in 1930 the Soviet director Sergei Eisenstein argued for a square frame, which would make compositions along horizontal, vertical, and diagonal directions equally feasible. But, in the early 1930s, the Hollywood Academy of Motion Picture Arts and Sciences established the so-called **Academy ratio** of 1:1.33 (for reasons of sound and exhibition conditions). This was standardized throughout the world, and most of the frames reproduced in this book are in Academy ratio.

At present, the 1:1.33 ratio is seldom employed in 35-mm filmmaking. The most common ratios are *widescreen* ones. Historically, widescreen ratios have ranged from 1:1.66 to almost 1:4 (for Gance's triptychs). Since the 1960s, a few formats have dominated widescreen use: the 1:2.35 ratio standardized by the CinemaScope process during the 1950s, the 1:1.66 ratio popular in Europe, the updated Academy ratio of 1:1.85, and the 1:2.2 ratio currently standard for 70-mm presentations.

The simplest way to create a widescreen image is by masking it at some point in the production or exhibition process. The frame from Jean-Pierre Melville's *Le*

Fig. 6.32

Fig. 6.33

Fig. 6.34

Fig. 6.35

*Samourai* (Fig. 6.33) was masked during filming or printing. Alternatively, a "full-frame" image may be recorded on the print and then masked during projection.

Another way to create a widescreen image is by using an **anamorphic** process. Here the image is horizontally "squeezed," either during filming or in printing. A special lens is necessary to unsqueeze the image during projection. Figure 6.34, from Jean-Luc Godard's *Made in USA*, shows the image on the 35-mm film strip, while Figure 6.35 shows the image as projected on the screen. The aspect ratio is 1:2.35, that of CinemaScope previously and that of most anamorphic processes today. (Godard's film was photographed in Techniscope, a popular European process; the most frequently used process in the U.S. is anamorphic Panavision.)

Fig. 6.36

Fig. 6.37

Fig. 6.38

Fig. 6.39

Today studio films are often shot in one format but shown in others. For example, *Die Hard* was filmed in anamorphic 35 mm, and some prints were exhibited in the corresponding 1:2.35 ratio. A squeezed frame is shown in Figure 6.36. Wide-masked 70-mm prints were also made from the 35-mm negative, and Figure 6.37 shows that here the aspect ratio is closer to 1:2.2. (As a result, the anamorphic frame contains a bit more material on each side of the image.)

Widescreen cinema, either masked or anamorphic, has important effects. Compositionally, the screen becomes a band or strip, emphasizing horizontal compositions. The format was initially associated with genres of spectacle—Westerns, travelogues, musicals, historical epics—in which sweeping settings were important. But directors quickly learned that widescreen has value for more intimate subjects too. Figure 6.38, from Kurosawa's *Red Beard*, shows how an anamorphic process (Tohoscope, the Japanese equivalent of CinemaScope) can be used to create significant foreground and background areas in a confined setting.

In some widescreen compositions, the director will draw the audience's attention to only one area of the image. A common solution is to isolate a figure slightly off center (Fig. 6.39, from John Huston's *Heaven Knows, Mr. Allison*; Fig. 6.40, from John McTiernan's *Die Hard*). More original is Kurosawa's attempt in *Red Beard* to cue us to notice the growing friendship between a little boy and girl. As an intern and nurse look on in the lower right of Figure 6.41, the frame is filled mostly with quilts hanging out to dry. But in a gap between them, in the middle left, we can see the boy's hand extend a bunch of lollipops to the girl. (Figure 6.41 is also an excellent example of the flattening effects achieved by a very long telephoto lens. Rather than receding into the distance, the quilts look squashed together and stacked up. Contrast the greater depth in a similar composition in Figure 5.51.)

Fig. 6.40

Fig. 6.41

Fig. 6.42

The director also may use the widescreen format to multiply points of interest, as Otto Preminger does in *Advise and Consent*. Preminger avoids Kurosawa's telephoto effects and instead uses wide-angle lenses, which permit great depth of field and an exaggeratedly hollow-looking space. In scenes in the Senate chamber and committee rooms, Preminger peppers the shot with the faces of many characters. Our eye shuttles around the frame according to who is speaking, who is facing us, and who reacts to the speaker's words (Fig. 6.42).

On occasion, widescreen processes have attempted to "surround" viewers by activating their peripheral vision. Cinerama, introduced commercially in 1952, presents us with the rectangular screen slightly curved on the edges, a tactic that increases our sense of immersion in the image. Originally a process involving three separate frames projected side by side, Cinerama later became another anamorphic process, with the image squeezed onto a single frame.

More recently a process called OMNIMAX has been introduced and is featured in several science museums in the United States. In a specially built auditorium, the audience sits in reclining seats and faces up toward a dome-shaped screen. The screen is designed to cover the entire field of vision and give the image a greater sense of depth. Films made for such presentations are shot with anamorphic lenses but in this case lenses that compress the image from top to bottom as well as from side to side.

A comparable approach to engaging peripheral vision comes with various experiments in 360° cinema (seen at various world's fairs and international expositions, as well as at Disneyland and Disney World). In wraparound cinema ratios, the frame runs in a complete circle around the audience.

As we noted in Chapter 1 (p. 22), widescreen films shown in the theater may differ markedly from what we see on television. Many films shown on television are

Fig. 6.43

Fig. 6.44

Fig. 6.45

Fig. 6.46

adapted by the "pan-and-scan" technique, which selects from the wide-film image a portion that fills the roughly 1:1.33 format of the television screen. Thus in *Advise and Consent*, a single shot in the original (Fig. 6.43) becomes two shots in the video version (Figs. 6.44 and 6.45).

Today, widescreen films are often shot with eventual television presentation in mind. The camera viewfinder in Figure 6.46 frames a 1:1.85 image overall, but it also marks out a wider format within that. The portions visible at the top and bottom of the viewfinder will be recorded on the film. In some cases, the "full-frame" image may be on the print shown in the theater, but an aperture plate in the projector will mask out the top and bottom areas. Or the film may be printed in one format for theater projection and in another for transfer to video. Figure 6.47 is a 70-mm frame from *Good Morning Vietnam*, printed for showing in about a 1:1.85 format, and Figure 6.48 shows the corresponding video image. While the film image includes slightly more material on the sides, the squarer video image has a little more information at the bottom.

The rectangular frame, while by far the most common, has not prevented filmmakers from experimenting with other frame shapes. This has usually been done by attaching variously shaped **masks** over either the camera's or the printer's lens to block the passage of light. Masks were quite common in the silent cinema. A moving circular mask that opens to reveal or closes to conceal a scene is called an **iris**. In *La Roue*, Gance employed a variety of circular and oval masks (Fig. 6.49). In Figure 6.50, a shot from Griffith's *Intolerance*, most of the frame is boldly blocked out to leave only a thin vertical slice, emphasizing the soldier's fall from the tower. A number of directors in the sound cinema have revived the use of irises and masks. In *The Magnificent Ambersons* (Fig. 6.51), Orson Welles uses an iris to close a scene; the old-fashioned device adds a nostalgic note to the sequence.

Finally, we should mention experiments with *multiple-frame* imagery. In this process, two or more different images, each with its own frame dimensions and shape, appear within the larger frame. From the early cinema onward, this device has been used to present scenes of telephone conversations; Figure 6.52, from Philips Smalley's 1913 film *Suspense*, provides an example. The device was revived for phone conversations in *Bye Bye Birdie* and other 1960s widescreen comedies. More adventurous is a scene in Gance's *Napoleon*, where as many as nine rectangular images within the frame suggest the frenzy of a dormitory pillow fight (Fig. 6.53). Multiple-frame imagery is also useful for building suspense, as Brian De Palma has shown in such films as *Sisters* and *Blow-Out*. We gain a godlike omniscience as we watch two or more actions at exactly the same moment. In Robert Aldrich's *Twilight's Last Gleaming*, the moments before a guided missile are about

Fig. 6.47

Fig. 6.48

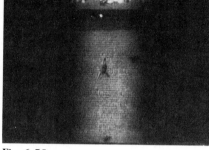

Fig. 6.49

Fig. 6.50

Fig. 6.51

to be launched are made more tense by splitting the frame into several images and giving us an unrestricted range of knowledge. Some portions of the frame show the desperate men who have commandeered a missile silo, some show the reactions of officials in Washington, and some simply depict, from various camera angles, the eerily rising missiles themselves.

As usual, the filmmaker's choice of screen format can be an important factor in shaping the viewer's experience. Frame size and shape can guide the spectator's attention. It can be concentrated through compositional patterns or masking, or it can be dispersed by use of various points of interest or sound cues. The same possibilities exist with multiple-frame imagery, which must be carefully coordinated either to focus the viewer's notice or to send it ricocheting from one image to another.

Fig. 6.52

## ■ ONSCREEN AND OFFSCREEN SPACE

Whatever its shape, the frame makes the image finite. The film image is bounded, limited. From an implicitly continuous world, the frame selects a slice to show us. Even in those early films so heavily dependent on theater, the characters enter the image *from* somewhere and go off *to* another area—**offscreen space**. Even in an abstract film, we cannot resist the sense that the shapes and forces that burst into the frame come from somewhere. If the camera leaves an object or person and moves elsewhere, we will assume that the object or person is still there, outside the frame.

Noël Burch has pointed out six zones of offscreen space: the space beyond each of the four edges of the frame, the space behind the set, and the space behind

Fig. 6.53

Fig. 6.54

Fig. 6.55

Fig. 6.56

Fig. 6.57

Fig. 6.58

Fig. 6.59

the camera. It is worth considering how many ways a filmmaker can imply the presence of things in these zones. A character can direct looks or gestures at something offscreen. As we shall see in Chapter 8, sound can offer potent clues about offscreen space. And, of course, something from offscreen can protrude partly into the frame. Virtually any film could be cited for examples of all these possibilities, but attractive instances are offered by films that utilize offscreen space for surprise effects.

In William Wyler's *Jezebel* the heroine, Julie, greets some friends in medium shot (Fig. 6.54), when suddenly a huge fist holding a glass appears in the center foreground (Fig. 6.55). Julie looks off at its owner and comes forward, the camera retreating slightly to frame her with the man who had toasted her (Figs. 6.56 and 6.57). The intrusion of the hand abruptly signals us to the man's presence; Julie's glance, the camera movement, and the sound track confirm our new awareness of the total space. The director has used the selective powers of the frame to exclude something of great importance and then introduced it with startling effect.

More systematically, D. W. Griffith's *Musketeers of Pig Alley* makes use of sudden intrusions into the frame as a motif developing across the whole film. When a gangster is trying to slip a drug into the heroine's drink, we are not aware that the Snapper Kid has entered the room until a plume of his cigarette smoke wafts into the frame (Fig. 6.58). At the film's end, when the Snapper Kid receives a payoff, a mysterious hand thrusts into the frame to offer him money (Fig. 6.59). Griffith has thus exploited the surprise latent in our sudden awareness that figures are offscreen.

The use of the fifth zone of offscreen space, that behind the set, is of course common; characters go out a door and are now concealed by a wall or a staircase. Somewhat rarer is the sixth zone—the offscreen space behind and near the camera. One famous example occurs in Jean Renoir's *Rules of the Game*, in the context of a shot in which characters virtually explode into the frame from offscreen space. André and Robert are embroiled in a fistfight; during the melee, André is flung back onto and over a divan (Fig. 6.60). Then magazines start flying at him from over the top of the frame, from "behind us," as it were (Fig. 6.61). In such ways the director can turn the necessary limitations of the frame edge to advantage.

## ■ ANGLE, LEVEL, HEIGHT, AND DISTANCE OF FRAMING

The frame implies not only space outside itself but also a position from which the material in the image is viewed. Most often, of course, such a position is that of the camera filming the event, but this need not always be true. In an animated film

Fig. 6.60

Fig. 6.61

Fig. 6.62

the position implied by the drawn frames is not necessarily the same position that the camera occupies during the making of the film; shots in an animated film may be framed as high or low angles, or long shots or close-ups, all of which simply result from the perspective of drawings selected to be photographed. Still, in what follows, we shall continue to speak of "camera angle," "camera level," "camera height," and "camera distance," with the understanding that these terms refer simply to what we see on the screen and need not always conform to what occurred during production.

Fig. 6.63

**Angle.**   The frame implies an **angle of framing** with respect to what is shown. It thus positions us at some angle onto the shot's mise-en-scene. The number of such angles is infinite, since there is an infinite number of points in space that the camera might occupy. In practice, we typically distinguish three general categories: the straight-on angle, the high angle, and the low angle. The straight-on angle is the most common. Figure 6.62 shows a straight-on angle from Straub and Huillet's *Chronicle of Anna Magdalena Bach*. The high angle positions us "looking down" at the material within the frame, as in Figure 6.63, a shot from *Ivan the Terrible*. The low-angle framing positions us as "looking up" at the framed material (as in Fig. 6.64, again from *Ivan the Terrible*).

Fig. 6.64

**Level.**   We can also distinguish the degree to which the framing is "level." This ultimately bears on the sense of gravity governing the filmed material and the frame. Assume that we are filming telephone poles. If the framing is level, the horizontal edges of the frame will be parallel to the horizon of the shot and perpendicular to the poles. If horizon and poles are at diagonal angles, the frame is **canted** in one manner or another. The canted frame is relatively rare, although a few films make heavy use of it, such as Carol Reed's *The Third Man* (see Fig. 6.65).

**Height.**   Sometimes it becomes important to specify the sense that the framing gives us of being stationed at a certain *height*. Camera angle is, of course, related to height in a certain sense (to frame from a high angle entails being at a higher vantage point than the material in the image), but camera height is not simply a matter of camera angle. For instance, the Japanese filmmaker Yasujiro Ozu often positions his camera close to the ground to film characters or objects on the floor (see Plates 7, 14, and 15). Note that this is not a matter of camera angle, for the angle is straight-on; we still see the ground or floor. Filming from such a low height with a straight-on angle is an important quality of Ozu's visual style, as we shall see in Chapter 10.

Fig. 6.65

*Canted frame*

*long shot*

*plans américien*

Fig. 6.66

Fig. 6.67

Fig. 6.68

*medium shot*

*M close up*

Fig. 6.69

Fig. 6.70

**Distance.** Finally, the framing of the image stations us not only at certain angle and height and on a level plane or at a cant but also with respect to distance. Framing supplies a sense of being far away from or close to the mise-en-scene of the shot. This aspect of framing is usually called camera distance. In what follows, we shall use the standard measure—the scale of the human body—but any other filmed material would do as well. The examples are all from Carol Reed's *Third Man.*

In the **extreme long shot**, the human figure is barely visible (Fig. 6.66). This is the framing for landscapes, bird's-eye views of cities, and other extensive entities. In the **long shot**, figures are more prominent, but the background still dominates (Fig. 6.67). The **plan américain** ("American shot") is very common in Hollywood cinema. Here, as in Figure 6.68, the human figure is framed from the knees up. This shot permits a nice balance of figure and surroundings. Shots at the same distance of nonhuman subjects are called **medium long shots.**

The **medium shot** frames the human body from the waist up (Fig. 6.69). Gesture and expression now become more visible. The **medium close-up** frames the body from the chest up (Fig. 6.70). The **close-up** is traditionally the shot showing just the head, hands, feet, or a small object; it emphasizes facial expression, the details of a gesture, or a significant object (Fig. 6.71). The **extreme close-up** singles out a portion of the face (eyes or lips), isolates a detail, magnifies the minute (Fig. 6.72).

Note that the size of the photographed material within the frame is as important as any real "camera distance." From the same "camera distance," you could film a long shot of a person or of King Kong's elbow. We would not call the shot in

Fig. 6.71

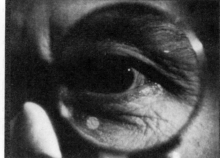

Fig. 6.72

Figure 6.73 (from *La Passion de Jeanne d'Arc*) a close-up just because only Jeanne's head appears in the frame; the framing is that of a long shot because in scale her head is relatively small. (If the framing simply adjusted downward, her whole body would be visible.) In judging camera distance, the relative proportion of the material framed provides the basic determinant.

Fig. 6.73

Common confusions exist about framing. First, categories of framing are obviously matters of degree. There is no universal measure of camera angle or distance; no precise cut-off point distinguishes between a long shot and an extreme long shot, or a slightly low angle and a straight-on angle. Moreover, filmmakers are not bound by terminology; they rightly do not worry if a shot does not fit into traditional categories. Nevertheless, the overall concepts are clear enough to be workable. It is not of great importance whether the shot that cuts John Wayne off slightly above his waist is to be called a "true" medium shot or a "true" medium close-up. What is important is that we recognize how that framing functions in that particular film and that we notice when it reappears.

**Functions of framing.** Another problem is more important. Sometimes we are tempted to assign absolute meanings to angles, distances, and other qualities of framing. It is tempting to believe that framing from a low angle automatically "says" that a character is powerful and that framing from a high angle presents him or her as dwarfed and defeated. Verbal analogies are especially seductive: a canted frame seems to mean that "the world is out of kilter."

Fig. 6.74

The analysis of film as art would be a lot easier if technical qualities automatically possessed such hard-and-fast meanings, but individual films would thereby lose much of their uniqueness and richness. The fact is that framings have no absolute or general meanings. In *some* films angles and distances carry such meanings as mentioned above, but in other films—probably most films—they do not. To rely on such formulas is to forget that meaning and effect always stem from the total film, from its operation as a system. The context of the film will determine the function of the framings, just as it determines the function of mise-en-scene, photographic qualities, and other techniques. Consider three examples.

At many points in *Citizen Kane*, low-angle shots of Kane do convey his looming power, but the lowest angles in the film occur at the point of Kane's most humiliating defeat—his miscarried gubernatorial campaign. In this context the low angle functions to isolate Kane against an empty background (Fig. 6.74). Note that angles of framing affect not only our view of the main figures but also the background against which those figures may appear.

Fig. 6.75

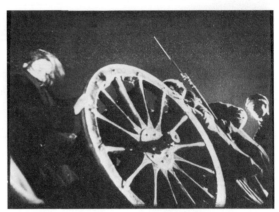

Fig. 6.76

Fig. 6.77

If the cliché were correct, Figure 6.75, a shot from *North by Northwest*, would express the powerlessness of Van Damm and Leonard. In fact, Van Damm has just decided to eliminate his mistress by pushing her out of a plane, and he is saying: "I think that this is a matter best disposed of from a great height." The angle and distance of Hitchcock's shot wittily prophesy how the murder is to be carried out.

The world is hardly out of kilter in the shot from Eisenstein's *October* shown in Figure 6.76. The canted frame dynamizes the effort of pushing the cannon.

These three examples should demonstrate that we cannot reduce the richness of cinema to a few recipes. We must, as usual, look for the *functions* the technique performs in the particular *context* of the total film.

Camera distance, height, level, and angle often take on clear-cut narrative functions. Camera distance can establish or reestablish settings and character positions, as we shall see in the next chapter when we examine the editing of the first sequence of *The Maltese Falcon*. A framing can isolate a narratively important detail—the tears of Henriette in *A Day in the Country* (Fig. 6.77), the snips of Jeanne's hair in *La Passion de Jeanne d'Arc* (Fig. 6.78).

Framing also contributes to cueing a shot as "subjective." In Chapter 3, we saw that a film's narration may present story information with some degree of psychological depth (p. 66), and one option is a perceptual subjectivity that renders what a character sees or hears. When a shot's framing prompts us to take it as a character's vision, we call it an optically subjective shot, or a **point-of-view shot** (abbreviated as POV shot). In Figure 6.79, a shot from Curtis Bernhardt's *Possessed*, the distance and the angle furnish cues which impel us to read the shot as through the eyes of a patient being brought into a hospital on a stretcher.

Less obviously, camera distance and angle can situate us in one area of the narrative's space. The angle and distance of Figure 6.80, a shot from *Sergeant York*, do not show the preacher from any specific character's vantage point, but we are generally situated in the congregation's position. (An alternative distance and angle might view the preacher from a high angle and from the rear.) A canted framing may serve the narrative function of marking certain shots or sequences as distinctly different from the rest of the film. Note the canted framing in Figure 6.81, a shot from a montage sequence in *The Roaring Twenties*, showing a routine action rather than a specific moment.

Framings may serve the narrative in yet other ways. Across an entire film the repetitions of certain framings may associate themselves with a character or situa-

Fig. 6.78

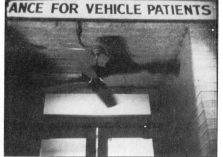

Fig. 6.79

Fig. 6.80

Fig. 6.81

tion. That is, framings may become motifs unifying the film. In *The Maltese Falcon* Casper Gutman is frequently photographed from a low angle emphasizing his grotesque obesity. Throughout *La Passion de Jeanne d'Arc* Dreyer returns obsessively to extreme close-up shots of Jeanne.

Or, certain framings in a film may stand out by virtue of their rarity. The ominously calm effect of the shot of the birds descending on Bodega Bay (in Hitchcock's film *The Birds*) arises from the abrupt shift from straight-on medium shots to an extreme long shot from very high above the town (see Figs. 7.26 and 7.27). In a film composed primarily of long shots and medium shots, an extreme close-up will obviously have considerable force. Similarly, the early scenes of Ridley Scott's *Alien* generally include few shots representing any character's point of view. But when Caine approaches the alien egg, we see close views of it as if through his eyes, and the creature that attaches itself to his face leaps straight out at the camera. This sudden switch to framings that restrict us to one character's range of knowledge emphasizes the main turning point in the plot.

Even within a single sequence, we can note how camera angle, level, and distance change significantly. In the final sequence from Hitchcock's *Saboteur*, at the top of the Statue of Liberty, the hero is holding the coatsleeve of the saboteur, who dangles precariously. The sleeve's stitching starts to tear. Hitchcock cuts from extreme long shots, high- and low-angled, canted this way and that, of the statue to extreme close-ups of the threads ripping out one by one. The scene's suspense derives principally from the drastic difference between the broad view (emphasizing the saboteur's danger) and the near-microscopic enlargement (his fate literally hangs by a thread).

Fig. 6.82

Fig. 6.83

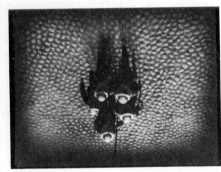

Fig. 6.84

But framings do not function only to emphasize narrative form. They can have their own intrinsic interest as well. Close-ups can bring out textures and details we might otherwise ignore. We can see the smallest surreptitious gestures of a pickpocket in the medium close-up from Robert Bresson's *Pickpocket* (Fig. 6.82); a series of similar close shots makes up a dazzling, balletlike scene in this film. Long shots can permit us to explore expansive spaces; much of the visual delight of Westerns, of *2001*, or of *Seven Samurai* arises from long shots that make huge spaces manifest.

Our eye also enjoys the formal play presented by unusual angles on familiar objects, as when René Clair in *Entr'acte* frames a ballerina from straight below, transforming the figure into an expanding and contracting flower (Fig. 6.83). In *La Passion de Jeanne d'Arc* the upside-down framings (Fig. 6.84) are not motivated as a character's point of view; they exist as an exploration of framing in its own right. "By reproducing the object from an unusual and striking angle," writes Rudolf Arnheim, "the artist forces the spectator to take a keener interest, which goes beyond mere noticing or acceptance. The object thus photographed sometimes gains in reality, and the impression it makes is livelier and more arresting."

Framing may be used for comic effect, as Charlie Chaplin, Buster Keaton, and Jacques Tati have all shown. We have seen how in *Our Hospitality*, Keaton stages many gags in depth; now we can see that well-chosen camera angles and distances are also vital to the gags' success. For example, if the scene shown in Figure 5.57 were shot from the side and in extreme long shot, we would not see so clearly that the two parts of the train are on parallel tracks. Moreover, we could not see the engineer's unconcerned posture, which indicates his failure to realize what has happened. Similarly, the use of framing to create offscreen space is vital to the gag shown in Figures 5.66 and 5.67. Here the gag is laid out in time rather than space: first Willie tugs on the rope, then an unseen effect of that tug becomes visible as the Canfield son hurtles past and disappears, and finally Willie reacts and is himself dragged down into the abyss below the frameline. Try to imagine these moments and others in *Our Hospitality* framed in a different way, and you will see how our reaction to Keaton's humor depends on the careful combination of mise-en-scene and framing.

Similarly, in Tati's *Play Time* mise-en-scene and camera position cooperate to create humorous visual patterns. At one point, M. Hulot turns around to discover that a doorman locking a door has suddenly sprouted "horns" (the door handles; see Plate 3). The visual pun issues from the precisely chosen camera angle and distance. Later in the film, a waiter is pouring champagne for a group of ladies (see Plate 4). But the camera angle and the positions of the figures carefully conceal most of the glasses, so that the waiter seems to be watering the flowers on the ladies' hats. We cannot classify all the nonnarrative functions of framing; we can only suggest that camera distance, angle, height, and level have the constant possibility of sharpening our perception of purely visual qualities.

## ◼ THE MOBILE FRAME

All of the features of framing we have examined are present in every framed image. Paintings, photographs, comic strips, and other images all furnish instances of aspect ratios, in-frame and out-of-frame relations, angle, height, level, and distance of the frame's vantage point. But there is one resource of framing that is specific to cinema (and video). In film it is possible for the frame to *move* with respect to the framed material. **"Mobile framing"** means that within the confines of the image we see, the framing of the object changes. Since the framing orients us to the material in the image, we often see ourselves as moving *along with* the frame. Through such framing we may approach the object or retreat from it, circle it or move past it. The mobile frame may thus produce changes of camera height, distance, angle, or level *within* the shot.

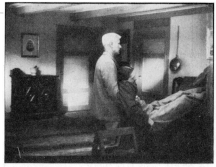

Fig. 6.85

**Types of mobile framing.** We usually refer to the ability of the frame to be mobile as "camera movement." Very often the term is accurate, for usually mobility of framing is achieved by moving the camera physically during production. The camera, as we know, is usually attached to a support while filming, and this support may be designed to move the camera. There are several kinds of camera movement, each one of which creates a specific effect onscreen.

The **pan** (short for "panorama") movement rotates the camera on a vertical axis. The camera as a whole does not displace itself. On screen, the pan gives the impression of a frame horizontally scanning space. It is as if the camera "turns its head" right or left. In Figures 6.85 and 6.86, shots from Dreyer's *Ordet*, the camera pans right to keep the figures in frame as they cross a room.

The **tilt** movement rotates the camera on a horizontal axis. It is as if the camera's "head" were swiveling up or down. Again, the camera as a whole does not change its position. On screen, the tilt movement yields the impression of unrolling a space from top to bottom or bottom to top. Vera Chytilova's *Daisies* combines a rack focus with a tilt: the camera focuses initially on the burning streamers in the foreground (Fig. 6.87) and then racks focus while tilting down to the women in the background (Fig. 6.88).

Fig. 6.86

Fig. 6.87

Fig. 6.88

Fig. 6.89

Fig. 6.90

In the **tracking** (or **dolly** or *trucking*) **shot** the camera as a whole does change position, traveling in any direction along the ground—forward, backward, circularly, diagonally, or from side to side. Figures 6.89 and 6.90 show two stages of a tracking shot in Welles's *Magnificent Ambersons*; note how the figures have remained in the same basic relationship to the frame, while the background has shifted.

In the **crane shot** the camera is lifted off the ground and can travel not only forward and backward, in and out, but also up and down. Variations of the crane shot are helicopter and airplane shots, which allow the camera to travel great distances above the ground. The mourning scene in *Ivan the Terrible* begins with a crane down from a high view of the bier (Fig. 6.91) to a lower position, ending with a framing on Ivan seated at the bier's base (Fig. 6.92).

Such framing movements are the most common, but virtually any kind of camera movement can be imagined (somersaulting, rolling, gyroscopic, etc.). Only a few camera movements might be mistaken for each other. The pan resembles a lateral tracking shot, and the tilt resembles a vertical crane shot. But a little practice makes the difference easy to spot. In both the pan and the tilt, the body of the camera does not change position; it simply swivels left or right, up or down. For example, in Figure 6.85 the framing is fairly close to the central man, showing him in profile. If the camera were tracking along with him, it would remain alongside him—yet Figure 6.86 shows him at a greater distance and from behind—indicating that the camera has turned but not moved along with the character. In the lateral tracking shot and the vertical crane shot, the camera is moved horizontally or vertically, as if you watched the countryside from a moving car or a city from a moving glass elevator. As we shall see, though, types of camera movements can be combined.

Camera movements have held an appeal for filmmakers and audiences since the beginnings of cinema. Why? Visually, camera movements have several arresting effects. They tend to increase information about the space of the image. Objects' positions become more vivid and sharp than in stationary framings. New objects or figures are usually revealed. Tracking shots and crane shots supply continually changing perspectives on passing objects as the frame continually shifts its orientation. Objects appear more solid and three-dimensional when the camera arcs (i.e, tracks along a curved path) around them. Pan and tilt shots present space as continuous, both horizontally and vertically.

Moreover, it is usually impossible not to see camera movement as a substitute for *our* movement. It is not just that objects swell or shrink; we seem to approach or retreat from them. This is not, of course, the case in a literal sense: we never forget that we are watching a film in a theater. But camera movement provides

Fig. 6.91

Fig. 6.92

Fig. 6.93

several powerful cues for a convincing substitute movement. Indeed, so powerful are these cues that filmmakers often make camera movements *subjective*—motivated narratively to represent the view through the eyes of a moving character. That is, camera movement can be a powerful cue that we are watching a POV shot. Narratively subjective or not, the roving camera eye, the mobile framing of the shot, acts as a surrogate for our eye and our attention. Camera movement illustrates very well how the image frame defines our view of a scene.

In certain circumstances our view may be explicitly identified with that of the camera itself. A bumpy, jiggling image usually implies that the camera was **hand held,** that the operator did not anchor the machine on a tripod, but instead trusted his or her body to act as the support. In Figure 6.93 Don Pennebaker hand holds the camera during the filming of his *Keep on Rocking*. This sort of camera movement became common in the late 1950s, with the growth of the *cinéma-vérité* documentary. Soon the device appeared in fiction filmmaking. Often the hand-held camera functions as a special form of subjective point of view, as in Figure 6.94, from Samuel Fuller's *The Naked Kiss*. Sometimes the hand-held shot serves to remind the viewer of the presence of the camera filming the scene. In commercial film production today, the cinematographer can use the gyroscopically balanced Steadi-

Fig. 6.94

Fig. 6.95

Fig. 6.96

Fig. 6.97

Fig. 6.98

Fig. 6.99

cam. This is a camera mount that attaches the camera to the operator's body and allows him or her to see the framing in any position on a video monitor. The Steadicam can produce images as smooth or as bumpy as desired.

Camera movement is the most common way of making the frame mobile, but it is not the only way. In animation filming, the camera seldom moves from one position, but through the drawing of individual "cels" frame by frame, the animator can create the effect of camera movement, as in this pan shot from *The Old Grey Hare* (Figs. 6.95–6.97). Alternatively, a mobile frame effect can be achieved by photographing a still picture or a stopped frame of film and gradually enlarging or reducing any portion of that image, as is frequently done in optical printing. Iris masking can open up to reveal a vista or close down to isolate a detail. Finally, the zoom lens, as we have already mentioned, can be used to provide a mobile framing.

The differences between the laboratory or zoom sorts of mobile framing and some kinds of mobile framing created by camera movement during filming are difficult to illustrate on the printed page. No one will think an iris-in or a circular tracking shot is a zoom. But how, for instance, can we as viewers distinguish between a zoom-in and a forward tracking shot, or a crane shot back and a change in framing created on the optical printer? In general, animation, special effects, and the zoom lens make the frame mobile by reducing or blowing up some portion of the image. Although the tracking shot and the crane shot do enlarge or reduce portions of the frame, this is not *all* that they do. In the genuine camera movement static objects in different planes pass one another at different rates, displaying *different aspects* to us; backgrounds gain depth. Consider two pairs of frames from Alain Resnais's *La Guerre est finie*. Figures 6.98 and 6.99 are both portions of a tracking shot. Note how the street sign has not simply been enlarged; its orientation and angle has somewhat changed with respect to the camera's vantage point. The wall has lost none of its volume or solidity. With the zoom and optical printer enlargement, however, static objects display the *same* aspects and remain in the same positions relative to each other. Perspective relations change, too: backgrounds look flatter and more squeezed (Figs. 6.100 and 6.101). In sum, when the camera moves, we sense our own movement through the space; when the lens zooms, a bit of the image is magnified or demagnified.

So far, we have isolated these different sorts of mobile framings in fairly pure states. But filmmakers frequently combine such framings within a single shot: the camera may track and pan at the same time or crane up while zooming. Still, every instance can be identified as a combination of the basic types.

**Functions of frame mobility.** Our catalog of the types of mobile framings is of little use without a consideration of how such framing strategies function systematically within films. How does mobile framing relate to cinematic space? To cinematic time? How do mobile framings create certain patterns of their own? Such questions demand that we examine how mobile framing interacts with the form of the film.

Fig. 6.100

1. *The mobile frame and space.* The mobile frame has enormous impact on space, considerably affecting onscreen and offscreen space. A forward tracking shot or zoom moves onscreen space offscreen. Other camera movements and optical effects may reveal fresh offscreen areas. In many films the camera moves back from a detail and brings something unexpected into the shot's space. This is what happens in our earlier example from *Jezebel* (Figs. 6.54 through 6.57); after the hand with the glass intrudes into close-up, the camera tracks back to frame the man standing in the foreground. The mobile frame also continually affects the distance, angle, height, and level of the framing. A track-in may change the distance from long shot to close-up; a crane up may change the angle from a low one to a high one. It is useful to think of frame mobility as a way of controlling *spatial changes.*

Fig. 6.101

We can, in general, ask several questions of how the mobile frame relates to space. Are the frame's movements dependent on figure movement? For example, one of the commonest functions of camera movement is **reframing.** If a character moves in relation to another character, very often the frame will slightly adjust to the movement. In *Open City*, when Ricci is in Pina's apartment, he changes position slightly as he sits on the table edge, and the frame shifts slightly to accommodate his movement. Reframing can be an art unto itself, as in *His Girl Friday*, which strives to balance its compositions through reframing. When Hildy moves, the camera pans right to reframe her; when Walter swivels in his chair, the camera reframes leftward—each time guiding our attention and maintaining a balanced composition (see Figs. 6.102–6.104). Since reframings are motivated by figure movement, they tend to be relatively unnoticeable; practice is needed to spot them. When you do start to notice them, you may be surprised at how frequently they appear; the classical narrative cinema often uses them.

Reframing is only one way that the mobile frame may be dependent on figure movement. The camera may also move to follow figures or moving objects. A pan may keep a racing car centered; a tracking shot may follow a character from room to room; or a crane shot may pursue a rising balloon. In such cases frame mobility

Fig. 6.102

Fig. 6.103

Fig. 6.104

Fig. 6.105

Fig. 6.106

Fig. 6.107

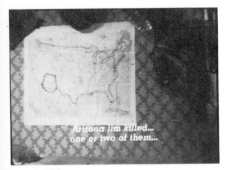

Fig. 6.108

Fig. 6.109

Fig. 6.110

functions primarily to keep our attention fastened on the subject of the shot, and it subordinates itself to that subject's movement.

Following shots can become quite complex. Michelangelo Antonioni's *Cronaca di un amore (Story of a Love Affair)* contains many scenes in which several characters are present. Typically the camera follows one figure moving to meet another, then follows the second character's movement to another spot, where he or she meets someone else, then traces the third character's movement, etc. The card-party sequence in *Cronaca* is a superb example of the camera's restlessly following character after character in rapid succession.

Still, the mobile frame need not be subordinate to the movement of figures at all. It can move independently of them, too. Often, of course, the camera moves away from the characters to reveal something of significance to the narrative. The most banal examples are movements that point out an overlooked clue, a sign that comments on the action, an unnoticed shadow, or a clutching hand. The moving camera can establish a locale the characters will eventually enter. This is what happens at the start of Otto Preminger's *Laura*, when the camera glides through Waldo Lydecker's sitting room, establishing him as a man of wealth and taste, before fastening on the detective MacPherson. In Renoir's *Crime of M. Lange* the moving camera characterizes Lange by leaving him and panning around to survey the objects in his room—six-guns, Western hats, a map with Arizona outlined— (Figs. 6.105–6.110). Lange is shown to be a fantasist, living in the world of Western lore he draws on for his cowboy stories.

Sometimes, though, we can be thrown off guard by a movement that only *apparently* establishes a space for action, as in the opening of Kenji Mizoguchi's *Forty-Seven Ronin*. After a static shot of the courtyard of a castle, we cut to another view of the courtyard, now seen from within the corridor of the castle. The camera inches laterally along the corridor, its gaze fastened on the utterly empty courtyard. Surely, we expect, someone or something will enter that courtyard. Sure enough, voices are heard as the camera continues slowly to track right. But then, after what seems like minutes, the camera pans right to reveal men standing in the corridor and talking. We have been misled; the real action was occurring in the corridor, offscreen, and the camera's sidewise trajectory deliberately excluded the action. Moreover, this camera movement establishes unoccupied space as important to the film, as it will prove in ensuing scenes.

Whether dependent on figure movement or independent of it, the mobile frame can profoundly affect how we perceive the space within the frame and offscreen. Different sorts of camera movements create different conceptions of space. In *Last Year at Marienbad* Resnais often employs a rectilinear tracking shot that moves

**Fig. 6.111**

into corridors and through doorways, turning a fashionable resort hotel into a maze. Alfred Hitchcock has produced some of the most famous single camera movements in film history: a track-and-crane shot that moves from a high-angle long shot of a ballroom over the heads of the dancers to an extreme close-up of a drummer's blinking eyes (*Young and Innocent*), an especially tricky combination track-*out* and zoom-*in* to plastically distort the shot's perspective (used in *Marnie* and *Vertigo*). (The device reappears in *Jaws* by Steven Spielberg, when Sheriff Brody at the beach suddenly realizes that a child has been killed.) In films such as *The Red and the White, Agnus Dei,* and *Red Psalm* Miklós Jancsó has specialized in very lengthy camera movements that roam among groups of people moving across a plain. His shots use all of the resources of tracking, panning, craning, zooming, and racking focus, to guide our perception of spatial relations.

For his film *La Région centrale* Michael Snow built the machine pictured in Figure 6.111. Since all of the moving arms could pivot the camera in several ways in response to a remote-control device, the machine produced a varied series of rotational camera movements—everything from elaborate corkscrew spiralings to huge, Ferris-wheel spins. Snow set up his machine in a barren Canadian landscape, and the film that resulted transforms that landscape into a series of uniquely mobile views. A set of variations on the possibilities of the camera's speed and direction of movement provided the basis of this film's abstract form. This is an example of how one filmic technique can largely determine the form of a long (over three hours) and complex film.

All of these examples illustrate various ways in which frame mobility affects our perception of space. Of any mobile framing we can ask: How does it function to reveal or conceal offscreen space? Is the frame mobility dependent on figure movement or independent of it? What particular trajectory does the camera pursue? Such questions will best be answered by considering how spatial effects of the camera movement function with respect to narrative or nonnarrative form.

2. *The mobile frame and time.* Frame mobility involves time as well as space, and filmmakers have realized that our sense of duration and rhythm is affected by the mobile frame. The importance of duration in camera movement, for example, can be sensed by comparing two Japanese directors, Yasujiro Ozu and Kenji Mizoguchi. Ozu prefers short, unidirectional camera movements, as in *Early Summer* and *The Flavor of Green Tea over Rice*. Mizoguchi, on the other hand, cultivates the leisurely, drawn-out tracking shot, often combining it with panning. That camera movements simply take less time in Ozu's films than in Mizoguchi's constitutes a major difference between the two directors' styles. More broadly, since a camera

movement occupies duration, it can create an arc of expectation and fulfillment all its own. Shortly, we shall see how this happens in a long-take camera movement in the opening of Welles's *Touch of Evil*.

The velocity of frame mobility is important, too. A zoom or a camera movement may be relatively slow or fast. Richard Lester started a fad in the 1960s with the use of very fast zoom-ins and -outs with such films as *A Hard Day's Night*. In comparison, one of the most impressive early camera movements, D. W. Griffith's monumental crane shot into Belshazzar's feast in *Intolerance*, gains majesty and suspense through its inexorably slow descent toward the immense set pictured in Figure 5.10.

In general, a camera movement may create significant effects of its own. If the camera pans quickly away from an event, we may be prompted to wonder what has happened—a manifestation of the curiosity effect discussed in Chapter 2. If the camera abruptly tracks back to show us something in the foreground which we had not expected, we are taken by surprise. If the camera slowly moves in on a detail, gradually enlarging it but delaying the fulfillment of our expectations, the camera movement has contributed to suspense. In a narrative film, the velocity of mobile framing can be motivated by narrational needs: a quick track-in to a significant object or a slow craning out from figures in a landscape can underline key pieces of story information.

Sometimes the speed of the mobile framing functions rhythmically. In Will Hindle's *Pastorale d'été* a gentle, bouncing rhythm is created by zooming in and slightly tilting up and down in time to Honegger's music. Often musical films make use of the speed of camera movement to underline qualities of a song or dance. During the "Broadway Rhythm" number in *Singin' in the Rain*, the camera cranes quickly back from Gene Kelly several times and the speed of the movement is timed to match the rhythm of the lyrics. Frame velocity can also create expressive qualities—a camera movement can be fluid, staccato, hesitant, and so forth. In short, the duration and velocity of the mobile frame can significantly control our perception of the shot over time.

3. *Patterns of mobile framing.* The mobile frame can create its own specific motifs within a film. Consider, for example, how Alfred Hitchcock's *Psycho* begins and ends with a forward movement of the frame. At the beginning, the camera pans right and zooms in on a building in a cityscape; repeated forward movements finally carry us under a window blind and into the darkness of a cheap hotel room. The camera's movement inward, the penetration of an interior, is repeated throughout the film, often motivated as subjective point of view as when various characters move deeper and deeper into Norman Bates's mansion. The next-to-last shot of the film shows Norman sitting against a blank white wall, while we hear his interior monologue; the camera again moves forward into a close-up of his face. This shot is the climax of the forward movement initiated at the start of the film; the film has traced a movement into Norman's mind. Another film that relies heavily on a pattern of forward, penetrating movements is *Citizen Kane*, which depicts the same inexorable drive toward the revelation of a secret.

Other kinds of movements can repeat and develop across a film. Max Ophuls's *Lola Montès* uses both 360° tracking shots and constant upward and downward crane shots to contrast the circus arena with the world of Lola's past. Films as otherwise different as Jean Renoir's *Grand Illusion* and Fritz Lang's *Big Heat* share the habit of beginning a sequence on a relatively close shot of an object and then

Fig. 6.112                Fig. 6.113                Fig. 6.114

tracking back to situate that object in a dramatic context—sometimes with startling
results. In Michael Snow's ⟷ (usually called *Back and Forth*) the constant
panning to and fro across a classroom, Ping-Pong fashion, determines the basic
formal pattern of the film; it comes as a surprise when near the very end, the
movement suddenly becomes a repeated tilting up and down. In these and many
other films the mobile frame sets up marked repetitions and variations.

In these examples, repetitions and variations of camera-movement motifs
interact with the film's narrative or nonnarrative form. By way of summary we can
look at two films that illustrate possible relations of the mobile frame to narrative
form. These two films constitute a pertinent contrast in that one uses the mobile
frame in order to strengthen and support the narrative, whereas the other—para-
doxical as it sounds—subordinates narrative form to an overall frame mobility.

Jean Renoir's *Grand Illusion* is a war film in which we almost never see the
war. The staples of the genre—heroic charges, doomed battalions—are absent.
World War I remains permanently offscreen. Instead, Renoir concentrates on how
national and social-class relations are affected by war. Maréchal and Boeldieu are
both French; Rauffenstein is a German. Yet the aristocrat Boeldieu has more in
common with Rauffenstein than with the mechanic Maréchal. The film's narrative
form traces the death of the Boeldieu-Rauffenstein upper class and the precarious
survival of Maréchal and his pal Rosenthal—their flight to Elsa's farm, their
interlude of peace there, and their final escape back to France and presumably
back to the war as well.

Within this framework, camera movement has several functions, all directly
supportive of the narrative. First, and least unusual, is its tendency to adhere to
figure movement. When a character or vehicle moves, Renoir often pans or tracks
to follow. The camera follows Maréchal and Rosenthal walking together after their
escape; it tracks back when the prisoners are drawn to the window by the sound
of marching Germans below. But it is the movements of the camera *independent* of
figure movement that make the film more unusual.

When the camera moves on its own in *Grand Illusion*, we are conscious of it
actively interpreting the action, creating suspense or giving us information of which
the characters are ignorant. For example, when a prisoner is digging in the escape
tunnel and pulls on the string to signal to be pulled out, the camera frames the
can being tugged over (Fig. 6.112), then pans left to reveal that the characters do
not notice it (Figs. 6.113 and 6.114). Camera movement thus helps create a

Fig. 6.115

Fig. 6.116

Fig. 6.117

Fig. 6.118

Fig. 6.119

Fig. 6.120

somewhat unrestricted narration. Sometimes, in fact, the camera is such an active agent that Renoir will use repeated camera movements to create specific patterns of narrative significance. One such pattern is the movement to link characters with details of their environment. Sometimes a sequence begins on a close-up of some detail, and the camera moves back to anchor this detail in its larger spatial and narrative context. When Renoir begins the scene of Boeldieu and Maréchal's discussion of escape plans with a close-up of a caged squirrel (Fig. 6.115) before tracking back to reveal the men (Fig. 6.116) beside the cage, the narrative parallel is apparent.

More complicated is the scene of the Christmas celebration at Elsa's, which begins on a close-up of the crèche and tracks back to show, in several stages, the interplay of reactions among the characters. Such camera movements are not simply decoration; their habit of beginning on a scenic detail before moving to the larger context makes narrative points economically, constantly emphasizing relationships among elements of Renoir's mise-en-scene. So does the rarer track-*in* to a detail at the *end* of a scene, as when after Boeldieu's death, Rauffenstein goes to cut the geranium, the one flower in the prison (Fig. 6.117), and Renoir tracks in to a final close shot of the flower pot (Fig. 6.118).

Characters are tied to their environment by some even more ambitious moving-camera shots, which function to stress important narrative parallels. In the first scene, as Maréchal leaves the officers' bar (Fig. 6.119), Renoir pans and tracks left from the door to reveal pinups (on the right in Fig. 6.120) and a poster (Fig. 6.121). One scene later, in the German officers' bar, a similar camera movement (this time in the opposite direction) leaves the characters and explores, on its own, a similar collection of decorations (Figs. 6.122–6.124). Through his camera movements Renoir indicates a similarity between the two warring sides, blurring their national differences and stressing common desires. The camera movements *as movements*, repeated in a systematic pattern, create the narrative parallel.

Or consider how two parallel tracking shots compare the war of the aristocrats and the war of the lower-class people. We are introduced to Rauffenstein's new position as commander of a prisoner-of-war camp through a lengthy tracking shot that begins on a cross (ironic, since the chapel has been commandeered as a bivouac) and tracks along whips, spurs, weapons, and gloves to a servant preparing Rauffenstein's gloves and finally to Rauffenstein himself (Figs. 6.125 through 6.132). In this shot Renoir presents, wordlessly, the military mystique of grace on the battlefield that characterizes the aristocrat's war. But, late in the film, a parallel shot criticizes this. Again the shot begins on an object—a picture of Elsa's dead

Fig. 6.121

Fig. 6.122

Fig. 6.123

Fig. 6.124

Fig. 6.125

Fig. 6.126

Fig. 6.127

Fig. 6.128

Fig. 6.129

Fig. 6.130

Fig. 6.131

Fig. 6.132

Fig. 6.133

Fig. 6.134

Fig. 6.135

Fig. 6.136

Fig. 6.137

Fig. 6.138

Fig. 6.139

husband (Fig. 6.133)—and tracks back to reveal pictures of other of Elsa's relatives as she recites offscreen where they were killed. The camera tracks left (Fig. 6.134) to the kitchen table, where the child Lotte sits alone (Fig. 6.135) as Elsa explains offscreen: "Now the table is too large." That Elsa's war has none of Rauffenstein's glory is conveyed chiefly through a parallel created by the repeated camera movement. (Note that camera movement works together with mise-en-scene here as the narrative parallel is reinforced by the subtle use of objects as motifs—the crucifixes in Figs. 6.125 and 6.135, the photographs in Figs. 6.126 and 6.133, and the tables that end both shots.)

Another function of moving the camera independently of figure movement is to link characters with one another. Again and again in the prison camps, the camera moves to join one man to another, spatially indicating their shared condition. When the prisoners ransack the collection of women's clothes, one man decides to dress up in them, and when he appears, a stillness falls over the men; Renoir tracks silently over the prisoners' faces, each one registering a reticent longing. In the scene of the prison vaudeville show, the men learn that the French have recaptured a city; the camera moves among them as they begin defiantly to sing the "Marseillaise." Renoir presents the shot as a celebration of spatial unity, tracking right from the musicians (Fig. 6.136) along the singing performers (Figs. 6.137 and 6.138) to a pair of worried German guards (Fig. 6.139). The camera then pans left to reveal a row of the audience of prisoners on their feet, singing (Fig. 6.140). The camera tracks forward past the musicians again (Fig. 6.141), then pans quickly left to face the entire audience (Fig. 6.142). This very complex camera movement circulates among the prisoners as they join together in defiance of their captors.

Fig. 6.140

Fig. 6.141

Fig. 6.142

Fig. 6.143

Fig. 6.144

Fig. 6.145

In Elsa's cottage as well as in the prison, camera movement links characters. Recall the shot that moves from Elsa and Rosenthal inside through the window to Maréchal outside. The culmination of the linking movement comes near the film's end, when Renoir pans from the Germans on one side of the border (Fig. 6.143) to the distant French escapees on the other (Figs. 6.144 and 6.145); even on this scale, Renoir's camera refuses to honor national divisions.

A remark of André Bazin's is pertinent here: "Jean Renoir found a way to reveal the hidden meaning of people and things without destroying the unity that is natural to them." In such ways as these, camera movement in *Grand Illusion* functions as an active agent in creating the film's drama; in its ability to place emphasis and make comparisons, the camera work is as important as the mise-en-scene. The camera carves into space to create connections that enrich the film's narrative form. Renoir has found imaginative ways to make the mobile frame sustain and elaborate a system of narrative relationships.

In Michael Snow's *Wavelength* the relation of narrative to the mobile frame is almost exactly the inverse. Instead of supporting narrative form, frame mobility dominates narrative, even deflecting our attention from narrative. The film begins with a long-shot framing of a loft apartment, facing one wall and window (Fig. 6.146). In the course of the film the camera zooms in abruptly a short distance, then holds that framing; it zooms in a bit more, then holds that (Fig. 6.147); and so on. By the end of the film a photograph of ocean waves on the distant wall fills the frame in close-up.

Thus *Wavelength* is structured primarily around a single kind of frame mobility—the zoom-in. Its pattern of progression and development is not a narrative one, but that of an exploration, through deliberately limited means, of how the

Fig. 6.146

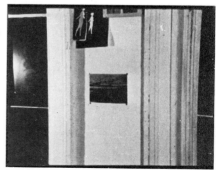

Fig. 6.147

zoom transforms the space of the loft. The sudden zooms create frequent abrupt shifts of perspective relations. In excluding parts of the room, the zoom-in also magnifies and flattens what we see; every change of focal length gives us a new set of spatial relations. The zoom places more and more space offscreen. The sound track, for the most part, reinforces the basic formal progression by emitting a single humming tone that rises consistently in pitch as the zoom magnifies more and more.

Within *Wavelength*'s basic pattern, though, there are two contrasting subsystems. The first is a series of colored tints that plays across the image as abstract blocks of color; these tints often work against the depth represented in the shot of the loft. The second subsystem is a narrative one. At various intervals characters enter the loft and carry on certain activities (talking, listening to the radio, making phone calls). There is even a mysterious death, possibly a murder (note the body on the floor, Fig. 6.148). But the narrative events remain unexplained in cause-effect terms and inconclusive as to closure (although at the film's end we do hear a sound that resembles a police siren). Furthermore, none of these actions swerves the mobile framing from its predetermined course. The jerkily shifting and halting zoom continues, even when it will exclude important narrative information; the continuing trajectory of the framing remains central. Thus *Wavelength* pulls in bits and pieces of narrative, but these fragments of action remain secondary; they function within the temporal progression of the zoom.

From the standpoint of the viewer's experience, *Wavelength*'s use of frame mobility arouses, delays, and gratifies unusual expectations. What plot there is arouses curiosity (What are the people up to? What has led to the man's death, if he does die?) and surprise (the apparent murder). But in general, a story-centered suspense is replaced by a *stylistic* suspense: What will the zoom eventually frame? From this standpoint, the colored tints and even the plot work with the spasmodic qualities of the zoom to delay the forward progress of the framing. When the zoom finally reveals its target, our stylistic anticipations have come to fulfillment. The film's title stands revealed as a multiple pun, referring not only to the steadily rising pitch of the sound track but also to the distance which the zoom had to cross in order to reveal the photo—a "wave length."

*Grand Illusion* and *Wavelength* illustrate, in different ways, how frame mobility can guide and shape our perception of a film's space and time. Frame mobility may be motivated by larger formal concerns, as in Renoir's film, or it may itself become the principal formal concern, motivating other systems, as in Snow's film. What is important to realize is that by attention to how filmmakers utilize the mobile frame within specific contexts, we can gain a fuller understanding of how our experience of a film is created.

## DURATION OF THE IMAGE: THE LONG TAKE

In our consideration of the film image, we have emphasized spatial qualities—how photographic transformations can alter the properties of the image, how framing defines the image for our attention. But cinema is an art of time as well as of space, and we have seen already how mise-en-scene and frame mobility operate in temporal as well as spatial dimensions. What we need to consider now is how the duration of the shot affects our understanding of it.

Fig. 6.148

Fig. 6.149                     Fig. 6.150

There is a tendency to consider the shot as recording "real" duration. A runner takes three seconds to clear a hurdle; if we film the runner, our projected film will also consume three seconds—or so the assumption goes. One film theorist, André Bazin, made it a major tenet of his aesthetic that cinema records "real time." (See Notes and Queries for a discussion of Bazin's position.) What must be noted, though, is that the relation of shot duration to the time consumed by the filmed event is not so simple.

First, obviously, the duration of the event on the screen may be manipulated by adjustments in the camera's or printer's drive mechanism, as we discussed earlier in this chapter. "Slow motion" or "fast motion" may present the runner's jump in twenty seconds or two. Second, narrative films often permit no simple equivalence of "real duration" with screen duration. As Chapter 3 pointed out (p. 60), story duration can differ considerably from plot duration and screen duration.

Consider a shot from Ozu's *Only Son*. It is well past midnight, and we have just seen a family awake and talking; this shot shows a dim corner of the family's apartment, with none of the characters onscreen (Fig. 6.149). But soon the light changes. The sun is rising. By the end of the shot it is morning (Fig. 6.150). This transitional shot consumes about a minute of screen time. It plainly does not record the "real" duration of the story events—that duration would be at least five hours. To put it another way, by manipulating screen duration, the film's plot has condensed a story duration of several hours into a minute or so. In the next chapter we shall examine how editing one shot with another can expand or contract screen duration, but we ought to recognize that it is just as possible to manipulate screen duration *within a single shot* as well. There need be no one-to-one correspondence between the onscreen duration of the shot and the duration of the story events represented.

## ■ THE LONG TAKE

Every shot has some measurable screen duration, but in the history of cinema, directors have varied considerably in their choice of short or lengthy shots. In general, early cinema (1895–1905) tended to rely on shots of fairly long duration. With the emergence of continuity editing in the period 1905–16, shots became shorter. In the late teens and early twenties, an American film would have an average shot length of about five seconds. After the coming of sound, the average stretched to around 10 seconds.

But throughout the history of the cinema, some filmmakers have consistently preferred to utilize shots of greater duration than the average. In various countries in the mid-1930s there was a tendency to increase the length of the shots, and this tendency continued throughout the next 20 years. The causes of this change are complex and not fully understood, but film scholars agree that the use of unusually lengthy shots—**long takes**, as they are called—constitutes a major resource for the filmmaker. ("Long take" is not the same as "long shot"; the latter term refers to the apparent distance between camera and object. As we saw in examining film production (p. 15), a **take** is one run of the camera that records a single shot. (Calling a shot of notable length a "long take" rather than a "long shot" prevents ambiguity, since the latter term refers to a distanced framing, not to shot duration.) In the films of Jean Renoir, Kenji Mizoguchi, Orson Welles, Carl Dreyer, Andy Warhol, or Miklós Jancsó a shot may go on for several minutes, and it would be impossible to analyze these films without an awareness of how the long take can contribute to a film's form and style.

Formally, it is often useful to consider the long take as a large-scale part of a film. In a film with 500 shots, each shot is part of a sequence, which in turn belongs to a larger whole—as a brick is part of a wall, a wall is part of a whole building. But in a film consisting of 14 shots, things are different; the shot becomes a major part within the whole, as, say, a wall of poured concrete is a large-scale, complete unit of the entire building. The long take promotes the single shot to a role of great formal significance.

For such reasons, we can regard the long take as an alternative to a series of shots. The director may choose to present a scene in one or a few long takes or to present the scene through several shorter shots. Sometimes a director builds the entire film out of long takes, as Miklós Jancsó frequently does. His films (for example, *Winterwind, Agnus Dei, Red Psalm*) often present an entire scene in only one shot—a device known by the French term *plan-séquence*, or "shot sequence." Other directors choose to present certain scenes through long takes and other scenes through sequences composed of shorter shots. Within the context of a film built on long takes, editing can have a considerable force. André Bazin pointed out that *Citizen Kane* oscillates between quite lengthy shots (many of the dialogue scenes) and very short ones (in the "News on the March" sequence and other sequences). Hitchcock, Mizoguchi, Renoir, and Dreyer often vary shot duration, depending on the scene's function in the entire film. Thus a film may present a rich interplay between the long take and editing.

If the long take often replaces editing, it should surprise no one that the long take is frequently allied to the mobile frame. The long take may use panning, tracking, craning, or zooming to present continually changing vantage points that are comparable in some ways to the shifts of view supplied by editing. Very often frame mobility breaks the long-take shot into significant smaller units. In Mizoguchi's *Sisters of Gion*, one long take begins with Omocha and the older man seated (Fig. 6.151). Preparing to lure him into becoming her patron, she moves to the opposite end of the room, the camera following her (Figs. 6.152 and 6.153). Now a second phase of the scene occurs: she starts to appeal to his sympathy. He comes over to console her (Figs. 6.154 and 6.155); the camera moves into a tighter shot of the two as he succumbs to her advances (Fig. 6.156). Though there is no cutting, the camera and figure movements have demarcated important stages of the scene's action.

This example also illustrates perhaps the most important consequence of the long take. The Mizoguchi shot reveals a complete internal logic—a beginning,

Fig. 6.151

Fig. 6.152

Fig. 6.153

Fig. 6.154

Fig. 6.155

Fig. 6.156

Fig. 6.157

Fig. 6.158

Fig. 6.159

middle, and end. As a large-scale part of a film, the long take can have its own formal pattern, its own development, its own trajectory and shape. Suspense develops; we start to ask how the shot will continue and when it will end.

The classic example of how the long take can constitute a formal pattern in its own right is the opening sequence of Welles's *Touch of Evil*. The shot begins with a close-up of a hand setting the timer of a bomb (Fig. 6.157). The camera tracks immediately right to follow first the shadow and then the figure of an unknown assassin planting the bomb in a car (Figs. 6.158 and 6.159).

Fig. 6.160

Fig. 6.161

Fig. 6.162

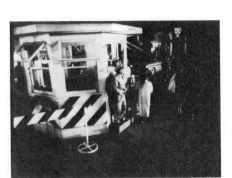

Fig. 6.163

Fig. 6.164

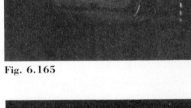

Fig. 6.165

Fig. 6.166

Fig. 6.167

Fig. 6.168

The camera cranes up to a high angle as the assassin flees and the victims arrive and set out in the car (Fig. 6.160). As the car goes around the corner, the camera circles the block, rejoins the car, and tracks back to follow it (Fig. 6.161).

The car passes Vargas and his wife, Susan, and the camera starts to follow them. The camera loses the car and tracks diagonally backward with the couple as they move through the crowd (Fig. 6.162).

The shot continues as the camera tracks until both the occupants of the car and Susan and Vargas again meet, this time at the border post. A brief scene with the border guard ensues (Figs. 6.163 and 6.164).

After tracking left with the car, the camera again encounters Susan and Vargas (Fig. 6.165) and tracks forward toward them. The shot ends as Susan and Vargas are about to kiss (Fig. 6.166). Their embrace is interrupted by the offscreen sound of an explosion. The couple turns to stare (Fig. 6.167). The next shot shows the car in flames (Fig. 6.168).

This opening shot makes plain most of the features of the long take. It offers an alternative to building the sequence out of many shots, and it stresses the cut that finally comes (the sudden cut on the sound of the explosion to the burning car). Most important, the shot has its own internal pattern of development. We expect that the bomb shown at the beginning will explode at some point, and we wait for that explosion through the duration of the long take. The shot establishes the geography of the scene (the border between Mexico and the United States), and the camera movement, alternately picking up the car and Vargas and Susan, weaves together two separate lines of narrative cause and effect that intersect at the border station. Vargas and Susan are thus drawn into the action involving the bombing. Our expectation is fulfilled when the end of the shot coincides with the explosion (offscreen) of the bomb. The shot has guided our response by taking us through a suspenseful process of narrative development. The long take's ability to present, in a single chunk of time, a complex pattern of events moving toward a goal makes shot duration as important to the image's effect as photographic qualities and framing are.

## SUMMARY

The film shot, then, is a very complex formal unit. Mise-en-scene fills the image with material, arranging setting, lighting, costume, and figure behavior within the formal context of the total film. Within that same formal context, the filmmaker also controls the cinematographic qualities of the shot—how the image is photographed and framed, how long the image lasts on the screen.

You can sensitize yourself to these cinematographic qualities in much the same way that you worked on mise-en-scene. Trace the progress of a single technique—say, camera angle—through an entire film. Become conscious of when a shot begins and ends, observing how the long take may function to shape the film's form. Watch for camera movements, especially those that follow the action (since those are usually the hardest to notice). In short, once we are aware of cinematographic qualities, we can move to an understanding of their various possible functions within the total film.

Yet film art offers still other possibilities for choice and control. Chapters 5 and 6 have focused on the shot. The filmmaker may also juxtapose one shot with another through editing, and that is the subject of Chapter 7.

## NOTES AND QUERIES

### ■ GENERAL WORKS

Carl L. Gregory's *Motion Picture Photography* (New York: New York Institute of Photography, 1920; rev. ed., 1927) is a comprehensive work on silent cinematography techniques. The standard contemporary references are *The American Cine-*

*matographer Manual* (Hollywood: A.S.C., 1966); H. Mario Raimondo Souto, *The Technique of the Motion Picture Camera* (New York: Hastings House, 1967); Russell Campbell, *Photographic Theory for the Motion Picture Cameraman* (New York: Barnes, 1970), and *Practical Motion Picture Photography* (New York: Barnes, 1970); Leslie J. Wheeler, *Principles of Cinematography*, 4th ed. (New York: Morgan & Morgan, 1969); and Joseph V. Mascelli, *The Five C's of Cinematography* (Hollywood: Cine/Grafic, 1965). An excellent introduction to all phases of 8-mm and 16-mm cinematography is David Cheshire, *The Book of Movie Photography* (New York: Knopf, 1979). For historical information, see Brian Coe, *The History of Movie Photography* (London: Ash & Grant, 1981); Leonard Maltin, *The Art of the Cinematographer* (New York: Dover, 1978); and David Bordwell, Janet Staiger, and Kristin Thompson, *The Classical Hollywood Cinema: Film Style and Mode of Production to 1960* (New York: Columbia University Press, 1985). *American Cinematographer* and *The Journal of the Society of Motion Picture and Television Engineers* continually publish articles on the subject. A detailed introduction to lens optics is Sidney Ray's *The Lens in Action* (New York: Hastings House, 1976). Laboratory work is discussed in L. Bernard Happé's *Your Film and the Lab* (New York: Hastings House, 1974). Alternative points of view on cinematography may be found in Stan Brakhage, "A Moving Picture Giving and Taking Book," *Film Culture* 41 (Summer 1976): 39–57; Dziga Vertov, *Kino-Eye: The Writings of Dziga Vertov*, ed. Annette Michelson (Berkeley: University of California Press, 1984); and Maya Deren, "An Anagram of Ideas on Art, Form, and Film," and "Cinematography," in George Amberg, ed., *The Art of Cinema* (New York: Arno, 1972).

## ■ COLOR VERSUS BLACK AND WHITE

Though today most films are shot on color stock and most viewers have come to expect that movies will be in color, color enjoys no absolute superiority over black and white. At many points in film history, each type of film stock has been used to carry different meanings. In 1930s and 1940s American cinema, color tended to be reserved for fantasies (for example, *The Wizard of Oz*), historical films or films set in exotic locales (*Becky Sharp, Blood and Sand*), or very lavish musicals (*Meet Me in St. Louis*). Black and white was then considered more "realistic." But now that most films are in color, filmmakers can call on black and white to suggest a historical period (as witnessed by two such different films as Straub and Huillet's *Chronicle of Anna Magdalena Bach* and Bogdanovich's *Paper Moon*). Such rules of thumb as "color for realism" have no universal validity; as always, it is a matter of context, the function of color or black-and-white tonalities within a specific film.

For more data on the principles of color photography, see Society of Motion Picture and Television Engineers, *Elements of Color in Professional Motion Pictures* (New York: SMPTE, 1957); De Maré, *Color Photography* (Baltimore: Penguin, 1968); Joseph S. Friedman, *The History of Color Photography* (London: Focal Press, 1968); and Andreas Feininger, *Successful Color Photography* (Englewood Cliffs, N.J.: Prentice-Hall, 1969). Color in the cinema has not received as much discussion as it should. A brief but well-illustrated history of color in motion pictures may be found in Roger Manvell, ed., *The International Encyclopedia of Film* (New York: Crown, 1972); this article demonstrates conclusively that radically different color ranges can all be accepted as "realistic." A basic history is R. T. Ryan, *A History of Motion Picture Color Technology* (New York: Focal Press, 1977). The most influential early process is considered in Fred E. Basten's *Glorious Technicolor: The Movies' Magic Rainbow* (San Diego, Calif.: A. S. Barnes, 1980).

See also Edward Branigan, "Color and Cinema: Problems in the Writing of History," *Film Reader* **4** (1979): 16–34. Journals publishing articles on color cinematography include *The Journal of the Society of Motion Picture and Television Engineers* and *American Cinematographer*. Film theorists have debated whether color film is artistically more impure than black and white. One argument against color may be found in Rudolf Arnheim, *Film as Art* (Berkeley: University of California Press, 1967). How is Arnheim's argument disputed by V. F. Perkins in *Film as Film* (Baltimore: Penguin, 1972)?

Filmmakers have discussed the relative advantages and disadvantages of color. Believing that color evokes definite emotions, Rouben Mamoulian claimed that the director must develop "a complete chromatic plan for the film." (See Rouben Mamoulian, "Color and Light in Films," *Film Culture* **21** [Summer 1960]: 68–79.) Carl Dreyer agreed, stressing the necessity for the director to plan the color scheme to flow smoothly, "which creates the effect of persons and objects being in constant motion and causes the colors to glide from one place to another in changing rhythms, creating new and surprising effects when they collide with other colors or melt into them" ("Color Film and Colored Films," *Dreyer in Double Reflection* [New York: Dutton, 1973], pp. 168–173).

For Stan Brakhage, cinema must break down our normal sense of color, as "closed-eye vision" produces purely subjective tonalities: "I am stating my given ability, prize all above pursuing, to transform the light sculptured shapes of an almost dark-blackened room to the rainbow-hued patterns of light without any scientific paraphernalia" (Brakhage, *Metaphors on Vision* [New York: Film Culture, 1963]). The filmmaker who theorized most extensively about color was Sergei Eisenstein. See especially "Color and Meaning," in *The Film Sense* (New York: Harcourt, Brace, 1947), pp. 113–153.

For general discussion of the aesthetics of film color, see: Raymond Durgnat, "Colours and Contrasts," *Films and Filming* **15**, 2 (November 1968): 58–62; and William Johnson, "Coming to Terms with Color," *Film Quarterly* **20**, 1 (Fall 1966): 2–22. Two essays on Jean-Luc Godard exemplify how the analyst can examine a film's color system: Paul Sharits, "Red, Blue, Godard," *Film Quarterly* **19**, 4 (Summer 1966): 24–29; and Edward Branigan, "The Articulation of Color in a Filmic System," *Wide Angle* **1**, 3 (1976): 20–31. The latter contains an excellent bibliography.

## ■ PERSPECTIVE AND THE CINEMA

On the history of perspective in painting, see John White, *The Birth and Rebirth of Pictorial Space* (New York: Harper, 1972); E. H. Gombrich, *Art and Illusion* (Princeton, N.J.: Princeton University Press, 1969); Lee Baxandall, *Painting and Experience in Fifteenth Century Italy* (New York: Oxford University Press, 1972); William Ivins, *On the Rationalization of Sight* (New York: Da Capo, 1973); Lawrence Wright, *Perspective in Perspective* (London: Routledge & Kegan Paul, 1983); Samuel Y. Edgerton, Jr., *The Renaissance Rediscovery of Linear Perspective* (New York: Harper & Row, 1975). Psychological aspects are discussed in Margaret A. Hagen, ed., *The Perception of Pictures*, 2 vols. (New York: Academic Press, 1980). A handy and informative guide is Fred Dubery and John Willats, *Perspective and Other Drawing Systems* (New York: Van Nostrand Reinhold, 1983).

We have already seen how the motion picture camera can transform the filmed scene in ways that manipulate perspective. Today film theorists are asking to what extent the medium of cinema is necessarily bound up with that system of monocular perspective that gave birth to the camera. Some argue that Renaissance perspective issues from a specific social and political conception of the world—an ideology—that makes the world seem neatly objectified for the eye of the independent observer. If this is valid, the cinema may be in similar ways tied to a social and ideological position by the very nature of its machinery.

To analyze this position takes us beyond the scope of an introductory text. Yet since the issue is important to contemporary thinking about cinema, the interested reader can go to several places to find the argument set out in more detail. The crucial sources in English are Jean-Pierre Baudry, "Ideological Effects of the Basic Cinematographic Apparatus," *Film Quarterly* **28**, 2 (Winter 1974–75): 39–47; Daniel Dayan, "The Tutor-Code of Classical Cinema," *Film Quarterly* **28**, 1 (Fall 1974); 22–31; and Stephen Heath, "Narrative Space," in *Questions of Cinema* (Bloomington: Indiana University Press, 1982). See also William C. Wees, "The Cinematic Image as a Visualization of Sight," *Wide Angle* **4**, 3 (1980): 28–37; Noël Carroll, "Address to the Heathen," *October* **23** (Winter 1982): 109–125; Stephen Heath, "Le Père Noël," *October* **26** (Fall 1983): 78–91; Noël Carroll, "A Reply to Heath," *October* **27** (Winter 1983): 97–101; and David Bordwell, *Narration in the Fiction Film* (Madison: University of Wisconsin Press, 1985), chapters 1 and 6.

## ■ SPECIAL EFFECTS

Part of the reason that major film studios tout themselves as "the magic factories" is that special-effects cinematography demands the complexity and expense that only a big firm can support. Special effects—rear projection, matte work, superimposition, and other procedures—require the time, patience, and rehearsal afforded by control over mise-en-scene. It is, then, no surprise that Méliès, the first person to exploit fully the possibilities of studio filmmaking, excelled at special-effects cinematography. Nor is it surprising that when UFA, the gigantic German firm of the 1920s, became the best-equipped film studio in Europe, it invested heavily in new special-effects processes. Similarly, as Hollywood studios grew from the mid-teens on, so did their special-effects departments. Engineers, painters, photographers, and set designers collaborated to contrive fantastic visual novelties. In these "magic factories" most of the history of special effects has been made.

But such firms were not motivated by sheer curiosity. The costs of elaborate back projection and matte work were usually investments. First, expensive as they were, such tricks often saved money in the long run. Instead of building a huge set, one could photograph the actors through a glass with the setting painted on it. Instead of taking cast and crew to the North Pole, one could film them against a back projection. Second, special effects made certain film genres possible. The historical epic—whether set in Rome, Babylon, or Jerusalem—was unthinkable unless special effects were devised to create huge vistas and crowds. The fantasy film, with its panoply of ghosts, flying horses, and invisible or incredibly shrinking people, demanded the perfection of superimposition and matte processes. The science-fiction genre could scarcely exist without a barrage of special effects. Science-fiction films have produced many of the newest special-effects innovations (*Metropolis*'s Schüfftan process, *2001*'s front projection and multiple mattes, *Tron*'s computer-generated settings). For the major studios, the "factory" principle was responsible for the "magic." The major early work on the subject is Raymond Fielding's *The Technique of Special Effects Cinematography* (New York: Hastings House, 1974). See also Harold Schechter and David Everitt, *Film Tricks: Special Effects in the Movies* (New York: Dial, 1980) and Christopher Finch's lavishly illustrated *Special Effects: Creating Movie Magic* (New York: Abbeville, 1984).

Illuminating case studies can be found in Linwood G. Dunn and George E. Turner, eds., *The ASC Treasury of Visual Effects* (Hollywood: American Society of Cinematographers, 1983). Articles on particular films' use of special effects appear regularly in *American Cinematographer* and *Cinefex*.

## ■ ASPECT RATIO

In Jean-Luc Godard's film *Contempt*, the director Fritz Lang (playing himself) laments that "CinemaScope is good only for filming funerals and snakes." *Contempt*, of course, is an anamorphic widescreen film (though it uses the Franscope widescreen system).

The aspect ratio of the film image has been debated since the inception of cinema. The Edison-Lumière ratio (1:1.33) was not generally standardized until 1911, and even after that other ratios were explored. Many cinematographers believed that 1:1.33 was the perfect ratio (perhaps not aware that it harks back to the "golden section" of academic painting). With the large-scale innovation of widescreen cinema in the early 1950s, cries of distress were heard. Most camera operators hated it. Lenses often were not sharp, lighting became more complicated, and as Lee Garmes put it: "We'd look through the camera and be startled at what it was taking in." Yet some directors—Nicholas Ray, Akira Kurosawa, Samuel Fuller, François Truffaut, Jean-Luc Godard—created unusual and fascinating compositions in the widescreen ratio. The systems are surveyed in Robert E. Carr and R. M. Hayes's exhaustive book, *Wide Screen Movies: A History and Filmography of Wide Gauge Filmmaking* (Jefferson, N.C.: McFarland, 1988). The most detailed defense of the aesthetic virtues of the widescreen image remains Charles Barr's "Cinemascope: Before and After," *Film Quarterly* **16**, 4 (Summer 1963): 4–24. To what extent does Barr's argument rest on an assumption that new technological possibilities create new formal and functional possibilities? See *The Velvet Light Trap* **21** (1985) for several articles on the history and aesthetics of widescreen cinema, including an article on Barr's essay and second thoughts by Barr. See Notes and Queries for Chapter 1 (p. 28) for sources on widescreen film on video.

## ■ THE SUBJECTIVE SHOT

In films we sometimes find the camera, through its positioning and movements, inviting us to see events "through the eyes" of a character. Some directors (Howard Hawks, John Ford, Kenji Mizoguchi, Jacques Tati) seldom use the subjective shot, but others (Alfred Hitchcock, Alain Resnais) use it constantly. As Figure 6.94 indicated, Samuel Fuller's *Naked Kiss* starts with shocking subjective shots:

> We open with a direct cut. In that scene, the actors utilized the camera. They held the camera; it was strapped on them. For the first shot, the pimp has the camera strapped on his chest. I say to [Constance] Towers, "Hit the camera!" She hits the camera, the lens. Then I reverse it. I put the camera on her, and she whacks the hell out of him. I thought it was effective. (Quoted in Eric Sherman and Martin Rubin, *The Director's Event* [New York: Signet, 1969], p. 189.)

Historically, filmmakers began experimenting with the "first-person camera" or the "camera as character" quite early. *Grandma's Reading Glass* (1901) features subjective point-of-view shots. Keyholes, binoculars, and other apertures were often used to motivate optical point of view. In 1919 Abel Gance used many subjective shots in *J'accuse*. The 1920s saw many filmmakers taking an interest in subjectivity, seen in such films as Jean Epstein's *Coeur fidèle* (1923) and *La Belle nivernaise* (1923), E. A. Dupont's *Variety* (1925), F. W. Murnau's *The Last Laugh* (1924), with its famous drunken scene, and Abel Gance's *Napoleon* (1928). Some believe that in the 1940s the subjective shot—especially the subjective camera movement— got completely out of hand in Robert Montgomery's *Lady in the Lake* (1946). For almost the entire film the camera represents the vision of the protagonist, Philip Marlowe; we see him only when he glances in mirrors. "Suspenseful! Unusual!" proclaimed the advertising. "YOU accept an invitation to a blonde's apartment! YOU get socked in the jaw by a murder suspect!"

The history of the technique has teased film theorists into speculating about whether the subjective shot evokes identification from the audience. Do we think we *are* Philip Marlowe? Theorists in the silent era thought that we might tend to identify with that character whose position the camera occupies. But recent film theory is reluctant to make this move. *The Lady in the Lake* fails, Albert Laffay claims, because "by pursuing an impossible perceptual assimilation, the film in fact inhibits symbolic identification" (quoted in Christian Metz, "Current Problems in Film Theory," *Screen* **14**, 1/2 [Spring/Summer 1973]: 47). François Truffaut claims that we identify with a character not when we look *with* the character but when the character looks *at us*. "A subjective camera is the negation of subjective cinema. When it replaces a character, one cannot identify oneself with him. The cinema becomes subjective when the actor's gaze meets that of the audience" (in Peter Graham, *The New Wave* [New York: Viking, 1968], p.93). All of these claims remain murky; we need to study more seriously how the subjective shot functions within a film. A start is made in chapter 5 of Edward Branigan's *Point of View in the Cinema: A Theory of Narration and Subjectivity in Classical Film* (New York: Mouton, 1984).

## ■ CAMERA MOVEMENT AND ZOOM

The visual effects of camera movement have been discussed in Raymond Durgnat, "The Restless Camera," *Films and Filming* **15**, 3 (December 1968): 14–18, and David Bordwell, "Camera Movement and Cinematic Space," *Ciné-tracts* **1**, 2 (Summer 1977): 19–26.

A statement of the classical Hollywood cinema's position on camera movement may be found in Herb A. Lightman, "The Fluid Camera," *American Cinematographer* **27**, 3 (March 1946): 82, 102–103: "The intelligent director or cinematographer moves the camera only when the demands of the filmic situation motivate that movement." Compare the Soviet filmmaker Dziga Vertov: "I am kino-eye, I am a mechanical eye. . . . Now and forever, I free myself from human immobility, I am in constant motion" ("Kinoks: A Revolution," in *Kino Eye: The Writings of Dziga Vertov*, cited earlier, p. 17). For a historical treatment, see Jon Gartenberg, "Camera Movement in Edison and Biograph Films, 1900–1907," *Cinema Journal* **19**, 2 (Spring 1980): 1–16.

The Steadicam hand-held process, which uses complex gyroscopes to compensate for any tremble or jitter, has become a favorite way to save money on complex tracking shots. Cinematographer Allen Daviau also used the device in George Miller's episode of *The Twilight Zone* to create the impression of an airplane lurching during a storm. "I said to Garrett [Brown], 'Can you adjust your gyros to make it an unsteady cam?' . . . And I said to John Toll, hand holding his camera, 'Take the darn thing and shake it' " (*Moviemakers at Work*, ed. David Chell [Redmond, Wash.: Microsoft Press, 1987], p. 28).

Since creating frame mobility by means of the zoom lens has become a common shooting technique today, recent discussions have compared zooming (usually unfavorably) with camera movement. See Arthur Graham, "Zoom Lens Techniques," *American Cinematographer* **44**, 1 (January 1963): 28–29; Paul Joannides, "The Aesthetics of the Zoom Lens," *Sight and Sound* **40**, 1 (Winter 1970–71): 40–42; and Stuart M. Kaminsky, "The Use and Abuse of the Zoom Lens," *Filmmakers Newsletter* **5**, 12 (October 1972): 20–23. To what extent do these three authors agree about the "proper" utilization of the zoom? The most thorough historical and aesthetic discussion is John Belton, "The Bionic Eye: Zoom Esthetics," *Cineaste* **9**, 1 (Winter 1980–81): 20–27.

Hitchcock's *Vertigo* innovated the combination of zooming in and tracking out, which has since become a cliché. Discussing his use of this device in *Le Samourai*, Jean-Pierre Melville remarked, "Instead of simply resorting to the now almost classical technique of a track back compensated by a zoom forward, I used the same movement but with stops." (Quoted in Rui Nogueira, ed., *Melville* [New York: Viking, 1971], p. 130.) The effect is not unlike the spasmodic flattening of depth in *Wavelength*. On this latter film, see William C. Wees, "Prophecy, Memory and the Zoom: Michael Snow's *Wavelength* Re-Viewed," *Ciné-tracts* 14/15 (Summer/Fall 1981): 78–83.

## ■ "REAL TIME" AND THE LONG TAKE

When the camera is running, does it record "real time"? If so, what artistic implications follow from that?

It was André Bazin who took the theoretical initiative in viewing cinema as an art which depends on "real time." Like photography, Bazin argued, cinema is a *recording process*. The camera registers, photochemically, the light reflected from the object. Like the still camera, the movie camera records space. But unlike the still camera, the movie camera can also record *time*. "The cinema is objectivity in time. . . . Now, for the first time, the image of things is likewise the image of their duration, change mummified as it were" (*What Is Cinema?* vol. 1 [Berkeley: University of California Press, 1966], pp. 14–15). On this basis, Bazin saw editing as an intrusive interruption of the "natural" continuity of duration. He thus praised long-take directors such as Jean Renoir, Orson Welles, William Wyler, and Roberto Rossellini as artists whose styles respected concrete moment-to-moment life.

Bazin should be praised for calling our attention to the possibilities latent in the long take at a time when other film theorists considered it "theatrical" and "uncinematic." Yet the problem of "real time" in film seems more complicated than Bazin thought. The most productive avenues which Bazin's ideas opened up have involved the analysis of different directorial *styles* rather than analysis of the most "realistic" ways to shoot a scene. That is, analysts no longer tend to ask whether Renoir's long takes are more faithful to reality than Eisenstein's short shots; we ask instead about the shots' different formal functions in each director's films. Incidentally, Eisenstein himself—*before* Bazin—proposed shooting an entire scene from *Crime and Punishment* in one long take. See "Mise-en-shot," in Vladimir Nizhny, *Lessons with Eisenstein* (New York: Hill and Wang, 1969), pp. 93–139. Representative stylistic analyses include V. F. Perkins, "*Rope*," *The Movie Reader* (New York: Praeger, 1972), pp. 35–37; David Thomson, *Movie Man* (New York: Stein and Day, 1967); Brian Henderson, "The Long Take," in *A Critique of Film Theory* (New York: Dutton, 1980); and Barry Salt, "Statistical Style Analysis of Motion Pictures," *Film Quarterly* **28**, 1 (Fall 1974): 13–22.

# THE RELATION
# OF SHOT TO SHOT:
# EDITING

Since the 1920s, when film theorists began to realize what editing can achieve, it has been the most widely discussed film technique. This has not been all to the good, for some writers have mistakenly found in editing the key to good cinema (or even *all* cinema). Yet some films, particularly in the period before 1904, consist of only one shot and hence do not depend on editing at all. Films of various periods contain several shots but do not rely heavily on editing for their stylistic effect. Experimental films sometimes de-emphasize editing by making each shot as long as the amount of film a camera will hold, as with Michael Snow's *La Région centrale* and Andy Warhol's *Eat*, *Sleep*, and *Empire*. Such films are not necessarily less "cinematic" than others that rely heavily on editing.

Still, one can see why editing has exercised such an enormous fascination for film aestheticians, for as a technique it is very powerful. The ride of the Klan in *The Birth of a Nation*, the Odessa Steps sequence in *Potemkin*, the "degradation of the gods" episode in *October*, the shower murder in *Psycho*, the train crash in *La Roue*, the diving sequence of *Olympia*, the "News on the March" segment of *Citizen Kane*—all of these celebrated moments derive much of their effect from editing. Perhaps more important, however, is the power of editing to dominate an entire film's stylistic system, becoming a key to the film's overall construction and effect. If editing is not the most important film technique, it contributes considerably to the form and effect of a film.

Fig. 7.1

Fig. 7.2

Fig. 7.3

Fig. 7.4

# WHAT EDITING IS

Editing may be thought of as the coordination of one shot with the next. We need to distinguish how editing is done in production from how editing appears on the screen to viewers. As we have seen, in film production a shot is one or more frames in series on a continuous length of film stock. The film editor joins shots, the end of one to the beginning of another.

This junction may be made in several ways. A **fade-out** may gradually darken the end of shot A to black, and a **fade-in** may accordingly lighten shot B from black. A **dissolve** may briefly superimpose the end of shot A and the beginning of shot B, as at the beginning of *The Maltese Falcon* (Figs. 7.1–7.3). In a **wipe,** one image replaces another as a moving boundary line crosses the screen, as in *Seven Samurai* (Fig. 7.4). Here both images are briefly on the screen at the same time, but they do not blend, as in a dissolve. The most common means of joining two shots, however, is the **cut,** which in film production is usually made by splicing two shots together by means of cement or tape. Some filmmakers "cut" during shooting by planning or trusting that the film will emerge from the camera ready for final showing; in such cases the physical junction from shot to shot is accomplished in the act of filmmaking. Such "editing in the camera," however, is rare; cutting after shooting is the norm.

As viewers, we perceive a shot as an uninterrupted segment of screen time, space, or graphic configurations. Fades, dissolves, and wipes are perceived as

Fig. 7.5

Fig. 7.6

Fig. 7.7

Fig. 7.8

*gradually* interrupting one shot and replacing it with another. Cuts are perceived as *instantaneous* changes from one shot to another. Consider an example of cutting, four shots from the first attack on Bodega Bay in Alfred Hitchcock's film *The Birds* (see Figs. 7.5 through 7.8):

1. *Medium shot, straight-on angle.* Melanie, Mitch, and the Captain standing by the restaurant window talking. Melanie on extreme right, bartender in background (Fig. 7.5).
2. *Medium close-up.* Melanie looking to screen left by Captain's shoulder. She looks to right (out offscreen window) up, as if following with eyes. Pan right with her as she turns to the window and looks out (Fig. 7.6).
3. *Extreme long shot.* Melanie's point of view. Gas station across street, phone booth in left foreground. Birds dive-bomb attendant, right to left (Fig. 7.7).
4. *Medium close-up.* Melanie, profile. Captain moves right into shot, blocking out bartender; Mitch moves right into extreme foreground. All in profile look out window (Fig. 7.8).

Each of these four shots presents a different segment of time, space, and graphic materials. The first shot shows three people talking. An instantaneous change—a **cut**—shifts us to a medium close-up shot of Melanie. (Hitchcock could have utilized a fade, dissolve, or wipe instead, with a slower change from shot to shot, or he could have handled the scene as one continuous shot, as we shall see presently.) In the second shot, space has changed (Melanie is isolated and larger in the frame), time is continuous, and the graphic configurations have changed (the arrangements of the shapes and colors vary). Another cut takes us instantly to what she sees. The gas station shot (Fig. 7.7) presents a very different space, a successive bit of time, and a different graphic configuration. Another cut returns us to Melanie (Fig. 7.8), and again we are shifted instantly to another space, the next slice of time, and a different graphic configuration. Thus the four shots are joined by three cuts.

Now let us consider alternative ways of presenting the *Birds* scene without editing. Imagine a camera movement that frames the four people talking, tracks in to Melanie as she turns, pans to the window to show the dive-bombing gull, and pans back to catch Melanie's expression. This would constitute one shot, for we would not have the disjunctions afforded by editing; the camera movements, no matter how fast, would not present the marked and abrupt shifts that cuts produce. Now imagine a deep-space composition that presents Mitch in the foreground, Melanie and the window in the middle ground, and the gull attack in the distance. Again, the scene could now be played in one shot, for we would have no abrupt change of time or space of graphics; the movements of the figures would not yield that disjunction of the screen material that is provided by editing. In this sequence, then, Hitchcock could have presented the action in a single shot (e.g., through a camera movement or a deep-space composition). Instead, he presents it in *more* than one shot—that is, through editing.

Once you become aware of editing, it is easy to notice, not only because it is such a prevalent technique but also because the disjunctions of space, time, and graphics wrought by editing leap to the attentive eye. Both the instantaneous disjunction of the cut and the more gradual disjunction of the fade, dissolve, or wipe usually mark off shots quite plainly.

## DIMENSIONS OF FILM EDITING

What is the scope of this technique? Editing offers the filmmaker four basic areas of choice and control:

1. Graphic relations between shot A and shot B
2. Rhythmic relations between shot A and shot B
3. Spatial relations between shot A and shot B
4. Temporal relations between shot A and shot B

Graphic and rhythmic relationships are present in the editing of any film. Spatial and temporal relationships are usually absent in the editing of abstract and many associative films but are present in the editing of films built out of nonabstract images (that is, the great majority of motion pictures). Let us trace the range of choice and control in each area. In each case the discussion will apply to all means of joining shots, but most of our examples will be drawn from the most common editing technique—cutting.

### ■ GRAPHIC RELATIONS BETWEEN SHOT A AND SHOT B

The four shots from *The Birds* may be considered purely as graphic configurations, as patterns of light and dark, line and shape, volumes and depths, movement and stasis—*independent of* the shot's relation to the time and space of the story. For instance, Hitchcock has not drastically altered the overall brightness from shot to shot. But he could have cut from the uniformly lit second shot (Fig. 7.6, Melanie turning to the window) to a shot of the gas station swathed in darkness. Moreover, Hitchcock has usually kept the most important part of the composition in the center of the frame (compare Melanie's position in the frame with that of the gas station in Fig. 7.7). He could, however, have cut from a shot in which Melanie was in, say, upper frame left to a shot locating the gas station in the lower right of the frame.

Hitchcock has also played off certain color differences. Melanie's hair and outfit make her a predominantly yellow and green figure, whereas the shot of the gas station is dominated by drab bluish grays set off by touches of red in the gas pumps. Alternatively, Hitchcock could have cut from Melanie to another figure composed of similar colors. Furthermore, the movement in Melanie's shot—her turning to the window—does not blend into the movements of either the attendant or the gull in the next shot, but Hitchcock could have echoed Melanie's movement in speed, direction, or frame placement by movement in the next shot. In short, editing together any two shots permits the interaction, through similarity and difference, of the *purely pictorial* qualities of those two shots. The four aspects of mise-en-scene (lighting, setting, costume, and the behavior of the figures in space and time) and most cinematographic qualities (photography, framing, and camera mobility) all furnish potential graphic elements. Thus every shot provides possibilities for purely graphic editing, and every cut creates some sort of graphic relationship between two shots.

Though abstract films depend heavily on the graphic dimension of editing, most filmmaking has subordinated it to other areas of control. Yet at one level we perceive all film images as configurations of graphic material, and every film manipulates those configurations. Indeed, even in a film that is not pure abstraction, graphic editing can be a source of profound interest to filmmaker and audience.

Graphics may be edited to achieve smooth continuity or abrupt contrast. The filmmaker may link shots by graphic similarities, thus making what we can call a **graphic match.** Shapes, colors, tones of light or dark, or the direction or speed of movement in shot A may be picked up in the composition of shot B. For example, in *Seven Samurai*, after the samurai have first arrived at the village, an alarm sounds and they race to discover its source. The director, Akira Kurosawa, cuts together six shots of different running samurai, which he dynamically "matches" by means of composition, lighting, figure movement, and panning camera movement (Figs. 7.9–7.14). In the "Beautiful Girl" song in Stanley Donen and Gene Kelly's *Singin' in the Rain* amusing graphic matches are achieved through dissolves from one fashionably dressed woman to another, each figure posed and framed quite similarly from shot to shot. Such precise graphic matching is, of course, relatively rare, but a general graphic continuity from shot A to shot B (keeping the center of interest at frame center, retaining the overall lighting level, avoiding strong color clashes from shot to shot) is typical of the classical narrative cinema.

Yet shots need *not* be graphically continuous, if the filmmaker so chooses. Orson Welles frequently strives for a clash from shot to shot, as in *Citizen Kane* when the dark long shot of Kane's bedroom is followed by the bright opening title of the "News on the March" reel. Similarly, in *Touch of Evil*, Welles dissolves from a shot of Menzies looking out a window on frame right (Fig. 7.15) to a shot of Susan Vargas looking out a different window on frame left (Fig. 7.16); the clash is further accentuated by contrasting screen positions of the window reflections. Alain Resnais's *Night and Fog* began something of a fad by utilizing an extreme but apt

Fig. 7.9

Fig. 7.10

Fig. 7.11

Fig. 7.12

Fig. 7.13

Fig. 7.14

Fig. 7.15

Fig. 7.16

graphic conflict: color footage of an abandoned concentration camp is cut together with black-and-white newsreel shots of the camps in the period 1942–45. (Even here, though, Resnais found striking graphic similarities in shape, as when a tracking shot of fence posts graphically matches a low-angle shot of marching Nazi legs.)

Later in the sequence from *The Birds* that was discussed above, Hitchcock puts graphic conflict to good use. Gasoline spurting from the pump has flowed across the street to a parking lot, and Melanie, along with several other people at the restaurant window, has seen a man accidentally set the gasoline alight. His car ignites, and an explosion of flame engulfs him. What we see next is Melanie watching helplessly as the flame races along the trail of gas toward the station. Hitchcock cuts the shots as shown in Figures 7.17–7.27:

| | | | |
|---|---|---|---|
| 30. | (ls) | High angle. Melanie's POV. Flaming car, spreading flames. | 73 frames |
| 31. | (mcu) | Straight-on angle. Melanie, immobile, looking off left, mouth open. | 20 frames |
| 32. | (ms) | High angle. Melanie's POV. Pan with flames moving from lower right to upper left of trail of gasoline. | 18 frames |
| 33. | (mcu) | as 31. Melanie, immobile, staring down (center). | 16 frames |
| 34. | (ms) | High angle. Melanie's POV. Pan with flames moving from lower right to upper left. | 14 frames |
| 35. | (mcu) | as 31. Melanie, immobile, looking off right, staring, aghast. | 12 frames |
| 36. | (ls) | Melanie's POV. Gas station. Flames rush in from right. Mitch, sheriff, and attendant run out left. | 10 frames |
| 37. | (mcu) | as 31. Melanie, immobile, stares off extreme right. | 8 frames |
| 38. | (ls) | as 36. Melanie's POV. Cars at station explode. | 34 frames |
| 39. | (mcu) | as 31. Melanie covers her face with her hands. | 33 frames |
| 40. | (els) | Extreme high angle on city, flaming trail in center. Gulls fly into shot. | |

In graphic terms, Hitchcock has exploited two possibilities of contrast. First, although each shot's composition centers the action (Melanie's head, the flaming trail), the movements thrust in different directions. In shot 31 Melanie looks to the lower left, whereas in shot 32 the fire moves to the upper left. In shot 33 Melanie is looking down center, whereas in the next shot the flames still move to the upper left; and so on. More important—and what makes the sequence impossible to recapture on the printed page—is the crucial contrast of mobility and stasis. The shots of the flames present movement of both subject (the flames rushing along the gas) and of the camera (which pans to follow). But the shots of Melanie could almost be "stills," since they are absolutely static; she does not turn her head within the shots, and the camera does not move in or away from her. Interestingly too, instead of showing her turning to watch the flames, Hitchcock presents only static stages of her action, and so we must infer the progress of her attention. Such clashes of one direction with another and of movement with stasis constitute very powerful means of utilizing the graphic possibilities of editing. We shall examine some other means later.

## ■ RHYTHMIC RELATIONS BETWEEN SHOT A AND SHOT B

Each strip of film—each shot—is necessarily of a certain length. That length can be determined by the filmmaker. When we consider the absolute lengths of shot A and shot B, measured in frames, feet, or meters, we are considering the most basic *rhythmic* potential of editing. The physical length of any shot corresponds to a measurable duration onscreen. As we know, at "sound speed" 24 frames last one second in projection. A shot can be as short as a frame, or it may be thousands of frames long, running for many minutes when projected. Editing thus opens the possibility of controlling the rhythmic succession of shots by adjusting their *screen duration*. The filmmaker may construct a steady rhythm by making all of the shots

Fig. 7.17    Shot 30

Fig. 7.18    Shot 31

Fig. 7.19    Shot 32

Fig. 7.20    Shot 33

Fig. 7.21    Shot 34

Fig. 7.22    Shot 35

Fig. 7.23    Shot 36

Fig. 7.24    Shot 37

Fig. 7.25    Shot 38

Fig. 7.26    Shot 39

Fig. 7.27    Shot 40

approximately the same length. An accelerating rhythm may arise from successively shorter shots; a spasmodic, irregular rhythm may be produced by a combination of shots of widely different lengths. Now these cases are somewhat oversimplified, since cinematic rhythm as a whole derives from not only editing but other film techniques as well. The filmmaker also relies on mise-en-scene, camera position and movement, and the overall context to determine the editing rhythm. Nevertheless, the lengths of the successive shots contribute considerably to what we intuitively recognize as a film's tempo or "pace."

Consider how Hitchcock handles the rhythm of the first gull attack in *The Birds*. Shot 1, the medium shot of the group talking (Fig. 7.5), consumes 996 frames, or about 41 seconds. But shot 2 (Fig. 7.6), which shows Melanie looking, is much shorter—309 frames (almost 13 seconds). Even shorter is shot 3 (Fig. 7.7), which is only 55 frames (about 2⅓ seconds). The fourth shot (Fig. 7.8)—of Melanie joined by Mitch and the Captain—lasts only 35 frames (about 1½ seconds). Clearly Hitchcock is accelerating the rhythm at the beginning of what will be a tense sequence. In what follows, Hitchcock makes the shots fairly short, but subordinates the length of the shot to the internal rhythm of the dialogue and the movement in the images. As a result, shots 5 through 29 (not illustrated here) have no fixed pattern of lengths. But once the essential components of the scene have been established, Hitchcock again emphasizes editing rhythm, as can be seen in shots 30 through 40 (Figs. 7.17 through 7.27). In presenting Melanie's horrified realization of the flames racing from the parking lot to the gas station, this series of shots climaxes the rhythmic acceleration of the sequence. As the description on p. 212 shows, after the shot of the spreading flames (no. 30, Fig. 7.17), each shot decreases in length by two frames, from 20 frames (⅘ of a second) to 8 frames (⅓ of a second). Two shots, 38 and 39, then punctuate the sequence with almost identical durations (a little less than 1½ seconds). Shot 40 (Fig. 7.27), a long shot that lasts over 600 frames, functions as both a pause and a suspenseful preparation for the next savage bird attack. In this scene variations in rhythm lead us to expect changes in narrative action.

What is the point of all these numbers? The theater viewer cannot, of course, count frames, but does *feel* and *recognize* the accelerating cutting in this sequence. In general, by controlling editing rhythm, the filmmaker controls the amount of time we have to grasp and reflect on what we see. Rhythmic editing can thus be a source of surprise (as through an unexpected series of rapid shots) or of suspense (as when several short shots prolong the expectations by reiterating information we already have). In the *Birds* sequence, Hitchcock's editing impels the viewer's perception to move at a faster and faster pace. The necessity of quickly inferring the progress of the fire and Melanie's changes in position becomes an essential factor in the rising excitement of the scene.

Hitchcock is not, of course, the only director to utilize rhythmic editing. Such possibilities were initially explored before 1923 by such directors as D. W. Griffith (especially in *Intolerance*) and Abel Gance. In the 1920s the Hollywood cinema, the Soviet montage school, and the French "impressionist" filmmakers explored the rhythmic possibilities of series of short shots. When sound films became the standard, pronounced rhythmic editing survived not only in musical comedies and fantasies such as René Clair's *A Nous la liberté* and *Le Million*, Rouben Mamoulian's *Love Me Tonight*, and Busby Berkeley's dance sequences in *42nd Street* and *Footlight Parade* but also in dramatic films such as Lewis Milestone's *All Quiet on the Western Front*. In classical Hollywood cinema the rhythmic use of dissolves became crucial to the "montage sequence," which we shall discuss shortly. To this day, rhythm is recognized as a fundamental resource of the editor, as witness not only the vogue of fast cutting in the 1960s (for example, Richard Lester's films starring the Beatles) but also the ubiquitous television soft drink commercials and music videos cut to the beat of a song.

## ■ SPATIAL RELATIONS BETWEEN SHOT A AND SHOT B

Editing usually serves not only to control graphics and rhythm but to construct film space as well. Exhilaration in this newly discovered power can be sensed in the writings of such filmmakers as the Soviet director Dziga Vertov: "I am Kino-eye. I am builder. I have placed you . . . in an extraordinary room which did not exist until just now when I also created it. In this room there are twelve walls, shot by me in various parts of the world. In bringing together shots of walls and details, I've managed to arrange them in an order that is pleasing" (Annette Michelson, ed., *Kino-Eye: The Writings of Dziga Vertov* [Berkeley: University of California Press, 1984], p. 17). Such elation is understandable. Editing lets an omiscient range of knowledge become visible as omnipresence, the ability to move from one spot to any other. Editing permits the filmmaker to relate *any* two points in space through similarity, difference, or development.

One may, for instance, start with a shot that establishes a spatial whole and follow this with a shot of a part of this space. This is what Hitchcock does in shot 1 and shot 2 of the *Birds* sequence described above (Figs. 7.5–7.6): a medium long shot of the group of people followed by a medium shot of only one, Melanie. Such analytical breakdown is a very common editing pattern, especially in classical continuity editing.

One may, alternatively, construct a whole space out of component parts, as Hitchcock also does in later shots of the *Birds* sequence. Note that in shots 30–39 (Figs. 7.17–7.26) we do not see a single establishing shot including Melanie *and* the gas station. In production the restaurant window need not have been across from the station at all; they could have been filmed in different cities or countries. (It is likely that, shooting "out of continuity," Hitchcock filmed the restaurant shots on a sound stage and the gas station shots in an outdoor set.) Yet we are compelled to "see" Melanie as being across the street from the gas station. The bird cry offscreen and the mise-en-scene (the window and Melanie's sideways glance) contribute considerably, but it is primarily the editing that creates the spatial whole of restaurant-and-gas-station.

Such spatial manipulation through cutting is fairly common. In films compiled from newsreel footage, for example, one shot might show a cannon firing, and another shot might show a shell hitting its target; we infer that the cannon fired the shell (though the shots may show entirely different battles). Again, if a shot of a speaker is followed by a shot of a cheering crowd, we assume a spatial coexistence. The possibility of such spatial manipulation was examined by the Soviet filmmaker Lev Kuleshov, who is said to have come up with a series of "experiments" in constructing spatial relations by eliminating establishing shots. The most famous of these involved the cutting of neutral shots of an actor's face with other shots (variously reported as shots of soup, nature scenes, a dead woman, a baby). The result was that the audience immediately assumed not only that the actor's expression changed but also that the actor was reacting to things present in the same space as himself. Similarly, Kuleshov cut together shots of actors, "looking at each other" but on Moscow streets miles apart, then meeting and strolling together— and looking at the White House in Washington. Though films' use of such cutting predates Kuleshov's work, his careful study of this possibility has caused film scholars to call "the Kuleshov effect" any series of shots that *in the absence of an establishing shot* creates a spatial whole by joining disparate spatial fragments. Carl Reiner's *Dead Men Don't Wear Plaid* is a recent example of a film relying on the Kuleshov effect, since it cuts together shots taken in the present with footage from films of the 1940s.

In contrast to such types of editing that build up a single locale, editing can also juxtapose two or more distinctly separate locales. In *Intolerance* D. W. Griffith cuts from ancient Babylon to Gethsemane, from France in 1572 to America in 1916. Such parallel editing, or **crosscutting,** is a common way films construct heterogeneous spaces.

More radically, the editing can present spatial relations as being ambiguous and uncertain. In Carl Dreyer's *La Passion de Jeanne d'Arc*, for instance, we know only that Jeanne and the priests are in the same room; because the neutral white backgrounds and the numerous close-ups provide no orientation to the entire space, we can seldom tell how far apart the characters are or precisely who is beside whom. We shall see later how *October* and *Last Year at Marienbad* create similar spatial discontinuities.

## ■ TEMPORAL RELATIONS BETWEEN SHOT A AND SHOT B

Like other film techniques, editing can control the time of the action denoted in the film. In a narrative film especially, editing usually contributes to the plot's manipulation of story time. You will recall that Chapter 3 pointed out three areas in which plot time can cue the spectator to construct the story time: order, duration, and frequency. Our *Birds* example (Figs. 7.5–7.8) shows how editing reinforces all three areas of control.

First, there is the *order* of presentation of events. The men talk, then Melanie turns away, then she sees the gull swoop, then she responds. Hitchcock's editing presents these story events in the 1-2-3-4 order of his shots. But he could have shuffled the shots into a different order: transposing shot 2 and shot 3 would be least unusual, but it is possible to put them in any order at all, even reverse (4-3-2-1). This is to say that the filmmaker may control temporal succession through the editing.

As we saw in Chapter 3, such manipulation of events leads to changes in story-plot relations. We are most familiar with such manipulations in *flashbacks*, which present one or more shots out of their presumed story order. In *Hiroshima mon amour*, for instance, Resnais cuts from a shot of the hand of the protagonist's Japanese lover to a shot of the hand of her German lover years earlier (with memory motivating the violation of temporal order). The rarer *flashforward* also breaks the presumed order of story events, by juxtaposing a shot of the "present" with a shot of a future event before returning to the present (as in the foreshadowings of death in *Don't Look Now* and *Love Affair, or the Case of the Missing Switchboard Operator*). Such edited manipulations of temporal order can become very complex, as in Straub's *Not Reconciled* and Resnais's *Last Year at Marienbad*, which interweave several different time schemes. We may assume, then, that if a series of shots traces a 1-2-3 order in the presentation of story events, it is because the filmmaker has chosen to do that, not because of any necessity of following this order.

Editing also offers ways for the filmmaker to alter the "natural" *duration* of story events as presented in the film's plot. In our sample sequence, it is true, the duration of the story events is presented whole: Melanie's act of turning consumes a certain length of time, and Hitchcock does not alter the duration of the event in his editing. Nevertheless, he could have omitted any or all of the duration of the event. Imagine cutting from shot 1 (the men talking and Melanie standing by) to a shot of Melanie already turned and looking out the window. The time it took her to turn to the window would be eliminated by the cut. Thus editing can create a temporal **ellipsis.**

**Elliptical editing** presents an action in such a way that it consumes less time on the screen than it does in the story. The filmmaker can create an ellipsis in three principal ways. Suppose that a director wants to show a man climbing a flight of stairs, but does not want to show the entire duration of his climb. Most simply, the director could use a conventional *"punctuation"* shot change, such as a dissolve or a wipe or a fade; in the classical filmmaking tradition, such a device signals that some time has been omitted. In our example, the director could simply dissolve from a shot of the man starting at the bottom to a shot of him reaching the top. Alternatively, the filmmaker could show the man at the bottom of the staircase and let him walk up out of the frame, hold briefly on the empty frame, then cut to an empty frame of the top of the stairs and let the man enter the frame. The *empty frames* on either side of the cut cover the elided time. Finally, the filmmaker can create an ellipsis by means of a *cutaway:* a shot of another event elsewhere that will not last as long as the elided action. In our example, the director might start with the man climbing but then cut away to a woman in her apartment. We could then cut back to the man, much further along in his ascent.

In our *Birds* example, Hitchcock could also have altered the duration of the action in yet another way—by *expansion*. For example, he might have extended shot 1 so as to include the beginning of Melanie's act of turning, then shown her beginning to turn in shot 2 as well. This would have prolonged the action, stretching it out past its story duration. The Russian filmmakers of the 1920s made frequent use of temporal expansion through such **overlapping editing**, and no one mastered it more thoroughly than Sergei Eisenstein. In *Strike*, when factory workers bowl over a foreman with a large wheel hanging from a crane, three shots expand the action. In *October* Eisenstein overlaps several shots of rising bridges in order to stress the significance of the moment. In *Ivan the Terrible* friends pour golden coins down on the newly crowned Ivan in a torrent that seems never to cease. In all of these sequences the duration of the action is prolonged through noticeably overlapping the movements from shot to shot.

Returning once more to the temporal relations in the *Birds* segment, we note that in the story Melanie turns to the window only once and the gull swoops only once. And Hitchcock presents these events on the screen the same number of times that they occur in the story. But, of course, Hitchcock could have repeated any of these shots. Melanie could have been shown turning to the window several times; this would be not merely overlapping a phase of an action but rather full-scale repetition. If this sounds peculiar, it is doubtless because we are overwhelmingly accustomed to seeing a shot present the action only once. Yet its very rarity may make repetition a powerful editing resource. In Bruce Conner's *Report* there is a newsreel shot of John and Jacqueline Kennedy riding a limousine down a Dallas street; the shot is systematically repeated, in part or in whole, again and again, building up tension in our expectations as the shot seems to move by tiny increments closer to the moment of the inevitable assassination. We shall see a similar strategy of repetition at work in segments of *Last Year at Marienbad*. Thus *frequency* is another area of choice and control that, like order and duration, gives the filmmaker considerable temporal possibilities in editing.

Graphics, rhythm, space, and time, then, are at the service of the filmmaker through the technique of editing. Our brief survey should suggest that the potential range of these areas of control is virtually unlimited. Yet most films we see make use of a very narrow set of editing possibilities—so narrow, indeed, that we can speak of a dominant editing style throughout Western film history. This is what is usually called **continuity editing,** and because of its prevalence we will examine it. But the most familiar way to edit a film is not the only way to edit a film, and so we will also consider some alternatives to continuity editing.

## CONTINUITY EDITING

Editing might appear to present a dilemma to the filmmaker. On one hand, the physical break between one shot and another may seem to have a disturbing effect, interrupting the viewer's flow of attention. But on the other hand, editing is undeniably a primary means for constructing a film. How can one use editing and yet control its potentially disruptive force? This problem (though not stated in these terms) first confronted filmmakers around 1900–10. The solution eventually adopted was to plan the cinematography and mise-en-scene with a view to editing the shots according to a specific system. The purpose of the system was *to tell a story* coherently and clearly, to map out the chain of characters' actions in an undistracting way. Thus editing, supported by specific strategies of cinematography and mise-en-scene, was used to ensure *narrative continuity.* So powerful is this style that, even today, a director or editor in narrative filmmaking is expected to be thoroughly familiar with it. How does this stylistic system work?

The basic purpose of the continuity system is to control the potentially disunifying force of editing by establishing a smooth flow from shot to shot. All of the possibilities of editing we have already examined are bent to this end. First, graphics are kept roughly similar from shot to shot. The figures are balanced and symmetrically deployed in the frame; the overall lighting tonality remains constant; the action occupies the central zone of the screen. Second, the rhythm of the cutting is usually made dependent on the camera distance of the shot: long shots are left on the screen longer than medium shots, and medium shots are left on longer than close-ups. (Sometimes, in scenes of physical action like the fire in *The Birds,* markedly accelerated editing rhythms may be present, regardless of the shot scale.) Since the continuity style seeks to present a narrative action, however, it is chiefly through the handling of space and time that editing furthers narrative continuity.

### ■ SPATIAL CONTINUITY: THE 180° SYSTEM

In the continuity style the space of a scene is constructed along what is called variously the **"axis of action,"** the "center line, " or the "180° line." The scene's action—a person walking, two people conversing, a car racing along a road—is assumed to project along a discernible, predictable line. Consequently, the filmmaker will plan, film, and edit the shots to establish this center line as clearly as possible. The camera work and mise-en-scene in each shot will be manipulated to establish and reiterate the 180° space. A bird's-eye view (Fig. 7.28) will clarify the system.

This bird's-eye view shows A and B conversing. The axis of action is that imaginary line connecting the two people. Under the continuity system, the director

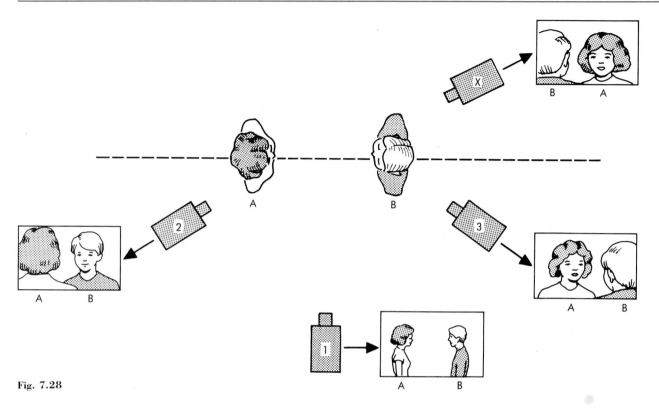

Fig. 7.28

would arrange the mise-en-scene and camera placement so as to establish and sustain this line. The camera can be put at any point as long as it stays on the same *side* of the line (hence the 180° term). A typical series of shots would be: (1) a medium shot of A and B; (2) a shot over A's shoulder, "favoring" B; (3) a shot over B's shoulder, favoring A. But to cut to a shot from camera position "X" would be considered a violation of the system because it *crosses* the axis of action. Indeed, one handbook on film directing calls shot X flatly "wrong." To see why, we need to examine what this 180° system does.

*It ensures some common space from shot to shot.* As long as the axis of action is not crossed, portions of the space will tally from shot to shot. In our example, assume that there is a wall with pictures and shelves behind A and B. If we follow shot 1 with shot 2, not only will one side of B reappear as a common factor but so will at least part of the wall, the pictures, and shelves. We are thus oriented to the space presented in shot 2: it is simply part of the space of shot 1, observed from a new position. But if we follow shot 1 with shot X, we see both a new side of B and an entirely different background (another wall, a door, or whatever). A defender of traditional continuity would claim that this disorients us; has B moved to another locale? Thus the 180° rule generates a common area from shot to shot, which stabilizes space and orients the viewer within the scene.

*It ensures constant screen direction.* Assume now that A is walking left to right; A's path constitutes the axis of action. As long as our shots do not cross this axis, cutting them together will keep the screen direction of A's movement constant, from left to right. But if we *cross* the axis and film a shot from the other side, not only will the background change but also A will now appear on the screen as moving from *right to left.* Such a cut could be disorienting.

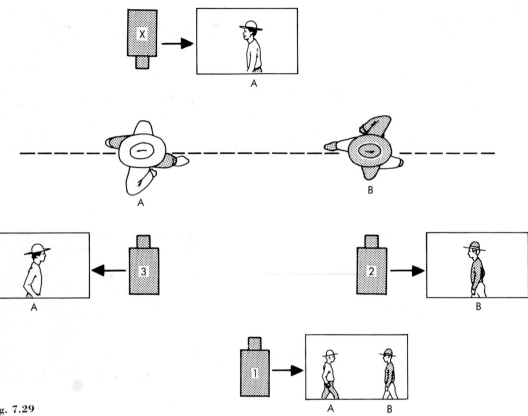

Fig. 7.29

Consider a similar situation to that in Figure 7.28, a standard scene of two cowboys meeting for a shootout on a town street (Fig. 7.29). A and B again form the 180° line, but here A is walking from left to right and B is approaching from right to left, both seen in the shot taken from camera position one. A closer view, from camera position two, shows B still moving from right to left. A third shot, from camera position three, shows A walking, as he had been in the first shot, from left to right. But imagine that this third shot was instead taken from position X, on the opposite side of the line. He is now seen as moving from right to left. Has he taken fright and turned around while the second shot, of B, was on the screen? The filmmakers may intend that we understand that he is still walking toward his adversary, but it could be difficult for us to figure this out. Such breaks in continuity can be confusing. Even more disorienting would be crossing the line while establishing the same shootout situation. If the first shot shows A walking from left to right and the second shot shows B (from the other side of the line) also walking left to right, we would probably not be able to tell whether they were walking toward each other. The two cowboys would seem to us to be walking in the same direction at different points on the street, as if one were following the other. We would very likely be startled if they suddenly came face to face within the same shot. Though we shall examine some stratagems for getting "across the line," it is enough for now to see that adhering to the 180° system ensures consistent screen direction from shot to shot. (We shall see in our examination of *Stagecoach* in Part IV that not all violations of screen direction are necessarily confusing.)

**Fig. 7.30    Shot 1a**

**Fig. 7.31    Shot 1b**

**Fig. 7.32    Shot 2**

It should be obvious that the 180° system prides itself on delineating space clearly. The viewer always knows where the *characters* are in relation to one another and to the setting. More important, the viewer always knows *where he or she is* with respect to the story action. The space of the scene, clearly and unambiguously unfolded, does not jar or disorient, because such disorientation, it is felt, will distract the viewer from the material at hand: the narrative chain of causes and effects. We saw in Chapter 3 that the classical Hollywood mode of narrative subordinates time, motivation, and other factors to the cause-effect sequence. We also saw how mise-en-scene and camera position and movement may function to present narrative material. Now we can note how continuity editing also works to subordinate space to causality. On the basis of the 180° principle, the continuity system has developed a repertory of tactics for building a smoothly flowing space subordinate to the narrative. Let us consider a concrete example, the opening of John Huston's film *The Maltese Falcon*.

**Fig. 7.33    Shot 3**

The action begins in the office of Sam Spade. Note that in the first two shots this space is established in several ways. First, there is the office window (shot 1a, Fig. 7.30) from which the camera tilts down to reveal Spade (shot 1b, Fig. 7.31) rolling a cigarette. As Spade says, "Yes, sweetheart?" shot 2 (Fig. 7.32) appears. This is important in several respects. It is what would be called an **establishing shot,** delineating the overall space of the office: the door, the intervening area, the desk, and Spade's position. Note also that shot 2 establishes a 180° line between Spade and his secretary, Effie; Effie could be A in Figure 7.28, and Spade could be B. In this scene, we will always be on the same side of this 180° line.

Once laid out for us in the first two shots, the space is analyzed into its components. Shots 3 (Fig. 7.33) and 4 (Fig. 7.34) show Spade and Effie talking. Because the 180° line established at the outset is adhered to (each shot presents the two from the same side), we know their location and spatial relationships. In cutting to medium shots of the two, however, Huston relies on two other common tactics within the 180° system. The first is the **shot/reverse shot**. Once the 180° line has been established, we can show first one end point of the line, then the other, cutting back and forth (here from Effie to Spade). A reverse shot is not literally the "reverse" of the first framing; it is simply a shot of the opposite end of the axis of action. In our bird's-eye-view diagram (Fig. 7.28), shots 2 and 3 form a shot/reverse-shot pattern, just as Figures 7.33 and 7.34 do here.

**Fig. 7.34    Shot 4**

The second tactic Huston uses here is the **eyeline match**. That is, shot A presents someone looking at something offscreen; shot B shows us what is being looked at. In neither shot are *both* looker and object present. (The shots from *The*

Fig. 7.35   Shot 5a                                    Fig. 7.36   Shot 5b

*Birds* of Melanie watching the bird attack and the fire also create eyeline matches.) This is a simple idea but a powerful one, since the *directional* quality of the eyeline creates a strong spatial continuity. To be looked at, an object must be near the looker. (The eyeline match presumably created the effects Kuleshov identified in his construction of false spaces through editing. That is, the expressionless actor seems to be looking at whatever is in the next shot, and the audience assumes that the actor is reacting accordingly.)

Within the 180° system, the eyeline match, like constant screen direction, can stabilize space. Note how in shot 3, Effie's glance off right reiterates Spade's position even though he is not onscreen. And though Spade does not look up and create another eyeline match in shot 4, the camera position remains adamantly on the same side of the axis of action (indeed, the position is virtually identical to that in shot 1b). Thus the breakdown of the scene's space is completely consistent, this consistency ensured by adherence to the 180° system. Thanks to the shot/reverse-shot pattern and the eyeline match, even though the two characters are not in the same frame, we are always certain of their whereabouts.

Such spatial clarity is reaffirmed in shot 5, which presents the same space as in shot 2. The office is thus shown again (shot 5a, Fig. 7.35), when the new character, Brigid O'Shaughnessy, enters (shot 5b, Fig. 7.36). Shot 5 is what is called a **reestablishing shot,** since it reestablishes the overall space that was analyzed into shots 3 and 4. The pattern, then, has been *establishment/breakdown/ reestablishment*—one of the most common patterns of development of space in the classical continuity style.

Let us pause to examine how this pattern has functioned to advance the narrative. Shot 1 has partially established the space of the office but has, more importantly, emphasized the protagonist of the story by linking him to the sign on the window. Offscreen sound and Spade's "Yes, sweetheart?" motivate the cut to shot 2. This establishing shot firmly anchors shot 1 spatially. It also introduces the source of the offscreen sound—the new character, Effie. The cut has occurred at precisely the moment when Effie enters. We are thus unlikely to notice the cut, because our expectations lead us to want to see what happens next. The space near the door has been shown when the cause-effect chain makes it important, not before and not after. Shots 3 and 4 present the conversation between Spade and Effie, and the shot/reverse shot and the eyeline match reassure us as to the characters' locations. We may not even notice the cutting, since the style works to emphasize the dramatic flow of the scene—what Effie says and how Spade reacts. In shot 5 the overall view of the office is presented again, precisely at the moment when a

Fig. 7.37    Shot 6a          Fig. 7.38    Shot 6b

new character is about to enter the scene, and this situates *her* firmly in the space. Thus the narrative—the dialogue, the entrance of new characters—is emphasized by adhering to the 180° system. The editing subordinates space to action.

We can trace the same procedures—with one additional variation—in the shots that follow. In shot 5 Brigid O'Shaughnessy enters Spade's office. Shot 6 presents another angle on the two of them as she comes toward him (shot 6a, Fig. 7.37) and sits down in front of his desk (shot 6b, Fig. 7.38). Again, the 180° line is observed, though the line no longer runs from Spade to the doorway; it now runs from Spade to the client's chair by his desk. Once established, this new line will not be violated.

The one extra factor here is a third tactic for ensuring spatial continuity—the **match on action,** a very powerful device. Assume that a figure starts to stand up in shot 1. We can wait until the character is standing up and has stopped moving before cutting to shot 2. But we can instead show the figure's movement *beginning* in shot 1, and then we can cut to shot 2, which shows the continuation of the movement. We would then have a match on action, the editing device that carries a movement across the break between two shots.

To appreciate the skill involved in making a match on action, it helps to realize that most films are shot with a single camera. In production, all the shots that will be taken from the same position will be filmed one immediately after the other. Then all the shots to be taken from another camera position will be made. (This is simply another instance of the general practice of shooting out of continuity.) In filming shots whose action will be matched at the editing stage, it is possible that the first shot, the one in which the movement starts, will be filmed hours or days apart from the second, in which the movement is continued. Thus matching action is not simply a matter of cutting together two complete versions of the same scene from different vantage points. The process involves keeping detailed notes about matters of camera work, mise-en-scene, and editing so that all the details can be fitted together in the assembly phase of production.

In the *Maltese Falcon* scene the cut from shot 5 (Fig. 7.36) to shot 6 (Fig. 7.37) uses a match on action, the action being Brigid's walk toward Spade's desk. Again, the 180° system aids in concealing the match, since it keeps screen direction constant. As one would expect, the match on action is a tool of narrative continuity. It takes a practiced eye to spot a smooth match on action; so powerful is our desire to follow the action flowing across the cut that we ignore the cut itself. The similarity of movement from shot to shot holds our attention more than the differences resulting from the cut.

Fig. 7.39    Shot 7

Fig. 7.40    Shot 8

Fig. 7.41    Shot 9

Fig. 7.42    Shot 10

Fig. 7.43    Shot 11

Fig. 7.44    Shot 12

Fig. 7.45    Shot 13

Fig. 7.46    Shot 14

Fig. 7.47    Shot 15

Fig. 7.48    Shot 16a

Fig. 7.49    Shot 16b

Fig. 7.50    Shot 17

Except for the match on action, the editing in the rest of the scene uses the same tactics we have already seen. When Brigid sits down, a new axis of action has been *established* (shot 6b). This enables Huston to break down the space into closer shots (shots 7–13, Figs. 7.39 through 7.45). All of these shots use the shot/reverse-shot tactic: first one point on the 180° line, then the other. (Note the shoulders in the foreground of shots 7, 8, and 10—Figs. 7.39, 7.40, and 7.42.) Here again, the editing of space presents the dialogue action simply and unambiguously. Beginning with shot 11, Huston's cuts also create eyeline matches: Brigid looks off right at Spade (shot 11, Fig. 7.43); Spade looks off left at Brigid (shot 12, Fig. 7.44); Brigid looks off left toward the door (shot 13, Fig. 7.45); Archer, just coming in, looks off right at them (shot 14, Fig. 7.46); and they both look off at him (shot 15, Fig. 7.47). The 180° rule permits us always to know who is looking at whom.

We must also ask about the function of the analytical cutting here. Huston could have played the entire conversation in one long take, remaining with shot 6b (Fig. 7.38). Why has he broken the conversation into seven shots? Most evidently, the analytical breakdown controls our attention, ensuring that we will look at Brigid and Spade at exactly the moment Huston wants us to. In the long take and the more distant framing, Huston would have to channel our attention in other ways (perhaps through composition or sound). Furthermore, the shot/reverse-shot pattern emphasizes the development of Brigid's story and Spade's reaction to it. As she gets into details, the cutting moves from over-the-shoulder reverse shots (Figs. 7.39, 7.40) to framings that isolate Brigid (Figs. 7.41 and 7.43) and eventually one that isolates Spade (Fig. 7.44). These shots come at the point when Brigid, in an artificially shy manner, tells her story, and the medium close-ups arouse curiosity about whether she is telling the truth. The shot of Spade's reaction (Fig. 7.44) cues us to suspect that he is skeptical. In short, the analytical editing cooperates with framing and figure behavior to focus our attention on Brigid's tale and to let us study her performance and Spade's response.

Fig. 7.51

When Archer enters, the breakdown of the space ceases momentarily, and Huston *reestablishes* the space with a long shot (shot 16a, Fig. 7.48) that integrates Archer into it (shot 16b, Fig. 7.49). (Compare shots 16b and 6a [Figs. 7.49 and 7.37] to see how almost exactly the same camera position earlier established Brigid's entrance.) Archer sits down on Spade's desk, establishing a new axis of action which governs the cut to the next shot (shot 17, Fig. 7.50); here Brigid is on one end of the axis, Spade and Archer on the other). The rest of the scene's editing analyzes this newly established set of relationships without ever crossing the line.

The viewer is not supposed to notice all this. Throughout, the shots present space to emphasize the cause-and-effect flow—the characters' actions, entrances, dialogue, reactions. The editing has economically organized space to convey narrative continuity. The continuity system, in exactly these terms, remains in force today; virtually any narrative film you may see will draw upon the 180° system of editing.

There are some refinements in this system. If a director arranges several characters in a circular pattern, say, sitting around a dinner table, then the axis of action will probably run between the characters of greatest importance at the moment. In Figures 7.51 and 7.52, from *Bringing Up Baby*, the important interaction is occurring between the two men, so we can cut from one side of the woman in the foreground to the other side in order to get consistent shot/reverse shots. When one man leaves the table, however, a semicircular arrangement of figures in space is created, so that a new axis of action can be established. Now we can get

Fig. 7.52

Fig. 7.53

Fig. 7.54

shot/reverse-shot exchanges running down the length of the table (Figs. 7.53, 7.54). As in the *Maltese Falcon* scene, this passage reminds us that in the course of a scene the 180° line may shift as the characters move around in the setting.

Another felicity in the 180° system is the **cheat cut.** Sometimes a director may not have perfect continuity from shot to shot because he or she has composed each shot for specific reasons. Must the two shots match perfectly? Again, narrative motivation decides the matter. Given that the 180° system emphasizes narrative causality, the director has some freedom to "cheat" mise-en-scene from shot to shot. Consider two shots from William Wyler's *Jezebel*. Neither character moves during either shot, but Wyler has blatantly cheated the position of Julie: in the first shot the top of her head is even with the man's chin (Fig. 7.55), but in the second shot she seems to have grown several inches (Fig. 7.56). Yet the great majority of viewers would not notice the discrepancy since it is the dialogue that is of paramount importance in the scene; here again, the similarities between shots outweigh the differences of position. Moreover, a change from a straight-on angle to a slightly high angle helps hide the cheat. There is, in fact, a cheat in the *Maltese Falcon* scene, too, between shots 6b and 7; in 6b (Fig. 7.38), as Spade leans forward, the back of his chair is not anywhere near him, yet in shot 7 (Fig. 7.39), it has been cheated to be just behind his left arm. Here again, the primacy of the narrative flow overrides such a cheat cut.

In several of our examples so far, continuity editing has proved itself well suited for portraying the interactions of two or more characters. But the same techniques can be used when a character is alone. Hitchcock's *Rear Window*

Fig. 7.55

Fig. 7.56

Fig. 7.57          Fig. 7.58

includes many scenes of the solitary photographer Jeff watching events occurring in an apartment across the courtyard from him. Hitchcock uses a standard pattern: he cuts from a shot of Jeff looking at something offscreen to a shot of what Jeff sees. (Since usually there is no establishing shot, the Kuleshov effect operates here.) Thus shot/reverse-shot and eyeline-match cutting are central to the film's effect. More specifically, Hitchcock uses a variety of eyeline-match editing known as *point of view cutting*. Shot 1 (Fig. 7.57) shows Jeff looking out his window, and shot 2 (Fig. 7.58) is a shot of what he sees—from his optical POV. (We have already discussed POV framings in Chapter 6, p. 178, and we have seen an instance of POV cutting in the *Birds* sequence discussed on pp. 208–209.) Now we are in a position to see how this is consistent with the 360° continuity system. The second shot is taken from a position *on* the axis of action, from the end point Jeff occupies (see Fig. 7.59).

*POV cutting*

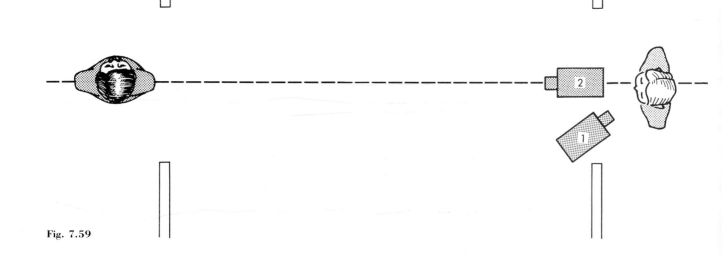

Fig. 7.59

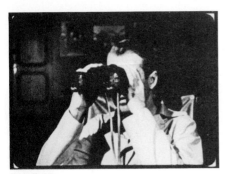

Fig. 7.60

Fig. 7.62

Fig. 7.63

As *Rear Window* goes on, the subjectivity of the POV shots intensifies. Becoming more eager to examine the details of his neighbor's life, Jeff begins to use binoculars and a photographic telephoto lens to magnify his view. By using shots taken with lenses of different focal lengths, Hitchcock can show how each new tool enlarges what Jeff can see (see Figs. 7.60–7.63). Even though Jeff is alone for much of the film, Hitchcock's cutting adheres to spatial continuity rules and exploits their POV possibilities in order to arouse curiosity and suspense.

Can the director ever legitimately cross the axis of action? Yes. A scene occurring in certain settings—in a doorway or on a staircase, for instance—may "break the line." Also, having the actors or the camera move across the line may create a new axis of action; this in turn permits the filmmaker to cut to shots that would normally be out of continuity. (Since a violation of continuity can occur *only* at a cut, a camera movement cannot break continuity.) But the most usual way of crossing the line is by taking one shot from *on the line itself* and using that as a transition. If, say, in shot 1 a car is moving from left to right, shot 2 could be a *head-on* or *tails-on* shot (that is, the car would be moving directly toward or directly away from the viewer). Then one could cut to shot 3, showing the car moving from right to left. Without the shot taken *on* the axis of action, a cut from 1 to 3 would violate continuity, but shot 2 serves as a transition to permit the crossing of the line. This is relatively rare in a dialogue scene but is more common in sequences of chases and outdoor physical action.

Continuity editing illustrates how editing can endow the film's narration with a great range of knowledge; a cut can take us to any point on the correct side of the axis of action. Editing can also create omniscience, that godlike knowledge that some films seek to present. The outstanding technical device here is **crosscutting,** first extensively explored by D. W. Griffith in his last-minute-rescue scenes. Crosscutting gives us an unrestricted knowledge of causal, temporal, or spatial information by alternating shots from one line of action in one place with shots of other events in other places. Crosscutting thus creates some spatial discontinuity, but it binds the action together by creating a sense of cause and effect and temporal simultaneity. For example, in Fritz Lang's *M*, while the police seek the child murderer, gangsters prowl the streets looking for him as well, and we also occasionally see the murderer himself. The different lines of action are tied together by the causal process of the pursuit and by a sense of simultaneity. In most cases, crosscutting gives us a range of knowledge greater than that of any one character. (We know that the gangsters are after the murderer, but the police and the murderer do not.) Crosscutting also builds up suspense, as we form expectations that are only gradually clarified and fulfilled. It may also create parallels, and Lang exploits this possibility by suggesting analogies between the police and the crooks. Whatever other functions it may have, though, crosscutting remains primarily a means of presenting narrative actions that are occurring in several locales at roughly the same time.

All the devices of spatial continuity illustrate how film technique draws the spectator into an active process. We assume that setting, character movement, and character position will be consistent and coherent. Our prior knowledge of filmic conventions lets us form strong expectations about what shot will follow the one we are seeing. We also make inferences on the basis of cues, so that when Brigid and Spade look off left we infer that someone is entering the room and we expect to see a shot of that person. What makes the continuity system "invisible" is its ability to draw on a range of skills that we have learned so well that they seem automatic. This makes spatial continuity editing a powerful tool for the filmmaker who wishes to reinforce habitual expectations and a central target for the filmmaker who wants to use film style to challenge or change our normal viewing activities.

## ■ TEMPORAL CONTINUITY: ORDER, FREQUENCY, DURATION

In the classical continuity system, time, like space, is organized according to the development of the narrative. We know that the plot's presentation of the story typically involves considerable manipulation of time. Continuity editing seeks to support and sustain this temporal manipulation.

Recall, to get specific, our distinction among temporal order, frequency, and duration. Continuity editing typically presents the story events in a 1-2-3 order (e.g., Spade rolls a cigarette, then Effie comes in, then he answers her, etc.). The only violation of this order is a flashback, signaled by a cut or dissolve. Furthermore, classical editing also typically presents only *once* what happens *once* in the story; in continuity style, it would be a gross mistake for Huston to repeat the shot of, say, Brigid sitting down (Fig. 7.38). (Only a flashback would motivate the repetition of a scene already witnessed.) So chronological sequence and "one-for-one" frequency are the most common methods of handling order and frequency in the continuity style of editing. What of duration?

In the classical continuity system, story duration is seldom expanded (that is, screen time is seldom made greater than story time). Usually, duration is in complete continuity (plot time equaling story time) or is elided (story time being greater than plot time). Let us first consider complete continuity, the most common possibility. Here a scene occupying five minutes in the story also occupies five minutes when projected on the screen. The first scene of *The Maltese Falcon* has three cues for such temporal continuity. First, the narrative progression of the scene has no gaps. Every movement by the characters and every line of dialogue is presented. There is also the sound track. Sound issuing from the story space (what we shall later call "diegetic" sound) is a standard indicator of temporal continuity, especially when (as in this scene) the sound "bleeds over" each cut. Finally, there is the match on action between shots 5 and 6. So powerful is the match on action that it creates both spatial *and* temporal continuity. The reason is obvious: if an action carries across the cut, the space and time are assumed to be continuous from shot to shot. (Our look at *Last Year at Marienbad* in Chapter 10 will show that this is only an assumption, not a universal truth.) In all, an absence of ellipses in the story action, diegetic sound overlapping the cuts, and matching on action are three primary indicators that the duration of the scene is continuous.

Sometimes, however, a second possibility will be explored: *temporal ellipsis*. The ellipsis may, of course, omit seconds, minutes, hours, days, years, or centuries. Some ellipses are of no importance to the narrative development and so are concealed. To take a common example: a classical narrative film typically does not show the entire time it takes a character to dress, wash, and breakfast in the morning. Shots of the character going into the shower, putting on shoes, or frying an egg might be edited so as to eliminate the unwanted bits of time, with the plot presenting in seconds a process that might have taken an hour in the story. As we saw on p. 217, empty frames and cutaways are frequently used to cover short temporal ellipses.

But other ellipses are important to the narrative. The viewer must recognize that time has passed. For this task the continuity style has built up a varied repertory of devices. Most often, dissolves, fades, or wipes are used to indicate an ellipsis between shots. Thus from the last shot of one scene we dissolve, fade, or wipe to the first shot of the next scene. (The Hollywood "rule" is that a dissolve indicates a brief time lapse and a fade indicates a much longer one.) In some cases contemporary practice substitutes a cut for such transitions. For example, in *2001* Kubrick cuts directly from a bone spinning in the air to a space station orbiting the earth, one of the boldest graphic matches in narrative cinema. The cut eliminates thousands of years of story time.

In other cases it is necessary to show a large-scale process or a lengthy period—a city waking up in the morning, a war, a child growing up, the rise of a singing star. Here classical continuity uses another device for temporal ellipsis: the **montage sequence.** (This should not be confused with the concept of "montage" in Sergei Eisenstein's film theory.) Brief portions of a process, informative titles (for example, "1865" or "San Francisco"), stereotyped images (e.g., the Eiffel Tower), newsreel footage, newspaper headlines, and the like, can be swiftly joined by dissolves and music to compress a lengthy series of actions into a few moments. We are all familiar with the most clichéd montage ellipses—calendar leaves fluttering away, newspaper presses churning out an Extra, clocks ticking portentously—but in the hands of deft editors such sequences become small virtuoso pieces in themselves. Slavko Vorkapich's montages of American life in *Mr. Smith Goes to Washington*, Jack Killifer's tracing of a society across two decades in *The Roaring Twenties*, and Edward Curtis's brutal depictions of a gangster's rise in *Scarface* illustrate the powers of the device. The montage sequence is still utilized in Hollywood films, though it tends to be more restrained stylistically than in the 1930s and 1940s. *Jaws*, for example, simply uses a series of unmatched shots of vacationers arriving at the beach to indicate a time shift to the beginning of the tourist season. Music is still used as an accompaniment, however, as when the opening montage of *9 to 5* depicts three women going to work, or when *Tootsie* shows the hero's rise to success as a soap-opera star.

In sum, the continuity style uses the temporal dimension of editing primarily for narrative purposes. Through prior knowledge, the spectator expects the editing to present story events in chronological order, with only occasional rearrangement through flashbacks. The viewer expects that editing will respect the frequency of story events. And the viewer assumes that actions irrelevant to story causality will be omitted or at least abridged by judicious ellipses. At least, this is how the classical Hollywood continuity system has conceived storytelling. Like graphics, rhythm, and space, time is organized to permit the unfolding of cause and effect, the arousal of curiosity, suspense, and surprise. But there are many alternatives to the continuity style of editing, and these are worth a look.

# ALTERNATIVES TO CONTINUITY EDITING

## ■ GRAPHIC AND RHYTHMIC POSSIBILITIES

Powerful and pervasive as it is, the continuity style remains only *one* style, and many filmmakers have explored other editing possibilities. One alternative to such emphasis is to grant the graphic and rhythmic dimensions greater weight. That is, instead of joining shot 1 to shot 2 primarily on the basis of the spatial and temporal functions that the shot fulfills in presenting a story, you could join them on the basis of purely graphic or rhythmic qualities—independent of the time and space they represent. In the nonnarrative film of abstract form, graphic and rhythmic dimensions come to the fore. In films such as *Anticipation of the Night, Scenes from under Childhood, Western History,* and others, Stan Brakhage has explored purely graphic means of joining shot to shot: continuities and discontinuities of light, texture, and shape motivate the editing. Interested in the very surface of the film itself, Brakhage has scratched, painted on the image, even taped moth wings to it, in search of abstract graphic combinations. Similarly, parts of Bruce Conner's *Cosmic Ray, A Movie,* and *Report* cut together newsreel footage, old film clips, leader, and black frames on the basis of graphic patterns of movement, direction, and speed. Many filmmakers have completely subordinated the space and time presented in each shot to the rhythmic relations among shots. "Single-frame" films (in which each shot is only one frame long) are the most extreme examples of this overriding rhythmic concern; two famous examples are Robert Breer's *Fist Fight* and Peter Kubelka's *Schwechater.*

The preeminence of graphic and rhythmic editing in nonnarrative cinema is not, however, as recent a phenomenon as these examples might suggest. As early as 1913, some painters were contemplating the pure-design possibilities offered by film, and many works of the European avant-garde movements of the 1920s combined an interest in abstract graphics with a desire to explore rhythmic editing. The results were as diverse as Man Ray's *Emak Bakia,* Henri Chomette's *Cinq Minutes de cinéma pur,* Germaine Dulac's *Thème et variations,* Hans Richter's *Ghosts before Breakfast,* and Walter Ruttmann's *Berlin: Symphony of a Great City.* Perhaps the most famous of these is the Fernand Léger–Dudley Murphy film *Ballet mécanique* (see Chapter 4, p. 107). In Chapter 9 we shall see how *Ballet mécanique* juxtaposes its shots on the basis of graphic and rhythmic qualities.

Important as the graphic and rhythmic possibilities of editing have been to the nonnarrative film, their powers have not been wholly neglected in the narrative film. Although the continuity style seeks an overall graphic continuity, this is usually subordinated to the concern with mapping narrative space and tracing narrative time. Some narrative filmmakers, however, at times subordinate narrative concerns to graphic pattern. The most famous examples are probably the films for which Busby Berkeley choreographed elaborate dance numbers. In *42nd Street, Golddiggers of 1933, Footlight Parade, Golddiggers of 1935,* and *Dames,* the narrative periodically grinds to a halt and the film presents intricate dances that are arranged, shot, and edited with a concern for the pure configuration of dancers and background.

More complexly related to the narrative is the graphic editing of Yasujiro Ozu. Ozu's cutting is often dictated by a much more precise graphic continuity than we find in the classical continuity style. In *An Autumn Afternoon* Ozu cuts from one

Fig. 7.64

Fig. 7.65

Fig. 7.66

Fig. 7.67

Fig. 7.68

Fig. 7.69

man drinking *sake* (Fig. 7.64) directly to another (Fig. 7.65) caught in almost exactly the same position, costume, and gesture. Later in the film, he cuts from one man to another (Figs. 7.66 and 7.67), keeping the composition very similar across the cut. Even a beer bottle (a different one in each shot) sits precisely in the same position on frame left, its label in a constant position as well. In *Ohayu* Ozu uses color for the same purpose, cutting from laundry on a line to a domestic interior and matching on a red shape in the upper left of each shot (a shirt, a lamp). (See Plates 14 and 15.)

Graphic continuity is, of course, a matter of degree, and in narrative films the spectrum runs from Hollywood's general graphic continuity to Ozu's precise matching, with two shots like these from Eisenstein's *Ivan the Terrible*, Part I, coming somewhere in the middle. (See Figs. 7.68 and 7.69.) The lighting (darkness on frame left, brightness on frame right) and the triangular shape on frame right of shot 1 are picked up in shot 2, with Anastasia's head and body now closely matching the tapering chair. If such graphic editing motivates the entire film's form, however, narrative will be dissolved, and the film will become more abstract in form.

Some narrative films have momentarily subordinated spatial and temporal editing factors to rhythmic ones. In the 1920s both the French "impressionist" school and the Soviet avant-garde frequently made narrative secondary to purely rhythmic editing. In such films as Abel Gance's *La Roue*, Jean Epstein's *Cœur fidèle* and *La Glace à trois faces*, and Ivan Mosjoukin's *Kean*, accelerated editing renders the tempo of an onrushing train, a whirling carousel, a racing automobile, or a drunken dance. In Epstein's *Fall of the House of Usher* a poetic sequence of Usher strumming a guitar and singing organizes the length of the shots in accord with a songlike pattern of verse and refrain. Kuleshov's *The Death Ray* and, as we shall see, Eisenstein's *October* occasionally make rhythm dominate narrative space and time. More recently, we can find rhythmic editing momentarily predominant in narrative films as varied as the Busby Berkeley musicals, Rouben Mamoulian's *Love Me Tonight*, René Clair's *Le Million*, several films of Ozu and Hitchcock, Resnais's *Last Year at Marienbad* and *Muriel*, and Godard's *Pierrot le fou*. As we saw with graphics, rhythmic editing may override the spatial and temporal dimensions; when this happens, narrative becomes proportionately less important.

Fig. 7.70

Fig. 7.71

## ■ SPATIAL AND TEMPORAL DISCONTINUITY

Nonnarrative films, of course, implicitly attack the continuity style at its center, for that style is founded on the cogent presentation of a story. But what of *narrative* alternatives to the continuity system? How can one tell a story without use of the continuity rules? Let us sample some ways particular filmmakers have created distinct editing styles by use of what might be considered spatial and temporal discontinuities.

One obvious spatial discontinuity consists of violating or ignoring the 180° system. In *Jeanne Dielman, 23 quai du Commerce, 1080 Bruxelles*, Chantal Akerman often films the protagonist's daily housework from positions perpendicular to a wall; cutting these shots together yields sharp 90° changes of angle (Figs. 7.70 and 7.71). The editing choices of filmmakers Jacques Tati and Yasujiro Ozu are based on what we might call 360° space. Instead of an axis of action that dictates that the camera be placed within an imaginary semicircle, these filmmakers work as if the action were not a line but a point at the center of a circle and as if the camera could be placed at any point on the circumference. In *Mr. Hulot's Holiday*, *Play Time*, and *Traffic* Tati systematically films from almost every side; edited together, the shots present multiple spatial perspectives on a single event. Similarly, Ozu's scenes construct a 360° space that produces what the continuity style would consider grave editing errors. Ozu's films often yield no consistent background spaces and no consistent screen direction; the eyeline matches are out of joint and the only consistency is the *violation* of the 180° line. One of the gravest sins in the classical continuity style is to match on action while breaking the line, yet Ozu does this comfortably in *Early Summer* (see Figs. 7.72 and 7.73).

Explaining in more detail how Akerman, Tati, Ozu, and others rigorously construct such 360° edited space would be out of place here. (See Part IV for further discussion of Ozu's *Tokyo Story*.) We can, however, pause to note a very important consequence of such spatially discontinuous editing. The defender of classical continuity would claim that spatial continuity rules are necessary for the clear presentation of a narrative. But anyone who has seen a film by Ozu or Tati

Fig. 7.72

Fig. 7.73

30° rule

Fig. 7.74

Fig. 7.75

Fig. 7.76

Fig. 7.77

can testify that no narrative confusion arises from their continuity "violations." Though the spaces do not flow as smoothly as in the Hollywood style (this is indeed part of the films' fascination), the cause-effect chains remain intelligible. The inescapable conclusion is that the continuity system is only *one* way to render a narrative. Historically, this system has been the dominant one, but aesthetically it has no priority over other styles.

There are two other noteworthy devices of discontinuity. In *Breathless* Jean-Luc Godard violates conventions of spatial, temporal, and graphic continuity by his systematic use of the **jump cut**. Though this term is often loosely used, its primary meaning is this. When two shots of the same subject are cut together but are not sufficiently different in camera distance and angle, there will be a noticeable jump on the screen. Classical continuity avoids such jumps by generous use of shot/reverse shots and by the "30° rule" (advising that every camera position be varied by at least 30° from the previous one). But an examination of shots from *Breathless* suggests the consequences of Godard's jump cuts. Between the end of one shot of Michel and his friend and the beginning of the next shot of them, they have moved several feet and some story time has elapsed (Figs. 7.74 and 7.75). Between the first shot of Patricia riding in the car and the second, the background has changed and some story time has elapsed (Figs. 7.76 and 7.77). These cuts, far from flowing smoothly, function to disorient the spectator.

A second prevalent violation of continuity is that created by the **nondiegetic insert**. Here the filmmaker cuts from the scene to a metaphorical or symbolic shot that is not part of the space and time of the narrative. Clichés abound here. In Fritz Lang's *Fury* housewives gossiping are juxtaposed to shots of clucking hens. More complex examples occur in the films of Eisenstein and Godard. In Eisenstein's *Strike* the massacre of workers is intercut with the slaughter of a bull. In Godard's *La Chinoise*, a character tells an anecdote about the ancient Egyptians who, he claims, thought that "their language was the language of the gods." As he says this (Fig. 7.78), Godard cuts in two close-ups of gold relics from the tomb of King Tutankhamen (Figs. 7.79 and 7.80). As nondiegetic inserts, coming from outside the story world, they construct a running, often ironic, commentary on the action, and they prompt the spectator to search for implicit meanings. (Do the relics corroborate or challenge what Henri says?)

Though both the jump cut and the nondiegetic insert can be utilized in a narrative context, both tend to somewhat weaken narrative continuity—the first by abrupt gaps, the second by suspension of story action altogether. It is no accident that both devices have been prominently used by the contemporary filmmaker most associated with the challenge to classical narrative, Jean-Luc Godard. In Part IV we shall examine the nature of this challenge by analyzing *Tout va bien*.

There are still other alternatives to classical continuity, especially in the temporal dimension. Although the classical approach to order and frequency of story events may seem the most natural, it is only the most familiar. Story events do not have to be edited in 1-2-3 order. Not only flashbacks but flashforwards are possible. In Resnais's *La Guerre est finie*, scenes cut in conventional continuity are interrupted by images that may represent flashbacks, or fantasy episodes, or even future events. Editing can also play with variable frequency for narrative purposes; the same event can be shown repeatedly. In *La Guerre est finie*, the same funeral is depicted in different hypothetical ways (the protagonist is present, or he is not). Again, Godard offers a striking example of how editing can manipulate both order and frequency. In *Pierrot le fou*, Marianne and Ferdinand flee an apartment as gangsters arrive. Godard scrambles the order of the shots: first, Ferdinand jumps

Fig. 7.78

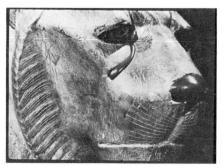
Fig. 7.79

Fig. 7.80

into the car as Marianne pulls away; then the couple are seen back in the apartment; then the car races down a street; then Marianne and Ferdinand climb onto a rooftop; and so on. Moreover, Godard plays with frequency by repeating one story action—Ferdinand jumping into the car—but showing it *differently* each time. Such manipulation of editing blocks our normal expectations about story time and forces us to concentrate on the very process of assembling the film's story.

The editing may also take liberties with story duration. Although complete continuity and ellipsis are the most common ways of rendering duration, expansion—stretching a moment out, making screen time greater than story time—remains a distinct possibility. Truffaut uses such expansions in *Jules et Jim* to underscore narrative turning points (Catherine lifting her veil or jumping off the bridge). In Chabrol's *La Femme infidèle*, when the outraged husband strikes his wife's lover with a statuette, Chabrol overlaps shots of the victim falling to the floor. On one hand, then, discontinuities of temporal order, duration, and frequency can become perfectly intelligible in a narrative context. On the other hand, in the jump cut and the nondiegetic insert, such temporal dislocations can also push away from traditional notions of "story" altogether and create ambiguous relations among shots.

As an example of the power of spatial and temporal discontinuities in editing, we shall look at a single example: Sergei Eisenstein's *October*.

## ■ DISCONTINUITY EDITING: *OCTOBER*

For many Soviet filmmakers of the 1920s, editing was a major means of organizing the entire form of the film; it did not simply serve the narrative progression, as in the continuity system. Sergei Eisenstein's early films—*Strike, Potemkin, October, Old and New*, and the unfinished *Que Viva Mexico!*—all constitute attempts to make certain editing devices the fundamental principles of constructing a film. Rather than subordinate his editing patterns to the mapping out of a story, Eisenstein conceives of these films as editing constructions. As a Marxist, Eisenstein believed that the law of the dialectical conflict and synthesis of opposites could provide principles of dynamic editing. Thus he deliberately opposed himself to continuity editing; he sought out and exploited what Hollywood would call discontinuities. He staged, shot, and cut his films for the maximum *collision* from shot to shot, sequence to sequence, since he believed that only through being forced to synthesize such conflicts does the viewer participate in a dialectical process. Eisenstein sought to make the collisions and conflicts not only perceptual but also emotional and intellectual. His aim was nothing less than to alter the audience's total consciousness.

To this end, Eisenstein "wrote" his film by a juxtaposition of shots. No longer bound by conventional dramaturgy, Eisenstein's films roam freely through time and space to construct an intricate pattern of images calculated to stimulate the viewer's senses, emotions, and thinking. He dreamed of filming Marx's *Das Kapital*, of writing an essay by means of film editing. Needless to say, the intricacy of Eisenstein's editing cannot be wholly conveyed here; even a single sequence of an Eisenstein film is properly the subject of a chapter in itself. Let us, however, briefly indicate how Eisenstein uses editing discontinuities in a short sequence from *October*.

The sequence is the third one in the film (and comprises no fewer than 125 shots!). The story action is simple. The Provisional Government has taken power in Russia after the February Revolution, but instead of withdrawing from World War I, the government has continued to support the Allies. This maneuver has left the Russian people no better off than under the czar. Now in classical Hollywood cinema, this story might be shown through a "montage sequence" of newspaper headlines smoothly linked to a scene wherein a protagonist complains that the Provisional Government has not changed a thing. *October*'s protagonist, though, is not one person, but the entire Russian people, and the film does not usually use dialogue scenes to present its story points. Rather, *October* seeks to go beyond a simple presentation of story events by making the audience actively *interpret* those events. To this end, the film confronts the audience with a disorienting and disjunctive set of images.

The sequence begins with shots showing the Russian soldiers on the front casting down their rifles and fraternizing freely with their German "enemies"— talking, drinking, laughing together (Fig. 7.81). Eisenstein then cuts back to the Provisional Government, where a flunky extends a document to an unseen ruler (Fig. 7.82); this document pledges the government to aid the Allies. The soldiers' fraternization is suddenly disrupted by a bombardment (Fig. 7.83). The soldiers run back to the trenches and huddle as dirt and bomb fragments rain down on them. Eisenstein then cuts to a series of shots of a cannon being lowered off a factory assembly line. For a time the narration crosscuts these images with the soldiers on the battlefield (Figs. 7.84 and 7.85). In the last section of the sequence, the shots of the cannon are crosscut with hungry women and children standing in breadlines in the snow (Fig. 7.86). The sequence ends with two titles: "All as before . . ."/"Hunger and war."

What are the consequences of this editing construction? Rhythmically the sequence is striking, especially in the bombing section, where the shots are only around 15 frames long. Of more interest here, however, are the various graphic, temporal, and spatial editing strategies used by Eisenstein.

Graphically, there are some continuities and many strong discontinuities. When the soldiers fraternize, many shots closely resemble one another graphically, and one shot of a bursting bomb is graphically matched in its movement with men bustling into a trench. But the graphic *dis*continuities are more noteworthy. Eisenstein cuts from a laughing German soldier facing right to a menacing eagle statue (facing left) at the government headquarters (Figs. 7.87 and 7.88). There is a bold jump cut from the flunky bowing to him standing up (Figs. 7.89 and 7.90). A static shot of rifles thrust into the snow cuts to a long shot of a bursting shell (Figs. 7.91 and 7.92). When the soldiers race back to the trenches, Eisenstein often opposes their direction of movement from shot to shot. Moreover, the cutting contrasts shots of the men crouching in the trenches looking *upward* with shots of the cannon

Fig. 7.81

Fig. 7.82

Fig. 7.83

Fig. 7.84

Fig. 7.85

Fig. 7.86

Fig. 7.87

Fig. 7.88

Fig. 7.89

Fig. 7.90

Fig. 7.91

Fig. 7.92

slowly *descending* (Figs. 7.84 and 7.85). In the last phase of the sequence, Eisenstein juxtaposes the misty, almost completely static shots of the women and children with the sharply defined, dynamically moving shots of factory workers lowering the cannon. Such graphic discontinuities recur throughout the film, especially in scenes of dynamic action, and stimulate perceptual conflict in the audience. To watch an Eisenstein film is to submit oneself to such percussive, pulsating graphic editing.

Eisenstein also makes vigorous use of temporal discontinuities. The sequence as a whole is opposed to Hollywood rules in its refusal to present the order of events unambiguously. Does the crosscutting of battlefield and government, factory and street indicate simultaneous action? (Consider, for example, that the women and children are seen at night, whereas the factory appears to be working in the daytime.) It is simply impossible to say if the battlefield events take place before or after or during the women's vigil. Eisenstein has sacrificed the delineation of 1-2-3 order so that he can present the shots as emotional and conceptual units.

Duration is likewise variable. The soldiers fraternize in relative continuity, but the Provisional Government's behavior is elided drastically; this permits Eisenstein to identify the government as the unseen cause of the bombardment that ruptures the peace. At one point, Eisenstein utilizes one of his favorite devices, a temporal expansion: there is an overlapping cut as a soldier drinks from a bottle. (Later in *October*, such durational expansions create the famous bridge-raising sequence.) At another point, the gradual collapse of the women and children is elided. We see them standing, then later lying on the ground. Even frequency is made discontinuous: it is difficult to say if we are seeing *several cannons* lowered off the assembly line or only one descending cannon shown *several times*. Again, Eisenstein seeks a specific *juxtaposition* of elements, not obedience to a temporal chain. Editing's manipulation of order, duration, and frequency subordinates straightforward story time to specific logical relationships. Eisenstein creates these relationships by juxtaposing disparate lines of action through editing.

Spatially, the *October* sequence runs from rough continuity to extreme discontinuity. Although at times the 180° rule is respected (especially in the shots of women and children), never does Eisenstein start a section with an establishing shot. Reestablishing shots are rare, and usually the major components of the locales are never shown in one shot. Moreover, these three locales are built up from close-ups (of the rifles, the cannon, the women's feet). In all, then, the classical continuity of space is broken by the intercutting of the different locales. To what end? By violating space in this manner, the film invites us to make emotional and conceptual connections. For example, crosscutting to the Provisional Government makes it the source of bombardment, a meaning reinforced by the way the first explosions are followed by the jump cut of the government flunky.

More daringly, by cutting from the crouching soldiers to a descending cannon, Eisenstein powerfully depicts the men visually crushed by the war-making apparatus of the government. This is reinforced by a *false* eyeline match from soldiers looking upward, *as if* at the lowering cannon—false because of course the two elements are in entirely separate settings (Figs. 7.84 and 7.85). By then showing the factory workers lowering the cannon (Fig. 7.93), the cutting links the oppressed soldiers to the oppressed proletariat. Finally, as the cannon hits the ground, Eisenstein crosscuts images of it with the shots of the starving families of the soldiers and the workers. They too are shown as crushed by the government machine; as the cannon wheels come slowly to the floor, we cut to the women's feet in the snow, and the

Fig. 7.93

machine's heaviness is linked by titles ("one pound," "half a pound") to the steady starvation of the women and children. Although all of the spaces are in the story, such discontinuities make the sequence a commentary on the story by the plot.

In all, then, Eisenstein's spatial editing, like his temporal and graphic editing, constructs correspondences, analogies, and contrasts that *interpret* the story events. The interpretation is not simply handed to the viewer; rather, the editing discontinuities force the viewer to work out the interrelations. Like the rest of *October*, this sequence suggests that there are powerful alternatives to the principles of classical continuity.

## SUMMARY

When any two shots are joined, we can ask several questions:

1. How are the shots graphically continuous or discontinuous?
2. What rhythmic relations are created?
3. Are the shots spatially continuous? If not, what creates the discontinuity? (Crosscutting? Ambiguous cues?) If the shots are spatially continuous, how does the 180° system create the continuity?
4. Are the shots temporally continuous? If so, what creates the continuity? (For example, matches on action?) If not, what creates the discontinuity? (Ellipsis? Overlapping cuts?)

More generally, we can ask the same question we have asked of every film technique. How does this film's editing *function* with respect to the film's narrative or nonnarrative form? Does the film utilize editing to lay out the narrative space, time, and cause-effect chain in the manner of classical continuity? Or does the film utilize other editing patterns that enter into a different interplay with the narrative? If the film is not a narrative one, how does editing function to engage our formal expectations?

Some practical hints: You can learn to notice editing in several ways. If you are having trouble noticing cuts, try watching a film or television show and tapping with a pencil each time a shot changes. Once you recognize editing easily, watch any film with the sole purpose of observing one editing aspect—say, the way space is presented or the control of graphics or time. Sensitize yourself to rhythmic editing by noting cutting rates; tapping out the tempo of the cuts can help. Watching 1930s and 1940s American films can introduce you to classical continuity style; try to predict what shot will come next in a sequence. (You will be surprised at how often you are right.) When you watch a film on video, try turning off the sound; editing patterns become more apparent this way. When there is a violation of continuity, ask yourself what purpose it serves. When you see a film that does not obey classical continuity principles, search for its unique editing patterns. If it is feasible, sit down at an editor or viewer or use the slow-motion, freeze, and reverse controls on a videocassette machine to analyze a film sequence as this chapter has done. (Almost any film will do.) In such ways as these, you can considerably increase your awareness and understanding of the power of editing.

## NOTES AND QUERIES

### ■ WHAT EDITING IS

An overview of the work of the film editor may be found in "Prime Cut," *Film Comment* **13,** 2 (March–April 1977): 6–29. Professional reflections include Dai Vaughan, *Portrait of an Invisible Man: The Working Life of Stewart McAllister, Film Editor* (London: British Film Institute, 1983); Ralph Rosenblum, *When the Shooting Stops . . . The Cutting Begins: A Film Editor's Story* (New York: Penguin, 1980); Edward Dmytryk, *On Film Editing* (Boston: Focal Press, 1984); and Kristin Thompson and David Bordwell, "From Sennett to Stevens: An Interview with Editor William Hornbeck," *The Velvet Light Trap* **20** (Summer 1983): 34–40. An amusing essay on the powers of editing is William K. Everson, "Movies out of Thin Air," *Films in Review* **6,** 4 (April 1955): 171–180.

General discussions of film editing may be found in Rudolf Arnheim, *Film as Art* (Berkeley: University of California Press, 1967), pp. 87–102; Erwin Panofsky, "Style and Medium in the Moving Pictures," in Daniel Talbot, ed., *Film: An Anthology* (Berkeley: University of California Press, 1970), pp. 15–32; Béla Balázs, *Theory of the Film* (New York: Dover, 1970), pp. 118–138; Noël Carroll, "Toward a Theory of Film Editing," *Millennium Film Journal* **3** (1978): 79–99. We await an authoritative history of film editing, but at least one historical pattern has been sketched in André Bazin, "The Evolution of the Language of Cinema," in *What Is Cinema?* vol. 1 (Berkeley: University of California Press, 1967), pp. 23–40.

Editing has often been seen as an alternative to mise-en-scene and camera work. Instead of cutting to a close-up of the hero's face, we can have him come closer to the camera, or we can track into a close-up. Early film theory argued that editing was more inherently "cinematic" than the more "theatrical" technique of mise-en-scene; see in this connection Arnheim, Panofsky, and Balázs, cited above. But the aesthetic prominence of editing was disputed by the film theorist André Bazin, who argued that editing ruptures and falsifies the spatiotemporal continuum of reality. (See not only the Bazin essay cited above but also "The Virtues and Limitations of Montage," pp. 41–52 of the same volume.) Bazin claimed that concrete reality is better respected by cinematography and mise-en-scene techniques. This debate has been taken up by others. See Charles Barr, "CinemaScope: Before and After," *Film Quarterly* **16,** 4 (Summer 1963): 4–24; David Thomson, *Movie Man* (New York: Stein and Day, 1967), pp. 84–91; Christian Metz, *Film Language* (New York: Oxford University Press, 1974), pp. 31–91; Brian Henderson, "Two Types of Film Theory," in *A Critique of Film Theory* (New York: Dutton, 1980).

Professional filmmakers' views of editing are invariably interesting. Roberto Rossellini and Jean Renoir, in a famous interview with André Bazin, minimize it ("Cinema and Television," *Sight and Sound* [Winter 1958–59]: 26–29). Alfred Hitchcock, in an equally famous interview with François Truffaut, swears by it (*Hitchcock* [New York: Simon & Schuster, 1967], *passim*). For Jean-Luc Godard, "editing can restore to actuality that ephemeral grace neglected by both snob and filmlover, or can transform chance into destiny" ("Montage My Fine Care," *Godard on Godard* [New York: Viking, 1972], p. 39). For V. I. Pudovkin, "Editing is the basic creative force, by power of which the soulless photographs (the separate shots) are engineered into living, cinematographic form" (*Film Technique* [New York:

Grove, 1960], p. 25). An editor has recalled that John Ford shot so little footage that Ford would not have to involve himself in editing: "By and large, the film that an editor would get would almost *have* to go into the picture. After the shooting, [Ford] would often go off to his boat and not come back until after the picture was cut" (Peter Bogdanovich, *John Ford* [Berkeley: University of California Press, 1968], p. 9).

## ■ DIMENSIONS OF FILM EDITING

Very little has been written on graphic aspects of editing. See Vladimir Nilsen, *The Cinema as a Graphic Art* (New York: Hill & Wang, 1959); Sergei Eisenstein, "The Dramaturgy of Film Form," in Richard Taylor, ed., *Selected Works, Vol. 1: Writings 1922–1934* (Bloomington: Indiana University Press, 1988), pp. 161–180; and Jonas Mekas, "An Interview with Peter Kubelka," *Film Culture* **44** (Spring 1967): 42–47.

What we are calling rhythmic editing comprises the categories of "metric" and "rhythmic" montage discussed by Eisenstein in "The Fourth Dimension in Cinema," in *Selected Works, Vol. 1*, pp. 181–194. For a sample analysis of a film's rhythm, see Lewis Jacobs, "D. W. Griffith," in *The Rise of the American Film* (New York: Teachers College Press, 1968), chapter 11, pp. 171–201. Television commercials are useful to study for rhythmic editing, for their selection of highly stereotyped imagery permits the editor to cut the shots together in a rapid rhythm matched to the rhythm of the jingle on the sound track.

For a good discussion of spatial and temporal editing, see Noël Burch, *Theory of Film Practice* (Princeton, N.J.: Princeton University Press, 1981), especially pp. 3–16, 32–48; and Vladimir Nizhny, *Lessons with Eisenstein* (New York: Hill & Wang, 1962), pp. 63–92.

The Kuleshov experiments have been variously described. The two most authoritative accounts are in V. I. Pudovkin, *Film Technique* (New York: Grove, 1960), *passim*, and Ronald Levaco, trans. and ed., *Kuleshov on Film: Writings of Lev Kuleshov* (Berkeley: University of California Press, 1974), pp. 51–55. For attacks on the Kuleshov effect, see André Bazin, "The Virtues and Limitations of Montage," *What Is Cinema?*, pp. 44–52.

## ■ CONTINUITY EDITING

For a historical discussion of continuity editing, see Chapter 11 and the chapter's bibliography. The hidden selectivity that continuity editing can achieve is well summarized in a remark of Thom Noble, who edited *Fahrenheit 451* and *Witness*: "What usually happens is that there are maybe seven moments in each scene that are brilliant. But they're all on different takes. My job is to try and get all those seven moments in and yet have it look seamless, so that nobody knows there's a cut in there." (Quoted in David Chell, ed., *Moviemakers at Work* [Redmond, Washington: Microsoft Press, 1987], pp. 81–82.)

Since the continuity system was guided by explicit "rules," many sources enumerate the principles of continuity. See Karel Reisz and Gavin Millar, *The Technique of Film Editing* (New York: Hastings House, 1973); Daniel Arijohn, *A Grammar of the Film Language* (New York: Focal Press, 1978); and Edward Dmytryk, *On Screen Directing* (Boston: Focal Press, 1984). Older but still informative sources include Sidney Cole, "Film Editor," in Oswell Blakeston, ed.,

*Working for the Films* (London: Focal Press, 1947), pp. 152–160; Anne Bauchens, "Cutting the Film," in Nancy Naumburg, *We Make the Movies* (New York: Norton, 1937), pp. 199–215; and Lewis Herman, *A Practical Manual of Screen Playwriting for Theater and Television Films* (New York: Meridian, 1974), pp. 93–165. Our diagram of a hypothetical axis of action has been adapted from Edward Pincus's concise discussion in his *Guide to Filmmaking* (New York: Signet, 1969), pp. 120–125. Pat P. Miller explains how to avoid discontinuities in *Script Supervising and Film Continuity* (Boston: Focal Press, 1986).

Recent scholarship has begun increasingly to analyze the continuity style. See Raymond Bellour, "The Obvious and the Code," *Screen* **15,** 4 (Winter 1974/5): 7–17; Vance Kepley, Jr., "Spatial Articulation in the Classical Cinema: A Scene from *His Girl Friday,*" *Wide Angle* **5,** 3 (1983): 50–58; André Gaudreault, "Detours in Film Narrative: The Development of Cross-Cutting," *Cinema Journal* **19,** 1 (Fall 1979): 35–59; and William Simon, "An Approach to Point of View," *Film Reader* **4** (1979): 145–151. More theoretical consideration of the shot/reverse-shot device was initiated by Jean-Pierre Oudart in "Cinema and Suture," *Screen* **18,** 4 (Winter 1977/78): 35–47. Oudart's ideas are discussed in Daniel Dayan, "The Tutor-Code of Classical Cinema," *Film Quarterly* **28,** 1 (Fall 1974): 22–31; Stephen Heath, *Questions of Cinema* (Bloomington: Indiana University Press, 1982); and David Bordwell, *Narration in the Fiction Film* (Madison: University of Wisconsin Press, 1985), chapter 6.

Literally thousands of films can be studied for their use of continuity editing, but here are a few familiar ones: *Bringing Up Baby* (Hawks, 1938); *Trouble in Paradise* (Lubitsch, 1932); *The Wizard of Oz* (Fleming, 1939); *Singin' in the Rain* (Donen-Kelly, 1952); *Mildred Pierce* (Curtiz, 1945); *Roaring Twenties* (Walsh, 1939); *White Heat* (Walsh, 1949); *Winchester 73* (Mann, 1950); *The Philadelphia Story* (Cukor, 1940); *The General* (Keaton, 1927); *Mr. Smith Goes to Washington* (Capra, 1939). In all of these films, watch for occasional violations of the continuity rules. The second scene of *Mr. Smith* is especially instructive in this regard; is there a pattern or reason behind Capra's frequent continuity breaks, or are they simply errors? Are the continuity rules obeyed in such non-American films as *Children of Paradise* (Carné, 1945); *The Blue Angel* (von Sternberg, 1930); *M* (Lang, 1931); and *Persona* (Bergman, 1965)?

### ■ ALTERNATIVES TO CONTINUITY EDITING

Eisenstein remains the chief source in this area. An exceptionally introspective filmmaker, he bequeathed us a rich set of ideas on the possibilities of nonnarrative editing; see the essays in *Selected Works, Vol. I.* For further discussion of editing in *October*, see the essays by Annette Michelson, Noël Carroll, and Rosalind Krauss in the special "Eisenstein/Brakhage" number of *Artforum* **11,** 5 (January 1973): 30–37, 56–65, and Marie-Claire Ropars, "The Overture of *October*," *Enclitic* **2,** 2 (Fall 1978): 50–72, and **3,** 1 (Spring 1979): 35–47. The writings of another Russian, Dziga Vertov, are also of interest; see Annette Michelson, ed., *Kino-Eye: The Writings of Dziga Vertov* (Berkeley: University of California Press, 1984). Good discussions of Vertov's montage practice are Stephen Crofts and Olivia Rose, "An Essay toward *Man with a Movie Camera*," *Screen* **18,** 1 (Spring 1977): 9–58, and Seth R. Feldman, *Evolution of Style in the Early Work of Dziga Vertov* (New York: Arno, 1977). For a detailed consideration of Godard's play with continuity cues, see Jacques Aumont, "This Is Not a Textual Analysis (Godard's *La Chinoise*)," *Camera Obscura* 8-9-10 (1982): 131–161. On Ozu's manipulation of discontinuities, see David Bordwell, *Ozu and the Poetics of Cinema* (Princeton, N.J.: Princeton University Press, 1988); Kristin Thompson, "*Late Spring* and Ozu's Unreasonable Style," in *Breaking the Glass Armor: Neoformalist Film Analysis* (Princeton, N.J.: Princeton University Press, 1988), pp. 317–352; and Edward Branigan, "The Space of *Equinox Flower*," *Screen* **17,** 2 (Summer 1976): 74–105.

Experimental and avant-garde cinema have taken the largest steps toward constructing alternatives to the continuity style. David Curtis's *Experimental Cinema* (New York: Delta, 1971) and Jean Mitry's *Le Cinéma Experimental* (Paris: Seghers, 1974) provide general overviews of the history of experimental film. On the "New American Cinema" there are several sources: Gregory Battcock, ed., *The New American Cinema* (New York: Dutton, 1967); P. Adams Sitney, *Visionary Film*, 2d ed. (New York: Oxford University Press, 1978); and P. Adams Sitney, ed., *Film Culture Reader* (New York: Praeger, 1970). Journals like *Millennium Film Journal* and *Afterimage* provide continuing coverage of experimental cinema. A shot-by-shot analysis of *Ballet mécanique* may be found in Standish Lawder, *The Cubist Cinema* (Berkeley: University of California Press, 1975).

# EIGHT

## SOUND
## IN THE CINEMA

---

### THE POWERS OF SOUND

---

Many people tend to think of sound as simply an accompaniment to the real basis of cinema, the moving images. These viewers assume that the people and things pictured on the screen just produce an appropriate noise. But as we have seen, in the process of film production the sound track is recorded separately from the images and can be manipulated independently.

Consider some of the advantages of sound for a film. First, it engages another sense mode: our visual attention can be accompanied by an aural attention. (Even before recorded sound was introduced in 1926, the "silent" cinema recognized this by its use of accompaniment by orchestra, organ, or piano.) Second, sound can *actively shape how we interpret the image.* In one sequence of *Letter from Siberia,* Chris Marker demonstrates the power of sound to alter our perception of images. Three times Marker plays the same footage—a shot of a bus passing a car on a city street, three shots of workers paving a street. But each time the footage is accompanied by a completely different sound track. Compare the three versions tabulated alongside the sequence (Table 8.1). The verbal differences are emphasized by the sameness of the images; the audience will interpret the same images differently, depending on the sound track.

The *Letter from Siberia* sequence also demonstrates a third advantage of sound. Film sound can direct our attention quite specifically within the image. When the commentator describes the "blood-colored buses," we will look at the bus and not at the car. When Fred Astaire and Ginger Rogers are executing an intricate step, chances are that we watch their bodies and not the silent nightclub spectators

244

| Table 8.1 | *LETTER FROM SIBERIA* FOOTAGE | | |
|---|---|---|---|
| IMAGES | FIRST COMMENTARY | SECOND COMMENTARY | THIRD COMMENTARY |
| <br>**Fig. 8.1** | Yakutsk, capital of the Yakutsk Autonomous Soviet Socialist Republic, is a modern city in which comfortable buses made available to the population share the streets with powerful Zyms, the pride of the Soviet automobile industry. In the | Yakutsk is a dark city with an evil reputation. The population is crammed into blood-colored buses while the members of the privileged caste brazenly display the luxury of their Zyms, a costly and uncomfortable car at best. Bending | In Yakutsk, where modern houses are gradually replacing the dark older sections, a bus, less crowded than its London or New York equivalent at rush hour, passes a Zym, an excellent car reserved for public utilities departments on account of its scarcity. |
| <br>**Fig. 8.2** | joyful spirit of socialist emulation, happy Soviet workers, among them this picturesque denizen | to the task like slaves, the miserable Soviet workers, among them this sinister-looking Asiatic, | With courage and tenacity under extremely difficult conditions, Soviet workers, among them this Yakut |
| <br>**Fig. 8.3** | of the Arctic reaches, apply themselves | apply themselves to the primitive labor | afflicted with an eye disorder, apply themselves to |
| <br>**Fig. 8.4** | to making Yakutsk an even better place to live.<br><br>Or else: | of grading with a drag beam.<br><br>Or simply: | improving the appearance of their city, which could certainly use it. |

**Fig. 8.5**

looking on (see production still from *Swing Time*, Fig. 8.5). In such ways, sound can guide us through the images, "pointing" to things to watch. This possibility becomes even more complex when you consider that the sound cue for some visual element may *anticipate* that element and relay our attention to it. Suppose we have a close-up of a man in a room and we hear the creaking of a door opening; if the next shot shows the door, now open, the viewer will likely focus his or her attention on that door, the source of the offscreen sound. In an opposite way, if the next shot shows the door still closed, the viewer will likely ponder his or her interpretation of the sound. (Maybe it wasn't a door, after all?) Thus the sound track can clarify image events, contradict them, or render them ambiguous. In all cases, the sound track can enter into an active relation with the image track.

This example of the door opening suggests a fourth advantage of sound: it cues us to form expectations. If we hear a door creaking, we anticipate that someone has entered a room and that we will see that person in the next shot. But, if the film draws upon conventions of the horror genre, the camera might stay on the man, staring fearfully. We would then be in suspense as to the appearance of the monster offscreen. Horror and mystery films often utilize the power of sound from an unseen source to engage the audience's interest, but all types of films can take advantage of this aspect of sound.

Moreover, as V. F. Perkins has pointed out, sound brings with it a new sense of the value of silence. "Only with colour as an available resource can we regard the use of black-and-white photography as the result of a conscious artistic decision. Only in the sound film can a director use silence for dramatic effect" (*Film as Film*, p. 54). In the context of sound, silence takes on a new expressive function.

A final advantage: sound bristles with as many creative possibilities as editing. Through editing, one may join shots of any two spaces to create a meaningful

CLARITY; CONTRADICT;
REWDER AMBIGUOUS

EXPECTATIONS X

power of silence

relation. Similarly, the filmmaker can mix any sonic phenomena into a whole. With the introduction of sound cinema, the infinity of visual possibilities was joined by the infinity of acoustic events.

## FUNDAMENTALS OF FILM SOUND

### ■ ACOUSTIC PROPERTIES

To pursue in detail the acoustic processes that produce sound would take us on a long detour. (See Notes and Queries for reading on the subject.) We should, however, isolate some qualities of sound as we perceive it. These qualities are familiar to us from everyday experience.

**Loudness.** Perceived sound results from vibrations in air; the amplitude of the vibrations produces our sense of volume. Film sound constantly manipulates volume. For example, in many films a long shot of a busy street is accompanied by loud traffic noises, but when two people meet and start to speak, the loudness of the noise drops. Or a dialogue between a soft-spoken character and a blustery one is characterized as much by the difference in volume as by the substance of the talk. Needless to say, loudness is also affected by perceived distance; often the louder the sound, the closer we take it to be. Some films exploit radical changes in volume for shock value, as when a quiet scene is interrupted by a very loud noise.

**Pitch.** The frequency of sound vibrations governs pitch, or the perceived "highness" or "lowness" of the sound. Pitch is the principal way we distinguish music from other sounds in the film, but it has more complex uses. When a young boy tries to speak in a man's deep voice and fails (as in *How Green Was My Valley*), the joke is based primarily on pitch. In the coronation scene of *Ivan the Terrible*, Part I, a court singer with a deep bass voice begins a song of praise to Ivan, and each phrase rises dramatically in pitch—which Eisenstein emphasizes in the editing, with successively closer shots of the singer coinciding with each vocal change. When Bernard Herrmann obtained the effects of unnatural, birdlike shrieking in Hitchcock's *Psycho*, even many musicians could not recognize the source: violins played at extraordinarily high pitch.

**Timbre.** The harmonic components of a sound give it a certain "color" or tone quality—what musicians call timbre. When we call someone's voice nasal or a certain musical tone mellow, we are referring to timbre. Again, filmmakers manipulate timbre continually. Timbre can help articulate portions of the sound track; for instance, timbre differentiates musical instruments from one another. Timbre also "comes forward" on certain occasions, as in the clichéd use of oleaginous saxophone tones behind seduction scenes. More subtly, in the opening sequence of Rouben Mamoulian's *Love Me Tonight* people pass a musical rhythm from object to object—a broom, a carpet beater—and the humor of the number springs in part from the very different timbres of the objects.

As the fundamental components of film sound, loudness, pitch, and timbre usually interact to define the sonic texture of a film. At the most elementary level, loudness, pitch, and timbre enable us to distinguish among all of the sounds in a film; we recognize different characters' voices by these qualities, for example. But at a more complex level, all three interact to add considerably to our experience of the film. Both John Wayne and James Stewart speak slowly, but Wayne's voice tends to be deeper and gruffer than Stewart's querulous drawl. This difference works to great advantage in *The Man Who Shot Liberty Valance*, where their characters are sharply contrasted. In *The Wizard of Oz* the disparity between the public image of the Wizard and the old charlatan who rigs it up is marked by the booming bass of the effigy and the old man's higher, softer, more quavering voice. *Citizen Kane* offers a wide range of sound manipulations. Echo chambers alter timbre and volume, and a motif is formed by the inability of Kane's wife Susan to sing pitches accurately. Moreover, in *Citizen Kane* shifts between times and places are covered by continuing a sound "thread" and varying the basic acoustics. A shot of Kane applauding dissolves to a shot of a crowd applauding (a shift in volume and timbre); Leland beginning a sentence in the street cuts to Kane finishing the sentence in an auditorium, his voice magnified by loudspeakers (a shift in volume, timbre, and pitch). Such examples suggest that the elementary properties of sound afford a rich set of possibilities for the filmmaker to explore.

### ■ SELECTION AND COMBINATION

Sound in the cinema takes three forms: *speech*, *music*, and *noise* (also called *sound effects*). Occasionally a sound may share categories—is a scream speech or noise? is electronic music also noise?—and filmmakers have freely exploited these ambiguities. (In *Psycho*, when a woman screams, we expect to hear a human voice and instead hear "screaming" violins.) Nevertheless, in most cases the distinctions hold. Now that we have an idea of the role of acoustic properties, we must consider how speech, music, and noise are selected and combined for specific functions within films.

The creation of the sound track resembles the editing of the image track. Just as the filmmaker may select from several shots the best image, he or she may choose what exact bit of sound from this or that source will best serve the purpose. And, just as the filmmaker may link or superimpose images, so may he or she join any two sounds end to end or one "over" another (as with commentary "over" music). Though we are not usually as aware of the manipulation of the sound track, it demands as much selection and control as does the visual track.

*Selection* of the desired sound is a necessary step in the process. Normally, our perception filters out irrelevant stimuli and retains what is most useful at a particular moment. As you read this, you are attending to words on the page and (to various degrees) ignoring certain stimuli that reach your ears. But if you close your eyes and listen attentively to the sounds around you, you will become aware of many previously unnoticed sounds—distant voices, the wind, footsteps, a radio playing. As any amateur recordist knows, if you set up a microphone and tape recorder in a "quiet" environment, all of those normally unnoticed sounds suddenly become obtrusive. The microphone is unselective; like the camera lens, it does not automatically achieve the desired result. Sound studios, camera blimps to absorb motor noise, directional and shielded microphones, sound engineering and editing, and libraries of stock sounds all exist so that a film's sound track may be carefully controlled through selection. Unless a filmmaker actually *wants* to record all of the ambient noise of a scene, simply holding out a microphone while filming will rarely suffice.

Fig. 8.6

*continuing sonic elements*

Because our normal perception is linked to our choices about what to pay attention to, the director's selection of the sounds in a film can control the audience's choices and thus guide the audience's perception. In one scene from Jacques Tati's *Mr. Hulot's Holiday* vacationers at a resort hotel are relaxing (Fig. 8.6). In the foreground guests quietly play cards; in the depth of the shot, Mr. Hulot is frantically playing Ping-Pong. Early in the scene, the guests in the foreground are murmuring quietly, but Hulot's Ping-Pong game is louder; the sound cues us to watch Hulot. Later in the scene, however, the same Ping-Pong game makes *no* sound at all, and our attention is drawn to the muttering card players in the foreground. The presence and absence of the sound of the Ping-Pong ball guides our expectations. If you start to notice how such selection of sound shapes our perception, you will also notice that filmmakers often use sound to shift our attention.

Such examples depend not only on selection but also on the filmmaker's *combining* of various sonic elements. It is the mixing of sounds in a specific pattern that constitutes the sound track as we know it. We have already seen that mixing is a careful and deliberate production procedure. It can also be a flexible process, since in modern filmmaking, a dozen or more separate tracks may be recorded and later mixed. The mixer can control the volume and duration of each sound precisely. What we must now notice is what functions the particular mix can have in the total film. Obviously the mix can range from very dense (e.g., a scene containing the babble of voices, the sounds of footsteps, Muzak, and plane engines at an airport) to total silence, with most cases falling in between. In addition, the filmmaker may create a mix in which each sound modulates and overlaps smoothly with the others, or one that is composed of much more abrupt and startling contrasts.

The possibilities of combining sounds are well illustrated by the final battle sequence of Akira Kurosawa's *Seven Samurai*. In a heavy rain, marauding bandits charge into a village defended by the villagers and the samurai. The torrent and wind form a constant background noise throughout the scene. Before the battle, the conversation of the waiting men, footsteps, and the sound of swords being drawn are punctuated by long pauses in which we hear only the drumming rain. Suddenly distant horses' hooves are heard offscreen. This draws our attention from the defenders to the attackers. Then Kurosawa cuts to a long shot of the bandits; their horses' hooves become abruptly louder. (This is typical of the scene: the closer the camera is to a sound source, the louder the sound.) When the bandits burst into the village, yet another sound element appears—the bandits' harsh battle cries, which increase steadily in volume as they approach. The battle begins. The muddy, storm-swept mise-en-scène and rhythmic cutting gain impact from the way in which the incessant rain and splashing are explosively interrupted by brief noises—the screams of the wounded, the splintering of a fence one bandit crashes through, the whinnies of horses, the twang of one samurai's bowstring, the gurgle of a speared bandit, the screams of women when the bandit chieftain breaks into their hiding place. The sudden intrusion of certain sounds marks abrupt developments in the battle. Such frequent surprises heighten our tension, since the narration frequently shifts us from one line of action to another. The scene climaxes after the main battle has ended. Offscreen horses' hooves are cut short by a new sound—the sharp crack of a bandit's rifle shot, which fells one samurai. A long pause, in which we hear only the driving rain, emphasizes the moment. The samurai furiously throws his sword in the direction of the shot and falls dead into the mud. Another samurai races toward the bandit chieftain, who has the rifle; another shot cracks out and he falls back, wounded; another pause, in which only the relentless rain is heard. The wounded samurai kills the chieftain. The other samurai gather. At the scene's end, the sobs of a young samurai, the distant whinnies and hoofbeats of now riderless horses, and the rain all fade slowly out. The relatively dense mix of this sound track (accomplished entirely without music) gradually introduces sounds to turn our attention to new narrative elements (hooves, battle cries) and then goes on to modulate these sounds smoothly into a harmonious whole. This whole is then punctuated by abrupt sounds of unusual volume or pitch associated with crucial narrative actions (the archery, women's screams, the gunshots). Overall, the combination of many sounds enhances the unrestricted, objective narration of this sequence, which shows us what happens in various parts of the village, rather than confining us to the experience of a single participant.

The choice and combination of sonic materials also affect the film as a whole. This is most readily seen by examining how the filmmaker can use a musical score. Sometimes the filmmaker will select preexisting pieces of music to accompany the images, as Bruce Conner has done in using portions of Respighi's *Pines of Rome* as the sound track for *A Movie*. In other cases the music will be composed for the film, and here the filmmaker and the composer make several choices. The meter, rhythm, melody, harmony, and instrumentation of the music can strongly affect the viewer's emotional reactions. In addition, a melody or musical phrase can be associated with a particular character, setting, situation, or idea. By manipulating such motifs, the filmmaker can subtly compare scenes, trace out patterns of development, and suggest implicit meanings.

A convenient example is furnished by Georges Delerue's score for François Truffaut's *Jules and Jim*. Overall, the music reflects the Paris of 1912–33, during which the action takes place; many of the melodies resemble works by Debussy and Erik Satie, two of the most prominent French composers of that era. Virtually the entire score consists of waltzes, which unify the film by giving a gentle rhythm to most scenes.

More specifically, musical themes are associated with particular aspects of the narrative. For example, Catherine's constant search for happiness and freedom outside conventional boundaries is conveyed by her singing the "Tourbillon" ("whirlwind") song, which says that life is a constant changing of romantic partners. Settings are also evoked in musical terms. One tune is heard every time the characters are in a café. As the years go by, the tune changes from a mechanical player-piano rendition to a jazzier version played by a black pianist.

The characters' relations become more strained and complicated over time, and the score reflects this in its development of certain motifs. A lyrical melody is first heard when the three characters visit the countryside and bicycle to the beach. This "idyll" waltz will recur at many points when the characters reunite, but as the years pass it will become slower in tempo and more sombre in instrumentation. Another motif that reappears in different guises is a "dangerous love" theme associated with Jim and Catherine. This grave, shimmering waltz is first heard when he visits her apartment and watches her pour a bottle of vitriol down the sink. (The acid, she says, is "for lying eyes.") Thereafter, this theme, which resembles one of Satie's *Gymnopédies* for piano, is used to underscore Jim and Catherine's vertiginous love affair: at times it accompanies scenes of passion, but at other times it accompanies their growing disillusionment and despair.

The most varied theme is a mysterious woodwind phrase first heard when Jules and Jim encounter a striking ancient statue. Later they meet Catherine and discover that she has the statue's face; a repetition of the musical motif confirms the comparison. Throughout the film, this brief motif is associated with the enigmatic side of Catherine. In the later scenes, this motif is developed in an intriguing way.

The bass line (played on harpsichord or strings) that softly accompanied the woodwind tune now comes to the fore, creating a relentless, often harsh pulsation. This "menace" waltz underscores Catherine's fling with Albert and accompanies her final vengeance on Jim: driving her car, with him as passenger, into the river.

Once musical motifs have been selected, they can be combined to evoke associations. During Jim and Catherine's first intimate talk after the war, the bass-line-dominated version of the "Catherine" waltz is followed by the love theme, as if the latter could drown out the menacing side of Catherine's character. The love theme accompanies long tracking shots of Jim and Catherine strolling through the woods. But at the scene's end, as Jim bids Catherine farewell, the original woodwind version of her theme recalls her mystery and the risk he is running by falling in love with her.

A similar sort of blending can be found in the film's final scene. Catherine and Jim have drowned, and Jules is overseeing the cremation of their bodies. As shots of the coffins dissolve into detailed shots of the cremation process, the "enigma" motif segues into its sinister variant, the "menace" motif. But as Jules leaves the cemetery and the narrator comments that Catherine had wanted her ashes to be cast to the winds, the music glides into a sweeping string version of the "whirlwind" waltz. The film's musical score thus concludes by recalling the three sides of Catherine that attracted the men to her: her mystery, her menace, and her vivacious openness to experience. In such ways, a musical score can create, develop, and associate motifs that enter into the film's overall formal system.

## DIMENSIONS OF FILM SOUND

We have now seen what sounds consist of and how the filmmaker can take advantage of the widely different kinds of sounds available. In addition, the way in which the sounds relate to other film elements gives them several other dimensions. First, because sound occupies a duration, it has a *rhythm.* Second, sound can relate to its perceived source with greater or lesser *fidelity.* Third, sound conveys a sense of the *spatial* conditions in which it occurs. And fourth, the sound relates to visual events that take place in a specific time, and this relationship gives sound a *temporal* dimension. These categories begin to reveal that sound in film is actually a very complex thing; let's look at each category briefly.

### ■ RHYTHM

For our purposes, a sound's rhythm will be defined by its speed and its regularity. The reverberating note of a large gong may go on for many seconds and seem slow in rhythm to the perceiver, while a sudden sneeze occupies only an instant. And, whatever their speeds, sounds can come with greater or lesser regularity. In a gangster film, a machine gun's fire would make a very regular sound, while the sporadic reports of pistols would come at irregular intervals. These qualities may be combined in different ways: a film's sound may be slow and irregular, fast and regular, and so on. Moreover, all three types of sound on the sound track have their own rhythmic possibilities independent of one another. The gasping voice of a character who lies dying has a slower rhythm than the voice of a racetrack announcer. Music obviously may have different rhythms in a film. Finally, sound

effects also vary in rhythm (compare the plodding hooves of a farmhorse and a cavalry company riding at full speed).

But even this simple definition of rhythm as speed and regularity is complicated by the fact that the movements in the images themselves have a rhythm as well, distinguished by the same variable principles of speed and regularity. In addition, the editing has a rhythm; as we have seen, a succession of short shots helps create a fast rhythm, whereas shots held longer slow down the editing's rhythm.

In most cases the rhythms of editing, of movement within the image, and of sound do not function separately. Possibly the most common tendency is for the filmmaker to match visual and sonic rhythms to each other. An obvious example is the typical dance sequence in a musical; here the figures move about at a rhythm determined by the music. But variation is always possible. In the "Waltz in Swing Time" number in *Swing Time*, the dancing of Astaire and Rogers moves quickly in time to the music. But no fast cutting accompanies this scene. Indeed, there is no cutting at all within the dance, for the scene consists of a single long take from a long-shot distance. Another example of close coordination between screen movement and sound comes in the animated films of Walt Disney in the 1930s. Mickey Mouse and the other Disney characters often move in exact synchronization with the music, even when they are not dancing. (This nondance matching of movement with music in fact came to be known as "Mickey Mousing.")

The filmmaker may choose to create a disparity among the rhythms of sound, editing, and image. One way of accomplishing this is to keep the source of the sound offscreen and to show something else onscreen. Toward the end of John Ford's *She Wore a Yellow Ribbon*, the aging cavalry captain, Nathan Brittles, watches his troop ride out of the fort just after he has retired; he regrets leaving the service and desires to go with the patrol. The sound of the scene consists of two elements: the cheerful title song sung by the departing riders, and the quick hoofbeats of their horses. Yet only a few of the shots show the horses and singers, who move at a rhythm matched to the sound. Instead, the scene concentrates our attention on Brittles, standing almost motionless by his own horse. (The moderate rate of cutting lies between these two rhythms.) The contrast of fast rhythm of sound with the shots of the solitary Brittles functions expressively, to emphasize his regret at having to stay behind for the first time in many years.

Several great directors have used music that might seem to have a rhythm inappropriate for the visuals. At intervals in *Four Nights of a Dreamer* Robert Bresson includes shots of a large, floating nightclub cruising the Seine. The boat's movement is slow and smooth, yet the sound track consists of lively calypso music. (Not until a later scene do we discover that the music comes from the boat.) The strange combination of fast music with the slow passage of the boat creates a langorous, mysterious effect. Jacques Tati does something similar in *Play Time*. In a scene outside a Parisian hotel, tourists climb aboard a bus to go to a nightclub; as they file slowly up the steps, raucous, jazzy music begins. The music again startles our expectations because it seems inappropriate to the images. In fact, it belongs with the next scene, in which some carpenters awkwardly carrying a large plate-glass window seem to be dancing to the music. By starting the fast music over an earlier scene of slower visual rhythm, Tati creates a comic effect and prepares for a transition to a new space.

Chris Marker has carried this contrast between image and sound rhythms to what may be its logical limit, in *La Jetée*. This film is made up almost entirely of still shots; except for one tiny gesture, all movement within the images is eliminated. Yet the film has a narrator, music, and sound effects of a generally dynamic rhythm.

The result is not at all "uncinematic," but rather it has great effectiveness because of the originality of the concept and the care and consistency with which this juxtaposition of rhythms is carried through the whole structure of the film.

These examples suggest some of the ways in which rhythms may be combined. But of course most films also vary their rhythms from one point to another. A change of rhythm may function to shift our expectations. In a famous sequence Sergei Eisenstein develops the sound from slow tempos to fast and back to slow: the battle on the ice in *Alexander Nevsky*. The first 12 shots of the scene show the Russian army prepared for the attack of the German knights. The shots are of moderate, even length, and they contain very little movement. The music is comparably slow, consisting of short, distinctly separated chords. Then, as the German army rides into sight over the horizon, both the visual movement and the tempo of the music increase quickly, and the battle begins. At the end of the battle Eisenstein creates another contrast with a long passage of slow, lamenting music and little movement.

## ■ FIDELITY

By fidelity we do not mean the quality of recording. Here we are speaking of whether the sound is faithful to the source as we conceive it. If a film shows us a barking dog and the sound track has a barking noise, that sound is faithful to its source; the sound maintains fidelity. But if the sound of a cat meowing accompanies the picture of the barking dog, there enters a disparity between sound and image— a lack of fidelity. Fidelity has nothing to do with what originally made the sound during filming. As we have seen, the filmmaker may manipulate sound independently of image; accompanying the image of a dog with the meow is no more difficult than accompanying the image with a bark. Note, however, that fidelity is purely a matter of our expectations. In production the bark or meow might be created electronically or by an animal imitator. Fidelity involves conventional expectations about sources, not knowledge of where the filmmaker actually obtained the sound.

A play with fidelity most commonly functions for comic effect. Jacques Tati is one of the directors most skillful at employing various degrees of fidelity. In *Mr. Hulot's Holiday* much comedy arises from the opening and closing of a dining-room door. Instead of simply recording a real door, Tati inserts a twanging sound like a plucked cello string each time the door swings. Aside from being amusing in itself, this sound functions to emphasize the rhythmic patterns created by waiters and diners passing through the door. Another master of comically unfaithful sound is René Clair. In several scenes of *Le Million* sound effects occur that are not faithful to their sources. When the hero's friend drops a plate, we hear not shattering crockery, but the clash of cymbals. Later, during a chase scene, when characters collide, the impact is portrayed by a heavy bass drum beat. Similar manipulations of fidelity commonly occur in animated cartoons.

But as with low- or high-angle framings, we have no recipe that will allow us to interpret every manipulation of fidelity as comic. Some nonfaithful sounds have serious functions. In Hitchcock's *The Thirty-Nine Steps* a landlady discovers a corpse in an apartment. A shot of her screaming face is accompanied by a train whistle; then the scene shifts to an actual train. Though the whistle is not a faithful sound for an image of a screaming person, it provides a striking transition.

Finally, in some special cases fidelity may be manipulated by a change in volume. A sound may seem unreasonably loud or soft in relation to other sounds in the film. Curtis Bernhardt's *Possessed* alters volume in ways that are not faithful to the sources. The central character is gradually falling deeper into mental illness. In one scene she is alone, very distraught, in her room on a rainy night, and the narration restricts us to her range of knowledge. But sound devices enable the narration to achieve subjective depth as well. We begin to hear things as she does; the ticking of the clock and dripping of raindrops gradually magnify in volume. Here the shift in fidelity functions to suggest a psychological state, a movement from the character's heightened perception into sheer hallucination.

## ■ SPACE

Sound has a spatial dimension because it comes from a *source*, and that source may be characterized by the space it occupies. If the source of a sound is a character or object in the story space of the film, we call the sound **diegetic.** The voice of the characters, sounds made by objects in the story, or music represented as coming from instruments in the story space are all diegetic sound. Diegetic sound is often hard to notice as such. It may seem to come from the "world" of the film naturally, as when characters speak lines of dialogue. But as we saw with the example of the Ping-Pong game in *Mr. Hulot's Holiday*, the filmmaker may manipulate diegetic sound in ways that are not at all realistic. Because many of the jokes in *Mr. Hulot's Holiday* and other Tati films are based on funny noises, his films are good specimens for an initial study of sound.

On the other hand there is **nondiegetic** sound, which is represented as coming from a source outside the story space. Familiar examples of such sound are easy to find. Music added to enhance the film's action is the most common type of nondiegetic sound; when a character is climbing a sheer cliff and tense music comes up, we do not expect to see an orchestra perched on the side of the mountain. Viewers understand that the "movie music" is a convention and does not issue from the space of the story. The same holds true for the so-called omniscient narrator, the disembodied voice that gives us information but does not belong to any of the characters in the film. Orson Welles speaks the nondiegetic narration in his own film *The Magnificent Ambersons*, for example. Nondiegetic sound effects are also possible. In *Le Million* various characters all pursue an old coat with a winning lottery ticket in the pocket. They converge backstage at the opera and begin racing and dodging around one another, tossing the coat to their accomplices. But instead of putting in the sounds coming from the actual space of the chase, Clair fades in the sounds of a football game. Because the maneuvers of the chase do look like a football game, with the coat serving as ball, this enhances the comedy of the sequence. We hear a crowd cheering and a whistle's sound; yet we do not assume that the characters present are making these sounds (so this is not a manipulation of fidelity, as with the earlier examples from *Le Million*). The nondiegetic sounds create comedy by making a sort of audiovisual pun.

As with fidelity, the distinction between diegetic and nondiegetic sound does not depend on the real source of the sound in the filmmaking process. Rather, it depends on our understanding of the conventions of film viewing. We know that certain sounds are represented as coming from the story world, while others are represented as a commenting intervention from outside the space of the story events. Such viewing conventions are so common that we usually do not have to think about which type of sound we are hearing at any moment—*unless* the film's narration plays with conventions and uses a sound whose source puzzles or surprises us.

What are the possibilities of diegetic sound? We know that the space of the narrative action is not limited to what we can see on the screen at any given moment. If we know that several people are present in a room, we can see a shot that shows only one person without assuming that the other people have dropped out of the story. We simply have a sense that those people are offscreen. And if one of those offscreen people speaks, we still assume that the sound is coming from part of the story space. Thus diegetic sound can be either *onscreen* or *offscreen*, depending on whether its source is within the frame or outside the frame.

Simple examples will illustrate this. A shot shows a character talking, and we hear the sound of his or her voice; another shows a door closing, and we hear a slam; a person plays a fiddle, and we hear its notes. In each case the source of the sound is in the story—diegetic—and visible within the frame—onscreen. But the shot may show only a person listening to a voice without the speaker being seen; another shot might show a character running down a corridor and the sound of an unseen door slamming; lastly, an audience is shown listening while the sound of a fiddle is heard. In all of these instances, the sounds come from within the story—again diegetic—but are now in a space outside the frame—offscreen.

This may seem a trivial distinction at first, but we know from Chapter 6 how powerful offscreen space can be. Offscreen sound can suggest space extending in various directions beyond the visible action. In *American Graffiti*, a film that plays heavily on the distinction between diegetic and nondiegetic music, offscreen sounds of car radios often suggest that all of the cars on a street are tuned to the same radio station. Offscreen sound may also control our expectations about offscreen space. In *His Girl Friday* Hildy goes into the press room to write her final story. As she chats with the other reporters, a loud clunk comes from an unseen source. Hildy glances off left, and immediately a new space comes to our attention, though we have not seen it yet. She walks to the window and sees a gallows being prepared for an execution. Here offscreen sound initiates the discovery of fresh space. As these examples indicate, offscreen diegetic sound usually functions to make narration less restricted, since it gives us story information about events in two different spaces at once.

A brilliant use of a similar device comes in John Ford's *Stagecoach*. The stagecoach is desperately fleeing from a band of Indians. The ammunition is running out, and all seems lost until a troop of cavalry suddenly arrives. Yet Ford does not create the situation this baldly. He shows a medium close-up of one of the men, Hatfield, who has just discovered that he is down to his last bullet (Fig. 8.7). He glances off right and raises his gun (Fig. 8.8). The camera pans right to a woman, Lucy, praying. During all this, orchestral music, including bugles, plays nondiegetically. Unseen by Lucy, the gun comes into the frame from the left as Hatfield

Fig. 8.7

Fig. 8.8

Fig. 8.9

Fig. 8.10

Fig. 8.11

prepares to shoot her to prevent her being captured by the Indians (Fig. 8.9). But before he shoots, an offscreen gunshot is heard, and Hatfield's hand and gun drop down out of the frame (Fig. 8.10). Then the bugle music becomes somewhat more prominent. Lucy's expression changes as she says, "Can you hear it? Can you hear it? It's a bugle. They're blowing the charge" (Fig. 8.11). Only then does Ford cut to the cavalry itself racing toward the coach. Rather than focusing on the mechanics of the rescue, the film's narration uses offscreen sound to restrict our vision to the initial despair of the passengers and their growing hope as they hear the distant sound. The sound of the bugle also emerges imperceptibly out of the nondiegetic music. Only Lucy's line tells us that this is a diegetic sound that signals their rescue, at which point the narration becomes far less restricted.

There are other possibilities for diegetic sound. Often a filmmaker uses sound to represent what a character is thinking. We hear the character's voice speaking his or her thoughts even though that character's lips do not move; presumably other characters cannot hear these thoughts. Here the narration uses sound to achieve subjectivity, giving us insight into the mental subjectivity of the character. Such "spoken thoughts" are comparable to mental images on the visual track. A character may also remember words, snatches of music, or events as represented by sound effects; in this case the technique is comparable to a visual flashback. This device is so common that we need to distinguish between *internal* and *external* diegetic sound. External diegetic sound is that which we as spectators take to have a physical source in the scene. Internal diegetic sound is that which comes only from the mind of a character; it is subjective. (Nondiegetic and internal diegetic sounds are often called **sound over** because they do not come from the real space of the scene.)

In the Laurence Olivier version of *Hamlet*, for example, the filmmaker presents Hamlet's famous soliloquies as interior monologues. Hamlet is the source of the thoughts we hear represented as speech, but the words are only in his mind, not in his objective surroundings. A more complex use of internal diegetic sound occurs in Wim Wenders's *Wings of Desire*. Dozens of people are reading in a large public library. As the camera tracks along past them, we hear their thoughts as a murmur of many voices in many languages. The technique is varied when the camera moves into the library section devoted to musical scores. Here the subjective sound becomes a dense choir of instruments and singing voices, representing the different musical pieces the readers are studying. Incidentally, this sequence also constitutes an interesting exception to the general rule that no characters can hear internal diegetic sound. The film's premise is that Berlin is patrolled by invisible angels who can tune in to humans' thoughts. This is a good example of how the conventions of a genre (here, the fantasy film) and the film's specific narrative context can modify a traditional device.

To summarize: Sound may be diegetic (in the story space) or nondiegetic (outside the story space). If it is diegetic, it may be onscreen or offscreen, and internal ("subjective") or external ("objective").

One characteristic of diegetic sound is the possibility of suggesting the *distance* of its source. Volume is one simple way to give an impression of distance. A loud sound tends to seem near; a soft one, more distant. The horses' hooves in the *Seven Samurai* battle and the bugle call from *Stagecoach* exemplify how changing volume suggests changing distance.

In addition to volume, timbre may suggest the texture and dimensions of the space within which a sound supposedly exists. In *The Magnificent Ambersons* the conversations that take place on the baroque staircase have an echoing effect, giving the impression of huge, empty spaces around the characters. The skillful filmmaker will pay attention to the quality of the sound, taking advantage of the possibilities of variation from shot to shot.

In recent years technical developments have added the possibilities of stereo and other multichanneled systems to the filmmaker's range. Speakers for each track may be placed at the sides of the screen and even behind the audience. This means that the sound can suggest location not only in terms of distance (volume, resonance) but also by specifying *direction*. In stereo versions of David Lean's *Lawrence of Arabia*, for example, the approach of planes to bomb a camp is first suggested through a rumble occurring only on the right side of the screen. Lawrence and an officer look off right, and their dialogue identifies the source of the sound. Then, when the scene shifts to the besieged camp itself, the stereo sound slides from channel to channel, reinforcing the visual depiction of the planes swooping over-head. The *Star Wars* series has expanded on this device to suggest space vehicles whizzing not only from side to side but even above and behind the spectators. Multiple channels make it possible to delineate space precisely.

In general, the spatial relations of sounds in films are clearly diegetic or nondiegetic. But because film is such a complex art form, involving the combination of so many elements, some films blur the distinctions between diegetic and non-diegetic sound, as we saw in the cavalry-rescue scene of *Stagecoach*. Since we are used to placing the source of a sound easily, a film may cheat our expectations.

A simple example of this comes at the beginning of Mel Brooks's *Blazing Saddles*, when we hear what we think is nondiegetic musical accompaniment, until the hero rides past Count Basie and his orchestra playing in the middle of the prairie. This joke depends on a simple reversal of our expectations about the convention of nondiegetic music. More complex is a moment in *The Magnificent Ambersons* when Welles creates an unusual interplay between the diegetic and nondiegetic sounds. A prologue to the film outlines the background of the Amberson family and the birth of the son, George. We see a group of townswomen gossiping about the marriage of Isabel Amberson, and one predicts that she will have "the worst spoiled lot of children this town will ever see." This scene has involved diegetic dialogue. After the last line, the nondiegetic narrator resumes his description of the family history. Over a shot of the empty street, he says: "The prophetess proved to be mistaken in a single detail merely; Wilbur and Isabel did not have *children*. They had only one." But at this point, still over the shot of the street, we hear the gossiper's voice again: "Only one. But I'd like to know if he isn't spoiled enough for a whole carload." After her line, a pony cart comes up the street, and we see George for the first time. In this exchange the woman seems to reply to the narrator, even though we must assume that she cannot hear what he says. After all, she is a character in the story and he is not. Here Welles playfully departs from conventional usage to emphasize the arrival of the story's main character.

This example from *The Magnificent Ambersons* juxtaposes diegetic and non-diegetic sounds in an ambiguous way. In other films a single sound may be ambiguous because it seems to fall with equal logic into either category. This is often true in the films of Jean-Luc Godard. He narrates some of his films, but sometimes he seems also to be present in the story space just offscreen. Godard does not claim to be a character in the action, yet the characters on the screen sometimes seem to hear him. In an early scene in *Two or Three Things I Know about Her* Godard's voice introduces the actress Marina Vlady and describes her, then does the same with the character that Vlady plays, Juliette Janson. He speaks in a whisper, and we are not sure whether she can hear him or not. Later in the scene she gives answers to questions seemingly asked by someone offscreen. Yet we do not hear the questions themselves and do not know if Godard is asking them from his position behind the camera as director. We are never sure whether Godard is nondiegetic narrator or diegetic character; in the latter case, his role would have to be something like "director/narrator of *Two or Three Things I Know about Her*." This uncertainty is important for Godard, since in some of his films an uncertainty as to diegetic or nondiegetic sound sources enables him to stress the conventionality of traditional sound usage.

The distinction between diegetic and nondiegetic sound is important not as an end in itself but as a tool for understanding particular films, as we shall see when we examine *A Man Escaped*.

## ■ TIME

Sound relates temporally to filmic images in three ways: through story time, plot time, and screen duration. As we saw in Chapter 4, story time is usually the longest and includes the time of events that we infer as having happened earlier than the events we witness. Plot time shows us selected events but only refers to others; thus it usually covers a shorter span than the complete story events. And screen duration, or viewing time, equals the length of the film itself.

Sound offers one way for the filmmaker to create complex relations among these three types of time, for the time of the sound track may or may not be the same as that of the image. The matching of sound with image in terms of our viewing time creates **synchronous sound.** When a sound is synchronized with the image, we hear it at the same time as we see the source produce the sound on the screen. Most dialogue between characters is matched so that the lips of the actors move at the same time that we hear the appropriate words.

When the sound does go out of synchronization during a viewing (e.g., through an error in projection), the result is quite distracting. But some imaginative film-makers have obtained good effects by using out-of-sync, or **asynchronous,** sound. One such example occurs in a scene in the musical by Gene Kelly and Stanley Donen, *Singin' in the Rain*. The story is set in the early days of sound in Hollywood; a famous pair of silent screen actors have just made their first talking picture, *The Dueling Cavalier*. Their film company previews the film for an audience at a theater. In the earliest days of "talkies," sound was often recorded on a phonograph record to be played along with the film; hence the chances of the sound's getting out of synchronization with the picture were much greater than they are today. This is what happens in the preview of *The Dueling Cavalier*. As the film is projected, it slows down momentarily, but the record keeps running. From this point all the sounds come several seconds before their sources are seen in the image. A line of dialogue begins, *then* the actor's lips move. A woman's voice is heard when a man moves his lips and vice versa. The humor of this disastrous preview in *Singin' in the Rain* depends on our realization that the sound and image are supposed to be matched but actually occur separately.

A lengthier example of a play with our expectations about synchronization comes in Woody Allen's film *What's Up Tiger Lily?* Allen has taken an Oriental spy film and dubbed a new sound track on, but the English-language dialogue is not a translation of the original; rather, it creates a new story in comic juxtaposition with the original images. Much of the humor results from our constant awareness that the words are not perfectly synchronized with the actors' lips. Allen has turned the usual problems of the dubbing of foreign films into the basis of his comedy.

Synchronization relates to *viewing* time. But what of *plot* time? If the sound takes place at the same time as the image in terms of the story events, it is **simultaneous sound;** if the sound occurs earlier or later than the story events of the image, the sound is **nonsimultaneous.** Nonsimultaneous sound is one way the film can give us information about story events without showing them to us, as in a sonic flashback. Similarly, the frequency of a single story event can be multiplied if we hear the sound of it repeated as a motif later in the film. Sound provides a major way for the plot to manipulate our grasp of story events.

Most of the time a film's sound is simultaneous, with image and sound both in the present. We are familiar with this form from countless dialogue scenes, musical numbers, chase scenes, and so forth. We shall call this simultaneous diegetic sound **simple diegetic.**

But scenes with nonsimultaneous sound are relatively familiar as well. Diegetic sound can occur in a time either earlier or later than the time of the image. In either case we shall call it **displaced diegetic sound.** As we saw earlier, both types of diegetic sound can have either an external or an internal source.

As these categories suggest, temporal relationships in the cinema are complex. To help distinguish them, Table 8.2 sums up the possible temporal and spatial relationships that can exist between image and sound.

| Table 8.2 | TEMPORAL RELATION OF SOUND IN CINEMA | |
|---|---|---|
| | SPACE OF SOURCE | |
| TEMPORAL RELATION | DIEGETIC (STORY SPACE) | NONDIEGETIC (NONSTORY SPACE) |
| 1. Sound from *earlier* in story than image | Displaced diegetic: sound flashback; image flashforward; sound bridge | Sound marked as past put over images (e.g., sound of a Winston Churchill speech put over images of Britain today) |
| 2. Sound *simultaneous* in story with image | Simple diegetic: *External:* dialogue, effects, music *Internal:* thoughts of character heard | Sound, marked as simultaneous with images, put over images (e.g., a narrator describing events in the present tense) |
| 3. Sound from *later* in story than image | Displaced diegetic: sound flashforward; image flashback with sound continuing in the present; sound bridge; character narrates earlier events | Sound marked as later put over images (e.g., reminiscing narrator of *The Magnificent Ambersons*) |

**Diegetic sound.**   Because the first and third of these possibilities are comparatively uncommon, we start by commenting on the second option.

2. *Sound simultaneous in story with image.* This is by far the most common temporal relation which sound has in most fiction films. Noise, music, or speech that comes from the space of the story is almost invariably occurring at the same time as the image. As we have already seen (p. 256), this sort of simple diegetic sound can be either external (objective) or internal (subjective).

1. *Sound earlier in story than image.* Here the sound comes from an earlier point in the story action and is thus "displaced." A clear example occurs at the end of Joseph Losey's *Accident.* Over a shot of a driveway gate, we hear a car crash. The sound represents the crash that occurred at the *beginning* of the film. Now if there were cues that the sound was internal—that is, that a character was recalling it—it would not strictly be coming from the past, since the memory of the sound would be occurring in the present. But here no character is remembering the scene, so we have a fairly pure case of a "sonic flashback." In this film, an unrestricted narration makes an ironic final comment on the action.

Sound may belong to an earlier time than the image in another way. The sound from one scene may linger briefly while the image is already presenting the next scene. This is called a **sound bridge.** Near the end of *Ivan the Terrible*, Part I, a herald announces to a crowd that Ivan has just gone into exile in Alexandrov. His voice continues for a few seconds over the fades that lead to the new scene: Ivan, much later, in exile in Alexandrov. Sound bridges of this sort may create smooth transitions by setting up expectations that are quickly confirmed.

Other sound bridges can make our expectations more uncertain. In Tim Hunter's *River's Edge*, three high-school boys are standing outside school, and one of them confesses to having killed his girlfriend. When his pals scoff, he says, "They don't believe me." There is a cut to the dead girl lying in the grass by the river, while on the sound track we hear one of his friends respond to him by calling it a crazy story that no one will believe. For an instant we cannot be sure whether a new scene is starting or we are seeing a cutaway to the corpse, which will be followed by a shot that returns to the three boys at school. But the shot dwells on the dead girl, and after a pause we hear, with a different sound ambiance: "If you brought us. . . ." Then there is a cut to a shot of the three youths walking through the woods to the river, as the same character continues, ". . . all the way out here for nothing. . . ." The friend's remark about the crazy story belongs to an earlier time than the shot of the corpse, and it is used as an unsettling sound bridge to the new scene.

3. *Sound later in story than image.* Displaced diegetic sound may also occur at a later time than that depicted by the images. Here we may take the images as occurring in the past and the sound as occurring in the present or future. A simple example occurs in many trial dramas: the testimony of a witness in the present is heard on the sound track, while the image presents a flashback to an earlier event. The same effect occurs when the film employs a reminiscing narrator, as in John Ford's *How Green Was My Valley.* Aside from a glimpse at the beginning, we do not see the protagonist Huw as a man, only as a boy, but his narration accompanies the bulk of the plot, which is set in the distant past. Huw's voice on the sound track creates a strong nostalgia for the past and constantly reminds us of the pathetic decline that the characters will eventually suffer.

*Sound bridge*

*River's Edge*

Since the late 1960s, it has become somewhat common for the sound from the next scene to begin while the images of the last one are still on the screen. Like the instances mentioned above, this transitional device is called a *sound bridge*. In Wim Wenders's *American Friend*, a nighttime shot of a little boy riding in the back seat of a car is accompanied by a harsh metallic whirring. There is a cut to a railroad station, where the timetable board flips through its metal cards listing times and destinations. Since the sound comes from the space of the later scene, the portion that accompanies the earlier scene is displaced.

If the sound bridge is not immediately identifiable, it can surprise or disorient the audience, as in the *American Friend* transition. A more recognizable sonic lead-in can create more clear-cut expectations about what we will see in the next scene. Federico Fellini's *8½* takes place in a town famous for its health spa and natural springs, and several scenes have shown an outdoor orchestra playing to entertain the tourists and guests. Midway through the film, a scene ends with the closing of a window on a steam bath. Near the end of the shot, we hear an orchestral version of the song "Blue Moon." There is a cut to an orchestra playing the tune in the center of the town's shopping area. Even before the new scene has established the exact locale of the action, we can reasonably expect that the musical bridge is bringing us back to the public life of the spa.

One could also have a sound flashforward; the filmmaker could, say, use the sounds that belong with scene 5 to accompany the images in scene 2. Such a technique is rare, but occasionally Jean-Luc Godard uses it. In *Band of Outsiders*, the sound of a tiger's roar is heard as sound "over," not as sound "off," several scenes before we see the tiger. A more ambiguous case can be found in Godard's *Contempt*. A husband and wife quarrel, and the scene ends with her swimming out to sea while he sits quietly on a rock formation. On the sound track we hear her voice, closely miked, reciting a letter in which she tells him she has driven back to Rome with another man. Since the husband has not yet received the letter, and perhaps the wife has not yet written it, the letter and its recitation presumably come from a later point in the story. Here the sound flashforward sets up strong expectations which a later scene confirms: we see the wife and the husband's rival stopping for gas on the road. In fact we never see a scene in which the husband receives the letter.

**Nondiegetic sound.** Most nondiegetic sound has no relevant temporal relationship to the story. When "mood" music comes up over a tense scene, it would be irrelevant for us to ask if it is happening at the same time as the images, since the music has no relation to the space of the story. But occasionally the filmmaker may use a type of nondiegetic sound that does have a defined temporal relationship to the story. For example, Orson Welles's narration in *The Magnificent Ambersons* speaks of the action as having happened long ago, in a different era of American history.

## ■ SUMMARY

All of these temporal categories offer us ways of making important distinctions in films—especially when we are dealing with complex or unusual films that play with our expectations about sounds.

Fritz Lang's *Secret beyond the Door*, for example, depends on the contrast of two types of internal speech: the character's mind reacts to immediate situations (simple diegetic) and reflects on past events (displaced diegetic). In the first third of the film, the heroine's wedding is about to take place. Since the plot has begun

American Friend

in the middle of the action, we are curious to learn the circumstances leading up to her marriage. She recalls those circumstances in an interior monologue in the present tense. When we see the past in flashbacks, the voice belongs to a later time (internal displaced diegetic); over the present-time scenes of the wedding itself, the same monologue is simultaneous (internal simple diegetic). We must mentally unscramble the story events being given to us out of order, understand how the heroine's words relate to both past and present simultaneously, and form expectations about how this marriage will turn out. Because the narration in *Secret beyond the Door* is severely limited to the range of the heroine's knowledge, access to her ongoing reactions to events is vital to our understanding of the story.

We will not, of course, be mentally putting each sound we hear in a film into these categories (although in learning to listen for sound it might be helpful to do so once or twice for a whole film). But, by becoming more aware of them, we are less likely to take a film's sound track for granted. Instead, we may be able to notice much more complex uses of sound. One such use comes early in Alain Resnais's *Providence*, during a courtroom scene. As the film begins we see a mysterious house and a hunt for a wounded old man. Now we are plunged into the middle of a courtroom examination of a witness. These abrupt transitions give us little time to form expectations. Apparently a prosecutor is questioning a young man accused of the mercy killing of the old man during the hunt. The young man justifies his act by saying the man was not only dying but turning into an animal as well. (We had seen the man's hairy face and clawlike hands, so now we begin to see the links between the scenes.) The prosecutor pauses, astonished: "Are you suggesting some kind of actual metamorphosis?" He pauses again, and a man's voice whispers, "A werewolf." The prosecutor then asks, "A werewolf, perhaps?" and the questioning continues. The whispered words startle us, and we cannot account for them. Are they the prosecutor's thoughts? (But it does not sound like his voice.) Are they whispered by an unseen character offscreen? Are they perhaps even nondiegetic, coming from outside the story world? Only much later in the film do we find out whose voice whispered these words, and why. The whole opening of *Providence* provides an excellent extended case of how disorienting an ambiguity of sound sources can be when the filmmaker departs from conventional usage.

## FUNCTIONS OF FILM SOUND: *A MAN ESCAPED*

Robert Bresson's *A Man Escaped (Un Condamné à mort c'est échappé)* shows how a variety of sound techniques can function throughout an entire film. The narrative takes place in France in 1943. Fontaine, a Resistance fighter arrested by the Germans, has been put in prison and condemned to die. But while awaiting his execution, he works at an escape plan, loosening the boards of his cell door and making ropes. Just as he is ready to put his plan in action, a boy, Jost, is put into his cell. Deciding to trust that Jost is not a spy, Fontaine reveals his plan to him, and they are both able to escape.

Throughout the film, sound has many important functions. As in all of his films, Bresson emphasizes the sound track, rightly believing that sound may be just as "cinematic" as the images. At certain points in *A Man Escaped*, Bresson even lets his sound techniques dominate the image; in ways we shall examine, we are compelled to *listen*. Indeed, Bresson is one of a handful of directors who create a complete interplay between sound and image.

A key factor in guiding our perception of the film is the commentary spoken over by Fontaine himself. The voice-over is displaced, since it occurs at a time later than the images. But it could be either internal or external displaced diegetic sound. We never learn whether he is reciting these events mentally or telling them to someone.

Fontaine's narration has multiple functions. First, the commentary helps clarify the action. Certain temporal cues suggest how long Fontaine spends in prison. As we see him working at his escape plan, his voice-over tells us, "One month of patient work and my door opened." At other points he gives us additional indications of time. His commentary is particularly important during the final escape scene, where the action occupies only 15 minutes of viewing time and the lighting is so dim as to allow only glimpses of the action itself. Yet Fontaine's voice calmly tells us of the hours he and Jost spend on each stage of their progress.

We receive other vital information through the commentary. Sometimes the narration simply states facts: that the pin Fontaine obtains came from the women's wing of the prison or that certain prison officials' quarters were at various places in the building. More strikingly, Fontaine often tells what his thoughts had been. After being beaten and put in his first cell, he wipes the blood from his face and lies down; on the track we hear his voice say: "I'd have preferred a quick death." Often the actor does not register such thoughts visually. At some points the sound even corrects an impression given by the image. After Fontaine has been sentenced to death, he is led back to his cell and flings himself down on the bed. We might take him to be crying, but the commentary says, "I laughed hysterically. It helped." Thus the commentary adds a degree of depth to the film's narration by sometimes allowing us insights into Fontaine's mental states (though we never hear his thoughts at the moment they occur, but only as recalled after the fact).

Yet at first much of the commentary may seem unnecessary, since it often tells us something that we can also see in the image. In one scene Fontaine wipes the blood from his face, and his voice tells us, "I tried to clean up." Again and again in the film Fontaine describes his actions as we see him perform them or just before or after them. But this use of sound is not redundantly supporting the visuals. One major function of the past-tense commentary and even the apparently redundant remarks is to emphasize the prison events as having *already* happened. Instead of simply showing a series of events in the present, the commentary places the events in the past. Indeed certain phrases emphasize the fact that the commentary is a remembering of events. As we see Fontaine lie down in his cell after having been beaten, his commentary says, "I believe that I gave up and wept," as if the passage of time has made him uncertain. After meeting another prisoner, Fontaine narrates, "Terry was an exception; he was allowed to see his daughter. I learned this later." Again we sense that the meeting we see on the screen occurred at a point in the past.

Because of this difference in time between image and commentary, the narrative indicates to us that Fontaine will eventually escape rather than be executed. (The title also indicates this.) The final *effect* of the narrative cause-effect chain is known. As a result, our suspense is centered on the *cause*—not *whether* Fontaine will escape, but *how* he will escape. The film guides our expectations, first of all, toward the minute details of Fontaine's work to break out of prison. The commentary and the sound effects draw our attention to tiny gestures and ordinary objects that become crucial to the escape. Second, the narrative stresses that work alone is not enough, that Fontaine and the other prisoners can survive, both mentally and physically, only through their efforts to help one another. Fontaine receives much aid from his fellow prisoners: his neighbor, Blanchet, gives him a blanket to make his ropes; another prisoner who also tries to escape, Orsini, provides vital information about how to get over the walls. Finally, Fontaine himself must extend trust and aid to his new cellmate, Jost, by taking him along in spite of suspicions that he may be a spy planted by the Germans.

The interplay between the sounds and images in *A Man Escaped* does not pertain solely to the commentary. The ability to focus our attention on details works with sound effects as well. In the long middle portion of the film, in which Fontaine works on breaking through his door and making the implements of escape, this focus on details becomes particularly prominent. A close-up shows Fontaine's hands sharpening a spoon handle into a chisel; the loud scraping sound intensifies our perception of this detail. We also hear distinctly the rubbing of the spoon against the boards of the door, the ripping of cloth with a razor to make ropes, even the swish of straw against the floor as Fontaine sweeps up slivers of wood.

This intense concentration of our attention on details follows a general pattern in the narration of *A Man Escaped*. The narration is unusually restricted. We learn nothing at all that Fontaine does not know, and indeed at times we know less than he does. When he attempts to escape from the car in the opening scene, the camera holds on his empty seat rather than moving to follow him and show his recapture. Sound aids in restricting our knowledge by controlling what we see. As Fontaine looks around his cell for the first time, he names the items it contains—a slop bucket, a shelf, a window. *After* he mentions each, the camera moves to give us a glimpse of it. At another point Fontaine hears a strange sound outside his cell. He moves to the door, and we see what he sees in a point-of-view shot through the peephole in his door; a guard is winding the crank of a skylight in the hall. For the first time Fontaine becomes aware of the skylight, which eventually becomes his escape route. At another point Fontaine's neighbor, Blanchet, falls down during their daily walk to empty their slop buckets. We first hear the sound of his fall as the camera remains on a medium shot of Fontaine reacting in surprise; then there is a cut to Blanchet as Fontaine moves to help him up. Thus the sound anticipates, limits, and guides our expectations.

At times, sound in *A Man Escaped* goes beyond controlling the image—sometimes it partially *replaces* it. Some of the film's scenes are so dark that sound must carry the burden of letting us know what the action is. After Fontaine falls asleep in prison for the first time, there is a fade-out. While the screen is still dark, we hear his voice-over saying, "I slept so soundly, my guards had to awaken me." This is followed by the loud sound of a bolt and hinge. The light let in by the door allows us to see a faint image of a guard's hand shaking Fontaine, and we hear a voice tell him to get up. In general, the film contains many fade-outs in which the sound of the next scene begins before the image. By putting sound over a black screen or dark image, Bresson allows the sound track an unusually prominent place in his film.

The reliance on sound culminates in the final escape scene. During much of the last 15 or 20 minutes of the film, the action takes place outdoors at night. There are no establishing shots to give us a sense of the space of the roofs and walls Fontaine and Jost must scale. We get glimpses of gestures and settings, but often sound is our main guide to what is happening. This has the effect of intensifying the spectators' attention greatly. We must strain to understand the action from what we can glimpse and hear. We judge the pair's progress from the church bells heard tolling the hour; the train outside the walls serves to cover the noise they make; each strange noise suggests an unseen threat to the escape. In one remarkable shot Fontaine stands in almost total darkness by a wall, listening to the footsteps of a guard walking up and down offscreen. Fontaine knows that he must kill this man if his escape is to succeed. We hear his voice-over explaining where the guard is moving and mentioning how hard his own heart is beating. There is little movement. All we see is Fontaine's dim outline and a tiny reflection of light in his eye. Again, throughout this scene the sound concentrates our attention on the reactions and gestures of the characters rather than on the simple cause-effect sequence of the story action.

We have discussed how a filmmaker controls not only what we hear, but also the qualities of that sound. Bresson has achieved a considerable variety in *A Man Escaped*. Every object in the film is assigned a distinct pitch. The volumes of sounds range from very loud to almost inaudible, as the opening scene illustrates. The first few shots of Fontaine riding to prison in a car are accompanied only by the soft hum of the motor. But as a streetcar blocks the road, Fontaine seeks to use the streetcar's uproar to conceal his dash from the car. The moment Fontaine leaps from the car, Bresson eliminates the streetcar noise, and we hear running feet and gunshots off. Later, in the final escape, the film alternates sounds off (trains, bells, bicycle, and so on) with stretches of silence. The film's sparse sound mix effectively isolates specific sounds for our attention.

Certain sounds not only are very loud but also have an echo effect added to give them a distinctive timbre. The voices of the German guards as they give Fontaine orders are reverberant and harsh compared to the voices of the French prisoners. Similarly, the noises of the handcuffs and bolts of the cell doors are magnified for the same echo effect. These manipulations suggest Fontaine's own perceptual subjectivity. Thus our reactions to Fontaine's imprisonment are intensified through the manipulation of timbre.

These devices all help focus our attention on the details of Fontaine's prison life. But there are other devices that help unify the film and sustain its narrative and thematic development. These are the sound **motifs,** which come back at significant moments of the action; they often call attention to Fontaine's interactions with the other prisoners, since the men depend on one another.

One set of sound motifs emphasizes the space outside Fontaine's cell. We see a streetcar in the opening scene, and the bell and motor of a streetcar are heard offscreen every time Fontaine speaks to someone through his cell window. We are always aware of his goal of reaching the streets beyond the walls. During the second half of the film the sounds of trains also become important. When Fontaine is first able to leave his cell and walk in the hall unobserved, we hear a train whistle. It returns at other moments when he leaves his cell clandestinely, until the train provides the noise to cover the sounds Fontaine and Jost make during their escape. The daily gathering of the men to wash in a common sink becomes associated with running water; at first, the faucet is seen, but later Bresson shoots the actions of the prisoners in closer shots, with the sound of the water offscreen.

Some sound motifs become associated with defiance of the prison rules. Fontaine uses his handcuffs to tap on the wall to signal his neighbors; he coughs to cover the sound of scraping (the coughs also become signals between the men); Fontaine defies the guards' orders and continues to talk to the other men. There are other sound motifs in the film (bells, guns, whistles, children's voices), which share the different functions already noted: characterizing Fontaine's escape, calling our attention to details, and guiding what we notice.

Yet another motif involves the only nondiegetic sound in the film, passages from a Mozart mass. The music is motivated clearly enough; the film's narrative refers continually to religious faith. Fontaine tells another prisoner that he prays but does not expect God to help him if he does not work for his own liberty. But the pattern of the actual uses of the music is less clear. We may be unable at first to form any satisfactory expectations about it, and its recurrences are likely to take us by surprise. After it is heard over the credits, the music does not return for some time. Its first use over the action occurs during the first walk Fontaine takes with the men to empty their slop buckets. As the music plays, Fontaine's commentary explains the routine: "Empty your buckets and wash, back to your cell for the day." The juxtaposition of ceremonial, baroque church music with the emptying of slop buckets in a prison is an incongruous one. Yet the contrast is not ironic. Not only are these moments of movement important to Fontaine's life in the prison but they also provide his main means of direct contact with other prisoners. The music, which comes back seven more times, emphasizes the narrative development: Fontaine meets the other men, wins their support, and finally plans to share his escape. The music reappears whenever Fontaine makes contact with another prisoner (Blanchet, Orsini) who will affect his final escape. Later washing scenes have no music; these are scenes in which Fontaine's contact is cut off (Orsini decides not to go along). The music returns as Orsini attempts his own escape plan. He fails but is able to give Fontaine vital information he will need in his own attempt. The music reappears when Blanchet, once opposed to Fontaine's plan, contributes his blanket to the rope making. Eventually the music becomes associated with the boy, Jost; it plays again as Fontaine realizes that he must either kill Jost or take him along. The final use of music comes over the very end of the film, as the two leave the prison and disappear into the night. The nondiegetic music has traced Fontaine's progress in his relations with the other men on whom his endeavor depends.

The musical motif constitutes the only major intervention of a relatively unrestricted narrational element—the principal moments when we move briefly outside of our limitation to Fontaine's knowledge. Thus the music is crucial in suggesting a general implicit meaning beyond what Fontaine tells us explicitly. If we follow the pattern of the music's recurrences, we might interpret the motif as suggesting the importance of trust and interdependence among the people of the prison. It is not simply the conventional "mood" music that accompanies the action of many films. Indeed, its very incongruence as an accompaniment to mundane actions should cue us to seek an implicit meaning of this type.

Let us look at a brief scene from *A Man Escaped* in order to see how silence and shifts between sounds that are internal and external, diegetic and displaced diegetic, guide our expectations. The four shots indicated by Figures 8.12 through 8.22 in Table 8.3 constitute the scene in which the boy Jost is put into Fontaine's cell.

The use of silence and the oscillations between Fontaine's internal and external speech dominate the scene. We have not seen Jost before and do not know what is happening as the scene begins. Fontaine's internal commentary tells us that a new threat has appeared. Offscreen footsteps and Fontaine's gaze indicate that someone has entered his room, but the camera lingers on Fontaine. Bresson delays the cut to the newcomer for a surprisingly long time. (This first shot is as long as the other three shots combined.) The delay serves multiple functions. It restricts the narration considerably; we do not know to what Fontaine is reacting in the first shot. Our access to his mental state through the commentary only hints at the threat: the "he" referred to could be either a guard or another prisoner. This is one of the many small moments of suspense the narration creates.

| Table 8.3 | SOUND AND SILENCE IN *A MAN ESCAPED* | | |
|---|---|---|---|
| SHOT | VOICE | EFFECTS | ACTION/CAMERA |
| (1) 27 sec  Fig. 8.12 | F. (over): But then once again . . . | Lock rattles off<br><br>Rattle continues off | F. turns |
|  Fig. 8.13 | . . . I thought I was lost. | Footsteps off | F. turns head left<br><br>Watches off left, turning head<br><br>Moves left and slightly forward; camera pans with his actions |
|  Fig. 8.14 | (Over): In French and German uniform, he looked repulsively filthy. | Lock closing off<br>One retreating footstep off | Catches door as it closes |
|  Fig. 8.15 | (Over): He seemed barely sixteen. | Echoing of locks and doors, off<br><br>Two footsteps, off | |

| Table 8.3 | SOUND AND SILENCE IN *A MAN ESCAPED* (continued) | | |
|---|---|---|---|
| SHOT | VOICE | EFFECTS | ACTION/CAMERA |

Fig. 8.16

F. (aloud): Are you German?

(2) 10 sec

Fig. 8.17

French? What is your name?

Jost lifts head, looks off right

Fig. 8.18

Jost: Jost, François Jost.

F. (over): Had they planted a spy?

(3) 10 sec

Fig. 8.19

F. (over): Did they think I was ready to talk?

F. lowers eyes

| Table 8.3 | SOUND AND SILENCE IN *A MAN ESCAPED* (continued) | | |
| --- | --- | --- | --- |
| SHOT | VOICE | EFFECTS | ACTION/CAMERA |

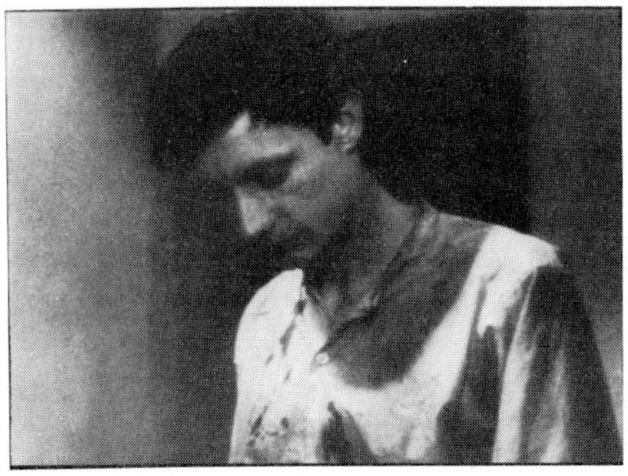

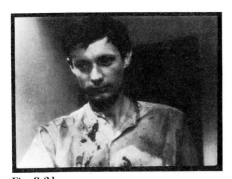

**Fig. 8.20**

|  |  | Sound of one footstep (F.'s) on cell floor | F. moves left and forward; camera pans to follow |

**Fig. 8.21**

(4) 7 sec

|  | F. (aloud): Give me your hand, Jost. |  | F. stretches right arm out |

**Fig. 8.22**
Dissolve

|  |  | Sound of Jost rising | Jost stands, they shake hands |
|  | F. (aloud): There isn't much room. |  | F. looks right |
|  |  | Shoes against floor | They both look around |

The fact that we wait to see Jost also functions to emphasize the importance of his appearance; it directs our expectations to Fontaine's reaction (conveyed largely through his displaced diegetic narration) rather than to the new character. By the time we actually see Jost, we know that Fontaine feels threatened by him and disturbed by his part-German uniform. The first words Fontaine speaks externally emphasize his doubt. Rather than stating a decisive attitude, he simply seeks information. Again his internal commentary returns as he makes clear the dilemma he is in: Jost may be a spy planted by the prison officials. Yet his words to Jost contrast with this inner doubt as he shakes hands and begins to converse in a friendly fashion. Thus the interplay of external diegetic and internal displaced diegetic voice allows the filmmaker to present contrasting psychological aspects of the action.

The sound effects differentiate significant actions and develop the narrative progression. Fontaine's footstep is heard as he moves toward Jost after his initial reserve; Jost's rising accompanies their first gesture of trust, the handshake; finally, their shoes scrape against the floor as they relax and begin to speak of their situation.

This scene is very brief, but the combination of many different types of sound in a few shots indicates the complexity of the film's sound track. Regardless of whether we consider that sound track realistic or unrealistic, we can see it as a part of the entire film, functioning in interaction with other techniques and with narrative form. Bresson uses sounds that are recognizable to us but which come at carefully chosen moments. Through his control of what sounds we hear, what qualities these sounds have, and what relationships exist among those sounds and between sound and image, he has made this technique an important factor in sharing our experience of the film.

## SUMMARY

As usual, both extensive viewing and intensive scrutiny will sharpen your capacity to notice the functioning of film sound. You can get comfortable with the analytical tools we have suggested by asking several questions about a film's sound:

1. What sounds are present—music, speech, noise? How are loudness, pitch, and timbre used? Is the mixture sparse or dense? Modulated or abruptly changing?
2. Is the sound related rhythmically to the image? If so, how?
3. Is the sound faithful or unfaithful to its perceived source?
4. *Where* is the sound coming from? In the story's space or outside it? Onscreen or offscreen?
5. *When* is the sound occurring? Simultaneously with the story action? Before? After?
6. How are the various sorts of sounds organized across a sequence or the entire film? What patterns are formed, and how do they reinforce aspects of the film's overall formal system (narrative or nonnarrative)?

Practice at trying to answer such questions will familiarize you with the basic uses of film sound. As always, though, it is not enough to name and classify. These categories and terms are most useful when we take the next step and examine how the types of sound we identify *function* in the total film.

## NOTES AND QUERIES

For material on how sound is created in film production, see Notes and Queries to Chapter 1.

# THE POWER OF SOUND

"The most exciting moment," claims Akira Kurosawa, "is the moment when I add the sound. . . . At this moment, I tremble." Wide-ranging discussions of the effects of film sound may be found in two special issues of journals: "Cinema/Sound," *Yale French Studies* **60** (1980), and "On the Soundtrack," *Screen* **25,** 3 (May–June 1984), and in an anthology edited by John Belton and Elizabeth Weis, *Film Sound: Theory and Practice* (New York: Columbia University Press, 1985). Critical analyses of sound in particular films and filmmakers include Noël Carroll, "Lang, Pabst, and Sound," *Ciné-tracts* **5** (Fall 1978): 15–23; Kristin Thompson, *Eisenstein's "Ivan the Terrible": A Neoformalist Analysis* (Princeton, N.J.: Princeton University Press, 1981), pp. 203–260; Alan Williams, "Godard's Use of Sound," *Camera Obscura* 8–9–10 (1982): 193–208; and Lindley Handlon's *Fragments: Bresson's Film Style* (Rutherford, N.J.: Fairleigh Dickinson University Press, 1986), with chapters on sound in *Mouchette* and *Lancelot du Lac*. A detailed study of the "sound designer" for *American Graffiti* and *Apocalypse Now* is "Walter Murch—Making Beaches out of Grains of Sand," *Cinefex*, no. 3 (December 1980): 42–56.

As the *Letter from Siberia* example suggests, documentary filmmakers have experimented a great deal with sound. For other examples, see Basil Wright's *Song of Ceylon* and Humphrey Jennings's *Listen to Britain* and *Diary for Timothy*. Analyses of sound in these films may be found in Paul Rotha, *Documentary Film* (New York: Hastings House, 1952), and Karel Reisz and Gavin Millar's *Technique of Film Editing* (New York: Hastings House, 1968), pp. 156–170. Voice-over narration is discussed in Bill Nichols, "Documentary Theory and Practice," *Screen* **17,** 4 (Winter 1976/77): 34–48, and Eric Smoodin, "The Image and the Voice in the Film with Spoken Narration," *Quarterly Review of Film Studies* **8,** 4 (Fall 1983): 19–32; the most detailed study is Sarah Kozloff's *Invisible Storytellers: Voice-Over Narration in American Fiction Film* (Berkeley: University of California Press, 1988). Experimental and nonnarrative films also exploit unusual aspects of sound; see Norman McLaren's "Notes on Animated Sound," *Film Quarterly* **7,** 3 (Spring 1953): 223–229 (an article on hand-*drawn* sound tracks), and Robert Russell and Cecile Starr, *Experimental Animation* (New York: Van Nostrand, 1976).

# SILENT FILM VERSUS SOUND FILM

On the transition from silent to sound in American cinema, see Harry M. Geduld, *The Birth of the Talkies: From Edison to Jolson* (Bloomington: Indiana University Press, 1975); Alexander Walker, *The Shattered Silents* (New York: Morrow, 1979); Nancy Wood, "Towards a Semiotics of the Transition to Sound: Spatial and Temporal Codes," *Screen* **25,** 3 (May–June 1984): 16–24; and chapter 23 of David Bordwell, Janet Staiger, and Kristin Thompson, *The Classical Hollywood Cinema: Film Style and Mode of Production to 1960* (New York: Columbia University Press, 1985).

Some film aestheticians protested against the coming of "talkies," feeling that sound film spoiled a pristine mute art. In the bad sound film, René Clair claimed, "the image is reduced precisely to the role of the illustration of a phonograph record, and the sole aim of the whole show is to resemble as closely as possible the play of which it is the 'cinematic' reproduction. In three or four settings there take place endless scenes of dialogue which are merely boring if you do not understand English but unbearable if you do" (*Cinema Yesterday and Today* [New York: Dover, 1972], p. 137). Rudolf Arnheim, who saw the artistic potential of cinema as its inability to reproduce reality perfectly, asserted that "the introduction

272/ SOUND IN THE CINEMA

of the sound film smashed many of the forms that the film artists were using in favor of the inartistic demand for the greatest possible 'naturalness' (in the most superficial sense of the word)" (*Film as Art* [Berkeley: University of California Press, 1957], p. 154).

It is easy to find such beliefs anachronistic, but we must recall that many early sound films relied simply on dialogue for their novelty; both Clair and Arnheim welcomed sound effects and music but warned against talkiness. In any event, the inevitable reaction eventually came. André Bazin constructed a lengthy, influential argument in favor of the greater realism of both sound and image possible in the sound cinema. See his essays "The Evolution of the Language of Cinema," "In Defense of Mixed Cinema," and "Theatre and Cinema," all to be found in *What Is Cinema?* vol. 1 (Berkeley: University of California Press, 1967). See also V. F. Perkins, *Film as Film* (Baltimore: Penguin, 1972); Erwin Panofsky, "Style and Medium in the Motion Pictures," in Gerald Mast and Marshall Cohen, eds., *Film Theory and Criticism* (New York: Oxford University Press, 1974), pp. 151–169; and Siegfried Kracauer, *Theory of Film* (New York: Oxford University Press, 1965), in which Kracauer remarks, "Films with sound live up to the spirit of the medium only if the visuals take the lead in them" (p. 103). As we have seen, however, the creation of realism is only one of many functions sound can perform in a film.

## ■ FILM MUSIC

Of all the kinds of sound in cinema, music has been most extensively discussed. The literature is voluminous, and with a recent surge of interest in film composers, many more recordings of film music have become available. A survey of the field, with bibliography and discography, may be found in Harry Geduld, "Film Music: A Survey," *Quarterly Review of Film Studies* **1,** 2 (May 1976): 183–204. Basic introductions to music useful for film study include William S. Newman, *Understanding Music* (New York: Harper, 1961); Leonard B. Meyer, *Emotion and Meaning in Music* (Chicago: University of Chicago Press, 1956); and Deryck Cooke, *The Language of Music* (New York: Oxford University Press, 1962). Classic studies of film music are Roger Manvell, *The Technique of Film Music* (New York: Hastings House, 1957); Kurt London, *Film Music* (New York: Hastings House, 1970); Aaron Copland, "Film Music," in *What to Listen for in Music* (New York: Signet, 1957), pp. 152–157; and Hanns Eisler's attack on Hollywood film scoring, *Composing for the Films* (London: Dobson, 1947). More recent works include Tony Thomas, *Music for the Movies* (New York: A. S. Barnes, 1973); Roy M. Prendergast, *Film Music: A Neglected Art* (New York: Norton, 1977); Mark Evans, *Soundtrack: The Music of the Movies* (New York: Da Capo, 1979); and Claudia Gorbman, *Unheard Melodies: Narrative Film Music* (Bloomington: Indiana University Press, 1987). See also Chuck Jones, "Music and the Animated Cartoon," *Hollywood Quarterly* **1,** 4 (July 1946): 364–370. Music for silent films is discussed in Charles Hofmann, *Sounds for Silents* (New York: DBS Publications/Drama Book Specialists, 1970).

Despite the bulk of material on film music, there have been fairly few analyses of music's functions in particular films. The most famous (or notorious) is Sergei Eisenstein's "Form and Content: Practice," in *The Film Sense* (New York: Harcourt, Brace, 1942), pp. 157–216, which examines sound/image relations in a sequence from *Alexander Nevsky*. (See also Thompson, *Eisenstein's "Ivan the Terrible,"* cited above.) Recent analysis of film music has been done by Claudia Gorbman in such detailed studies as "Music as Salvation: Notes on Fellini and Rota," *Film Quarterly* **28,** 2 (Winter 1974–75): 17–25; "*Cleo from Five to Seven:* Music as Mirror," *Wide*

*Angle* **4,** 4 (1981): 38–49; and in several chapters of her book *Unheard Melodies,* cited above. For other sensitive and scrupulous work on film music, see two essays by Royal S. Brown: "Music and *Vivre sa vie,*" *Quarterly Review of Film Studies* **5,** 3 (Summer 1980); 319–333; and "Herrmann, Hitchcock, and the Music of the Irrational," *Cinema Journal* **21,** 2 (Spring 1982): 14–49.

## ■ DIMENSIONS OF FILM SOUND

The categories of sound suggested in the chapter conform to the distinctions most film analysts currently make, but the overall system and some of the terms are of our devising. Many other schemes for understanding film sound have been proposed. See Siegfried Kracauer, *Theory of Film* (New York: Oxford University Press, 1965), pp. 102–156; Claudia Gorbman, "Teaching the Sound Track," *Quarterly Review of Film Studies* **1,** 4 (November 1976): 446–452; Béla Balázs, *Theory of the Film* (New York: Dover, 1970), pp. 194–241; Raymond Spottiswoode, *A Grammar of the Film* (Berkeley: University of California Press, 1951), 173–197; Noël Burch, *Theory of Film Practice* (New York: Praeger, 1973), pp. 90–104. Each of these schemes offers tools for analyzing how sound interacts with the image.

Stereophonic and other sound recording and reproducing systems are discussed in Stephen Handzo, "A Narrative Glossary of Film Sound Technology," in Weis and Belton, *Film Sound: Theory and Practice.* See also Michael Arick, "The Sound of Money: In Stereo!" *Sight and Sound* **57,** 1 (Winter 1987–88): 35–42.

## ■ DUBBING AND SUBTITLES

People beginning to study cinema may express surprise (even annoyance) that films in foreign languages are usually shown with subtitled captions translating the dialogue. Why not, some viewers ask, use "dubbed" versions of the films, i.e., versions in which the dialogue has been translated into the audience's tongue and recorded on prints of the films? In many countries dubbing is very common. (Italy has a tradition of dubbing almost every imported film.) Why, then, do most people who study movies prefer subtitles?

There are several reasons. Dubbed voices usually have a bland "studio" sound. Elimination of the original actors' voices wipes out an important component of their performance. (Partisans of dubbing ought to look at dubbed versions of English-language films to see how a performance by Katharine Hepburn, Orson Welles, or John Wayne can be hurt by a voice that does not fit the body.) With dubbing, all of the usual problems of translation are multiplied by the need to synchronize specific words with specific lip movements. Most important, with subtitling viewers still have access to the original sound track. By eliminating the original voice track, dubbing simply destroys part of the film.

# NINE

# STYLE AS A
# FORMAL SYSTEM:
# SUMMARY

At the beginning of Part II, we saw how the different parts of a film relate to one another within the dynamic system we call its *form*. We have already examined one major aspect of a film's form: its organization into a categorical, rhetorical, abstract, associational, or narrative structure. Now, having examined each category of techniques of the film medium, we may go on to see how these techniques interact to create another formal system of the film, its *style*. These two systems—style and narrative/nonnnarrative form—in turn interact within the total film. At this point we can recall the diagram we introduced at the start of Part III:

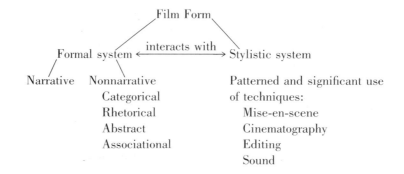

No single film uses all the technical possibilities we have discussed. First, historical circumstances limit the choices that filmmakers have open to them. Before 1928, for example, most filmmakers did not have the choice of using synchronized dialogue. Even today, when the range of technical choices seems far broader, there are still limits. Filmmakers cannot use the now obsolete orthochromatic film stock of the silent era, although in some respects it was superior to contemporary stocks. Similarly, a successful system for creating three-dimensional cinema images without the necessity for spectators to wear "3D" glasses has not yet been invented. Second, even within a given production situation, the filmmaker must choose what techniques to employ in his or her film. Typically, the filmmaker makes certain technical choices and adheres to them throughout the film. For instance, a filmmaker will characteristically use three-point lighting, or continuity editing, or diegetic sound across the film. One segment might stand out as varying from the film's normal usage, but in general a film tends to rely on consistent usage of certain techniques. The film's style results from a combination of historical constraints and deliberate choice.

The spectator has a relation to style as well. Although we are seldom conscious of the fact, we tend to have expectations about style. If we see two characters in a long shot, we expect a cut-in to a closer view. If the actor walks rightward, as if about to leave the frame, we expect the camera to pan or track right to keep the person in the shot. If a character speaks, we expect to hear diegetic sound that is faithful to its source.

Like other kinds of expectations, stylistic ones derive both from our experience of the world generally (people talk, they don't tweet) and our experience of film and other media. The specific film's style can confirm our expectations, or modify them, or cheat or challenge them. Many films use techniques in ways that conform to our expectations. For example, the conventions of the classical Hollywood cinema and specific genres provide a firm basis for reinforcing our prior assumptions. Other films ask us to readjust our expectations somewhat. Keaton's *Our Hospitality* accustoms us to expect deep-space manipulations of figures and objects, while Renoir's *Grand Illusion* builds up specific expectations about the likelihood of camera movements. Still other films make highly unusual technical choices, and to follow them we must construct stylistic expectations to which we are unaccustomed. The editing discontinuities in Eisenstein's *October* and the use of minute offscreen sounds in Bresson's *Man Escaped* ask us to notice stylistic manipulation. In other words, a director directs not only the cast and crew; a director directs us, directs our attention, shapes our reaction; and the director's technical decisions make a difference in what we perceive and how we respond.

We can speak not only of the individual *film*'s style but also of the *filmmaker*'s style. Then at least part of what we refer to are the particular techniques that person typically employs and the unique ways these techniques relate to one another in his or her films. When we discussed sound in *A Man Escaped*, we characterized Bresson as a director who makes sound particularly important in his films; we analyzed several important ways in which sound related to image in *A Man Escaped*. This use of sound is one aspect of Bresson's unique style. Similarly, we looked at *Our Hospitality* in terms of how its comic mise-en-scene is organized around a consistent use of long shots; this is part of Keaton's style in other films too. Both Bresson and Keaton have distinctive filmmaking styles, and we can become familiar with those styles by analyzing the way in which they utilize techniques within whole filmic systems. Finally, we can also speak of a *group style*—the consistent use of techniques across the work of several filmmakers. We can speak of a German expressionist style, or a Soviet montage style. In Part V, we will consider some significant group styles that have emerged in film history.

Style, then, is that formal system of the film that organizes film techniques. Any one film will tend to rely on particular technical options in creating its style, and these are both constrained by history and chosen by the filmmaker. The spectator may not consciously notice film style, but it nonetheless makes an important contribution to the film's ongoing effect and overall meaning. We may also extend the term "style" to describe the characteristic use of techniques made by a single filmmaker or group of filmmakers.

## ANALYZING FILM STYLE

As viewers we register the effects of film style but seldom notice it. If we want to understand how these effects are achieved, we need to look and listen more carefully than we usually do. Since the previous four chapters have shown how we can pay attention to stylistic features, we can now set forth four steps in analyzing style.

1. *Determine the organizational structure of the film, its narrative or nonnarrative formal system.*

The first step is to understand how the film is put together as a whole. If it is a narrative film, it will draw on all the principles we have discussed in Chapters 2 and 3. That is, it will have a plot that cues us to construct a story; it will manipulate causality, time, and space; it will have a distinct pattern of development from opening to closing; it may use parallelism; its narration will choose between restricted and more unrestricted knowledge at various points. If the film is not a narrative, the analyst should seek to understand its organization according to appropriate formal principles. (See Chapters 2 and 4.) Is the film unified as a set of categories, or an argument, or a stream of associations? Or is it structured by an abstract set of technical features? In understanding either narrative or nonnarrative form, making a segmentation is indispensable. Grasping the logic that underlies the whole film puts the analyst in a position to situate techniques with respect to their placement and purpose.

2. *Identify the salient techniques used.*

Here the analyst will draw upon our survey of technical possibilities in Chapters 5 through 8. You need to be able to spot things which most viewers don't consciously notice—color, lighting, framing, cutting, sound, and so on. Once you notice them, you can identify them as techniques—as nondiegetic music, or as a low-angle framing.

But noting and naming are only the beginning of stylistic analysis. The analyst must develop an eye for *salient* techniques. Saliency will partly be determined by what techniques the film relies heavily on. In addition, what is salient depends on the analyst's purpose. If you want to show that a film's style is typical of one approach to filmmaking, you may focus on how the technique conforms to stylistic expectations. The 180° editing of *The Maltese Falcon* is not obvious or emphasized, but the adherence to rules of classical continuity is a characteristic aspect of the film's style. (Our purpose in Chapter 7 was to show that the film is typical in this respect.) If, however, you want to stress unusual qualities of the film's style, you can concentrate on the more unexpected technical devices. Bresson's use of sound in *A Man Escaped* is unusual, representing choices that few filmmakers would make. (It was the originality of these sonic devices that we chose to stress in Chapter 8.) From the standpoint of originality, costume in *A Man Escaped* is not as salient a stylistic feature as sound because it is more in accord with conventional practice. Guided by an overall purpose and an awareness of expectations about style, the analyst can concentrate on salient techniques.

3. *Trace out patterns of techniques within the whole film.*

Once you have identified salient techniques you can notice how they are patterned. Techniques will be repeated and varied, developed and paralleled, across the whole film or within a single segment. Chapters 5 through 8 have shown how this occurs in some films.

You can "zero in" on stylistic patterns in two ways. First, you can reflect upon your responses. If a scene begins with a track-in, do you expect that it will end with a track-out? If you see a character looking left, do you assume that someone or something is offscreen and will be revealed in the next shot? If you feel a mounting excitement in an action scene, is that traceable to a quickening tempo in the music or to accelerating editing?

The second tactic for noticing stylistic patterns is to look for the ways in which style reinforces patterns of nonnarrative or narrative organization. In any film, "punctuation" between segments utilizes stylistic features (fades, cuts, dissolves, color shifts, musical bridges). A scene in a narrative film will usually have a dramatic pattern of encounter, conflict, and outcome, and the style will often reflect this, with the cutting becoming more marked and the shots coming closer to the characters as the scene progresses. As we saw in *Grand Illusion*, style may create associations between situations (the camera movements suggesting the prisoners' unity) or reinforce parallels (the tracking shots comparing Rauffenstein's war trophies and Elsa's). Later we shall see how style can also reinforce the organization of nonnarrative films.

Sometimes, however, stylistic patterning will not respect the nonnarrative or narrative structure of the film. Style can claim our attention in its own right. Since most stylistic devices have several functions, a technique may interest the analyst for different reasons. In Plates 14 and 15, a cut from a washline to a living room acts as a transition between scenes. But the cut is of more interest for other reasons, since we do not expect that a narrative film will treat objects as flat patches of color to be compared across shots. Such attention to graphic play is a convention of abstract form. Here, in a passage from Ozu's *Ohayu*, a stylistic choice "comes forward" because it goes beyond its narrative function. Even here, though, stylistic patterns continue to call on the viewer's expectations and to draw the spectator into a dynamic process. And, if stylistic patterns do swerve off on their own, we still need a sense of the film's narrative or nonnarrative organization in order to show how and when that happens.

4. *Propose functions for the salient techniques and the patterns they form.*

Here the analyst looks for the role that style plays in the film's overall form. Does the use of camera movement tend to create suspense by delaying the revelation of story information, as in the opening of *Touch of Evil?* Does the use of discontinuous editing create a narrational omniscience, as in the sequence we analyzed in *October?* Does the arrangement of the shot tend to make us concentrate on a particular detail (as in Figure 5.50, the shot of Anne's face in *Day of Wrath*)? Does the use of music or noise create surprise?

A direct route to noticing function is to notice the effects of the film. Style may enhance *emotional* aspects of the film. Rapid cutting in *The Birds* evokes shock and horror, while the Mozart music in *A Man Escaped* ennobles the routine of emptying slop buckets. Style also shapes *meaning*. For example, in *Grand Illusion* the contrast between Rauffenstein and Elsa is heightened by Renoir's parallel tracking shots. What is most important, however, is not to "read" isolated elements atomistically, taking them out of context. As we argued on p. 178, a high angle does not automatically mean "inferiority," just as a low angle does not automatically mean "power." There is no dictionary to which you can turn to look up the meaning of a specific stylistic element. Instead the analyst must scrutinize the whole film, the patterns of the techniques in it, and the specific effects of film form. Meaning is only one type of effect, and there is no reason to expect that every stylistic feature will possess a distinct significance. One part of a director's job is to direct our attention and, for this reason, style will often function simply *perceptually*—to get us to notice things, to emphasize one thing over another, to misdirect our attention, to clarify, intensify, or complicate our understanding of the action.

One way to sharpen our sense of the functions of specific techniques is to *imagine alternatives* and reflect on what differences would result. Suppose the director had made a different technical choice; how would this create a different effect? *Our Hospitality* creates its gags by putting two or more elements into the same shot and letting us observe the comic juxtaposition. Suppose Keaton had instead isolated each element in a single shot and then linked the two elements by editing. The meaning might be the same, but the perceptual effects would vary: instead of a simultaneous presentation that lets our attention shuttle to and fro, we would have a more "programmed" pattern of building up the gags and paying them off. Or, suppose that Huston had handled the opening scene of *The Maltese Falcon* as a single take with camera movement. How would he then have drawn our attention to Brigid O'Shaughnessey's and Spade's facial reactions, and how would this have affected our expectations? By focusing on effects and imagining alternatives to the technical choices that were made, the analyst can gain a sharp sense of the particular functions of style in the given film.

The rest of this chapter provides a series of illustrations of how we can analyze film style. Our specimens are the films whose narrative and nonnarrative systems were analyzed in Chapters 3 and 4: *Citizen Kane* (narrative form), *Olympia*, Part 2 (categorical form), *The River* (rhetorical form), *Ballet mécanique* (abstract form), and *A Movie* (associational form). Our analyses are the results of following all four steps in stylistic analysis, but because the two earlier chapters have discussed the films' organizational structures, we will concentrate here on identifying salient techniques, locating patterns, and proposing some functions for style in each case.

## STYLE IN *CITIZEN KANE*

In looking at *Citizen Kane*'s narrative, we discovered that the film is organized as a search: a detectivelike figure, the reporter Thompson, tries to find the significance of Kane's last word, "Rosebud." But even before Thompson appears as a character, we, the spectators, are invited to ask questions about Kane and to seek their answers. The very beginning of the film sets up a mystery. The fade-in reveals a "No Trespassing" sign; in a series of craning movements upward, the camera travels over a set of fences, all matched graphically in the slow dissolves that link the shots. There follows a series of shots of a huge estate, always with the great house in the distance (Fig. 9.1). (This sequence depends largely on special effects; the house itself is a series of paintings, combined through matte work with three-dimensional miniatures in the foreground.) The gloomy lighting, the deserted setting, and the ominous music give the opening of the film the eerie uncertainty that we associate with mystery stories. These shots are connected by dissolves; the camera gradually seems to shift closer to the house, though there is no camera movement. From shot to shot the foreground changes—from a golf course to a dock, and so forth—yet the single lighted window remains in almost exactly the same position on the screen. Graphically matching the window from shot to shot already focuses our attention on it; we assume (rightly) that whatever is in that room will be important in initiating the story.

Fig. 9.1

This pattern of our penetration into the space of a scene returns at other points in the film. Again and again, the camera moves toward things that might reveal the secrets of Kane's character. In the scene in which Thompson goes to interview Susan Alexander, the camera begins not on the reporter but on the poster of Susan on the nightclub wall; then in a spectacular crane shot the camera moves up the wall, over the roof, through the "El Rancho" sign, and over to the skylight. At that point a dissolve and a crack of lightning shift the scene inside to another craning movement down to Susan's table (though during the production, some of the apparent camera movements in the film were created in the laboratory using special effects; see Notes and Queries). These two scenes have some striking similarities. Each begins with a sign ("No Trespassing" and the publicity poster), and each moves us into a building to reveal a new character. The first scene uses a series of shots, whereas the second depends more on camera movement; but these different techniques are working in similar directions to create a pattern that becomes part of the film's style. Thompson's second visit to Susan repeats the crane shots of the first. The second flashback of Jed Leland's story begins with another movement into a scene. The camera is initially pointed at the wet cobblestones of a street, then tilts up and tracks in toward Susan coming out of a drugstore; only then does the camera pan right to reveal Kane standing, splashed with mud, on the curb. This pattern of movement into the story space not only carries through the narrative's search pattern but uses film technique consistently to create curiosity and suspense.

As we have seen, films' endings often contain variations of their beginnings. Toward the end of *Citizen Kane*, Thompson gives up his search for Rosebud. But after the reporters leave the huge storeroom of Xanadu, the camera begins to move over the great expanse of Kane's collections. It cranes forward high above the crates and piles of objects (Fig. 9.2), then moves down to center on the sled from Kane's childhood. Then there is a cut to the furnace, and the camera again moves in on the sled as it is tossed into the fire. At last we are able to read the word "Rosebud" on the sled. The ending continues the pattern set up at the beginning; the film techniques create a penetration into the story space, probing the mystery of the central character. But, after our glimpse of the sled, the film reverses the pattern. A series of shots linked by dissolves leads us back outside Xanadu, the camera travels down to the "No Trespassing" sign again, and we are left to wonder whether this discovery really provides a resolution to the mystery about Kane's character.

Fig. 9.2

Our study of *Kane*'s organization in Chapter 3 also showed that Thompson's search was, from the standpoint of narration, a complex one. At one level, our knowledge is restricted principally to what Kane's acquaintances know. Within the flashbacks, the style reinforces this by avoiding crosscutting or other techniques that would move toward a more unrestricted range of knowledge. Many of the

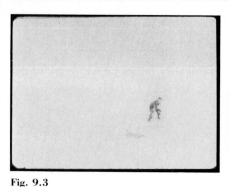

Fig. 9.3

Fig. 9.4

Fig. 9.5

Fig. 9.6

*Welles' maintain objective perspective*

flashback scenes are shot in fairly static long takes, strictly confining us to what participants in the scene could witness. When the youthful Kane confronts Thatcher during the *Inquirer* crusade, Welles could have cut away to the reporter in Cuba sending Kane a telegram or could have shown a montage sequence of a day in the life of the paper. Instead, because this is Thatcher's tale, Welles handles the scene in a long take showing Kane and Thatcher in a face-to-face standoff, which is then capped by a close-up of Kane's cocky response.

We have also seen that the film's narrative requires us to take each narrator's version as objective within his or her limited knowledge. Welles reinforces this by avoiding shots that suggest optical or mental subjectivity. (Contrast Hitchcock's optical point-of-view angles in *The Birds* and *Rear Window*, pp. 208–216 and 227.) Welles utilizes deep-focus cinematography that yields an external perspective on the action. The shot in which Kane's mother signs her son over to Thatcher is a good example of this. Several shots precede this one, introducing the young Kane. Then there is a cut to what at first seems a simple long shot of the boy (Fig. 9.3). But the camera tracks back to reveal a window; Kane's mother appears at the left of the frame, calling to him (Fig. 9.4). Then the camera continues to track back, into another room (Fig. 9.5). Mrs. Kane and Thatcher sit at a table in the foreground to sign the papers, while Kane's father remains standing farther away at the left, and the boy plays in the distance (Fig. 9.6). Welles eliminates cutting here. The shot becomes a complex unit unto itself, like the opening of *Touch of Evil* discussed in Chapter 6. Most Hollywood directors would have handled this scene in shot/ reverse shot, but Welles keeps all of the implications of the action simultaneously before us. The boy, who is the subject of the discussion, remains framed in the distant window through the whole scene; his game leads us to believe that he is unaware of what his mother is doing. The tensions between the father and mother are conveyed not only by the fact that she excludes him from the discussion at the table but also by the overlapping sound; his objections to signing his son away to a guardian mix in with the dialogue in the foreground, and even the boy's shouts (ironically, "The Union Forever!") can be heard in the distance. The framing also emphasizes the mother in much of the scene. This is her only appearance in the film; the suggestion of her tenseness and controlled emotions helps motivate the many effects that follow from her action here. We have had little introduction to the situation prior to this scene, but the combination of sound, cinematography, and mise-en-scene conveys the complicated action with an overall objectivity.

Every director directs our attention, but Welles does so in unusual ways. *Kane* offers a good example of how a director chooses between alternatives. By giving up

Fig. 9.7

Fig. 9.8

cutting, Welles cues our attention by using deep-space mise-en-scene (figure be-havior, lighting, placement in space) and sound. We can watch expressions because the actors play frontally (Fig. 9.6); the framing emphasizes certain figures by putting them in the foreground or in dead center (Fig. 9.7); and our attention bounces from one character to another as they speak lines. Even if Welles avoids the classical Hollywood convention of cutting in such scenes, he still uses film techniques to prompt us to make the correct assumptions and inferences.

*Kane*'s narration also embeds the narrators' objective but restricted versions within broader contexts. Thompson's investigation links the various tales, so we learn substantially what he learns. Yet he must not become the protagonist of the film, for that would remove Kane from the center of interest. Welles makes a crucial, salient stylistic choice here. By the use of low-key selective lighting and patterns of staging and framing, Thompson is made virtually unidentifiable. His back is to us, he is tucked into the corner of the frame, and he is usually in darkness. The stylistic handling makes him the neutral investigator, less a character than a channel for information.

More broadly still, we have seen that the film encloses Thompson's search within a more omniscient narration. Our discussion of the opening shots of Xanadu is relevant here: film style is used to convey a high degree of non-character-centered knowledge. But when we enter Kane's death chamber, the style also suggests the narration's ability to plumb characters' minds: we see the possibly subjective shots of snow covering the frame (for example, Fig. 9.8). Later in the film, the camera movements occasionally remind us of the broader range of narrational knowledge. For instance, during the first version of Susan's opera premiere (in Leland's story, Segment 6), the camera cranes up from the stage to reveal something neither Leland nor Susan could know about—stagehands panning her performance. The final sequence, which partially answers the mystery of "Rosebud," also uses a vast camera movement to give us an omniscient perspective: the camera cranes over objects from Kane's collection, moving forward in space but backward through Kane's life to concentrate on his earliest memento, the sled. A salient technique again conforms to pattern by giving us knowledge no character will ever possess.

In looking at the development of the narrative form of *Citizen Kane*, we saw how Kane changes from an idealistic young man to a friendless recluse. The film sets up a contrast between Kane's early life as an editor and his later withdrawal from public life after Susan's opera career fails. This contrast is most readily apparent in the mise-en-scene, particularly the settings of the *Inquirer* office and Xanadu. The *Inquirer* office is initially an efficient but cluttered place. When Kane takes over, he creates a casual environment by moving in his furnishings and living in his office. The low camera angles tend to emphasize the office's thin pillars and low ceilings, which are white and evenly, brightly lit. Xanadu, on the other hand, is huge and sparsely furnished. The ceilings are too high to be seen in most shots, and the few furnishings stand far apart. The lighting often strikes figures strongly from the back or side (such as the shot of Kane descending a great staircase, in Fig. 5.25), creating a few patches of hard light in the midst of general darkness.

The contrast between the *Inquirer* office and Xanadu is also created by the sound techniques associated with each. Several scenes at the newspaper (Kane's initial arrival and his return from Europe) involve a dense sound mix with a babble of overlapping voices; the timbre of these sounds is comparatively "flat." In Xanadu the conversations are very different. Kane and Susan speak their lines to each other slowly, with pauses between; their voices have an echo effect that combines with the setting and lighting to convey a sense of vast, empty spaces.

The transition from Kane's life at the *Inquirer* to his eventual seclusion at Xanadu is suggested by a change in the mise-en-scene at the *Inquirer;* while Kane is in Europe, the statues he sends back begin to fill up his little office. This hints at Kane's growing ambitions and declining interest in working personally on his newspaper. This change culminates in the last scene in the *Inquirer* office: Leland's confrontation with Kane. The office is being used as a campaign headquarters; with the desks pushed aside and the employees gone, the room looks larger and emptier than it had in earlier scenes there. Welles emphasizes this by placing the camera at floor level and shooting from a very low angle (see Fig. 6.74). The Chicago *Inquirer* office, with its vast, shadowy spaces, also picks up this pattern; deep-focus photography and rear projection exaggerate the depth of the scene, making the characters seem very far apart (as in later conversation scenes in the huge rooms of Xanadu).

Contrast the Kane-Leland scene with one near the end of the film. The reporters invade Kane's museumlike storeroom at Xanadu. Though the echo of Xanadu conveys its cavernous quality, the reporters transform the setting briefly by the same sort of dense, overlapping dialogue that characterized the early *Inquirer* scenes and the scene after the newsreel. By bringing together these reporters and Kane's later environment, the film creates one final strong contrasting parallel that points up the change Kane underwent in his career.

Parallelism is indeed an important feature of *Citizen Kane*, and most of the salient techniques work to create parallels in the ways we have already seen. For example, the use of deep focus and deep space to pack many characters into the frame can create significant similarities and contrasts. Late in Thatcher's account (Segment 4), a scene presents Kane's financial losses in the Depression; he is forced to sign over his newspaper to Thatcher's bank. The scene opens on a close-up of Kane's manager, Bernstein, reading the contract. He lowers the paper to reveal Thatcher, now much older, seated opposite him. We hear Kane's voice off, and Bernstein moves his head slightly (the camera reframes a little); we see that Kane is pacing beyond them in a huge room (see Fig. 6.17). The scene is a single take in which the dramatic situation is created by the arrangement of the figures and the image's depth of field. The lowering of the contract recalls the previous scene, in which we first get a real look at the adult Kane as Thatcher puts down the newspaper that has concealed him. There Thatcher had been annoyed, but Kane could defy him. Now Thatcher has gained control and Kane paces restlessly, still defiant, but stripped of his power over the *Inquirer* chain. The use of a similar device to open these two scenes sets up a contrasting parallel between them.

Fig. 9.9

Fig. 9.10

Editing patterns can also suggest similarities between scenes, as when Welles compares two scenes in which Kane makes a major effort to win popular support. In the first scene, Kane is running for governor and makes a speech at a mammoth rally. The main organizational principle of this scene involves editing that shows one or two shots of Kane speaking, then one or two close shots of small groups of characters in the audience (Emily and their son, Leland, Bernstein, Gettys), then another shot of Kane. The cutting establishes the characters who are important for their hopes for Kane. Boss Gettys is the last to be shown in the scene, and we expect him to retaliate against Kane's denunciation. After his defeat, Kane sets out to make Susan an opera star and thus justify his interest in her to the public. In the scene which parallels Kane's election speech, Susan's debut, the organization of shots is similar to that of the political rally. Again the figure on the stage, Susan, serves as a pivot for the editing: one or two shots of her are followed by a few shots of the various listeners (Kane, Bernstein, Leland, the singing teacher), then back to Susan, and so on (Figs. 9.9 and 9.10). General narrative parallels and specific stylistic techniques articulate two stages of Kane's power quest: first on his own, then with Susan as his proxy.

As we have seen in Chapter 8, music can bring out parallels. For example, Susan's singing is causally central to the narrative. Her elaborate aria in the opera *Salammbo* contrasts sharply with the other main diegetic music, the little song about "Charlie Kane." In spite of the differences between the songs, there is a parallel between them, in that both relate to Kane's ambitions. The "Charlie Kane" song seems silly, but its lyrics clearly show that Kane intends it as a political song, and it does turn up later as campaign music. In addition, the chorus girls who sing the song wear costumes with Rough Rider hats and boots, and they carry toy rifles; Kane's desire for war with Spain has shown up even in this apparently simple farewell party for his departure to Europe. When Kane's political ambitions are dashed, he tries to create a public career for his wife instead, but she is incapable of singing grand opera. Again, the songs create narrative parallels between different actions in Kane's career.

As we saw in examining *Citizen Kane*'s narrative, the newsreel is a very important sequence; it provides a "map" to the upcoming plot events. Because of its importance, Welles sets off the style of this sequence from the rest of the film by using distinctive techniques here which do not appear elsewhere in *Citizen Kane*. Also, we need to believe that this is a real newsreel in order to motivate Thompson's search for the key to Kane's life. The realistic newsreel sequence also helps establish Kane's power and wealth, which will be the basis of much of the upcoming action.

Fig. 9.11                                    Fig. 9.12

Welles uses several techniques to achieve the look and sound of an actual
newsreel of the period. Some of these are fairly simple: the music used is that of
actual newsreels, and the insert titles, outmoded in regular narrative films, were
still a convention in newsreel films. But beyond this, Welles employs a number of
subtle cinematographic techniques to achieve a "documentary" quality. Since some
of the footage in the newsreel is supposed to have been taken in the silent period,
he uses several different film stocks to make it appear that the different shots have
been assembled from widely different sources. Some of the footage has been printed
so as to achieve the jerkiness of silent film run at sound speed. Welles has also
scratched and faded this footage to give it the look of old, worn film. This, combined
with the make-up work, creates a remarkable impression of documentary footage
of Kane with Teddy Roosevelt, Adolf Hitler (Fig. 9.11), and others. In the later
scenes of Kane being wheeled around his estate, the hand-held camera, the slats
and barriers (Fig. 9.12), and the high angle imitate the effects of a newsreel reporter
surreptitiously filming Kane. All of these "documentary" conventions are enhanced
by the use of a narrator whose booming voice also mimics the commentary typical
in newsreels of the day.

One of *Citizen Kane*'s outstanding formal features is the way its plot manipulates story time (a process motivated, as we have seen, by Thompson's inquiry and
the order in which he interviews the narrators). Various techniques assist in the
manipulation of order and duration. The shift from a narrator's present recounting
to a past event is often reinforced by a "shock" cut. Shock cuts create some jarring
juxtaposition—usually both a sudden shift to a higher sound volume and a considerable graphic discontinuity. Several examples are found in *Citizen Kane:* the abrupt
beginning of the newsreel after the deathbed shot, the shift from the quiet conversation in the newsreel projection room to the lightning and thunder outside the El
Rancho, and the sudden appearance of a screeching cockatoo in the foreground as
Raymond's flashback begins. Such transitions create surprise and sharply demarcate
one portion of the plot from another.

The transitions that skip over or drastically compress time are less abrupt.
Recall, for instance, the languid images of Kane's sled being gradually covered by
snow. A more extended example is the breakfast-table montage (Segment 6) that
elliptically traces the decline of Kane's first marriage. Starting with the newlyweds'
late supper, rendered in a track-in and a shot/reverse-shot series, the sequence
moves through several brief episodes, consisting of shot/reverse-shot exchanges
linked by whip pans. (A **whip pan** is a very rapid pan that creates a blurring
sidewise motion across the screen; it is usually used as a transition between scenes.)
In each episode, Kane and Emily become more sharply hostile. The segment ends

by tracking away to show the surprising distance between them at the table. The music reinforces the sequence's development as well. The initial late supper is accompanied by a lilting waltz. At each transition to a later time, the music changes. A comic variation of the waltz follows its initial statement, then a tense one; then horns and trumpets restate the Kane theme. The final portion of the scene, with a stony silence between the couple, is accompanied by a slow, eerie variation on the initial theme. The dissolution of the marriage is stressed by this theme-and-variations accompaniment. A similar sort of temporal compression and sonic elaboration can be found in the montage of Susan's opera career (Segment 7).

Our brief examination of *Citizen Kane*'s style has pointed out only a few of the major patterns in the film. You will be able to find others: the musical motif associated with Kane's power: the "K" motif appearing in Kane's costumes and in Xanadu's settings; the way the decor of Susan's room in Xanadu reveals Kane's attitude toward her; the changes in the acting of individuals as their characters age in the course of the story; and the playful photographic devices, such as the photos that become animated or the many superimpositions during montage sequences. *Citizen Kane* is rich in such formal patterns.

## STYLE IN *OLYMPIA*, PART 2

Although the Nazi government financed and guided Leni Riefenstahl's filmmaking in the 1936 Olympic Games, she also had to conform to the regulations of the International Olympic Committee. Thus, in *Olympia*, she was limited in what sorts of film techniques she could employ. Cameras could not, of course, get so close to the athletes during the competition that they would be distracting. Riefenstahl overcame this limitation by creating a variety of ingenious camera devices that could compensate by allowing her camera crew to film from a distance and from unusual angles. In this way, the solution to technical problems ended by enhancing the stylistic variety of the film.

The enormous stadium and other Olympic facilities built in and around Berlin for the games reflected the effort of the Nazi government to impress the rest of the world. In a sense, then, the settings were planned with the camera in mind. But Riefenstahl and her colleagues had little control over the arrangement of the actual events; the mise-en-scene was largely unstaged. Still, Riefenstahl knew ahead of time where and when each event was to take place, and she was able to plan out the cinematography in detail. And after shooting, her control of editing and the addition of a sound track contributed powerfully to the final effect of the film.

Although the mise-en-scene of the film was largely controlled by the Olympic officials rather than by the filmmakers, there is evidence of manipulation in certain scenes. The events of Segment 1—morning jogging, a sauna bath, swimming, and exercising—are arranged for the camera. The joggers run in perfect formation past the camera, and athletes outside their club smile and show off. Segment 5, showing the enormous group of women doing synchronized calisthenics before the stadium, could hardly have been filmed without the event's being staged to some degree. And certainly the final moments of the film were completely staged: the stadium with its ring of searchlights seems to be a model, and the rows of moving flags are arranged for the camera rather than for any audience present within the scene (Fig. 4.22). This drive to shape our response rather than simply record the events will be far more evident in Riefenstahl's use of other filmic techniques.

Fig. 9.13

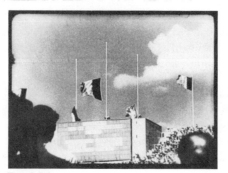

Fig. 9.14

Fig. 9.15

The many cameras filming the games had to be set up in such a way as to avoid interfering with the athletes' concentration. Some cameras were placed in pits dug at a distance from the track and field events. Cameras with telephoto lenses caught the action from a distance, and lens length becomes an important trait of the film's style; we often see the athletes' bodies moving in front of a flat-looking backdrop of slightly out-of-focus faces (see Fig. 4.7). The effect is particularly apparent when the cameras are outfitted with extremely long lenses to capture a detail; in the close view of Glen Morris, for example, the crowd far behind him appears as barely discernible blobs of black and white (Fig. 4.13). Such shots contrast with the views of athletes against the sky, taken from low angles that eliminate the crowd (Figs. 4.9 and 4.21). As we saw in Chapter 4, the move toward the low-angle sky shots formed part of one pattern of development; they occurred toward the end of the gymnastics (Segment 2) and diving (Segment 11) events.

Other techniques of framing add variety and interest to the whole. A very low placement of a row of yachts within the frame (Fig. 9.13) makes for a striking composition and emphasizes the sky motif once again. Some framings emphasize the juxtaposition of foreground and background planes in depth, as when a branch and the distant stadium carry through the nature motif (Fig. 4.6), or when French cyclist medal winners watch their flags being raised (Fig. 9.14). Finally, a number of special effects are used. A superimposition creates a subjective effect of speed as a cyclist races for the finish line (Fig. 4.16). In the pentathlon segment, optical printing permits shots of a scoreboard to seem to flip over to reveal a new shot— an interesting transitional device.

With such a great amount of footage of different types at her disposal, Riefenstahl faced a huge editing task. In fact, the film was not released until 1938, two years after the games were held, partly because of the enormity of this post-shooting phase. But the many hours of film also offered the potential for dynamic graphic and rhythmic juxtapositions. *Olympia*, Part 2, contains a great range of editing techniques. Some moments exploit graphic similarities, as when a whole series of panning shots of different runners leaving the starting point in the pentathlon are strung together. But graphic discontinuity becomes important in other segments. The diagonals formed by the parallel bars in one shot (Fig. 9.15) contrast with those in the next shot (Fig. 9.16). We have seen how this kind of low-angle composition against the sky links the gymnastics and diving segments, reinforcing the film's pattern of development. Graphic discontinuity also performs the function of creating a comparison between these two segments. Many shots of the divers contain opposed directions, culminating in the spectacular finale, when one by one

Fig. 9.16

Fig. 9.17

Fig. 9.18

Fig. 9.19

Fig. 9.20

Fig. 9.21

eleven divers leap into space, with virtually every cut shifting the diver's take-off point from one side of the frame to the other (Figs. 9.17 and 9.18). Combined with a quick cutting rhythm, such graphic playfulness creates an exhilarating ending for this subsegment.

The editing rhythms also cover a considerable range. Although the shots tend to follow a moderate or quick pattern, there are occasional lengthy shots. Riefenstahl holds, for example, on a shot of a gymnast changing and holding a series of positions on the rings (Figs. 9.19 and 9.20). His slow, controlled movements, combined with the telephoto lens that places him against the distant crowd, create a sense of tension within a single shot. Similarly, some shots of the cross-country riding event linger over the amusing attempts of riders to persuade recalcitrant horses over a jump, or over the losers floundering about after falling into a water jump. Riefenstahl tends to save quick editing rhythms for the most dynamic moments. The rowing races contain some quick alternations between shots of the shells skimming through the water and of the crowd cheering them on. Most spectacularly, the diving sequence gradually builds up its editing pace. A quick barrage of varied shots makes us lose track of the concrete space and time of the event—we come to see a series of bodies soaring through space. Riefenstahl cuts in some shots backward, so that the divers fly *upward,* and one shot is even upside down and backward (Fig. 9.21). As divers move in all directions, gravity seems to be defied, and the sense of birdlike motion is enhanced.

The sound track of *Olympia* is simple but powerful. Romantic, Wagnerian-style music by Herbert Windt accompanies many events and is especially important during those early and late segments when the announcer is not giving us information about the events. This music cues us to react in certain ways: slow, majestic music for the opening in the woods; lighter rhythms for the exercise portions of Segment 2; grandiose, exhilarating music for the diving scene. For the sake of variety, a few scenes have no music, concentrating on the narrator's voice (as with the field-hockey portion of Segment 7). That voice itself cues us how to respond, and it is crucially important to the personalized, narrative segments in the central part of the film. In the pentathlon and decathlon, the narrator sets up suspense by cueing us to watch certain athletes; his slightly hushed voice suggests that he, too, is awaiting the outcomes of the contests (even though the sound track was added long after those outcomes were known). Occasionally there are effects that supposedly come from the space of the events—crowds cheering, wind, and so on—but the film concentrates on music and the narrator's words to guide our attention.

We saw in Chapter 4 how *Olympia*, Part 2, creates referential and explicit meanings that have to do with the Olympic Games themselves, while its more implicit and symptomatic meanings arise from the ideology of its Nazi backers. The film's style is especially important in embodying the symptomatic meanings. The grandiose settings, and the framing and editing patterns that turn the athletes into superhuman beings, support elements of the Nazi mythology of the supremacy of certain races. Framing also brings out the regimentation of the events. The Wagnerian music picks up on current official German views of acceptable artistic style. Luckily these ideas have little currency for us today, and a modern audience is unlikely to respond to *Olympia* in the same way that Germans might have in the late 1930s. But the style's functions of demarcating the film's categories and tracing out patterns of development demonstrate how a filmmaker can create variety and maintain interest in a film with categorical form.

## STYLE IN *THE RIVER*

As we saw in Chapter 4, *The River*'s formal development depends on a simple argument: the Mississippi Valley was beautiful in the past and the people's strength made it productive; that strength and productivity damaged the land; now, with programs like the Tennessee Valley Authority, that strength can be used to repair the damage while enhancing the valley's productivity. Stylistic systems in the film help create this argument. Motifs of camera work, sound, and editing create the parallels we have noted among the various segments and work to suggest that by the end of the film, the TVA has helped re-create a situation similar to the pristine nature we saw at the beginning. But the film also sets up great contrasts between segments showing the country's beauty and strengths and those showing the problems created by careless exploitation of resources. Differences in the use of filmic techniques strengthen the contrasts; hence the film's persuasive power.

*The River* includes a large amount of information—a summary of decades of American history, explanations of the causes of erosion and flooding, a description of the situation in 1937, and a look at the activities of the TVA. Yet we are able to keep all these matters straight and see the relations among them because of the film's clear form and its stylistic repetitions. For example, some segments begin by combining camera work and editing to show us landscapes against a cloudy sky. The very first shots after the prologue introduce this motif, with mountains against

Fig. 9.22

Fig. 9.23

Fig. 9.24

the sky. At the beginning of Segment 3, we see low-height shots of the mule teams against more clouds, and again in Segment 4, we first see the pine forests against the sky (Fig. 4.25). This sets up an expectation that such sky shots are associated with the beauty and strength of the Mississippi Valley, and the filmmakers use this association later to draw parallels. During the flood in Segment 6 and the description of the problems flooding causes, such framings are less prominent. But, after the introduction of the TVA, they return. We see men going to work, framed in low angle against the sky (Fig. 9.22), and just after this one shot begins on a hillside against the sky (Fig. 9.23), then tilts down to reveal the model town (Fig. 9.24). Thus the film satisfies our expectations about this visual motif by bringing it back in association with the new beauty and strength created by the TVA. This repetition also ties the ending back to the beginning, suggesting the return to an idyllic land, and seeming to confirm the film's argument that the TVA was the right solution to the problem.

By way of contrast, other scenes either eliminate this motif or vary it considerably. Thus Segment 4, on the Civil War, begins with a printed announcement quoting Robert E. Lee's surrender statement, with flames superimposed over the writing. This is very different from the earlier segments' openings, marking Segment 4 off as introducing the problems with which the film will deal. As we saw in Chapter 4, the segment devoted to erosion and flooding also contrasts with the earlier scenes by showing stumps against fog (Fig. 4.26)—an obvious contrast with the cloud-filled shots of trees (Fig. 4.25).

*The River* uses a wide range of rhythms within its editing and sound track to create parallels and contrasts. Virgil Thomson's famous musical score plays a more active role than do the scores of most documentary films, and the mixing of voice and music has been very carefully done to enhance the images they accompany. After the prologue, a fanfare introduces the mountain-and-cloud shots, and then the authoritative narrator's voice enters, all combining to suggest the stateliness and splendor of nature in the Mississippi Valley. Later scenes employ faster rhythms, as when a bouncy version of "Hot Time in the Old Town Tonight" plays over shots of logs rushing down chutes into the river; the quick tempo of the movement within the shot matches the music. Here the music is very important in cueing us how to react. We might take the logging to be destructive, but the style suggests that this industry is part of the building of American strength.

But in the next scene, Segment 6, the filmmakers create a contrast. Now we are cued to take the logging activities as having harmful side effects. Here a long series of shots creates a slow, inexorable rhythm building up to the turbulent,

Fig. 9.25

Fig. 9.26

Fig. 9.27

Fig. 9.28

Fig. 9.29

dangerous movements of the flood waters. The segment begins with slow shots of the fog-shrouded stumps (Fig. 4.26), with little movement. Rhythmic, threatening, dissonant chords make up the musical accompaniment. The narrator speaks more slowly and deliberately; dissolves, rather than straight cuts, connect the shots, slowing down the visual rhythm still further. Then the segment begins to build up tension. One shot shows a stump with icicles on it and, instead of going on to other stumps, as the sequence had been doing, the next shot is a cut-in to emphasize the icicles dripping (Fig. 9.25). A sudden dissonant trumpet chord signals us to expect some threat arising from this tiny movement. Then, in a series of close shots of the earth, we see more and more water gathering, first in trickles (Fig. 9.26), later in streams, washing the unprotected soil away. By now the sound is very rhythmic: quiet tom-tom-like drum beats punctuate the shots, and the narrator begins giving dates, one over each shot: "Nineteen-three" (Fig. 9.26); "Nineteen-seven" (Fig. 9.27); "Nineteen-thirteen" (Fig. 9.28); "Nineteen-sixteen" (Fig. 9.29); and so on, up to 1937. By the "1916" shot (Fig. 9.29), we see a small waterfall forming, and in successive shots the creeks become rivers swelling over their banks. As the storm and flood sequence builds up, brief shots of lightning bolts are intercut with shots of raging water. Here the dramatic music becomes overwhelmed by loud sirens and whistles. The stylistic techniques have combined to build up to a climax of rising tension, convincing us of the flood's threat. Were we not to grasp that threat, both factually and emotionally, the film's overall argument would probably affect us less. As you watch the film, look and listen for other rhythmic combinations of voice, music, editing, and movement. You will find a great variety and subtlety in the way *The River* uses such combinations.

Fig. 9.30

Fig. 9.31

Fig. 9.32

Aside from such uses of style to draw us into comparisons between different segments of its form, *The River* employs techniques on a small scale to enhance each individual scene's impact on us. Since the film does not present a narrative with continuing characters and action, it needs neither to use the continuity editing system nor to keep its style unobtrusive. For example, graphic discontinuity may create a striking transition; Lorentz cuts from a shot of a mud-filled, mule-drawn sledge moving from right to left (Fig. 9.30) to a similarly framed shot of a plow going from left to right (Fig. 9.31). This cut leads from the first portion of Segment 3, on the building of the dike, to a new portion on cotton farming. The differences between these shots suggest the transition, but their similarities might also lead us to expect some connection between these two topics.

Camera work can function in an equally striking way. *The River* uses canted framings occasionally, as when we see a montage sequence of workers loading cotton bales onto a steamboat (Fig. 9.32). The off-balance composition makes the bales seem to roll downhill almost effortlessly. Combined with sprightly banjo music, this series of shots cues us to take the scene as a positive depiction of the South's productivity in earlier years. (The cues discourage us from, say, considering whether these black workers are slaves—an important issue in southern history but one which the film does not make pertinent to its subject matter and argument.)

Such small-scale techniques enhance *The River*'s emotional impact on us, and, as we saw in Chapter 4, appeals to our emotions play a large part in rhetorical form. If a film can make us feel strongly about its subject, we may be more inclined to accept its arguments as valid. *The River* demonstrates just how important style can be to rhetorical form. Even today, when the issues around which Pare Lorentz built his arguments are no longer topical, the film still can affect us emotionally with its powerful uses of film style.

## STYLE IN *BALLET MÉCANIQUE*

When we first analyzed *Ballet mécanique* in Chapter 4, we necessarily looked at some aspects of its style—its short bursts of shots, its swinging camera movements, its graphic discontinuities. Style is crucial to abstract organization of form. Indeed, we often refer to the emphasis on abstract qualities of recognizable objects as "stylization." But, now that we have surveyed the techniques of the film medium, we can be more specific about how style functions in *Ballet mécanique*.

Fig. 9.33

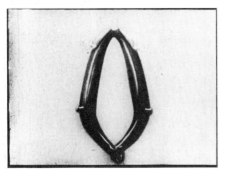

Fig. 9.34

The film uses many stylistic devices in its attempt to give a dancelike rhythm to inanimate objects and a machinelike rhythm to humans. We have seen how most of the objects are familiar, even mundane, things from everyday life. Yet even within the shots, the mise-en-scene takes them out of their familiar context and makes us see them in a new way. For example, many of the shots show faces or objects against black or white backgrounds (Figs. 4.38 and 4.43). In a few cases, the backgrounds themselves have abstract white and black patterns, as in the shot of the swinging ball near the end of Segment 2 (Fig. 9.33). In *Ballet mécanique*, even make-up, which we usually associate with films involving characters, acts to render abstract relations more prominent: in the shot of the woman's profile (Fig. 4.38), heavy make-up combines with her lack of expression and stiff swiveling movement to point up her resemblance to a mannequin. Figure movement also can function in abstract ways. The swinging or turning objects—especially the machine movements in Segment 4—emphasize the "mechanical ballet" pattern; conversely, human figure movement imitates that of the machines.

The cinematographic properties of the shot heighten these functions and add new abstract qualities to their mise-en-scene. Any framing creates a composition, of course, but the filmmaker can emphasize or de-emphasize the abstract qualities of shapes on the flat space of the screen. In *Ballet mécanique*, shot scale often makes shape a very prominent element of the shot. The film has a great proportion of medium close-ups, close-ups, and even extreme close-ups. In combination with the blank backgrounds, such close framings function to isolate and draw attention to shapes: the round hat (Fig. 4.43), the zerolike horse collar (Fig. 9.34), the round profile (Fig. 4.38). Such close framings also make texture easier to discern, as with the shiny pans and bottles.

Other aspects of framing work in similar ways. Masks change the screen's shape to emphasize one portion, as with the repeated shots of a woman's eye (Fig. 4.33). The film uses a great variety of framings, as with the upside-down shot of the swinging woman in Segment 1 (Fig. 4.31) and later, in Segment 6, the rows of swinging pans that also appear upside down (Fig. 4.40). Special effects can organize the small-scale form of a whole segment, as in number 2, where shots through a prism predominate, and then recur as a motif in later portions. Finally, mobile framing functions prominently in the creation of the film's rhythm. The short, regular pans in the upside-down shot of the swinging woman begin this process, and we see other instances later, as in the rapid succession of brief, repetitive pan shots of fairground-ride cars in Segment 3.

Editing is a very important technique for creating abstract relations in *Ballet mécanique*. This film provides a good example of how filmmakers may work entirely outside the continuity editing system and create interesting, highly organized patterns between shots. Although many visual motifs continue to be repeated through the film—especially circular objects—there is relatively little graphic matching. One of the film's most striking and amusing moments, though, does depend on a precise graphic match. In Segment 2 we see an extreme close-up of a woman's wide-open eyes (Fig. 9.35); she closes them, leaving her heavily made-up eyes and brows as dark crescents against her white skin. A cut presents us with the same composition, now upside down (Fig. 9.36 shows the last frame of the first shot and the first frame of the next); the eyes and brows are now reversed, but in identical positions. When the eyes pop open (Fig. 9.37), we are momentarily surprised to find their positions switched—the match is so close as to make the cut almost invisible. (This effect is enhanced by a quick cutting rate that does not allow us to really examine the shots closely.) Humorous touches like this occur throughout

*Ballet mécanique* and make it as enjoyable to watch now as it must have been when it was first shown over sixty years ago.

Graphic matches like this, however, are rare in the film. Usually we must recognize the similarities of shapes even though other shots come between them. Thus in Segment 5, the "dance" of intertitles and pictures, the large zero (Fig. 9.38) and the horse collar (Fig. 9.34) are graphically similar, and each recurs in many shots. Yet they are never juxtaposed in a graphic match; other elements, like the woman's masked eye or fragments of the intertitle sentence, always come in between shots of these two motifs. On the other hand, a great many cuts contrast elements through strong graphic discontinuity. The circle and triangle alternation that recurs so regularly is one obvious example of this. True, the shapes are both white, and both are seen against black backgrounds. But the difference in their shapes is what we notice most readily in these passages. Such an obvious contrast cues us to look for others.

Graphic contrast works along with rhythmic editing. In the hat-shoe alternation in Segment 7 (Fig. 4.43), we see the striking differences in shape right away. But, as the lengthy series of short shots continues, we notice variations. About a third of the way through, the directions are switched: the shoe protrudes in from the left briefly, and the hat also flips. Then they return to their original positions and the editing rhythm accelerates. By the end, the shots are so short that we seem almost to see a single white object pulsating—rapidly changing shape from round to elongated and back again. (Here the filmmakers are exploiting the same apparent-motion phenomenon that makes us see motion in a strip of slightly different still images—the effect that makes cinema itself possible; see Chapter 1.)

Even when there are no specific graphic similarities or contrasts present, editing can suggest other comparisons to us. By placing a shot of a woman's eye next to a machine, or by punctuating a washerwoman's repeated motions with a rhythmically rotating machine part, the film creates a metaphorical similarity. Such repeated comparisons help to organize the overall development of the film's form.

In combination, rhythmic figure movement, rhythmic framing mobility, and rhythmic editing function to suggest the "dance" of objects. It is difficult to resist seeing the quick shots of mannequins' legs (Fig. 4.42) in Segment 7 as such a dance, even though most of the individual shots contain no movement. This passage differs greatly from the simple shot of the woman swinging that we saw at the beginning. Yet, without any use of language beyond the title itself to direct our expectations, *Ballet mécanique* has employed film techniques to guide us to see a similarity between two such contrasting moments. Random objects seem to belong together, and a mechanical rhythm pulses through objects and humans alike. Such is the power of abstract form.

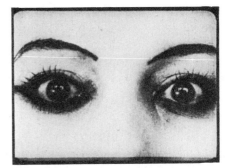

Fig. 9.35

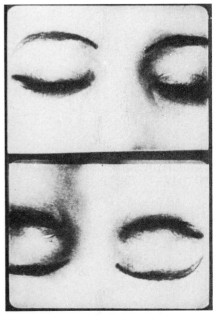

Fig. 9.36

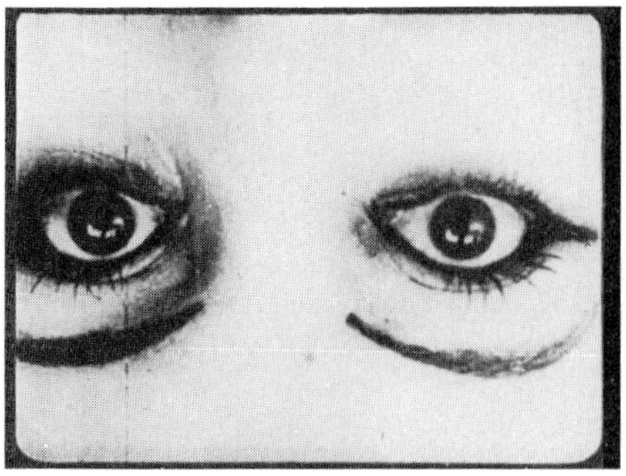

Fig. 9.37

![O](Fig. 9.38)

Fig. 9.38

## STYLE IN *A MOVIE*

We have already seen that the overall form of Bruce Conner's *Movie* is associational. In this context, film style fulfills three general types of functions. On a local level, individual techniques enhance the links between different objects and draw us to form expectations on the basis of the comparison. Second, the style offers us cues as to how to respond, emotionally and intellectually. And, across the whole film, stylistic techniques help break the form into parts and create relations among those parts.

Conner controlled neither the original mise-en-scene nor the cinematography of the films from which he took the shots for *A Movie* nor the composition of the music that forms its sound track. Yet, by selection and arrangement, he made use of these elements as they already existed, and we can find techniques of mise-en-scene, camera work, sound, and editing all at work in fulfilling the three types of functions.

Perhaps the most noticeable characteristic of the mise-en-scene of *A Movie* is its great variety. By choosing material from so many different film genres, Conner cues us to seek more and more generalized associations to explain the links among the objects we see. Galloping cowboys and Indians from a fiction film, atomic-bomb blasts from documentary, and nudie shots from pornography do not add up to a story or an argument, and we must find some common association, like aggressivity and disaster, to make sense of this barrage of heterogeneous images.

Our ability to follow the comparisons being made from shot to shot also depends on the fact that Conner found similar types of mise-en-scene elements from different films and juxtaposed them, putting a stock-car crash next to a race-car crash or a water-skier's fall next to a surfer's wipe-out. *A Movie* also makes use of the mise-en-scene of its different shots to guide our emotional reaction. The plane crashes or firing-squad shots evoke horror, while the more quietly ominous sections of the film contain some images of considerable beauty, such as the first shot of the *Hindenburg* floating over a city (Fig. 4.48). Mise-en-scene elements contribute to the overall form of the film, since visual motifs are repeated and varied. As we saw in Chapter 4, motifs from Segments 2 and 3 are picked up again in the fourth and final part.

Cinematography works in similar ways in *A Movie*. On the one hand, there is a great variety in the types of techniques found in the original footage: wartime aerial photography of planes being fired upon, panning documentary shots that follow race cars and motor boats, and more static framings of staged scenes, as in the pornography shots. Again, this variety enhances the contrasts among elements and encourages us to make comparisons on a very general level. Yet *A Movie* also uses as motifs the similar types of cinematography found in different films. Thus the series of different plane disasters at the beginning of Segment 4 all use aerial photography, and this links them with the aerial shots of the *Hindenburg* early in Segment 3. Cinematography can also enhance emotional response. The series of panning shots of crashing race cars late in Segment 2 builds up a relatively regular rhythm of disasters, a pattern soon to be intensified in later parts of the film. Similarly, the long tilt with the old car that falls over a cliff at the end of this segment (Figs. 9.39 and 9.40) emphasizes the length of that fall and provides an emotional climax to the series of car crashes.

At a few points in *A Movie*, Conner also manipulates cinematography by using laboratory-made special effects to alter shots. A few shots in Segment 4 begin or

Fig. 9.39

Fig. 9.40

Fig. 9.41

Fig. 9.42

Fig. 9.43

Fig. 9.44

Fig. 9.45

end with black masks that move to reveal or conceal the mise-en-scene of the shot; for example, the brief series of shots of the buckling suspension bridge begins with such a mask moving aside (Fig. 9.41). Such moments stress Conner's own manipulation of the found footage and perhaps function similarly to the repeated insertions of the titles "Movie," "Bruce Conner," and so on, at other points in the film. There is also a brief series of shots early in Segment 4 that are linked by dissolves and optically printed zoom-ins that enlarge the frames. From the planes in front of the pyramid (Fig. 4.55), a dissolve moves us to the beginning of the first volcano shot (Fig. 9.42). You can see the edges of this frame as Conner prints it small at first, then optically enlarges it frame by frame to achieve a zooming effect (Fig. 9.43). After a straight cut to a closer volcano shot (also with an optical zoom-in), there is a dissolve to the coronation (Fig. 9.44), which is also optically enlarged (Fig. 9.45), followed by another dissolve to the burning *Hindenburg*, and a final dissolve and zoom-in to a group of moving tanks. In a film that usually manipulates the original shots only through editing and sound, this brief segment stands out by contrast. The effect of the quick dissolves and zooms is partly to seem to move us in toward the disasters and other scenes. But, more strikingly, each scene seems to emerge out of the previous one—the volcano "coming forward" from the pyramid, the church official blending briefly with the smoke of the volcano and growing larger, and so on. This series creates a very strong linkage among the disparate elements, enhancing our sense of the inevitable, rhythmic flow of this set of ominous images.

Sound is crucial to *A Movie*'s various effects. In Chapter 4 we saw how the divisions between Segments 2, 3, and 4 coincide with pauses between parts of Respighi's *Pines of Rome*. The considerable differences in tone among those parts also give us strong cues as to how to react to the images. The shots that open Segment 3—the women carrying totems, the *Hindenburg*, the acrobats—take on their eerie, slightly ominous quality almost solely because of the musical accompaniment. Moreover, the music intensifies our emotional response: while the series of disasters in Segment 4 are horrendous in themselves, the slow, ponderous, driving music links them all into one plunging, apocalyptic rush.

The sound is all nondiegetic, of course, and we hear no voices or sound effects from the individual scenes. Yet Conner has edited his shots very carefully to create corresponding rhythms in image movement, cutting, and music. For example, the frenzied build-up of the fast passage in *The Pines of Rome* toward the end of Segment 2 accompanies the series of race-car crashes. Blaring, dissonant notes begin to punctuate the music at regular intervals, and Conner times these to coincide with the individual car crashes, considerably enhancing their visual effectiveness. Later, in Segment 4, the shot of the flute player (Fig. 4.56) coincides with a passage of flute and oboe music, so that we almost sense for a moment that the sound has become diegetic. This impression enhances the idyllic quality of these exotic shots, just before the return to the disaster footage. Thus, although Conner chose an existing piece of music, he has tailored it closely to his images and used it to help create the tone and form of *A Movie*. (Significantly, *The Pines of Rome* itself uses associational form; it is a tone poem that uses musical imagery to suggest impressions of a place or situation. In this case, Respighi was trying to depict musically various famous spots in Rome. Such music strongly cues emotional and conceptual responses, and Conner has exploited these qualities.)

Editing was the only technique in *A Movie* that Conner controlled completely, and it is the source of many spectacular effects. Of course, the basic associational comparisons are made by cutting together series of shots from different sources. But Conner does not stop with just juxtaposing objects by cutting. He exploits the graphic, spatial, and temporal relations between shots as well. Some cuts use principles of continuity to fit together shots that really could not be in the same space, thus creating an "impossible" continuity that gives the film much of its humor. We can see now that the joke of the submarine officer "looking" at the bikini-clad woman (Figs. 4.50 and 4.51) comes from the fact that it is a false eyeline match. Similarly, the various racing horses, elephants, and tanks in the first part of Segment 2 are linked partly by their common screen direction. Most of the movement is from left to right on the screen, or coming directly toward the camera—two directions that would cut together "correctly" in the continuity system. Thus we can imagine all these vehicles and animals racing along together in some vast space—yet the obvious impossibility of the juxtaposition makes this notion funny. Later, in Segment 3, Conner varies this technique by cutting together various

Fig. 9.46

Fig. 9.47

water skiers and motor boats, some with similar directions of movement, some with opposed directions, but all compared through the general similarities of the series of shots.

Graphic matches can create comparisons through editing. During the same series of fast movements cut together in Segment 2, we see first a shot of a wagon moving over the camera (Fig. 9.46), then a graphically similar shot from a low camera height of a tank hurtling toward the camera (Fig. 9.47). Combined with the quick tempo of the editing rhythm, such moments contribute to the dynamic sense of exhilaration that this segment generates. By finding similarities of this type between shots taken from different sources, Conner also enhances the associational links between shots: stylistic links cue us to find emotional and conceptual links as well.

The overall formal organization of *A Movie*, with its initial humor and its development toward a threatening tone and ultimate disaster, depends heavily on the repeated use of film techniques. With editing to juxtapose elements, mise-en-scene and cinematography to emphasize the similarities and contrasts among them, and music to suggest and unify the changing tone, this short film can elicit a wide range of responses from the viewer. Here, as in all the types of nonnarrative form, we can see that style plays a crucial role in the total form of a film.

This concludes our discussion of film form and film technique. As we have emphasized, no single set of rules will allow you to understand every film automatically. Any film creates a unique form from an interplay of overall structure and film style, and each individual element (each formal part or stylistic technique) functions according to its place within that system. Analyzing the nature of that formal system and the functions of individual devices is the goal of the critic; Part IV of this book consists of a series of analyses showing how a critic may understand the workings of widely differing kinds of films.

## NOTES AND QUERIES

### ■ THE CONCEPT OF FILM STYLE

Sometimes the concept of style is used evaluatively, to imply that something is inherently good ("Now that's got real style!"), but we are using it descriptively: all films have style. For discussion of the concept of style in various arts, see Monroe C. Beardsley, *Aesthetics: Problems in the Philosophy of Criticism* (New York: Harcourt, Brace & World, 1958); J. V. Cunningham, ed., *The Problem of Style* (Greenwich, Conn.: Fawcett, 1966); and Berel Lang, ed., *The Concept of Style* (Philadelphia: University of Pennsylvania Press, 1979).

Pioneering studies of style in the cinema are Erwin Panofsky, "Style and Medium in the Moving Pictures" (originally published in 1934), in Daniel Talbot, ed., *Film: An Anthology* (Berkeley: University of California Press, 1970), pp. 13–32; Raymond Durgnat, *Films and Feelings* (Cambridge, Mass.: MIT Press, 1967); and Raymond Bellour, "Pour une stylistique du film," *Revue d'esthétique* **19**, 2 (April–June 1966): 161–178. Many of the works cited in Notes and Queries to chapters in Part III offer concrete studies of aspects of film style.

An entire book has been written on the production of *Citizen Kane*, shedding much light on how its style was created: Robert L. Carringer's *The Making of Citizen Kane* (Berkeley: University of California Press, 1985). Among other things, Carringer reveals the degree to which Welles and his collaborators used special effects for many of the film's scenes.

# CRITICAL ANALYSIS
# OF FILMS

Criticism is not an activity limited to those people who write articles or books about films. Any person who seeks actively to understand a film he or she sees is engaged in a process of criticism. You may be unsure, for example, why one scene was included in a film; your search for the function of that scene in the context of the whole is a first step in a critical examination. People who discuss a film they have seen are participating in criticism.

Up to this point, we have looked at concepts and definitions that should enable a filmgoer to analyze a film systematically. The critic approaches a film already knowing that formal patterns, such as repetitions and variations, will likely be important and should be examined. The critic will also be alert for principles of narrative and nonnarrative form, and she or he will watch for salient uses of the various film techniques. The critic will also ground his or her claims in specific evidence from the film.

So far, we have looked at all of the techniques that constitute a film; we have laid out the basic principles that govern a film's formal system. Many detailed examples and analyses of several entire films have shown how elements of a film function in an overall system. But the only way to gain an ability to analyze films critically is through practice—in both viewing films critically and reading analyses by other critics. For this reason, we conclude our look at films as formal systems with a series of brief sample essays on individual films.

An analyst usually scrutinizes a film with some sort of purpose in view. You may want to understand a film's perplexing aspects, or reveal the process that created a pleasurable response, or convince someone that the film is worth seeing. Our sample analyses have two primary purposes. First, we want to illustrate how film form and film style work together in a variety of films. Secondly, we seek to provide models of short critical analyses, exemplars of how an essay might illuminate some aspects of a film's workings. Because an analyst is limited by his or her purposes, there is little chance of "getting everything," of accounting for every facet of a film. As a result, these analyses do not exhaust the films. You might study any one of them and find many more points of interest than we have been able to present here. Indeed, whole books can be and have been written about single films without exhausting the possibilities for enriching our experience of those films.

# TEN

# FILM CRITICISM: SAMPLE ANALYSES

Each of the five major sections of this chapter emphasizes different aspects of various films. First, we discuss four classical narrative films: *His Girl Friday*, *Stagecoach*, *North by Northwest*, and *Hannah and Her Sisters*. Since such films are very familiar to most viewers, it is important to study closely how they work.

Next, we move to four films that represent various alternatives to classical norms. The first two films in this section rely on ambiguity to create their effects. *Day of Wrath* and *Last Year at Marienbad* do not have as clear-cut a narrative chain of cause and effect as do the more classical films. They also tend to use film technique in equivocal and unsettling ways. The next film we examine, *Tokyo Story*, uses selective deviations from classical stylistic norms in order to create a unique, highly unified system. The last example, *Innocence Unprotected*, is far more eclectic, using a collage of fiction and nonfiction to reflect on cinema's social and political implications.

Documentary films can be constructed in various ways, and the third section considers two examples. Although *High School* purports to be a neutral description of a situation, it nonetheless illustrates how the filmmaker's formal and stylistic choices can create strong spectator effects and a particular range of explicit and implicit meanings. By contrast, *Man with a Movie Camera* makes no pretense of objectivity and instead flaunts the manipulative powers of the film medium.

We may not think of cartoons as susceptible to close analysis, but our fourth section demonstrates that animated film offers intriguing formal and stylistic challenges. Three significant short films reveal the range of possibilities available in drawn animation.

Finally, we move to analyses that emphasize social ideology. Our first example, *Meet Me in St. Louis*, is a film that accepts a dominant ideology and quietly reinforces the audience's belief in that ideology. By contrast, *Tout va bien* takes an explicitly radical position and challenges the audience to reflect consciously on the ideas set forth.

We could have emphasized different aspects of any of these films. *Meet Me In St. Louis*, for example, is a classical narrative film and could be considered from that perspective. Similarly, *Man with a Movie Camera* could be seen as offering an alternative to classical continuity editing. And any of the films represents an ideological position which could be analyzed. Our choices suggest only certain angles of approach; your own critical activities will discover many more.

Those activities are the focus of the appendix to this part. There we suggest some ways in which you can prepare, organize, and write a critical analysis of a film. We draw on the previous sample analyses for various strategies that you can apply in your own writing.

## THE CLASSICAL NARRATIVE CINEMA

### ■ *HIS GIRL FRIDAY*

> 1940. Columbia. Directed by Howard Hawks. Script by Charles Lederer from the play *The Front Page* by Ben Hecht and Charles MacArthur. Photographed by Joseph Walker. Edited by Gene Harlick. Music by Morris W. Stoloff. With Cary Grant, Rosalind Russell, Ralph Bellamy, Gene Lockhart, Porter Hall.

The dominant impression left by *His Girl Friday* is that of speed: it is often said to be the fastest sound comedy ever made. Let us therefore "slow it down" analytically. By breaking the film into parts and seeing how the parts relate to one another logically, temporally, and spatially, we can suggest how classical narrative form and specific film techniques are used to create this unique, whirlwind experience.

*His Girl Friday* is built on the common unit of classical narrative cinema: the scene. Typically marked off by editing devices such as the dissolve, fade, or wipe, each scene presents a distinct segment of space, time, and narrative action. We can locate 13 such scenes in *His Girl Friday*, set in the following locales: (1) the *Morning Post* offices; (2) the restaurant; (3) the Criminal Courts pressroom; (4) Walter's office; (5) Earl Williams's cell; (6) the pressroom; (7) a precinct jail; (8) the pressroom; (9) the sheriff's office; (10) the street outside the prison; (11) the pressroom; (12) the sheriff's office; (13) the pressroom. All of these scenes are marked off by dissolves except for the transition between 8 and 9, which is simply a cut.

Within these scenes, smaller units of action occur. Note, for example, that scene 1, occupying almost 14 minutes of screen time, introduces almost all of the major characters and sets two plot lines in motion. Or, consider scene 13: almost every major character appears in it, and it runs for about 33 minutes! We can, then, conveniently break several long scenes into smaller parts on the basis of changing character interactions. Thus scene 1 comprises: (a) the introduction to the newspaper office; (b) the first conversation between Hildy and Bruce; (c) Walter's discussion of the past with Hildy; (d) Walter's conference with Duffy about the Earl Williams case; (e) Hildy's telling Walter that she's remarrying; and (f) Walter's introduction to Bruce. To grasp the construction of other lengthy scenes, you may divide them into similar segments. It may be, in fact, that the somewhat "theatrical" feel of the film comes from its practice of segmenting its scenes by character entrances and exits (rather than, say, by frequent shifts of locale). In any event, the developing patterns of character interaction contribute a great deal to the hubbub and speed of the film.

The scenes function, of course, to advance the narrative action. As we saw in Chapter 3 (pp. 70–71), classical Hollywood cinema often constructs a narrative around characters with definite traits who want to achieve specific goals. The clash of these characters' contrasting traits and conflicting goals propels the story forward in a step-by-step process of cause and effect. *His Girl Friday* has two such cause-effect chains:

1. *The romance.* Hildy Johnson wants to quit newspaper reporting and settle down with Bruce Baldwin. This is her initial goal. But Hildy's editor and ex-husband, Walter Burns, wants her to continue as his reporter and to remarry him (his goal). Given these two goals, the characters enter into a conflict in several stages. First, Walter lures Hildy by promising a nest egg for the couple in exchange for her writing one last story. But Walter also plots to have Bruce robbed. Learning of this, Hildy tears up her story. Walter continues to delay Bruce, however, and eventually wins Hildy through her renewed interest in reporting. She changes her mind about marrying Bruce and stays with Walter.

2. *Crime and politics.* Earl Williams is to be hanged for shooting a policeman. The city's political bosses are relying on the execution to ensure their reelection. This is the goal shared by the mayor and the sheriff. But Walter's goal is to induce the governor to reprieve Williams and thus unseat the mayor's party at the polls. Through the sheriff's stupidity, Williams escapes and is concealed by Hildy and Walter. In the meantime, a reprieve does arrive from the governor, but the mayor bribes the messenger into leaving. Williams is discovered, but the messenger returns with the reprieve in time to save Williams from death and Walter and Hildy from jail. Presumably the mayor's machine will be defeated at the election.

The crime-and-politics line of action is made to depend on events in the romance line at several points: Walter uses the Williams case to lure Hildy back to him, Hildy chases the Williams story instead of returning to Bruce, Bruce's mother reveals to the police that Walter has concealed Williams, and so on. More specifically, the interplay of the two lines of action alters the goals of various characters. In Walter's case, inducing Hildy to write the story fulfills his goals of embarrassing the politicos and of tempting Hildy back. Hildy's goals are more greatly altered: after she destroys her article, her decision to cover Earl Williams's jailbreak marks her acceptance of Walter's goal, and her later willingness to hide Williams and her indifference to Bruce's plea firmly establish her goals as linked to Walter's. In this way the interaction of the two plot lines advances Walter's goals but radically alters Hildy's.

Within this general framework, the cause-effect sequencing is very complex and deserves a closer analysis than space permits here. But consider, for example, the various ways in which Walter's delaying tactics (involving his confederates Duffy, Louie, and Angie) set up short-term chains of cause and effect in themselves. Also interesting is the way Bruce is steadily shouldered out of the romance plot, becoming more and more passive as he is shuttled in and out of precinct jails. In this regard Earl Williams undergoes a parallel experience as he is manipulated by Hildy, the sheriff, the psychologist, and Walter. We could also consider the function of the minor characters, such as Molly Malloy (Williams's platonic sweetheart),

Bruce's mother, the other reporters, and especially Pettibone, the delightful emissary from the governor. Perhaps most important, note how the scenes "hook into" each other. An event at the end of one scene is seen as a cause leading to an effect, that is, the event that begins the next scene. For example, at the end of the first scene, Walter offers to take Bruce and Hildy to lunch; scene 2 starts with the three of them arriving at the restaurant. This exemplifies the famous "linearity" of classical narrative: almost every scene ends with a "dangling cause," the effect of which is shown at the beginning of the next scene. In *His Girl Friday*, this linear pattern helps keep the plot action moving rapidly forward, "setting up" each new scene quickly at the end of the previous one.

The cause-and-effect logic of the film illustrates yet another principle of classical narrative structure: closure. No event is uncaused. (Even when Pettibone arrives, he is no deus ex machina, for we know that the governor is under pressure to decide about the case.) And, more important, both lines of action are clearly resolved at the end. Williams is saved and the politicians are disgraced. Bruce, having gone home with mother, leaves Walter and Hildy preparing for a second honeymoon no less hectic than their first.

So much for causality. What of narrative time? Classical Hollywood cinema typically subordinates time to the narrative's cause-effect relations, and one common way is to set a deadline for the action. Thus a temporal goal is wedded to a causal one, and the time becomes charged with cause-effect significance. The deadline is, of course, a convention of the newspaper genre, already adding a built-in time (and suspense) factor. But in *His Girl Friday* each of the two plots has its own deadlines as well. The mayor and sheriff face an obvious deadline: Earl Williams must be hanged before next Tuesday's election and before the governor can reprieve him. In his political strategizing Walter Burns faces the other side of the same deadline: he wants Williams reprieved. What we might not expect is that the romance plot has deadlines as well. Bruce and Hildy are set to leave on a train bound for Albany (and for marriage) at four o'clock that very day. Walter's machinations keep forcing the couple to postpone their departure. Add to this the fact that when Bruce comes to confront Hildy and Walter, he exits with the defiant ultimatum: "I'm leaving on the nine o'clock train!" (Hildy misses that train as well.) The temporal structure of the film, then, depends on the cause-effect sequence. If Earl Williams were to be hanged next month, or if the election were two years off, or if Bruce and Hildy were planning a marriage at some distant future date, the sense of dramatic pressure would be entirely absent. The numerous and overlapping deadlines under which all of the characters labor have the effect of squeezing together all the lines of action and sustaining the breathless pace of the film.

Another aspect of *His Girl Friday*'s patterning of time reinforces this pace. Though the plot presents events in straightforward chronological order, it takes remarkable liberties with story duration. Of course, since the action consumes about nine hours (from around 12:30 P.M. to around 9:30 P.M.), we expect that certain portions of time *between scenes* will be eliminated. And so they have been. What is unusual is that the time *within* scenes has been accelerated. At the start of the very first scene, for example, the clock in the *Post* office reads 12:36; after 12 minutes of screen time have passed, the clock in the *Post* office reads 12:57. It's important to note that there have been no editing ellipses in the scene; the story duration has simply been compressed. If you clock scene 13, you will find even more remarkable acceleration; people leave on long trips and return in less than 10 minutes. Again, the editing is continuous: it is story time that "goes faster" than screen time. Add to this temporal compression the frenetically rushed dialogue and the occasionally accelerated rhythmic editing (for example, the reporters' cries just before Williams's capture), and we have a film that often proceeds at breakneck pace.

Space, like time, is here subordinate to narrative cause and effect. Hawks's camera moves unobtrusively to reframe the characters symmetrically in the shot. (Watch any scene silent to observe the subtle "balancing act" that goes on during the dialogue scenes. An example is shown in Figs. 6.87 to 6.89). Straight-on camera angles predominate, varied by an occasional high-angle shot down on the prison courtyard or on Williams's cell. Lighting is generally high key, except for the morbid Gothic silhouettes of the gallows and of Earl Williams's cell bars. (Why, we might ask in passing, does the prison receive this visual emphasis in the camera angle and the lighting?) The restriction of the action to very few locales might seem a handicap, but the patterns of character placement are remarkably varied and functional: Walter's persuading Hildy to write the story is interesting from this standpoint, as the two pace in a complete circuit around the desk and Walter assumes dynamic and comic postures. And spatial continuity in the editing antic-ipates each dramatic point by judiciously cutting to a closer shot or smoothly matching on action so that we watch the movements and not the cuts. Virtually every scene, especially the restaurant episode and the final scene, offers many fine examples of classical continuity editing. In all, space is used to delineate the flow of the cause-effect sequence.

We might highlight for special attention one specific item of both sound and mise-en-scene. It is "realistic" that newspapermen in 1939 should use telephones, but *His Girl Friday* makes the phone integral to the narrative. Walter's duplicity demands phones: at the restaurant he pretends to be summoned away to a call; he makes and breaks promises to Hildy via phones; he directs Duffy and other minions by phone. More generally, the pressroom is equipped with a veritable flotilla of phones, enabling the reporters to contact their editors. And, of course, Bruce keeps calling Hildy from the various police stations in which he continually finds himself. The telephones thus constitute a communications network that permits the narrative to be relayed from point to point.

But Hawks also visually and sonically orchestrates the characters' use of the phones. There are many variations. One person may be talking on the phone, or several may be talking *in turn* on different phones, or several may be talking *at once* on different phones, or a phone conversation may be juxtaposed with a conversation elsewhere in the room, and so on. In scene 11, there is a "polyphonic" effect of reporters coming in to phone their editors, each conversation overlapping with the preceding one. Later, in scene 13, while Hildy frantically phones hospitals, Walter screams into another phone. And when Bruce returns for Hildy, a helter-skelter din arises that eventually sorts itself into three soundlines: Bruce begging Hildy to listen, Hildy obsessively typing her story, and Walter yelling into the phone for Duffy to clear page one ("No, no, leave the rooster story—that's human interest!"). Like much in *His Girl Friday*, the telephones warrant close study for the complex and various ways in which they are integrated into the narrative, and for their contribution to the rapid tempo of the film.

## ■ *STAGECOACH*

1939. Walter Wanger Productions (released through United Artists). Directed by John Ford. Script by Dudley Nichols, from the short story "Stage to Lordsburg," by Ernest Haycox. Photographed by Bert Glennon. Edited by Dorothy Spencer and Walter Reynolds. Music by Richard Hageman, W. Franke Harling, John Leipold, Leo Shuken, Louis Gruienberg. With John Wayne, Claire Trevor, Thomas Mitchell, Andy Devine, George Bancroft, Donald Meek, Louise Platt, John Carradine, Berton Churchill.

Film theorist André Bazin has written of John Ford's *Stagecoach*: "*Stagecoach* (1939) is the ideal example of the maturity of a style brought to classic perfection. . . . *Stagecoach* is like a wheel, so perfectly made that it remains in equilibrium on its axis in any position." This effect results from the film's concentration on the creation of a tight narrative unity, with all of its elements serving that goal.

As in *His Girl Friday*, the plot takes place over a short time—two days. Ford's narrative takes the word "stagecoach" (a coach traveling in stages, stopping along the way) literally and makes this the basis of its narrative divisions. Thus the film's action is the progression of a stagecoach from its starting point to its destination, with the major scenes occurring at the places where the coach stops for meals and rest. Instead of a detailed segmentation of the film, a broader breakdown of the large-scale parts of the journey lets us bring out important aspects of the form's development:

First day

1. Cavalry receives word of Indian uprising.
2. In Tonto, the passengers board the stagecoach.
3. Conversations during the first part of the journey.
4. First stage stop: noon dinner and word that there will be no escort.
5. Conversations during the second part of the journey.
6. Second stage stop: night. Lucy's baby is born; Ringo proposes to Dallas.

Second day

7. Morning: departure from the second stage stop.
8. Conversations during the third part of the journey.
9. Third stage stop: passengers discover burned ferry, float coach across river, are attacked and chased by Indians, and are rescued by the cavalry.
10. Arrival at Lordsburg; Ringo has his shoot-out with the Plummer brothers.
11. Ringo and Dallas depart for Ringo's ranch.

The perfect balance of one part against another is apparent in this outline. At the very beginning and end, short scenes take place among the buttes of Monument Valley. Initially we see the cavalry riding and bringing the news that Geronimo is on the warpath; at the end, a single shot shows Ringo and Dallas riding through the valley toward their new life together. The film's second part takes place in the town of Tonto, where the passengers board the coach. The journey ends in sequence 10, which reverses the second part; here the passengers disembark in Lordsburg, their destination. Here also the various goals these characters had set up for themselves are resolved.

Between these two points of departure and arrival, there are three sequences of travel along the road (parts 3, 5, and 8), each culminating in the arrival at one of the three stages, or stops, along the way. During the first stop, at Dry Fork, the passengers eat their noon meal. At the second, Apache Wells, they spend the night. The departure the next morning parallels the previous day's departure from the town; the pattern of parts 5–6 repeats that of parts 3–4.

As before, the departure scene leads to a new traveling phase, part 8. But after two repetitions of the travel-stage-stop pattern, the narrative introduces a major variation. When the coach arrives at the outpost for the third and final stage, East Ferry, the characters find it burnt by Indians. The coach crosses the river and goes on toward Lordsburg, but our expectation of a major scene at this point is not disappointed. In the formal position of the third stage stop, the Indian attack occurs. After the chase and rescue, an ellipsis moves the narrative directly to Lordsburg, eliminating the last part of the journey.

The initial departure from Tonto (Segment 2) establishes the goals of most of the characters. Lucy Mallory is traveling to join her husband, who is in the cavalry. Mr. Peacock, a whiskey salesman, is on his way home to join his wife in Kansas City. The two leaders of the group are the driver, Buck, who also is going home to his family in Lordsburg, and the marshal, Curly, who goes along as guard to try to capture the Ringo Kid.

Two "undesirables"—Doc Boone, the local drunk, and Dallas, a prostitute—leave town on the same stagecoach, driven out by the "respectable" elements of the town. Doc and Dallas have no definite goal, except to find a place where they will be allowed to stay. The gambler, Hatfield, also joins the group with no long-term goal of his own; he seeks to protect Lucy Mallory on her journey.

The narrative marks two characters off by having them board the coach later. Having stolen the payroll money deposited in his bank, Gatewood hails the coach on the street and gets in. Gatewood's goal is to escape undetected. A short while after the coach leaves Tonto, it meets Ringo, who wants to get to Lordsburg to avenge himself on the Plummer brothers. He joins the group, under arrest by Curly.

Most of the significant causal developments in the plot come in the scenes at the two stage stops. In the first (Segment 4), the seating pattern at the table defines the social relationships. Within the group, Ringo and Dallas are both shunned as outcasts and hence thrown together. Mr. Peacock defines himself as the weakling of the group by being the only one to vote to return to Tonto when they discover that no cavalry escort will be available beyond that stop.

The second stage stop (Segment 6) is the most important scene during the journey for its development of character relationships. Doc Boone and Dallas, the two undesirables, earn the admiration of the others by helping deliver Lucy's baby. At this point Ringo proposes marriage to Dallas.

Between the major sequences in the towns, the stages, and the Indian attack come three sequences of traveling through Monument Valley (parts 3, 5, and 8), each consisting of a number of similar short scenes. Each scene begins with a long shot or extreme long shot of the coach; most of these are accompanied by the distinctive "stagecoach" musical motif. Several times, especially early in each sequence, this long shot is followed by a medium shot of the driver's seat, with Curly and Buck talking. These shots give snatches of exposition. For example, we learn that Curly is sympathetic to Ringo's revenge motives and that he is suspicious of Gatewood.

Each short scene also contains one or more shots inside the coach, with the passengers making conversation or exchanging glances. These interchanges tend to reestablish character traits and relations rather than move the action forward. Gatewood complains constantly; Boone filches drinks from Peacock's sample bag; Hatfield does courteous little favors for Lucy's comfort. Several motifs enter into these characterizations. Boone's liquor contrasts with the canteen the women drink from, and the two valises belonging to Gatewood and Peacock also set up a contrast. The development of the characters' attitudes toward one another is also apparent. Before the birth of Lucy's baby, the other characters ignore Dallas; in later scenes they are relatively kind to her.

These numerous short scenes, strung together within the travel sequences, function to give a sense of the coach's progression. Dissolves link most of them, indicating the passage of time and space. Unlike *His Girl Friday*, *Stagecoach* has

Fig. 10.1

Fig. 10.2

almost no scenes that end with dangling causes that "hook" over into the beginning of the next scene. Causes are introduced, but these tend to disappear for long stretches of the action. Thus early in the film Curly mentions that he sympathizes with Ringo's desire for revenge. This sympathy emerges only in the final scene, in which Curly lets Ringo go have his shoot-out with the Plummers. Because most or all of the nine characters are present in almost every scene of the journey, *Stagecoach* has little need for dangling causes; there are few transitions from one set of characters in one locale to another set in another locale. The coach's journey itself provides the forward development of the narrative.

Much of the richness of *Stagecoach*'s narrative comes from the mixing of numerous characters with separate, sometimes contradictory goals. The rapid resolutions of the characters' goals on the arrival at Lordsburg gives a strong sense of closure. Lucy learns that her husband, reported to have been wounded by Indians, is safe; Peacock survives his wound; Gatefield is arrested. Thus most of the strongly positive and negative characters are taken care of.

Other characters have had to prove their worth in the course of the action. Hatfield is a notorious gambler but proves himself to be a "gentleman" by protecting Lucy and dying in the battle with the Indians. Doc Boone has sobered up in order to deliver Lucy's baby; he also stands up to the Plummers in the tavern before the shoot-out. Indeed, at the end of the film the marshal offers Boone a drink. He replies, "Just one," suggesting that even he has been reformed somewhat by his experiences on the trip.

The last section of the narrative focuses primarily on the fates of Dallas and Ringo. Ringo had entered the action last of all the passengers; now his goal of revenge determines the last portion of the plot, after most of the other characters have gone their ways. Dallas, who had no definite goal of her own, has gained one in her love for Ringo. His victory over the Plummers and the marshal's decision not to send him back to jail lead to the final resolution. Both Dallas and Ringo go free to start their new life together. The final long shot of their wagon moving along the road through Monument Valley recalls the beginning and the many long shots of the coach.

The style of *Stagecoach* helps create the repetitions and variations of this narrative action. We have indicated the repeated pattern of establishing long shots of the coach, interspersed with closer shots within the coach; these latter shots pick up the eyelines and gestures of the characters' conversations. We have already analyzed one outstanding use of offscreen sound in *Stagecoach*, in Chapter 8 (p. 255); you might examine other uses of sound in the film, along with their functions.

One aspect of the film's style is particularly outstanding: its use of deep space and deep focus. As we shall see in more detail in Chapter 11, the style of filming in Hollywood during the 1930s was generally a "shallow-," or "soft-focus" style. A few American films in the late 1930s began to experiment with deep focus, and *Stagecoach* was one of them. A number of shots in the second stage-stop sequence use deep focus along the corridor outside Lucy's room, as when Ringo watches Dallas go out into the yard (Fig. 10.1) or outside when he follows her (Fig. 10.2). Welles claimed to have watched *Stagecoach* many times before making *Citizen Kane*, the film usually credited with having introduced deep-focus photography; the similarities of lighting, mise-en-scene, and camera manipulations are apparent from these stills. Ford's cinematographer used wide-angle lenses to keep several planes in focus and to exaggerate perspective. The deep-focus shots make use of strong backlighting, which picks out Dallas and Ringo in the dark hallway and yard. The lighting is very different from the flat lighting used in most other scenes. This pattern of patches of light in darkness returns again in the Lordsburg sequence, when the plans the couple has made at the stage stop are finally made possible.

On the whole, Ford's editing style remains within the Hollywood continuity system. But it is worth noting that *Stagecoach*'s editing is not always as "perfectly classical" as Bazin maintains. For example, the Indian attack violates screen direction. At times the coach and Indians move across the screen from left to right. At others they move right to left. Sometimes Ford uses a heads-on or tails-on shot to cross the line, in the accepted manner, but at other times he does not. At one point, Ringo starts to leap down onto the horses' backs to retrieve a lost rein. His leap begins in medium long shot, from right to left (Fig. 10.3). In the next shot he is moving left to right (Fig. 10.4).

These deviations show that violations of continuity rules do not always confuse the audience. The narrative context tells us that there is only one coach and one band of Indians chasing it in a straight line across a flat desert. As long as the filmmaker has sufficiently established the space and the moving elements, changes in screen direction should not be perplexing. It is usually only when we are uncertain about who is present and where the figures are in relation to one another that the violation of screen direction becomes confusing.

In spite of such lapses, *Stagecoach* remains an outstanding example of that classical unity of form and style that Bazin identified with 1930s Hollywood. Our discussions of *North by Northwest* and *Hannah and Her Sisters* will show that the same tendency has continued up to the present.

Fig. 10.3

Fig. 10.4

## ■ *NORTH BY NORTHWEST*

1959. MGM. Directed by Alfred Hitchcock. Script by Ernest Lehman. Photographed by Robert Burks. Edited by George Tomasini. Music composed by Bernard Herrmann. With Cary Grant, Eva Marie Saint, James Mason, Leo G. Carroll, Jesse Royce Landis.

Hitchcock long insisted that he made thrillers, not mystery films. For him, creating a puzzle was less important than generating suspense and surprise. While there are important mystery elements in films like *Notorious* (1946), *Stage Fright* (1950), and *Psycho* (1960), *North by Northwest* stands as almost a pure example of Hitchcock's belief that the mystery element can serve as merely a pretext for intriguing the audience. The film's tight causal unity enables Hitchcock to create an engrossing plot that obeys the norms of classical filmmaking. This plot is presented through a narration that continually emphasizes suspense and surprise.

Like most spy films, *North by Northwest* has a complex plot, involving two major lines of action. In one line, a gang of spies mistakes advertising-agency executive Roger Thornhill for an American agent, George Kaplan. Although the spies fail to kill him, he becomes the chief suspect in a murder which the gang commits. He must flee the police while trying to track down the real George Kaplan. Unfortunately, Kaplan does not exist; he is only a decoy invented by the United States Intelligence Agency (USIA). Thornhill's pursuit of "Kaplan" leads to the second line of action: his meeting and falling in love with Eve Kendall, who is really the mistress of Philip Van Damm, the spies' leader. The spy-chase line and the romance line further connect when Thornhill learns that Eve is actually a double agent, secretly working for the USIA. He must then rescue her from Van Damm, who has discovered her identity and has resolved to kill her. In the course of all this, Thornhill also discloses the spies' clandestine operation: they are smuggling government secrets out of the country in pieces of sculpture.

From even so bare an outline it should be evident that the film's plot presents many conventional patterns to the viewer. There is the search pattern, seen when Thornhill sets out to find Kaplan. There is also a journey pattern: Thornhill and his pursuers travel from New York to Chicago and then to Rapid City, South Dakota, with side excursions as well. In addition, the last two-thirds of the plot is organized around the romance between Thornhill and Eve. Moreover, each pattern develops markedly in the course of the film. In the course of his search, Thornhill must often assume the identity of the man he is trailing. The journey pattern gets varied by all the vehicles Thornhill uses—cabs, train, pickup truck, police car, bus, ambulance, and airplane.

Most subtly, the romance line of action is constantly modified by Thornhill's changing awareness of the situation. When he believes that Eve wants to help him, he starts to fall in love with her. But then he learns that she sent him to the murderous appointment at Prairie Stop, and he becomes cold and suspicious. When he discovers her at the auction with Van Damm, his anger and bitterness impel him to humiliate her and make Van Damm doubt her loyalty. Only after the USIA chief, the "Professor," tells him that she is really an agent does Thornhill realize that he has misjudged and endangered her. Each step in his growing awareness alters his romantic relation to Eve.

This intricate plot is made unified and comprehensible by other familiar strategies. It has a strict time scheme, comprising four days and nights (followed by a brief epilogue on a later night). The first day and a half take place in New York; the second night on the train to Chicago; the third day in Chicago and at Prairie Stop; and the fourth day at Mount Rushmore. The timetable is neatly

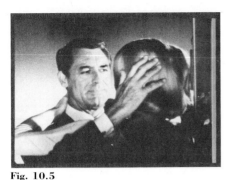

Fig. 10.5

Fig. 10.6

established early on when Van Damm, having abducted Roger as "Kaplan," announces, "In two days you're due at the Ambassador East in Chicago, and then at the Sheraton Johnson Hotel in Rapid City, South Dakota." This itinerary prepares the spectator for the shifts in action that will occur in the rest of the film. Apart from the time scheme, the film also unifies itself through the characterization of Thornhill. He is initially presented as a resourceful liar when he steals a cab from another pedestrian. Later, he will have to lie in many circumstances to evade capture. Similarly, Roger is established as a heavy drinker, and his ability to hold his liquor will enable him to survive Van Damm's attempt to make him kill himself when driving while drunk.

A great many motifs are repeated and help make the film cohere. Roger is constantly in danger from heights: his car hangs over a cliff, he must sneak out on the ledge of a hospital, he must clamber up Van Damm's modernistic clifftop house, and he and Eve wind up dangling from the faces on Mount Rushmore. Thornhill's constant changing of vehicles also constitutes a motif which Hitchcock varies. A more subtle example is the motif which conveys Thornhill's growing suspicion of Eve. On the train, when they kiss, his hands close tenderly around her hair (Fig. 10.5). But in her hotel room, when she tries to embrace him after his narrow escape from death, his hands freeze in place, as if he fears touching her (Fig. 10.6).

But narrative unity by itself cannot explain the film's strong emotional appeal. In Chapter 3's discussion of narration, we used *North by Northwest* as an example of a "hierarchy of knowledge" (pp. 65–67). We suggested that as the film progresses, sometimes we are restricted only to what Roger knows, whereas at other times we know significantly more than he does. At still other moments, our range of knowledge, while greater than Roger's, is not as great as that of other characters. Now we are in a position to see how this constantly changing process helps create suspense and surprise across a whole film.

The most straightforward way in which the film's narration controls our knowledge is through the numerous *optical point-of-view* (POV) shots Hitchcock employs. This device yields a degree of subjective depth—we see what a character sees more or less as she or he sees it—but more importantly here, the optical POV shot restricts us only to what that character learns at that moment. Hitchcock gives almost every major character a shot of this sort. The very first optical POV we see in the film is taken from the position of the two spies who are watching Roger apparently respond to the paging of George Kaplan (Figs. 10.7 and 10.8). Later, we view events through the eyes of Eve, of Van Damm, of his henchman Leonard, and even of a clerk at a ticket counter.

Fig. 10.7

Fig. 10.8

Fig. 10.9

Fig. 10.10

Nevertheless, by far the greatest number of POV shots are attached to Thornhill. Through his eyes we see his approach to the Townsend mansion, the mail he finds in the library, his drunken drive along the cliff, and the airplane that is "crop dusting where there ain't no crops." Some of the most extreme uses of optical POV, such as an advancing truck or a trooper's fist coming toward the camera, give us Roger's experience directly (Figs. 10.9 and 10.10).

Thornhill's optical POV shots function within a narration that is often restricted not only to what he *sees* but to what he *knows*. The plane attack at Prairie Stop, for example, is confined wholly to Roger's range of knowledge. Hitchcock could have cut away from Roger waiting by the road in order to show us the villains plotting in their plane, but he does not. Similarly, when Roger is searching George Kaplan's room and gets a phone call from the two henchmen, Hitchcock could have used crosscutting to show the villains phoning from the lobby. Instead, we learn that they are in the hotel no sooner than Roger does. And when Thornhill and his mother hurry out of the room, Hitchcock does not use crosscutting to show the villains in pursuit. This makes it more startling when Roger and his mother get on the elevator and discover the two men there already. In scenes like these, confining us to Thornhill's range of knowledge sharpens the effect of surprise.

Sometimes the effect of surprise comes from the film's restricting us to Roger's range of knowledge and then giving us information that he does not at the moment have. On page 65 we suggested that this sort of surprise occurs when the plot shifts us from Roger's escape from the United Nations murder to the scene at the USIA office, where the staff discuss the case. At this point we learn that there is no George Kaplan—something that Roger will not discover for many more scenes to come. A similar effect occurs during the train trip from New York to Chicago. During several scenes, Eve Kendall helps Thornhill evade the police. Finally, they are alone and relatively safe in her compartment. At this point the narration shifts the range of knowledge. A message is delivered to another compartment. Hands unfold a note: "What do I do with him in the morning?" The camera then moves back to show us Leonard and Van Damm reading the message. Now we know that Eve is not merely a sympathetic stranger but someone working for the spy ring. Again, Roger will learn this much later. In such cases, the move to a more unrestricted range of information lets the narration put us a notch higher than Thornhill in the hierarchy of knowledge.

We have already quoted Hitchcock's remarks to the effect that in general he prefers to evoke suspense rather than surprise (see pp. 65–66). Suspense is created by giving the spectator more information than the character has. In the scenes we have just mentioned, once the effect of surprise has been achieved, the narration can use our superior knowledge to build suspense across several sequences. After the audience knows that there is no George Kaplan, every attempt by Thornhill to find him will generate suspense about whether he will discover the truth. Once we learn that Eve is working for Van Damm, her message to Roger on behalf of "Kaplan" will make us uncertain as to whether Roger will fall into the trap.

In these examples, suspense arises across a series of scenes. Hitchcock also uses unrestricted narration to build up suspense within a single scene. His handling of the UN murder differs markedly from his treatment of the scene showing Roger and his mother in Kaplan's hotel room. In the hotel scene, Hitchcock refused to employ crosscutting to show the spies' pursuit. At the UN, however, he crosscuts between Roger, who is searching for Townsend, and Valerian, one of the thugs following him. Just before the murder, a rightward tracking shot establishes Valerian's position in the doorway (something of which Roger is wholly unaware). Here crosscutting and camera movement widen our frame of knowledge and create suspense as to the scene's outcome.

Fig. 10.11

The sequence in Chicago's Union Station is handled very similarly. Here crosscutting moves us from Roger shaving in the men's room to Eve talking on the phone. Then another lateral tracking shot reveals that she is talking to Leonard, who is giving her orders from another phone booth. We now are certain that the message she will give Roger will endanger him, and the suspense is increased accordingly. (Note, however, that the narration does not reveal the conversation itself. As often happens, Hitchcock conceals certain information for the sake of further surprises.)

Fig. 10.12

Thornhill's knowledge expands as the lines of action develop. On the third day, he discovers that Eve is Van Damm's mistress, that she is a double agent, and that Kaplan doesn't exist. He agrees to help the Professor in a scheme to clear Eve of any suspicion in Van Damm's eyes. When the scheme (a faked shooting in the Mount Rushmore restaurant) succeeds, Roger believes that Eve will leave Van Damm. Once more, however, he has been duped (as we have). The Professor insists that she must go off to Europe that night on Van Damm's private flight. Roger resists, but he is knocked out and held captive in a hospital. His escape leads to the final major sequence of the film. Here the narrative resolves all its lines of action, and the narration continues to expand and contract our knowledge for the sake of suspense and surprise.

Fig. 10.13

The ending comprises almost three hundred shots and runs for several minutes, but we can conveniently divide the sequence into three subsegments.

In the first subsegment, Roger arrives at Van Damm's house and reconnoiters. He clambers up to the window and learns from a conversation between Leonard and Van Damm that the piece of sculpture they bought at the auction contains microfilm. More important, he watches Leonard inform Van Damm that Eve is an American agent. This action is conveyed largely through optical POV shots as Roger watches in dismay (Figs. 10.11 and 10.12) (see also Figs. 3.1–3.3, p. 67). At two moments, as Leonard and Van Damm face one another, the narration gives us optical POV shots from each man's standpoint (Figs. 10.13 and 10.14), but these are enclosed, so to speak, within Roger's ongoing witnessing of the situation. For the first time in the film, Roger has more knowledge of the situation than any other character. He knows how the smuggling has been done, and he discovers that the villains intend to murder Eve.

The second phase of the sequence can be said to begin when Roger enters Eve's bedroom. She has gone back downstairs and is sitting on a couch. Again, Hitchcock emphasizes the restriction to Thornhill's knowledge by means of optical

Fig. 10.14

Fig. 10.15

Fig. 10.16

Fig. 10.17

POV shots—now high-angle ones appropriate to his position at the balcony (Figs. 10.15 and 10.16). In order to warn Eve, he uses his ROT monogrammed matchbook (a motif set up on the train as a joke). He tosses the matchbook down toward Eve. (This initiates still more suspense when Leonard sees it, but he unconcernedly puts it in an ashtray on the coffee table.) When Eve notices the matchbook, Hitchcock varies his handling of optical POV from the first subsegment. There he was willing to show us the face-off between Van Damm and Leonard (Figs. 10.13 and 10.14). Now he does not show us Eve's eyes at all. Instead, through Roger's eyes, we see her back stiffen; we *infer* that she is looking at the matchbook (Fig. 10.17). Again, though, Roger's range of knowledge is the broadest, and his optical POV "encloses" another character's. On a pretext Eve returns to her room, and Roger warns her not to get on the plane.

As the spies make their way to the landing field outside, Roger starts to follow. Now Hitchcock's narration shifts again to show Van Damm's housekeeper spotting Roger's reflection in a television set. As earlier in the film, we know more than Roger does, and this generates suspense when she walks out—and returns with a pistol aimed at him.

The third subsegment takes place outdoors. Eve is about to get in the plane when a pistol shot distracts the spies' attention long enough for her to grab the statuette and race to the car Roger has stolen. This portion of the sequence confines us to Eve's range of knowledge, accentuating it with shots from her optical POV. The pattern of surprise interrupting a period of suspense—here, Roger's escape from the house interrupting Eve's tense walk to the plane—will dominate the rest of the sequence.

The last portion of the sequence depicts the chase across the faces of Mount Rushmore. Some crosscutting informs us of the spies' progress in following the couple, but on the whole the narration restricts us to what Eve and Thornhill know. As usual, some moments are heightened by optical POV shots, as when Eve watches Roger and Valerian roll down what seems to be a sheer drop. At the climax, Eve is dangling over the edge while Roger is clutching one of her hands and Leonard grinds his foot into Roger's other hand. It is a classic, not to say conventional, situation of suspense. Again, however, the narration reveals the limits of our knowledge. A rifle shot cracks out and Leonard falls. The Professor has arrived and captured Van Damm, and a marksman has shot Leonard. Once more, a restricted range of knowledge has enabled the narration to spring a surprise.

The same effect gets magnified at the very end. In a series of optical POV shots, Roger pulls Eve up from the brink. But this gesture is made continuous, in both sound and image, with that of him pulling her up to a train bunk. The narration ignores the details of their rescue in order to cut short the suspense of Eve's plight. Such a self-conscious transition is not completely out of place in a film that has taken time for offhand jokes. (During the opening credits, Hitchcock himself is shown being shut out of a bus. As Roger strides into the Plaza Hotel, about to be plunged into his adventure, the Muzak is playing "It's a Most Unusual Day.") This concluding twist shows once again that Hitchcock's moment-by-moment manipulation of our knowledge yields a constantly shifting play between the probable and the unexpected, between suspense and surprise.

## ◼ HANNAH AND HER SISTERS

> 1986. Orion Pictures. Directed and written by Woody Allen. Photographed by Carlo Palma. Edited by Susan E. Morse. With Woody Allen, Michael Caine, Mia Farrow, Carrie Fisher, Barbara Hershey, Lloyd Nolan, Maureen O'Sullivan, Daniel Stern, Max von Sydow, Dianne Wiest.

In the three films we have looked at so far, one person or a couple function as the protagonists of the film. Yet many Hollywood films use multiple protagonists. A recent example is Woody Allen's *Hannah and Her Sisters*, which examines the psychological traits and interactions among a group of characters. We shall see that creating several protagonists does not necessarily make a film any less "classical" in its form and style.

The early portions of *Hannah and Her Sisters* make it difficult to tell which characters will be the most important. The initial credits give little clue, since the ten actors' names are given in alphabetical order. As the narrative progresses, we eventually discover that five of these actors play major roles, and they are not always the best known of the group. Even once the action begins, we have to wait for a considerable time before we can sort out who the protagonists are: the three sisters and Hannah's current husband and ex-husband. We gradually realize that they are the main characters partly because they appear in more scenes than the five minor characters do, and partly because they are the ones whose thoughts we occasionally hear on the sound track.

The film's refusal to single out a protagonist functions to emphasize the characters' psychological traits and the development of those traits across time. A clue to the film's strategy comes in the scene where Mickey remembers how his marriage to Hannah ended; his final remark is, "Boy, love is really unpredictable." After this line, a cut shifts the scene to the opera, where Holly is sitting in a box seat with the architect David. The last time we had seen her, she was upset because she thought David was more attracted to April than to her; now it turns out she was wrong, and for a while it seems that her relationship with David is progressing well. Yet after this scene, David will abruptly begin dating April. Indeed, all the main characters' relationships demonstrate in one way or another the truth of Mickey's remark.

The unpredictability of the characters' changing relationships arises from the fact that so many of the characters are equally prominent, or at least seem so at first. For example, for much of the film, Hannah's husband Elliot cannot decide whether to stay with her or leave her and marry her sister Lee. Since Lee is a major character—even a little more prominent than Hannah—it seems plausible that Elliot and Lee could end up together. This is also made plausible by the fact that her relationship with Frederick seems to be ending anyway. Yet Lee eventually marries another man, a professor whom we barely see, and Elliot remains with

Fig. 10.18

Fig. 10.19

Fig. 10.20

Fig. 10.21

Fig. 10.22

Fig. 10.23

Fig. 10.24

Fig. 10.25

Hannah. The final romance between Mickey and Holly is likely to come as a surprise, since the two are hardly ever seen together; the flashback to their one disastrous date makes it appear impossible that they would fall in love. Thus the use of a group of characters roughly equivalent in prominence helps create unpredictable action. Moreover, as we shall see, each character's goals change radically in the course of the plot, making it even more difficult for us to sense how each line of action will turn out.

Even the film's style reinforces the idea that all the characters are important. Rather than using shot/reverse shot to cut back and forth between the characters as they converse, most scenes employ relatively little editing. When the characters are not moving, the camera usually keeps them together in a balanced framing, and when they move, the camera pans to keep them onscreen. In the opening scene, for example, a single shot shows Hannah and Holly talking as they set the table (Fig. 10.18), and the only cut occurs when April enters (Fig. 10.19); she quickly moves to the table, with the camera panning to frame all three women (Fig. 10.20). Later, the dinner itself is handled in one long take (Fig. 10.21), as the father, mother, and Hannah all give little speeches. This tactic continues through most of the film, as in the scene (Fig. 10.22) where four characters are lined up during a conversation. Much later, Hannah discusses Holly's play (Fig. 10.23), and the camera simply pans back and forth (Fig. 10.24) as the two women move around the kitchen (Fig. 10.25). In all these cases, the ordinary Hollywood film would use editing to call our attention to certain lines or reactions. Here Allen presents the characters as a group.

Among the few scenes that use quick cutting and shot/reverse shots are those involving Mickey. The quick cutting shows the progress of the various tests in brief montage sequences, and the shot/reverse shots show him talking with minor characters: his various doctors (Figs. 10.26 and 10.27) or his colleague at the television office. This different stylistic treatment sets Mickey apart as being a more isolated character. When he is with other major characters, the scenes are handled with longer takes and balanced framing, such as the flashback when Hannah and Mickey discuss artificial insemination with their friends (Fig. 10.28), a scene that is handled in one take, or the final shot of the film (Fig. 10.29). Thus in general the film's style participates in the effort to make all the main characters seem equal in importance.

Fig. 10.26

The film's unusually large group of protagonists and secondary characters could create problems for moving from scene to scene. As a result, Allen uses three distinctive tactics for moving smoothly among the characters and lines of action.

First, the plot is organized around holiday parties. The story duration runs across two years, and three of the major scenes take place on Thanksgiving. The opening scene occurs at one such party, and here we meet all the protagonists except Mickey. The first climax, the resolution of the Lee-Elliot-Hannah triangle, takes place at another party, one year later. Finally, the denouement is set at the third Thanksgiving party, and here all five protagonists are present for the first time.

A second tactic for moving among various characters is Allen's use of intertitles before scenes. Of the twenty-two scenes in the film, sixteen begin with intertitles, somewhat in the style of American silent films. These are of various sorts, so that it is usually difficult to predict how they will relate to the scene. The first title says, "God, she's beautiful," and it leads into the opening party scene; this same

Fig. 10.27

Fig. 10.28

Fig. 10.29

line is spoken immediately by Elliot, as we hear his thoughts on the sound track. As the second scene begins, a title appears, reading, "We all had a terrific time." This time the line is not spoken until well into the scene between Lee and Frederick, when she speaks it aloud as part of a longer speech. Later, the intertitle's line may not be spoken at all, as when "The anxiety of the man in the booth" leads into the scene of Mickey having a series of tests in a hospital. One intertitle is a quotation from a poem, which Lee reads aloud near the end of the scene; another quotes Tolstoi, but no one speaks the text within the scene. These intertitles create a small-scale curiosity, coaxing us to ask how the line will apply to the upcoming scene. The intertitles also help signal new scenes and thus indicate that the plot will switch from one line of action to another.

A third device for moving across plot lines is the use of cyclical patterns of action. For example, Mickey usually appears in every third scene. The film's first scene involves the party, the second shows Lee at home with Frederick, and the third introduces Mickey at the television studio where he works. Next comes the scene with Holly and April catering a party; the fifth scene shows Elliot pretending to meet Lee by accident in the street and going with her to a book shop. Then, in the sixth, Mickey visits his doctor. This pattern continues through the film, with one scene dealing with Mickey followed by two scenes (or in one case three) with some combination of the other characters. Moreover, at least one of the three sisters appears in every one of these other scenes. Thus, although a scene may not relate directly to the ones that precede and follow it, we still have a sense that the plot is dealing with the various characters in turn, and that the lines of action are progressing in a parallel fashion.

These rather unusual storytelling devices are imbedded in a context of far more familiar ones. *Hannah and Her Sisters* remains within the classical tradition in several respects. For one thing, the plot relies upon a strong cause-effect sequence. This is especially evident when early scenes motivate actions to come. For example, early in the first party scene, Lee remarks to her sisters that their mother has not been drinking. Nothing more is said about this here, but the dialogue sets up the later scene where Hannah has to visit her parents when her mother has been drinking heavily. Another instance of careful motivation is the series of scenes near the end, when Mickey and Holly meet and begin to fall in love. This twist has been prepared for in the earlier flashback to their first date. At the end of that scene, Mickey remarked that he had always had "a little crush" on Holly. We know that she has given up drugs, which he had objected to; she is also now interested in the kind of jazz music he likes, since she is looking at jazz records when he sees her. Most important, both characters have changed in the meantime: Holly with her successful writing, Mickey with his newfound optimism.

Similarly, though the film may have more protagonists than the standard Hollywood film does, they still function to unify the action and to drive it forward. Complex though the characters may seem to be, each is actually given only a few traits, and each behaves in a fashion consistent with those traits.

The opening party scene assigns one or more traits to each of the ten characters. As the film begins, Elliot is expressing his desire for Lee but also struggling to convince himself that this desire should be suppressed. Indeed, all of Elliot's voice-over thoughts are presented in the form of a sort of interior dialogue in which he argues with himself. Throughout the film his major trait will be his indecision, which he sums up in the scene where he talks to his psychologist. Ultimately it will be Lee who ends their affair and convinces Elliot to stay with Hannah. Lee herself is characterized mainly by her beauty, on which both Elliot and Hannah comment. At one point she mentions, however, that she enjoyed a book Elliot had loaned her; this sets up one of her major traits, her attraction to men who teach her about art and culture. Frederick has been an intellectual mentor for her, Elliot seduces her with poetry and music, and she ultimately marries a professor she meets while taking college courses. Holly's desire to act, her flightiness, and her former drug addiction are all quickly stressed, and both she and April talk about having come to the party hoping to meet attractive single men. The parents are characterized as nostalgic, reliving their past glories in the theater, and the mother apparently has a drinking problem. Hannah is revealed to be competent, domestically oriented, and successful: as dinner begins, her parents tell how she has cooked the huge meal and has recently acted the lead in Ibsen's play *A Doll's House.*

Even the two absent characters are mentioned, with their basic traits laid out. When Lee mentions having seen Mickey, Hannah remarks, "God, Mickey's such a hypochondriac! I wonder how he'd handle it if there was ever anything really wrong with him." Her speculation sets up the later action, when we witness Mickey's panic at the thought that he really has cancer. Similarly, early in the scene Holly remarks to Hannah that Frederick has not come with Lee to the party, and calls him "depressive"; she also says that she thought Lee was moving out, which sets up the idea that Lee's relationship with Frederick is in trouble. Shortly thereafter, Lee mentions to Elliot that Frederick has sold a painting. Thus by the time we see Frederick in person we know basic facts about him, and he acts very much as we would expect him to. Virtually all of the film's action harks back to character traits concisely established in this first scene.

During approximately the first third of the film, the five protagonists develop goals consistent with their original traits. After we have seen Mickey wandering anxiously around his apartment and then Holly at the opera with David, we seem to know what all the characters want. Elliot wants to have an affair with Lee, and by now he has begun actively to pursue her by giving her the book of poetry. Holly wants to be a successful actress and also to find an attractive man, and she seems to be on her way to achieving the second goal. Mickey thinks he has a brain tumor and simply wants to survive. ("Look, I'll make a deal with God. Let it just be my ear. I'll go deaf, I'll go deaf in one ear and blind in one eye, maybe. . . . ") Hannah's goal is less clear, but she seems to be working to keep her parents' marriage stable; this is in keeping with Hannah's position as the stable center around which the rest of the action revolves. She is the only character who seems completely content with her circumstances, and hence her goals simply involve dealing with threats to her family's situation. Lee's goal is also vague, but we know she is aware of Elliot's interest in her, and we sense that she is attracted to him. Later, when Elliot and she begin their affair, her goal will be to get Elliot to leave Hannah and marry her.

These goals would seem to be enough to sustain the entire film. Yet, in keeping with the principle of unpredictability, the characters one by one alter their goals or formulate entirely new ones over the next stretch of the film. Elliot, who has succeeded in starting the affair with Lee, now struggles to decide between divorcing Hannah or staying with her. Hannah says that she wants to have another baby, and she also tries to solve whatever problem is alienating Elliot from her. Mickey, who discovers that he does not in fact have cancer, suddenly becomes very depressed and sets out to find the meaning of life. Holly discovers that David has dropped her for April and realizes that she will never succeed as an actress; she abruptly attempts a career as a writer. Lee decides to leave Frederick, saying, "I want a less complicated life, Frederick. I want a husband, maybe even a child, before it's too late." It seems apparent that this is her goal, whether or not the man she marries is Elliot. These various new goals are the ones that carry the action through to the end of the film. Interestingly, the characters alter their goals at different rates: some are still working on their original goals while others have already switched goals. Thus the two cycles of goals do not seem so schematic as they might when we list them here.

All these goals are achieved in some fashion during the two climactic sequences, the second Thanksgiving party and the series of brief scenes between Mickey and Holly. The third Thanksgiving party, introduced by the title "One year later," serves mainly to confirm that all the main characters are now happily situated. Mickey's dialogue with Holly also reiterates the notion of the unpredictability of love; he says, "I was talking to your father before, and I was telling him, it's ironic, I used to always have Thanksgiving with Hannah, and I never thought I could love anybody else, and here it is years later, and I'm married to you, and completely in love with you. The heart is a very, very resilient little muscle." He then suggests she write a story based on that idea, adding, "How're you going to top that?" She responds, "Mickey, I'm pregnant," adding one more surprise to the plot. By the way, the music that the father is playing offscreen on the piano is "In Love Again," the same song that the jazz musician Bobby Short had sung during Holly and Mickey's first date. At that time Holly had disliked it; now it returns as a motif to link the two scenes, stressing again how unpredictable it had been that these two would ever fall in love. This musical motif is one more example of how *Hannah and Her Sisters*, despite its distinctive innovations, draws on the principles of the classical Hollywood cinema to create a unified narrative.

# NARRATIVE ALTERNATIVES TO CLASSICAL FILMMAKING

## ■ *DAY OF WRATH (VREDENS DAG)*

1943. Palladium Film, Denmark. Directed by Carl Dreyer. Script by Dreyer, Mogens Skot-Hansen, and Poul Knudsen; based on the play *Anne Pedersdotter* by Hans Wiers-Jenssen. Photographed by Karl Andersson. Edited by Edith Schluessel and Anne Marie Petersen. Music by Poul Schierbeck. With Lisbeth Movin, Thorkild Roose, Sigrid Neiiendam, Preben Lerdorff Rye, Anna Svierkier.

The films analyzed so far pose few difficulties for viewers who like their movies straightforward and easy to digest. But several films we will be examining from this point onward are not so clear in their form and style. In these films our uncertainty becomes central. In films like *Day of Wrath*, the questions we ask often do not get definite answers; endings do not tie everything up; film technique does not always function to "invisibly" advance the narrative. When analyzing such films, we should restrain ourselves from trying to answer all of the film's questions and to create neatly satisfying endings. Instead of ignoring peculiarities of technique, we should seek to examine how film form and style create uncertainty—seek to understand the cinematic conditions that produce ambiguity. *Day of Wrath*, a tale of witchcraft and murder set in seventeenth-century Denmark, offers a good test case.

Fig. 10.30                    Fig. 10.31

As a narrative film, *Day of Wrath* depends on cause-and-effect relations, but what strikes us immediately is its unusual number of parallels. The first half of the film centers on the fate of Herlofs Marthe, the old woman accused of witchcraft. In the course of this half, Herlofs Marthe's progress toward the stake is constantly paralleled to action involving the pastor Absalon; his new wife, Anne; his mother, Merete; and his son, Martin. After Herlofs Marthe is burned (in a scene whose use of offscreen sound is of outstanding interest), the second part of the film is concerned primarily with Absalon's family and especially with the growing love affair between Anne and Martin. Crosscutting parallels the young couple's idyll in nature with Absalon's solitude or his consolation of a dying friend. The crosscutting conveys minute similarities of gesture and difference of mood between these pairs of actions. After Absalon dies, apparently killed by Anne, Dreyer again uses crosscutting to parallel old Merete, sitting by the coffin, with Anne and Martin wrapped in the fog.

Among all the parallels in the film, one stands out particularly. Herlofs Marthe, the "witch" of the first part, is constantly compared to Anne, the "witch" of the second. From the start, Dreyer uses crosscutting to parallel Herlofs Marthe, fleeing from the mob, with Merete and particularly with Anne. In the course of the film, most of what we see of Herlofs Marthe's progress—the interrogations, torture, and execution—is seen through Anne's eyes. Anne becomes the central focus of the plot partly because optical point-of-view shots and eyeline-match cutting often restrict our knowledge to hers. The *Dies Irae* musical motif, associated with Herlofs Marthe's immolation, is scored in a brighter key when Anne and Martin are wandering through the forests. A motif of lighting repeats the parallel: often a shadow passes across Anne's face, exactly as the shadows of leaves tremble on Herlofs Marthe's face before she is burned (compare Figs. 10.30 and 10.31). Thus not only narrative form but also editing, sound, and lighting guide us to compare and contrast the old "witch" with the young one.

However clear such parallel relations may seem, the chains of narrative cause and effect lead us straight to ambiguities. The uncertainty revolves around the problem of witchcraft. The official whose hand writes and signs documents through-out the first third of the film assumes that witchcraft exists and threatens society. We are tempted to see this belief as simple superstition, the Church's means of oppression in this society. But things are not so simple. In the first sequence, a woman has sought out Herlofs Marthe for a potion. "This is sure to work," says Marthe. "It is herbs from under the gallows." And she adds, "There is power in evil." So perhaps she *is* a witch after all. But after she is captured and tortured,

Dreyer's mise-en-scene in the torture chamber depicts her as only a victimized old woman. And yet again, she curses her inquisitor, Laurentius, and he soon dies; she predicts that Anne will go to the stake, and Anne eventually does. Herlofs Marthe's "power" puts us in doubt as to whether certain narrative events have a natural or a supernatural cause.

An even stronger ambiguity hovers over the causes for crucial events involving Anne. In the course of the film, she displays the ability to summon Martin from a distance, to make Absalon fear for his life, and to kill Absalon by saying, "I wish you dead." What causes such events? Supernatural powers? The narrative does not explain how Anne could have acquired them. (There is the suggestion that her mother was a witch and "could call the quick and the dead," but this hardly constitutes a clear explanation of Anne's abilities.) Is, then, the cause sheerly psychological? Does Anne merely *believe* herself to be a witch? Are her "spells" successful only because she called for events that were likely to happen? (Martin may have been falling in love with her anyway, and the revelation of her hatred may have caused Absalon's heart attack.) As we shall see, her entire behavior does change as she becomes more deeply in love with Martin. Yet again, psychological states do not necessarily explain her power to call or kill from a distance. Up to the very end, the film refuses to specify the exact causes of Anne's actions— supernatural, psychological, or social. (Compare, in this regard, the very explicit causes that determine the characters' action in *His Girl Friday, North by Northwest,* or *Stagecoach.*) "Is Anne a witch?" is a question that *Day of Wrath* does not answer clearly.

The ambiguity surrounding witchcraft and its effects is stressed in Dreyer's handling of mise-en-scene as well. We have already seen how facial lighting compares Anne with Herlofs Marthe; we ought also to notice how lighting functions to cast an uncertain aura over Anne. When she first sees Martin, she steps into a patch of shadow. When she swears that she did not kill Absalon, a shadow falls across her face. Such lighting reminds us of the possibly supernatural sources of her power, even at moments when she seems most innocent.

Other aspects of mise-en-scene reinforce Anne's ambiguous status. Her deepening love for Martin is expressed through changes in her bodily movements—at first constrained, somewhat rigid, but later more sinuous, even catlike. We first see her wearing a prim, rectangular cap; later, with Martin, she wears a softly curving lace bonnet; still later, she simply lets her hair hang free. Props such as her embroidery pattern (depicting a young woman with a baby) and her drawing of an apple tree (Martin's poem had described a "young maiden in an apple tree") also convey her sexual blossoming.

Yet all of these motifs cut two ways. Anne may be impelled by desire or by sorcery. The most obvious manifestation of the ambiguity may be seen in her changing facial expressions, at once cunning and inviting. At one point, both Absalon and Martin seek to read her essence in her eyes, and they come to exactly opposite conclusions. To the old man, Anne's eyes are "childlike and innocent, so clear"; to Martin, they are "fathomless and mysterious . . . in the bottom, a trembling, quivering flame." Dreyer's mise-en-scene brings the ambiguity to the viewer's notice, compelling us to ask at almost every moment what motivates Anne's actions and how we are to understand her.

*Day of Wrath*'s final scene only partly dispels the uncertainties that run throughout the film. Absalon's funeral is beginning, and Martin has sworn to stand by Anne. Dreyer creates yet another narrative parallel by opening the scene with a lengthy circular tracking shot. By following the choirboys through the death room

Fig. 10.32

Fig. 10.33

Fig. 10.34

Fig. 10.35

Fig. 10.36

(Fig. 10.32), Dreyer establishes, in a long take, the entire space and all of the relevant characters' positions: the church elders (Fig. 10.33), the judge, Merete (Fig. 10.34), the coffin (Fig. 10.35), and Anne and Martin (Fig. 10.36). The attentive viewer will recall that a similar circular tracking shot previously introduced the torture-chamber scene and later the death of Laurentius as well; Dreyer uses the camera movement to parallel three somber interiors, all associated with the repressive power of the Church. In contrast to the "invisible" camera movements of most classical films, Dreyer emphasizes the camera movements as a motif, calling our attention to the parallel situations.

In the course of this scene, Merete publicly accuses Anne of witchcraft. Martin abandons her, and Anne breaks down, confessing to having been in the service of "the Evil One." Does this, then, settle the matter of her witchcraft?

Fig. 10.37

We know that in analyzing a film, it is useful to contrast the beginning with the ending. *Day of Wrath* begins with the image of a scroll unrolling, over which the medieval church melody *Dies Irae* plays nondiegetically. The scroll depicts and describes the terrible events that befall the sinful earth on Judgment Day (the "Day of Wrath" of the title). (See Fig. 10.37.) After Anne confesses, she looks upward—for help, for mercy? The scroll now returns to the screen, accompanied by the sweet solo voice of a choirboy, describing how the "bruised soul" will be lifted to heaven. In the eternal context of the scroll, Anne is apparently forgiven. Yet *what* she is forgiven for—seducing Martin, practicing witchcraft, accepting her society's definition of herself *as* a witch—is never stipulated. The scroll seems not to resolve the ambiguity so much as to postpone it. The final image of the film is a cross, but the cross is slowly transformed into the witch motif we saw earlier, during Herlofs Marthe's execution (Fig. 10.38). Presumably, the parallel with Herlofs Marthe is

Fig. 10.38

now complete: Anne will be burned. But the causes of certain events, the nature of witchcraft, the desires that motivate Anne—these remain, like her eyes, "fathomless and mysterious." *Day of Wrath* illustrates how a film may fascinate us not by its clarity but by its obscurity, not by fixed certainties but by teasing questions.

## ■ *LAST YEAR AT MARIENBAD (L'ANNÉE DERNIÈRE À MARIENBAD)*

> 1961. Précitel and Terrafilm, a French-Italian coproduction. Directed by Alain Resnais. Script by Alain Robbe-Grillet. Photographed by Sacha Vierney. Edited by Henri Colpi and Jasmine Chasney. Music by Francis Seyrig. With Delphine Seyrig, Giorgio Albertazzi, Sacha Pitoëff.

When *Last Year at Marienbad* was first shown in 1961, many critics offered widely varying interpretations of it. When faced with most films, these critics would have been looking for implicit meanings behind the plot. But, faced with *Marienbad*, their interpretations were attempts simply to describe the events that take place in the film's story. These proved difficult to agree on. Did the couple really meet last year? If not, what really happened? Is the film one of the characters' dreams or a mad imagining?

Typically, a film's plot—however simple or difficult—allows the spectator to construct the causal and chronological story mentally. But *Marienbad* is different; its story is impossible to determine. The film has only a plot, with no single consistent story for us to infer. This is because *Marienbad* carries the strategy of *Day of Wrath* to an extreme: it works entirely through ambiguities. As we watch the opening of the film, the events seem to be leading us toward a story, complicated though it might be. But then contradictions arise: one character says that an event occurred, specifying the time and place, but another character denies it. Because such contradictions are never resolved, we have no way of choosing which events are part of a causal series that would make up a potential story. The flow of the narration never supplies clear-cut story information.

*Marienbad* creates its ambiguity through contradictions on many different levels: the spatial, the temporal, and the causal. Within the same shot, impossible juxtapositions may occur in the mise-en-scene. At one point a track forward through a door reveals the shrub-lined promenade that is (sometimes) situated in front of the hotel. The people scattered across the flat expanse in the center cast long, dark shadows, yet the pointed trees that line the promenade cast none (Fig. 10.39). The sun is apparently simultaneously shining and not shining. Later in the film, there is a shot of the woman. (As none of the characters have names, we shall call her the Heroine, the lead male the Narrator, and the tall man the Other Man.) We see three images of her within the frame. Apparently two must be mirror reflections, yet the three images are facing in directions that make an arrangement of mirrors impossible (Fig. 10.40).

Settings shift in inconsistent ways between different segments of the film as well. The statue to which the couple frequently returns appears sometimes to be directly outside the French windows of the hotel (as in the fast track right as the Heroine leaves the Narrator and runs through these windows). At other times the statue is at a great distance. In some scenes the statue faces a lake; in others, the lake is behind it. In still other scenes the tree-lined promenade forms the background in shots of the statue. (Compare Figs. 10.41 and 10.42.) Within the hotel, things change as well, as the decoration of the Heroine's room becomes progressively

Fig. 10.39

Fig. 10.40

Fig. 10.41

Fig. 10.42

Fig. 10.43

more cluttered. New pieces of furniture appear, the gilded molding on the walls becomes more elaborate, and the decoration over the mantle is sometimes a mirror and sometimes a painting. The Narrator's frequent descriptions of the "vast hotel . . . baroque, dismal" and the "hallways crossing hallways" point up these impossible changes. His words cannot pin down the appearances of things, which frequently shift—as do the descriptions themselves, which the Narrator repeats many times, with different combinations of phrases.

Temporal relations are equally problematic. In one shot the Heroine stands by the window to the left of the bed in her room. The darkness of a nighttime exterior is visible, and the lights by the bed are lit. But when she moves left, with the camera panning, she reaches another window through which sunlight is visible. The type of lighting inside the room is also different in this new portion of the setting, yet no cut or ellipsis has occurred (Fig. 10.43).

Fig. 10.44                                      Fig. 10.45

Across the whole film, the temporal sequence of events is also uncertain. Supposedly the Narrator has returned to take the Heroine away after an agreed-on year's separation following their initial meeting. Yet in the scene at the end when they do leave together, the Narrator's voice is still describing this event as if it had taken place in the past—as if it were one of the things he is trying to recall to her mind. At the beginning of the film (which apparently coincides fairly closely with the Narrator's arrival at the hotel) the Heroine is watching a play called *Rosmer;* at the end, she stays away from the same performance in order to leave with the Narrator. (The actions of the Heroine and Narrator in this scene also duplicate those in the scene from *Rosmer* as we see it near the beginning of the film.) If the play occurs only once in the story, all of the events involved in the Narrator's attempt to convince the Heroine to leave take place between the two presentations of *Rosmer* in the plot. The temporal status of all of the events of the film becomes undeterminable.

*Marienbad* presents many varied combinations of ambiguous space, time, and causality. An action may carry from one time and space to a different time and space. This happens several times when "matches on action" cuts occur with a change in locale. The first such "match" gives us our first really contradictory cue in the film. A series of shots after the *Rosmer* performance shows small groups of guests standing around the hotel lobby; one medium shot frames a blond woman beginning to turn away from the camera (Fig. 10.44). In the middle of her turn, there is a cut to a different setting. The woman is dressed identically, and her position in the frame is matched precisely (Fig. 10.45). This cut also uses a device common throughout the film—a sudden start or cessation of loud organ music. The abrupt changes on the sound track accentuate the film's discontinuities and startling juxtapositions. A similar "match" on action occurs later as the Heroine walks with the Narrator down a hallway. In the first shot there are several people in the background; after the cut, the couple are alone in a different hallway—yet converse without a break.

The opposite of this pattern also occurs; that is, the space and time may remain constant, while different actions occur that contradict each other. Several times the camera begins a shot on one or more characters, moves away from them across considerable space, and picks up the same characters in a different locale. This happens as the Narrator confronts the Heroine after the first pistol-range segment. They stand in medium shot as he talks. Then the camera tracks away right, past a series of other people. It reaches the Narrator, who is now standing at the other end of the room, looking off right. A pan right reveals the Heroine coming in a door at the top of a flight of stairs. At several other points, the camera passes over characters who will reappear elsewhere at a later stage of the same shot.

*Marienbad* combines contradictions of space, time, and causality in many variations. The Narrator's voice-over account of events seems at first to make sense, but soon it comes into conflict with the image. In one shot (the night/day segment already mentioned), we see a "flashback," apparently illustrating the Narrator's account of a night he had seduced the Heroine. At first the images and his internal past-tense narration tally closely. But then discrepancies begin to creep in. He says that she went to the bed, yet in the image she remains standing by a wall made of mirrors near the door. He concedes, "It's true, there was a large mirror by the door . . . a huge mirror which you avoided." Yet the Heroine continues to move along the mirror, pressing herself closely to it. At other times the Narrator declares that entire sequences are false. We see the Other Man shoot the Heroine, apparently in jealousy over her affair with the Narrator. In the "present," the Narrator continues to describe the scene to the Heroine, trying to get her to remember it. But then he says, "That's not the right ending. It's you alive I must have." At other points he describes having entered the Heroine's bedroom and raped her, then denies that he had used force to seduce her. The images present several versions of the scene, with the Heroine sometimes cringing in fear, sometimes opening her arms in welcome. The Narrator's descriptions of the supposed events "last year" are unreliable, since he several times offers incompatible versions of scenes.

The film is careful not to give us clues to help establish clear connections. The title itself is purely arbitrary. It seems to imply that an important narrative event has occurred at a specific time and place. But in fact, the Narrator states several times that he had met the Heroine a year ago at Friedrichsbad. Only when she denies ever having been there does he reply, "Perhaps it was elsewhere . . . at Karlstadt, at Marienbad, or Baden-Salsa, or in this very room." Nor can we tell what the relationships among the characters are. The Narrator says that the Other Man is "perhaps" the Heroine's husband. He may also be her brother, friend, or lover, but we have no way of determining which. All of the characters invariably use the formal *vous* (you) to one another rather than the more intimate *tu*. As a result, we never get a sense of how close the Heroine's relationship to either of the two men is supposed to be.

*Marienbad* teases us to try to fit its parts into a coherent whole, yet at the same time it provides several indications that such a constructed unity is impossible. First, there is the statue beside which the couple often stands. The Narrator describes how they had discussed the figures of the man and woman in the statue, offering different interpretations. He says that the man is trying to keep the woman back from something dangerous, whereas she believes that the woman is pointing something out to the man. Each hypothesis is equally reasonable as an explanation for the gestures of the stone figures (as are still other explanations). The Narrator's voice-over says, "Both were possible," but goes on immediately to elaborate on his own explanation. Finally, he tells how the Heroine had insisted on identifying the statues: "You . . . began naming them—haphazardly, I think. Then I said, they might just as well be you and I or anyone. Leave them nameless, with more room for adventure." Yet the Heroine still persists in trying to interpret the statue and invent a story to go with it. Later, the Other Man offers a precise explanation of the statue as an allegorical figure representing Charles III. Here we have an apparently correct interpretation, for the Other Man seems to have special information that the others lack. But by this point in the film we are suspicious of everyone—perhaps he is only making it up. The statue resembles the film as a whole in several ways: its temporal and spatial situation shifts without explanation, and its meaning ultimately remains elusive.

Another clue to the ultimate undecidability of the film is offered by the locale. The ending of the film leaves the Heroine lost in the gardens of the hotel with the Narrator. The mazelike hotel and gardens suggest the windings of the narrative itself. The space, both inside and outside, is impossible; we can never reconstruct it. The Narrator's voice is heard over the ending, describing the locale: "The gardens of this hotel were in the French manner, without trees, without flowers, without plants, nothing. Gravel, stone, marble, straight lines setting rigid patterns of space, surfaces without mystery." The space as he describes it is stable and unambiguous; yet, as we have seen, contradictions abound in this apparently stable space. The Narrator goes on: "It seemed impossible—at first—to lose one's way there. At first. Among the stones, where you were, already, losing your way forever, in the quiet night, alone with me." This ease of losing one's way in a deceptively straightforward path applies to the spectator's attempts to construct the film's story as well. "At first" it seems possible to piece events together in a chronological fashion. Only gradually do we realize that the task is hopeless.

A major motif in the film is the game that the Other Man plays against several opponents, always winning easily. The game is not a symbol in the sense of representing some hidden meaning, but it does present yet a third image of impossibility. It is impossible to win the game without knowing the key. One onlooker suggests that perhaps the one who starts the round wins—but the Other Man wins whether he goes first or second. The Narrator struggles to learn the key, but the film offers no solution. Instead, the game helps to suggest to the spectator the nature of the film he or she is watching. The narrative, too, has no key that will enable us to find its hidden coherence; it is a game that we must lose. The whole structure of *Marienbad* is a play with logic, space, and time which does not offer us a single, complete story as a prize for winning this "game."

This is why *Marienbad* fascinates some people but frustrates others. Those who go expecting a comprehensible story and refuse to abandon that expectation may come away baffled and discouraged, feeling that the film is "obscure." But *Marienbad* broke with conventional expectations by suggesting, perhaps for the first time in film history, that a film could base itself entirely on a gamelike structure of causal, spatial, and temporal ambiguity, refusing to specify explicit meanings and teasing the viewer with hints about elusive implicit meanings. Critics have too often tried to find a thematic key to the film while ignoring this formal play. Much of *Marienbad*'s fascination for the spectator rests in the process of discovering its ambiguity. The film's Narrator gives us good guidance when he resists interpreting the statue. Of the film's characters and other devices we might also say, "Leave them nameless, with more room for adventure."

### ■ *TOKYO STORY (TOKYO MONOGATARI)*

1953. Shochiku/Ofuna, Japan. Directed by Yasujiro Ozu. Script by Ozu and Kogo Noda. Photographed by Yuharu Atsuta. With Chishu Ryu, Chieko Higashiyama, So Yamamura, Haruko Sugimura, Setsuko Hara.

We have seen how the classical Hollywood approach to filmmaking created a stylistic system ("continuity") in order to establish and maintain a clear narrative space and time. The continuity system is a specific set of guidelines which a filmmaker may follow. But some filmmakers do not use the continuity system. They develop an alternative set of formal guidelines, which allows them to make films that are quite distinct from classical narratives. Japanese director Yasujiro Ozu is one such

filmmaker. His approach to the interrelationships of time, space, and narrative structure differs greatly from that of most if not all other filmmakers. Although he is one of the greatest of all filmmakers, Ozu is less well known than some others because his films were seen only in Japan for many years. *Tokyo Story* was the first Ozu film to make a considerable impression in the West.

Ozu's approach to the creation of a narrative differs from that used in more classical films like *His Girl Friday* or *Stagecoach*. Instead of making narrative events the central organizing principle, Ozu tends to decenter narrative slightly. Spatial and temporal structures come forward and create their own interest. Sometimes we learn of important narrative events only indirectly; an ellipsis occurs at a crucial moment. The last portion of *Tokyo Story*, for example, involves a series of events surrounding the sudden illness and death of the grandmother of a family. Although the grandparents are the film's two central characters, we do not see the grandmother falling ill. We hear about it only when her son and daughter receive telegrams with the news. Similarly, the grandmother's death occurs between scenes; in one scene her children are gathered by her bedside, and in the next scene they are mourning her.

Fig. 10.46

Yet these ellipses are not evidence of a fast-paced film such as *His Girl Friday*, which must cover a lot of narrative ground in a hurry. On the contrary, the sequences of *Tokyo Story* often linger over details: the sad conversation between the grandfather and his friends in a bar as they discuss their disappointment in their children, or the grandmother's walk on a Sunday with her grandchild. The result is a shift in the balance of more classical narratives. Key narrative events are de-emphasized by means of ellipses, whereas narrative events that we do see in the plot are simple and understated.

Fig. 10.47

Accompanying this shift away from a presentation of the "dramatic" events of the narrative is a sliding away from narratively significant space. Scenes do not begin and end with shots that frame the most important narrative elements in the mise-en-scène. Instead of the usual transitional devices, such as dissolves and fades, Ozu typically employs a series of separate transitional shots linked by cuts. And these transitional shots often show spaces not directly connected with the action of the scene; the spaces are usually *near* where that action will take place. The opening of the film, for example, has five shots of the port town of Onomichi— the bay, schoolchildren, a passing train—before the sixth shot reveals the grandparents packing for their trip to Tokyo. Although a couple of important motifs make their first appearances in these first five shots, no narrative causes occur to get the action under way. (Compare the openings of *His Girl Friday* and *Stagecoach*.) Nor do these transitional shots appear only at the beginning. Several sequences in Tokyo start with shots of factory smokestacks, even though no action ever occurs in these locales.

Fig. 10.48

These transitions have only a minimal function as establishing shots. Sometimes the transitions do not establish space at all but tend to confuse the space of the upcoming scene. After the daughter-in-law, Noriko, gets a phone call at work telling her of the grandmother's illness, she goes and sits sadly at her desk. This scene ends on a medium shot of her; the only diegetic sound is the loud clack of typewriters. A nondiegetic musical transition comes up in this shot. Then there is a cut to a low-angle long shot of a building under construction; riveting noises replace the typewriters, with the music continuing. The next shot is another low angle of the construction site. A cut changes the locale to the clinic belonging to the eldest son, Dr. Hirayama. The sister, Shige, is present. The music ends and the new scene begins (see Figs. 10.46 through 10.49). In this segment, the two

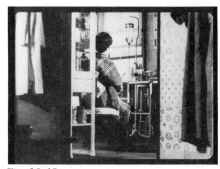
Fig. 10.49

shots of the construction site are not necessary to the action. The film does not give us any indication where the building under construction is. We might assume that it is outside Noriko's office, but the riveting sound is not audible in the interior shots.

As usual, we should look for the functions of such stylistic devices. It is hard to assign such transitional shots either explicit or implicit meanings. For example, someone might propose that the transitional shots symbolize the "new Tokyo" that is alien to the visiting grandparents from a village reminiscent of the old Japan. But often the transitional spaces do not involve outdoor locales, and some shots are within the characters' homes. A more systematic function, we suggest, is narrational, having to do with the flow of story information.

Ozu's narration alternates between scenes of story action and inserted portions that lead us to or away from them. As we watch the film, we start to form expectations about these "wedged-in" shots. Ozu emphasizes stylistic patterning by creating anticipation about when a transition will come and what it will show. The patterning can involve delaying our expectations and even some surprise. For example, early in the film Mrs. Hirayama, the doctor's wife, argues with her son, Minoru, over where to move his desk to make room for the grandparents. This issue is dropped, and there follows a scene of the grandparents' arrival. This ends on a conversation in an upstairs room; transitional music again comes up over the end of the scene. The next shot frames an empty hallway downstairs that contains Minoru's school desk, but no one is in the shot. An exterior long shot of children running along a ridge near the house follows; these children are not characters in the action. Finally, a cut back inside reveals Minoru at his father's desk in the clinic portion of the house, studying. Here the editing creates a very indirect route between two scenes, going first to a place where we expect a character to be (at his own desk) but is not; then the scene moves completely away from the action, outdoors. Only then, in the third shot, does a character reappear and the action continue. In these transitional passages, a kind of game emerges, one that asks us to form expectations not only about story action but about the editing and mise-en-scène.

Within scenes, Ozu's editing patterns are as systematic as those of Hollywood, but they tend to be sharply opposed to continuity rules. For example, Ozu does not observe the 180° line, or axis of action. Nor is his "violation" of these rules occasional, as Ford's is in *Stagecoach*. Ozu frequently cuts 180° across the line to frame the scene's space from the opposite direction. This, of course, violates rules of screen direction, since characters or objects on the right in the first shot will appear on the left in the second, and vice versa. At the beginning of a scene in Shige's beauty salon, the initial interior medium shot frames Shige from opposite the front door (Fig. 10.50). Then a 180° cut reveals a medium long shot of a woman under a dryer; the camera now faces the rear of the salon (Fig. 10.51). Another cut 180° presents a new long shot of the room, viewed toward the door again, and the grandparents come into the salon (Fig. 10.52). Rather than being an isolated violation of continuity rules, this is Ozu's typical way of framing and editing a scene.

Ozu is a master of matching on action, but he often does so in unusual ways. For example, as Noriko and the grandmother walk toward the door of Noriko's apartment, there is a 180° cut from a head-on view (Fig. 10.53) to a tails-on framing (Fig. 10.54). The women's movements are closely matched, but because the consistent camera height and distance create such similar framings, the effect at the cut is to make it seem momentarily that the pair "bumps into" themselves. (Their screen positions, left to right, are also abruptly reversed, something which is usually

Fig. 10.50

Fig. 10.51

Fig. 10.52

Fig. 10.53

Fig. 10.54

Fig. 10.55

Fig. 10.56

Fig. 10.57

considered an error in continuity.) A classical filmmaker would most likely avoid such an unusual cut, but Ozu uses it here and in other films as part of his distinctive style.

As these examples illustrate, Ozu does not restrict his camera and editing patterns to the semicircular space on one side of the axis of action. He cuts in a full circle around the action, usually in segments of 90° or 180°. This means that backgrounds change frequently, as is apparent in both previous examples. In a Hollywood film, backgrounds remain roughly consistent throughout much of the action, because the camera does not cross the axis of action to look at the fourth wall. Because surroundings change more frequently in *Tokyo Story*, they become more prominent in relation to the action; the viewer must pay attention to setting or become confused.

Fig. 10.58

The two strategies we have considered—the transitional shots that prolong or thwart the viewer's hypotheses, and the 360° space that asks us to notice surroundings—can work together, as when the grandparents visit a spa at Atami. The scene begins with a long shot along a hallway (Fig. 10.55). Latin-style dance music plays offscreen, and several people walk through the hall. The next shot (Fig. 10.56) is a long shot of another hallway upstairs, with a maid carrying a tray; two pairs of slippers are just visible by a doorway at the lower left. Next comes a medium long shot of a hallway by a courtyard (Fig. 10.57). More people bustle through. A medium shot of a mah-jongg game follows (Fig. 10.58); there is a loud sound of talking and moving pieces about. Then Ozu cuts 180° across the axis, framing another mah-jongg table (Fig. 10.59). The first table is now in the background,

Fig. 10.59

Fig. 10.60

Fig. 10.61

Fig. 10.62

Fig. 10.63

Fig. 10.64

viewed from the opposite side. The next cut returns to the medium long shot along the courtyard hallway (Fig. 10.60). In all of these shots, we have not yet seen the grandparents, who are the only major characters present at the spa. Finally, there is a medium shot of the two pairs of slippers by the door in the upper hallway (Fig. 10.61), suggesting that this is the grandparents' room. The panes of glass in the wall reflect the lively movement of the offscreen party, and the loud music and talk are still audible. A medium shot of the Hirayamas in bed, trying to sleep through the noise, finally reveals the narrative situation of the scene, and a conversation begins between the couple (Fig. 10.62). For seven shots the film slowly explores the space of the scene, gradually letting us discover the situation. The presence of the slippers in the second shot (Fig. 10.56) is almost unnoticeable; it hints that the grandparents are there, but the revelation of their whereabouts is then put off for several more shots.

In these ways Ozu draws our attention away from the strictly causal functions of space and makes space important in its own right. He does the same with the flat graphic space of the screen as well. See Figures 7.64 to 7.67 and Plates 14 and 15 for examples of graphic matches from Ozu films. The stylistic device is characteristic of Ozu; he seldom uses the graphic match for any narrative purpose. In *Tokyo Story* a conversation situation leads to a shot/reverse-shot pattern but again with cuts 180° across the axis of action. The two men speaking are framed so that each looks off right. (In Hollywood, upholders of the continuity system would claim that this implies that both are looking off toward the same thing.) Because they are positioned similarly in the frame, the result is a strong graphic carryover from one shot to another—a graphic match (Figs. 10.63 and 10.64). In this respect, Ozu's style owes something to abstract form (see Chapter 4, pp. 105–113 and Chapter 9, pp. 276–277). It is as if he sought to make a narrative film which would still make graphic similarities as evident as they are in an abstract film like *Ballet mécanique*.

The use of space and time in *Tokyo Story* is not willfully obscure, nor does it have a symbolic function in the narrative. Rather, it suggests a different relationship among space, time, and narrative logic than exists in the classical film. Space and time no longer simply function unobtrusively to create a clear narrative line; Ozu brings them forward and makes them into prominent aesthetic elements in their own right. Ozu does not eliminate narrative, but he opens it out. *Tokyo Story* and his other films allow other stylistic devices to exist independently alongside narrative. The result is that the viewer is invited to look at his films in a new way, to participate in a play of space and time.

## ■ *INNOCENCE UNPROTECTED (NEVINOST BEZ ZASTITE)*

1968. Avala Film, Yugoslavia. Directed by Dušan Makavejev, incorporating a film directed by Dragoljub Aleksic. Script by Makavejev. Photographed by Branko Perak and Stevan Miskovic. Edited by Ivanka Vukasovic. Music by Vojislav Dostic. With Dragoljub Aleksic, Ana Miloslavljevic, Vera Jovanovic, Bratoljub Gligorijviec, Ivan Zivkovic, Pere Milslavljevic.

Like *Last Year at Marienbad*, Dušan Makavejev's *Innocence Unprotected* (more correctly translated as *Innocent Unprotected*) diverges markedly from the norms of classical narrative filmmaking. In analyzing the film, it is useful to think of its form as a *collage*, an assemblage of materials taken from widely different sources. By playing up the disparities among the film's materials, the collage principle permits Makavejev to use film techniques and film form in fresh and provocative ways. The result is a film that examines the nature of cinema—particularly, cinema in a social and historical context.

The collage aspect of *Innocence Unprotected* stands out most strikingly in its use of a wide range of materials. In one sense it is a compilation film, drawn from at least four different sources. At the core is the original fiction film, "Innocence Unprotected," made by the Yugoslav acrobat Aleksic and his collaborators in 1942, under the German occupation. (Since we are dealing with two films of the same name, let us put Aleksic's film "Innocence Unprotected" in quotation marks and Makavejev's film *Innocence Unprotected* in italics.) A second source is the mass of social-political documentation from the same period: newsreels of Yugoslavian current events, German propaganda films, footage of contemporary newspaper headlines, and footage of contemporary posters. Third, there appear excerpts from another fiction film, the Soviet feature *Circus* (Grigori Alexandrov, 1936). Finally, Makavejev uses present-day footage of Aleksic and the surviving participants in the original production. The last three types of footage permit Makavejev to embed Aleksic's original film in a complex context, justifying Makavejev's subtitle: "A New Version of a Very Good Old Film."

The four strands—original film, documentary footage, other fiction footage, and present-day footage—function initially to compare several different styles and modes of filmmaking. We are forced to compare Aleksic's technically crude "Innocence Unprotected" (full of incorrect continuity editing and flat lighting) with the Hollywood norms of "technical perfection." By inserting newsreel footage into fictitious scenes, Makavejev also impels us to contrast fiction film with documentary. (When Nada, the heroine of "Innocence Unprotected," looks out a window, an eyeline match cut suggests that she "sees" the rubble of a bombed Belgrade.) The digressions in *Innocence Unprotected* often come from Makavejev's habit of breaking off one kind of footage to juxtapose it with another—a fictional scene with attack maps or animated cartoons, an interview interrupted by a fictional scene.

Perhaps most complicated of all are the comparisons we draw between Aleksic's old film "Innocence Unprotected" and the "new version," which Makavejev has "prepared, decorated, and supplied with comments." Aleksic's original was a fictional narrative shot in black and white. Makavejev has juggled sequences, inserted new footage, added commentative titles, toned the black and white in several hues, and even hand colored parts of certain shots. (See Plate 13 for an example of blue-black toning and hand coloring.) Thus we always see Aleksic's film at one remove, *through* Makavejev's interpretive framework. Moreover, in the present-day sections, which Makavejev has shot, the differences between the original and new versions function to contrast the past and the present. The participants are frantically energetic in the 1942 film; now, though still vital, they are elderly. The disparity of past and present is perhaps most amusingly indicated when we see Aleksic as a young man dangling from a plane by his teeth, and then, while the plane noise continues over the image, Makavejev's camera in the present tracks through a house to find Aleksic dangling by his teeth in his cellar.

Yet it would be rash to stress only the differences between the original "Innocence Unprotected" and the new version. The original film itself was something of a collage, drawing on newsreel footage of Aleksic's stunts. And Makavejev often imitates the editing discontinuities and musical effects found in Aleksic's 1942 original. At times Makavejev even hesitates to keep the two films separate, as when the credits for *Innocence Unprotected* include names of people who worked only on the original. In *Innocence Unprotected*, then, the juxtaposition of various strands of source material contrasts and likens various uses of film technique.

The strands do weave together but not in conventional ways. In films like *His Girl Friday*, we have little trouble in demarcating the separate scenes. But *Innocence Unprotected* (again like *Last Year at Marienbad*) is difficult to segment. This is because Makavejev has chopped into collage fragments whatever narrative unity Aleksic's first version had. But *Innocence Unprotected* does have a form, often more associational than narrative. Here is the breakdown we propose:

| | |
|---|---|
| Part 1: Introduction | Credits; explanatory prologue; introduction of surviving cast and crew |
| Part 2: "Innocence Unprotected" begins its narrative | Scene 1 of "Innocence Unprotected"; newsreel footage of German attack; Aleksic is introduced, then and now |
| Part 3: Production background | Financing; the film's success and the censorship; Serbia's place in Yugoslavia; the Occupation; credits of "Innocence Unprotected" |
| Part 4: "Innocence Unprotected" narrative continues | Scenes 2–8 of "Innocence Unprotected," interspersed with newsreels |
| Part 5: Souvenirs of Youth | (to be analyzed) |
| Part 6: Aleksic's strength | Scene 9 of "Innocence Unprotected" (Aleksic rescues Nada); Aleksic's stunts today; scene 10 of "Innocence Unprotected" (Aleksic escapes from police) |
| Part 7: Innocence protected | "Innocence Unprotected" narrative resolved (dance in cafe, lovers united); Aleksic cleared of criminal charges |

Fig. 10.65

The segmentation shows that this is no ordinary narrative film. Parts 2, 4, 6, and 7 emphasize the original narrative, but parts 1, 3, and 5 function principally to put the film into historical contexts. And every part is riddled with jokes, interruptions, and digressions. In this connection we might recall Eisenstein's notion of intellectual montage. (See the *October* example in Chapter 7, pp. 235–239.) By cutting freely from one kind of footage to another, Makavejev's collage form creates discontinuities that "free the action from time and space," as Eisenstein said of intellectual montage, in order to make abstract, ironic points. *Innocence Unprotected* presents us with a skeletal narrative form interrupted by parts that are organized around associationally linked topics.

Fig. 10.66

Fig. 10.67

Fig. 10.68

Fig. 10.69

Fig. 10.70

Fig. 10.71

As a concrete example, consider Part 5. We label this "Souvenirs of Youth" because that is the concept binding together a varied collection of material. The sequence begins in the present, with the original participants reflecting on their pasts. First, Aleksic and two collaborators stand on a roof used in the filming (Fig. 10.65). Next, Vera, the actress who portrayed the stepmother, recalls the beauty of her legs and performs a vaudeville song (Figs. 10.66 and 10.67). Then Pera, who played the butler in the original, stands before a memorial to heroism to sing a song about political fence sitting during the Occupation (Fig. 10.68).

The film now moves into the past, showing a newsreel of the boy King Peter reviewing his troops (Fig. 10.69). (Although a king, he had little power; Prince Paul actually ran the country before handing Yugoslavia over to Germany and fleeing.) Back to the present, with Aleksic bending a bar. ("This is a souvenir of my youth"; see Fig. 10.70). Now shots from *Circus* show a young woman shot from a cannon (Fig. 10.71). We learn that this film inspired Aleksic to build a similar cannon for one of his stunts (Fig. 10.72). Finally, news stories report how someone was killed by Aleksic's contraption (Fig. 10.73).

Fig. 10.72

The sequence's sources—songs, newsreels, a Russian musical—and the different periods discussed are not unified by narrative principles (cause-effect, temporal progression). Instead, associations pull the fragments loosely together: souvenirs from the youth of the participants in the film and from a period when their country was ruled by a child.

The "Souvenirs of Youth" segment also illustrates how the concepts emerging from the collage form tend to be overtly political ones. Makavejev's prologue announces: "This first Yugoslav talkie is not mentioned in our film histories because it was made during the Occupation." Makavejev situates Aleksic's "Innocence

Fig. 10.73

Unprotected" firmly within the ferment of Serbian nationalism. The success of Aleksic's film at the time is held to be a triumph for Serbian rights. More subtly, Makavejev's "decoration and commentary" turn Aleksic's film into an allegory of Yugoslav resistance to the Germans. When the uncle lunges toward Nada, Makavejev cuts in animated newsreel maps showing the German invasion. Nada, the unprotected innocent, becomes identified with native Yugoslavia, the uncle with the Nazis. By the same token, Aleksic emerges as a heroic, politicized figure. "We can all be proud of him," says Nada in "Innocence Unprotected," "but we underrate what is our own." While Aleksic breaks his chains in a stunt, Makavejev plays the Communist anthem, the *Internationale*, which refers to the world's workers arising and breaking their chains. In Part 6 Aleksic's prowess is celebrated in mock-heroic shots of him as a statue or a god. Here, as elsewhere, the nationalist allegory becomes ironic, but it nevertheless functions to make Makavejev's "decoration and commentary" frankly political.

Though this analysis has barely scratched the film's surface, we might end by posing the question of the title. Who is the innocent without protection? In Aleksic's 1942 film, it is the orphan Nada, rescued by Aleksic. But by comparing film styles, working out a unique form, and making general political points, Makavejev's "collage" strategy also suggests that Aleksic, the strong man who made the film, is something of an innocent, too. Over newsreel footage of blasted bodies we hear the characters in Aleksic's film singing a café tune. By situating the film in a political context, Makavejev suggests the implicit meaning that Aleksic and his crew were dangerously innocent, oblivious to the concrete political situation. All involved insist that they had no subversive intent, that they made the film only to get rich. They risked death at the hands of the Nazis to make a silly romance about an acrobat.

Yet despite the lack of political purpose, Makavejev makes the original "Innocence Unprotected" emerge as a genuinely subversive film. In the original, Aleksic's rescue of Nada culminates in a victory dance at a café ("our national dance"), and Makavejev hand colors one woman's dress the colors of the Serbian flag. No wonder Makavejev calls the original "a very good old film": the Germans banned it as subversive. The closing moments of *Innocence Unprotected* linger over the question of "innocence." We are told that many participants in the film fought in the Resistance and that Aleksic was exonerated after the war, since his film "had not told a single lie." The fiction film has become a document; the apolitical project has become political. Makavejev's use of style and form has revised the old film in ways that ask us to rethink cinema and its functions in history.

## DOCUMENTARY FORM AND STYLE

### ■ *HIGH SCHOOL*

1968. Produced and directed by Frederick Wiseman. Photographed by Richard Leiterman. Editor: Frederick Wiseman. Associate editor: Carter Howard. Assistant cameraman: David Eames.

Before the 1950s, most documentary filmmaking shot footage silent and added a voice-over commentary and postsynchronized music at the assembly stage. Lorentz's *The River* and Riefenstahl's *Olympia*, Part 2, analyzed in Chapters 4 and 9, are instances of this trend. After World War II, however, magnetic tape recording made it possible to record sound on location, and at the same period the demands of military and television users encouraged manufacturers to develop lightweight but sophisticated 16-mm cameras. These technological changes fostered a new approach to documentary filmmaking: *cinéma vérité* ("cinema truth"). In the 1950s and 1960s, many filmmakers began to use portable cameras and synchronized-sound recording equipment to capture spontaneous activity in a wide variety of situations—a political campaign (*Primary*, 1960), a legal case (*The Chair*, 1963), a folk singer's life (*Don't Look Back*, 1966), the tribulations of a Bible salesman (*Salesman*, 1969). Some filmmakers claimed that *cinéma vérité* was more objective than traditional documentary. Whereas the older trend had tended to use editing, music, and commentary to inject particular biases, the *cinéma-vérité* film, where voice-over commentary was minimized and the filmmaker was on the spot as the situation unfolded, could neutrally record the facts and let the audience draw its own conclusions.

Frederick Wiseman's *High School* is a good example of the *cinéma-vérité* approach. Wiseman received permission to film at Philadelphia's Northeast High School, and he acted as sound recordist while his cameraman shot footage in the hallways, classrooms, cafeteria, and auditorium of the institution. The film that resulted uses no voice-over narration and almost no nondiegetic music. Wiseman uses none of the facing-the-reporter interviews that television news coverage employs. In these ways, *High School* might seem to approach the *cinéma-vérité* ideal of simply presenting a slice of life. Yet if we analyze the film's form and style, we find that it still aims to achieve particular effects on the spectator, and it still suggests a specific range of meaning. Far from being a neutral transmission of the real world, *High School* shows how film form and style, even in *cinéma vérité*, transform the real world.

The *cinéma-vérité* film records reality in some sense, but like any film, it demands that the filmmaker select and arrange material. The filmmaker chooses not only the film's subject matter but also the events that he or she will photograph. The *cinéma-vérité* filmmaker also makes decisions on the spur of the moment, choosing when to start filming during a scene, what to keep in frame, and what sounds to record. There is selection in the editing phase as well; the 80 minutes of *High School* are culled from over 40 hours of raw footage. All these choices prevent the film from being a complete record of reality. The filmmaker also arranges the material, presenting it in a specific way that affects our experience. Although the *cinéma-vérité* filmmaker has surrendered control over what happens in front of the camera, she or he retains control over the film's structure, choosing what segment will follow another. The filmmaker can pick a camera position that will juxtapose various elements in the frame. (Consider Fig. 10.74, which frames the dean of discipline against the American flag; another angle, such as that of Fig. 10.79, does not make the flag visible.) The filmmaker also arranges shots through editing, by putting images and sounds into specific relations. Through selection and arrangement, the *cinéma-vérité* filmmaker utilizes film form and style no less than does a filmmaker who stages the action for the camera.

Fig. 10.74

*High School* contains 37 distinct segments, each one showing an episode of high-school life. Some segments, such as chorus rehearsal, are quite brief; others involve extensive dialogue. Formally, the film presents an interesting combination of structural types. In one respect, the form is categorical: the main category is high-school life, and the subcategories consist of typical activities—classes, student/teacher confrontations, sports activities, a pep rally, and so on. From another angle, the film's form can be seen to depend on narrative principles as well. Many of the episodes constitute little scenes fraught with conflict: the dean of discipline insists that a boy take an unjustified detention, an administrator argues with complaining parents, and so on. Nonetheless, the overall form of the film is not narrative. The film lacks continuing characters, causality (one action does not trigger the next), and temporality (we do not know the "real" order and duration of events shown in the film). Wiseman has realized that our prior knowledge and experience will help us fill in gaps. When one segment begins with the disciplinary dean saying, "What do you mean, you can't take gym?" we will draw on our own high-school memories to create a typical context around this scene. Finally, as we shall see, the film is associational in the way it arranges and links its parts. Thus *High School* presents typical categories of high-school life as fragments of narrative and organizes them by principles that are associational.

The way in which categorical, narrative, and associational strategies combine becomes clearer if we look at how Wiseman has selected and arranged his material. The film is not a full cross-section of high-school life. It omits many important aspects. We never see the home life of students and faculty, and strikingly, we never witness any conversations between students, either in class or outside it. Wiseman has concentrated on one aspect of high-school life: how the power of the authorities demands obedience from pupils and parents. The most common strategy we see is simple drilling. The classes consist of teachers lecturing, reading aloud, or leading the students in some regimented activity, such as calisthenics, cooking, musical performance, or language drill. The filmmaker's selectivity is especially evident in one segment, in which an English teacher uses a popular song to teach poetry. Wiseman shows her reading the text aloud and then playing the song on tape, but he omits the class discussion that came in between. At other times, the authorities exact obedience through cajolery and flattery: an administrator tells one girl that she could be a leader; the disciplinary dean coaxes the boy to take his punishment like a man. If conflict breaks out, a teacher or administrator is shown taking a hard line in order to exercise discipline or win a point. In this film, no one in authority ever loses an argument. Thus the narrative interest of each scene depends on our recognizing it as repeating the same pattern of the victory of authority. We come to expect that the disciplinary dean will argue down a fractious boy or that an administrator will force students to wear formal dress to the prom. Wiseman's selectivity also gives the neutral category of high-school life some of the expressive overtones we expect of associational form. One scene may depict a drum major's march while another portrays a history class, but the important thing is that we notice the regimented quality of each one.

The arrangement of parts in the overall film betrays the mixture of formal types as well. The film's first segment evokes sketchy narrative expectations. The opening shows views of streets, highways, and eventually the school, all filmed from a car or bus. It suggests that the day begins with someone (teacher? student?) coming to school. The next sequence, apparently during homeroom period, tends to confirm the hypothesis that the school day is starting. But as the film develops, there are no cues to demarcate phases of the day. Moreover, we see another homeroom period later, as well as several school assemblies, a simulated space flight, and other activities that would not all plausibly take place on a single day. By the last sequence, a teachers' meeting, we cannot be sure when this occurs— at the end of the day, the end of the semester, or at some other point. After the first two scenes, the sequences are not linked by any assumptions of chronology. What we see are simply categories within the topic high school, restricted to the sorts of face-to-face exercises of power that we have already mentioned.

In general, the film develops associatively. It mixes its scenes of drilling with more dramatic encounters, grouping several sequences around topics. For example, several scenes concentrate on how the school teaches about gender roles and sexuality. Sequence 15 shows a boys' health class being lectured on families; this is followed by a sequence showing an assembly of girls being lectured about sexual conduct. In Sequence 17, an administrator and a teacher explain why all female students must wear formal gowns to the senior prom. In Sequence 18, as a girls' gym class practices hanging from parallel rings, the teacher calls out, "We're feminine, let's go." Later in the film, three more sex-education classes are clustered together, reinforcing the idea that the school functions to create models of behavior that define masculinity and femininity. Another cluster of sequences involves college plans, while late in the film a string of sequences associates high-school education with the military. Here we can clearly see how powerfully the order of the sequences can shape our participation in the film. A soldier home on leave talks with a coach about a wounded friend who will never play soccer again. The next sequence, which simply shows a boys' gym class bouncing an enormous ball, encourages us to imagine these boys as future soldiers, some of whom may be killed or crippled. There follows a scene of a drum corps in the auditorium, again summoning up military comparisons. This is followed by the film's last scene, in which a female principal reads to the assembled teachers a letter from an ex-student about to go to Vietnam. The ordering of scenes thus encourages us to pick out aspects that the various scenes share—a basic convention of associational form. A film using this structure does not advance a specific *argument* about its subject (the form is not rhetorical), but the film may imply a broad *attitude* to its topic, as Conner's *A Movie* does (p. 122).

Associational qualities are strengthened by other means. For one thing, motifs reappear. Wiseman uses shots of the school hallway to demarcate the scenes. Details of student anatomy—hips and legs especially—reinforce the notion of docile bodies waiting, lining up, bent to assigned tasks. By contrast, the authorities are associated with hands. While talking to parents, one administrator makes a fist, and the framing emphasizes this with a close-up (Fig. 10.75); in the next sequence, the disciplinary dean's hand is treated in a similar framing (Fig. 10.76). Most strikingly, the transitions between scenes depend on associations. Some are simple repetitions, as when one teacher asks, "Are there any questions?" and we cut to another teacher asking, "Any questions?" Other transitions are more figurative. A teacher concludes "Casey at the Bat" with the line "Mighty Casey has struck out." Cut to a girl in gym class batting a ball. A Spanish teacher waves her arms, drilling

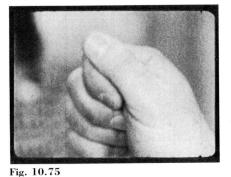

Fig. 10.75

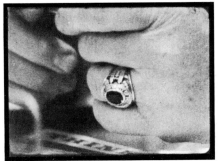

Fig. 10.76

Fig. 10.77

Fig. 10.78

Fig. 10.79

Fig. 10.80

the class in a pronunciation exercise (Fig. 10.77); cut to a percussion ensemble practicing, led by a teacher conducting them (Fig. 10.78). This effectively suggests the regimented nature of learning. Although the film does not supply cues for temporal order, it unifies itself through recurring motifs and transitions that reveal unexpected repetitions and similarities.

On the whole, the filmmaker's stylistic choices reinforce the overall structural features we have already mentioned. The segmentation into categories of school life is accomplished through editing and sound. Each sequence begins with an abrupt cut to a situation already in progress. Often the first shots are close-ups, so that the action is only gradually revealed. The associative aspects of the film's form also depend upon techniques that make the sort of surprising transitions we have already considered.

Within segments, the use of cinematography, editing, and sound supports the narrative aspects of the individual scenes. Even though Wiseman is filming unstaged situations, he adheres to principles of classical narrative style. The zoom lens permits the camera operator to situate someone in space and then isolate details (Figs. 10.79 and 10.80). More strikingly, *High School*'s scenes rely heavily on continuity editing which creates an axis of action and shot/reverse shot. In Figure 10.81, the blonde student is shown from the rear, at the far left edge of the frame; the next shot, Figure 10.82, cuts to a reverse angle on her that maintains the 180° line between her and the teacher. (Compare this cutting pattern with that in *The Maltese Falcon*, Figures 7.42 to 7.44.) When filming under confined conditions, however, a *cinéma-vérité* filmmaker cannot always obtain an establishing shot. In *High School*, this makes eyelines and screen direction crucial cues for spatial continuity. For example, when the English teacher reads "Casey at the Bat," she

Fig. 10.81

Fig. 10.82

Fig. 10.83

Fig. 10.84

is consistently intercut with shots of students looking to the left, even though no long shot shows all of them in the same space.

The use of continuity editing does more than give the scenes a narrative unity we can recognize from classical Hollywood conventions. Cutting from speaker to listener also lets Wiseman skip over intervals of real duration and conceal the breaks through offscreen sound. If we cut away from the teacher to a reaction shot of the pupil listening but keep the teacher's voice on the sound track, we can omit whole sentences before cutting back to the speaker. In the scene showing the English teacher studying the Simon and Garfunkel song, it is just such a use of cutaways and offscreen sound that allows Wiseman to omit the class discussion of the poem. The "invisible" ellipses that cutaways and offscreen sound can yield are constantly used in television news coverage, in which a cut to a nodding reporter typically conceals omissions in the speaker's talk.

Fig. 10.85

The absence of establishing shots and the reliance on eyelines can even create the sort of "imaginary geography" that Kuleshov discussed (see p. 215). We follow a teacher as he stalks the halls demanding passes. He turns (Fig. 10.83). There is a cut to a long shot of a girl walking down the corridor (Fig. 10.84). After the monitor has ordered some students to leave, he goes up to a door and peers in (Fig. 10.85). The offscreen music gradually grows louder, and we cut to a phonograph and a girls' gym class exercising, filmed to emphasize legs and torsos (Fig. 10.86). A close study of the shot reveals that the girl in Figure 10.84 is not in the hall that the teacher is patrolling. Moreover, since there is no establishing shot showing both teacher and students, we cannot know with certainty that the teacher actually looks in on the gym class. On this last point, if we recall the conditions of *cinéma-vérité* production, we realize that the music must have been added after

Fig. 10.86

the shot of the teacher was made. (If the music really was coming from the gym, there would have been a gap on the sound track when the filmmakers had to switch the camera off and go into the gym to film the students.) Thus both editing and sound create the Kuleshov effect, prompting us to connect two things that are not really adjacent. The stylistic function is to characterize the teacher as lecherous, ogling girls in the hallway and spying on them in gym class.

After analyzing how *High School* uses overall form and specific film techniques to guide our response, it may seem odd to suggest that the film is somewhat ambiguous. Yet reactions to the film varied. When *High School* was first shown to the Philadelphia Board of Education, many officials praised it. But critics from around the country have tended to see the film as criticizing the school and secondary education in general. Does this controversy mean that *cinéma vérité* has achieved the goal of a neutral capturing of reality, leaving meanings to the eye of each beholder?

We think that the varying reactions to the film illustrate how viewers can emphasize one sort of meaning over another. It is likely that school officials concentrated upon the film's *referential* and *explicit* meanings, treating it as a record of a single school (a sort of institutional home movie) and as a statement about the success of education—a sentiment made very explicit at the film's close, when the female principal reads a letter from the student about to go to Vietnam. Critics, however, offered an interpretation of the film that stressed an *implicit* meaning at odds with the explicit one. On this view, the school is shown as an oppressive bureaucracy. These critics could use our analysis to claim that the film's form and style, and its tactics of selection and arrangement, portray this institution as more concerned with inculcating obedience and conformity than with teaching critical thinking, independent action, and a sense of self-worth.

Fig. 10.87

This interpretation could gather further evidence from the use of rock-and-roll tunes to comment on the bleakness of high-school life as well as from the final scene, in which the soldier's letter is read. Here the film's development from educational discipline to military regimentation is capped by an overt link between school and army. The boy's letter urges people not to worry, and the motif of students as docile bodies returns: "I am not worth it. I am only a body doing a job." The scene also repeats the motif of the hand of authority when the camera racks focus during the administrator's reading (Figs. 10.87 and 10.88). From this interpretive stance, the film's final line—"When you get a letter like this, to me it means that we are very successful at Northeast High School. I think you will agree with me"—becomes ironic. (Irony, indeed, is often defined as exactly this sort of conflict between explicit and implicit meaning.) We could even suggest that the film's *symptomatic* meaning reinforces this interpretation. Depicting a school as a training ground for conformity is symptomatic of the period in which the film was made—1968, a time when many filmmakers were questioning both specific governmental policies, such as American involvement in Vietnam, and broader values of Western society. (These issues are more explicitly taken up in Godard/Gorin's *Tout va vien* [1971].)

Fig. 10.88

Frederick Wiseman's *High School* can be considered ambiguous in that its referential and explicit meanings run counter to its implicit and symptomatic ones. Nonetheless, the fact that the film can generate not vagueness but such a precise dispute about its range of meanings suggests that far from being a neutral record of the world "in front of" a camera and microphone, *cinéma vérité* is an active cinematic intervention *in* the world, another way of handling inevitable choices about form, style, and effect.

# ■ *MAN WITH A MOVIE CAMERA (CHELOVEK S KINOAPPARATOM)*

Made 1928, released 1929. VUFKU, Union of Soviet Socialist Republics. Directed by Dziga Vertov. Photographed by Mikhail Kaufman. Edited by Elizaveta Svilova.

In some ways, *Man with a Movie Camera* might seem to resemble *High School*. As a silent film, it necessarily avoids the use of music to guide our expectations (music, that is, controlled by the filmmaker, since in the theaters a piano or orchestra would have accompanied screenings). Moreover, the film does not employ intertitles to provide a commentary on the action, though most silent documentaries did use such titles. Yet, unlike *High School, Man with a Movie Camera* does not try to give the impression of being a straightforward, objective presentation of a reality captured, unaltered, on film. Instead, Dziga Vertov puts great emphasis on the manipulative power of editing and cinematography to shape a multitude of tiny scenes from everyday reality into a highly idiosyncratic documentary film.

Vertov's name is usually linked to the technique of editing; in Chapter 7 (p. 204), we quoted a passage in which he equated the filmmaker with an eye, gathering shots from many places and linking them creatively for the spectator. Vertov's theoretical writings (see the bibliography for Chapter 11, p. 405) also compare the eye to the lens of the camera, in a concept he termed the "kino eye." (*Kino* is the Russian word for "cinema," and one of his earlier films is called *Kino-Glaz*, or "Cinema-Eye.")

*Man with a Movie Camera* takes this idea—the equation of the filmmaker's eye with the lens of the camera—as the basis for the entire film's associative form. The film becomes a celebration of the documentary filmmaker's power to control our perception of reality by means of editing and special effects. The opening image shows a camera in close-up; through a double-exposure effect, we see the camera-man of the film's title (played by Vertov's regular cinematographer, Mikhail Kaufman) suddenly climb, in extreme long shot, onto the top of the giant camera (Fig. 10.89). He sets up his own camera on a tripod and films for a bit, then climbs down again. This play with shot scale within a single image emphasizes at once the power the camera has to alter reality in a seemingly magical way.

Many cinematographic special effects of this sort appear as a motif throughout the film. These are not intended to be unnoticeable, as in a science-fiction film. Instead, they flaunt the fact that the camera can alter everyday reality. Figure 10.90 shows a typical example, with Vertov filming an ordinary street scene but altering it by exposing each side of the image separately, with the camera canted in opposite

Fig. 10.89

Fig. 10.90

Fig. 10.91

Fig. 10.92

Fig. 10.93

Fig. 10.94

directions. Later Vertov uses a technique called **pixillation,** or single-frame animation with real objects. A crayfish on a plate "comes to life" and does a little dance in the course of the shot (Fig. 10.91). In another scene Vertov conveys the sound of a radio by superimposing several images—three of a dancer and one of a hand playing a piano—against a single black background (Fig. 10.92). This motif of virtuosic special effects culminates in the famous final shot (Fig. 10.93), where an eye is superimposed over the lens of the camera, staring straight out at us.

At several points in the film, the camera is also personified, linked by association through editing to the actions of human beings. One brief segment shows the camera lens focusing and then a blurry shot of flowers coming into sharp focus. This is followed immediately by a comic juxtaposition rapidly intercutting two elements: a woman's fluttering eyelids as she dries her face with a towel, and a set of venetian blinds opening and closing. Finally another shot shows the camera lens with a diaphragm closing and opening. A human eye is like venetian blinds, the lens is like an eye—all can open and close, admitting or keeping out light. Later, pixillation allows the camera to move by itself, as it comes out of its box, climbs onto the tripod, demonstrates how its various parts work (Fig. 10.94), and finally walks off on three legs. Such playfulness is far from the objective tone of *High School.*

*Man with a Movie Camera* belongs to a genre of documentaries that first became important during the 1920s: the "city symphony." There are many ways of making a film about a city, of course. One might use categorical form to lay out its geography or scenic attractions, as in a travelogue; rhetorical form could make arguments about aspects of city planning or government that need changing. A narrative might stress a city as the backdrop for many characters' actions, as in

Rossellini's *Rome, Open City* or Jules Dassin's semidocumentary crime drama *The Naked City*. Early city symphonies, however, established the convention of taking candid (or occasionally staged) scenes of city life and linking them, usually without commentary, through associations to create a set of shifting moods and attitudes in the viewer. Associational form is evident in such early examples of the genre as Alberto Cavalcanti's *Rien que les heures* (1926) and Walter Ruttmann's *Berlin, Symphony of a Great City* (1927). More recent films like Godfrey Reggio's *Koyaanisqatsi* (1983) and *Powaqqatsi* (1988) use similar techniques, avoiding voice-over narration in favor of a musical accompaniment that sets the tone for the juxtapositions of images.

In *Man with a Movie Camera*'s opening, we see a camera operator filming, then passing between the curtains of an empty movie theater, toward the screen. Then we see the theater opening, the spectators filing in, the orchestra preparing to play, and the film commencing. The film they and we then watch seems at first to be a city symphony of the type that lays out a typical day in the life of a town (as Ruttmann's *Berlin* does). We see a woman asleep, mannequins in closed shops, empty streets. Soon a few people appear, and the city wakes up. Indeed, much of *Man with a Movie Camera* follows a rough principle of development that progresses from waking up through work time to leisure time. But early in the waking-up portion we also see the cameraman again, setting out with his equipment, as if starting his work day. This action creates the first of many contradictions in the film. The cameraman now appears in his own film, and Vertov emphasizes this by cutting back immediately to the sleeping woman who had been the first thing we saw in the film-within-a-film.

Throughout *Man with a Movie Camera*, we will see the same actions and shots being filmed, edited, and viewed by the onscreen audience, all in jumbled order. Toward the end of the film, in fact, we see the audience in the theater watching the cameraman on the screen, filming from a moving motorcycle. Moreover, in this late portion of the film, many motifs from all the earlier parts of the day return, many now in fast motion; the simple time scheme is broken down and jumbled. Thus Vertov creates an impossible time scheme, once more emphasizing the extraordinary manipulative powers of the cinema. The film also refuses to show only one city, instead mixing footage filmed in Moscow, Kiev, and Riga, as if the cameraman hero can move effortlessly back and forth in space during this "day" of filming. Vertov's view of the cinema's relation to the cityscape is well conveyed in one shot which uses an extraordinary deep-focus composition to place the camera in the foreground, looming over the distant buildings as it pans madly about to capture various views on film (Fig. 10.95). In sum, *Man with a Movie Camera* may be a city symphony, but it goes beyond that genre as well.

Fig. 10.95

Apart from its exuberant celebration of the powers of cinema, Vertov's film contains many explicit and implicit meanings (some of which may be missed by viewers who do not read Russian). Explicitly, the film deals with both good and bad points of Soviet society a decade after the revolution. Many of the film's juxtapositions involve machines and human labor. At this stage in its history, the USSR was beginning a major push toward industrialization, and the mechanized factories are portrayed as fascinating places full of bustling movement, with the camera lingering over details of gleaming, moving machine parts (Fig. 10.96). The camera operator climbs a huge factory smokestack or swings suspended over a dam to capture all this activity. Workers are seen, not as oppressed, but as participating cheerfully in the country's growth, as when one young woman laughs and chats as she folds cigarette boxes on an assembly line.

Fig. 10.96

There are negative aspects to this society as well. Vertov turns occasionally to lingering class inequalities. Shots in a beauty shop suggest that some bourgeois values have survived the Revolution, and the leisure-time sequence near the end contrasts workers involved in outdoor sports with chubby women exercising in a weight-loss gym.

Another negative motif which crops up at an early point is that of drunkenness, which was a major social problem in the USSR. One of the first shots within the inner film shows a derelict sleeping outdoors, juxtaposed with a huge bottle advertising a café. A shop front which we repeatedly see advertises wine and vodka, and later there is a scene where the cameraman visits this bar. When he leaves, we see shots of workers' clubs, converted from former churches. The contrast between these two places where workers can spend their leisure time is made clear through associational crosscutting: a woman shooting at targets in one of the clubs seems to be shooting away bottles of beer that disappear (through stop motion) from a crate in the bar. During the 1920s, government officials instituted an official policy whose goal was to use the cinema and workers' clubs to replace both the tavern and the church in the lives of Soviet citizens. (Given that the government's biggest source of income came from its monopoly on vodka sales, the policy also aimed at making cinema a major alternative source of revenue.) Thus *Man with a Movie Camera* seems to be subtly promoting this policy by using playful camera techniques to make both the cinema and the clubs seem attractive.

Implicitly, *Man with a Movie Camera* can be seen as an argument for Vertov's view of the cinema. He opposed narrative form and the use of professional actors, preferring that films use the techniques of the camera and the editing table to create their effects upon the audience. (He was not entirely against controlling the mise-en-scene, and several scenes of this film—particularly the woman waking up and washing—clearly would have had to be arranged.) Throughout *Man with a Movie Camera*, associational juxtapositions compare the work of making a film with the other sorts of work depicted. The camera operator awakes and goes to work in the morning, like other workers. Like them, he uses a machine in his craft; the camera's crank is at various points compared with the crank on a cash register or with moving parts on factory equipment. (The moving parts of the projector in the theater also resemble parts of the factory machines we see in various sequences.)

Vertov further demonstrates how the film we (and the audience within the film) are watching is not a product of natural processes but of specific labor. We see the editor at work (Elizaveta Svilova, Vertov's wife and the actual editor of *Man with a Movie Camera*). Her gestures of scraping the film and putting cement on it with a brush to make a splice are cut in with shots in a beauty parlor, where a manicurist wields a nail file and a similar brush. At various times in the film we see many of the same shots in different contexts: on our screen, on the screen within the movie theater, in freeze frame, being filmed, being cut apart or spliced by the editor, in fast motion, and so on. We must therefore view them not only as little moments of captured reality but also as parts of a whole that is put together through much effort on the parts of these film workers. Finally, the camera operator has to resort to various means, sometimes dangerous, to obtain his shots; he not only climbs a huge smokestack but also crouches across the tracks to film an oncoming train and rides a motorcycle one-handed as he cranks the camera to capture the action of a race. Filmmaking is thus presented as a job or craft, rather than an elitist art form. Judging from the delighted reactions of the audience we see in the theater, Vertov hoped that the Soviet public would find his celebration of filmmaking interesting and entertaining.

This implicit meaning relates to a symptomatic meaning we can also see in the film. During the late 1920s, the Soviet authorities wanted films which would be easily understandable and would convey propagandistic messages to a far-flung, often illiterate populace. They were increasingly critical of filmmakers like Eisenstein and Vertov, whose films, though celebrating revolutionary ideology, were extremely complex. In Chapter 7 we saw how Eisenstein adopted a dense, discontinuous style of editing. While Vertov disagreed in many ways with Eisenstein, particularly over the latter's use of narrative form, both belonged to a larger stylistic movement called Soviet montage, whose history we shall examine in Chapter 11 (pp. 385–388). Both used very complex editing which they hoped would create predictable reactions in their audiences. With its contradictory time scheme and rapid editing (it contains over 1700 shots, more than twice what most Hollywood films of the same period had), *Man with a Movie Camera* is unquestionably a difficult film, especially for an audience unaccustomed to the conventions of filmmaking. Perhaps more Soviet spectators would have learned over time to enjoy such films as *October* and *Man with a Movie Camera* and to react to them with the delight evident in the audience in Vertov's film. Over the next few years, however, authorities increasingly criticized Vertov and his colleagues, limiting their ability to experiment with concepts like the "film eye." Vertov in particular was constrained in his later projects, but *Man with a Movie Camera* eventually came to be recognized, in the Soviet Union and abroad, as a classic use of associational form in the documentary mode.

## THE ANIMATED FILM

As we saw in Chapter 1, animated films are usually produced by a technique of photographing only one frame at a time, with slight changes in the mise-en-scene which create the illusion of movement on the screen. The mise-en-scene itself might consist of drawings, clay figures, computer-generated images on a monitor, or any number of other objects. Some animation is even created by painting directly onto the strip of film stock.

Animation yields complete control over the mise-en-scene. The filmmaker can design and draw literally anything, whether it resembles something in the real world or comes strictly out of his or her imagination. Thus there is a vast range of possibilities for animated films.

The three films we will be analyzing all use drawings. Two, *Clock Cleaners*, a Disney short, and *Duck Amuck*, made at Warner Bros., use the technique of **cel animation.** "Cel" is short for celluloid, and this name derives from the fact that typically the background, or scenery, for the shot is the only portion drawn on paper. The moving figures and objects are drawn on layers of clear plastic that can then be laid over the background. This system has strong advantages in saving time and labor. Although hundreds of slightly different drawings have to be done to create the movements, the same background can be used in all of them by laying new cels over it. Moreover, if only part of a figure is moving (say, Bugs Bunny's arm and head as he eats a carrot), that part can be rendered on one layer, which is redrawn and changed a bit each time, while the rest of the figure is on another cel which then is photographed repeatedly. Our third film, Robert Breer's *Fuji*, uses many separate drawings made on index cards and without cels overlaid but, as we shall see, it plays in an experimental way with conventions associated with traditional cel animation.

The three films are classics from the history of American drawn animation. Each one illustrates a different approach to this form of filmmaking. *Clock Cleaners* employs techniques of continuity and classical Hollywood filmmaking. *Duck Amuck* plays in a daring way with those techniques. And *Fuji* uses a mixture of live action and drawings to create a complex abstract form.

## ■ *CLOCK CLEANERS*

1937. Walt Disney Productions. Directed by Ben Sharpsteen.

*Clock Cleaners* is a narrative, but it does not adhere to the typical patterns of narrative development that we have observed at work in feature-length Hollywood films. Instead, it draws on a common strategy used in many slapstick shorts, both with live and animated comedians. That is, it sets up a basic situation and then has the characters perform a series of nearly self-contained skits or gags, building up in intensity as the film goes along. In this case, three familiar stars, Mickey Mouse, Goofy, and Donald Duck, all appear, but each is working in a different part of the huge clock tower. Thus they do not interact until near the end of the film. No overall pattern like a search or a journey helps the plot develop; though the characters could be said to share a general goal of cleaning the clock, they have not accomplished it by the end of the film, and our sense of narrative progression has more to do with their mishaps than with any work they may get done.

Because we already know the basic traits of the three stars from other cartoons, they can launch into their actions without any exposition beyond the fact, quickly established, that they are clock cleaners. Donald is irascible, and his scenes involve a fight with the clock's huge mainspring, which he has accidentally released from its tight coil. Mickey is kindly, but his efforts to eject a resting stork from the clock backfire. Goofy, whose main trait is defined by his name, unwittingly lets the clock's mechanical figures knock him silly and then performs a precarious dance high above the street. All these characters end up together, caught in the works of the clock at the final iris-out. Animation historian Leonard Maltin describes *Clock Cleaners* as typifying the narrative formula used in several Disney cartoons of the 1930s with these same three stars: "These superbly animated shorts featured the characters as a team that approached a given situation, then split up for solo episodes before coming together again at the finale."

As a result, *Clock Cleaners* has an episodic plot, but it develops as well, beginning with short, slightly risky predicaments and ending with a lengthy, dangerous climactic scene. First we see a brief scene where Donald accidentally loosens the clock's mainspring and gets caught inside the resulting tangle of metal bands. Then Mickey's struggles with the stork leave him dangling on a rope above the street, but the danger is only momentary. We return to Donald, who is flung from the spring into a gear, but he ends by falling on a platform inside the clock. Goofy's elaborate balancing act on ledges and ropes, however, puts both him and would-be rescuer Mickey in considerable peril—until both are tossed in to join Donald in the comparative safety of the clock's gears. Thus comic acceleration of danger and a final removal of that danger help create the film's narrative form.

In cel animation, costs rise when more movement and graphic detail is added to the shots. Of all the animation units in Hollywood during the heyday of the cartoon (roughly from the 1920s to the 1950s), Walt Disney Productions had the

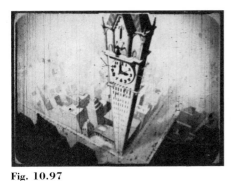

Fig. 10.97

Fig. 10.98

Fig. 10.99

Fig. 10.100

Fig. 10.101

Fig. 10.102

most lavish budgets, the best technical facilities, and the largest staff. While the Warner Bros. animation unit (which created Bugs Bunny, Daffy Duck, and Porky Pig, among others) and the Fleischer brothers (which created the Betty Boop and Popeye cartoons for Paramount) may have been equally imaginative, historians agree that Disney's animation was the most elaborate and virtuosic.

In *Clock Cleaners*, for example, the first shot inside the giant clock shows Mickey and the clock hands and numerals all visible, silhouetted against the translucent face. A tilt and crane move us to a high angle, revealing the huge gears and wheels of the clock's mechanism, with Goofy at work on a platform far below. This shot, full of separate, intricate movements, is typical of the Disney virtuosity. Similarly, the opening view of the city is detailed (Fig. 10.97), and the settings within the clock are drawn to suggest three-dimensional space, with shadows and textures.

Although *Clock Cleaners* is a fantasy, its space and time are created by using some of the familiar devices of live-action classical Hollywood films. The film's establishing shot (Fig. 10.97), for example, contains a zooming movement toward the central clock tower, and a dissolve leads into a closer shot of the mechanical figures. A tilt down then reveals Mickey on the clock's second hand, and another dissolve moves us closer to him. Finally, a third dissolve shifts the view inside the clock, and so on. Space is carefully laid out with continuity editing. Later, Donald battles the unruly mainspring of the clock, and there is a cut-in to his startled reaction as the end of the spring seems to talk back to him (Figs. 10.98 and 10.99). Toward the end, Mickey looks over to see Goofy in danger, staggering in a daze along a rope that is about to run out of a pulley and drop him. Again continuity editing makes the space and the situation clear, as one shot shows Mickey looking off to the left (Fig. 10.100), and the next shows the situation from his point of view (Fig. 10.101). Note how in the second shot, the drawing simulates the effects of a wide-angle lens, exaggerating depth so that Goofy appears tiny in the frame, and the rope and pulley appear large—emphasizing Mickey's realization of the danger.

*Clock Cleaners* also exploits some spatial possibilities that are unique to animation. When the mechanical figures strike the big clock bell with Goofy's head inside, the drawings convey his reaction by means of multiple overlapping images of his head (Fig. 10.102), which seems on the screen to vibrate wildly. Similarly, the characters' bodies are more flexible than those of real actors—as is evident in the running gag where they get their heads caught in a giant gear that jerks their bodies back and forth. (Such quick movements are fun to watch in slow motion, on an editing machine or video player, and such an exercise also gives us a better appreciation of the animators' skill.) Overall, however, we can say that Disney's cartoons of the late 1930s and 1940s often try for a relatively high degree of verisimilitude in the construction of consistent, three-dimensional space and continuous time. Such an approach was not universal, however, and a great deal of experimentation with bizarre and imaginative stylistic possibilities went on, even within Hollywood animation—as our next example demonstrates.

### ■ DUCK AMUCK

1953. Warner Bros. Directed by Charles M. (Chuck) Jones.

Cartoons made at other Hollywood studios often resembled those of Disney, in that they laid out space with continuity editing and used an accelerating gag structure in their narratives. But because cartoons were considered a genre of comic fantasy, they could also play with the medium. In Warner Bros. cartoons particularly, characters often spoke to the audience, or referred to the "bosses," the actual animators and studio executives. The tone of the films was also very different from that of Disney. The action was often faster and more violent. The main characters, like Bugs Bunny and Daffy Duck, were wisecracking cynics rather than endearing figures like Mickey Mouse.

The Warners animators tried many experiments over the years, but perhaps none was so extreme as *Duck Amuck*, now recognized as one of the masterpieces of American animation. Although it was made within the Hollywood system, it almost has the feel of an experimental film, because it explores various techniques of cel animation.

Fig. 10.103

The film seems at first to be a swashbuckler of the sort Daffy Duck had appeared in before (such as *The Scarlet Pumpernickel*, 1950). The credits are written on a scroll fastened to a wooden door with a dagger, and Daffy appears at the beginning as a dueling musketeer. But almost immediately he moves to the left and passes the edge of the painted background, which tapers off into white blankness (Fig. 10.103). Daffy is baffled and calls for scenery, then exits. A giant animated brush appears from offscreen and paints in a barnyard. When Daffy enters, still in musketeer costume, he is annoyed, but changes into a farmer's outfit. Such quick switches continue throughout the film, with the paintbrush and a pencil eraser adding and removing scenery, costumes, props, even Daffy himself, with dizzying frequency and illogic. At various times the sound cuts out, or the film seems to slip in the projector, so that we see the frameline in the middle of the screen, with Daffy's feet at the top and his head at the bottom.

All these tricks result in a strange narrative. Daffy repeatedly tries to *start* a narrative, and the unseen animator constantly thwarts those attempts. As a result, the film's principles of narrative progression are unusual ones. First, it gradually becomes apparent to us that the film is exploring various conventions and techniques of animation: painted backgrounds, sound effects, framing, music, and so on. Second, as in *Clock Cleaners*, the action accelerates, with the outrages perpetrated against Daffy becoming gradually worse, and his rage mounting in response to each new frustration.

Third, a mystery quickly surfaces, as we and Daffy both wonder who this perverse animator is and why he is tormenting Daffy. All three patterns culminate at the end, as the animator blasts Daffy with a bomb, then closes a door in his face as a cut moves us into a new space—the animation desk itself, where it is revealed that Bugs Bunny has been the "animator" playing all the tricks on Daffy. He grins at the audience: "Ain't I a stinker?" As in *Clock Cleaners*, the narrative

Fig. 10.104

Fig. 10.105

in *Duck Amuck* depends to a considerable extent on our already knowing the character traits of the two stars. Bugs and Daffy often costarred in other Jones cartoons, and invariably the calm, ruthless Bugs would get the better of the manic Daffy.

The style of *Duck Amuck* is just as unconventional as its narrative form. Because the action moves so quickly, we might fail on first viewing to note that, aside from the credits title and the "That's All, Folks!" logo, the film has only four shots—three of which come in quick succession at the end. The bulk of the cartoon contains no cutting of any sort, let alone the classical continuity editing used in *Clock Cleaners*. Yet the settings and situations change quickly as the paintbrush and pencil transform the onscreen space and Daffy moves in and out of the frame; often he appears against a stark white background (Fig. 10.104). All these techniques combine to create a floating, mutable, indefinable space quite different from the clearly established locales provided by continuity editing in *Clock Cleaners*.

Similarly, the temporal flow becomes warped as Daffy moves into and out of diegetic situations, launching into one narrative line only to find it cut short by the mystery animator. Daffy keeps assuming that he is at the beginning of the cartoon, but time is flowing inexorably by in the "outer" cartoon, *Duck Amuck* itself. At one point more than halfway through, he shouts, "All right! Let's get this picture started!" Immediately a "The End" title appears, but Daffy pushes it aside and tries to take charge: "Ladies and gentlemen, there will be no further delays, so I shall attempt to entertain you in my own inimitable fashion," going into a soft-shoe routine.

In the absence of editing, offscreen space becomes crucial in *Duck Amuck*, since many of the surprising transformations we witness come from outside the frame. Most important, the unknown animator occupies the space from which the camera photographs the scene—with the brush and pencil coming in from "under" the camera. Daffy enters and exits frequently, and the frame often moves to reveal or conceal new portions of the scenery. When the sound cuts out entirely, Daffy asks to get it back (Fig. 10.104), and we then hear a scratchy sound, as if from a phonograph playing offscreen. This unseen phonograph provides inappropriate noises—a machine gun when Daffy strums the guitar, a donkey's bray when he breaks it—in an elaborate joke on lack of fidelity on the sound track. The most spectacular gag involving offscreen space comes when the top of the frame seems to collapse, letting the "offscreen" space drip down onto Daffy like black syrup (Fig. 10.105). For a moment we have the contradictory situation of offscreen space (that is, the space we know *should* be invisible, beyond the frame edges) that we can see onscreen.

These and numerous other inventive moments in *Duck Amuck* set it apart from more conventional Hollywood animated films. Yet it also motivates its play with the medium through its adherence to comedy and its characters (Bugs mistreating Daffy, as usual). It is possible to go even further in exploring the medium of animation, and to depart from narrative altogether, as our final example will show.

## ■ *FUJI*

1974. Made by Robert Breer.

In contrast to smooth classical Hollywood animation, Robert Breer's film looks disjointed and crudely drawn. It begins without a title or credits, with a bell ringing three times over black leader. A cut leads, not to animated footage, but to a shaky, fuzzy shot through a train window, with someone's face and eyeglasses partially visible at the side in the extreme foreground; beyond we glimpse what might be rice paddies moving by. This shot and most of the rest of the film are accompanied by the clacking rhythmic sound of a train. More black leader creates a transition to a very different image: against a white background, two flat shapes, like keystones with rounded corners, alternate frame by frame, one red, the other green. The effect is a rapid flicker as the two colored shapes drift about the frame in a seemingly random pattern. Another stretch of black introduces a brief, fuzzy shot of a man in a dark suit running across the shot in a strange corridor of some sort. More black leader, and then, against a white background, a jagged line moves and changes shape, briefly coming together to form a crude tracing of the running man's movement, then collapsing quickly into an abstract line and reforming into a running man. During this shot, colors shift and change rapidly.

Within this brief series of images, Breer has aroused our curiosity about what kind of film we are watching, and he has also introduced most of the devices that will be varied across the film to create its principles of abstract form. For one thing, the regular clack and hum of the train sets up a rhythm which will govern the rhythm of the movement on the screen. A flicker effect in which images change every one or two frames will recur through much of the film. Even when the same shape remains on the screen for a longer stretch, its color and outline will often jump about every few frames. In *Fuji*, movements on the screen are seldom smooth; shapes jitter in a rough rhythm.

Such attempts to avoid smooth movement and to explore the perceptual possibilities offered by different types of abstract drawings are common in experimental animation. *Fuji* is distinctive, however, because of its juxtaposition of live-action footage and animated images that are obviously traced from the live-action frames. Here Breer is manipulating a technique commonly used in Hollywood cartoons, *rotoscoping*. The **rotoscope** is a machine used to project frames of live-action film, one at a time, onto a drawing board, so that they can be traced by an animator. The original purpose of rotoscoping was not to make the characters in the cartoon look exactly like those in the film, for in fact their appearances are often quite different. Rather, the motion of the animated character from frame to frame is usually smoother and more lifelike if traced from a live model. Disney's animated features, such as *Snow White and the Seven Dwarfs* and *Cinderella*, used extensive rotoscoping for their human characters.

Breer has thus taken a device intended to create smooth motion and used it in quite a different way. For one thing, he often rotoscopes only part of a figure, leaving it against a blank white background instead of tracing it onto a cel and combining it with painted scenery; in other cases he traces the background itself rather than the moving figures, as with the train interior that appears in various colors. He also photographs his rough pencil drawings, rather than tracing them neatly onto cels in ink, as a Hollywood animator would do. By changing the color so often and by moving from image to image so quickly, Breer's animation avoids all sense of smoothness. Most of the flickering images in *Fuji* are two frames long, and here Breer may be playing off the fact that in Hollywood cartoons, each set of cels is actually photographed for two frames in a row, to save time and labor. In the Hollywood films, of course, the movement still appears smooth and continuous on the screen, while Breer creates such noticeable differences between each pair of frames that the effect looks jerky.

Fig. 10.106

Perhaps most daringly, Breer includes bits of the original live-action footage from which he made his tracings—so that we are led to see many of the images in the film *as* tracings. For example, shortly after the opening images described above, we see flickering images that include single frames of blurry live-action footage of the train's interior (Fig. 10.106), alternating with single frames of parts of that same view in crude tracings of the conductor's body (Fig. 10.107). In effect, Breer has taken one of the most "realistic" of animation techniques, the rotoscope, and used it to create a dazzling, abstract exploration of movement and perception in cinema.

Fig. 10.107

The opening section of *Fuji* is based chiefly on shapes derived from train interiors. The second, lengthier section, which forms the remainder of the film, begins with a stylized series of views of a mountain—which, we assume from the title, is Mount Fuji. Again we see shifting colors and shapes, but as before, some of the footage seems to have been traced from live-action frames. The train sound continues, and as sparsely sketched buildings, bridges, poles, and fields move jerkily past in the foreground, we are likely to take this view to be one seen from a moving train (Fig. 10.108).

The mountain footage creates a sense of planes of depth, in that the objects in the middle ground—buildings, fields—pass by, while the distant object, the mountain, remains in the same spot. At times colors or abstract shapes appear for a frame or two, and we are likely to perceive them as being in the extreme foreground, "near the train" and thus visible only as a blurred flash. Yet, even though the mountain remains in the same spot, its simple black outline frequently shifts slightly, and the color changes constantly, with the sky now red, now blue. The smooth sense of motion that rotoscoped footage could create is undermined, and the "stable" mountain actually shimmers. In this way Breer simultaneously suggests realistic depth and flat, abstract shapes in the images.

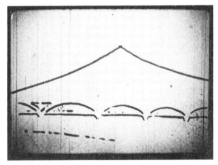

Fig. 10.108

To make this contrast between conventional animation and the abstract techniques of *Fuji* absolutely clear, Breer includes one "ordinary" rotoscoped motion: a paper-cup shape rolling in an arc against a white ground (Fig. 10.109). This shape, drawn with the simplest of perspective cues, is the only object in the film to move with this smoothness. We also, however, see it changing color, or seemingly superimposed over the more abstract, flickering images of the mountain. At other times, the cup shape is seen as just a flat blob of color. (Indeed, the rounded keystone shapes near the beginning are flat, nonperspectival versions of this cup.) At other points, the neat perspective renderings of the cup suddenly twist into skewed trapezoids or fold up into straight lines. Thus even the most conventional of animated movements can collapse in this pulsating, unstable space. With this and dozens of other devices, Breer explores and displays many of the perceptual tricks upon which drawn animation is based.

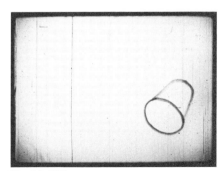

Fig. 10.109

## FORM, STYLE, AND IDEOLOGY

### ◼ *MEET ME IN ST. LOUIS*

> 1944. MGM. Directed by Vincente Minnelli. Script by Irving Brecher and Fred F. Finklehoffe, from the book by Sally Benson. Photographed by George Folsey. Edited by Albert Akst. Music by Hugh Martin and Ralph Blane. With Judy Garland, Margaret O'Brien, Mary Astor, Lucille Bremer, Leon Ames, Tom Drake.

Just over halfway through *Meet Me in St. Louis*, the father, Alonzo Smith, announces to his assembled family that he has been transferred to a new job and that they must move to New York City. "I've got the future to think about—the future for all of us. I've got to worry about where the money's coming from," he tells the dismayed group. These ideas of family and future, central to the form and style of the film, are used to create an ideological stance.

All of the films we have already analyzed could be examined for their ideological standpoints; any film combines formal and stylistic elements in such a way as to create an ideological stance, whether overtly stated or tacit. We have chosen to stress the ideology of *Meet Me in St. Louis* because it provides a clear example of a film that does not seek to change people's ways of thinking; instead, it tends to reinforce certain aspects of a dominant social ideology. In this case *Meet Me in St. Louis*, like most Hollywood films, seeks to uphold values of family unity and home life conceived of as "American."

*Meet Me in St. Louis* is set during the preparations for the Louisiana Purchase Exposition in St. Louis, with the fair itself becoming the culmination of the action. The film displays its form in a straightforward way, with a title card announcing each of its four sections with a different season, beginning with "Summer, 1903." In this way the film simultaneously suggests the passage of time (equated with the spring 1904 fair, which will bring the fruits of progress to St. Louis) and the unchanging cycle of the seasons.

The Smiths, living in a big Victorian house, form a large and closely knit family. The seasonal structure allows the film to show the Smiths at the traditional times of family unity, the holidays; we see them celebrating Halloween and Christmas. At the end, the fair becomes a new sort of holiday, the celebration of the Smiths' decision to remain in St. Louis.

The opening of the film quickly introduces the idea of St. Louis as a city on the boundary between tradition and progress. The fancy "candy-box" title card for Summer forms a vignette of white and red flowers around an old-fashioned black-and-white photo of the Smiths' house. As the camera moves in, color fades into the photo, and it "comes to life." Slow, subdued chords over the title card give way to a bouncy tune more in keeping with the onscreen movement. Horse-drawn beer wagons and carriages move along the road, but an early-model automobile (a bright red, which draws our eye) passes them. Already the motif of progress and inventions becomes prominent; it will develop quickly into the emphasis on the upcoming fair.

The Smiths' son, Lon, arrives home by bicycle; a dissolve inside to the kitchen continues the process of introduction. One by one we meet the family members as they go about their daily activities through the house. The camera follows the second youngest daughter, Agnes, as she goes upstairs singing "Meet Me in St. Louis." She encounters Grandpa, who takes up the song; the camera follows him for a brief time. The passage of the characters from room to room involves several very close matches on action as they pass through doors, yielding a smooth flow of movement that presents the house as full of bustle and music. Grandpa hears voices singing the same song; he moves to a window, and a high-angle shot from over his shoulder shows the second oldest sister, Esther, stepping out of a buggy. Her arrival brings the sequence full circle back to the front of the house.

The house remains the main image of family unity throughout most of the film. In the opening sequence, the family members return home one by one, until they all gather around the dinner table. Every section of the film begins with a similar candy-box title card and a move in toward the house. Aside from the expedition of the young people on the trolley to see the construction of the fair, the Christmas dance, and the final fairground sequence, the entire action of the film takes place in or near the Smith house. Although Mr. Smith's job provides the reason to move to New York, we never see him at his office. In the film's ideology the home appears to be a self-sufficient place; other social institutions become peripheral, even threatening.

This vision of the unified family within an idealized household places the women at the center of importance. The narration does not restrict our knowledge to a single character's range, but it tends to concentrate on what the Smith women know. Mrs. Smith, Rose, Tootie, and in particular Esther are the characters around which the narration is organized. Moreover, women are portrayed as the agents of stability; the action constantly returns to the kitchen, where the mother and maid, Katie, work calmly in the midst of small crises. The men, on the other hand, present the threat to the family's unity. Mr. Smith wants to take them to New York, thereby destroying their links with the past. Lon goes away to "the East," to college at Princeton. Only the grandfather, as representative of the older generation, sides with the women in their desire to stay in St. Louis. In general, the narrative's causality makes any departure from the home a threat—an example of how a narrative's principles of development can generate an ideological stance.

Within the family there are minor disagreements, but the members cooperate among themselves. The two older sisters, Rose and Esther, help each other in their flirtations. Esther is in love with the boy next door, John Truitt; marriage to him poses no threat to the family unity. Several times in the film she sits and watches him or gazes across at his house, without having to leave her own home. First she and Rose go out onto the porch to try to attract his attention; then she sits in the window to sing, "The Boy Next Door." Finally, much later, she sits in a darkened bedroom upstairs and sees John pull his shade just after they have become engaged. The romantic involvements of the older girls and the pranks of the younger pair become part of the pleasant round of small occurrences that make up the everyday life of the Smith family. The idea that girls might want to travel is not considered; similarly, education for the girls is presented as secondary to marriage.

Many stylistic devices build up a picture of a happy family life. The color contributes greatly to the lushness of the mise-en-scene. (See Plates 10 and 11.) The characters wear bright clothes, with Esther often in blue. She and Rose wear red and green, respectively, to the Christmas dance; this strengthens the association of the family unity with holidays and incidentally makes the sisters easy to pick out in the swirling crowd of pastel-clad dancers. (In Plate 11, the shot from the trolley scene, Esther is conspicuous because she is the only woman in black amidst the generally bright-colored dresses; a color need not be brighter than others to stand out.) The film was shot in Technicolor, which in the 1940s could render colors with extreme intensity and brightness. As a result, the hues of the costumes, the wallpaper of the house, Rose and Esther's red hair, and many other visual elements are conspicuous and attractive.

*Meet Me in St. Louis* is a musical, and music plays a large part in the family life. Songs come at moments of romance or at gatherings. Rose and Esther sing "Meet Me in St. Louis" in the parlor before dinner; the father is initially characterized as he returns from work and snaps at them, "For heaven's sake, stop that screeching!" At once we see him as both antimusic and antifair ("I wish everyone would meet at the fair and leave me alone"). Esther's other songs show that her romance with John Truitt is a safe and reasonable one; a woman does not have to leave home to find a husband—she can find him right in her own neighborhood ("The Boy Next Door") or by riding the trolley ("The Trolley Song"). Other songs accompany the two dances. Finally, Esther sings "Have Yourself a Merry Little Christmas" to Tootie, the youngest sister, after the Christmas dance. Here she tries to reassure Tootie that life in New York will be all right if the family can remain together.

But already there is a sense that such unity is in danger: "Someday soon we all will be together, if the Fates allow/Until then we'll have to muddle through somehow." We know already that Esther has achieved her goal and become engaged to John Truitt; if the Smiths do move to New York, she will have to decide between him and her family. By this point, the plot has reached an impasse; whichever way she decides, the old way of life will be destroyed. The narrative needs a resolution, and Tootie's hysterical crying in reaction to the song leads the father to reconsider his decision.

Tootie's destruction of the snow people after Esther's song is a striking image of the threat to family unity posed by the move to New York. As the winter season section opened, the children were building the snow people (and a dog) in the yard. In effect they had created a parallel to their own family, with statues of different sexes and sizes. At first these snow people were part of the comic scene in which Esther and Katie persuade Lon and Rose to go to the Christmas dance together. But when Tootie becomes hysterical at the prospect of leaving St. Louis, she runs down in her nightgown to smash the snow people. The scene is almost shocking, since Tootie seems to be killing the doubles of her own family. This strong moment is necessary because it motivates the father's change of mind; he realizes that his desire to move to New York threatens the family's internal ties. This realization leads to his decision to stay in St. Louis.

Two other elements of the mise-en-scene stand out because they present the comfortable life of the family; these motifs involve food and light. The Smiths live surrounded by food. In the initial scene the women are making ketchup, which is shortly served at the family dinner. After the scene in which Rose's boyfriend fails to propose to her by phone, the tensions are reconciled, and the maid serves large slices of corned beef.

In the Halloween scene the connection between the plentiful food and family unity becomes even more explicit. At first, the children gather around to eat cake and ice cream, but the father arrives home and makes his announcement about moving to New York. The family members depart without eating; only when they hear the mother and father singing at the piano do they gradually drift back to eat their cake. The words of the song, "Time may pass, but we'll be together," accompany their actions. The use of food as a motif associates the family's life in the house with plenty and with gatherings of the individuals into a group. At the fair in the last sequence, they decide to visit a restaurant together; the food motif returns at the moment of their reaffirmation of their life together in St. Louis.

The house is also ablaze with light much of the time. As the family sits together at dinner, the low evening sun sends bright yellow light in through the transparent white curtains behind the father's chair. Later, one of the loveliest scenes involves Esther's request that John accompany her through the downstairs to help her turn out the lights. This action is primarily accomplished in one long take, with the camera moving at ceiling height from room to room with the characters. At each pause, the brightly lit chandelier is framed in the upper portion of the screen (Plate 10). As the rooms darken and the couple moves out to the hall, the camera moves down to a height level with their faces. The shot contains a remarkable shift of tone. It begins with Esther's comically contrived excuse ("I'm afraid of mice") to keep John with her and develops gradually toward a genuinely romantic mood.

The Halloween sequence takes place entirely at night and makes light a central motif; the camera initially moves in toward the house's brightly lit yellow windows. Tense, slightly eerie music makes the house seem an island of safety in the darkness. As Tootie and Agnes go out to join the other children in playing tricks, they are silhouetted blackly against the flames of the bonfire the group has gathered around. At first the fire seems threatening, contradicting the earlier associations of light with safety and unity, but this scene actually fits in with the previous uses of light. Tootie is excluded from the group activities because she is "too little." After she proves herself worthy, she is allowed to help feed the flames along with the others. Note particularly the long track-back as Tootie leaves the fire to play her trick; the fire remains in the background of the shot, appearing as a haven she has left behind. The first sequence of the Halloween section of the film becomes a sort of miniature working out of the entire narrative structure; Tootie's position as a part of the group is abandoned as she moves away from the fire, then triumphantly affirmed as she returns to it.

Similarly, light plays an important part in the resolution of the threat to the family's unity. Late on Christmas Eve, Esther finds Tootie awake. They look out the window at the snow people standing in the yard below. A strip of yellow light falls across the snow from a different window, suggesting the warmth and safety of the house they plan to leave. Tootie's hysterical crying, however, leads the father to reconsider his decision. As he sits thinking, he holds the match, with which he was about to light his cigar, unnoticed in his hand until it burns him; combined with the slow playing of the "Meet Me in St. Louis" theme over, the flame serves to emphasize his abstraction and his gradual change of mind. As he calls his family down to announce his decision not to move, he turns up all the lights; the dim, bleak halls full of packing boxes become again the scene of busy activity as the family gathers. The lamps' glass shades are red and green, identifying the house with the appropriate Christmas colors. The announcement of the decision leads directly to the opening of the presents, as if to emphasize that staying in St. Louis will not create any financial hardship for the family.

As night falls in the final fair sequence, the many lights of the buildings come on, reflected in lakes and canals. Here the film ends, with the family gazing in awe at the view. Once more light signifies safety and family enjoyment. These lights also bring the other motifs of the film together. The father had originally wanted to move to New York as a provision for his family's future. In deciding to stay in St. Louis, he had told them, "New York hasn't got a copyright on opportunity. Why, St. Louis is headed for a boom that'll make your head swim. This is a great town." The fair confirms this; St. Louis allows the family to retain its unity and safety, and yet have all the benefits of progress. The film ends with the following comments by the characters:

Mother: There's never been anything like it in the whole world.
Rose: We don't have to come here in a train or stay in a hotel. It's right in our own home town.
Tootie: Grandpa, they'll never tear it down, will they?
Grandpa: Well, they'd better not.
Esther: I can't believe it. Right here where we live. Right here in St. Louis.

These lines do not *create* the film's ideology, which has been present in the narrative and stylistic devices throughout. The dialogue simply makes explicit what has been implicit all along.

The fair solves the problems of the future and family unity. The family is able to go to a *French* restaurant without going away from home. The ending also restores the father's position as at least the titular head of the family; only he is able to remember how to get to the restaurant and prepares to guide the group there.

Understanding a film's ideology typically involves analyzing how form and style create meaning. As Chapter 2 suggested, meaning can be of four general types: referential, explicit, implicit, and symptomatic. Our analysis of *Meet Me in St. Louis* has shown how all four types work to reinforce a social ideology—in this case, the values of tradition, home life, and family unity. The referential aspects of the film presuppose that the audience can grasp the difference between St. Louis and New York and that it knows about international expositions, American family customs, national holidays, and so on. These address the film to a specifically American audience. The explicit meaning of the film is formulated by the final exchange we have just considered, in which the small town is discussed as the perfect fusion of progress and tradition. We have also traced out how formal construction and stylistic motifs contribute to one major implicit meaning: the family and home as creating a "haven in a heartless world," the central reference point for the individual's life. What, then, of symptomatic meanings?

Speaking generally, the film expresses one tendency of many social ideologies in its attempt to "naturalize" social and cultural behavior. Chapter 2 mentioned that systems of value and belief may seem unquestionable to the social groups that hold them. One way that groups maintain such systems is to assume that certain things are beyond human choice or control, that they are simply natural. Historically, this habit of thought has often been used to justify oppression and injustice, as when minority groups or the poor or women are thought to be "naturally inferior." *Meet Me in St. Louis* participates in this general tendency, not only in its characterization of the Smith women (Esther and Rose are simply presumed to want husbands) but in the very choice of a white, upper-middle-class household as an emblem of American life. A more subtle naturalization is evident in the film's overall formal organization: the natural cycle of the seasons is harmonized with the family's life, and the conclusion of the plot takes place in spring, the period of renewal.

We can also focus on more historically specific symptomatic meanings. The film was released during 1944, late in World War II. The audience for this film would have consisted largely of women and children whose adult male relatives had been absent for extended periods, often overseas. It was also a time of rationing. Families were often forced apart, and the people who remained behind had to make considerable sacrifices for the war effort. At a period when many women had been required to work in defense plants, factories, and offices (and many were enjoying the experience), there appears a film which restricts the range of women's experiences to home and family, and yearns for a simpler time when family unity was prized. *Meet Me in St. Louis* can thus be seen as a symptom of a nostalgia for 1903 America; parents of young fighting men in a 1944 audience would remember this as the period of their own childhoods. The film suggests an ideal of family unity for the postwar future. The fact that the film was released around Thanksgiving would only have made its effect more poignant.

For the 1944 audience, the implication of all of these formal devices—seasons, motifs, songs, color, and the rest—is a reassuring one. If the women and others left at home can be strong and hold their families together against threats of disunity, harmony will eventually return. By setting forth this ideology at a time when so many people had been forced to leave home, *Meet Me in St. Louis* upholds dominant views instead of challenging them.

## ■ *TOUT VA BIEN*

> 1972. Coproduction of Anouchka Films, Vicco Films (France), and Empire Films (Italy). Directed by Jean-Luc Godard and Jean-Pierre Gorin. Script by Godard and Gorin. Photographed by Armand Marco. Edited by Kennout Peltier and Claudine Merlin. With Yves Montand, Jane Fonda, Yves Caprioi, Elizabeth Chauvin, Castel Costi, Anne Wiazemsky.

*Tout va bien* (which can be translated "Everything's just great") strongly criticizes certain features of the state of French society in 1972. It takes as its subject matter the repercussions of events four years before, around May 1968, a period of intense leftist activity among students and workers in France. The agitation had begun in March with university students protesting American involvement in Vietnam, as well as various university policies. Violent protests escalated in May, with workers' and teachers' unions supporting the students; a series of strikes, sit-ins, and demonstrations resulted. When a new general election was promised, many strikers went back to work, although pockets of resistance remained. In June, a student named Gilles Tautin was killed in a skirmish with police, and *Tout va bien* refers specifically to this event. Eventually, in late June, De Gaulle's party was reelected.

The events of May 1968 had lingering effects on leftist politics and the arts in France. Many artists, including Godard, became more radical. Before 1968 he had made films with leftist subjects, like *La Chinoise, Weekend,* and *Le Gai Savoir.* But he had always worked in a fairly conventional commercial production system. In 1968 many groups were trying to create alternative production systems, primarily cooperatives. Godard and his colleague, Jean-Pierre Gorin, formed a small cooperative, the Dziga-Vertov Group. (The group was named after the director of *The Man with a Movie Camera.* Political events in 1968 France had led to a renewed interest in the works of the Soviet filmmakers.) They made a number of films between 1968 and 1971, often short works shot on 16 mm, without stars or narratives. While these films were formally and politically interesting, they failed to reach a wide audience. By going outside the commercial production system, the Dziga-Vertov Group was also cut off from distribution, except on a small scale to film societies, student and worker groups, and other interested audiences. *Tout va bien* was a return to the conventions of commercial narrative filmmaking, but it also examines the political contradictions of leftists having to work within the very economic system that they are trying to change.

For this examination, Godard and Gorin took as their model one of the major Marxist artists of our century, the playwright Bertold Brecht. Brecht, too, had worked within the commercial theater and cinema in Germany and Hollywood, and he had written extensively on this subject. In fact, one of the main characters in *Tout va bien*, Jacques, refers at one point to Brecht's preface to his play, *The Rise and Fall of the City of Mahagonny*. There Brecht argues that each art form is controlled, not by the artists, but by larger social institutions. In a capitalist society, an artist may believe he or she is using the art form for personal expression, but he or she is actually producing artistic merchandise of a kind acceptable to the society. According to Brecht, there is no way to work outside this socially controlled art form, yet one can chip away at it from within, by introducing innovations into one's works. Brecht's own approach, he said, was accomplished through the "radical separation of the elements"; the words, music, and staging of his opera *Mahagonny* were not fused into a unified whole but kept rough and disunified—separate—to prevent the audience from being wholly absorbed in the illusionary aspects of the action. The audience would still be presented a story and characters but would simultaneously be aware of how the work's formal system was put together.

This approach suited Godard and Gorin's purposes because of its differences from that of the classical Hollywood cinema. There all the elements function in such a unified way to support the narration of story events that the audience is not encouraged to analyze *how* the film's form works. *Tout va bien* leads us to analyze both the political subject matter and the conventions of narrative filmmaking.

Because this approach is so different from the conventions of the films most of us are used to watching, we may have little in our filmgoing experience to prepare us to understand the form of *Tout va bien*. At first it may be difficult to watch and enjoy. (This is true of other Godard films as well, whether made with the Dziga-Vertov Group or not.) Part of the difficulty arises from our own assumptions that standard viewing habits constitute the *only* way to watch films. Thus an understanding and enjoyment of *Tout va bien* involves a willingness on the part of the spectator to learn and practice new viewing skills. These new viewing skills may lead to a new understanding of the film's ideological purpose as well.

Like Brecht in his operas, Godard and Gorin use principles of separation to create the overall form of *Tout va bien*. We can find three such principles at work in the film's form and style: *interruption*, *contradiction*, and *refraction*. These guide the stylistic devices as well as the overall formal organization. Let us look first at these principles of separation on a local level.

In a classical film, the cause-effect chain of narrative smoothly links scene to scene, and each event is thoroughly motivated. An interruption in the cause-effect series might confuse us as to how one event relates to others. Yet this is exactly how *Tout va bien* treats many scenes from the very beginning. We hear a man's and woman's voices talking about making a film, and a hand writes checks to cover the expenses of the film (as for an "international star" in Fig. 10.110). But credit titles with the stars' names (Fig. 10.111) and shots from the proposed film interrupt this check writing. Thus we see the preparation for the film and bits of the film itself at the same time, and the temporal relationships of the various shots are unclear. In a later scene during a strike in a meat factory, a female worker explains to the reporter, Susan, what special problems women face in their jobs (Fig. 10.112). This situation is interrupted twice by cuts to a shot of another woman facing the camera, reciting a radical song (Fig. 10.113). These two actions are not matched at the cut. They are not different stages of one scene, but alternative actions that interrupt and comment upon each other: in one line of action one worker speaks with quiet pathos, while in the other a second is strong and defiant.

These interruptions are important to the ideological meanings of *Tout va bien*. At another point, Susan tells her lover, Jacques, that she is no longer satisfied with

**Fig. 10.110**

**Fig. 10.111**

their relationship; they know only each other's personal lives but need to understand each other's work as well. This close connection between work and private life is one of the main explicit meanings in *Tout va bien*. As Susan speaks, the scene is interrupted by shots of each of them at work, emphasizing her point. There are many similar moments in the film, and in most cases they function, as in these examples, to undercut the narrative causality and to introduce ideological arguments. In this way, *Tout va bien* combines narrative and rhetorical form in almost equal doses.

Fig. 10.112

A second, related principle of separation of formal and stylistic elements is *contradiction*. One of *Tout va bien*'s most salient stylistic devices is discontinuity editing, and strongly discontinuous cuts create many small-scale spatial and temporal contradictions. In the classical Hollywood film, discontinuities are undesirable because they distract from a unified narrative. But because *Tout va bien* uses "impossible" matches and juxtapositions we, as viewers, must adjust our expectations and actively notice the construction of time and space. The film contains many mismatches: Susan sits down twice at the beginning of her conversation with Jacques (a temporal overlap); during the interview with the factory manager, he is pacing, then suddenly seated, then suddenly pacing again in three successive shots; at one point the manager breaks the window in order to urinate, but it is not broken two shots later. Such frequent small surprises keep us alert to the film's editing style.

Fig. 10.113

Other contradictions involve sound-image relationships. At one point Susan is sitting in the manager's office as a conversation seems to go on offscreen between Jacques and the manager (Fig. 10.114). Soon we hear her voice joining in the conversation, even though her lips are not moving. Is this a case of nonsimultaneous sound—a flashback? We never find out. In other scenes, groups of workers cluster around as one of them speaks, and we cannot pick out the source of the sound. Through both the editing and sound contradictions, we are forced to pay attention to style as well as subject matter. *Tout va bien* and other Godard films thus encourage very active viewing on the part of the spectator. We must analyze the film as we see it, or we will fail to understand and enjoy it.

Fig. 10.114

This emphasis on an active viewer carries through in the third principle of separation as well: *refraction*. By this we mean that *Tout va bien* draws our attention to media that stand between the depicted events and our perception of those events. We do not seem to see a series of "natural" events, as we might in a Hollywood-style film. Rather, *Tout va bien* takes the media as part of its topic and leads us to consider how these media function within society.

The jobs of two central characters explicitly represent the split between word and image. Susan is a radio reporter and broadcaster, while Jacques is a filmmaker forced to make commercials for a living. As we see them doing their work, the scenes underscore the point that the media manipulate the images and sounds we see. In the scene at Jacques's studio, there is a lengthy shot through a camera viewfinder of dancing women's legs, and we see technicians arranging the framing, the focus, the camera distance, and the mise-en-scene. A parallel shot occurs as Susan attempts to tape record an editorial; as she falters and has to go back, the recordist rewinds the tape with a garbled, speeded-up sound of her voice. These two scenes are crucial, for they display for us the same kinds of manipulations which *Tout va bien* itself uses throughout, and which it constantly calls to our attention.

Refraction also occurs in scenes that do not take the media as their explicit subject. When Susan interviews the woman worker, we hear neither of their voices;

rather, the scene is narrated in voice-over by one of the other women present (we do not learn which). When the workers' strike ends, we learn the news from a broadcaster's voice over an exterior shot of the factory. In such ways, Godard and Gorin emphasize the arbitrariness of their film's narration: it has the potential to be omniscient, since it can use voices and images from anywhere, yet it is also arbitrarily selective, even capricious, about what it tells us.

One final type of refraction comes from the film's concentration on production. Factory production is important in the narrative, and it is compared to filmmaking. Jacques is a film director within the narrative, but *Tout va bien* goes further and places its narrative within a framing device at beginning and end. The two voices that discuss how to go about making a film mention many of the formal conventions we take for granted in classical filmmaking: the necessity for romance, for conflict, for an ending, and so on. On the screen we see more than one version of the events described. When romance is mentioned, two separate takes show Susan and Jacques walking by a river, with the same action repeated slightly differently. Similarly, at the end we see two possible versions of the couple's meeting at a café: first he waits for her, then she for him.

These three principles of separation—interruption, contradiction, and refraction—are so pervasive in *Tout va bien* that we simply cannot watch it by applying conventions of ordinary film viewing. Some might simply give up and dismiss the film as "obscure." But if we accept the film's own terms and seek to find the principles of its form, we will of necessity rethink our view of traditional cinematic conventions.

These same principles of separation underlie the film's overall form as well. *Tout va bien* falls into five major parts, each of which contains a number of related segments:

1. The discussion of making the film, with hypothetical shots. (Everything before the first establishing shot of the factory exterior.)
2. The strike at the factory. (Ends with the radio announcement that the strike is over.)
3. Interview with Jacques and Susan at work; their argument about personal life and work. (Ends as she threatens to leave him.)
4. Rethinking of their positions. (Marked off by titles "Today 1–3"; ends with the long tracking shot in the department store.)
5. Discussion of how to end the film; song.

These five sections of the film are clearly marked off from each other; there is no dialogue hook or other smooth transition to show us immediately how each new section relates to the previous one. Again, we must take a more active role than usual in order to grasp the film's form.

We have seen that the beginning and ending place the narrative in a framing situation where two unseen people discuss how conventional films are financed and created. When the man says he wants to make a film, the woman tells him he needs money, and that means using stars. And, she says, "An actor won't accept a part without a story line . . . usually a love story." This points up the fact that in our society, narrative form is pervasive in theatrical films, and that this usually requires the sort of emphasis on personal and psychological causation typical of Hollywood cinema.

This scene also mentions genre expectations—"usually a love story." Thus when the stars—Yves Montand and Jane Fonda—appear, we may expect the conventions of a romance. Yet *Tout va bien* carries on its principles of separation by mixing its genre conventions. We do get some of the elements of a popular romance, as when we first see Fonda introduced in a studio, lit with glamorous three-point lighting (Fig. 10.115). Yet, in some scenes, Fonda's and Montand's characters are not treated as the center of the story. Many shots in the factory place them inconspicuously as part of a group, and much of the dialogue is spoken by the factory workers.

Fig. 10.115

Moreover, some of the stylistic devices Godard and Gorin employ are traditionally associated with documentary filmmaking rather than narrative romances. We are used to the interview format from documentary films, and in *Tout va bien* there are several long interviews where the characters face into the camera and seem to respond to questions from an offscreen interrogator. (Again, we never learn who this might be.) The union shop steward and factory manager both speak in very long takes, while the workers also speak but in series of shots edited together in discontinuous fashion. Later Susan and Jacques both describe their work to an unidentified questioner. (In none of these "interviews" do we ever hear any of the questions, but the characters seem to listen and respond.)

Fig. 10.116

The conventions of the documentary are constantly undercut, just as those of the romance are. The exterior shots of the factory show a real location, yet the area inside is highly stylized, with the side of the set cut away like a dollhouse (Fig. 10.116). In the interviews, the actors use a wide range of different acting styles; the manager uses broad, comic gestures to create a caricatural portrayal (Fig. 10.117), while Fonda and Montand speak in a quiet, naturalistic way. When we do see documentary-style shots of the factory's operations, we cannot take them as real because we see Jane Fonda and Yves Montand among the workers (Fig. 10.118); because they are stars, our attention is drawn to the staged nature of the scene.

Fig. 10.117

In these ways, conventions from one genre interrupt those of another. The disparity between the romance on the one hand and the realism of the documentary mode create a contradiction that weaves through the whole film. And the emphasis on *Tout va bien* as a "film about cinema" makes refraction an overriding principle as well.

Fig. 10.118

The film's pattern of development helps to give an overall unity to a set of elements which are very disunified on the local level. In Parts 1 and 5, the voices reflect on what it means to make a film in the modern French industry. In Part 2, two people who work in the French media are confronted with a radical group carrying on a strike in a factory, which leads them to reflect on how their own lives have become ideologically compromised. While both had been active in the political events of May 1968, they have since gotten into jobs that support the established media institutions of the country. They quarrel over this, but by the end seem to be working on solving their problems. As the woman's voice says in Part 5, "We'll simply say that He and She have begun to rethink themselves in historical terms." Thus the film avoids a completely closed ending but suggests a direction for progressive political action on a personal level.

As a result of the principles of separation we have discussed, rethinking becomes not just the film's subject matter but also a necessary process in watching *Tout va bien*. The narrative line involves the characters rethinking their lives. But, by framing this narrative within a discussion of filmmaking, the film implicitly reflects Godard and Gorin's own rethinking of their roles as filmmakers—how they can use narrative conventions and criticize them at the same time. And beyond even this, the spectator must rethink the process of watching a film. Thus in making a film with an ideological stance opposed to the contemporary social system of France, the filmmakers do not simply set forth a radical subject matter. They create a radical formal system for their film, one which might suggest not only new *things* to think about but new *ways* of thinking about them.

# APPENDIX:
# WRITING A CRITICAL ANALYSIS OF A FILM

The analyses in this chapter all exemplify a sort of writing characteristic of film criticism. It may be useful for us to conclude this part of the book by discussing some general choices and strategies open to the reader who wishes to write a film analysis for a course assignment, a published article, or some related purpose. This appendix does not seek to replace a good composition manual; we want simply to suggest some particular issues that come up in doing film analysis.

## ■ PREPARATION

As with any sort of writing, a film analysis requires that work be done before you sit down to write the piece. First, what sort of writing will the finished product be? Broadly speaking, your analysis will probably be some sort of *argumentative* essay. You will seek to present your opinion about the film and to back that opinion up with an argument. For instance, our analysis of *Stagecoach* (pp. 305–309) argues that Bazin was right to regard it as an example of tightly organized Hollywood classicism. Your planning of the essay will involve shaping your ideas and evidence into a rhetorical form.

Deciding on the film to be analyzed is probably not a great problem. Perhaps something about it attracted you, or you have heard that it is worth examining closely. More difficult is the process of thinking through in some detail what you want to say about the film. What do you find most intriguing or disturbing about the film? What makes the film noteworthy? Does it illustrate some aspect of filmmaking with special clarity? Does it have an unusual effect on the viewer? Do its implicit or symptomatic meanings seem to have particular importance?

Your answer to such questions will furnish the *thesis* of your analysis. The thesis, as in any piece of writing, is the central claim your argument advances. In our analysis of *His Girl Friday,* the thesis is that the film uses classical narrative devices to create an impression of rapid speed. In our discussion of *Man with a Movie Camera,* the thesis is that the film makes the viewer aware of how cinema manipulates the world we see on film.

Typically, your thesis will be a claim about the film's *functions,* its *effects,* or its *meanings* (or some mixture of all three aspects). For instance, we argue that the multiple protagonists in *Hannah and Her Sisters* allow Woody Allen to compare the characters' psychological development while keeping the film largely within the conventions of classical Hollywood cinema. In our discussion of *North by Northwest,* we concentrate more on how the film achieves the effects of suspense and surprise. The analysis of *Meet Me in St. Louis* emphasizes how technique carries implicit and symptomatic meanings.

The chemist who analyzes a compound breaks it into constituent elements. The orchestra conductor who analyzes a score takes it apart mentally in order to see how the melodies and motifs are organized. All analysis implies breaking something down into its component parts. Your thesis will be a general claim about the functions, effects, or meanings of the film. Your analysis will show how these arise from the interaction of the parts that make up the film's formal and stylistic systems.

In most cases, your argument will benefit if you begin with considerable preparatory work before actually beginning to write your piece. You can, as we suggest throughout Part II, make a segmentation of the film. Sometimes you will find it necessary for your argument to show your reader a scene-by-scene segmentation, as we do in the *His Girl Friday* discussion (p. 302). For other purposes, it may suffice only to show a more general breakdown into larger-scale sections, as we do in examining *Stagecoach* (p. 306) and *Innocence Unprotected* (p. 334). In still other cases, you may find it necessary to bring out a still finer-grained segmentation; we do this in considering the three subsegments of the final chase scene in *North by Northwest* (pp. 313–314). However much of your segmentation finally surfaces in your written analysis, we strongly recommend making a fairly detailed segmentation every time you examine a film. It will make the overall form clearer to you and thus enable you to spot the patterns of repetition, variation, and development that unify the film.

In examining a narrative film, it is usually a good idea to start by identifying the various causes and effects, the characters' goals, the principles of development, the degree of closure at the end, and other basic components of narrative form. In examining a nonnarrative film, you will need to be especially alert to its use of categorical, rhetorical, abstract, or associational principles. You probably noticed that nearly every one of our analyses includes, early on, a statement about the film's underlying formal organization. This provides a firm basis for more detailed analysis.

Another part of preparatory note taking involves jotting down accurate descriptions of various film techniques that are used. Here we can simply remind you of the suggestions for analyzing style that we set out in Chapter 9 (pp. 276–278). Once you have determined the overall organizational structure of the film, you can identify salient techniques, trace out patterns of techniques across the whole film, and propose functions for those techniques. The critic must not only be able to identify the techniques in isolation (Is this a case of three-point lighting? Is this a continuity cut?) but also be sensitive to context (What is the function of the technique *here*?) and to patterning (Does the technique repeat or develop across the film?).

Often beginning film analysts are uncertain as to what techniques are most relevant to their thesis. Sometimes they try to describe every single cut or pan or costume, and they wind up drowned in data. It is most fruitful to think in advance about what techniques stand out as most pertinent to the thesis that you want to prove. For example, the use of optical POV shots and crosscutting in *North by Northwest* is highly relevant to our general claim that Hitchcock achieves suspense and surprise by shifting from a restricted to an unrestricted range of knowledge. The color of the costumes, while relevant to some other thesis about the film, is not relevant to this one. Similarly, the editing in *Meet Me in St. Louis* would be interesting from the standpoint of another argument, but it is not central to the one that we are making, so it goes unmentioned.

Once you have a thesis, an awareness of the overall shape of the film, and a set of notes on the techniques relevant to your thesis, you are ready to plan the organization of your critical analysis.

## ■ ORGANIZATION AND WRITING

Broadly speaking, most argumentative writing has this underlying structure:

Introduction: Background
*Statement of thesis*

Body: Reasons to believe the thesis
Evidence and examples that support the thesis

Conclusion: Restatement of thesis and discussion of its broader implications

You will notice that all of our analyses in this part of the book adhere to this basic structure. The opening portion seeks to lead the reader into the argument to come, and the thesis is introduced at the end of this introduction. Where the introduction is brief, as in the *His Girl Friday* analysis, the thesis comes at the end of the first paragraph (p. 302). Where more background material is needed, the introduction is somewhat longer and the thesis is stated a little later. Examples are the *High School* essay, with the thesis coming at the end of the third paragraph (p. 337), and the *Tout va bien* analysis, with the thesis stated in part at the end of the fourth paragraph and modified at the end of the fifth (p. 360).

These last remarks depend on a principle which you already know but which no writer can ever afford to forget: the building block of any piece of writing is the paragraph. Each slot in the argumentative pattern outlined above will be filled by one or more paragraphs. The introduction is at least one paragraph, the body will be several paragraphs, and the conclusion will be one or two paragraphs.

Typically, the introductory paragraphs of a film analysis consist of little concrete evidence; this is a good place to introduce your reader to the general point you want to make. However, if you are adventurous, you may wish to start with a concrete piece of evidence—an intriguing scene or detail from the film—before you move quickly to state your thesis. (Our *Meet Me in St. Louis* piece uses this sort of opening.)

Writing a film analysis poses one particular problem of organization. Should the body of the argument follow the film's progress in chronological order, so that each paragraph deals with a scene or major part? In some cases this can work. We try it with our *Stagecoach* analysis, which traces out the symmetries that arise from the journey. By and large, however, you strengthen your argument by following a more conceptual structure of the sort indicated in our outline.

It is useful to think of the body of your essay as consisting of a series of *reasons* to believe the thesis, with those reasons buttressed by evidence and examples. An example is our analysis of *Day of Wrath*, which contends that ambiguity about Anne's causal powers is central to the film's effect. The first two paragraphs of the essay's body (p. 321) seek to show that Anne and Herlofs Marthe are paralleled. The next eight paragraphs seek to establish:

1. That Herlofs Marthe may be a witch (pp. 321–322)
2. That Anne may herself be a witch (p. 322)
3. That lighting evokes ambiguity around Anne (p. 322)
4. That her costumes reinforce this (p. 322)
5. That Anne's behavior also conveys this uncertainty (p. 322)
6. That the film's final scene refuses to settle the question of whether Anne is indeed a witch (pp. 322–323)

Each of these points constitutes a reason to accept the thesis.

The reasons may be of many sorts. Several of our analyses distinguish between reasons based upon the film's overall narrative form and reasons based upon stylistic choices. In our *Tout va bien* analysis we propose three types of separation (pp. 360–364), each of which supports the general claim about the importance of "separation of elements" in the film's organization. The essay on *Last Year at Marienbad* distinguishes aspects of space, time, and narrative causality before going on to discuss scenes in which all three combine to create uncertainty. In discussing *Meet Me in St. Louis*, we concentrate more on reviewing various motifs that create particular thematic effects. Here, as usual, preparation can save you time in the long run: as you start to formulate your thesis, it is a good idea to make a list of reasons that, suitably arranged, can form the body of your argument.

If you organize the essay conceptually rather than as a blow-by-blow résumé of the action, you may find it useful to acquaint your reader with the plot action at some point. A brief synopsis soon after the introduction may do the trick. (See, for example, our *North by Northwest* analysis, p. 310.) Alternatively, you may wish to cover basic plot material when you discuss segmentation, characterization, causal progression, or other topics. The crucial point is that the writer is not forced to follow the film's order. You can make the film subordinate to your argument about it.

Typically, each reason for the thesis becomes the topic sentence of a paragraph, with more detailed evidence displayed in the sentences that follow. In the *Day of Wrath* example, each main point is followed by specific examples of how lighting, or costume, or facial expression, or camera movement creates motifs that suggest an ambiguity about Anne's supernatural powers. It is here that the writer's detailed notes about salient scenes or film techniques will be useful. The writer can select the strongest and most vivid instances of mise-en-scene, cinematography, editing, and sound to back up the reason that the paragraph develops.

The body of the analysis can be made more persuasive by several other tactics. A paragraph that compares or contrasts this film with another can help you zero in on specific aspects that are central to your argument. (See, for example, our contrast between *Man with a Movie Camera* and *High School*, or the discussion of the three animated films.) You can also include a brief in-depth analysis of a single scene or sequence that drives your argumentative point home. We use this tactic in discussing the "Souvenirs of Youth" segment of *Innocence Unprotected* (pp. 335–336). As many of our analyses suggest, a close analysis of the film's ending can be a strong way to end the body of your analysis.

In general, the body of the argument should progress toward stronger or subtler reasons for believing the thesis. In discussing *High School*, we suggest that the filmmaker uses formal and stylistic choices to guide our response. Only then do we raise the question as to whether the film may still be considered somewhat ambiguous. This leads us to consider how the filmmaker's choices can be interpreted in different ways. This is a fairly complex point that would probably not come across if introduced early on. Only after the analysis has worked through more clear-cut matters is it possible to consider nuances of interpretation.

As for the ending: this is the occasion to restate the thesis (skillfully, not repeating previous statements word for word) and to remind the reader of the reasons to entertain the thesis. The ending is also an opportunity for you to try for a bit of eloquence, a telling quotation, a bit of historical context, or a concrete motif from the film itself. Again, in making preparatory notes it is wise to look for something that can create a vivid ending.

Just as there is no general recipe for understanding films or interpreting them, there is no formula for writing incisive and enlightening criticism. But there are basic principles and rules of thumb that govern good writing of all sorts. Only through writing, and constant rewriting, do those principles and rules come to seem second nature to the writer. By analyzing films, we come to a better understanding of the sources of our pleasure in them, and we are able to share that understanding with others. If we succeed, the writing itself can give pleasure to ourselves and our readers.

## NOTES AND QUERIES

### ■ SPECIMENS OF FILM ANALYSIS

Many of the critical studies we have cited in the Notes and Queries to Parts II and III repay attention as instances of film analysis. Here are some others that exemplify diverse approaches: David Bordwell, *The Films of Carl-Theodor Dreyer* (Berkeley: University of California Press, 1981); Noël Burch, "Fritz Lang: German Period," in Richard Roud, ed., *Cinema: A Critical Dictionary*, vol. 2 (New York: Viking, 1980), pp. 583–599 (on Fritz Lang's *M*); Noël Carroll, "Identity and Difference: From Ritual Symbolism to Condensation in *Inauguration of the Pleasure Dome*," *Millennium Film Journal* **6** (Spring 1980): 31–42; Mary Ann Doane, "*Gilda*: Striptease as Epistemology," *Camera Obscura* **11** (Fall 1983): 7–27; Philip Drummond, "Textual Space in *Un Chien andalou*," *Screen* **18**, 3 (Autumn 1977): 55–119; *Enclitic*, special number on textual analysis of film, **5**, 2, and **6**, 1 (Fall 1981 and Spring 1982); Lucy Fischer and Marcia Landy, " 'The Eyes of Laura Mars'— A Binocular Critique," *Screen* **23**, 3–4 (September–October 1982): 4–19; Annette Kuhn, "The Camera I—Observations on Documentary," *Screen* **19**, 2 (Summer 1978): 61–83; Thierry Kuntzel, "The Film-Work, 2," *Camera Obscura* **5** (1980): 7–68; Vlada Petrić, "Two Lincoln Assassinations by D. W. Griffith," *Quarterly Review of Film Studies* **3**, 3 (Summer 1978): 345–369; Philip Rosen, "Difference and Displacement in *Seventh Heaven*," *Screen* **18**, 2 (Summer 1977): 89–104; Bill Simon, " 'Reading' *Zorns Lemma*," *Millennium Film Journal* **1**, 2 (Spring–Summer 1978): 38–49; P. Adams Sitney, "The Rhetoric of Robert Bresson," in Sitney, ed., *The Essential Cinema* (New York: New York University Press, 1975), pp. 182–207; and Kristin Thompson, *Breaking the Glass Armor: Neoformalist Film Analysis* (Princeton, N.J.: Princeton University Press, 1988).

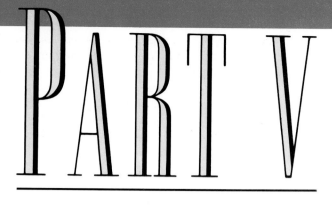

# FILM HISTORY

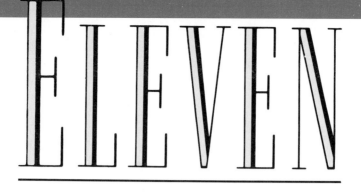

# FILM FORM
# AND
# FILM HISTORY

"Not everything is possible at all times." This aphorism of art historian Heinrich Wölfflin might serve as a slogan for the final chapter of this book. So far, our survey of film art has examined various formal and stylistic possibilities, and we have drawn our examples from the entire range of film history. But film forms and techniques do not exist in a realm outside human history. In particular historical circumstances, certain possiblities will be present while others are not. Griffith could not make films as Godard does, nor could Godard make films as Griffith did. This chapter asks: What are some ways in which film art has been treated in some particular historical contexts?

These contexts will be defined, first, by period and by nation. Although there are other equally good tools for tracing change, period and nation are standard ways of organizing historical problems. Second, in most of our cases, we shall look for what are typically called *film movements*. A film movement consists of:

1.  Films that are produced within a particular period and/or nation and that share significant traits of style and form.
2.  Filmmakers who operate within a common production structure and who share certain assumptions about filmmaking

There are other ways of defining a historical context (for example, biographical study, genre study), but the category of *movement* corresponds most closely to the emphasis of this book. The concepts of formal and stylistic systems permit us to compare films within a movement and to contrast them with films of other movements. Consequently, what follows seeks to identify and distinguish film movements by period and nation. Finally, we shall be concerned with Hollywood and selected alternatives. We shall trace the development of the commercial narrative cinema while contrasting to it other approaches to style and form.

Since a film movement consists of not only film but also the activities of specific filmmakers, we must go beyond noting stylistic and formal qualities. For each period and nation, we shall also sketch relevant factors that impinge on the cinema. These factors include the state of the film industry, artistic theories held by the filmmakers themselves, pertinent technological features, and elements of the socioeconomic context of the period. Such factors necessarily help explain how a particular movement began, what shaped its development, and what affected its decline. However brief, such material will also provide a context for particular films we have already discussed; for example, the following section on early cinema situates Lumière and Méliès in the work of their period.

Needless to say, what follows is drastically incomplete. The writing of serious film history is in its early stages, and we must often rely on secondary sources that will eventually be superseded. This chapter reflects only current states of knowledge; there are doubtless important films, filmmakers, and movements that await discovery. (A list of further readings may be found at the end of this chapter.) Moreover, there are many unfortunate omissions. Important filmmakers who do not relate to a movement (for example, Tati, Bresson, Kurosawa) are absent, as are certain important film movements (for example, French populist cinema of the 1930s, recent "structuralist" and underground cinema, and the materialist cinema of Godard, Straub, and Oshima). What follows simply seeks to show how the categories of film form and style could be applied to a few typical and well-known historical movements.

## EARLY CINEMA (1893–1903)

Because moving images depend on individual still pictures' appearing in rapid succession, the invention of films was not possible until certain technological developments had occurred. The invention of photography in 1826 began a series of discoveries that gradually made possible the creation of an illusion of movement. Early photographs required lengthy exposures (initially hours, later minutes) for a single image; this made photographed motion pictures, which need 12 or more frames per second, impossible. Faster exposures, of about $\frac{1}{25}$ second, became possible by the 1870s, but only on glass plates. Glass plates were not usable for motion pictures, since there was no practical way to move them through a camera or projector. In 1879 Eadweard Muybridge, an American photographer, did make a series of photographs of a running horse by using a series of cameras with glass plate film and fast exposure, but he was primarily interested in freezing phases of an action, not re-creating the movement by projecting the images in succession.

In 1882 another scientist interested in analyzing animal movement, the Frenchman Étienne-Jules Marey, invented a camera that recorded 12 separate images on the edge of a revolving disc of film. This was a step closer to the motion picture camera. In 1888 Marey built the first camera to use a long strip of flexible film, this time on paper. Again, the purpose was only to break down movement into a series of stills; the movements photographed lasted a second or less.

In 1889 Kodak introduced a flexible film base, celluloid (one type of which still forms the base of film stock today). With this base, and camera mechanisms to draw the film past the lens and expose it to light, the creation of lengthy series of frames became possible.

Projectors had existed for many years and had been used to show slides and other shadow entertainments. These "magic lanterns" were modified by the addition of shutters, cranks, and other devices to become early motion picture projectors.

One final device was needed if films were to be projected. Since the film stops briefly while the light shines through each individual frame, there had to be a mechanism to create an *intermittent* motion of the film. Marey used a Maltese cross gear on his 1888 camera, and this became a standard part of early cameras and projectors.

The combination of a flexible, transparent film base, fast exposure time, a mechanism to pull the film through the camera, an intermittent device to stop the film, and a shutter to block off light was achieved by the early 1890s. After several years, inventors working independently in many countries had developed several different film cameras and devices for showing films. The two most important firms were Edison in America and Lumière in France.

Thomas A. Edison's assistant, W. K. L. Dickson, developed a camera by 1893 that made short 35-mm films. Interested in exploiting these films as a novelty, Edison hoped to combine them with his phonograph to show sound movies. He had Dickson develop a peep-show machine, the *kinetoscope* (Fig. 11.1), to show these films to individual viewers.

Since Edison believed that movies were a passing fad, he did not develop a system to project films onto a screen. This was left to the Lumière brothers, Louis and Auguste. They invented their own camera independently; it also served as a contact printer and projector (Fig. 11.2). On December 28, 1895, the Lumière brothers held the first public showing of motion pictures projected on a screen, at the Grand Café in Paris. Thus, although the Lumières did not invent cinema, they largely helped to determine the specific form the new medium was to take. (Edison himself was soon to abandon kinetoscopes and form his own production company to make films for theaters.)

The first films were extremely simple in form and style. They usually consisted of a single shot with a fixed frame. A single action would occur, usually at long-shot distance. In the first film studio, Edison's Black Maria (Fig. 11.3), vaudeville

Fig. 11.1

Fig. 11.2

Fig. 11.3

Fig. 11.4

Fig. 11.5

entertainers, famous sports figures, and celebrities (for example, Annie Oakley) performed for the camera. A hinged portion of the roof opened to admit a patch of sunlight, and the entire building turned on a circular rail (visible in Figure 11.3) to follow the sun's motion. The Lumières, on the other hand, took their cameras out to parks, gardens, beaches, and other public places to film everyday activities or news events, as in their *Workers Leaving the Factory*, filmed on the street outside their own factory (see Fig. 11.4).

Although most films until about 1903 were of scenic places or noteworthy events, narrative form entered the cinema from the beginning as well. Edison staged comic scenes, like one copyrighted 1893 in which a drunken man struggles briefly with a policeman. The Lumières made a popular success with *L'Arroseur arrosé* (*The Waterer Watered*, 1895), also a comic scene, in which a boy tricks a gardener into squirting himself with a hose (see Fig. 5.7).

After the initial success of the new medium, filmmakers had to find more complex or interesting formal properties to keep the public's interest. The Lumières sent camera operators all over the world to show films and to photograph important events and exotic locales. But after making a huge number of films in their first few years, the Lumières diminished their output, and they ceased filmmaking altogether in 1905.

In 1896 Georges Méliès purchased a projector from the British inventor Robert William Paul and soon modified it for use as a camera as well. Méliès's first films resembled the Lumières' shots of everyday activities. But as we have seen, Méliès was also a magician, and he discovered the possibilities of simple special effects. In 1897 Méliès built his own studio. Unlike Edison's Black Maria, Méliès's studio was fashioned like a greenhouse, allowing the filming to utilize sunlight coming from any direction, so that the studio did not have to move with the sun (Fig. 11.5).

Méliès also began to build elaborate settings to create fantasy worlds within which his magical transformations could occur. From the simple filming of a magician performing a trick or two in a traditional stage setting, Méliès progressed to longer narratives with a series of "tableaux." (Each consisted of one shot—except when the transformations occurred. These were accomplished with cuts designed to be as imperceptible as possible on the screen.) He adapted old stories such as *Cinderella* (1899) or wrote his own. We have already seen how Méliès thereby became the first master of mise-en-scene technique (see Figs. 5.2–5.6). Méliès's films were extremely popular and were widely imitated. During this early period, films circulated freely from country to country.

The French phonograph company Pathé Frères switched increasingly to filmmaking from 1901 on, establishing production and distribution branches in many countries. Soon it was the largest film concern in the world, a position it retained until 1914, when the beginning of World War I forced it to cut back production. In England, several entrepreneurs managed to invent or obtain their own filmmaking equipment and made scenics, narratives, and trick films from 1895 into the early years of the twentieth century. Members of the "Brighton School" (including G. Albert Smith and James Williamson), as well as others like Cecil Hepworth, shot their films on location or on simple open-air stages. Their innovative films circulated abroad and influenced other filmmakers. Pioneers in other countries invented or bought equipment and were soon making their own films of everyday scenes or fantasy transformations.

From about 1904 on, narrative form became the most prominent type of filmmaking in the commercial industry, and the worldwide success of the cinema continued to grow. French, Italian, and American films—in that order—dominated world markets. Later, World War I was to restrict the free flow of films from country to country, and Hollywood was to emerge as the dominant industrial force in world film production. These factors contributed to the creation of distinct differences in the formal traits of individual national cinemas.

## THE DEVELOPMENT OF THE CLASSICAL HOLLYWOOD CINEMA (1908–1927)

Edison's determination to exploit the money-making potential of his company's invention led him to try to force competing filmmakers out of business by bringing patents-violation suits against them. One other company, American Mutoscope & Biograph, managed to survive by inventing cameras that differed from Edison's patents; others kept operating while Edison fought them in court. In 1908 Edison brought these other companies under his control by forming the Motion Picture Patents Company (MPPC), a group of ten firms based primarily in Chicago, New York, and New Jersey. Edison and Biograph were the only stockholders and patent owners. They licensed other members to make, distribute, and exhibit films.

The MPPC never succeeded in eliminating its competition. Numerous independent companies were formed throughout this period. Biograph's most important director from 1908 on, D. W. Griffith, formed his own company in 1913, as did other filmmakers. The United States government brought suit against the MPPC in 1912; in 1915 it was declared a monopoly.

After about 1910, film companies began to move permanently out to California (although some went to Florida and other locales). Eventually Hollywood, a small town on the outskirts of Los Angeles, became the site of much of the film production. Some historians claim that the independent companies moved west to avoid the harassment of the MPPC, but a few MPPC companies also made the move. Among the advantages of Hollywood were the climate, which permitted shooting year-round, and the great variety of terrains—mountains, ocean, desert, city—available for location shooting.

The demand for films was so great that no one studio could meet it. This was one of the factors that had led Edison to accept the existence of a group of other companies (although he tried to control them as much as possible through his licensing procedure). Before 1920, the American industry assumed the structure that would continue for years: a few large studios with individual artists under contract, and a peripheral group of small independent producers. In Hollywood, the studios developed a "factory" system, with each production under the control of the producer, who usually did not work on the actual making of the films. Even an independent director like Buster Keaton, with his own studio, had a business manager and distributed his films through a larger company, Metro.

Gradually, through the 1910s and 1920s the smaller studios merged to form the large firms which still exist today. Famous Players joined with Jesse L. Lasky and then formed a distribution wing, Paramount. By the late 1920s, most of the major companies existed—MGM (a merger of Metro, Goldwyn, and Mayer), Fox Film Corporation (merged with 20th Century in 1935), Universal, and Paramount. Though in competition with one another, these studios tended to cooperate to a degree, realizing that no one studio could satisfy the market.

Within this system of factorylike studios, and for reasons that are not yet clear, the American cinema became definitively oriented toward narrative form. One of Edison's directors, Edwin S. Porter, made some of the first films to utilize principles of narrative continuity and development (as opposed to the series of tableaux or the filmed vaudeville-style skits that made up early, preclassical narrative films). The first of these was *The Life of an American Fireman* (1902), which showed the race of fire fighters to rescue a mother and a child from a burning house. Although this film utilized several important classical narrative elements (a fireman's premonition of the disaster, a series of shots of the horse-drawn engine racing to the house), it still had not worked out the logic of temporal relations in cutting. Thus we see the rescue of the mother and child twice, from both inside and outside the house. Porter had not realized the possibility of intercutting the two locales within the action or matching on action to convey narrative information to the audience.

In 1903, Porter made *The Great Train Robbery*, an early prototype for the classical American film. Here the action develops with a clear linearity of time, space, and logic. We follow each stage of the robbery, the escape, and the final defeat of the robbers. In 1905, Porter also worked with a simple parallel narrative in *The Kleptomaniac*, contrasting the fates of a rich woman and a starving woman who are both caught stealing.

At about the same time, British filmmakers were working along similar lines. Indeed, many historians now believe that Porter derived some of his editing techniques from films like James Williamson's *Fire!* (1901) and G. A. Smith's *Mary Jane's Mishap* (1903). The most famous British film of this era was Lewin Fitzhamon's 1905 film *Rescued by Rover* (produced by a major British firm, Cecil Hepworth), which treated a kidnapping in a linear fashion similar to that of *The Great Train Robbery*. After the kidnapping, we see each stage of Rover's journey to fetch the child's father, and then of Rover and the father retracing the route to the kidnapper's lair.

In 1908, D. W. Griffith began his directing career. In the next five years, he was to make hundreds of one- and two-reelers (running around 15 and 30 minutes, respectively). These films created relatively complex narratives in short spans. Griffith probably was not the initiator of all the devices with which he has been credited, but he did give many techniques strong narrative motivation. For example, although a few other filmmakers had used simple last-minute rescues with cross-cutting between the rescuers and victims, Griffith is famous for developing and popularizing this technique. By the time he made *The Birth of a Nation* (1915) and *Intolerance* (1916), Griffith was creating lengthy sequences by cutting between several different locales. During the early teens, he also directed his actors in an unusual way, concentrating on subtle changes in facial expression. To catch such nuances, he moved his camera closer than the standard long-shot and *plan-américain* framings of earlier films, placing his actors in medium long or medium shot. Griffith's films were widely influential. In particular, his dynamic, rapid editing in the final chase scenes of *Intolerance* were to have a considerable impact on the Soviet montage style of the 1920s.

The refinement of narratively motivated cutting occurs in the work of a number of important filmmakers of the period. One of these was Thomas Ince, a producer and director responsible for many films between 1910 and the end of World War I. He devised a "unit system," whereby a single producer could oversee the making of numerous films. He also emphasized tight narratives, with no digressions or loose ends. *Civilization* (1915) and *The Italian* (1915) are good examples of films directed or supervised by Ince; he also supervised the popular Westerns of William S. Hart.

Fig. 11.6

Fig. 11.7

Another prolific filmmaker of this period (and later periods as well) was Cecil B. De Mille. Not yet engaged in the creation of historical epics, De Mille made a series of feature-length dramas and comedies. His *The Cheat* (1915) reflects important changes occurring in the studio style between about 1914 and 1917. During that period, the glass-roofed studios of the earlier period began to give way to studios dependent on artificial lighting rather than mixed daylight and electric lighting. *The Cheat* used spectacular effects of *chiaroscuro*, using only one or two bright sources of light and eliminating fill light. De Mille justified this effect to nervous exhibitors as "Rembrandt" lighting. This so-called Rembrandt, or "north," lighting was to become part of the classical repertoire of lighting techniques. *The Cheat* also greatly impressed the French impressionist filmmakers, who occasionally used similar stark lighting effects.

Like many American films of the teens, *The Cheat* also uses a linear pattern of narrative. The first scene (Fig. 11.6) introduces the stark lighting but also quickly establishes the Burmese businessman as a ruthless collector of objects; we see him burning his brand onto a small statue. The initial action motivates a later scene in which the businessman brands the heroine, who has fallen into his power by borrowing money from him (Fig. 11.7). *The Cheat* was evidence of the growing formal complexity of the Hollywood film.

The period 1909–17 saw the development of the basic continuity principles. Eyeline matches occur with increasing frequency from 1910 on. The match on action developed at about the same time and was in common use by 1916. It appears in such Douglas Fairbanks films as *The Mystery of the Leaping Fish* (1916) and *Wild and Woolly* (1917). Shot/reverse shot was used only occasionally between 1911 and 1915, but it became widespread by 1916–17; instances occur in such films as *The Cheat* (1915), *The Narrow Trail* (a William S. Hart Western of 1917), and Griffith's *A Romance of Happy Valley* (1918). During this period, only a small minority of films violated the axis-of-action rule in using these techniques.

By the 1920s, the continuity system had become a standardized style that directors in the Hollywood studios used almost automatically to create coherent spatial and temporal relations within narratives. A match on action could provide a cut to a closer view in a scene, as in *The Three Musketeers*, with Fairbanks (Figs. 11.8 and 11.9; Fred Niblo, 1921). A three-way conversation around a table would not be handled in a single frontal shot, as would have been the case a dozen years

Fig. 11.8

Fig. 11.9

Fig. 11.10

Fig. 11.11

Fig. 11.12

Fig. 11.13

Fig. 11.14

earlier. Note the clear spatial relations in Figures 11.10 through 11.14, shots from *Are Parents People?* (Malcolm St. Clair, 1925), as the daughter sits down at the table (Fig. 11.10), then looks back and forth in shot/reverse shot at her parents, seated at the ends of the table. Screen direction was usually respected, as in these cases. When an awkward match might have resulted from the joining of two shots, the filmmakers could cover it by inserting a dialogue title.

Keaton's *Our Hospitality* (1923), which we examined in Chapter 5, provides another example of a classical narrative. Keaton's mastery of classical form and style are evident in the carefully motivated recurrences of the various narrative elements and in the straightforward causal development from the death of Willie McKay's father in the feud to Willie's final resolution of the feud.

By the end of the silent period, in the late 1920s, the classical Hollywood cinema had developed into a sophisticated movement, but the Hollywood "product" was remarkably standardized. All of the major studios used the same production system, with a similar division of labor at each. Independent production became difficult. Keaton gave up his small studio in 1928 to go to MGM under contract; there his career declined, due partly to the incompatibility of his old working methods with the rigid production patterns of the huge studio. Griffith, Mary Pickford, Fairbanks, and Charles Chaplin were better off. Forming a distributing corporation of their own, United Artists, in 1919, they were able to continue independent production at small companies under their umbrella corporation, though Griffith's company soon failed, and the careers of Fairbanks and Pickford declined soon after the introduction of sound.

There were alternative kinds of films being made during these years—most of them in other countries. After examining these alternative movements, we shall return to a brief examination of the classical Hollywood cinema after the coming of sound.

## GERMAN EXPRESSIONISM (1919–1924)

At the start of World War I, the output of the German film industry was relatively insignificant, both within the country and internationally. Germany's 2000 movie theaters were playing mostly French, American, Italian, and Danish films. Although America and France banned German films from their screens immediately, Germany was not even in a solid enough position to ban French and American films—the theaters would have had little to show.

In order to combat imported competition, as well as to create its own propaganda films, the German government began to support the film industry. In 1916 film imports were banned except from neutral Denmark, whose film industry had close ties to that of Germany. Production increased rapidly; from a dozen small companies in 1911, the number grew to 131 by 1918. But government policy encouraged these companies to band together into cartels.

The war was unpopular with many in Germany, and rebellious tendencies increased after the success of the Russian Revolution in 1917. Widespread strikes and antiwar petitions were organized during the winter of 1916–17. In order to promote prowar films, the government, the Deutsche Bank, and large industrial concerns combined several small firms to create the large company UFA in late 1917; backed by these essentially conservative interests, UFA was a move toward a control of not only the German market but the postwar international market as well.

With this huge financial backing, UFA was able to gather superb technicians and build the best-equipped studios in Europe. These studios later attracted even foreign filmmakers (including the young Alfred Hitchcock). This led to coproductions in the 1920s between Germany and other countries, which helped spread German stylistic influence abroad.

In late 1918, with the end of the war, the need for overt militarist propaganda disappeared, and the German film industry concentrated on three types of films (although ordinary dramas and comedies continued to be made as well). One was the internationally popular genre that had appeared in the early teens, the adventure serial, featuring spy rings, clever detectives, or exotic settings. Second was a brief sex exploitation cycle, which dealt "educationally" with such topics as homosexuality and prostitution. Finally, UFA set out to copy the popular Italian historical epics of the prewar period.

This last type of film proved financially successful for UFA. In spite of continued bans and prejudice against German films in America, England, and France, UFA finally was able to break into the international market. In September 1919 Ernst Lubitsch's *Madame Dubarry*, an epic of the French Revolution, inaugurated the magnificent UFA Palatz theater in Berlin. This film helped reopen the world film market to Germany. Released as *Passion* in the United States, this film was extremely popular and won critical acclaim in various European countries as well; it was less enthusiastically received in France, where its premiere was considerably delayed by charges that it was anti-French propaganda. But it did well in most markets, and other Lubitsch historical films were soon exported. In 1923, he became the first German director to be hired by Hollywood.

Some small companies remained independent briefly; among these was Erich Pommer's Decla-Bioscop. In 1919, the firm undertook to produce an unconventional script by two unknowns, Carl Mayer and Hans Janowitz. These young writers wanted the film to be made in an unusually stylized way. The three designers assigned to the film—Hermann Warm, Walter Reimann, and Walter Röhrig—suggested that it be done in an *expressionist* style. As an avant-garde movement, expressionism had first been important in painting (starting about 1910) and had been quickly taken up in theater, then in literature, and in architecture. Now company officials consented to try it in the cinema, apparently believing that this might be a selling point in the international market.

This approach proved a valid one when this inexpensively made film, *The Cabinet of Dr. Caligari*, created a sensation in the United States, France, and other countries after its release in the early 1920s. Because of its success, other films in the expressionist style soon followed. The result was a stylistic movement in cinema that lasted several years.

The success of *Caligari* and other expressionist films meant that Germany's avant-garde remained largely within the industry. A few experimental filmmakers made abstract films, like Viking Eggeling's *Diagonal-symphonie* (1923), or Dada films influenced by the international art movement, like Hans Richter's *Ghosts before Breakfast* (1928). Big firms such as UFA (which absorbed Decla-Bioscop in 1921) as well as smaller companies invested in expressionist films because these films could compete with those of America. Indeed, by the mid-1920s, the German films were widely regarded as among the best in the world.

The first film of the movement, *Caligari*, is also one of the most typical examples. One of its designers, Warm, claimed, "The film image must become graphic art." *Caligari*, with its extreme stylization, was indeed like a moving expressionist painting or woodcut print. In contrast to French impressionism, which bases its style primarily on cinematography and editing, German expressionism depends heavily on mise-en-scene. Shapes are distorted and exaggerated unrealistically for expressive purposes. Actors often wear heavy makeup and move in jerky or slow, sinuous patterns. Most important, all of the elements of the mise-en-scene interact graphically to create an overall composition. Characters do not simply exist within a setting but rather form a visual element that merges with that setting. We have already seen an example of this in Figure 5.1; the character Cesare collapses in a stylized forest, with his body and outstretched arms echoing the shapes of the trees' trunks and branches.

Fig. 11.15

In *Caligari*, the expressionist stylization functions to convey the distorted viewpoint of a madman; we see the world as the hero does. This narrative function of the settings becomes explicit at one point, as the hero enters an asylum in his pursuit of Caligari. As he pauses to look around, he stands at the center of a pattern of radiating black and white lines that go across the floor and up the walls (Fig. 11.15). The world of the film is literally a projection of the hero's vision.

Later, as expressionism became an accepted style, filmmakers did not motivate expressionist style as the narrative point of view of mad characters. Instead, expressionism often functioned to create stylized situations for horror and fantasy stories (as with *Waxworks*, 1924, and *Nosferatu*, 1922) or historical epics (as with *The Nibelungen*, 1924). Some expressionism became less graphic and took on a more plastic, architectural style (see Fig. 11.16, from *Siegfried*, Part I of *The Nibelungen*). Both graphic and plastic varieties of expressionism depended greatly on their designers. In the German studios, a film's designer received a relatively high salary, third only after the director and the individual stars; a famous designer

Fig. 11.16

might even receive more money than the star of the film, a practice very different from that of other countries.

A combination of circumstances caused the disappearance of the movement. The rampant inflation of the early 1920s in Germany actually had favored expressionist filmmaking, partly by making it easy for German exporters to sell their films cheaply abroad. Inflation discouraged imports, however, for the tumbling exchange rate of the mark made foreign purchases prohibitively expensive. But in 1924 the U.S. Dawes Plan helped to stabilize the German economy, and foreign films came in more frequently, offering a degree of competition unknown in Germany for nearly a decade. Yet expressionist film budgets were climbing. The last major films of the movement, Murnau's *Faust* (1926) and Lang's *Metropolis*, were costly epics that helped drive UFA deeper into financial difficulty, leading Erich Pommer to quit and try his luck briefly in America. Other personnel were lured away to Hollywood as well. Murnau left after finishing his last German film, *Faust*, in 1926. Major actors (e.g., Conrad Veidt and Emil Jannings) and cinematographers (e.g., Karl Freund) went to Hollywood as well. Lang stayed on, but after the criticisms of *Metropolis*'s extravagance on its release in early 1927, he formed his own production company and turned to other styles in his later silent films. At the beginning of the Nazi regime in 1933, he, too, left the country.

Because of the stiffer competition from the Americans after 1924, the Germans also tried to imitate the American product; the resulting films, though often impressive, diluted the unique qualities of the expressionist style. Thus by 1927, expressionism as a movement died out. But as Georges Sadoul has pointed out, an expressionist tendency lingered on in many of the German films of the late 1920s and even into such 1930s films as Lang's *M* (1930) and *Testament of Dr. Mabuse* (1932). And because so many of the German filmmakers came to the United States, Hollywood films also displayed expressionist tendencies. Horror films such as *Son of Frankenstein* (1939) and *films noirs* have strong expressionist touches in their settings and lighting. Although the German movement lasted only about seven years, expressionism has never entirely died out as a trend in film style.

## FRENCH IMPRESSIONISM AND SURREALISM (1918–1930)

In France during the silent era, a number of film movements posed major alternatives to classical Hollywood narrative form. Some of these alternatives—abstract cinema, Dada filmmaking—are not specifically French and so will be discussed shortly as part of an international avant-garde. But two alternatives to the American mode remained quite localized. The first, impressionism, was an avant-garde style that nonetheless operated within the film industry. The impressionist filmmakers mostly started out by working for major French companies, and some of their avant-garde works proved financially successful. In the mid-twenties, most formed their own independent companies but remained within the mainstream commercial industry by renting studio facilities and releasing their films through established firms. The second alternative movement, surrealism, lay largely outside the film industry; allied with the surrealist movement in other arts, these filmmakers relied on their own means and private patronage. France in the 1920s thus offers a striking instance of how different film movements can coexist at the same time and place.

## ■ IMPRESSIONISM

World War I struck a serious blow to the French film industry as personnel were conscripted, film factories were shifted to wartime duties, and much export was halted. Yet since the two major firms, Pathé Frères and Léon Gaumont, also controlled circuits of theaters, they needed to fill vacant screens, and so in 1915 American films began increasingly to flood into France. Represented by Pearl White, Douglas Fairbanks, Chaplin and Ince films, De Mille's *The Cheat*, and William S. Hart (affectionately named "Rio Jim" by the French), the Hollywood cinema dominated the market by the end of 1917. After the war, French filmmaking never recovered: in the 1920s, French audiences saw eight times more Hollywood footage than domestic footage. The film industry tried in several ways to recapture the market—through imitation of Hollywood production methods and genres—but artistically the most significant move was the firms' encouragement of younger French directors: Abel Gance, Louis Delluc, Germaine Dulac, Marcel L'Herbier, and Jean Epstein.

These directors differed from their predecessors. The previous generation had regarded filmmaking as a commercial craft. More theoretical and ambitious, the younger filmmakers wrote essays proclaiming cinema to be an art comparable to poetry, painting, and (especially) music. Cinema should, they said, be purely itself and owe nothing to the theater or literature. (Here the impressionists drew heavily on symbolist poetic theory to define an art of suggestion and fleeting sensation.) Impressed by the verve and energy of the American cinema, the young theorists compared Chaplin to Nijinsky and the films of "Rio Jim" to *The Song of Roland*. Cinema should, above all, be (like music) an occasion for the artist to express feelings. Gance, Delluc, Dulac, L'Herbier, Epstein, and other more tangential members of the movement sought to put this aesthetic into practice as filmmakers.

Between 1918 and 1928, in a series of extraordinary films, the younger directors experimented with cinema in ways that posed an alternative to the dominant Hollywood formal principles. Given the centrality of emotion in their aesthetic, it is no wonder that the intimate psychological narrative dominated their filmmaking practice. The interactions of a few characters—often a love triangle (as in Delluc's *L'Inondation*, Epstein's *Cœur fidèle* and *La Belle nivernaise*, and Gance's *La Dixième symphonie*)—would serve as the basis for the filmmaker's exploration of fleeting moods and shifting sensations.

As in the Hollywood cinema, psychological causes were paramount, but the school gained the name "impressionist" because of its interest in making narrative form represent as fully as possible the play of a character's consciousness. The interest falls not on external physical behavior but on *inner* action. To a degree unprecedented in international filmmaking, impressionist films manipulate plot time and subjectivity. To depict memories, flashbacks are common; sometimes the bulk of a film will be a flashback. Even more striking is the films' insistence on registering characters' dreams, fantasies, and mental states. Dulac's *The Smiling Mme. Beudet* consists almost entirely of the main character's fantasy life, her imaginary escape from a dull marriage. Despite its epic length (over five hours), Gance's *La Roue* rests essentially on the erotic relations among only four people, and the director seeks to trace every development of each character's feelings. On the whole, then, impressionism's emphasis on personal emotion gives the films' narratives an intensely psychological focus.

The "impressionist" movement earned its name as well for its use of film style. The filmmakers experimented with ways of rendering mental states by new uses of cinematography and editing. In impressionist films, irises, masks, and superimpositions function as traces of characters' thoughts and feelings. In *Cœur fidèle*, the heroine looks out a window, and a superimposition of the foul jetsam of the waterfront conveys her dejection at having to work as a barmaid in a dockside tavern (Fig. 11.17). In *La Roue*, the image of Norma is superimposed over the smoke from a locomotive. To intensify the subjectivity, the impressionists' cinematography and editing present characters' perceptual experience, their optical "impressions." These films use point-of-view cutting—showing a shot of a character looking at something, then a shot of that thing, from an angle and distance replicating the character's vantage point. When a character in an impressionist film gets drunk or ill or dizzy, the filmmaker renders that experience through out-of-focus or filtered shots or vertiginous camera movements. Finally, the impressionists began experimenting with pronounced rhythmic editing to suggest the pace of an experience as a character feels it, moment by moment. During scenes of violence or emotional turmoil, the rhythm accelerates—the shots get shorter and shorter, building to a dynamic climax, sometimes with shots only a few frames long. In *La Roue* a train crash is presented in accelerating shots ranging from thirteen frames down to two, and a man's last thoughts before he falls from a cliff are rendered in a blur of many single-frame shots (the first known use of such rapid editing). In *Cœur fidèle* lovers at a fair ride in whirling swings, and Epstein presents their giddiness in a series of shots four frames, then two frames, long. Several impressionist films use a dance to motivate a markedly accelerated cutting rhythm. (Indeed, their comparison of cinema to music encouraged the impressionists to explore rhythmic editing.) In such ways subjective shooting and editing patterns function within impressionist films to reinforce the narrative treatment of psychological states.

**Fig. 11.17**

Impressionist film form created certain demands on film technology. Gance, the boldest innovator in this respect, used his epic *Napoléon* as a chance to try new lenses (even a 275-mm telephoto), multiple frame images (called "Polyvision"), and widescreen ratio (the celebrated triptychs; see Fig. 6.32). The most influential impressionist technological innovation was the development of new means of frame mobility. If the camera was to represent a character's eyes, it should be able to move with the ease of a person. Impressionists strapped their cameras to cars, carousels, and locomotive cowcatchers. For Gance's *Napoléon*, the camera manufacturer Debrie perfected a hand-held model that let the operator move on roller skates. Gance put the machine on wheels, cables, pendulums, and bobsleds. In *L'Argent*, L'Herbier had his camera gliding through huge rooms and even plummeting straight down toward the crowd from the dome of the Paris stock exchange (in an effort to convey the excitement of the traders as a group).

Such formal, stylistic, and technological innovations had given French filmmakers the hope that their films could win the popularity granted to Hollywood's product. During the 1920s, the impressionists had in fact operated somewhat independently; they had formed their own small production companies and had leased studio facilities from Pathé and Gaumont in exchange for distribution rights. But by 1929, foreign audiences had not taken to impressionism; its experimentation was attuned to elite tastes. Moreover, although production costs were rising, the impressionists (especially Gance and L'Herbier) became even more prodigal; as a result, filmmakers' companies either went out of business or were absorbed by the big firms. Two behemoth productions of the decade, *Napoléon* (1927) and *L'Argent* (1929), failed and were recut by the producers; they were among the last impressionist films released. With the arrival of the sound film, the French industry tightened its belt and had no money to risk on experiments. Thus impressionism as a distinct movement may be said to have ceased by 1929. But the influences of impressionist form—the psychological narrative, subjective camera work and editing—were more long lived. They continued to operate, for example, in the work of Alfred Hitchcock and Maya Deren, in Hollywood "montage sequences," and in certain American genres and styles (the horror film, *film noir*).

### ■ SURREALISM

Whereas the French impressionist filmmakers worked within the commercial film industry, the surrealist filmmakers relied on private patronage and screened their work in small artists' gatherings. Such isolation is hardly surprising, since surrealist cinema was a more radical movement, producing films that perplexed and shocked most audiences.

   Surrealist cinema was directly linked to surrealism in literature and painting. According to its spokesperson, André Breton, "surrealism" was "based on the belief in the superior reality of certain forms of association, heretofore neglected, in the omnipotence of dreams, in the undirected play of thought." Influenced by Freudian psychology, surrealist art sought to register the hidden currents of the unconscious, "in the absence of any control exercised by reason, and beyond any aesthetic and moral preoccupation." "Automatic" writing and painting, the search for bizarre or evocative imagery, the deliberate avoidance of rationally explicable form or style—these became features of surrealism as it developed in the period 1924–29. From the start, the surrealists were attracted to the cinema, especially admiring films that presented untamed desire or the fantastic and marvelous (for example, slapstick comedies, *Nosferatu*). In due time, painters such as Man Ray and Salvador Dali and writers such as Antonin Artaud began dabbling in cinema, while the young Spaniard Luis Buñuel, drawn to surrealism, became its most famous filmmaker.

   Surrealist cinema is overtly antinarrative, attacking causality itself. If rationality is to be fought, causal connections among events must be dissolved. *The Seashell and the Clergyman* (1928; scripted by Artaud, filmed by the impressionist Germaine Dulac) begins with the protagonist pouring liquids from flasks and then systematically breaking each one. In Dali–Buñuel's *Un Chien andalou (An Andalusian Dog,* 1928) the hero drags two pianos, stuffed with dead donkeys, across a parlor. In Buñuel's *L'Age d'or* (1930) a woman begins obsessively sucking the toes of a statue. Like *Last Year at Marienbad,* many surrealist films tease us to find a narrative logic that is simply absent. Causality is as evasive as in a dream. Instead, we find events juxtaposed for their disturbing effect. The hero gratuitously shoots a child (*L'Age d'or*), a woman closes her eyes only to reveal eyes painted on her eyelids (Ray's *Emak Bakia,* 1927), and—most famous of all—a man strops a razor and deliberately slits the eyeball of an unprotesting woman (*Un Chien andalou,* Fig. 11.18). An impressionist film would motivate such events as a character's dreams or hallucinations, but in these films character psychology is all but nonexistent. Sexual desire and ecstasy, violence, blasphemy, and bizarre humor furnish events that surrealist film form employs with a disregard for conventional narrative principles. The hope was that the free form of the film would arouse the deepest impulses of the viewer. Buñuel called *Un Chien andalou* "a passionate call to murder."

   The style of surrealist films is eclectic. Mise-en-scene is often influenced by surrealist painting. The ants in *Un Chien andalou* come from Dali's pictures, whereas the pillars and city squares of *The Seashell and the Clergyman* hark back to the Italian painter Giorgio de Chirico. Surrealist editing is an amalgam of some

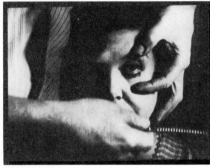

Fig. 11.18

impressionist devices (many dissolves and superimpositions) and some devices of the dominant cinema. The shocking eyeball slitting at the start of *Un Chien andalou* relies on some principles of continuity editing (and indeed on the Kuleshov effect). On the other hand, discontinuous editing is also commonly used to fracture any organized temporal-spatial coherence: in the same film, the heroine locks the man out of one room only to turn to find him already there with her. On the whole, surrealist film style refused to canonize any particular devices, since that would order and rationalize what had to be an "undirected play of thought."

The fortunes of surrealist cinema shifted with changes in the art movement as a whole. By late 1929, when Breton joined the Communist party, surrealists were embroiled in internal dissension about whether communism was a political equivalent of surrealism. Buñuel left France for a brief stay in Hollywood and then returned to Spain. The chief patron of surrealist filmmaking, the Vicomte de Noailles, supported Jean Vigo's *Zéro de Conduit* (1932), a film of surrealist ambitions, but then stopped sponsoring the avant-garde. Thus as a unified movement, French surrealism was no longer viable after 1930. Individual surrealists continued to work, however—the most famous being Buñuel, who continued to work in his own brand of the surrealist style for 50 years. His later films, such as *Belle de Jour* (1967) and *The Discreet Charm of the Bourgeoisie* (1972), continue the surrealist tradition.

## SOVIET MONTAGE (1924–1930)

In spite of the success of the Russian Revolution in 1917, the new Soviet government faced the difficult task of controlling all sectors of life. Like other industries, the film production and distribution systems took years to develop to a point where they could achieve a substantial output that served the aims of the new government.

Although the pre-Revolutionary Russian film industry had not figured prominently in world cinema, there were a number of private production companies operating in Moscow and Petrograd. These companies resisted the move made directly after the Revolution to nationalize all property, including private companies. With most imports cut off during the war, these companies had done quite well making films for the domestic market. Such film companies simply refused to supply films to theaters operating under the control of the government. In July 1918 the government's film subsection of the State Commission of Education put strict controls on the existing supplies of raw film stock. As a result, producers began hoarding their stock; many took all the equipment they could and fled to other countries. Some companies made films commissioned by the government, while hoping that the Reds would lose the Civil War and that things would return to pre-Revolutionary conditions.

In the face of shortages of equipment and difficult living conditions, a few young filmmakers made tentative moves that would result in the development of a national cinema movement. Dziga Vertov began working on documentary footage of the war; at age 20, he was placed in charge of all newsreels. Lev Kuleshov, teaching in the newly founded State School on Cinema Art, performed a series of experiments by editing footage from different sources into a whole that creates an impression of continuity. (In this sense, Kuleshov was perhaps the most conservative of the young Soviet filmmakers, since he was basically trying to systematize principles of editing similar to the continuity practices of the classical Hollywood cinema.) Even before they were able to make films, the young filmmakers were working at the first film school in the world and writing theoretical essays on the new art form. This grounding in theory would be the basis of the montage style.

In 1920 Sergei Eisenstein worked briefly in a train carrying propaganda to the troops in the Civil War; he returned that year to Moscow to work in the new workers' theater, the Proletkult. In May 1920 Vsevolod Pudovkin made his acting debut in a play presented by Kuleshov's State Film School. He had been inspired to go into filmmaking by seeing Griffith's *Intolerance*, which was first shown widely in Russia in 1919. American films, particularly those of Griffith, Douglas Fairbanks, and Mary Pickford, were a tremendous influence on the filmmakers of the emerging Soviet movement.

None of the important filmmakers of the montage style were veterans of the pre-Revolutionary industry. All came from other fields (for example, Eisenstein from engineering, Pudovkin from chemistry) and discovered the cinema in the midst of the Revolution's ferment. Those established filmmakers who did make films in the USSR in the 1920s tended to stick to older traditions. One popular director of the Czarist period, Yakov Protazanov, went abroad briefly after the Revolution but returned to continue making films whose style and form owed almost nothing to the theory and practice of the new filmmakers.

Protazanov's return coincided with a general loosening of government restrictions on private enterprise. In 1921 the country was experiencing tremendous difficulties, including a widespread famine. In order to facilitate the production and distribution of goods, Lenin instituted the New Economic Policy (NEP), which for a few years permitted private management of business. For film, this meant a sudden reappearance of film stock and equipment belonging to the producers who had not emigrated. By 1923 the government was able to create a Soviet monopoly on film production by nationalizing the industry permanently.

"Of all the arts, for us the cinema is the most important," Lenin stated in 1922. Since Lenin saw film as a powerful tool for education, the first films encouraged by the government were documentaries and newsreels such as Vertov's newsreel series *Kino-Pravda*, which began in May 1922. Fictional films were also being made from 1919 on, but it was not until 1923 that a Georgian feature, *Red Imps*, became the first Soviet film to compete successfully with the foreign films predominant on Soviet screens. (It was not until 1927 that the Soviet industry's income from its own films topped that of the films it had imported.)

The Soviet montage style displayed tentative beginnings in 1924, with Kuleshov's class from the State Film School filming *The Extraordinary Adventures of Mr. West in the Land of the Bolsheviks*. This delightful film, along with Kuleshov's next film, *The Death Ray* (1925), showed that Soviet directors could apply montage principles and come up with amusing satires or exciting adventures comparable to the Hollywood product.

Eisenstein's first feature, *Strike* (1924), was released early in 1925 and initiated the movement proper. His second, *Potemkin*, released later in 1925, was successful abroad and drew the attention of other countries to the new movement. In the next few years Eisenstein, Pudovkin, Vertov, and the Ukrainian Alexander Dovzhenko created a series of films that are classics of the montage style.

Eisenstein has written, "We all came to the Soviet cinema as something not yet existent. We came upon no ready-built city." The theoretical writings and filmmaking practice of these directors were based on editing. They all declared that a film does not exist in its individual shots but only in their combination through editing into a whole. We should remember here that since the primitive cinema, no national film style had yet appeared that depended on the long take; the great films that inspired Soviet filmmakers, like *Intolerance*, were based largely on editing juxtapositions.

Not all of the young theoreticians agreed on exactly how this editing was to be done. Pudovkin, for example, believed that shots were like bricks, to be joined together to build a sequence. Eisenstein disagreed, saying that the maximum effect would be gained if the shots did not fit together perfectly, if they created a jolt for the spectator; he also favored the juxtaposition of shots to create a concept, as we have already seen with his technique of "intellectual montage." Vertov disagreed with both theorists, favoring a "cinema-eye" approach to recording and shaping documentary reality.

Fig. 11.19

We have already seen examples of Soviet montage in our examination of a sequence from *October* (1928) in Chapter 7. Pudovkin's *Storm over Asia* (1928) provides a comparison. In one scene a British officer (as an imperial representative in Mongolia) and his wife dress in elegant clothes to attend a ceremony at a Buddhist temple. Pudovkin intercuts shots of the couple and their accessories (Figs. 11.19 and 11.20) with shots of the preparations at the temple (Figs. 11.21 and 11.22). By the use of montage, Pudovkin creates a parallelism that points up the absurdity of the British rituals. Other famous examples of Soviet montage style in this film are the moment when the hero knocks over a fish tank (rendered with many close shots of various phases of the action) and the "storm" finale, with fast cutting to convey the relentless sweep of the Mongolian troops.

Fig. 11.20

The Soviet approach to form set it apart from the cinemas of other countries. Soviet narrative films tended to downplay character psychology as a cause; instead, social forces provided the major causes. Characters were interesting for the way these social causes affected their lives. We have already mentioned (in Chapter 3) that films of the Soviet montage movement did not always have a single protagonist; large groups could form a collective hero, as in Eisenstein's films before *Old and New*. In keeping with this de-emphasis of individual personalities, Soviet filmmakers often avoided well-known actors, preferring to cast parts by searching out nonactors. This practice was called *typage*, since the filmmakers would search out an individual whose appearance seemed at once to convey the type of character he or she was to play. Except for the hero, Pudovkin used nonactors to play all of the Mongols in *Storm over Asia*.

Fig. 11.21

By the end of the 1920s, each of the major figures of this movement had made about four important films. The decline of the movement was not caused primarily, as in Germany and France, by industrial and economic factors. Instead, government political pressures exerted a strong control which discouraged the use of the montage style. By the late 1920s, Eisenstein and Dovzhenko were being criticized for their excessively formal and "esoteric" approaches. In 1929 Eisenstein went to Hollywood to study the new technique of sound; by the time he returned in 1932, the attitude of the film industry had changed. While he was away, a few filmmakers carried their montage experiments into sound cinema in the early 1930s. But the Soviet authorities, under Stalin's direction, encouraged filmmakers to create simple films that would be readily understandable to all audiences. Stylistic experimentation or nonrealistic subject matter was often criticized or censored.

This trend culminated in 1934, when the government instituted a new artistic policy called Socialist Realism. This dictated that all artworks must depict revolutionary development while being firmly grounded in "realism." The great Soviet directors continued to make films, occasionally masterpieces, but the montage

Fig. 11.22

experiments of the 1920s had to be discarded or modified. Eisenstein managed to continue his work on montage, but occasionally incurred the wrath of the authorities up until his death in 1948. As a movement, the Soviet montage style can be said to have ended by 1933, with the release of such films as Vertov's *Enthusiasm* (1931) and Pudovkin's *Deserter* (1933).

## SUMMARY: INTERNATIONAL STYLISTIC TRENDS OF THE LATE SILENT CINEMA

So far we have treated the three major alternative movements of the silent period—French, German, and Soviet—as largely separate from one another. That is how they began, but filmmakers in each country quickly became aware of the other movements. We have seen how German companies worked to break down bans and prejudices against their films in other countries. Soon German films were shown frequently in France and the USSR. Soviet films were exported later. (*Potemkin*, for example, was an enormous success in Berlin in 1926.) Often these films had to be shown at private cinema clubs in France and England, due to political resistance to things Soviet. There grew up, however, an international film culture that would have been aware of the major formal and stylistic traits of all three movements.

As a result, the filmmakers of each movement began to be influenced by the films of the other movements. Impressionism began in 1918 and German expressionism in 1920; by 1923–24, there were definite signs that the two groups of filmmakers had seen each other's work. Expressionist elements crop up in the mise-en-scène of French films, such as L'Herbier's *Don Juan et Faust* (1923) and *L'Inhumaine* (1924).

In turn, the Germans began to employ the subjective camera style developed by the French. Impressionist camera techniques are evident in a 1923 German film, *Die Strasse (The Street)*, which also employs expressionist set design in some of its scenes. F. W. Murnau created a sensation by rendering the hero's drunkenness in *The Last Laugh* (1924) with a hand-held camera, yet the French had already been doing this sort of thing for several years. Fritz Lang followed suit by mounting his camera on a swing for his 1926 *Metropolis*, subjectively rendering an explosion's impact on the hero.

The Russians were also seeing German films. One team of filmmakers, Grigori Kozintsev and Leonid Trauberg, was influenced by them; their films stand out from the majority of the Soviet films by their use of stylized sets, lighting, and acting as in *The Cloak* (1926). More important, several French impressionist films reached Russia by 1925. These included Jean Epstein's *Cœur fidèle* (1923) and excerpts from Gance's *La Roue* (1922). The latter film's most spectacular sequences involved fast rhythmic editing, some with series of single-frame shots. Direct influence is difficult to prove, but Eisenstein's editing changes considerably between *Potemkin* (1925) and *October* (1928); in the latter film, the editing is much faster, including series of two-frame shots. Pudovkin uses very fast montage in the last sequence of *Storm over Asia* (1928) as well.

By the late 1920s, the stylistic traits of German mise-en-scène, French cinematography and editing, and Soviet montage were being freely used by filmmakers of various countries. Dreyer's *La Passion de Jeanne d'Arc*, made in France in 1928, exemplifies this perfectly (Fig. 11.23, a production still). The film's set designer was Hermann Warm, who had collaborated on the designs of *Caligari* and other German films. Dreyer used elaborate swinging camera movements of the French style and assembled his scenes from close shots of parts of the action, somewhat in Soviet montage fashion. Other films that combine two or more of these stylistic tendencies are the German film *Überfall* (1928) and the French *Fall of the House of Usher* (1928).

The international style even made its way to Hollywood. Since so many filmmakers, particularly Germans, were hired by the American studios, the European traits began to show up in American films. F. W. Murnau's *Sunrise* (1927) was written by *Caligari*'s scriptwriter, Carl Mayer; it was an elaborate studio production for Fox Film Corporation, but aside from its familiar American stars, it might have been made in Germany.

One aspect of the European cinema that completely avoided national boundaries was the extreme avant-garde. The Dada movement, an anarchist anti-art group, began in Switzerland in the early 1920s and quickly spread to France and Germany. France's René Clair made one of the most important Dada films, *Entr'acte* (1924), to be shown in the intermission of a Dada ballet. Other Dada films included Marcel Duchamp's *Anemic Cinema* (1926) and Hans Richter's German film *Ghosts before Breakfast* (1928). These films resembled the surrealist films but carried their illogic to an even greater degree. If the surrealist films had a dreamlike, mystical quality, the Dada films showed objects in an anarchic revolt against conventional society. In *Entr'acte* a camel pulls a hearse in a chase through the streets of Paris; in *Ghosts before Breakfast* bowler hats fly off the heads of their respectable owners and cavort in the air.

Overall, the various national and international trends of the silent cinema had developed film art to a highly sophisticated level by the end of the 1920s. Since then, the introduction of sound and color have provided new stylistic possibilities, but no filmmakers have ever surpassed the intense theoretical study and variety of experiment that existed during this period.

Fig. 11.23

## THE CLASSICAL HOLLYWOOD CINEMA AFTER THE COMING OF SOUND

Contrary to accounts in most film histories, the introduction of sound technology was not a last-ditch gamble by a bankrupt Warner Bros. studio, nor did sound burst unexpectedly onto the scene. In fact, Warner Bros. was on firm financial ground and was in the process of investing a great deal of money to expand its facilities and holdings. One of these expansions was the investment (totaling only about one-fifth of the overall expansion by the studio) in a sound system using records in synchronization with film images. (Figure 11.24 shows an early projector with sound attachment.)

By releasing *Don Juan* (1926) with orchestral accompaniment and sound effects on disc, along with a series of sound vaudeville shorts, Warner Bros. began to popularize the idea of sound films. In 1927, *The Jazz Singer* (a part "talkie" with some scenes accompanied only by music) had a tremendous success, and the Warner Bros. investment began to pay.

The success of *Don Juan*, *The Jazz Singer*, and the shorts convinced other studios that sound contributed to profitable filmmaking. Unlike the early period of filmmaking and the Motion Pictures Patents Company, there was now no fierce

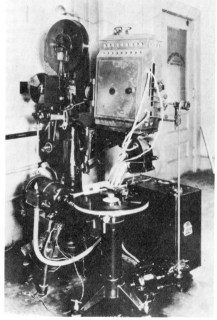
Fig. 11.24

Fig. 11.25

Fig. 11.26

competition within the industry. Instead, firms realized that whatever sound system the studios finally adopted, it would have to be compatible with the projection machinery set up in any theater. Eventually a sound-on-film rather than a sound-on-disc system became the standard and continues so to the present. (That is, as we saw in Chapter 1, the sound track is recorded on the strip of film alongside the image.) By 1930 most theaters in America were wired for sound.

For a few years, sound created a setback for Hollywood film style. The camera had to be put inside a sound booth so that its motor noise would not be picked up by the microphone. Figure 11.25 is a publicity still showing a setup for a dialogue scene in a 1928 MGM film. The camera operator can hear only through his earphones; obviously the camera cannot move except for short pans to reframe. The bulky microphone, on the table at the right, also did not move; the actors had to stay within a limited space if their speech was to register on the track. The result of such restrictions was a short phase of static films resembling stage plays.

Still, from the very beginning of sound filming, solutions were found for these problems. Sometimes several cameras, all in soundproof booths, would record the scene from different angles simultaneously. The resulting footage could be cut together to provide a standard analytical editing pattern in a scene, with all the sound synchronized perfectly. The whole camera booth might be mounted on wheels, or a scene might be shot silent and a sound track added later. Early sound films such as Rouben Mamoulian's *Applause* (1929) and René Clair's *Under the Roofs of Paris* (1930) demonstrate that the camera soon regained a great flexibility of movement. Later, smaller cases, enclosing only the camera body, replaced the cumbersome booths. These *blimps* (Fig. 11.26) permitted camerapersons to place the camera on movable supports. Similarly, microphones mounted on booms and hanging over the heads of the actors could also follow moving action without a loss of recording quality.

Once camera movement and subject movement were restored to the sound films, filmmakers continued to use many of the stylistic characteristics developed in Hollywood during the silent period. Diegetic sound provided a powerful addition to the system of continuity editing; a sound overlap could establish spaces outside the frame and could create temporal continuity.

Within the overall patterns of continuity style and classical narrative form, each of the large studios developed a distinctive approach of its own. Thus MGM, for example, became the prestige studio, with a huge number of stars and technicians under long-term contract. MGM lavished money on settings, costumes, and special effects, as in *The Good Earth* (1937), with its locust attack, or *San Francisco* (1936) in which the great earthquake is spectacularly re-created. Warner Bros., in spite of its success with sound, was still a relatively small studio and specialized in less expensive genre pictures. Its series of gangster films (*Little Caesar, Public Enemy*) and musicals (*Forty-Second Street, Golddiggers of 1933*) were among the studio's most successful products. Even lower on the ladder of prestige was Universal, which depended on imaginative filmmaking rather than established stars or expensive sets in its atmospheric horror films such as *Frankenstein* (1931) and *The Old Dark House* (1932).

One major genre, the musical, became possible only with the introduction of sound. (Indeed, the original intention of the Warners when they began their investment in sound equipment was the cheap circulation of vaudeville acts, which had previously toured the country live.) The form of most musicals involved separate numbers inserted into a linear narrative (although a few "revue" musicals simply strung together a series of numbers, with virtually no connecting narrative). One of the major studios, RKO, made a series of musicals starring Fred Astaire and Ginger Rogers; *Swing Time* (George Stevens, 1936) illustrates how a musical can be a classically constructed narrative. Like *Our Hospitality, Swing Time* contains a set of causally important motifs that recur to create a tight narrative. Fred comes from a family of gamblers, and his skill allows him to win a night club away from its owner—a bandleader who is also a gambler. Thus Fred wins Ginger, who works for the bandleader. As a gambler, the hero has a "lucky" quarter, the loss of which causes his initial meeting with Ginger. (The Ginger Rogers character is even named Penny, which links her immediately to the "lucky quarter" motif.) Here the musical numbers are motivated by the narrative. Initially Ginger works in a dancing school; although Fred is a professional dancer, he pretends to be a beginner to get to know her. When Ginger decides to marry the bandleader, Fred persuades her to dance one last romantic dance with him; this helps to motivate the final scene, in which Ginger chooses Fred instead of the bandleader. Stylistically, the musical numbers are set apart from the other scenes by a change in the rhythm of the editing; shots within musical numbers tend to be much longer.

During the 1930s, color film stocks became widely used for the first time. Photographic color had been around in various forms since 1908. In the 1920s, a few films had Technicolor sequences, but the process was too costly to use extensively. But by the mid-1930s, three-step Technicolor was proven to be economically feasible. After *Becky Sharp* (1935), a major all-color feature-length film, and *The Trail of the Lonesome Pine* (1936), studios began using Technicolor extensively. (See Plates 10 and 11, from *Meet Me in St. Louis*, for examples of Technicolor.)

Technicolor needed a great deal of light on the set, and the light had to favor certain hues. Thus, brighter lights specifically designed for color filmmaking were introduced. Some cinematographers began to use the new lights for black-and-white filming. These brighter lights, combined with the fast film stocks, made it easier to achieve greater depth of field by using more light and a smaller aperture. Many cinematographers stuck to the standard soft-focus style of the 1920s and 1930s, but others began to experiment.

By the late 1930s, there was a definite trend toward a deep-focus style. We have already seen an example in Ford's *Stagecoach* (1939; see Figs. 10.1 and

10.2). Mervyn Leroy's *Anthony Adverse* (1936), Alfred L. Werker's *The Adventures of Sherlock Holmes* (1939), and the Sam Wood–William Cameron Menzies *Our Town* (1940) also utilized deep focus to a considerable degree. But it was *Citizen Kane* that in 1941 brought deep focus strongly to the attention of spectators and film-makers alike. Welles's compositions placed the foreground figures very close to the camera and the background figures deep in the space of the shot. In some cases, the "deep-focus" image was actually achieved through process work such as matting and rear projection. Overall, *Citizen Kane* helped make the tendency toward deep focus a major part of classical Hollywood style in the next decade. Many films using the technique soon appeared. *Citizen Kane*'s cinematographer, Gregg Toland, worked on some of them, such as *The Little Foxes* (William Wyler, 1941).

With deep focus came a corresponding emphasis on the long take. Rather than setting up a conversation scene with the actors close together but in separate reverse shots, the filmmaker might now place them in depth in a single framing. The brightness of the light necessary for deep focus also tended to lend a hard-edged appearance to objects. Gauzy effects were largely eliminated, and much 1940s cinema became visually quite distinct from that of the 1930s. But the insistence on the clear narrative functioning of all these techniques remained strong. The classical Hollywood narrative modified itself over the years but did not change radically.

This has remained true until the present day. In the 1950s Hollywood responded to the invention of television (which competed with it for audiences) by introducing a series of technical innovations. Some of these (stereo, wide screen) have remained with us in one form or another. Others (3-D, Cinerama) have been used only sporadically in recent years. With the dwindling of the film audience, Hollywood has tended toward specialization. Where once it tried to lure the "family" audience, now it makes some films specifically for children, others specifically for college students, still others to be shown only in drive-ins.

But, in spite of these technical innovations and fashions in types of narrative form, the basic style of the classical Hollywood cinema remains. Continuity editing is still assumed to be the norm. The scene in *Jaws* (1975) where the young scientist visits the Brodys at home is handled very similarly to the restaurant sequence in *His Girl Friday;* both have three characters at a table and present the dialogue in a series of reverse shots. Similarly, you can spot shot/reverse shot, crosscutting, and other classical techniques at work in *Broadcast News* (1987), *Raising Arizona* (1987), and many other recent films. Clear, linear narrative remains the dominant factor in this type of filmmaking.

## JAPANESE CINEMA OF THE 1930s

Many countries' film production of the sound period is worthy of study and discussion. We have chosen to discuss Japan because it offers an especially interesting case of how a national cinema can both absorb and significantly modify conventions of classical Hollywood filmmaking.

Movies in Japan were from the start a foreign import: Edison films were shown in 1896, Lumière films a year later. At this time, Japan was eager to modernize itself and assimilate Western customs and knowledge. By 1920, there were hundreds of movie theaters, several small production companies, and two studios that would dominate the industry in a manner reminiscent of the U.S. "majors": Nippon

Katsudo Shashin (Japan Cinematograph Company), usually known as Nikkatsu; and the Shochiku Cinema Company. The demand was so great that production firms turned out films in a mass-production fashion similar to Hollywood's: the 1920s output averaged at least 700 films per year.

The Japanese gave this Western import some novel twists. A form of theater known as *rensa-geki* ("chain drama") used film freely, alternating live scenes on stage with film sequences. More significantly, there was the *benshi*, a live performer who accompanied the film screening in the theater by commenting on the action and playing all the vocal parts. These performers were enormously popular. There were *benshi* fan clubs, records, and even radio broadcasts. The Japanese thus initially treated cinema as a spectacle requiring a continuous verbal accompaniment, like the traditional theatrical forms of *kabuki* and puppet drama.

Chiefly under the leadership of Shochiku, the Japanese cinema eagerly studied and imitated American filmmaking. Chaplin, Griffith, Ince, Fairbanks, and other filmmakers were widely known and discussed. Studios ordered American equipment, hired Hollywood-trained Japanese actors and directors, and sent executives on visits to study U.S. production methods. Although very few Japanese films of the 1920s survive, most of them reveal an awareness of classical narrative construction and style. By 1930, Japanese directors had mastered the basic conventions of mainstream Western filmmaking. At the same time, the Japanese studios were cultivating specific genres that owed a good deal to their native culture. Following theatrical precedent, the Japanese divided films into two basic types: the *jidai-geki* (historical film, usually pre-1868) and the *gendai-geki* (film of contemporary life). Within the *jidai-geki*, the most popular genre was the *chambara*, or sword-fight movie. Hundreds of films in this popular genre were made every year. Within the *gendai-geki* category were many genres—the *haha-mono* ("mother-film"), the "tendency" film of social criticism, the *nansensu* ("nonsense" comedy), the *sarariman* ("salaryman") film about the life of office workers, and others. Some of these modern-life genres were modeled on American ones (Harold Lloyd films were popular *nansensu* sources), but others, such as the tendency film and the "salaryman" film, developed out of contemporary trends in Japanese fiction and journalism.

If the Japanese cinema had a golden age, many historians suggest that it was the 1930s. This was an era of great changes—severe economic depression, a rising tide of militaristic ideology and international aggression, the gradual emergence of a sound cinema, and the elimination of the *benshi*. Yet the very turbulence of the period seems to have contributed to an energetic film culture. Film magazines and books of film theory began to be published. The studios had perfected their own approach to the mass production of films in all genres, while foreign films were being imported and studied in large numbers. In form and style, the Japanese films of the 1930s exhibit a striking mixture of borrowings and innovations.

In general, the Japanese cinema of the 1930s employs principles of narrative structure modeled on those of classical Hollywood. Screenwriters would watch American films to learn how to construct a script. A typical *chambara* plot of the period consists of a clear cause-and-effect struggle, often involving a kidnapping or theft and always punctuated by frenzied sword fights. The climax is usually a pitched battle, in which the swordsman or his allies may be killed, but closure and triumph of virtue are usually ensured. The *gendai-geki* genre also employs a clear causal basis, with the delineation of interpersonal problems and the development toward a solution. Since Japanese fiction has traditionally favored a rambling and fragmentary approach to narrative form, the overall linear unity of Japanese films testifies to the importance of Hollywood's influence.

Certain aspects of narrative form, however, make Japanese films a little "looser" than the Hollywood model. There are fewer appeals to deadlines to unify the film, especially in the *gendai-geki*. Narration tends to be somewhat more overt, often superimposing an expository title over a scene of action. Before around 1935, filmmakers could count on the *benshi* to supply story information. The visual track could thus be less explicit. For example, the filmmaker might alternate shots of a character listening with dialogue titles proceeding from an offscreen character; this would pose no problem for the viewer, since the *benshi*'s mimicry would distinguish between the two characters. Most strikingly, the linearity of classical narrative might be broken by short scenes or transitions that rely more on associational principles. Dialogue between characters might be interrupted by a cutaway to an object associated with an absent character, or a scene might open on a series of shots that provide many details of setting. A Hollywood filmmaker might consider such shots digressions and snip them out, but for the Japanese such brief pauses in the narrative flow accumulated mood and emotional force. At such moments, some filmmakers sought to achieve the compressed suggestiveness of Japanese poetry.

Japanese filmmakers of the 1930s exhibited a comparable flexibility in their use of film technique. Although Japanese filmmakers usually adhere to classical continuity editing, they break the 180° line more often than would a Hollywood director. Some directors utilize 180° cuts, often establishing a scene from one side and then cutting in closer from the opposite side. There is also less concern for smooth and unnoticeable camera movements: a vigorous fight scene in a *chambara* might well be filmed in a bumpy, hand-held panning or tracking movement. The Japanese director makes far more use of location filming than would his American counterpart, and he seems to use wide-angle lenses much more often. The films also tend to create a deeper space than was common in American film before *Citizen Kane*. The *chambara* makes extensive use of movement straight toward the camera, as in Yoshiro Tsuji's *Mito Kōmon* (1932), in which a swordsman slays his enemies inside a room (Fig. 11.27) and then charges out at the viewer, slashing through the paper walls (Fig. 11.28). In general, Japanese film style is somewhat more varied in its choice of techniques, which often function to freshen up a stereotypical scene by appeal to suspense or surprise.

Fig. 11.27

Fig. 11.28

Many important directors worked at this period—Teinosuke Kinugasa, Tomu Uchida, Yasujiro Shimizu, Sadao Yamanaka, Mikio Naruse—but by common consent the two most significant were Kenji Mizoguchi and Yasujiro Ozu. Each one utilized particular norms of the Japanese cinema but also went beyond them to create a unique approach to film style. Mizoguchi, who worked in several genres, became most famous after two 1936 films, *Naniwa Elegy* and *Sisters of Gion*. His style utilized very long takes (a rare choice in a cinema that valued editing) and complicated camera movements. (We discuss a scene from *Sisters of Gion* in Chapter 6, p. 196.) By 1942, with his two-part film *Genroku Chushingura (The 47 Ronin)*, he was holding his shots for several minutes and employing a crane for sweeping high angles. Mizoguchi also extended his colleagues' use of deep space by an emphasis on deep focus which creates the sort of composition that Welles would later develop in *Citizen Kane*. (See Fig. 11.29, from *Naniwa Elegy*.) After World War II, Mizoguchi won international fame with *Ugetsu Monogatari* (1953) and *Sansho the Bailiff* (1954).

Yasujiro Ozu likewise gained international recognition in the postwar period, especially for *Tokyo Story* (1953; see pp. 328–332). But his first major films go back to the 1930s. He specialized in *gendai-geki* genres: *nansensu* comedies, *haha-*

Fig. 11.29

*mono* like *The Only Son* (1936), and salaryman films like *I Was Born, But . . .* (1932). His films extend the convention of the "poetic digression" by prolonging it and organizing it so as to cheat our expectations. In *The Only Son*, the son and his mother visit an old friend who runs a pork chop reataurant. Ozu cuts from the man washing his face to a washline full of clothes, then to a pump by the road. We might take these as signals that the scene is over. But Ozu cuts back to the restaurant sign, and we return to mother, son, and friend, already in the middle of a conversation. Similarly, most Japanese directors break the axis of action occasionally, but Ozu goes beyond random violations to create an alternative spatial system. As we saw in Chapter 10, he creates a 360° space for his scenes, slicing the space into multiples of 45°. Ozu's most obvious innovation was his use of a camera height that is consistently and strikingly lower than usual. This is not a "typically Japanese" choice (his fellow filmmakers were baffled), but one effect it has is to create a stylistic uniformity that lets the viewer concentrate on slight variations of shot composition.

The formal and stylistic variety of 1930s filmmaking gradually waned during the 1940s. In part this is attributable to tightening governmental control during the Pacific war and then to strict censorship during the U.S. Occupation. Whatever the cause, the ordinary Japanese film of the 1940s seems virtually identical to the classical Hollywood product. Ozu and Mizoguchi, however, revealed their commitment to their idiosyncratic methods in such works as the former's *Brothers and Sisters of the Toda Family* (1941), *There Was a Father* (1942), *Record of a Tenement Gentleman* (1947), and *Late Spring* (1949), and the latter's *Utamaro and His Five Women* (1946) and *Women of the Night* (1948). By the 1950s, the West had learned of the Japanese cinema, identifying it principally with another major director, Akira Kurosawa. Kurosawa's works hark back to the traditional genres: *Seven Samurai* (1954) and *Yojimbo* (1961) are *jidai-geki*; *Ikiru* (1952) and *I Live in Fear* (1955) recall the tendency film. But Kurosawa, who started as a script writer and assistant director in the 1930s, also acknowledges the influence of Western cinema, especially in the 1920s and 1930s. In mixing Western stylistic and dramaturgical principles with an urge for experimentation, Kurosawa continues the pluralistic tradition of the Japanese cinema of the golden era.

## ITALIAN NEOREALISM (1942–1951)

There is no definitive source for the term "neorealism," but it first appeared in the early 1940s in the writings of Italian critics as a way of describing filmmaking that sought to break free of the conventions of ordinary cinema. Some critics applied the term approvingly to French films of the 1930s, especially works by Jean Renoir. Other critics turned closer to home to praise films like Luchino Visconti's *Ossessione* (1942). Why was this a "new" realism? Under Mussolini, the motion picture industry had tended to concentrate on colossal historical epics and sentimental upper-class melodramas (nicknamed "white-telephone" films). Although significant documentary films were produced, filmmakers seldom left the lavish Cinecittà studios to set fictional stories in the context of contemporary life. After Mussolini's fall in 1943, as several filmmakers began to make films with the goal of revealing contemporary social conditions, the trend became the neorealist movement.

Economic, political, and cultural factors helped neorealism survive. Nearly all the major neorealists—Roberto Rossellini, Vittorio De Sica, Luchino Visconti, and others—came to the movement as experienced filmmakers. They knew one another, frequently shared scriptwriters and personnel, and gained public attention in the journals *Cinema* and *Bianco e Nero*. Before 1948 the neorealist movement had enough friends in the government to be relatively free of censorship. Small, independent production companies blossomed. There was even a correspondence between neorealism and an Italian literary movement of the same period modeled on the *verismo* of the previous century. Visconti's *Ossessione* (1942) and *La Terra Trema* (1947); Rossellini's *Open City* (1945), *Paisan* (1946), and *Germany Year Zero* (1947); De Sica's *Shoeshine* (1946) and *Bicycle Thief* (1948); and other works of Lattuada, Blasetti, De Santis, and Germi—the major Italian films of the 1940s—were supported to one extent or another, allied with the neorealist impulse.

Because of these factors, neorealism created a distinct approach to film style. By 1945 the fighting had destroyed most of Cinecittà, so studio settings were in short supply and sound equipment was rare. As a result, neorealist mise-en-scene relied on actual locales, and its photographic work tended toward the raw roughness of documentaries. Rossellini has told of buying bits of negative stock from street photographers, so that much of *Open City* was shot on different qualities of film stock.

Shooting on the streets and in private buildings made Italian camera operators adept at cinematography that avoided the "three-point" lighting system of Hollywood. (See Fig. 5.31.) Although neorealist films often featured famous stage or film actors, they also made use of nonactors, recruited for their realistic looks or behavior. For the adult "star" of *Bicycle Thief*, De Sica chose a factory worker: "The way he moved, the way he sat down, his gestures with those hands of a working man and not of an actor . . . everything about him was perfect." The Italian cinema had a long tradition of dubbing and the ability to postsynchronize dialogue permitted the filmmakers to work on location with smaller crews and to move the camera. With a degree of improvisational freedom in the acting and setting went a certain flexibility of framing and camera movement, well displayed in the death of Pina in *Open City*, the final sequence of *Germany Year Zero*, and the magnificent panning and tracking shots in *La Terra Trema*. The tracking shots through the open-air bicycle market in *Bicycle Thief* illustrate the possibilities which the neorealist director found in returning to location filming (Fig. 11.30).

No less influential was the neorealist sense of narrative form. Reacting against the intricately plotted white-telephone dramas, the neorealists tended to loosen up narrative relations. The earliest major films of the movement, such as *Ossessione*, *Open City*, and *Shoeshine*, contain relatively conventionally organized plots (albeit with unhappy endings). But the most formally innovative neorealist films tend to allow the intrusion of noncausally motivated ("accidental") details, such as the famous scene in *Bicycle Thief* in which the hero encounters a group of priests during a rain shower (Fig. 11.31). Although the causes of characters' actions are usually seen as concretely economic and political (poverty, unemployment, exploitation), the effects are often fragmentary and inconclusive. Rossellini's *Paisan* is frankly episodic, presenting six anecdotes of life in Italy during the Allied invasion; often we are not told the outcome of an event, the consequence of a cause. The ambiguity of neorealist films is also a product of a narration that refuses to yield an omniscient knowledge of events, as if the totality of reality is simply unknowable. This is especially evident in the films' endings. *Bicycle Thief* concludes with the worker and his son wandering down the street, their stolen bicycle still missing,

Fig. 11.30

Fig. 11.31

their future uncertain. Although ending with the defeat of the Sicilian fishermen's revolt against the merchants, *La Terra Trema* does not cancel the possibility that a later revolt will succeed. Neorealism's tendency toward a slice-of-life plot construction and unrestricted narration gave many films of the movement an open-ended quality quite opposed to the narrative closure of the Hollywood cinema.

As economic and cultural forces had sustained the neorealist movement, so they were prime causes of its cessation. When Italy began to prosper after the war, the government looked askance at films so critical of contemporary society. After 1949, censorship and state pressures began to constrain the movement. Large-scale Italian film production began to reappear, and neorealism no longer had the freedom of the small production company. Finally, the neorealist directors, now famous, began to pursue more individualized concerns: Rossellini's investigation of Christian humanism and Western history, De Sica's sentimental romances, Luchino Visconti's examination of upper-class milieux. Most historians date the end of the neorealist movement with the public attacks on De Sica's *Umberto D* (1951). Nevertheless, neorealist elements are still quite visible in the early works of Federico Fellini (*I Vitelloni*, 1954, is a good example) and of Michelangelo Antonioni (*Cronaca di un amore*, 1951); both directors had worked on neorealist films. The movement has exercised a considerable influence on individual filmmakers such as Satyajit Ray and on groups such as the French New Wave.

## THE NEW WAVE (1959–1964)

In the mid-1950s a group of young men who wrote for the Paris film journal *Cahiers du cinéma* made a habit of attacking the most artistically respected French filmmakers of the day. "I consider an adaptation of value," wrote François Truffaut, "only when written by a *man of the cinema*. Aurenche and Bost [the leading scriptwriters of the time] are essentially literary men and I reproach them here for being contemptuous of the cinema by underestimating it." Addressing 21 major directors, Jean-Luc Godard asserted, "Your camera movements are ugly because your subjects are bad, your casts act badly because your dialogue is worthless; in a word, you don't know how to create cinema because you no longer even know what it is." Truffaut and Godard, along with Claude Chabrol, Eric Rohmer, and Jacques Rivette, championed certain directors considered somewhat outdated (Jean Renoir, Max Ophuls) or esoteric (Robert Bresson, Jacques Tati). More important, the young men saw no contradiction in rejecting the French filmmaking establishment while loving blatantly commercial Hollywood. The young rebels of *Cahiers* claimed that in the works of certain directors—certain *auteurs* (authors)—artistry existed in the American cinema. An *auteur* managed to stamp his or her personality on genre and studio products, transcending the constraints of a mass-production system. Howard Hawks, Otto Preminger, Samuel Fuller, Vincente Minnelli, Nicholas Ray, Alfred Hitchcock—these were more than craftsmen. Each person's total output constituted a coherent world. Truffaut quoted Giraudoux, "There are no works, there are only *auteurs*."

Writing criticism did not, however, satisfy these young men. They itched to make films. Borrowing money from friends and filming on location, each started to shoot short films. By 1959 they had become a force to be reckoned with. In that year Rivette filmed *Paris nous appartient (Paris Belongs to Us);* Godard made *A*

*Bout de souffle (Breathless);* Chabrol made his second feature, *Les Cousins;* and in April Truffaut's *Les Quatre cent coups (The 400 Blows)* won the Grand Prize at the Cannes Festival. Godard treated it as a victory: "We won the day in having it acknowledged in principle that a film by Hitchcock, for example, is as important as a book by Aragon. Film *auteurs*, thanks to us, have finally entered the history of art."

The novelty and youthful vigor of these directors led journalists to nickname them *la nouvelle vague*—the "New Wave." Their output was staggering. All told, the five directors made 32 feature films between 1959 and 1966; Godard and Chabrol made 11 apiece! So many films must of course be highly disparate, but there are enough similarities of narrative form and cinematic style for us to identify a New Wave movement.

The most obviously revolutionary quality of the New Wave films was their casual look; to proponents of the carefully polished French "cinema of quality," the young directors must have seemed hopelessly sloppy. The New Wave directors had admired the neorealists (especially Rossellini) and in opposition to studio filmmaking, took as their mise-en-scene actual locales in and around Paris. Shooting on location became the norm. Similarly, glossy studio lighting was replaced by what Raoul Coutard called "light of day." The New Wave also encouraged its actors to improvise their lines, even if that might slow down the plot: *Breathless*'s bedroom scene was startling for many reasons but partly because of its rambling, repetitious dialogue.

Given such mise-en-scene, cinematography changed too. In general, the New Wave camera moves a great deal. It is often panning (sometimes 360°, as in *Jules and Jim*) and tracking, following characters or tracing out relations within a locale. Furthermore, shooting cheaply on location demanded flexible, portable equipment. Fortunately, Eclair had recently developed a lightweight camera that could be hand held. (That the Eclair had been used primarily for documentary work accorded perfectly with the "realistic" mise-en-scene of the New Wave.) New Wave films were intoxicated with the new freedom offered by the hand-held camera. In *The 400 Blows* the camera explores a cramped apartment and rides a carnival centrifuge. *Paris Belongs to Us* also contains hand-held-camera scenes within apartment locations. In *Breathless* the cinematographer held the camera while seated in a wheelchair to follow the hero along a complex path in a travel agency's office.

Along with the hand-held camera went an interest in the long take, which the New Wave directors admired in the work of American filmmakers such as Vincente Minnelli and Otto Preminger and in Japanese directors such as Kenji Mizoguchi. Figure 11.32 is from a long-take shot in *Breathless;* the hand-held camera moves back (Coutard held the camera while seated in a wheelchair) as the characters chat and stroll along a Paris street. The casual style of the New Wave resulted in occasional accidental intrusions by passersby, as with the man at the right, who glances at the actors.

One more quality of the New Wave style should be mentioned: its humor. These young men deliberately played with the medium. In Godard's *Band of Outsiders* the three main characters resolve to be silent for a minute, and Godard dutifully shuts off *all* the sound. In Truffaut's *Shoot the Piano Player* a character swears that he's not lying: "May my mother drop dead if I'm not telling the truth." Cut to a shot of an old lady keeling over. But most often the humor lies in intricate references to other films, Hollywood or European. These are homages to admired *auteurs:* Godard characters allude to *Johnny Guitar* (Ray), *Some Came Running* (Minnelli), and "Arizona Jim" (from Renoir's *Crime of M. Lange*). In *Les Carabiniers*

Fig. 11.32

Godard parodies Lumière, and in *Vivre sa vie* he "quotes" *La Passion de Jeanne d'Arc*. Hitchcock is frequently cited in Chabrol's films, and Truffaut's *Les Mistons* re-creates a shot from a Lumière short; compare Figure 11.33 with the frame from *L'Arroseur arrosé* (Fig. 5.7). Such homages even became in-jokes, as when New Wave actors Jean-Claude Brialy and Jeanne Moreau "walk on" in *The 400 Blows* or when a Godard character mentions "Arizona Jules" (combining names from *M. Lange* and *Jules and Jim*). Such gags, the New Wave directors felt, took some of the solemnity out of filmmaking and film viewing.

Fig. 11.33

New Wave films were narrative films, but as a group they were perhaps the most perplexing, discontinuous narratives that film viewers had seen since surrealist filmmaking. In general, causal connections became quite loose. Why does Michel, the hero of *Breathless*, behave as he does? Is there actually a political conspiracy going on in *Paris Belongs to Us?* Why is Nana shot at the end of *Vivre sa vie?* In *Shoot the Piano Player* the first sequence consists mainly of a conversation between the hero's brother and a man he accidentally meets on the street; the latter tells of his marital problems at some length, even though he has nothing to do with the film's narrative.

Moreover, the films often lack goal-oriented protagonists. The heroes may drift aimlessly, engage in actions on the spur of the moment, spend their time talking and drinking in a café or going to movies. New Wave narratives often introduce startling shifts in tone, jolting our expectations. In *Breathless*, Michel's comic monologue in the first scene as he drives along a road leads directly into his brutal murder of a policeman. When two gangsters kidnap the hero and his girlfriend in *Shoot the Piano Player*, the whole group begins a comic discussion of sex. Discontinuous editing—seen at its limit in Godard's jump cuts—further disturbs narrative continuity. Perhaps most important, the New Wave film typically ends ambiguously. In *Breathless*, Michel dies cursing his girlfriend, Patricia; looking out at us, her response is to rub her lip in the same Bogart-inspired gesture Michel himself has used, then to turn abruptly away. Antoine in *The 400 Blows* reaches the sea in the last shot, but as he moves forward, Truffaut zooms in and freezes the frame, ending the film with the question of where Antoine will go from here. In Chabrol's *Les Bonnes Femmes* and *Ophelia*, in Rivette's *Paris Belongs to Us*, and in nearly all of the work of Godard and Truffaut in this period, the looseness of the causal chain leads to endings that remain defiantly open and uncertain.

Curiously, despite the demands that the films place on the viewer and despite the critical rampages of the filmmakers, the French film industry was not hostile to the New Wave. The decade 1947–57 had been good to film production: the government supported the industry through enforced quotas, banks had invested heavily, and there was a flourishing business of international coproductions. But in 1957 cinema attendance fell off drastically (chiefly because television became more widespread). By 1959 the industry was in a crisis. The New Wave method of independent financing of low-budget films seemed to offer a good solution. New Wave directors shot films much more quickly and cheaply than did reigning directors. Moreover, the young directors helped one another out and thus reduced the financial risk by the established companies. Thus the French industry supported the New Wave through distribution, exhibition, and eventually production.

Indeed, it is possible to argue that by 1964, although each New Wave director had his or her own production company, the group had become absorbed into the French film industry. Godard made *Le Mépris (Contempt,* 1963) for a major commercial producer, Carlo Ponti; Truffaut made *Fahrenheit 451* (1966) in England for Universal; and Chabrol began turning out parodies of James Bond thrillers.

Dating the exact end of the movement is difficult, but most historians select 1964, when the characteristic New Wave form and style had already become diffused and imitated (by, for instance, Tony Richardson in his 1963 film *Tom Jones*). Certainly, after 1968 the political upheavals in France drastically altered the personal relations among the directors. Chabrol, Truffaut, and Rohmer became firmly entrenched in the French film industry, whereas Godard set up an experimental film and video studio in Switzerland, and Rivette began to create narratives of staggering complexity and length (such as *Out One*, originally about 12 hours long!). By the mid-1980s, Truffaut had died, Chabrol's films went largely unseen outside France, and Rivette's output had become esoteric. Rohmer retained international attention with his ironic tales of love and self-deception among the upper middle class (*Pauline at the Beach* [1982] and *Full Moon over Paris* [1984]), while Godard continued to attract notoriety with such films as *Passion* (1981) and his controversial retelling of the Old and New Testaments, *Hail Mary* (1983). In retrospect, the New Wave not only offered several original and valuable films but also demonstrated that renewal in the film industry could come from talented, aggressive young people inspired in large part by the sheer love of cinema.

## THE NEW GERMAN CINEMA (1966–1982)

The New German Cinema is not a stylistic movement in the sense that Italian neorealism and the French New Wave were. That is, it did not consist of a group of filmmakers using comparable stylistic traits. Rather, the term was coined to describe a surprising revival in the largely moribund German cinema by a number of young filmmakers who began working outside the traditional industry in the 1960s. These young filmmakers resorted to common production tactics, such as obtaining alternative financing and often banding together for mutual support in such matters as distribution. But each filmmaker had his or her own ideas about how films should be made, and as a result the "New German Cinema" consists of a tremendous variety of films.

The German film industry had emerged from the war in serious trouble. The Nazi government, after coming to power in 1933, had taken control of the industry. With the defeat of the Nazis, the industry itself virtually collapsed. Yet the occupying countries—the United States, England, France, and the USSR—dictated the types of films to be made. In the Soviet sector these were essentially Socialist Realist films (the same types of optimistic, pro-Soviet films that had become the official style in the USSR and had brought about the end of the montage movement).

In the Western sector, American control dominated. Strict censorship of German films was instituted, and the Americans took advantage of the situation to capture the bulk of the German market for their own imported films. The United States government outlawed import quotas, so that the Germans could not limit the number of American films that entered their market. Only a few interesting German films were made in the immediate postwar period. Some hinted at a socially critical, location-shot approach comparable to Italian neorealism. But, for the most part, the small number of German films made was escapist fare that avoided using anything from the Nazi period as subject matter.

After the division of the country into East and West Germany in 1949, the West German government attempted to stimulate production by offering credit guarantees. Although a greater number of films were made between 1950 and 1956, they continued to be undistinguished. After 1957, with the increasing competition from television, even this minor boom period ended. The industry reached a low point in 1961, when the prize given annually to the best German film shown at the Berlin Film Festival was not awarded—the judges could not find a film good enough to deserve it.

At the same time, a number of young filmmakers were making short films. Although they aspired to make feature-length productions, they were too untraditional in their approaches to get work within the industry. Short films were shown at a special annual festival at Oberhausen. At the 1962 festival a group of 26 filmmakers signed a key document, the Oberhausen Manifesto. In it they called for young filmmakers to replace the old:

> German short films by young auteurs, directors, and producers have in recent years received a great number of prizes at international festivals, and have met with approval by international critics. These works and their successes show that the future of the German cinema lies with those who have shown that they speak a new language of the cinema. As in other countries, so too in Germany the short film has become the training ground and laboratory for the feature film. We declare our intention to be the creation of the new German film.

As this passage indicates, these German filmmakers were familiar with the French New Wave—then only three years old. They knew of the *auteur* theory and that Truffaut, Godard, and others had begun by making shorts. Some of the signers of the Oberhausen Manifesto did in fact go on to become the first generation of New German filmmakers, the most prominent of them being Alexander Kluge (among whose most famous films are *Artists at the Top of the Big Top—Disoriented* [1967] and *Occasional Work of a Female Slave* [1973]).

Yet there are major differences between the New German Cinema filmmakers and those of the New Wave. The former had no central critical or theoretical position to lead them to employ similar approaches to film form. Instead, they primarily united around their common need to create a favorable production situation. Also, unlike the young French filmmakers, these Germans had little sense of their own country's cinema tradition. The great filmmakers of the twenties had gone into exile, the Nazi-period films were not shown, and there was little interest in current filmmaking. They had no national models, as the French had Bresson, Tati, Renoir, and Ophuls. Instead, the Germans had been brought up on American films, and they admired many of the same Hollywood *auteurs* that *Cahiers du cinéma* praised.

After the Oberhausen Manifesto, it took some time to convince the government to support alternative filmmaking. But in 1964 the Kuratorium junger deutscher Film (Board of Governors of Young German Film) was set up to provide interest-free loans to young, inexperienced directors. This action provided the breakthrough for the New German Cinema, which can be said to have begun in 1966 with the release of a number of important films, including Kluge's first feature, *Yesterday Girl*, Volker Schlöndorff's *Young Törless*, and Jean-Marie Straub and Danièle Huillet's *Not Reconciled*. A number of these films won prizes at major film festivals, and other countries became aware suddenly that something interesting was happening in Germany. The result was a tremendous euphoria among the German filmmakers, which was somewhat comparable to the effect in France when Truffaut's *400 Blows* had won at Cannes in 1959. In 1967, there were seasons devoted to

New German films in Mannheim, London, Rome, Paris, and other cities (although the films had not yet had an impact in America).

But the commercial German film industry saw the support for independent directors as a government subsidization of competition and lobbied successfully both to cut the Kuratorium's budget and to get a law passed limiting financing to those directors who had already made one successful film. As a result, government funding swung away from young directors toward more traditional commercial products. Moreover, even when young directors got production funding, they had trouble finding distributors and exhibitors willing to give up the more lucrative Hollywood imports and take a risk on somewhat experimental films by little-known directors.

Two solutions to these problems allowed the filmmakers to keep working. First, in 1971, thirteen of them formed the Filmverlag der Autoren. (*Verlag* means "publisher," and *autoren* means "authors"—note again the connection to the *auteur* theory.) This was an independent distribution company with shares owned by a number of key directors, including Kluge and Wim Wenders. Rainer Werner Fassbinder later bought shares as well. The company was well managed and became the main distributor for New German films within Germany.

The second solution involved television. TV had created competition for the film industry in Germany, as it had in other European countries. But because German television is state run and financed, it can show less popular films without worrying about ratings. In many European countries, television networks finance films, even if those films are to be shown theatrically before appearing on TV. Thus, in the late 1960s and 1970s, young directors could make a film that might show in only a few theaters but which would get backing from television.

The combination of control over their own distribution plus financing from national television gave the New German Cinema a sounder financial base, and many filmmakers turned out a great variety of films during the 1970s.

The year 1971 had proved a second turning point for the New German Cinema. Not only was the Filmverlag der Autoren founded, but a number of leading directors had major artistic and financial successes. After making a series of highly original but difficult experimental features in 1969 and 1970, Fassbinder made the film that first gained him international attention, *The Merchant of Four Seasons*. This began a period of his career when he made more accessible, socially critical films about contemporary German society. In the same year, Wim Wenders made his first feature, *The Goalie's Anxiety at the Penalty Kick*. Also in 1971, another major director of the group, Werner Herzog, began making *Aguirre, the Wrath of God*, which was released in 1972. Considered one of his best works, this epic of Spanish conquistadors on a mad search along the Amazon for the mythical El Dorado was one of the most popular of all the New German films. A tremendous hit in France, it is still frequently revived in the United States as well.

In spite of the high quality of some of these films, Germany itself had little interest in the New German Cinema. And, after the first flurry of exports and festival prizes in 1967, relatively few of the new films got extensive distribution abroad. But in 1974, with the increasingly favorable economic situation for production, the output increased. That year saw further enthusiastic recognition abroad. Fassbinder's *Ali—Fear Eats the Soul* won the Grand Prize at Cannes, and soon German films were being exported regularly.

The timing of the New German Cinema's increased output encouraged its success abroad. In the United States and elsewhere, "art-house" film theaters had grown up, specializing in showing foreign and independent films. French films had been popular in such theaters since the beginning of the New Wave. But, by the early 1970s, the New Wave had been over for some time, and the increasing demand for foreign films created a market receptive to the New German directors, whose work soon became the most widely shown foreign films in art cinemas. Fassbinder in particular became famous in the 1970s, and Herzog's films, such as *The Enigma of Kaspar Hauser* (1974) and *Stroszek* (1977), were also among the most successful imported films of the period. This made U.S. and European distributors anxious to discover more German filmmakers. Wenders's 1977 feature *The American Friend* introduced him to American audiences. As each new director was discovered, many of his or her past films were distributed abroad as well. In some cases, as with Fassbinder, this meant that many films appeared in a short time. To foreign audiences, it seemed that a sudden flood of new and exciting films was rushing out of Germany.

Stylistically, these films have little in common. The flamboyant camera movements and haunting, mysterious imagery of Herzog's *Aguirre, the Wrath of God* do not in the least resemble the restrained, almost motionless long takes and spare, black-and-white cinematography of Straub and Huillet's *The Chronicle of Anna Magdalena Bach* (see Figs. 5.49, 6.26, and 6.62). At most, one could perhaps characterize some of the filmmakers as sharing similar concerns in terms of subject matter. As an alternative group outside the mainstream film industry, many are leftist in their ideological outlook. Straub and Huillet are overtly Marxist, refusing to work on any sort of commercially oriented film. They work, somewhat as Godard did in the 1970s, with small production crews, making austere experimental films dealing with history; these go out to small audiences, often in nontheatrical viewing situations. Others, like Fassbinder, are leftist but less radically so. Fassbinder's films often deal with contemporary or recent German society from a critical perspective. But some of his films, especially late works like *The Marriage of Maria Braun* (1978) and *Lola* (1981), also sought a fairly wide, popular audience. Other filmmakers, like Wenders and Herzog, seem to have much less interest in social concerns, dealing instead with individual psychological studies and, in Herzog's case, mysticism.

Those filmmakers like Fassbinder who are interested in social concerns have worked in some distinctive genres that help characterize the New German Cinema. One group of films deals with the problems encountered by immigrant workers in Germany—the racism and alienation they experience (e.g., Fassbinder's *Katzelmacher* [1969] and *Ali—Fear Eats the Soul* [1973]). Another frequent subject involves the problems of older people, especially women. These films present sympathetic views of how the younger generation manipulates their elders (e.g., Fassbinder's *Mother Kusters Goes to Heaven* [1975]). A third group of films deals with women's concerns. The New German Cinema directors were the first large group to begin their work after the impact of the women's movement, and feminism plays a role in many films. Somewhat later in the period, a number of women directors began working; indeed, by 1978, a third of the German films at the Berlin Film Festival were by women directors. The most important of these to become known in the United States is Margaretha von Trotta (for example, *The German Sisters* [1981]).

By the late 1970s it was apparent that the filmmakers of the New German Cinema were becoming a less unified group. Many of its early practitioners were changing in much the same way that the French New Wave directors had in the mid-1960s—either going abroad or working for a more international and popular audience. Wenders came to America in the late 1970s to make *Hammett* (1982) and *Paris, Texas* (1984) and has worked in various countries since. Similarly, Herzog has worked in America, South America, and Europe, with backing from large American companies (20th Century–Fox financed his remake of the 1922 expressionist film, *Nosferatu* [1978]). Schlöndorff's *The Tin Drum* (1979) was one of the most successful foreign films ever brought to the United States, winning the Academy Award as best foreign film. On the other end of the scale, Straub and Huillet left Germany in the mid-1970s and now are based in Italy, making small, independent projects.

The 1982 death of the group's most prolific and popular director, Fassbinder, seemed to signal a sort of termination of the New German Cinema's first generation. With that event and the dispersion of the other directors to various countries and commercial or oppositional projects, the New German Cinema may well be said to have ended. But its accomplishments have endured, and there are no signs that the German industry will revert to its nadir of the late 1950s.

# BIBLIOGRAPHY
# FOR CHAPTER 11

## ■ GENERAL

Allen, Robert C., and Douglas Gomery. *Film History: Theory and Practice*. New York: Random House, 1985.

Bordwell, David. *Narration in the Fiction Film*. Madison: University of Wisconsin Press, 1985.

Branigan, Edward. "Color and Cinema: Problems in the Writing of History." *Film Reader* **4,** "Metahistory of Film" (1979): 16–34.

Cook, David A. *A History of Narrative Film*. New York: Norton, 1981.

Knight, Arthur. *The Liveliest Art*. New York: New American Library, 1957.

Luhr, William, ed. *World Cinema since 1945*. New York: Ungar, 1987.

MacGowan, Kenneth. *Behind the Screen*. New York: Dell, 1965.

"The Material History of Movies." Special number of *Quarterly Review of Film Studies* **3,** no. 1 (Winter 1978).

"Metahistory of Film." Special number of *Film Reader* **4** (1979).

Mitry, Jean. *Histoire du cinéma*. Vols. 1–3. Paris: Editions universitaires, 1967, 1969, 1973. Vols. 4–5. Paris: Jean-Pierre Delarge, 1980.

Nowell-Smith, Geoffrey. "Facts about Films and Facts of Films." *Quarterly Review of Film Studies* **1,** no. 3 (August 1967): 272–275.

Rotha, Paul. *The Film till Now*. London: Spring, 1967.

Sadoul, Georges. *Histoire générale du cinéma*. 6 vols. Paris: Denoël, 1973–77.

Salt, Barry. *Film Style and Technology: History and Analysis*. London: Starword, 1983.

Wölfflin, Heinrich. *Principles of Art History*. Translated by M. D. Hoffinger. New York: Dover, 1950.

## ■ EARLY CINEMA

Allen, Robert C. *Vaudeville and Film, 1895–1915: A Study in Media Interaction*. New York: Arno, 1980.

"Archives, Document, Fiction." Special number of *Iris* **2,** no. 1 (1984).

"Beginning . . . and Beginning Again." Special number on relationship of avant-garde and primitive film, *Afterimage* **8/9** (Spring 1981).

Burch, Noël. "Porter, or Ambivalence." *Screen* **19,** no. 4 (Winter 1978/79): 91–105.

Ceram, C. W. *Archaeology of the Cinema*. New York: Harcourt, Brace & World, 1965.

Chanan, Michael. *The Dream That Kicks: The Prehistory and Early Years of Cinema in Britain*. London: Routledge & Kegan Paul, 1980.

"Essays on D. W. Griffith." Special number of *Quarterly Review of Film Studies* **6,** no. 1 (Winter 1981).

Fell, John L., ed. *Film before Griffith*. Berkeley: University of California Press, 1983.

Hammond, Paul. *Marvelous Méliès*. New York: St. Martin's, 1975.

Hendricks, Gordon. *The Edison Motion Picture Myth*. Berkeley: University of California Press, 1961.

Kern, Stephen. *The Culture of Time and Space, 1880–1918*. Cambridge, Mass.: Harvard University Press, 1983.

Leyda, Jay, and Charles Musser, eds. *Before Hollywood: Turn-of-the-Century Film from American Archives*. New York: American Federation of the Arts, 1986.

Mayne, Judith. "Immigrants and Spectators." *Wide Angle* **5,** no. 2 (1982): 32–41.

Musser, Charles. "The Early Cinema of Edwin Porter." *Cinema Journal* **19,** no. 1 (Fall 1979): 1–38.

———. "The Nickelodeon Era Begins: Establishing the Framework for Hollywood's Mode of Representation." *Framework* **22/23** (Autumn 1983): 4–11.

Pratt, George, ed. *Spellbound in Darkness*. Greenwich, Conn.: New York Graphic Society, 1973.

Spehr, Paul C. *The Movies Begin*. Newark, N.J.: Newark Museum, 1977.

Thompson, Kristin, and David Bordwell. "Linearity, Materialism, and the Study of Early American Cinema." *Wide Angle* **5,** no. 3 (1983): 4–15.

## ■ CLASSICAL HOLLYWOOD CINEMA (1908–1927)

Balio, Tino, ed. *The American Film Industry*. Madison: University of Wisconsin Press, 1976.

Bordwell, David, Janet Staiger, and Kristin Thompson. *The Classical Hollywood Cinema: Film Style and Mode of Production to 1960*. New York: Columbia University Press, 1985.

Brownlow, Kevin. *The Parade's Gone By.* New York: Knopf, 1968.

"Economic and Technological History." Special number of *Cinema Journal* **18**, no. 2 (Spring 1979).

Hampton, Benjamin. *History of the American Film Industry.* New York: Dover, 1970.

Jacobs, Lewis. *The Rise of the American Film.* New York: Teachers College Press, 1968.

Koszarski, Richard. "Maurice Tourneur: The First of the Visual Stylists." *Film Comment* **9**, no. 2 (March–April 1973): 24–31.

Pratt, George. *Spellbound in Darkness.* Greenwich, Conn.: New York Graphic Society, 1973.


### ■ GERMAN EXPRESSIONISM

Barlow, John D. *German Expressionist Film.* Boston: Twayne, 1982.

Bronner, Stephen Eric, and Douglas Kellner, eds. *Passion and Rebellion: The Expressionist Heritage.* South Hadley, Mass.: J. F. Bergin, 1983.

Bucher, Felix, ed. *Germany.* New York: A. S. Barnes, 1970.

Eisner, Lotte. *F. W. Murnau.* Berkeley: University of California Press, 1973.

———. *Fritz Lang.* New York: Oxford University Press, 1977.

———. *The Haunted Screen.* Berkeley: University of California Press, 1969.

Elsaesser, Thomas. "Social Mobility and the Fantastic: German Silent Cinema." *Wide Angle* **5**, no. 2 (1982): 14–25.

Kracauer, Siegfried. *From Caligari to Hitler.* Princeton, N.J.: Princeton University Press, 1947.

Miesel, Victor H., ed. *Voices of German Expressionism.* Englewood Cliffs, N.J.: Prentice-Hall, 1970.

Myers, Bernard S. *The German Expressionists.* New York: Praeger, 1963.

Selz, Peter. *German Expressionist Painting.* Berkeley: University of California Press, 1957.

Titford, John S. "Object-Subject Relationships in German Expressionist Cinema." *Cinema Journal* **13**, no. 1 (Fall 1973): 17–24.

Tudor, Andrew. "Elective Affinities—the Myth of German Expressionism." *Screen* **12**, no. 3 (Summer 1971): 143–150.

Willett, John. *Expressionism.* New York: McGraw-Hill, 1970.

———. *The New Sobriety: Art and Politics in the Weimar Period, 1917–1933.* London: Thames & Hudson, 1978.


### ■ FRENCH IMPRESSIONISM

Abel, Richard. *French Cinema: The First Wave, 1915–1929.* Princeton, N.J.: Princeton University Press, 1984.

———. *French Film Theory and Criticism, 1907–1939.* Vol. 1. Princeton, N.J.: Princeton University Press, 1988.

Bordwell, David. *French Impressionist Cinema: Film Culture, Film Theory, and Film Style.* New York: Arno, 1980.

Brownlow, Kevin. *NAPOLEON: Abel Gance's Classic Film.* New York: Knopf, 1983.

Clair, René. *Cinema Yesterday and Tomorrow.* New York: Dover, 1972.

King, Norman. *Abel Gance: A Politics of Spectacle.* London: British Film Institute, 1984.

Liebman, Stuart. "French Film Theory, 1910–1921." *Quarterly Review of Film Studies* **8**, no. 1 (Winter 1983): 1–23.

Martin, Marcel. *France.* New York: A. S. Barnes, 1971.

Sadoul, Georges. *The French Cinema.* London: Falcon Press, 1952.


### ■ SOVIET MONTAGE

Bowlt, John, ed. *Russian Art of the Avant-Garde.* New York: Viking, 1973.

Carynnyk, Mario, ed. *Alexander Dovzhenko: Poet as Filmmaker.* Cambridge, Mass.: MIT Press, 1973.

Christie, Ian. "Soviet Cinema—Making Sense of Sound." *Screen* **23**, no. 2 (July–August 1982): 34–49.

Eisenstein, S. M. *S. M. Eisenstein: Writings,* Vol. 1, 1911–1934. Edited and translated by Richard Taylor. Bloomington: Indiana University Press, 1988.

Fuelop-Miller, René. *The Mind and Face of Bolshevism.* New York: Harper & Row, 1965.

Kepley, Vance. *In the Service of the State: The Cinema of Alexander Dovzhenko.* Madison: University of Wisconsin Press, 1986.

Kuleshov, Lev. *Kuleshov on Film.* Edited and translated by Ronald Levaco. Berkeley: University of California Press, 1974.

Leyda, Jay. *Kino,* 3d ed. Princeton, N.J.: Princeton University Press, 1983.

Lodder, Christina. *Russian Constructivism.* New Haven, Conn.: Yale University Press, 1983.

Michelson, Annette. "Man with a Movie Camera: From Magician to Epistemologist." *Artforum* **10**, no. 7 (March 1972): 60–72.

Nilsen, Vladimir. *The Cinema as a Graphic Art.* New York: Hill & Wang, 1959.

Petrić, Vlada. *Constructivism in Film: The Man with a Movie Camera—A Cinematic Analysis.* London: Cambridge University Press, 1987.

Pudovkin, V. I. *Film Technique and Film Acting.* New York: Grove, 1960.

Schnitzer, Luda, Jean Schnitzer, and Marcel Martin, eds. *Cinema and Revolution.* New York: Hill & Wang, 1973.

Taylor, Richard. *The Politics of the Soviet Cinema, 1917–1929.* Cambridge: Cambridge University Press, 1979.

Taylor, Richard, and Ian Christie. *The Film Factory: Russian and Soviet Cinema in Documents, 1896–1939.* Cambridge, Mass.: Harvard University Press, 1988.

Thompson, Kristin. "Early Sound Counterpoint." *Yale French Studies* **60** (1980): 115–140.

Vertov, Dziga. *Kino-Eye: The Writings of Dziga Vertov.* Edited by Annette Michelson, translated by Kevin O'Brien. Berkeley: University of California Press, 1984.

Youngblood, Denise. *Soviet Cinema in the Silent Era, 1918–1935.* Ann Arbor: UMI Research Press, 1985.

## ■ THE CLASSICAL HOLLYWOOD CINEMA AFTER THE COMING OF SOUND

Balio, Tino, ed. *The American Film Industry.* Madison: University of Wisconsin Press, 1976.

Bordwell, David, Janet Staiger, and Kristin Thompson. *The Classical Hollywood Cinema: Film Style and Mode of Production to 1960.* New York: Columbia University Press, 1985.

Gomery, Douglas. *The Hollywood Studio System.* New York: St. Martin's, 1986.

Koszarski, Richard, ed. *Hollywood Directors, 1914–1940.* New York: Oxford University Press, 1976.

Maltby, Richard. *Harmless Entertainment: Hollywood and the Ideology of Consensus.* Metuchen, N.J.: Scarecrow Press, 1983.

Silver, Alain, and Elizabeth Ward. *Film Noir: An Encyclopedic Reference to the American Style.* Woodstock, N.Y.: Overlook Press, 1979.

Sklar, Robert. *Movie-Made America: A Cultural History of American Movies.* New York: Vintage, 1976.

Walker, Alexander. *The Shattered Silents: How the Talkies Came to Stay.* New York: Morrow, 1979.

## ■ JAPANESE CINEMA

Anderson, Joseph L., and Donald Richie. *The Japanese Film: Art and Industry.* Rev. ed. Princeton, N.J.: Princeton University Press, 1982.

Andrew, Dudley, and Paul Andrew. *Kenji Mizoguchi: A Guide to References and Resources.* Boston: G. K. Hall & Co., 1981.

Bock, Audie. *Japanese Film Directors.* Tokyo: Kodansha, 1978.

Bordwell, David. "Our Dream Cinema: Western Historiography and Japanese Film." *Film Reader* 4 (1979): 45–62.

———. *Ozu and the Poetics of Cinema.* Princeton: Princeton University Press, 1988.

Burch, Noël. *To the Distant Observer: Form and Meaning in the Japanese Cinema.* Revised and edited by Annette Michelson. Berkeley: University of California Press, 1979.

Cohen, Robert. "Mizoguchi and Modernism: Structure, Culture, Point of View." *Sight and Sound* **47,** no. 2 (1978): 110–118.

Richie, Donald. *Ozu: His Life and Films.* Berkeley: University of California Press, 1974.

## ■ ITALIAN NEOREALISM

Armes, Roy. *Patterns of Realism.* New York: A. S. Barnes, 1970.

Bazin, André. "Cinema and Television." *Sight and Sound* **28,** no. 1 (Winter 1958–59): 26–30.

———. *What Is Cinema?* Vol. 2. Berkeley: University of California Press, 1971.

Brunette, Peter. *Roberto Rossellini.* New York: Oxford University Press, 1987.

Leprohon, Pierre. *The Italian Cinema.* New York: Praeger, 1972.

Liehm, Mira. *Passion and Defiance: Film in Italy from 1942 to the Present.* Berkeley: University of California Press, 1984.

Marcus, Millicent. *Italian Film in the Light of Neorealism.* Princeton, N.J.: Princeton University Press, 1986.

Overbey, David, ed. *Springtime in Italy: A Reader on Neo-Realism.* London: Talisman, 1978.

Pacifici, Sergio J. "Notes toward a Definition of Neorealism." *Yale French Studies* **17** (Summer 1956): 44–53.

## ■ THE NEW WAVE

Armes, Roy. *The French Cinema since 1946.* Vol 2. New York: A. S. Barnes, 1970.

Brown, Royal S., ed. *Focus on Godard.* Englewood Cliffs, N.J.: Prentice-Hall, 1972.

Burch, Noël, "Qu'est-ce que la Nouvelle Vague?" *Film Quarterly* **13,** no. 2 (Winter 1959): 16–30.

*Camera Obscura.* Special number on Godard, no. 8-9-10 (Fall 1982).

Godard, Jean-Luc. *Godard on Godard.* New York: Viking, 1972.

Graham, Peter, ed. *The New Wave.* Garden City, N.Y.: Doubleday, 1968.

Insdorf, Annette. *François Truffaut.* New York: William Morrow, 1979.

Marie, Michel. "The Art of the Film in France since the 'New Wave.'" *Wide Angle* **4,** no. 4 (1981): 18–25.

Monaco, James. *The New Wave: Truffaut, Godard, Chabrol, Rohmer, Rivette.* New York: Oxford University Press, 1976.

Mussman, Toby, ed. *Jean-Luc Godard.* New York: Dutton, 1968.

## ■ THE NEW GERMAN CINEMA

Corrigan, Timothy. *New German Cinema: The Displaced Image.* Austin: University of Texas Press, 1983.

Eden, Peter, et al. *Fassbinder.* New York: Tanam Press, 1981.

Elsaesser, Thomas. *New German Cinema: A History.* New Brunswick, N.J.: Rutgers University Press, 1989.

"New German Cinema." Special number of *New German Critique,* no. 24–25 (Fall/Winter 1981–82).

"New German Cinema." Special number of *Persistence of Vision,* no. 3 (Fall 1985).

"New German Cinema." Special number of *Wide Angle* **3,** no. 4 (1980).

Phillips, Klaus, ed. *New German Filmmakers: From Oberhausen through the 1970s.* New York: Ungar, 1984.

Rayns, Tony, ed. *Fassbinder.* Rev. ed. London: British Film Institute, 1979.

Rentschler, Eric. *West German Film in the Course of Time.* Bedford Hills, N.Y.: Redgrave, 1984.

Roud, Richard. *Jean-Marie Straub.* New York: Viking, 1972.

Sandford, John. *The New German Cinema.* London: Eyre Methuen, 1980.

Walsh, Martin. *The Brechtian Aspect of Radical Cinema.* London: British Film Institute, 1981.

"West German Film in the 1970s." Special number of *Quarterly Review of Film Studies* **5,** no. 2 (Spring 1980).

# GLOSSARY

**abstract form** A type of filmic organization in which the parts relate to each other through such visual and sonic qualities as shape, color, rhythm, and direction of movement.

**Academy ratio** The standardized shape of the film frame established by the Academy of Motion Picture Arts and Sciences. In the original 1930 ratio, the frame was 1⅓ times as wide as it was high (1:1.33); recently the width was changed to 1.85 times the height (1:1.85).

**aerial perspective** A cue for suggesting represented depth in the image by presenting objects in the distance less distinctly than those in the foreground.

**anamorphic lens** A lens for making widescreen films using regular *Academy ratio* frame size. The camera lens takes in a wide field of view and squeezes it onto the frame, and a similar projector lens unsqueezes the image onto a wide theater screen.

**angle of framing** The position of the frame in relation to the subject it shows: above it, looking down (a high angle); horizontal, on the same level (a straight-on angle); looking up (a low angle). Also called "camera angle."

**animation** Any process whereby artificial movement is created by photographing a series of drawings (see also *cel animation*), objects, or computer images one by one. Small changes in position manipulated to create the illusion of movement.

**aspect ratio** The relationship of the frame's height to its width. The standard *Academy ratio* for many years was 1:1.33.

**associational form** A type of organization in which the film's parts are juxtaposed to suggest similarities, contrasts, emotions, and expressive qualities.

**asynchronous sound** Sound that is not matched temporally with the movements occurring in the image, as when dialogue does not correspond to lip movements.

**auteur** The presumed or actual "author" of a film, usually identified as the director. Also sometimes used in an evaluative sense to distinguish good filmmakers (*auteurs*) from bad ones.

**axis of action** In the *continuity editing* system, the imaginary line that passes from side to side through the main actors, defining the spatial relations of all the elements of the scene as being to the right or left. The camera is not supposed to cross the axis at a cut and thus reverse those spatial relations. Also called the "180° line." (See also *180° system*.)

**backlighting** Illumination cast onto the figures in the scene from the side opposite the camera, creating a thin outline of highlighting on those figures.

**boom** A pole upon which a microphone can be suspended above the scene being filmed and which is used to change the microphone's position as the action moves about.

**camera angle** See *angle of framing*.

**canted framing** A view in which the frame is not level; either the right or left side is lower than the other, causing objects in the scene to appear slanted out of an upright position.

**categorical form** A type of filmic organization in which the parts treat distinct types of subject matter.

**cel animation** Animation that uses a series of drawings on pieces of celluloid, called "cels" for short; slight changes between the drawings combine to create an illusion of movement.

**cheat cut** In the *continuity editing* system, a cut which involves continuous time from shot to shot, but which mismatches the positions of figures or objects.

**cinematography** A general term for all the manipulations of the film strip by the camera in the shooting phase and by the laboratory in the developing phase.

**close-up** A framing in which the scale of the object shown is relatively large; most commonly a head seen from the neck up, or an object of a comparable size that fills most of the screen.

**closure** The degree to which the ending of a narrative film reveals the effects of all the causal events and resolves (or "closes off") all lines of action.

**continuity editing** A system of cutting to maintain continuous and clear narrative action by matching screen direction, position, and temporal relations from shot to shot. For specific techniques of continuity editing, see *axis of action, crosscutting, cut-in, establishing shot, eyeline match, match on action, reestablishing shot, screen direction, shot/reverse shot*.

**crane shot** A shot with a change of framing accomplished by having the camera above the ground and moving through the air in any direction.

**crosscutting** Editing that alternates shots of two or more lines of action occurring in different places, usually simultaneously.

**cut** 1. In filmmaking, the joining of two strips of film together with a splice. 2. In the finished film, an instantaneous change from one framing to another (or, in rare cases, an instantaneous change only of time; see *jump cut*).

**cut-in**   An instantaneous shift from a distant framing to a closer view of some portion of the same space.

**deep focus**   A use of the camera lens and lighting that keeps both the close and distant planes being photographed in sharp focus.

**deep space**   An arrangement of mise-en-scene elements so that there is a considerable distance between the plane closest to the camera and the one farthest away.

**depth of field**   The measurements of the closest and farthest planes in front of the camera lens between which everything will be in sharp focus; a depth of field from 5 to 16 feet, for example, would mean everything closer than 5 feet and farther than 16 feet would be out of focus.

**diegesis**   In a narrative film, the world of the film's story. The diegesis includes events that are presumed to have occurred and actions and spaces not shown onscreen. See also *diegetic sound*, *nondiegetic insert*, *nondiegetic sound*.

**diegetic sound**   Any voice, musical passage, or sound effect presented as originating from a source within the film's world. See also *nondiegetic sound*.

**direct sound**   Music, noise, and speech recorded from the event at the moment of filming; opposite of *postsynchronization*.

**discontinuity editing**   Any alternative system of joining shots together using techniques unacceptable within *continuity editing* principles; these would include mismatching of temporal and spatial relations, violations of the *axis of action*, and concentration on graphic relationships. See also *elliptical editing*, *graphic match*, *intellectual montage*, *jump cut*, *nondiegetic insert*, *overlapping editing*.

**displaced diegetic sound**   Sound that originates within the represented space of the story but which occurs at a time earlier or later than the images that it accompanies.

**dissolve**   A transition between two shots during which the second image gradually appears as a superimposition until the two images are evenly blended, and then the first image gradually disappears.

**distance of framing**   The apparent distance of the frame from the mise-en-scene elements. Also called "camera distance" and "shot scale." See also *close-up, extreme close-up, extreme long shot, medium close-up, medium shot, plan américain*.

**distribution**   One of the three branches of the film industry; the process of supplying the finished film to the places where it will be shown. See also *exhibition, production*.

**dolly**   A camera support with wheels, used in making *tracking shots*.

**dubbing**   The process of replacing part or all of the voices on the sound track in order to correct mistakes or rerecord dialogue. See also *postsynchronization*.

**duration**   In a narrative film, the aspect of temporal manipulation that involves the time span presented in the *plot* and assumed to operate in the *story*. See also *frequency, order*.

**editing**   1. In filmmaking, the task of selecting and joining camera takes. 2. In the finished film, the set of techniques that govern the relations among shots.

**ellipsis**   1. In a narrative film, the shortening of *plot* duration achieved by omitting intervals of *story* duration. 2. The omission of intervals of story and plot duration in the *viewing time*, usually accomplished by *elliptical editing*.

**elliptical editing**   Shot transitions that omit parts of an event, causing an *ellipsis* in plot and story duration.

**establishing shot**   A shot with a distant framing that shows the spatial relations among the important figures, objects, and setting in a scene.

**exhibition**   One of the three areas of the film industry; the process of showing the finished film to audiences. See also *distribution, production*.

**exposure**   The adjustment of the camera mechanism in order to control how much light strikes each frame of film passing through the aperture.

**external diegetic sound**   Sound represented as coming from a physical source within the story space and which we assume characters in the scene can also hear. See also *internal diegetic sound*.

**extreme close-up**   A framing in which the scale of the object shown is very large; most commonly, a small object or a part of the body.

**extreme long shot**   A framing in which the scale of the object shown is very small; a building, landscape, or crowd of people would fill the screen.

**eyeline match**   A cut obeying the *axis of action* principle, in which the first shot shows a person looking off in one direction and the second shows a nearby space containing what he or she sees. (If the person looks to the left, the following shot should imply that the looker is offscreen right.)

**fade**   1. *Fade-in:* A dark screen that gradually brightens as a shot appears. 2. *Fade-out:* A shot gradually darkens as the screen goes black. (Occasionally fades brighten to pure white or to some blank color.)

**fill light**   Illumination from a source less bright than the *key light*, used to soften deep shadows in a scene. See also *three-point lighting*.

**film noir**   "Dark film," a term applied after World War II by French critics to a type of American film, usually in the detective or thriller genre, with low lighting and a sombre mood.

**film stock**   The strip of material upon which a series of still photographs are registered; it consists of a clear base coated on one side with a light-sensitive emulsion.

**filter**   A piece of glass or gelatin placed in front of the camera or printer lens to alter the quality or quantity of light striking the film in the aperture.

**flashback**   An alteration of story order in which the plot moves back to show events that take place earlier than the one already shown.

**flashforward**   An alteration of story order in which the plot presentation moves forward to future events, then returns to the present.

**focal length**   The distance from the center of the lens to the point at which the light rays meet in sharp focus. The focal length determines the perspective relations of the space represented on the flat screen. See also *normal lens, telephoto lens, wide-angle lens.*

**focus** The degree to which light rays coming from the same part of an object through different parts of the lens reconverge at the same point on the film frame, creating sharp outlines and distinct textures.

**following shot** A shot with framing that shifts to keep a moving figure onscreen.

**form** The general system of all relationships among the parts of a film.

**frame** A single image on the strip of film. When a series of frames are projected onto a screen in quick succession, an illusion of movement is created by the spectator.

**framing** The use of the edges of the film frame to select and to compose what will be visible onscreen.

**frequency** In a narrative film, the aspect of temporal manipulation that involves the number of times any *story* event is shown in the *plot*. See also *duration, order.*

**frontal lighting** Illumination directed into the scene from a position near the camera.

**function** The role or effect of any element within the film's form.

**gauge** The width in millimeters of the film strip.

**genres** Various types of films which audiences and filmmakers recognize by their familiar narrative conventions. Common genres are musical, gangster, and Western films.

**graphic match** At a cut, a strong similarity of compositional elements (e.g., color, shape) between the two shots.

**hand-held camera** The use of the camera operator's body as a camera support, either holding it by hand or using a harness.

**hard lighting** Illumination that creates stark contrasts between the lighted and shadowed areas of the scene.

**height of framing** The distance of the camera above the ground, regardless of its angle to the horizontal.

**ideology** A relatively coherent system of values, beliefs, or ideas shared by some social group and often taken for granted as natural or inherently true.

**intellectual montage** The juxtaposition of a series of images to create an abstract idea not present in any one image.

**internal diegetic sound** Sound represented as coming from the mind of a character within the story space. Although we can hear it, we assume the other characters cannot. See also *external diegetic sound.*

**interpretation** The viewer's activity of analyzing the implicit and symptomatic meanings suggested in a film. See also *meaning.*

**iris** A round, moving *mask* that can close down to end a scene (iris-out) or emphasize a detail, or it can open to begin a scene (iris-in) or to reveal more space around a detail.

**jump cut** An elliptical cut that from shot to shot either keeps the same framing on a background with the figures instantaneously changing or keeps the figure constant and changes the background. See also *ellipsis.*

**key light** In the three-point lighting system, the brightest illumination coming into the scene. See also *backlighting, fill light, three-point lighting.*

**lens** A shaped piece of transparent material (usually glass) with either or both sides curved to gather and focus light rays. Most

camera and projector lenses place a series of lenses within a metal tube to form a compound lens.

**linearity** In a narrative, the clear motivation of a series of causes and effects that progress without significant digressions, delays, or irrelevant actions.

**long shot** A framing in which the scale of the object shown is small; a standing human figure would appear nearly the height of the screen.

**long take** A shot that continues for an unusually lengthy time before the transition to the next shot.

**mask** An opaque screen placed in the camera or printer that blocks part of the frame off and changes the shape of the photographed image, leaving part of the frame a solid color. As seen on the screen, most masks are black, although they can be white or colored.

**masking** In exhibition, stretches of black fabric that frame the theater screen. Masking may be adjusted according to the *aspect ratio* of the film to be projected.

**match on action** A continuity cut which places two different framings of the same action together at the same moment in the gesture, making it seem to continue uninterrupted.

**matte shot** A type of *process shot* in which different areas of the image (usually actors and setting) are photographed separately and combined in laboratory work.

**meaning** 1. *Referential meaning:* Allusion to particular pieces of shared prior knowledge outside the film which the viewer is expected to recognize. 2. *Explicit meaning:* Significance presented overtly, usually in language and usually near the film's beginning or end. 3. *Implicit meaning:* Significance left tacit, for the viewer to discover upon analysis or reflection. 4. *Symptomatic meaning:* Significance which the film divulges, often "against its will," by virtue of its historical or social context.

**medium close-up** A framing in which the scale of the object shown is fairly large; a human figure seen from the chest up would fill most of the screen.

**medium long shot** A framing at a distance which makes an object about four or five feet high appear to fill most of the screen vertically. See also *plan américan,* the special term for a medium long shot depicting human figures.

**medium shot** A framing in which the scale of the object shown is of moderate size; a human figure seen from the waist up would fill most of the screen.

**mise-en-scène** All the elements placed in front of the camera to be photographed: the settings and props, lighting, costumes and make-up, and figure behavior.

**mixing** Rerecording two or more sound tracks and combining them into one.

**mobile frame** The effect on the screen of moving camera, a *zoom lens,* or certain *special effects;* the framing shifts in relation to the scene being photographed. See also *crane shot, pan, tilt, tracking shot.*

**montage** 1. A synonym for *editing.* 2. An approach to editing developed by the Soviet filmmakers of the 1920s; it emphasizes dynamic, often discontinuous, relationships between shots and the juxtaposition of images to create ideas not present in either one by itself. See also *discontinuity editing, intellectual montage.*

**montage sequence**   A segment of a film that summarizes a topic or compresses a passage of time into brief symbolic or typical images; the segment is often set off by the use of filmic techniques that contrast with the treatment in the other segments.

**motif**   An element in a film that is repeated in a significant way.

**motivation**   The justification given in the work for the presence of an element. This may be an appeal to the viewer's knowledge of the real world, to genre conventions, to narrative causality, or to a stylistic pattern within the film.

**narration**   The process through which the *plot* conveys or withholds *story* information. The narration can be more or less restricted to character knowledge and more or less deep in presenting characters' mental perceptions and thoughts.

**narrative form**   A type of filmic organization in which the parts relate to each other through a series of causally related events taking place in a specific time and space.

**nondiegetic insert**   A shot or series of shots cut into a sequence, showing objects represented as being outside the space of the narrative.

**nondiegetic sound**   Sound, such as mood music or a narrator's voice, represented as being from a source outside the space of the narrative.

**nonsimultaneous sound**   Sound that comes from a source in time either earlier or later than that of the images it accompanies.

**normal lens**   A lens that shows objects without severely exaggerating or reducing the depth of the scene's planes. In 35-mm filming, a normal lens is 35 to 50 mm. See also *telephoto lens*, *wide-angle lens*.

**offscreen sound**   Simultaneous sound from a source assumed to be in the space of the scene but in an area outside the space visible onscreen.

**offscreen space**   The six areas blocked from being visible on the screen but still part of the space of the scene: to each side and above and below the frame, behind the set, and behind the camera.

**180° system**   The continuity approach to editing dictates that the camera should stay on one side of the action to ensure consistent spatial relations between objects to the right and left of the frame. The 180° line is the same as the *axis of action*. See also *continuity editing*, *screen direction*.

**order**   In a narrative film, the aspect of temporal manipulation that involves the sequence in which the chronological events of the *story* are arranged in the *plot*. See also *duration*, *frequency*.

**overlap**   A cue for suggesting represented depth in the film image by placing closer objects partly in front of more distant ones.

**overlapping editing**   Consecutive cuts that repeat part or all of an action, thus expanding its plot and viewing duration.

**pan**   A camera movement with the camera body turning to the right or left on a stationary tripod; on the screen, it produces a mobile framing which scans the space horizontally.

**pixillation**   A form of animation in which three-dimensional objects, often people, are made to move in staccato bursts through the use of stop-motion cinematography.

**plan américain**   A framing in which the scale of the object shown is moderately small; the human figure seen from the shins to the head would fill most of the screen. (This is sometimes referred to as a *medium long shot*, especially when human figures are not shown.)

**plot**   In a narrative film, all the events that are directly presented to us, including their causal relations, chronological order, duration, frequency, and spatial locations. Opposed to *story*, which is the viewer's imaginary construction of all the events in the narrative. See also *duration*, *ellipsis*, *frequency*, *order*, *viewing time*.

**point-of-view shot**   (POV shot) A shot taken with the camera placed approximately where the character's eyes would be, showing what that character would see; usually cut in before or after a shot of the character looking.

**postsynchronization**   The process of adding sound to images after they have been shot and assembled. This can include *dubbing* of voices, as well as inserting diegetic music or sound effects. It is the opposite of *direct sound*.

**process shot**   Any shot involving rephotography to combine two or more images into one, or to create a special effect; also called "composite shot." See also *matte shot*, *rear projection*, *special effects*.

**production**   One of the three branches of the film industry; the process of creating the film. See also *distribution*, *exhibition*.

**racking focus**   Shifting the area of sharp focus from one plane to another during a shot; the effect on the screen is called "rack focus."

**rate**   In shooting, the number of frames exposed per second; in projection, the number of frames thrown on the screen per second. If the two are the same, the speed of the action will appear normal, while a disparity will create slow or fast motion.

**rear projection**   A technique for combining a foreground action in a studio with a background action filmed earlier, by projecting the background from behind onto a screen, against which the new action is filmed.

**reestablishing shot**   A return to a view of an entire space after a series of closer shots following the *establishing shot*.

**reframing**   Short panning or tilting movements to adjust for the figures' movements, keeping them onscreen or centered.

**rhetorical form**   A type of filmic organization in which the parts create and support an argument.

**rhythm**   The perceived rate and regularity of sounds, series of shots, and movements within the shots.

**rotoscope**   A machine that projects live-action motion picture film frames one by one onto a drawing pad so that an animator can trace the figures in each frame to achieve more realistic movement in a cartoon.

**scene**   A segment in a narrative film that takes place in one time and space, or which uses crosscutting to show two or more simultaneous actions.

**screen direction**   The right-left relationships in a scene, set up in an establishing shot and determined by which characters and objects are on which side of the frame and by the directions of the characters' movement and eyelines. *Continuity editing* will attempt to keep these directions consistent between shots. See also *axis of action*, *180° system*.

**segmentation**   The process of dividing a film into parts for analysis.

**sequence**  Term commonly used for a moderately large segment of a film, involving one complete stretch of action. In a narrative film, often equivalent to a *scene*.

**shallow focus**  A restricted *depth of field*, which keeps only those planes close to the camera in sharp focus; the opposite of *deep focus*.

**shot**  1. In shooting, one uninterrupted run of the camera to expose a series of frames. Also called a *take*. 2. In the finished film, one uninterrupted image from a single static or mobile framing.

**shot/reverse shot**  Two shots edited together that alternate characters, typically in a conversation situation. In *continuity editing*, characters in one framing usually look left, in the other framing, right.

**side lighting**  Lighting coming from one side of a person or object, usually in order to create a sense of volume, to bring out surface tensions, or to fill in areas left shadowed by light from another source.

**simple diegetic sound**  Sound represented as coming from a source within the story and simultaneous temporally with the image it accompanies.

**simultaneous sound**  Sound that is represented as occurring at the same time as the images it accompanies.

**size diminution**  A cue for suggesting represented depth in the image by showing objects that are farther away as smaller than foreground objects.

**soft lighting**  Illumination that avoids harsh bright and dark areas, creating a gradual transition from highlights to shadows.

**sound bridge**  The sound coming from one scene while the image shows another scene. If scene A shows a nightclub and scene B a factory, a sound bridge could continue the nightclub sound after scene B had already started. Or a sound bridge could present the sound of the factory just before the nightclub scene had ended.

**sound over**  Any sound that is not represented as being directly audible within the space and time of the images on the screen: nonsimultaneous diegetic, simultaneous displaced diegetic, and nondiegetic sounds. See also *displaced diegetic sound, nondiegetic sound, nonsimultaneous sound.*

**space**  In film, there are types of represented three-dimensional space: the story space, plot space, and viewing (or onscreen) space. In addition, there is the flat, or graphic, space of the screen.

**special effects**  A general term for various photographic manipulations that create fictitious spatial relations in the shot, such as a *superimposition*, a *matte shot*, and *rear projection*.

**story**  In a narrative film, all the events that we see and hear, as well as all those that we infer or assume to have occurred, including their presumed causal relations, chronological order, duration, frequency, and spatial locations. Opposed to *plot*, which is the film's actual presentation of certain events in the narrative. See also *duration, ellipsis, frequency, order, viewing time.*

**storyboard**  A tool used in planning film production, consisting of drawings of individual shots or phases of shots with descriptions written below each drawing. Usually pinned on a wall and resembling a comic strip in appearance.

**style**  The repeated and salient uses of film techniques characteristic of a single film or a group of films (for example, a filmmaker's work or a national movement).

**superimposition**  The exposure of more than one image onto the same film strip.

**synchronous sound**  Sound that is matched temporally with the movements occurring in the images, as when dialogue corresponds to lip movements.

**take**  In filmmaking, the shot produced by one uninterrupted run of the camera; one shot in the final film may be chosen from among several takes of the same action.

**technique**  Any aspect of the film medium that can be chosen and manipulated in making a film.

**telephoto lens**  A lens of long focal length that affects a scene's perspective by enlarging distant planes and making them seem close to the foreground planes. In 35-mm filming, a lens of 75-mm length or more. See also *normal lens, wide-angle lens.*

**three-point lighting**  A common arrangement using three directions of light on a scene: from behind the subjects (*backlighting*), from one bright source (*key light*), and from a dimmer source opposite the key light (*fill light*).

**tilt**  A camera movement with the camera body swiveling upward or downward on a stationary support; it produces a mobile framing that scans the space vertically.

**top lighting**  Lighting coming from above a person or object, usually in order to outline the upper areas of the figure or to separate it more clearly from the background.

**tracking shot**  A camera movement with the camera body moving through space horizontal to the ground on a moving support; on the screen, it produces a mobile framing that travels through space forward, backward, or to one side.

**underlighting**  Illumination from a point below the figures in the scene.

**unity**  The degree to which a film's parts relate systematically to each other and provide motivations for all the elements used.

**variation**  In film form, the return of an element with notable changes.

**viewing time**  The length of time it takes to watch a film when it is projected at the appropriate speed.

**whip pan**  An extremely fast movement of the camera from side to side, which causes the image to blur into a set of indistinct horizontal lines briefly. Often an imperceptible cut will join two whip pans to create a trick transition between scenes.

**wide-angle lens**  A lens of short focal length that affects a scene's perspective by distorting straight lines near the edges of the frame and by exaggerating the distance between foreground and background planes. In 35-mm filming, a wide-angle lens is 30 mm or less. See also *normal lens, telephoto lens.*

**wipe**  A transition between shots in which a line passes across the screen, eliminating the first shot as it goes and replacing it with the next one.

**zoom lens**  A lens with a focal length that can be changed during a shot; a shift toward the *telephoto* range enlarges the image and flattens its planes together, giving an impression of moving into the scene's space, while a shift toward the *wide-angle* range does the opposite.

# ALTERNATIVE FILMS

In the Preface we suggest that instructors can easily replace our major examples with other comparable films. Here is a list of some alternative films which could be shown in class to illustrate each of the chapters that introduce the major formal and stylistic categories. There are many other films that would serve equally well. Some teachers may wish to assign their students a critical paper along the lines of Chapter 10's Sample Analyses, and many of these titles would be appropriate for that purpose as well.

We have included films from a variety of rental price ranges.

### ■ CHAPTER 3

*Hiroshima, Mon Amour* (Alain Resnais)
*Destiny* (Fritz Lang)
*The Ceremony* (Nagisa Oshima)
*8½* (Federico Fellini)
*Anatomy of a Murder* (Otto Preminger)
*How Green Was My Valley* (John Ford)
*Love Affair, or The Case of the Missing Switchboard Operator* (Dušan Makaveyev)
*Stage Fright* (Alfred Hitchcock)
*Meshes of the Afternoon* (Maya Deren)
*Un Chien andalou* (Luis Buñuel)
*Man with a Movie Camera* (Dziga Vertov)
*Berlin, Symphony of a Great City* (Walter Ruttmann)
*L'Étoile de mer* (Man Ray)
*Scorpio Rising* (Kenneth Anger)
*Dog Star Man* (Stan Brakhage)
*Breathdeath* (Stan Van Der Beek)
*Entr'acte* (René Clair)
*Rose Hobart* (Joseph Cornell)
*Unsere Afrikareise* (Peter Kubelka)
*À Propos de Nice* (Jean Vigo)

### ■ CHAPTER 4

Categorical form:
*Every Day except Christmas* (Lindsay Anderson)
*Thursday's Children* (Lindsay Anderson)
*Let There Be Light* (John Huston)
Films by Frederick Wiseman—e.g., *Law and Order, Hospital*

Abstract form:
*Bridges-Go-Round* (Shirley Clarke)
*Motion Painting #1* (Oskar Fischinger)
*Nine Variations on a Dance Theme* (Hilary Harris)
*Fist Fight* (Robert Breer)
*A Study in Choreography for the Camera* (Maya Deren)
*The Very Eye of Night* (Deren)
*Dom* (Jan Lenica and Walerian Borowczyk)

Rhetorical form:
*The Plow That Broke the Plains* (Pare Lorentz)
*Harvest of Shame* (David Lowe)
*Smoke Menace* (John Taylor)
*London Can Take It* (Harry Watt and Humphrey Jennings)
*The Spanish Earth* (Joris Ivens)
*Prelude to War* (Frank Capra)

Associational form:
*Cosmic Ray* (Bruce Conner)
*Report* (Bruce Conner)
*To Parsifal* (Bruce Baillie)
*Mass for the Dakota Sioux* (Baillie)
*Song of Ceylon* (Basil Wright)

### ■ CHAPTER 5

*The General* (Buster Keaton)
*Foolish Wives* (Erich Von Stroheim)
*Ivan the Terrible* (Sergei Eisenstein)
*Trouble in Paradise* (Ernst Lubitsch)
*Play Time* (Jacques Tati)
*Shanghai Express* (Josef von Sternberg)

### ■ CHAPTER 6

*Rules of the Game* (Jean Renoir)
*Ugetsu Monogatari* (Kenji Mizoguchi)
*The Four Horsemen of the Apocalypse* (Rex Ingram)
*Sunrise* (F. W. Murnau)
*Touch of Evil* (Orson Welles)
*For a Few Dollars More* (Sergio Leone)

*Breathless* (Jean-Luc Godard)
*Cronaca di un amore* (Michelangelo Antonioni)
*Vampyr* (Carl Theodor Dreyer)
*Metropolis* (Fritz Lang)

### ■ CHAPTER 7

*My Man Godfrey* (Gregory La Cava)
*His Girl Friday* (Howard Hawks)
*Bringing Up Baby* (Howard Hawks)
*The Freshman* (Sam Taylor and Fred Neumeyer)
*Wild and Woolly* (John Emerson)
*Potemkin* (Sergei Eisenstein)
*Mother* (Vsevolod Pudovkin)
*Mr. Hulot's Holiday* (Jacques Tati)

*M* (Fritz Lang)
*Lady from Shanghai* (Orson Welles)
*Stray Dog* (Akira Kurosawa)

### ■ CHAPTER 8

*Mr. Hulot's Holiday* (Jacques Tati)
*M* (Fritz Lang)
*Le Million* (René Clair)
*Providence* (Alain Resnais)
*The Conversation* (Francis Ford Coppola)
*Love Me Tonight* (Rouben Mamoulian)
*Letter from Siberia* (Chris Marker)
*The Long Goodbye* (Robert Altman)

# CREDITS

Frame enlargements and production stills not in the public domain were obtained from a variety of sources. In the following listing, the boldface numbers are the figure references. In addition, the following abbreviations are used: WCFTR (Wisconsin Center for Film and Theater Research) and MOMA (Museum of Modern Art Film Stills Archive).

**1.9** courtesy WCFTR; **1.10** copyright 1962, British Lion Pictures; **1.13–1.14** courtesy WCFTR; **1.15** from the collection of MOMA; **1.16** courtesy Pennebaker, Inc.

**3.1–3.3** copyright Metro-Goldwyn-Mayer, Inc. 1959.

**4.42** from the collection of MOMA; **4.46–4.59** courtesy Bruce Conner.

**5.8–5.9** from the collection of MOMA; **5.12** courtesy Images, Inc.; **5.24, 5.28** copyright 1958, Universal Pictures, Inc.; **5.25–5.27** courtesy WCFTR; **5.30, 5.32** courtesy WCFTR; **5.31** courtesy Toho Films; **5.32** courtesy WCFTR; **5.33** copyright 1950, Universal Pictures, Inc.; **5.34** copyright 1932, Paramount Pictures, Inc.; **5.38–5.39** courtesy New Yorker Films; **5.40** courtesy New Yorker Films; **5.46** courtesy WCFTR; **5.47** courtesy New Yorker Films; **5.53–5.66** courtesy Macmillan Audio–Brandon.

**6.3** courtesy Palladium Films; **6.4, 6.7** copyright Samuel Goldwyn, Inc., 1941 and 1938; **6.8** courtesy Toho Films; **6.10** courtesy WCFTR; **6.11–6.12** copyright 1962, Toho Films; **6.13–6.14** courtesy Ernie Gehr; **6.16** courtesy WCFTR; **6.20, 6.25** from the collection of MOMA; **6.26** courtesy New Yorker Films; **6.27** courtesy Macmillan Audio-Brandon; **6.30–6.31** courtesy WCFTR; **6.32** from the collection of MOMA; **6.33** courtesy WCFTR; **6.36–6.37** copyright 1988, Twentieth Century Fox Film Corporation; **6.38, 6.41** copyright 1962, Toho Films; **6.46** from the collection of the Museum of Modern Art; **6.47–6.48** copyright 1987, Touchstone Pictures, Inc.; **6.49–6.51, 6.54–6.57** courtesy WCFTR; **6.62** courtesy New Yorker Films; **6.53–6.72, 6.74** courtesy WCFTR; **6.75** copyright 1959, Metro-Goldwyn-Mayer, Inc.; **6.79–6.81** courtesy WCFTR; **6.85–6.86** courtesy Palladium Films; **6.17–6.18** courtesy Macmillan Audio–Brandon; **6.89–6.90** courtesy WCFTR; **6.93** courtesy Pennebaker, Inc.;

**6.95–6.101** courtesy WCFTR; **6.111** from the collection of MOMA; **6.112–6.145** courtesy Janus Films; **6.146–6.148** courtesy Michael Snow; **6.149–6.156** courtesy Macmillan Audio–Brandon; **6.157–6.168** copyright 1958, Universal Pictures, Inc.

**7.1–7.3** courtesy WCFTR; **7.4** copyright 1954, Toho Films; **7.5–7.8** copyright 1963, Universal Pictures, Inc.; **7.9–7.14** copyright 1954, Toho Films; **7.15–7.16** copyright 1958, Universal Pictures, Inc.; **7.17–7.27** copyright 1963, Universal Pictures, Inc.; **7.30–7.56** courtesy WCFTR; **7.57–7.58, 7.60–7.63** copyright 1954, Patron, Inc.; **7.64–7.67** courtesy New Yorker Films; **7.72–7.77** courtesy Macmillan Audio–Brandon; **7.78–7.80** courtesy Pennebaker Films.

**8.1–8.4** courtesy New Yorker Films; **8.5** from the collection of MOMA; **8.7–8.11** copyright 1939, United Artists; **8.12–8.22** courtesy New Yorker Films.

**9.1–9.12** courtesy WCFTR; **9.39–9.47** courtesy Bruce Conner.

**10.1–10.4** copyright 1939, United Artists; **10.5–10.17** copyright 1959, Metro-Goldwyn-Mayer, Inc.; **10.18–10.29** copyright 1986, Orion Pictures Corp.; **10.46–10.64** courtesy New Yorker Films; **10.65–10.73** courtesy Grove Press Films; **10.74–10.88** courtesy Zipporah Films; **10.97–10.102** copyright 1937, Walt Disney Productions; **10.103–10.105** copyright 1953, Warner Bros., Inc.; **10.110–10.118** courtesy New Yorker Films.

**11.1, 11.3–11.16** courtesy WCFTR; **11.17** from the collection of MOMA; **11.18–11.22** courtesy WCFTR; **11.24** from the collection of MOMA; **11.25–11.26** courtesy WCFTR; **11.32** courtesy Macmillan Audio–Brandon; **11.33** courtesy WCFTR.

**Plates 1 and 2** courtesy Pennebaker, Inc.; **3 and 4** copyright 1972, Walter Reade, Inc.; **7–9** courtesy New Yorker Films; **10 and 11** from the MGM release *Meet Me in St. Louis* © 1944, Loew's Incorporated. Copyright renewed in 1971 by Metro-Goldwyn-Mayer, Inc., courtesy MGM, Inc.; **12** courtesy Macmillan Audio–Brandon; **13** courtesy Grove Press Films; **14–16** courtesy Macmillan Audio–Brandon.

# INDEX